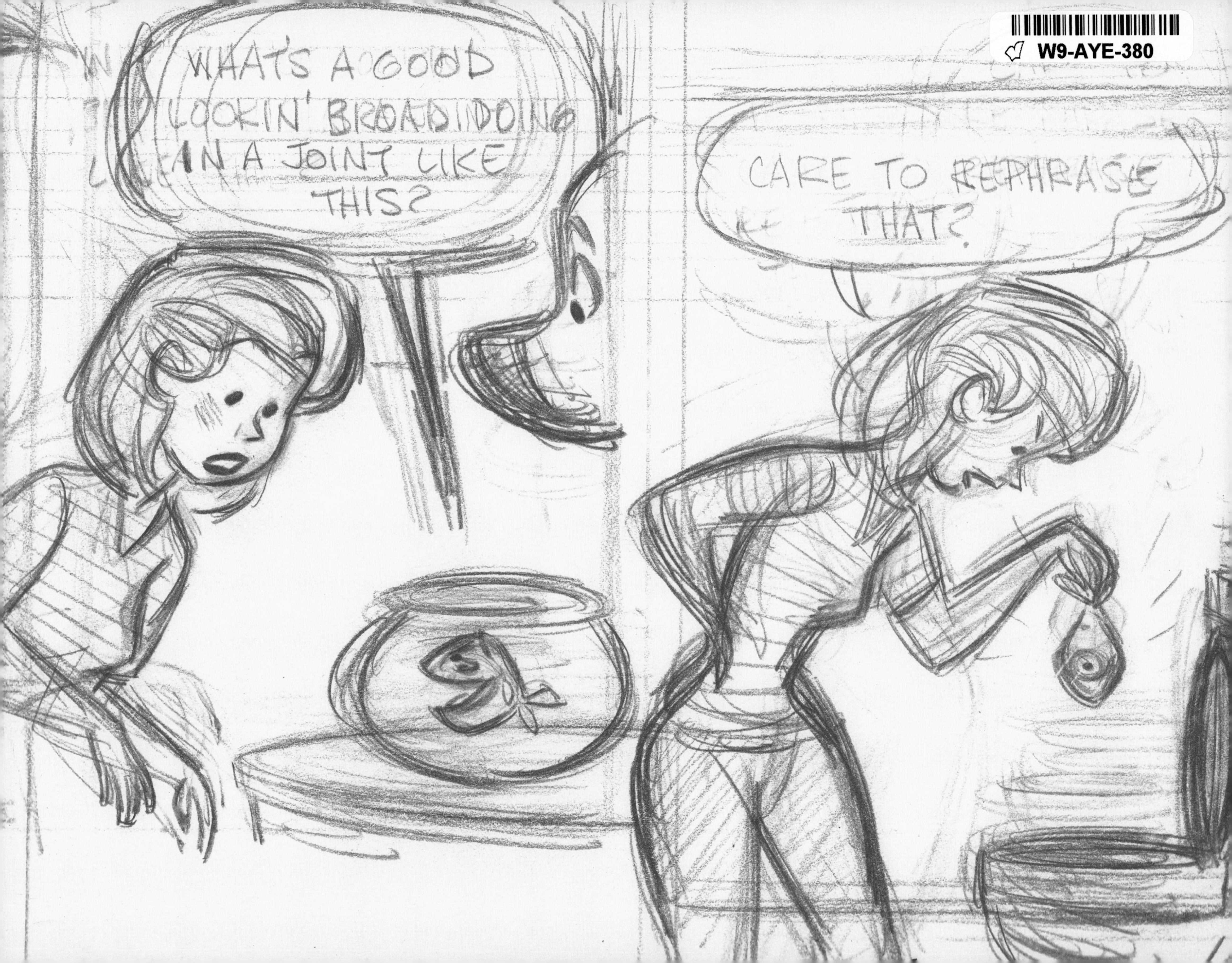
WHAT'S A GOOD LOOKIN' BROAD DOING IN A JOINT LIKE THIS?
CARE TO REPHRASE THAT?

MOLLY and the BEAR

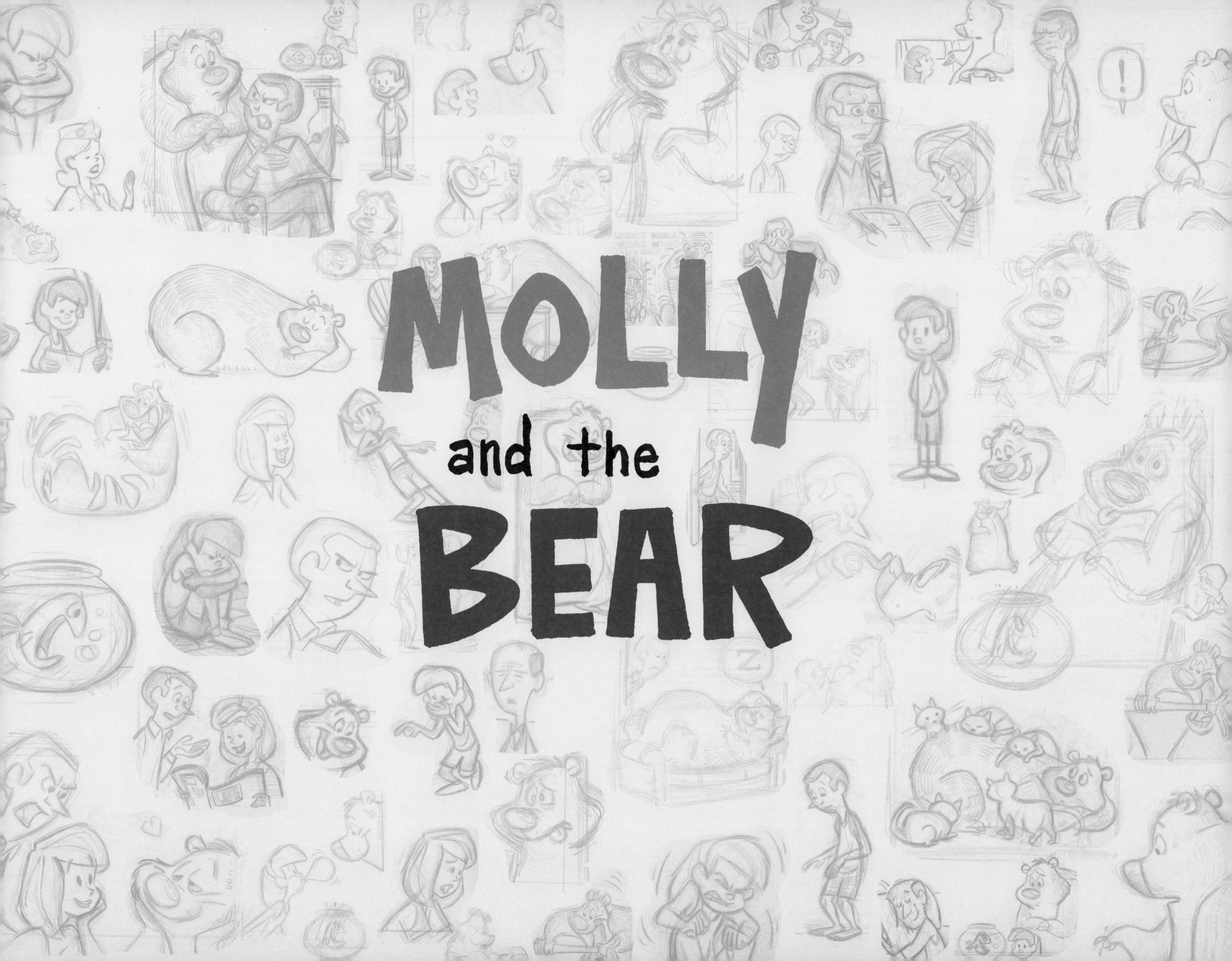

To my wonderful and tirelessly supportive parents. Thanks, Mom and Dad, for a lifetime of believing in me, and for always laughing at my early cartoons, even when they weren't that funny. I love you both!

FOR ABIGAIL!
BOB SCOTT 2017

MOLLY
and the
BEAR

BY BOB Scott

FOREWORD BY BRETT KOTH

BOOK DESIGN BY IAIN R. MORRIS

CAMERON + COMPANY

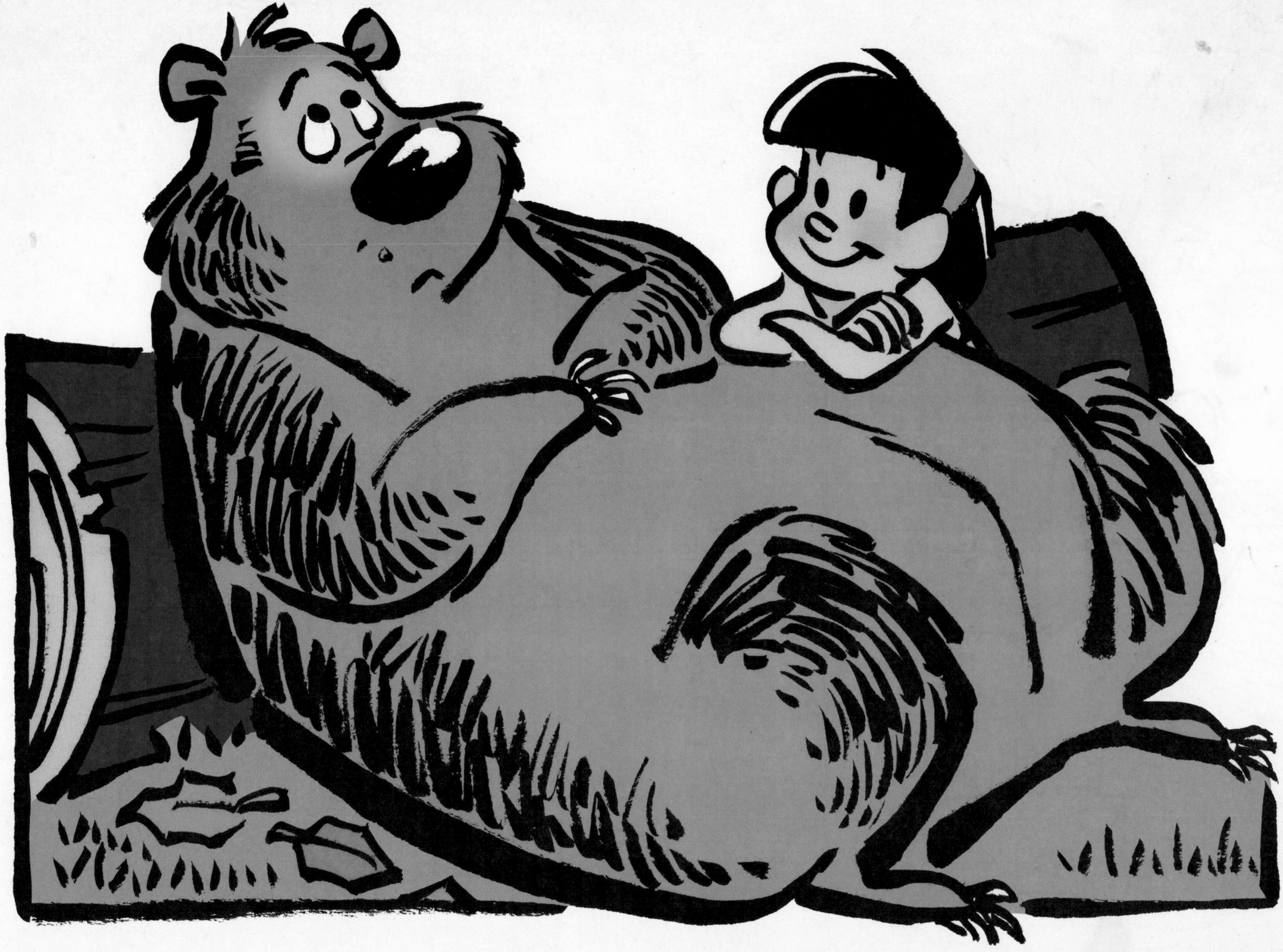

CONTENTS

FOREWORD

BY BRETT KOTH

Bob Scott is a kindred spirit. He and I are both certifiably nuts about comic strips and cartooning. "How nuts?," you ask? We met as students at Cal Arts, each got degrees in character animation, and then both promptly left the industry (and California) to work for Jim Davis in Muncie, Indiana, on a comic strip. "A hard decision to make?," you ask? Of course not! Decisions like that are easy when you're certifiable.

But Bob isn't just nuts about cartooning. As the work between these covers shows, he's pretty darn good at it, too. He's an amazing artist and animator—he couldn't do an ugly drawing to save his life—and when I look at his strips, I can always see the fun that he has doing them, because it shows through in every single panel. They're simply a delight to read.

One of my fondest memories of Bob is from almost thirty years ago: We're sitting in the conference room at Paws, Incorporated, just the two of us, under deadline and trying to write strip gags. We're going on very little sleep, and at this point are pretty punchy.

We have sharpened pencils, a stack of paper, and for some reason, a toy parrot that repeats back to you everything you say to it. And because there's work to be done, we're playing with the parrot. And we're already giggling like ninnies, when in the middle of all of this, Bob comes up with a gag. Probably the silliest, dumbest gag anyone's EVER written—and we both go absolutely helpless with laughter. I mean, we're crying, we're gasping for breath—the whole nine yards. And I remember thinking, "My God, we're getting PAID for this!"

Bob knows the gag—it involves a TV set—and it really was SO dumb that he debated whether or not he should even sketch it up. But he did (hey, he and the parrot and I were laughing at it), and to his utter amazement, it was approved, and saw print. To this day I think it's still my very favorite gag, because every time I think of it, it makes me laugh all over again. And Bob, my kindred spirit, wrote it.

Thank you, Bob. You really ARE nuts. And I mean that in the nicest possible way.

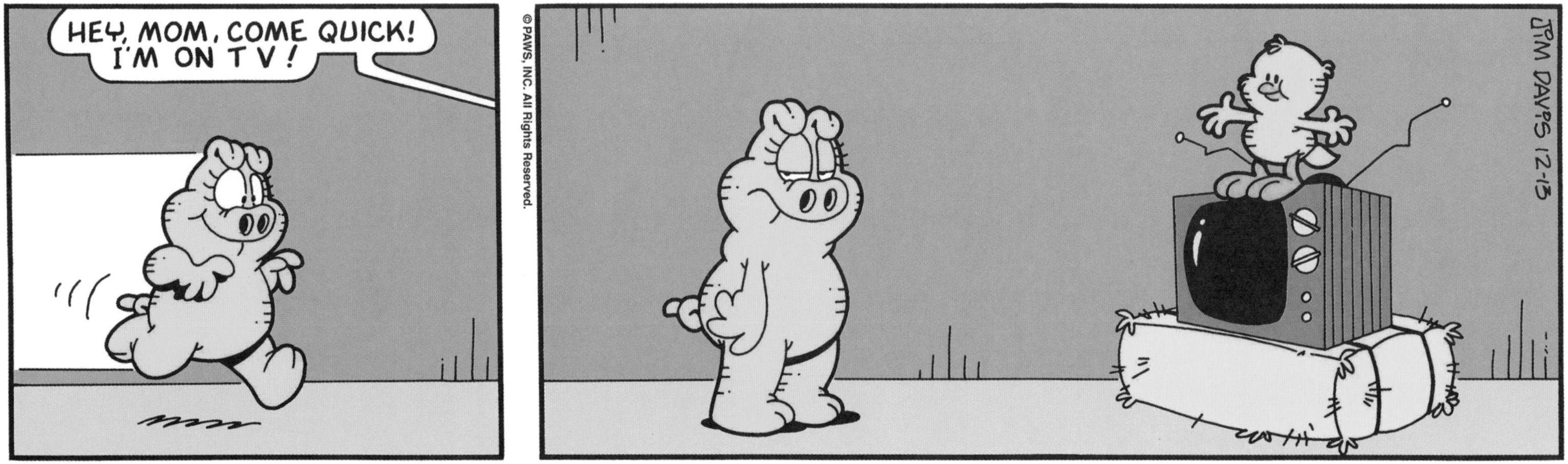
HEY, MOM, COME QUICK! I'M ON T V!
© PAWS, INC. All Rights Reserved.
JIM DAVIS 12-13

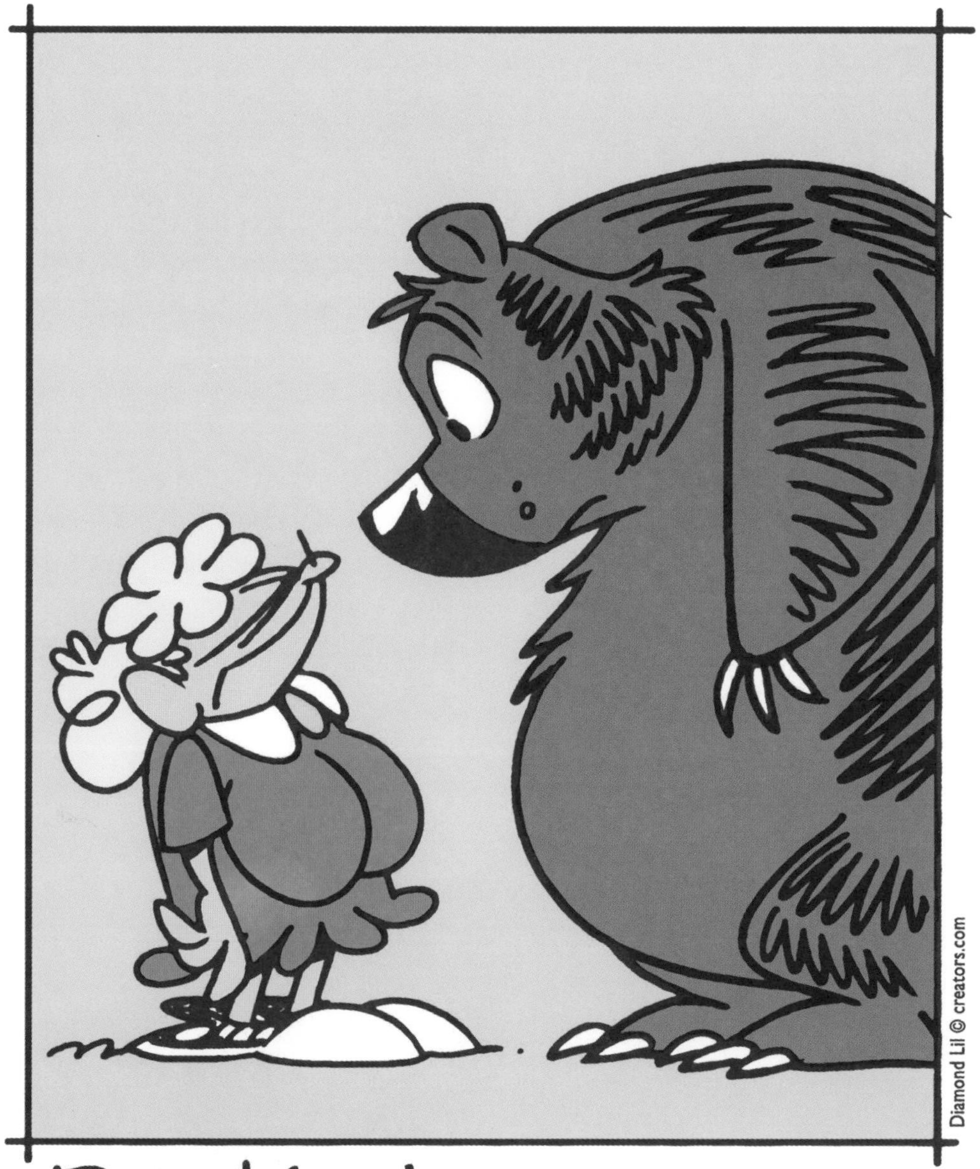
Diamond Lil © creators.com

BRETTKOTH

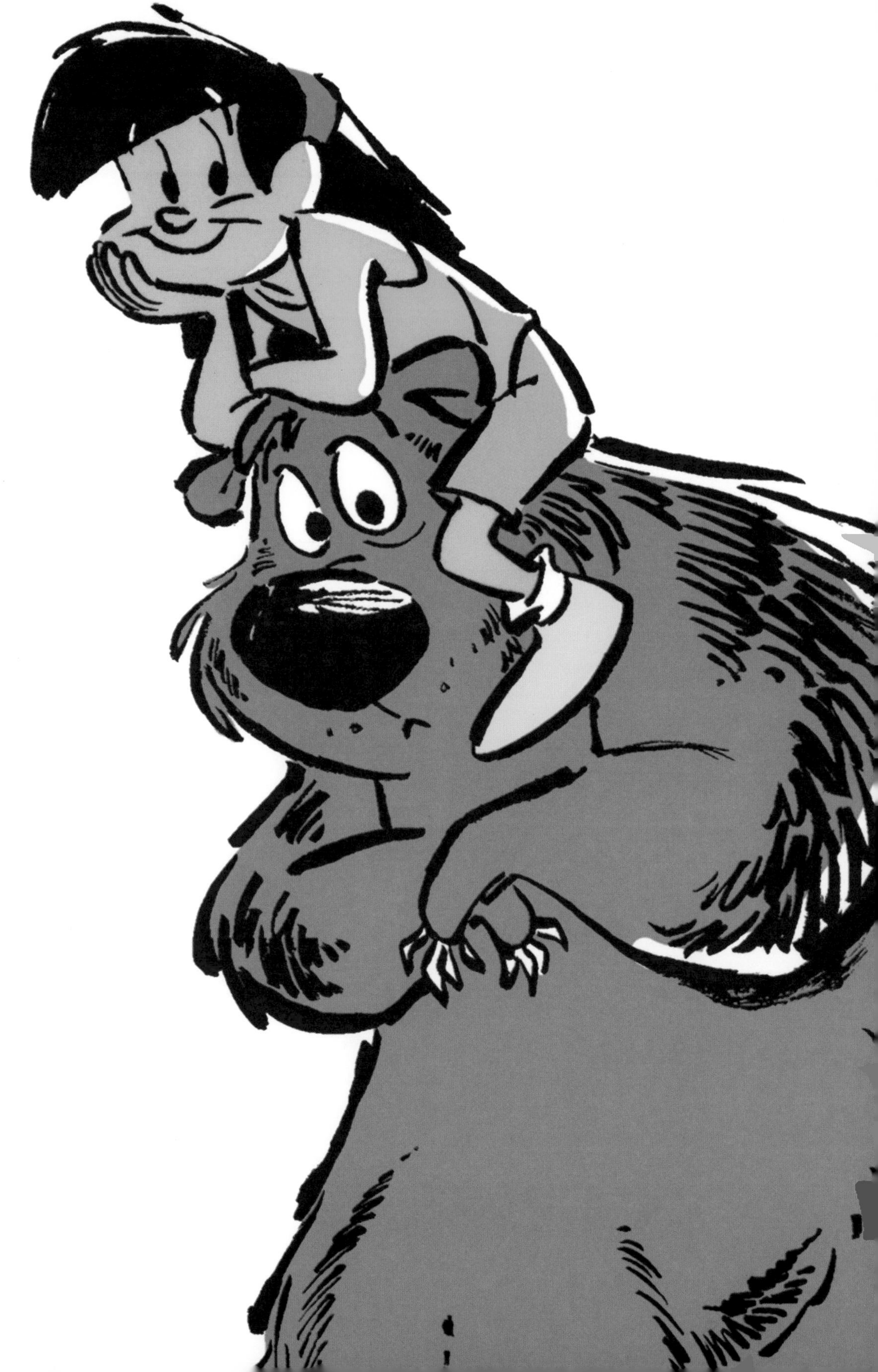

INTRODUCTION
BY BOB SCOTT

You've probably picked up this book wondering who or what is *Molly and the Bear*. You may be a fan of comic strips but are saying to yourself, "I've never heard of this one." No surprise there. *Molly and the Bear* is on the Web.

There are thousands and thousands of comics all over the Web, and you could search for years and still never find this one. Not to worry, it has been neatly organized and compiled into the very book you are now holding. Not all of them, mind you, but just my favorites of the hundreds I've drawn over the last seventeen years. I wanted to put my very best strips in this volume, so I've edited out false starts, strips I didn't think were funny, and others that for one reason or another I just wasn't happy with. Who knows if I'll ever have another book, so why not make this one the best it can be?

Holding a book of my own comic strips has been a long-standing dream for me, second only to having a successfully syndicated newspaper strip. Since I don't have the former, I've worked really hard to have the latter. To me, there is no better way to read comic strips than in print.

I hope you like the strips I've chosen. I've had so much fun drawing them. Long after this book is worn out and in a used-book store or worse, I'll have likely drawn hundreds of new strips. I get so much satisfaction from this art form that I don't think I'll ever quit. Maybe if I'm lucky and have the stamina, there will be a second volume of *Molly and the Bear*. Until then, I hope you're entertained by this one and that some of these strips give you a smile.

And afterwards you'll now know who Molly and the Bear are.

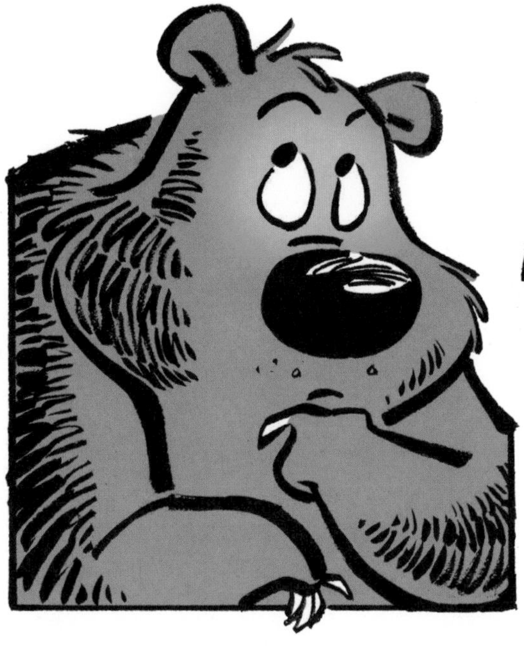

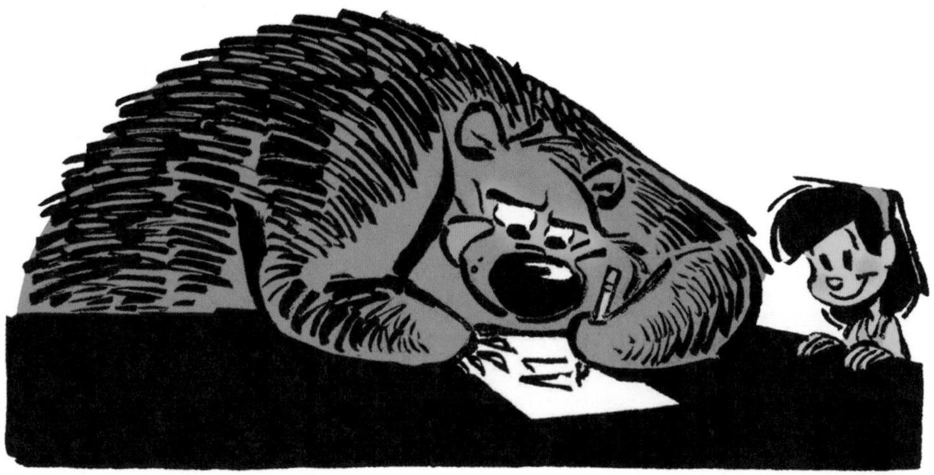

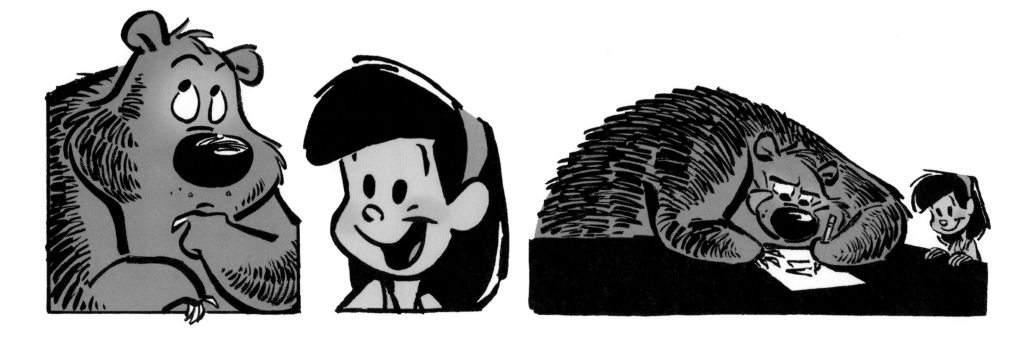

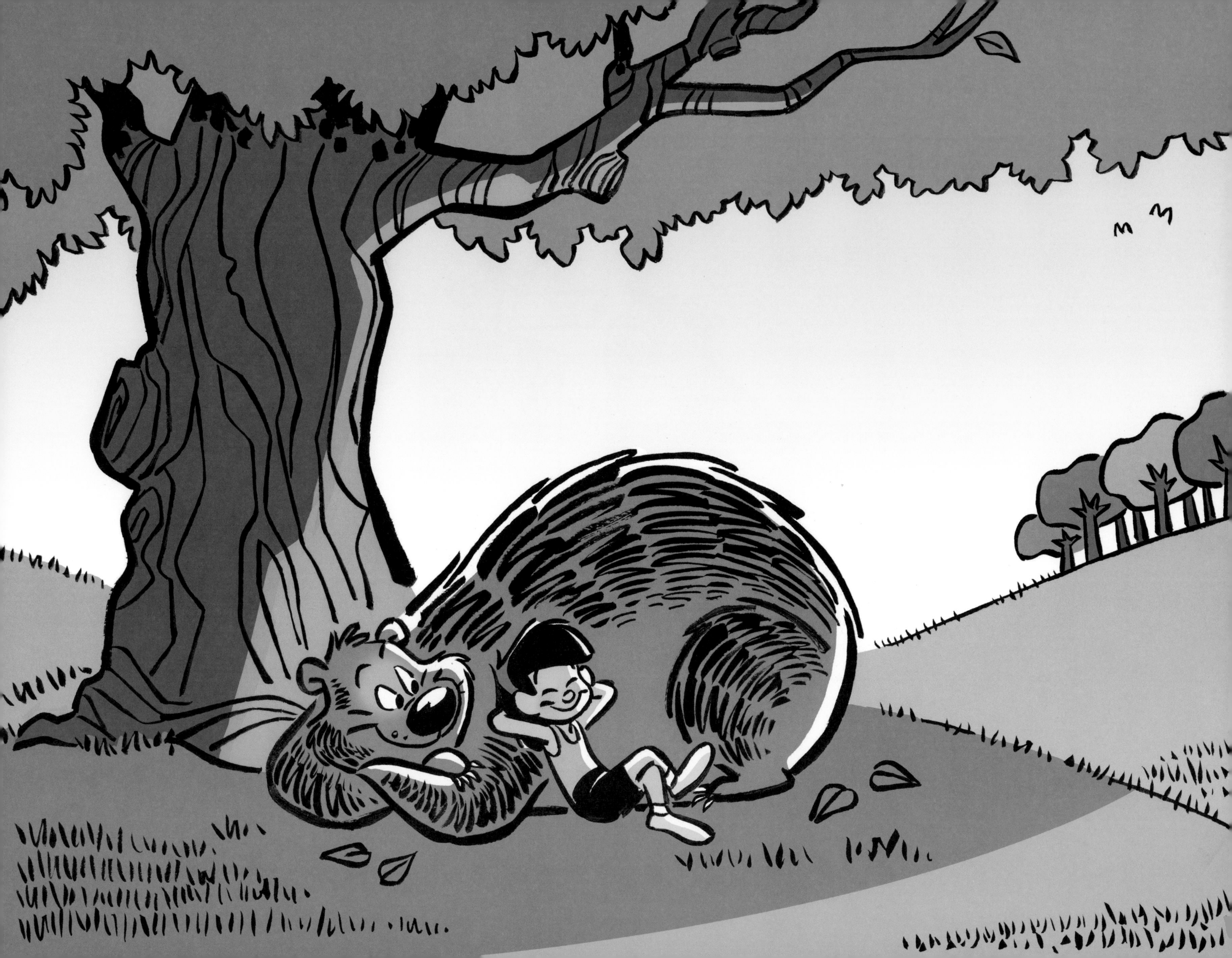

MY FAMILY ALBUM

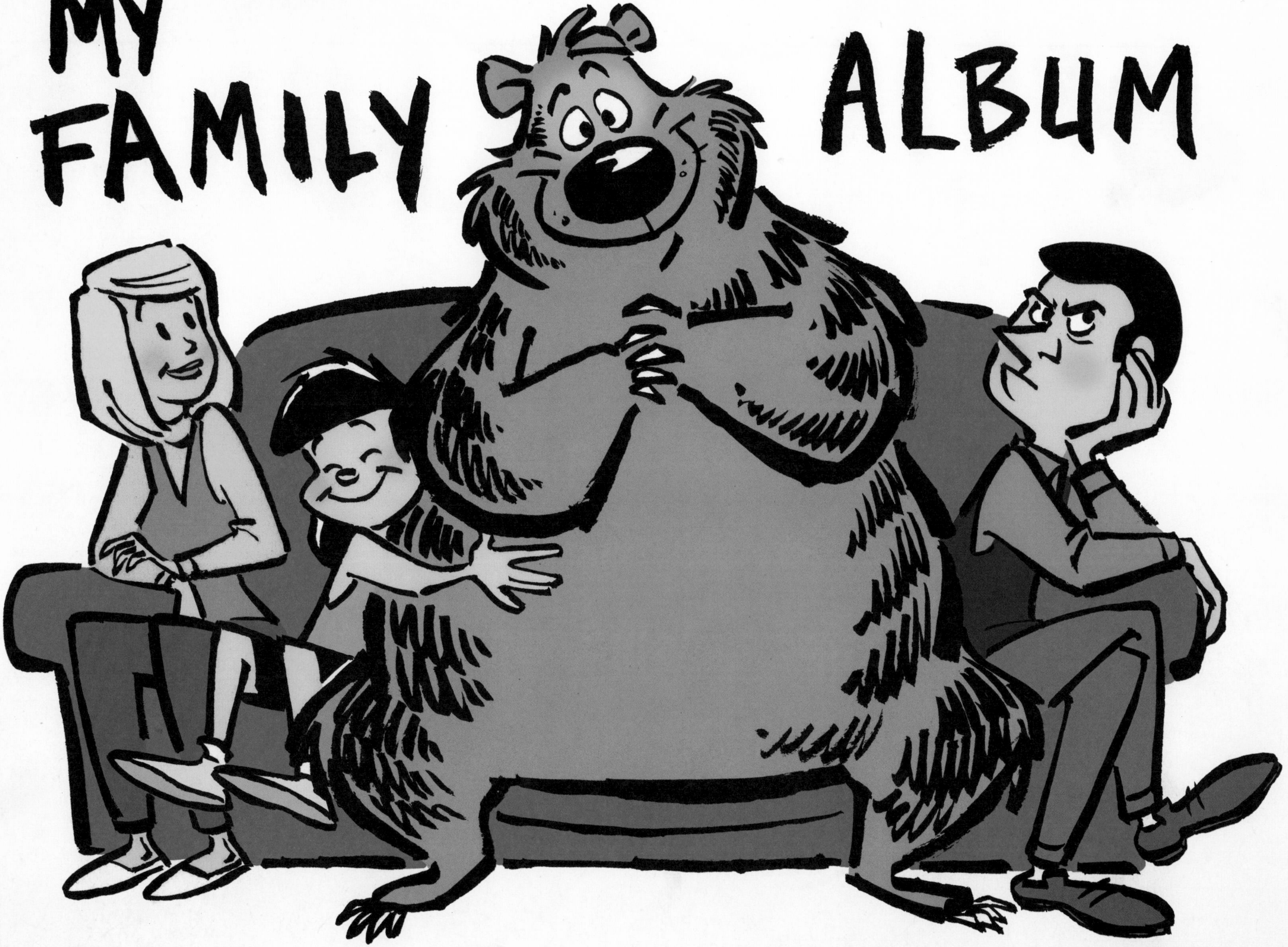

MOLLY

Molly looks like every other eleven-year-old girl in town. She goes to school, plays sports, and has a good life. But there is one difference. She has a nine-hundred-pound pet bear. Her boundless enthusiasm and encouraging nature make her the perfect person to shepherd the super-timid Bear along in life. She loves him thoroughly, and he reciprocates one hundred times over.

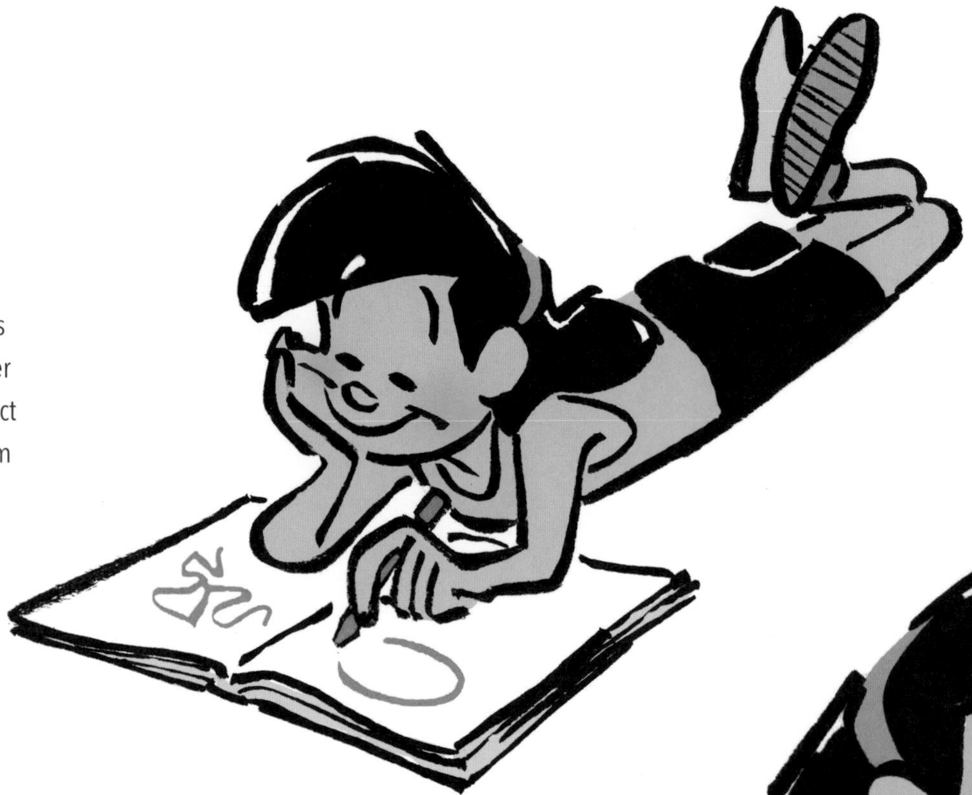

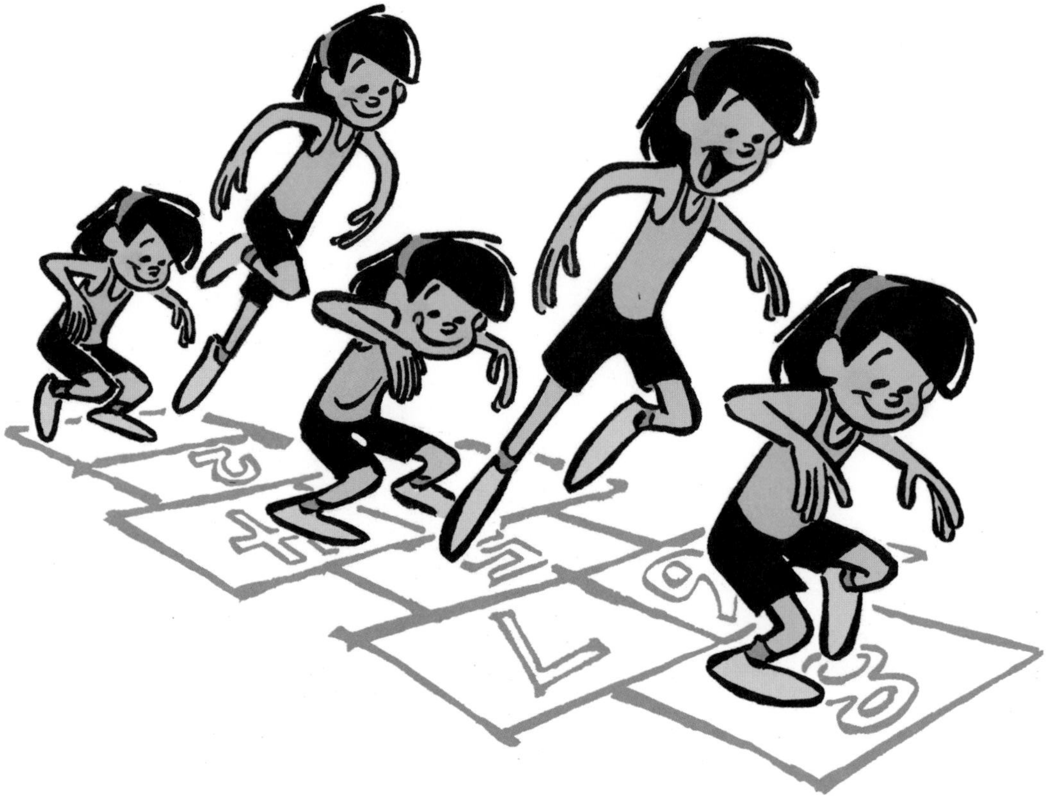

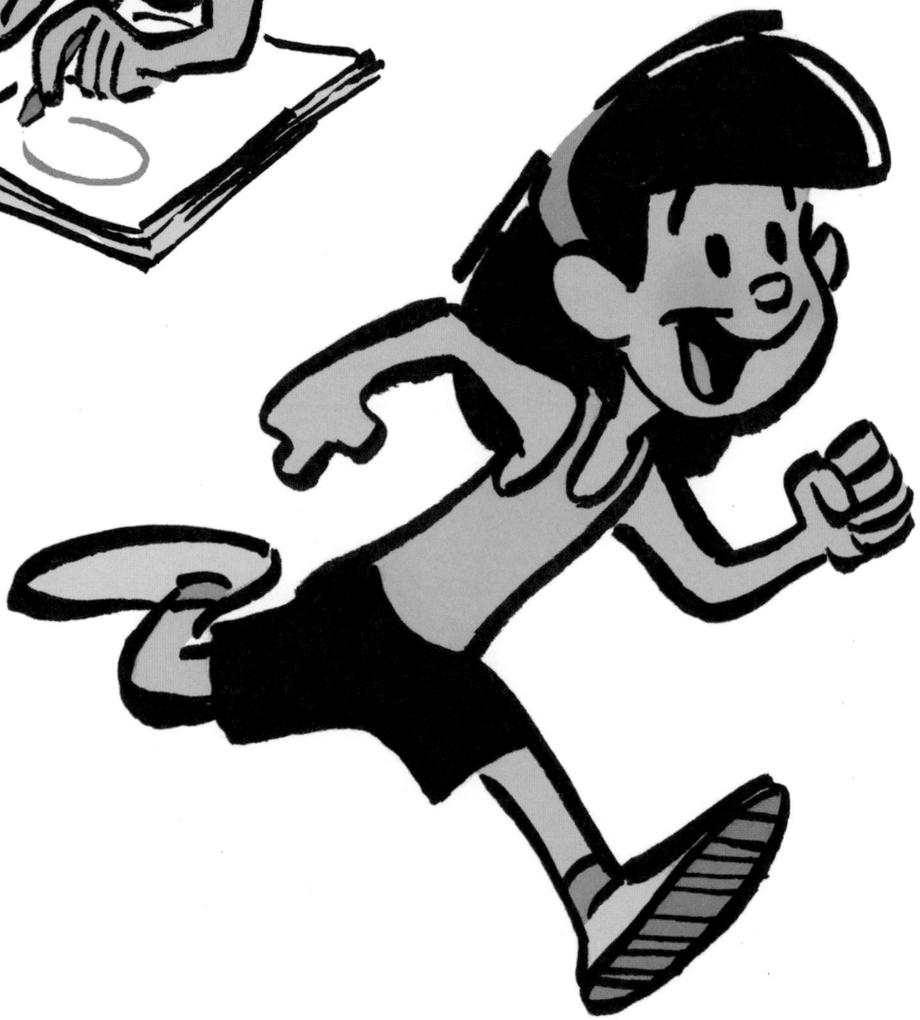

BEAR

What is a full-grown bear to do when the Great Outdoors is just one terror after another? Move to the suburbs. That is just what Bear decides. He now lives in Molly's house and they are inseparable BFFs. Poor Bear is mortally afraid of so many things, including spiders, swimming, and new situations. While clutching Molly's hand, Bear takes his first steps toward his brave new world.

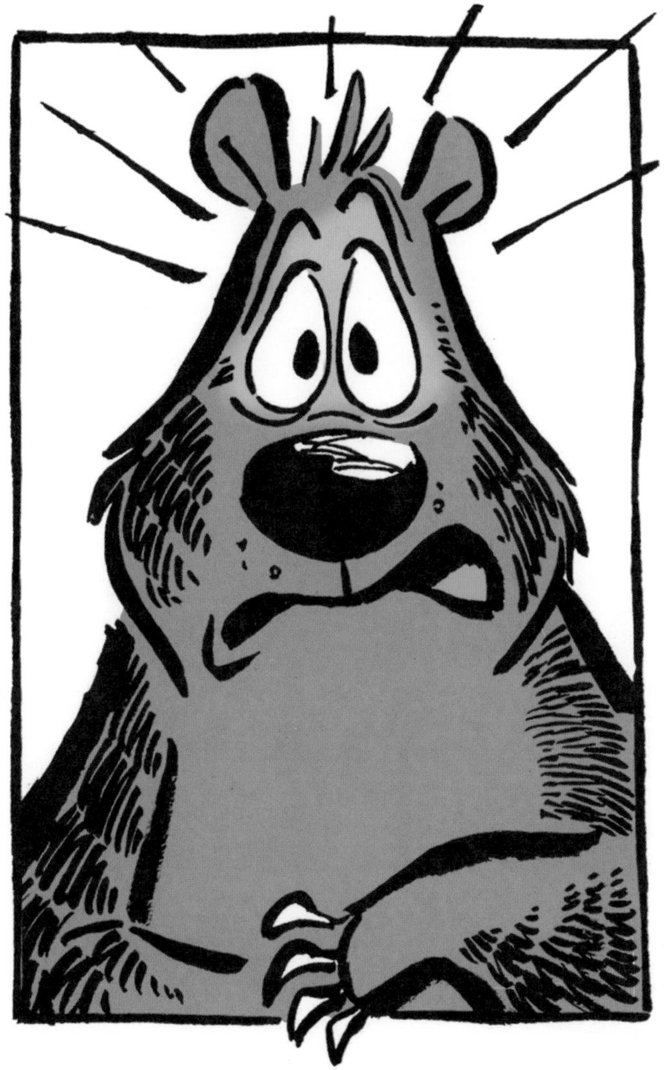

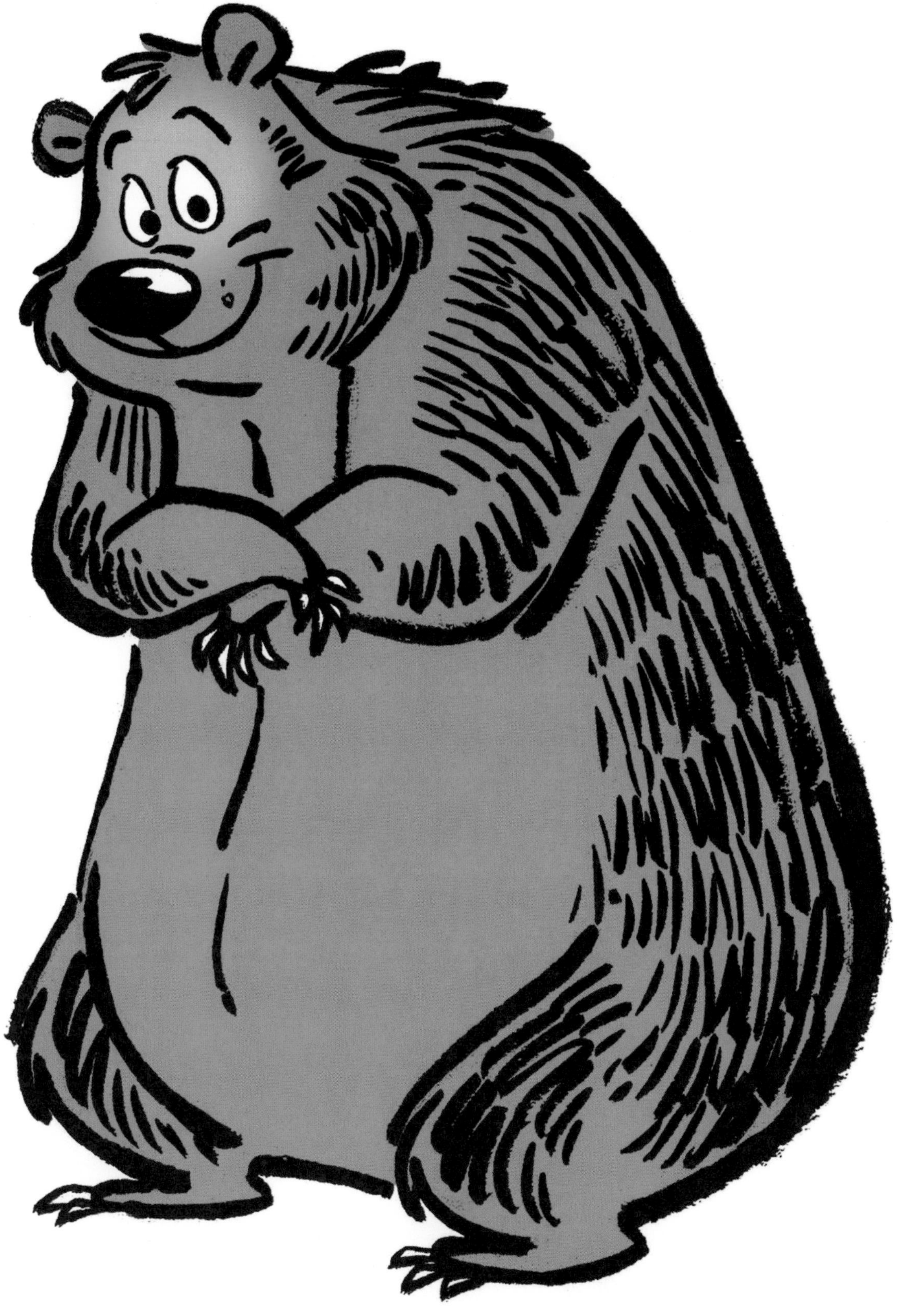

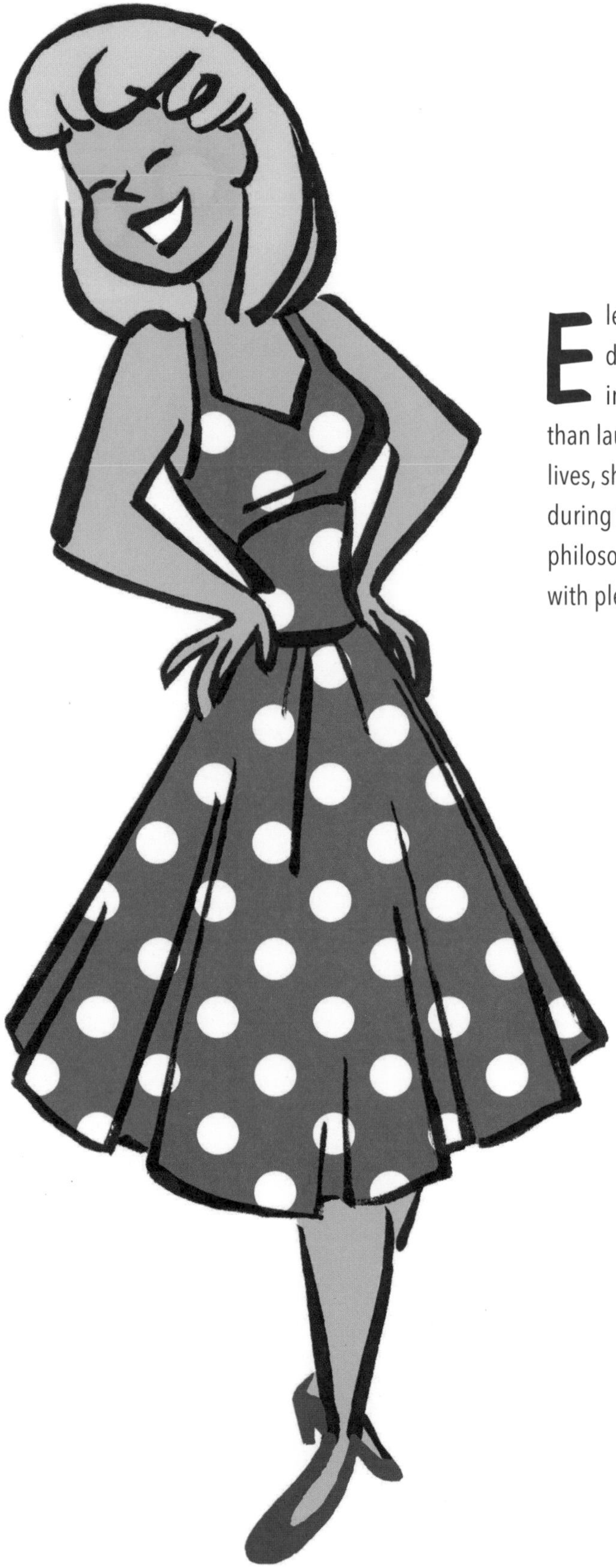

MOM

Eleven years ago, Mom said good-bye to her career and dedicated her days to her darling baby, Molly. She excels in her stay-at-home role but sometimes yearns for more than laundry and vacuuming. When Bear wanders into their lives, she's horrified at first, but soon is pleased to have company during the day. To Mom's delight, Bear turns out to be quite the philosophical conversationalist. In return, she keeps him supplied with plenty of honey and chocolate chip cookies.

DAD

For Dad, life before Bear was perfect. In those good old days, he came home from the office and was greeted by his loving wife and his daughter, who believed he was the center of the universe. All that changed when Bear moved in. Now Dad has to compete for his daughter's attention, his wife's time, and everything else he holds dear. Beneath it all, Bear likes Dad very much. Dad liking Bear? Not so much.

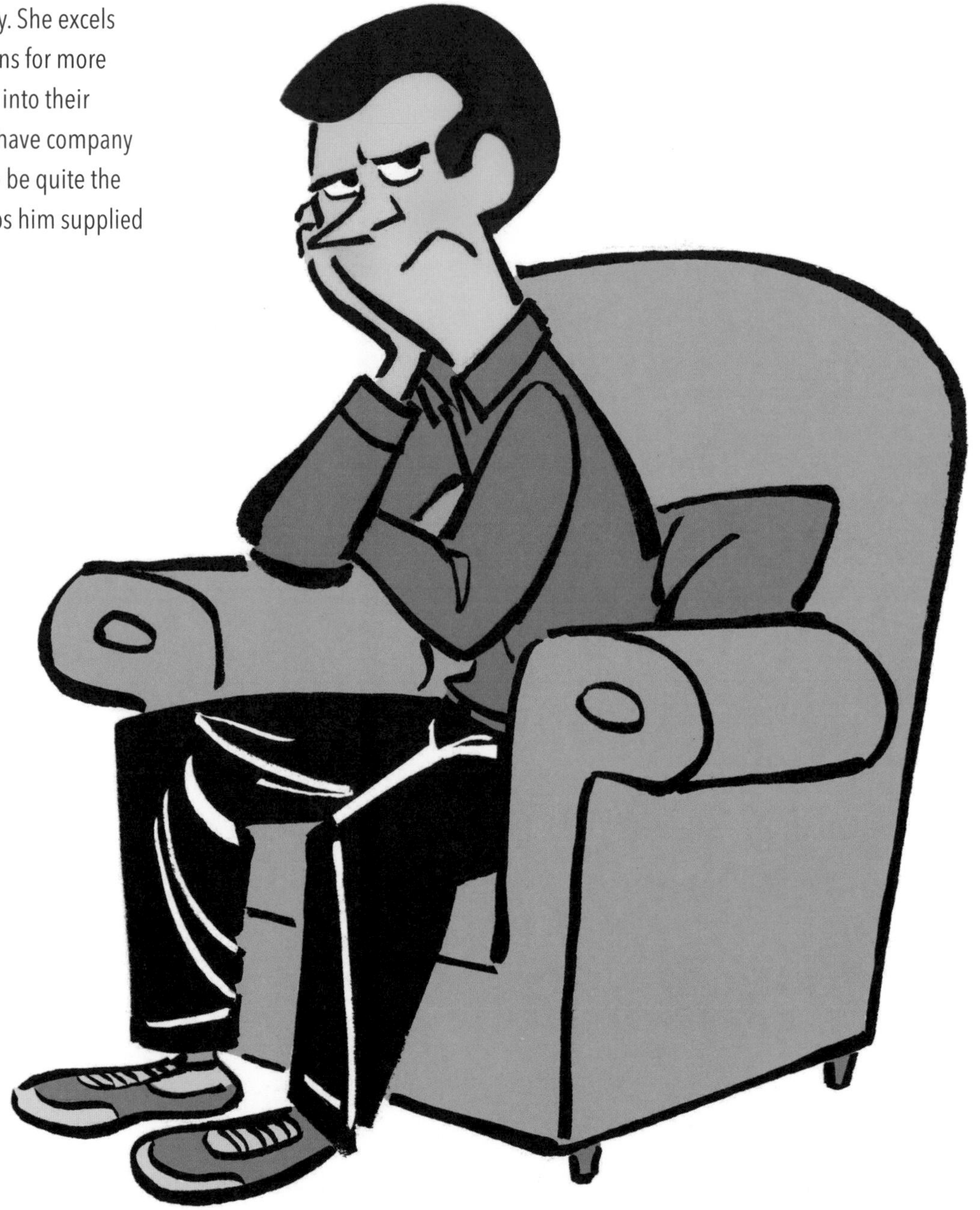

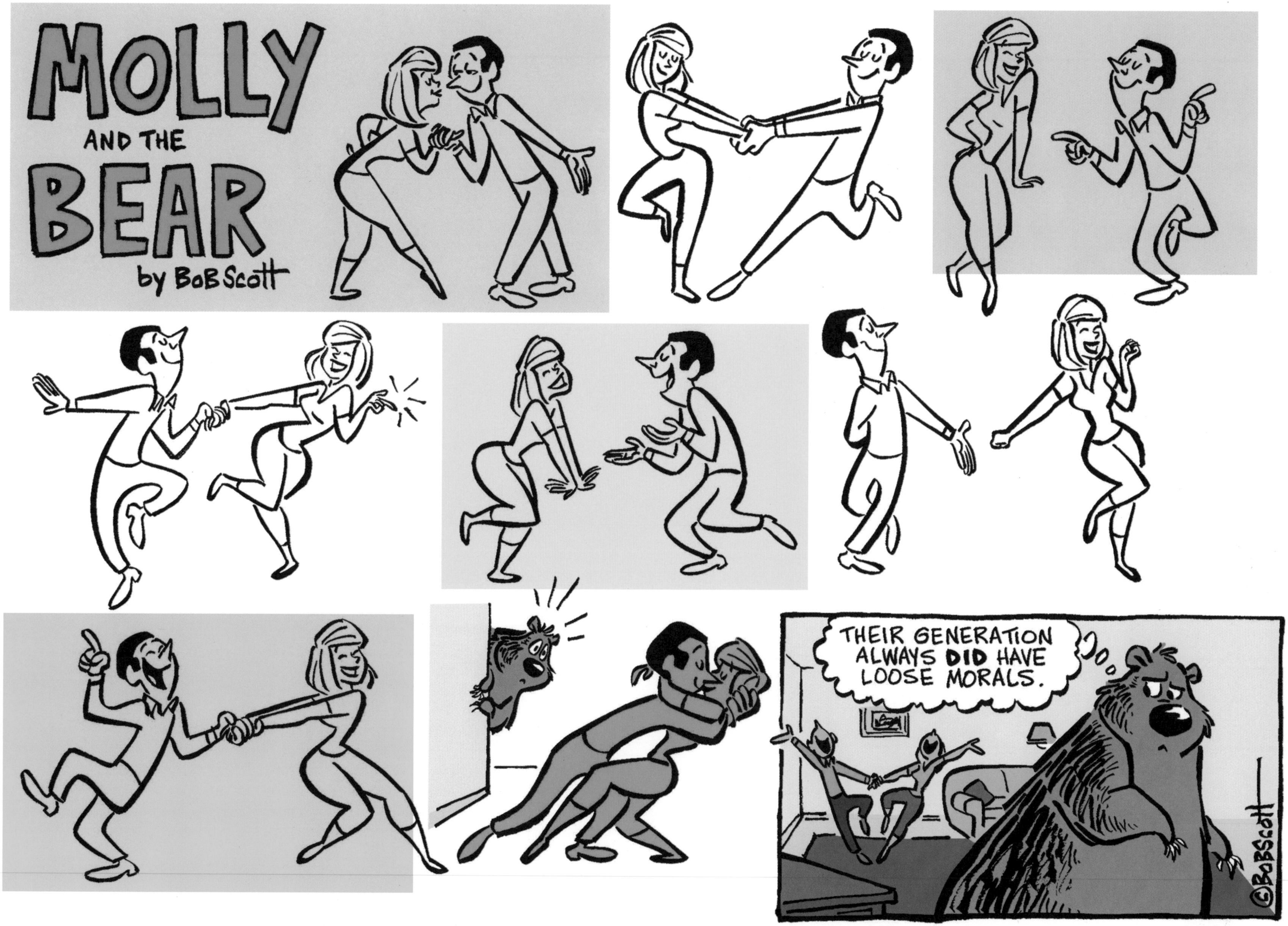
MOLLY
AND THE
BEAR
by BOB SCOTT
THEIR GENERATION ALWAYS DID HAVE LOOSE MORALS.
©BOBSCOTT

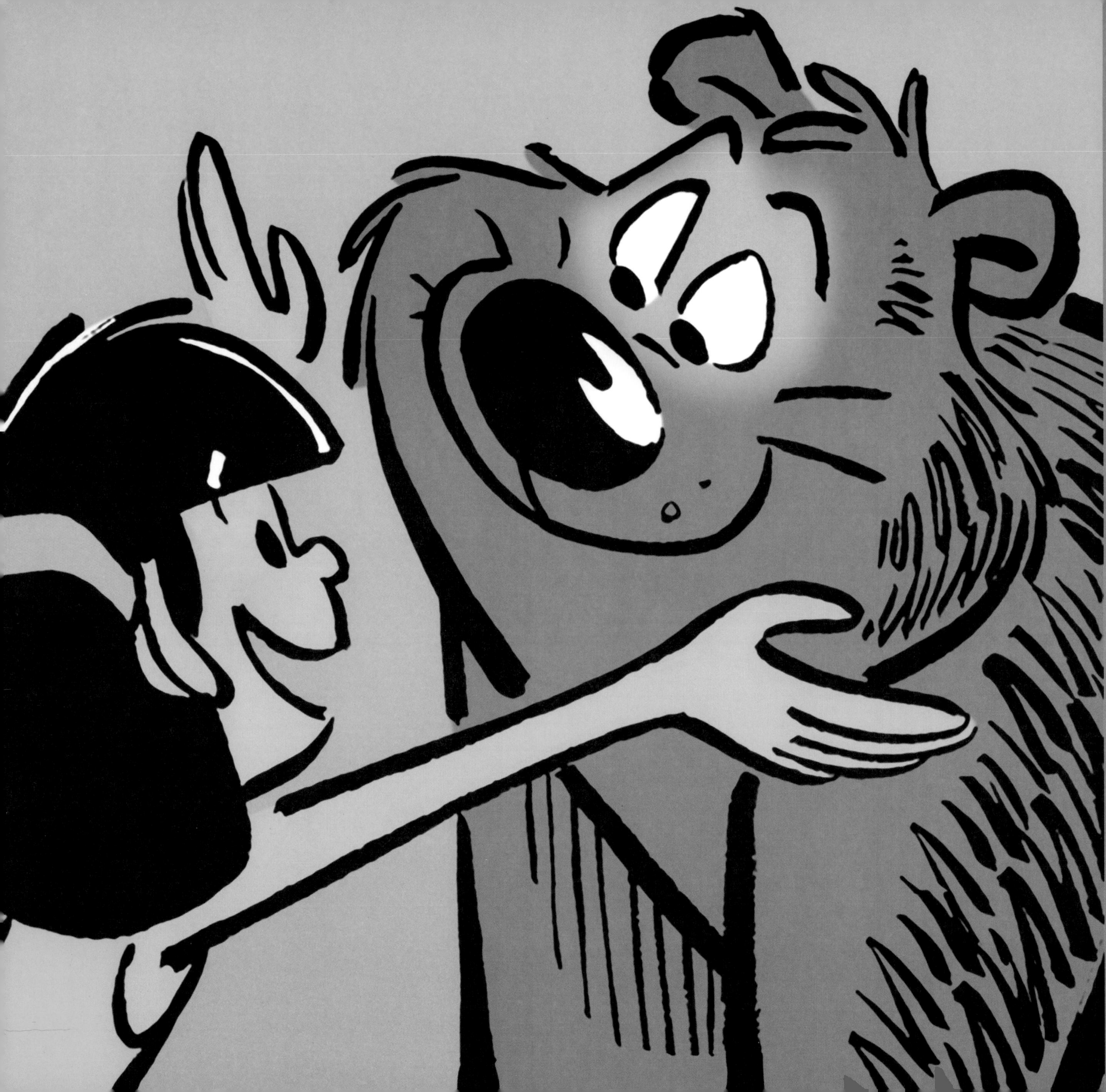

MOLLY
and the
BEAR
BY BOB SCOTT

THE STRIPS

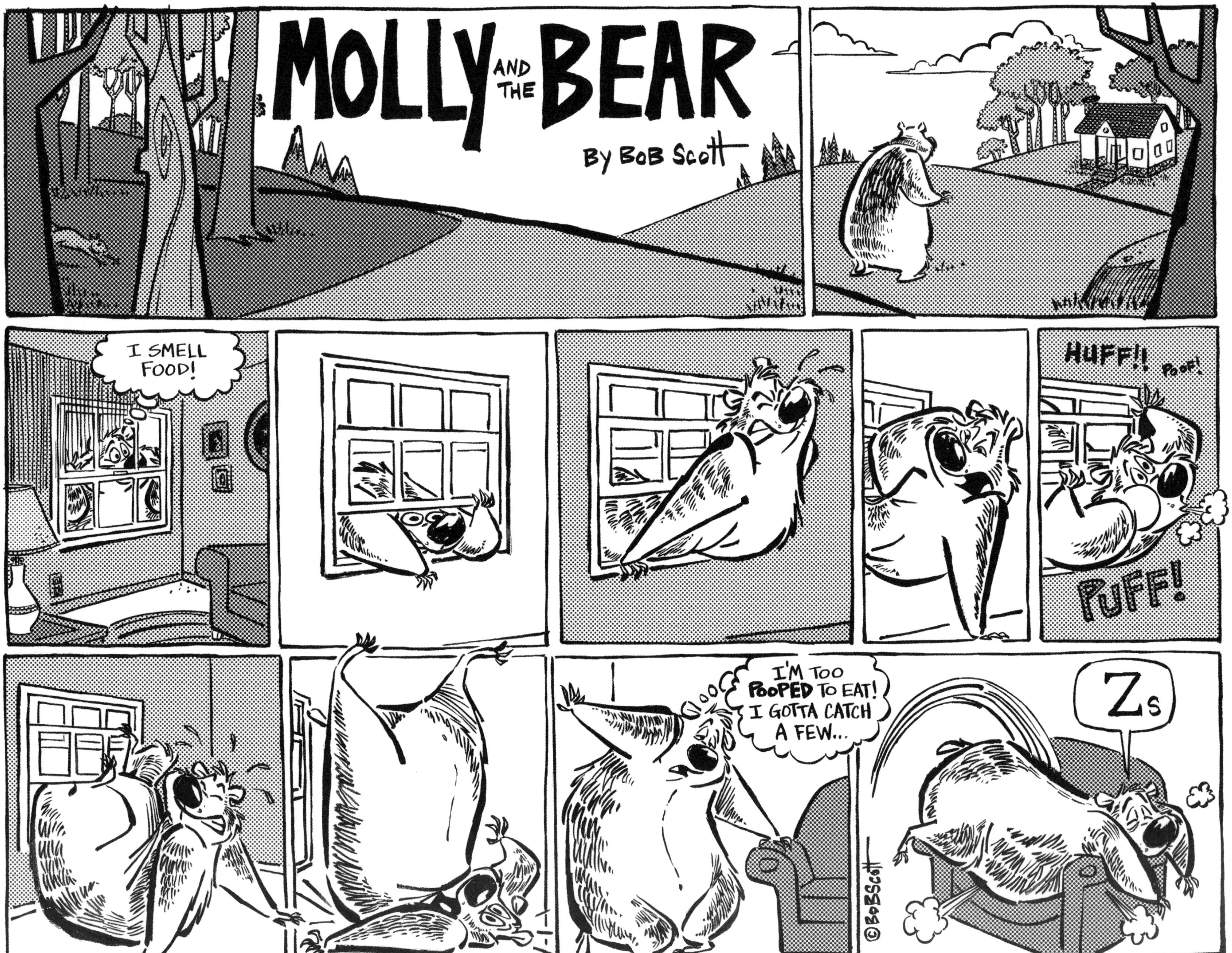
MOLLY AND THE BEAR
BY BOB SCOTT
I SMELL FOOD!
HUFF!!
POOF!
PUFF!
I'M TOO POOPED TO EAT! I GOTTA CATCH A FEW...
©BOBSCOTT
Zs

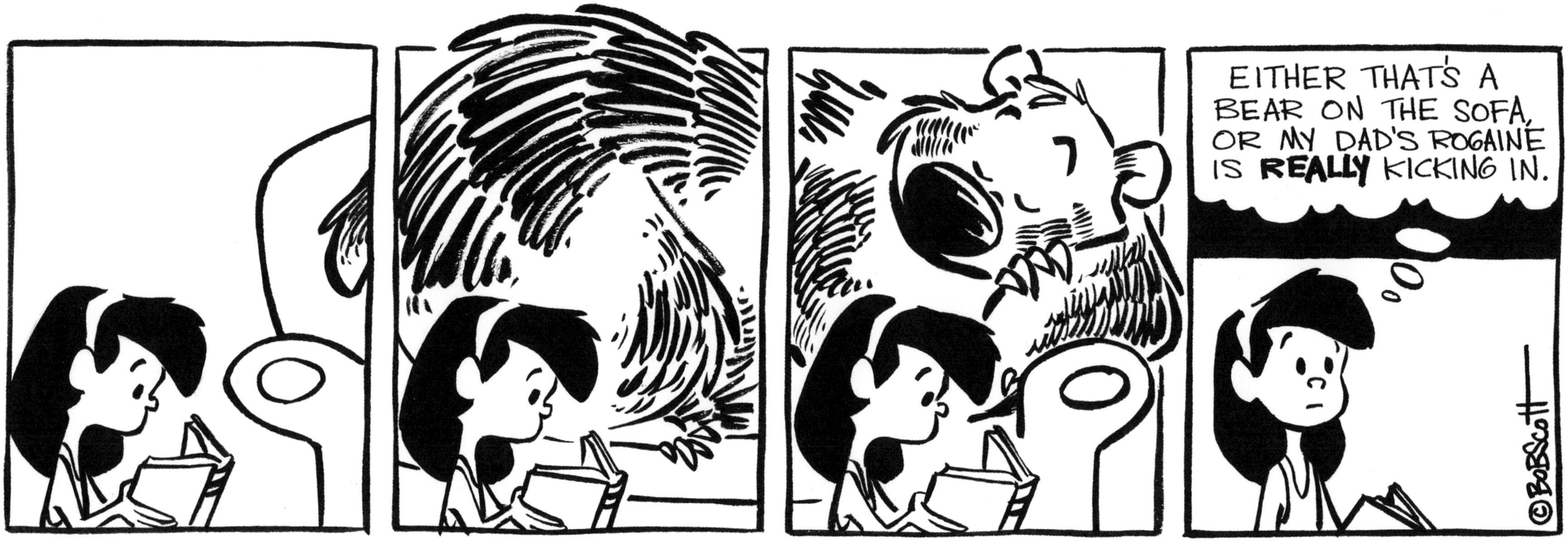
EITHER THAT'S A BEAR ON THE SOFA, OR MY DAD'S ROGAINE IS **REALLY** KICKING IN.
©BOBSCOTT

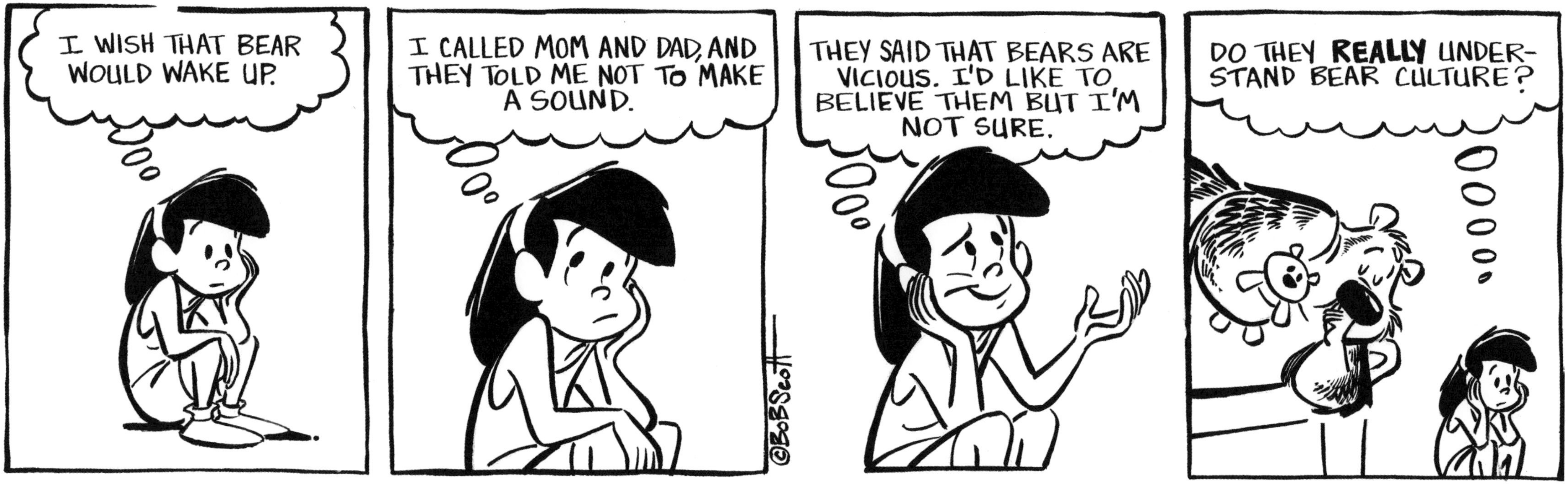
I WISH THAT BEAR WOULD WAKE UP.
I CALLED MOM AND DAD, AND THEY TOLD ME NOT TO MAKE A SOUND.
©BOBSCOTT
THEY SAID THAT BEARS ARE VICIOUS. I'D LIKE TO BELIEVE THEM BUT I'M NOT SURE.
DO THEY **REALLY** UNDERSTAND BEAR CULTURE?

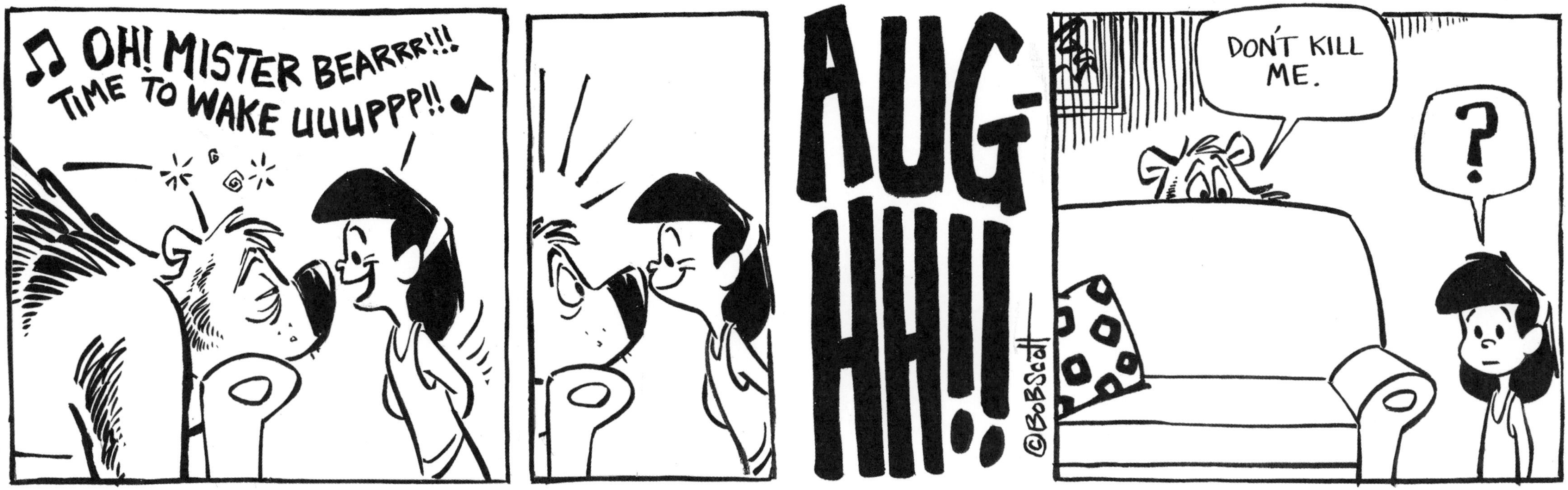
♫ OH! MISTER BEARRR!!! TIME TO WAKE UUUPPP!! ♪
AUG-HH!!!
©BOBSCOTT
DON'T KILL ME.
?

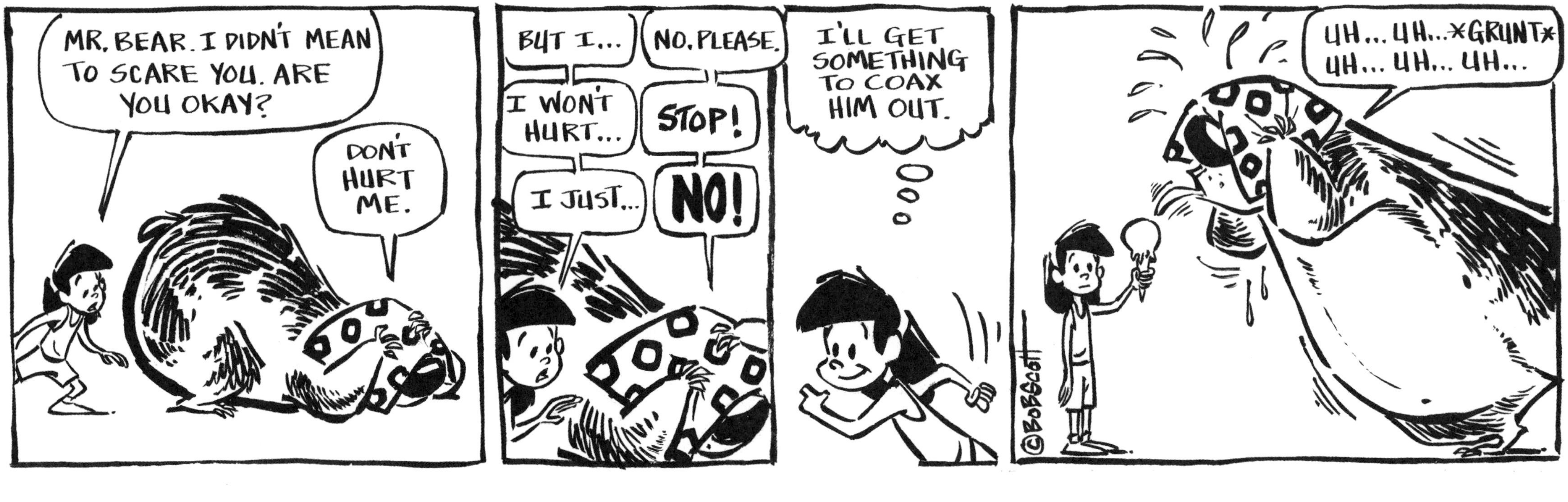
MR. BEAR. I DIDN'T MEAN TO SCARE YOU. ARE YOU OKAY?
DON'T HURT ME.
BUT I...
NO, PLEASE.
I WON'T HURT...
STOP!
I JUST...
NO!
I'LL GET SOMETHING TO COAX HIM OUT.
©BOBSCOTT
UH... UH... *GRUNT* UH... UH... UH...

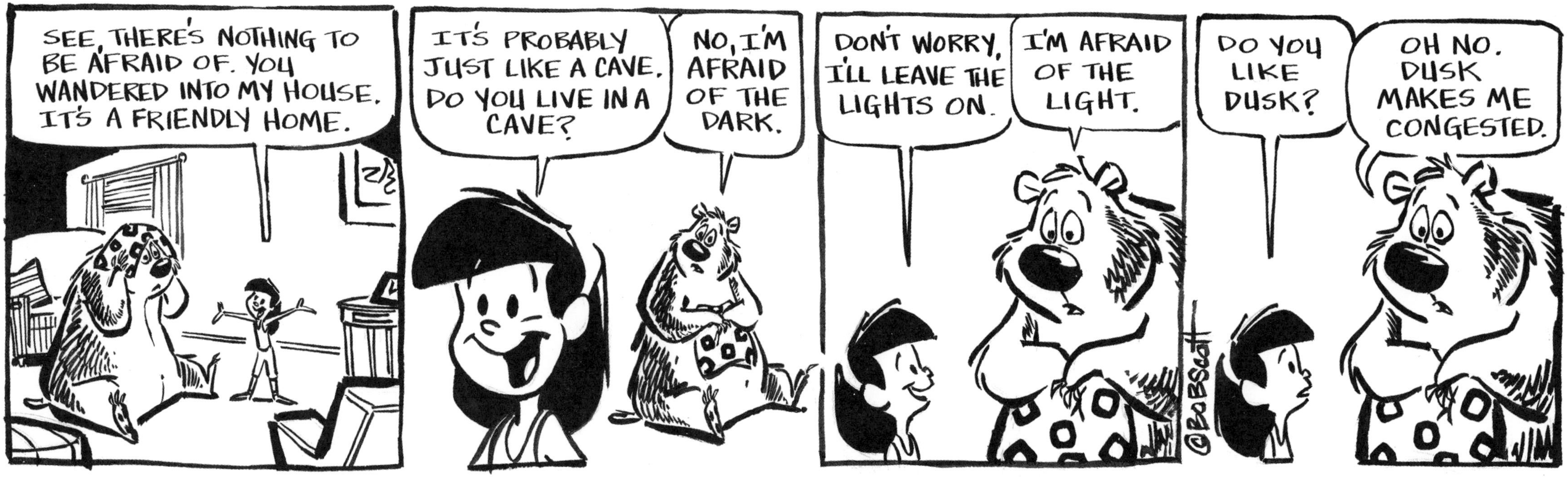
SEE, THERE'S NOTHING TO BE AFRAID OF. YOU WANDERED INTO MY HOUSE. IT'S A FRIENDLY HOME.
IT'S PROBABLY JUST LIKE A CAVE. DO YOU LIVE IN A CAVE?
NO, I'M AFRAID OF THE DARK.
DON'T WORRY, I'LL LEAVE THE LIGHTS ON.
I'M AFRAID OF THE LIGHT.
DO YOU LIKE DUSK?
OH NO. DUSK MAKES ME CONGESTED.
©BOBSCOTT

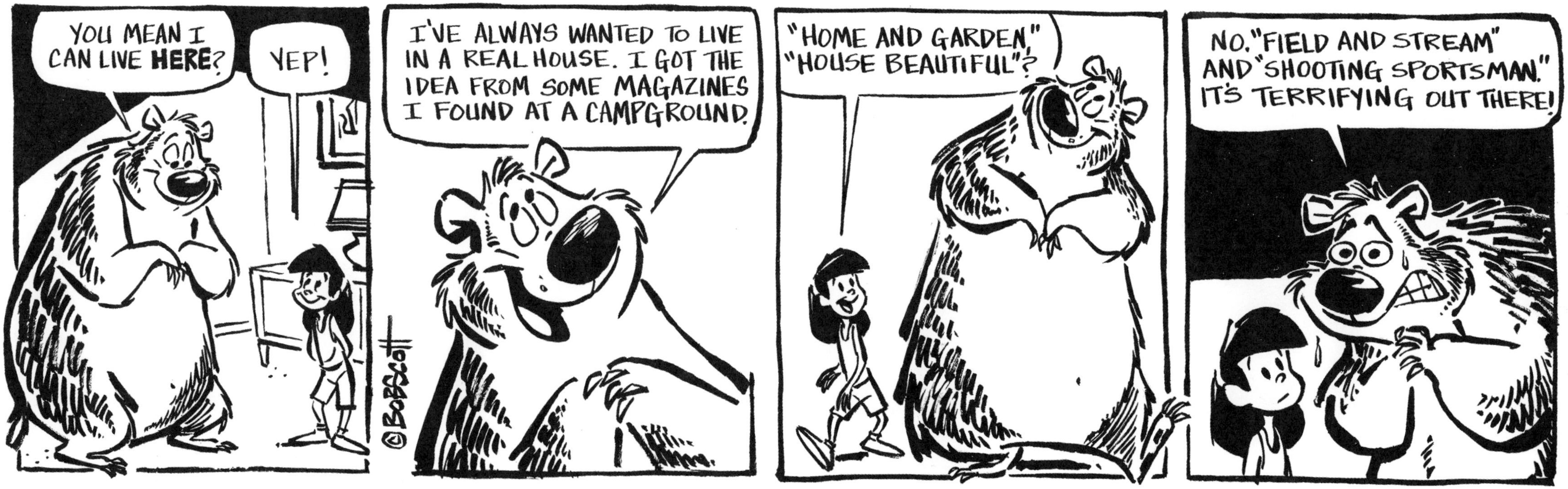
YOU MEAN I CAN LIVE **HERE**?
YEP!
©BOBSCOTT
I'VE ALWAYS WANTED TO LIVE IN A REAL HOUSE. I GOT THE IDEA FROM SOME MAGAZINES I FOUND AT A CAMPGROUND.
"HOME AND GARDEN," "HOUSE BEAUTIFUL"?
NO. "FIELD AND STREAM" AND "SHOOTING SPORTSMAN." IT'S TERRIFYING OUT THERE!

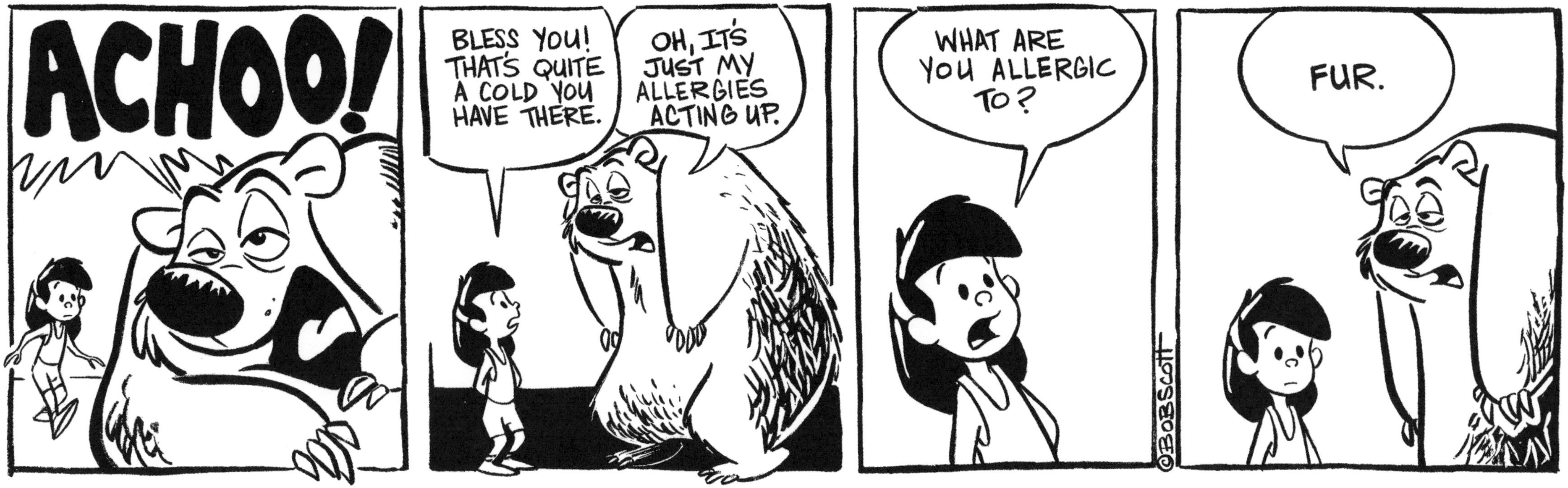
ACHOO!
BLESS YOU! THAT'S QUITE A COLD YOU HAVE THERE.
OH, IT'S JUST MY ALLERGIES ACTING UP.
WHAT ARE YOU ALLERGIC TO?
©BOBSCOTT
FUR.

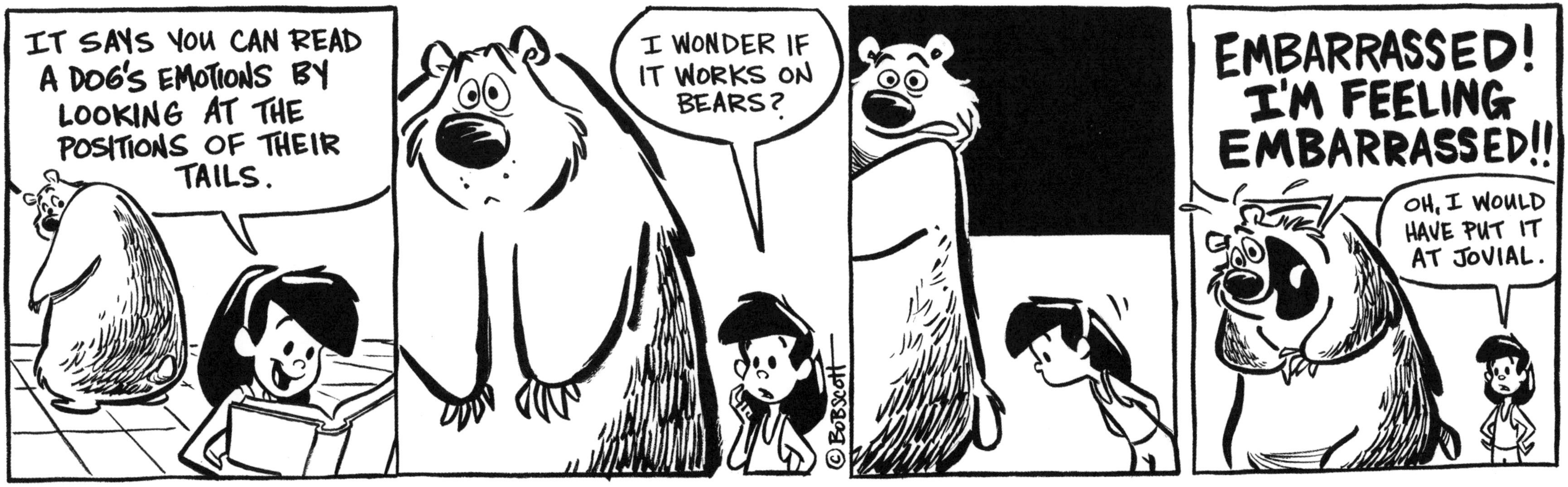
IT SAYS YOU CAN READ A DOG'S EMOTIONS BY LOOKING AT THE POSITIONS OF THEIR TAILS.
I WONDER IF IT WORKS ON BEARS?
©BOBSCOTT
EMBARRASSED! I'M FEELING EMBARRASSED!!
OH, I WOULD HAVE PUT IT AT JOVIAL.

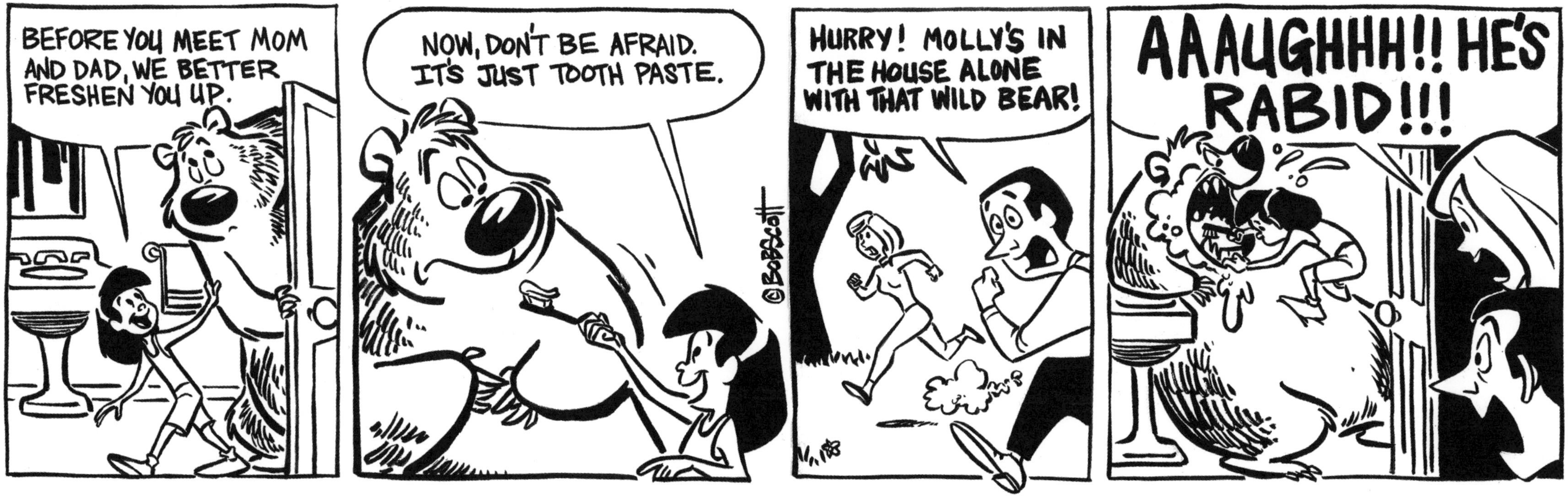
BEFORE YOU MEET MOM AND DAD, WE BETTER FRESHEN YOU UP.
NOW, DON'T BE AFRAID. IT'S JUST TOOTH PASTE.
© BOBSCOTT
HURRY! MOLLY'S IN THE HOUSE ALONE WITH THAT WILD BEAR!
AAAUGHHH!! HE'S RABID!!!

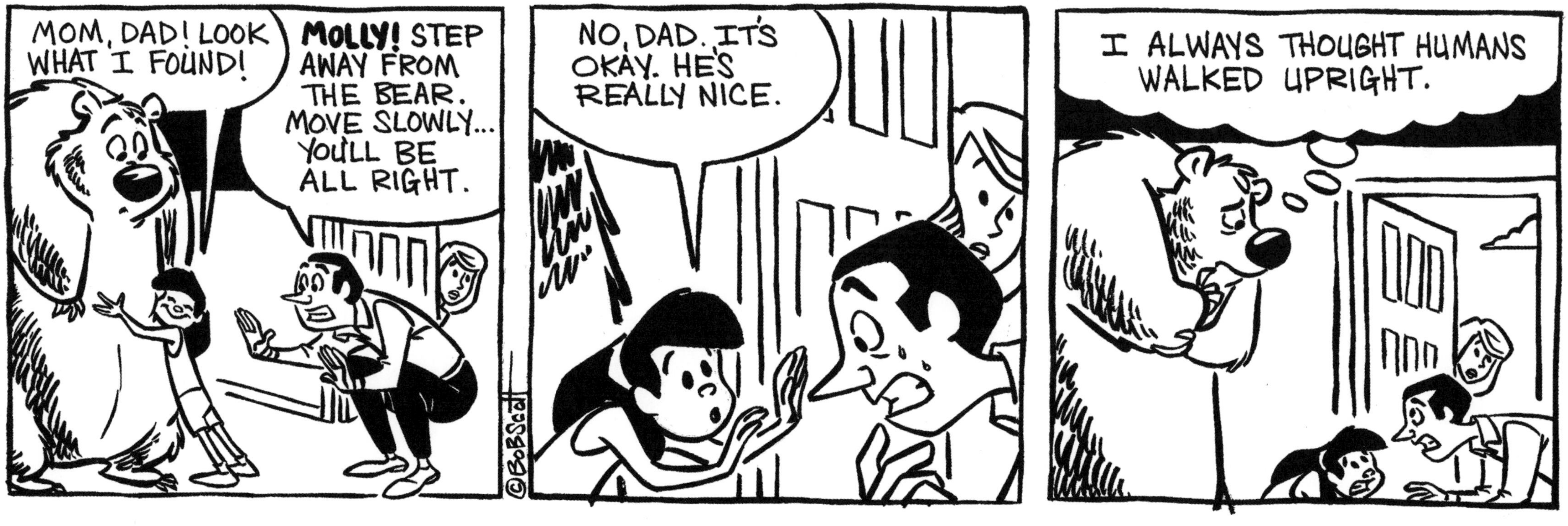
MOM, DAD! LOOK WHAT I FOUND!
MOLLY! STEP AWAY FROM THE BEAR. MOVE SLOWLY... YOU'LL BE ALL RIGHT.
© BOBSCOTT
NO, DAD. IT'S OKAY. HE'S REALLY NICE.
I ALWAYS THOUGHT HUMANS WALKED UPRIGHT.

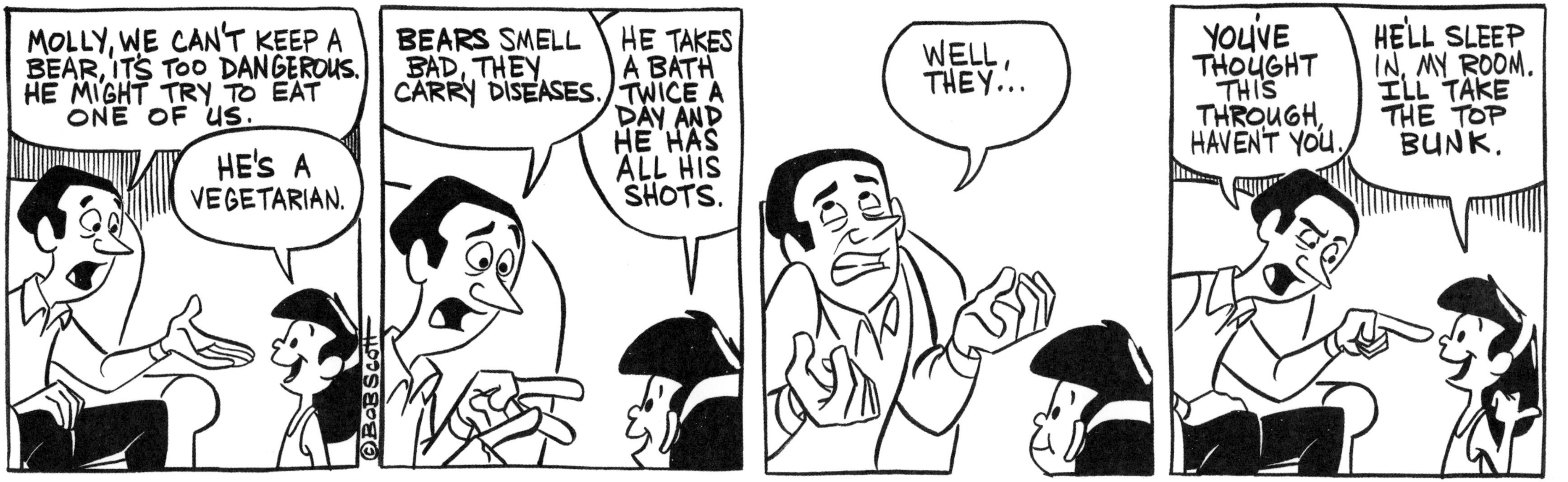
MOLLY, WE CAN'T KEEP A BEAR, IT'S TOO DANGEROUS. HE MIGHT TRY TO EAT ONE OF US.
HE'S A VEGETARIAN.
©BOBSCOTT
BEARS SMELL BAD, THEY CARRY DISEASES.
HE TAKES A BATH TWICE A DAY AND HE HAS ALL HIS SHOTS.
WELL, THEY...
YOU'VE THOUGHT THIS THROUGH, HAVEN'T YOU.
HE'LL SLEEP IN MY ROOM. I'LL TAKE THE TOP BUNK.

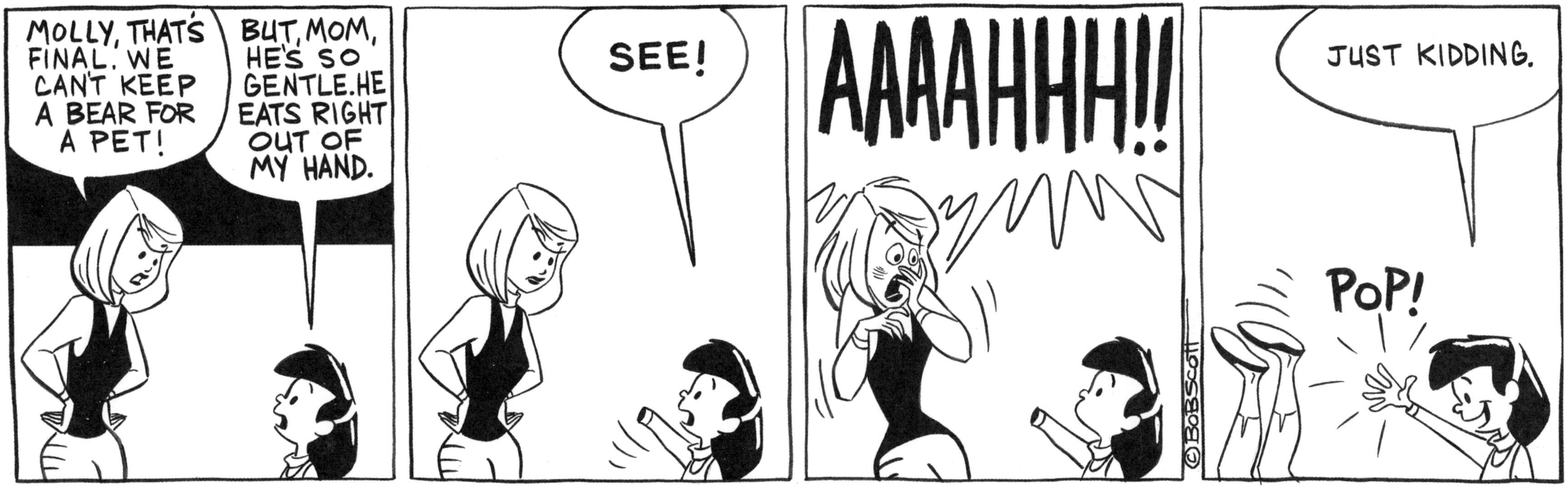
MOLLY, THAT'S FINAL. WE CAN'T KEEP A BEAR FOR A PET!
BUT, MOM, HE'S SO GENTLE. HE EATS RIGHT OUT OF MY HAND.
SEE!
AAAAHHH!!
©BOBSCOTT
JUST KIDDING.
POP!

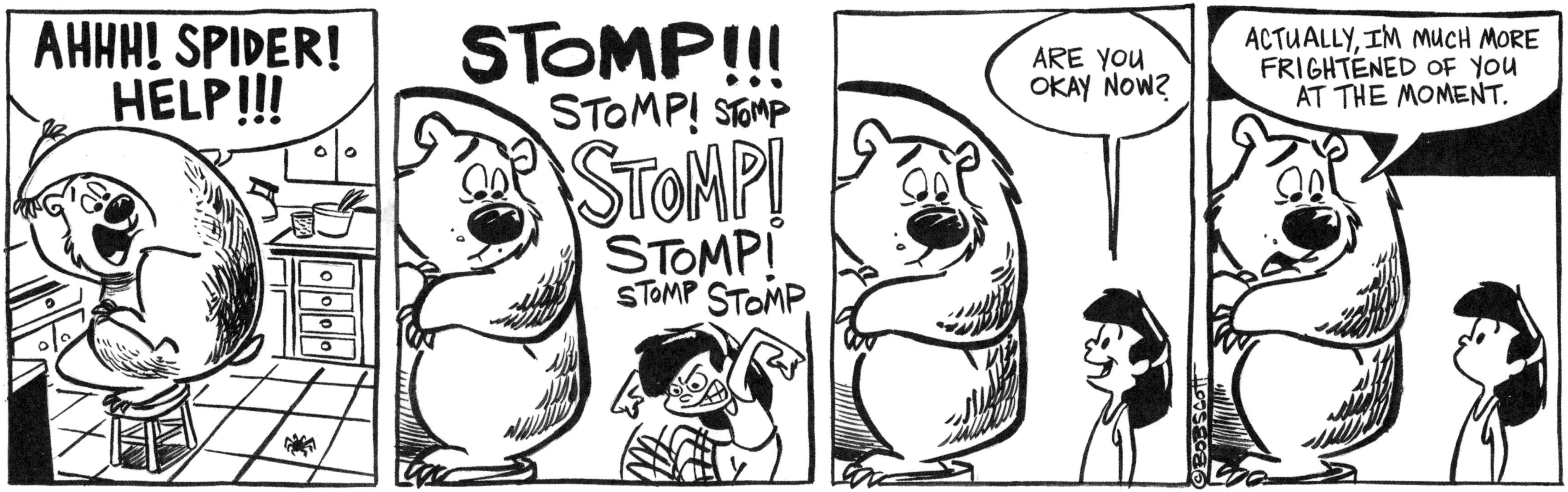
AHHH! SPIDER! HELP!!!
STOMP!!!
STOMP! STOMP
STOMP!
STOMP!
STOMP STOMP
ARE YOU OKAY NOW?
ACTUALLY, I'M MUCH MORE FRIGHTENED OF YOU AT THE MOMENT.
©BOBSCOTT

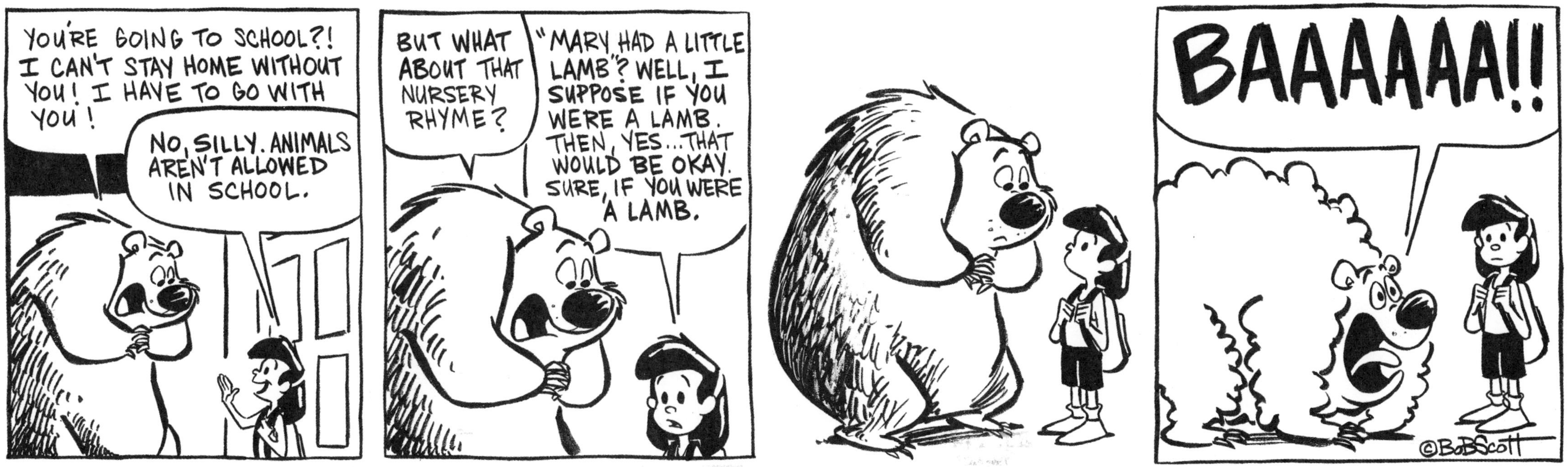
YOU'RE GOING TO SCHOOL?! I CAN'T STAY HOME WITHOUT YOU! I HAVE TO GO WITH YOU!
NO, SILLY. ANIMALS AREN'T ALLOWED IN SCHOOL.
BUT WHAT ABOUT THAT NURSERY RHYME?
"MARY HAD A LITTLE LAMB"? WELL, I SUPPOSE IF YOU WERE A LAMB. THEN, YES...THAT WOULD BE OKAY. SURE, IF YOU WERE A LAMB.
BAAAAAA!!
©BOBSCOTT

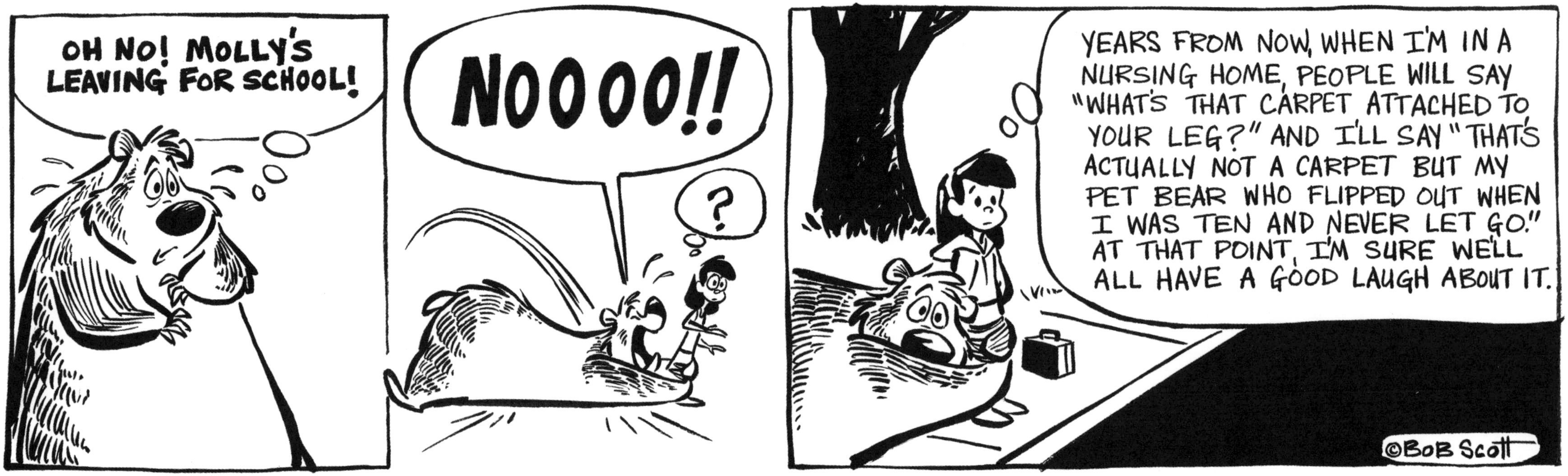
OH NO! MOLLY'S LEAVING FOR SCHOOL!
NOOOO!!
?
YEARS FROM NOW, WHEN I'M IN A NURSING HOME, PEOPLE WILL SAY "WHAT'S THAT CARPET ATTACHED TO YOUR LEG?" AND I'LL SAY "THAT'S ACTUALLY NOT A CARPET BUT MY PET BEAR WHO FLIPPED OUT WHEN I WAS TEN AND NEVER LET GO." AT THAT POINT, I'M SURE WE'LL ALL HAVE A GOOD LAUGH ABOUT IT.
©BOB SCOTT

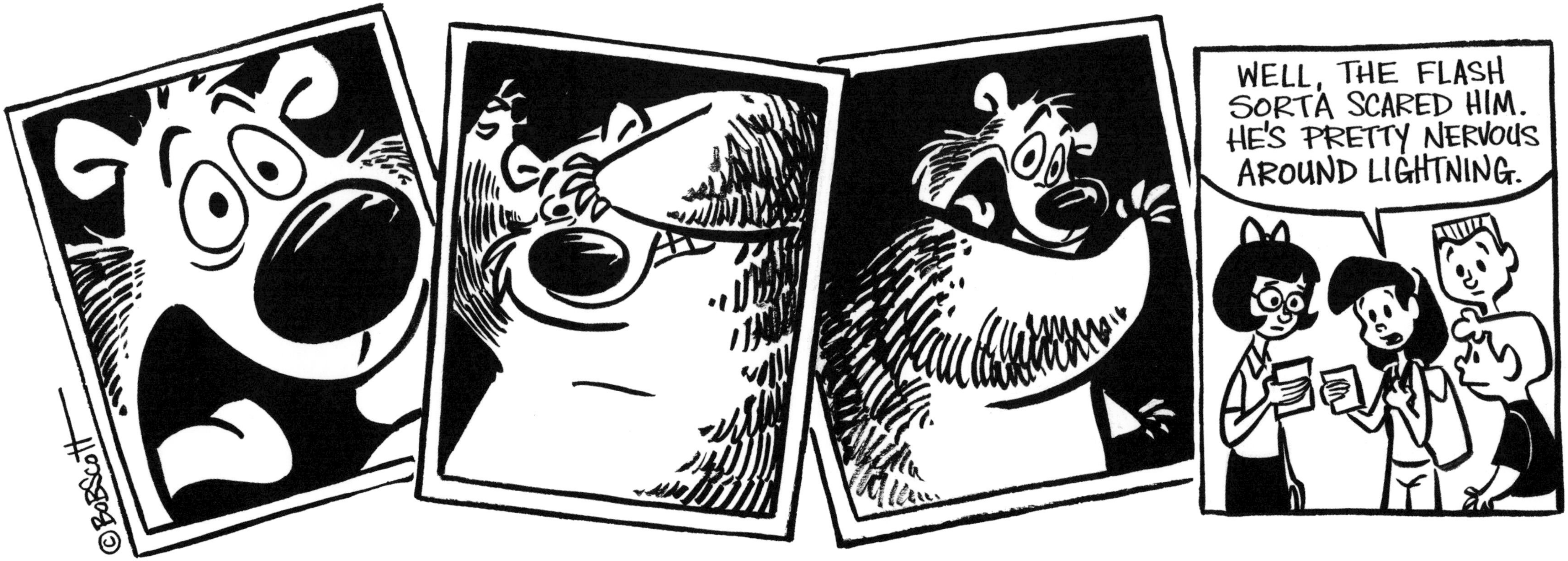
©BOBSCOTT
WELL, THE FLASH SORTA SCARED HIM. HE'S PRETTY NERVOUS AROUND LIGHTNING.

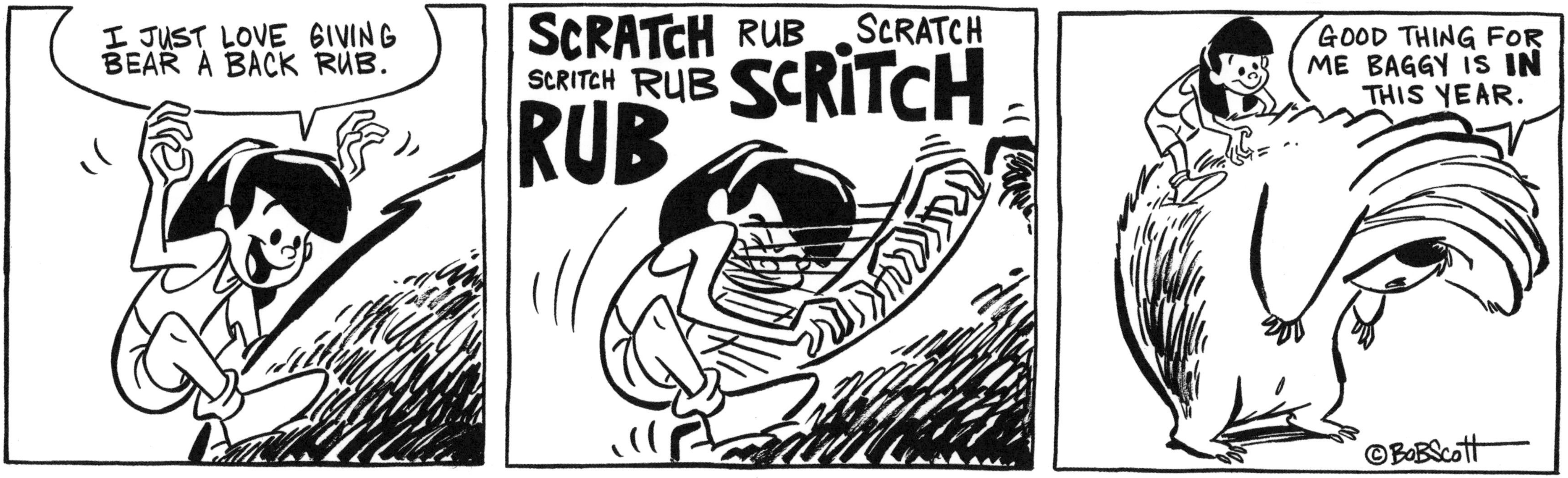
I JUST LOVE GIVING BEAR A BACK RUB.
SCRATCH RUB SCRATCH SCRITCH RUB SCRITCH RUB
GOOD THING FOR ME BAGGY IS **IN** THIS YEAR.
©BOBSCOTT

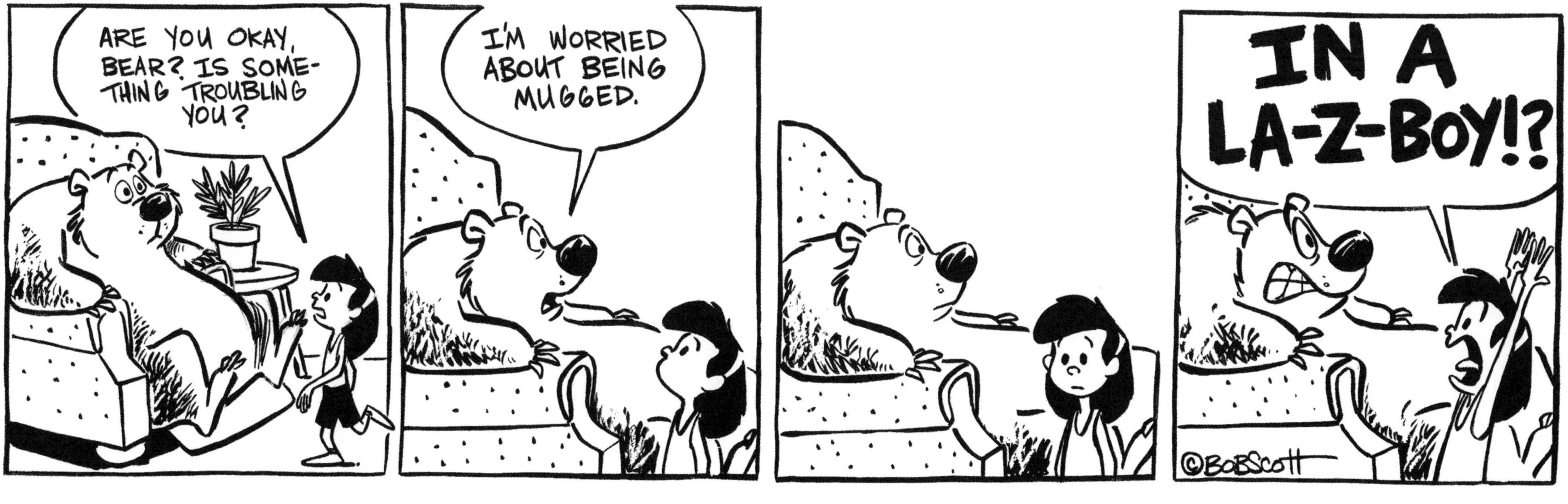
ARE YOU OKAY, BEAR? IS SOME-THING TROUBLING YOU?
I'M WORRIED ABOUT BEING MUGGED.
IN A LA-Z-BOY!?
©BOBSCOTT

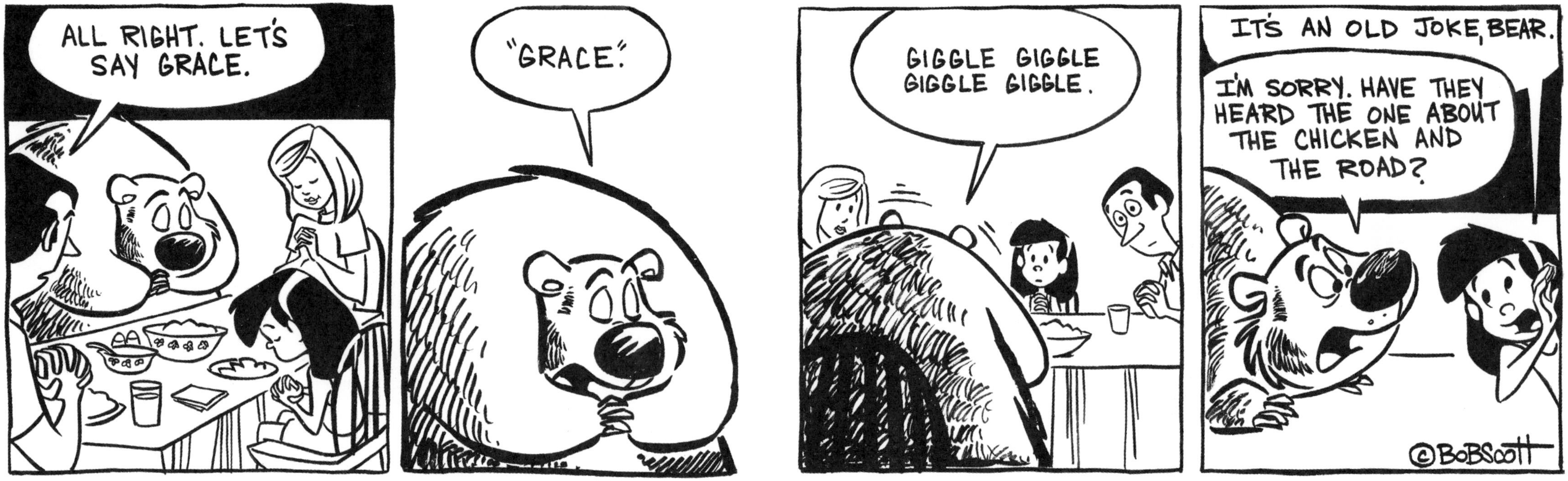
ALL RIGHT. LET'S SAY GRACE.
"GRACE."
GIGGLE GIGGLE GIGGLE GIGGLE.
IT'S AN OLD JOKE, BEAR.
I'M SORRY. HAVE THEY HEARD THE ONE ABOUT THE CHICKEN AND THE ROAD?
©BOBSCOTT

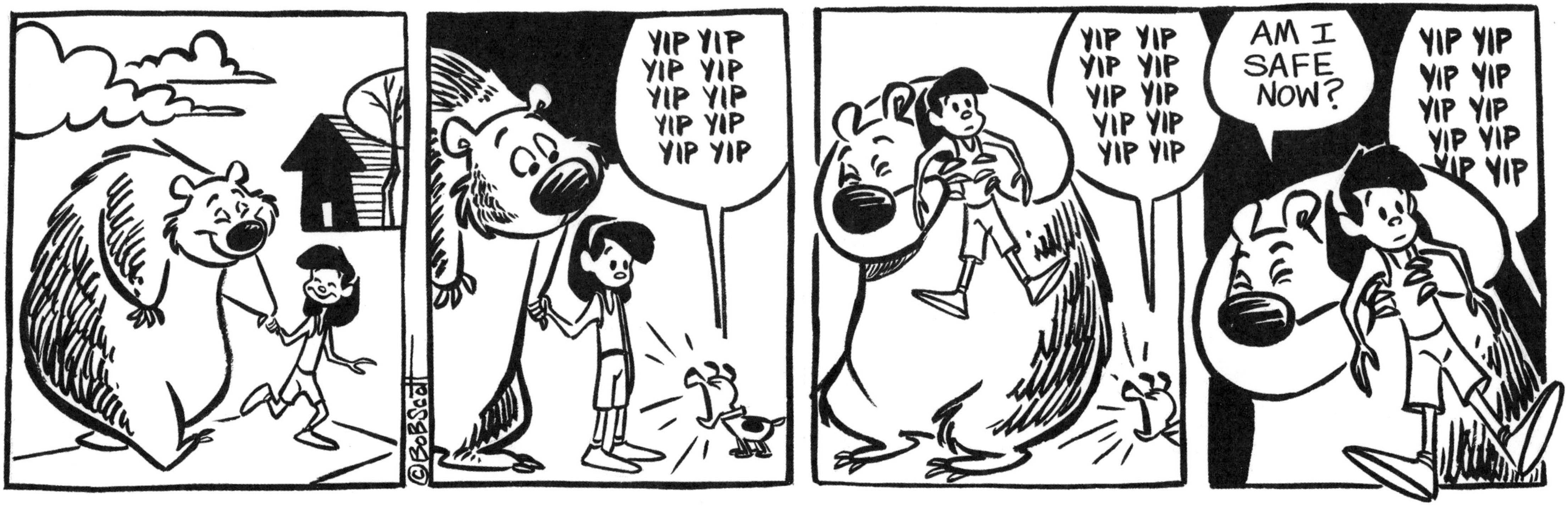
©BOBSCOTT
YIP YIP YIP YIP YIP YIP YIP YIP YIP YIP
YIP YIP YIP YIP YIP YIP YIP YIP YIP YIP
AM I SAFE NOW?
YIP YIP YIP YIP YIP YIP YIP YIP YIP YIP

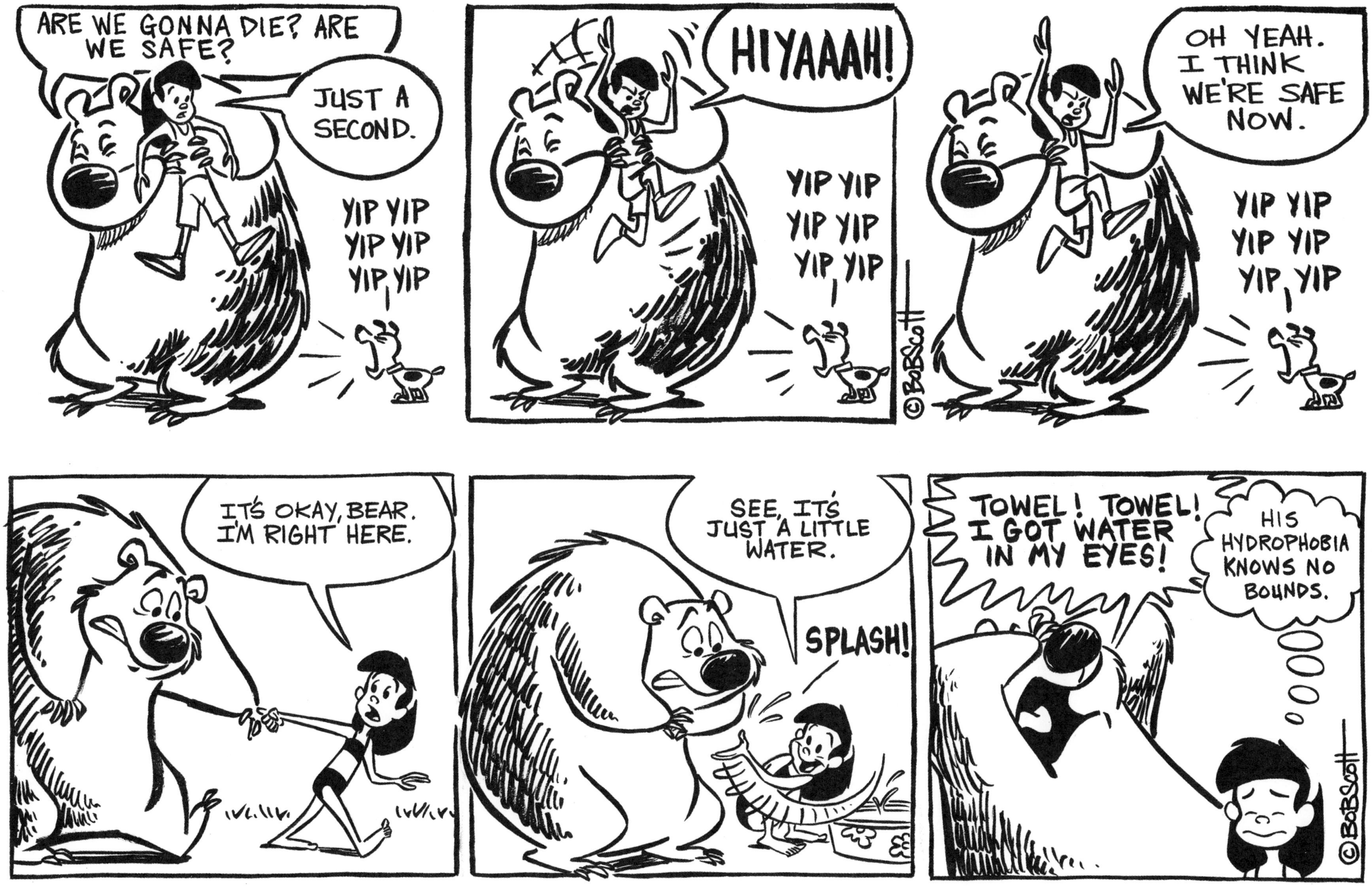
ARE WE GONNA DIE? ARE WE SAFE?
JUST A SECOND.
YIP YIP YIP YIP YIP YIP
HIYAAAH!
YIP YIP YIP YIP YIP YIP
©BoBScott
OH YEAH. I THINK WE'RE SAFE NOW.
YIP YIP YIP YIP YIP YIP
IT'S OKAY, BEAR. I'M RIGHT HERE.
SEE, IT'S JUST A LITTLE WATER.
SPLASH!
TOWEL! TOWEL! I GOT WATER IN MY EYES!
HIS HYDROPHOBIA KNOWS NO BOUNDS.
©BoBScott

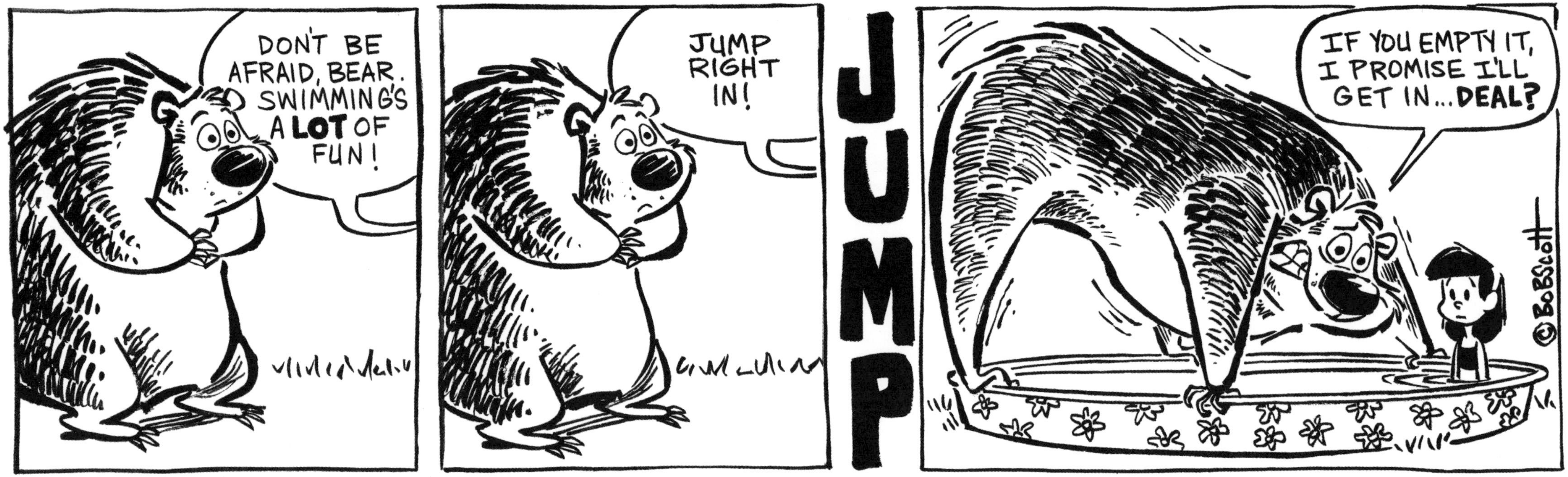
DON'T BE AFRAID, BEAR. SWIMMING'S A LOT OF FUN!
JUMP RIGHT IN!
JUMP
IF YOU EMPTY IT, I PROMISE I'LL GET IN... DEAL?
© BOBSCOTT

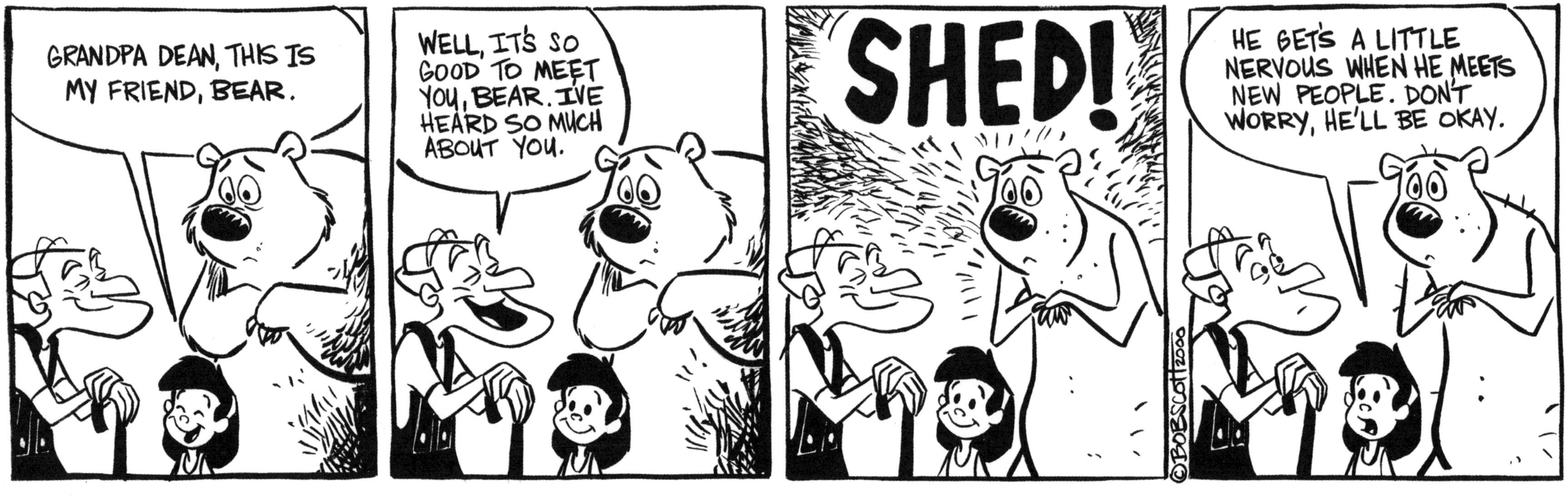
GRANDPA DEAN, THIS IS MY FRIEND, BEAR.
WELL, IT'S SO GOOD TO MEET YOU, BEAR. I'VE HEARD SO MUCH ABOUT YOU.
SHED!
©BOBSCOTT2000
HE GETS A LITTLE NERVOUS WHEN HE MEETS NEW PEOPLE. DON'T WORRY, HE'LL BE OKAY.

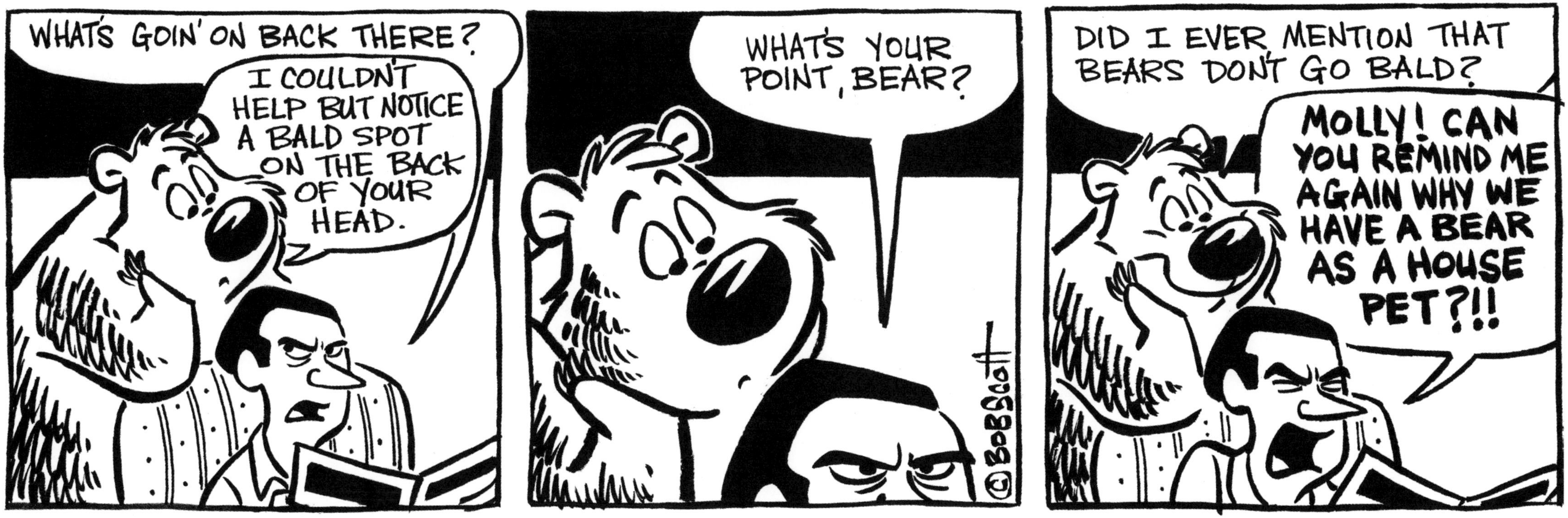
WHAT'S GOIN' ON BACK THERE?
I COULDN'T HELP BUT NOTICE A BALD SPOT ON THE BACK OF YOUR HEAD.
WHAT'S YOUR POINT, BEAR?
© BOBSCOTT
DID I EVER MENTION THAT BEARS DON'T GO BALD?
MOLLY! CAN YOU REMIND ME AGAIN WHY WE HAVE A BEAR AS A HOUSE PET?!!

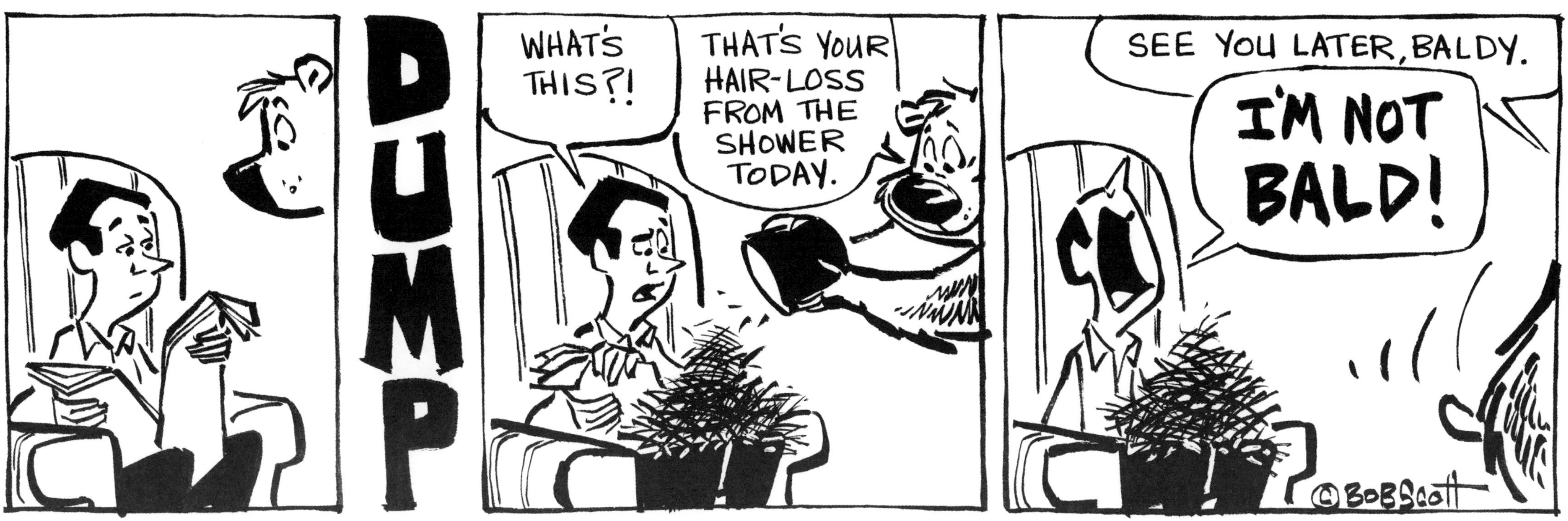
DUMP
WHAT'S THIS?!
THAT'S YOUR HAIR-LOSS FROM THE SHOWER TODAY.
SEE YOU LATER, BALDY.
I'M NOT BALD!
© BOBSCOTT

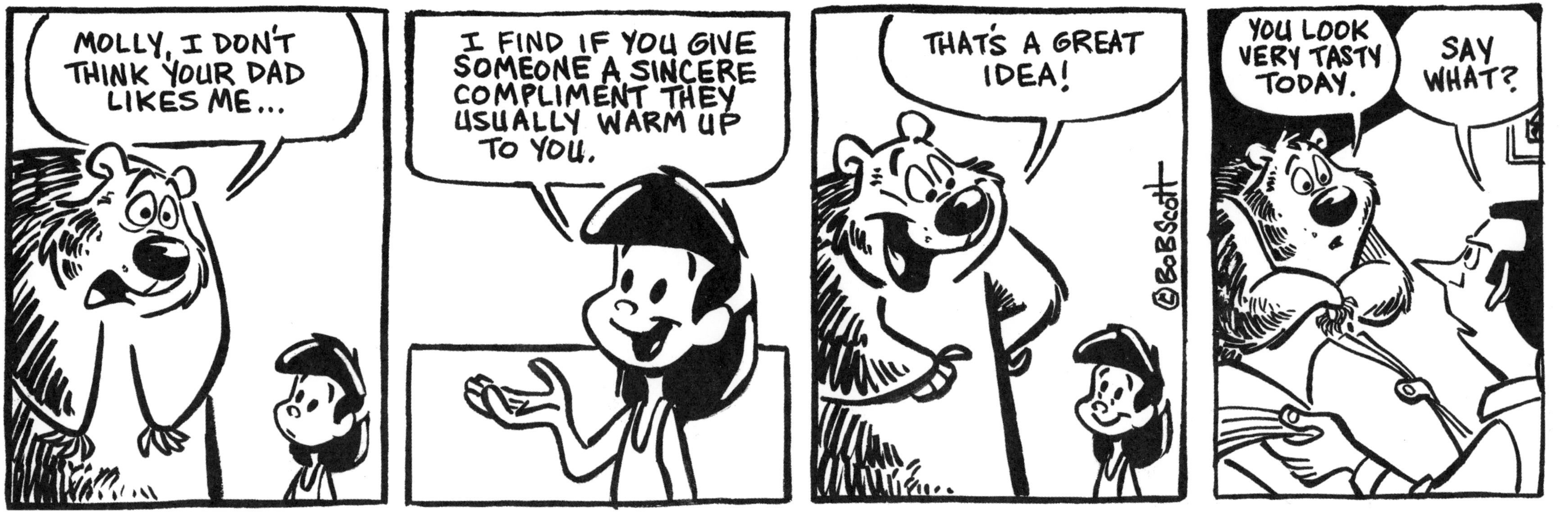
MOLLY, I DON'T THINK YOUR DAD LIKES ME...
I FIND IF YOU GIVE SOMEONE A SINCERE COMPLIMENT THEY USUALLY WARM UP TO YOU.
THAT'S A GREAT IDEA!
©BOBSCOTT
YOU LOOK VERY TASTY TODAY.
SAY WHAT?

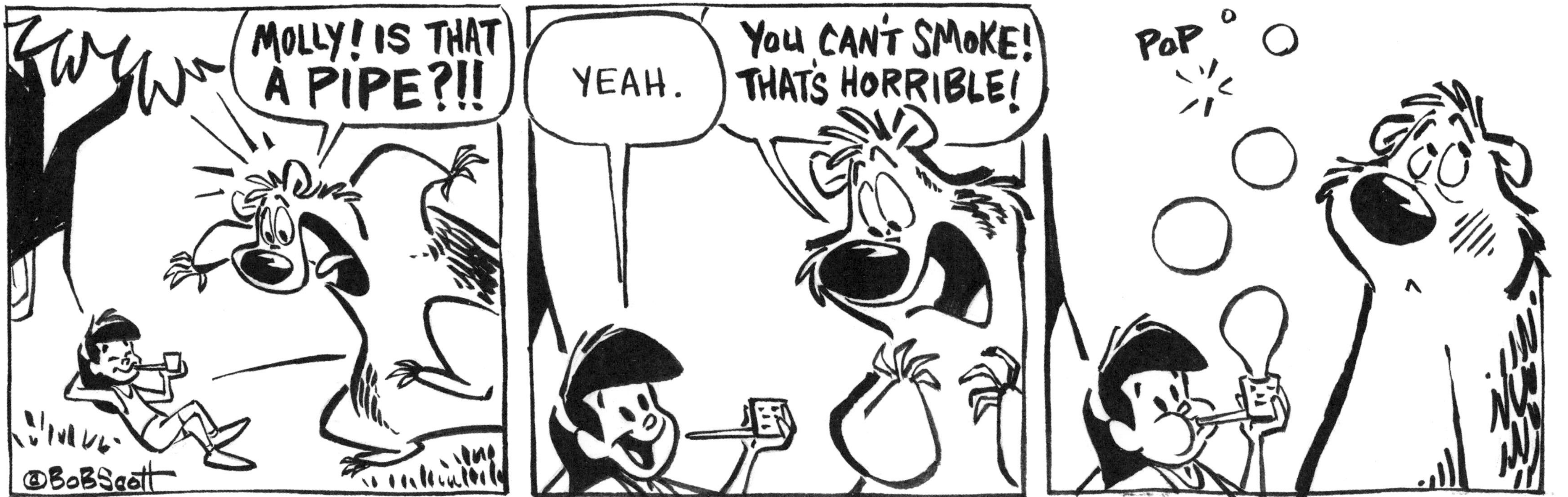
MOLLY! IS THAT A PIPE?!!
©BOBSCOTT
YEAH.
YOU CAN'T SMOKE! THAT'S HORRIBLE!
POP

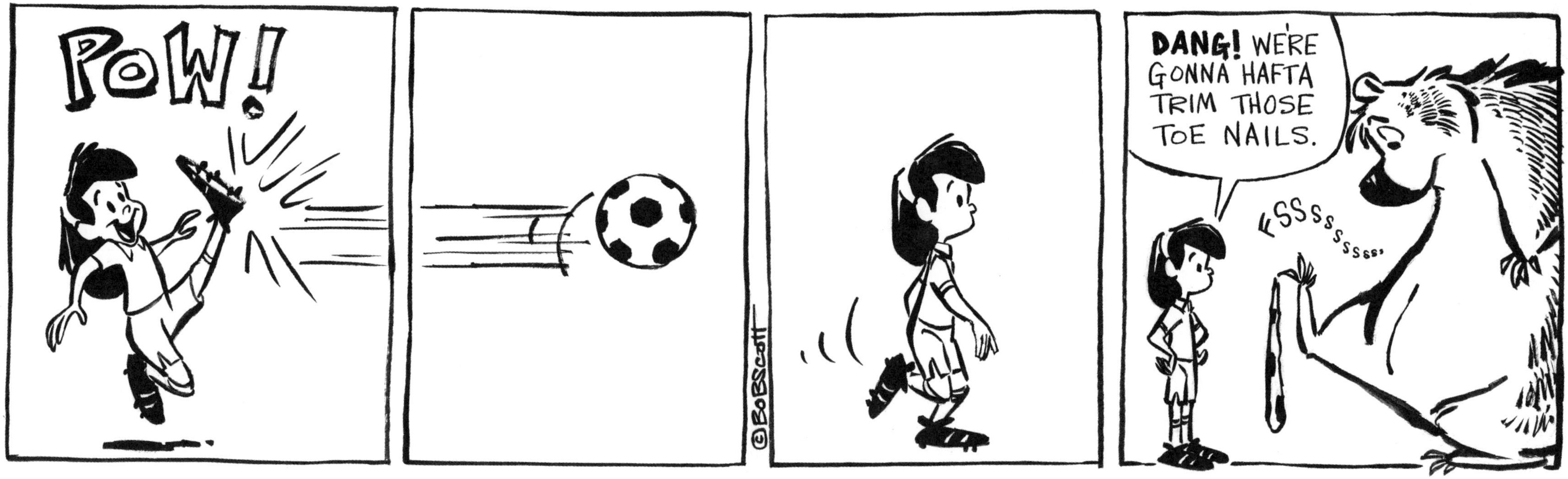
POW!
©BOBSCOTT
DANG! WE'RE GONNA HAFTA TRIM THOSE TOE NAILS.
FSSssssssss

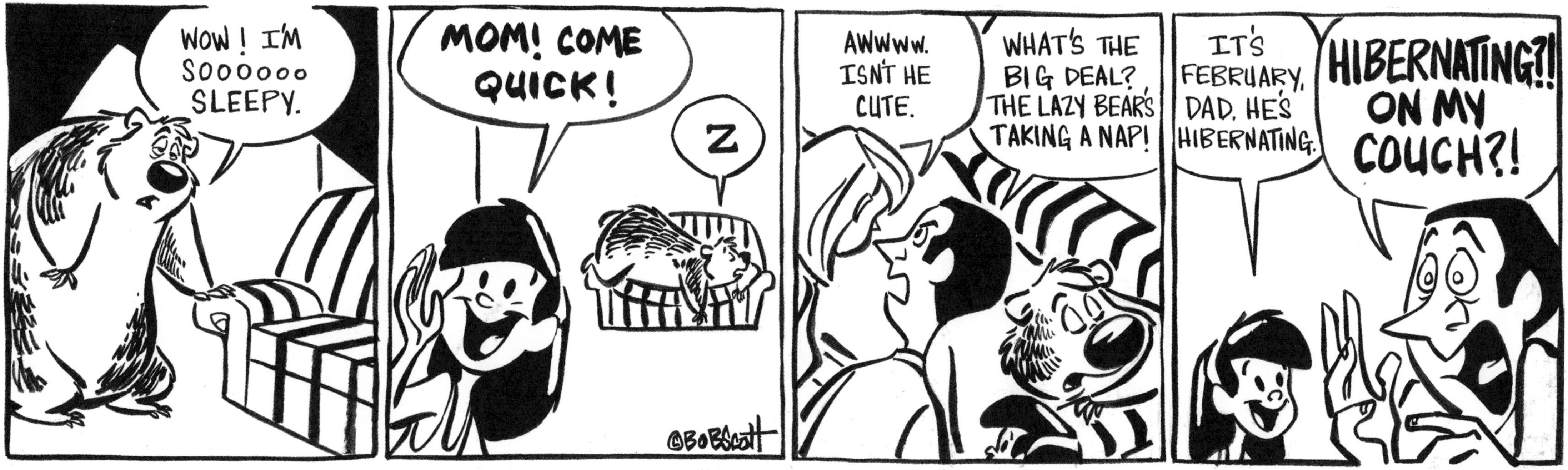
WOW! I'M SOOOOOO SLEEPY.
MOM! COME QUICK!
Z
©BOBSCOTT
AWWWW. ISN'T HE CUTE.
WHAT'S THE BIG DEAL? THE LAZY BEAR'S TAKING A NAP!
IT'S FEBRUARY, DAD. HE'S HIBERNATING.
HIBERNATING?! ON MY COUCH?!

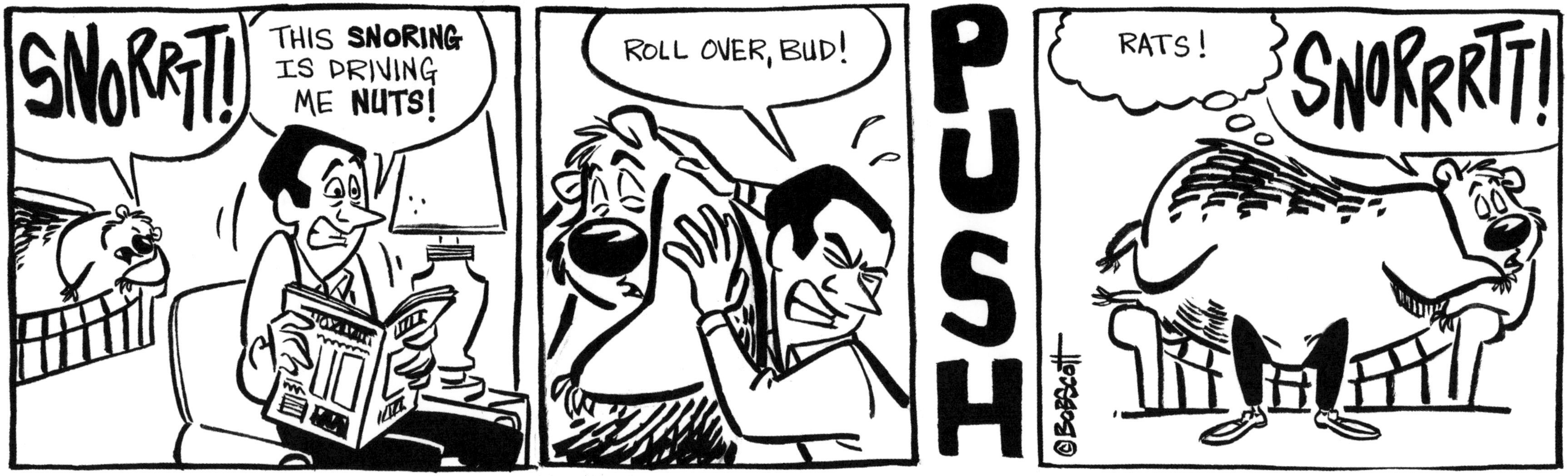
SNORRTT!
THIS SNORING IS DRIVING ME NUTS!
ROLL OVER, BUD!
PUSH
RATS!
SNORRRTT!
©BOBSCOTT

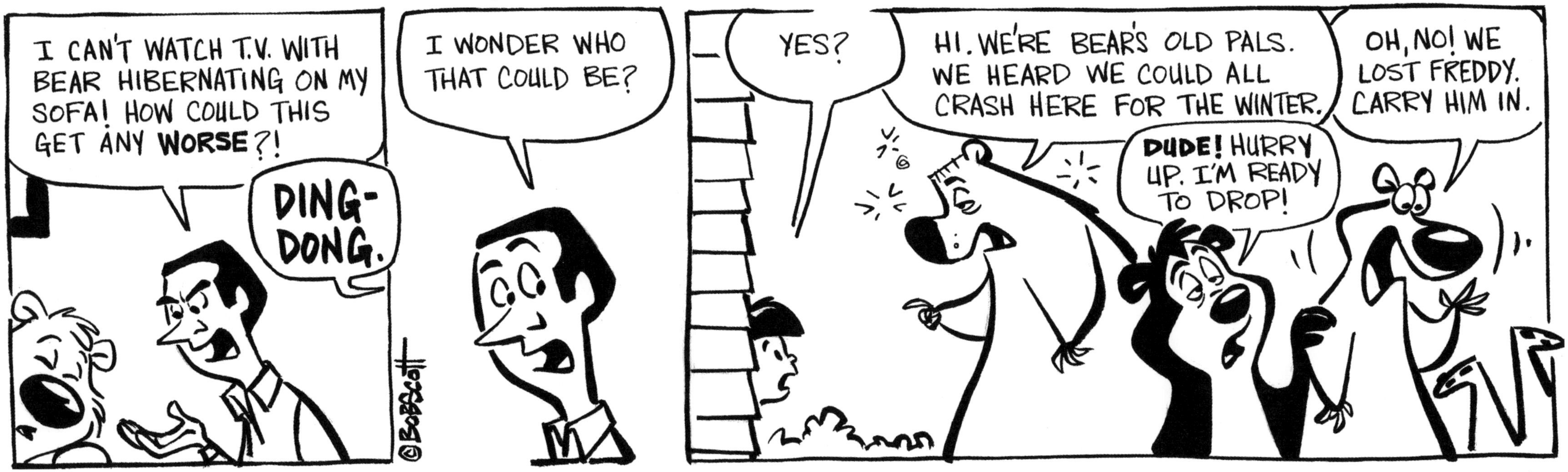
I CAN'T WATCH T.V. WITH BEAR HIBERNATING ON MY SOFA! HOW COULD THIS GET ANY WORSE?!
DING-DONG.
©BOBSCOTT
I WONDER WHO THAT COULD BE?
YES?
HI. WE'RE BEAR'S OLD PALS. WE HEARD WE COULD ALL CRASH HERE FOR THE WINTER.
DUDE! HURRY UP. I'M READY TO DROP!
OH, NO! WE LOST FREDDY. CARRY HIM IN.

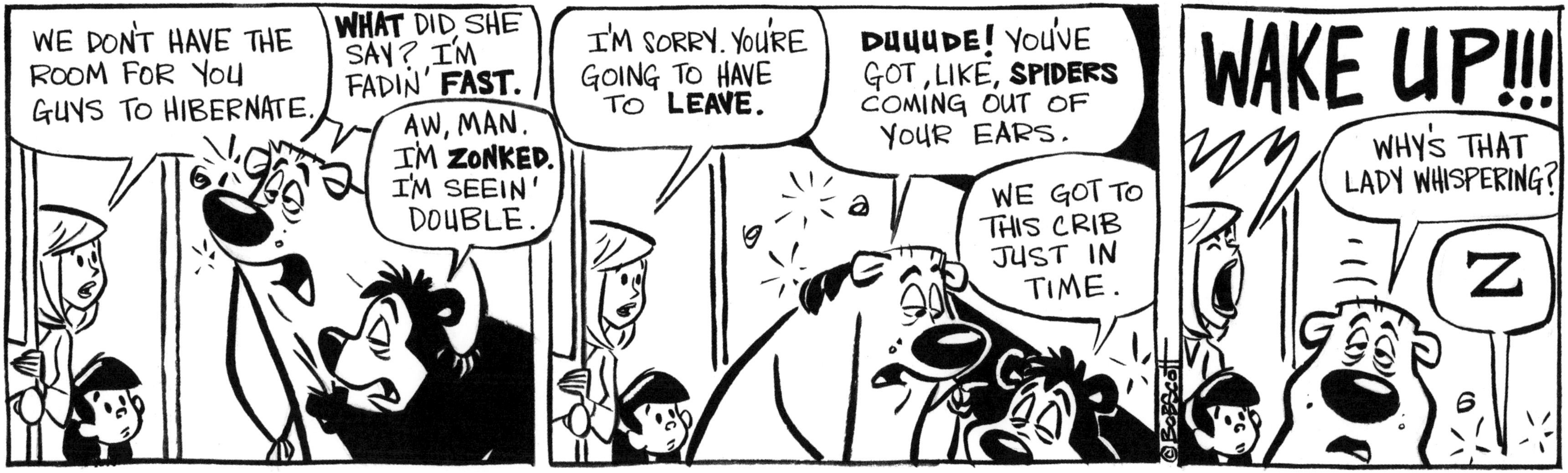
WE DON'T HAVE THE ROOM FOR YOU GUYS TO HIBERNATE.
WHAT DID SHE SAY? I'M FADIN' FAST.
AW, MAN. I'M ZONKED. I'M SEEIN' DOUBLE.
I'M SORRY. YOU'RE GOING TO HAVE TO LEAVE.
DUUUDE! YOU'VE GOT, LIKE, SPIDERS COMING OUT OF YOUR EARS.
WE GOT TO THIS CRIB JUST IN TIME.
©BOBSCOTT
WAKE UP!!!
WHY'S THAT LADY WHISPERING?
Z

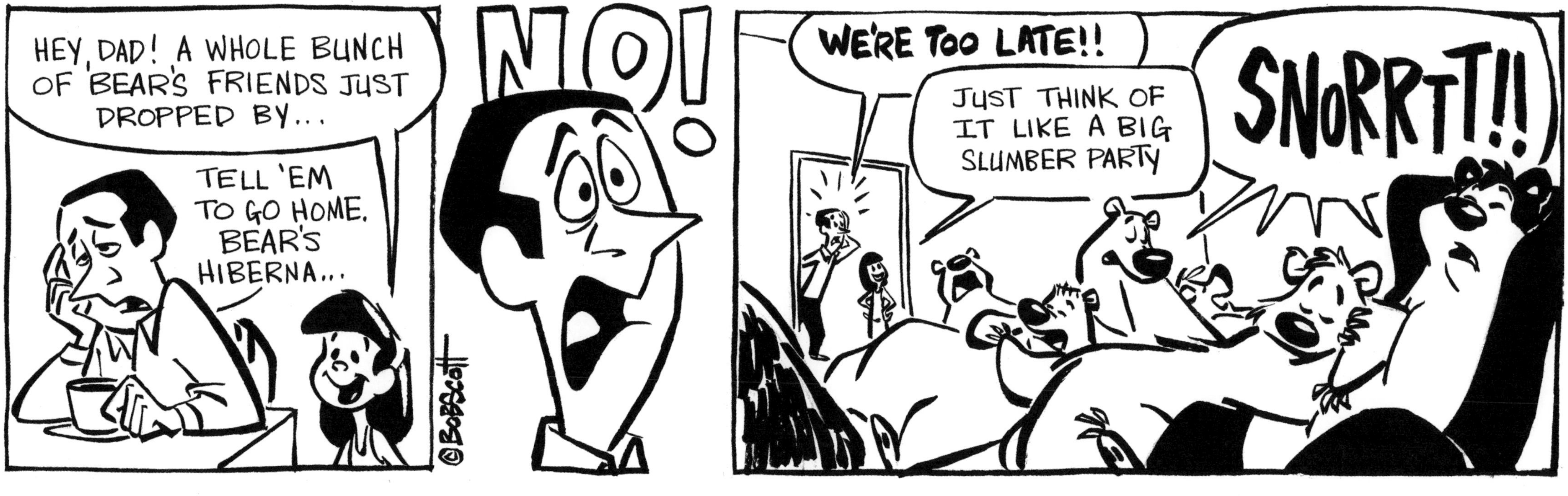
HEY, DAD! A WHOLE BUNCH OF BEAR'S FRIENDS JUST DROPPED BY...
TELL 'EM TO GO HOME. BEAR'S HIBERNA...
©BOBSCOTT
NO!
WE'RE TOO LATE!!
JUST THINK OF IT LIKE A BIG SLUMBER PARTY
SNORRTT!!

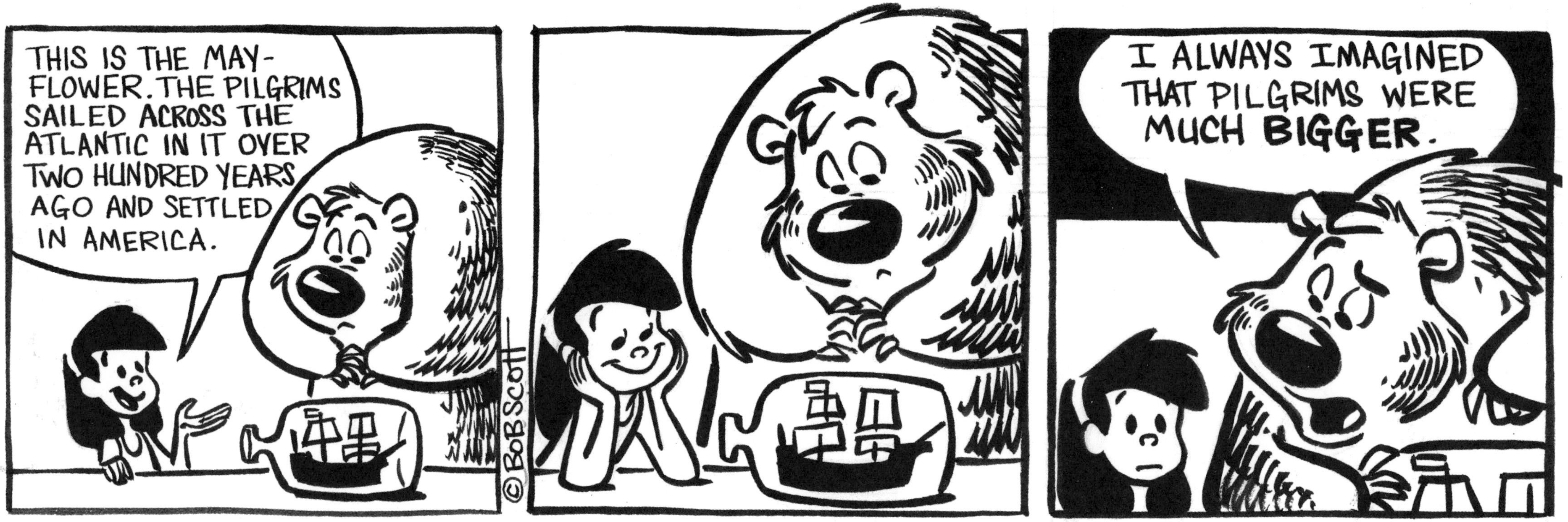
THIS IS THE MAY-FLOWER. THE PILGRIMS SAILED ACROSS THE ATLANTIC IN IT OVER TWO HUNDRED YEARS AGO AND SETTLED IN AMERICA.
© BOB SCOTT
I ALWAYS IMAGINED THAT PILGRIMS WERE MUCH **BIGGER**.

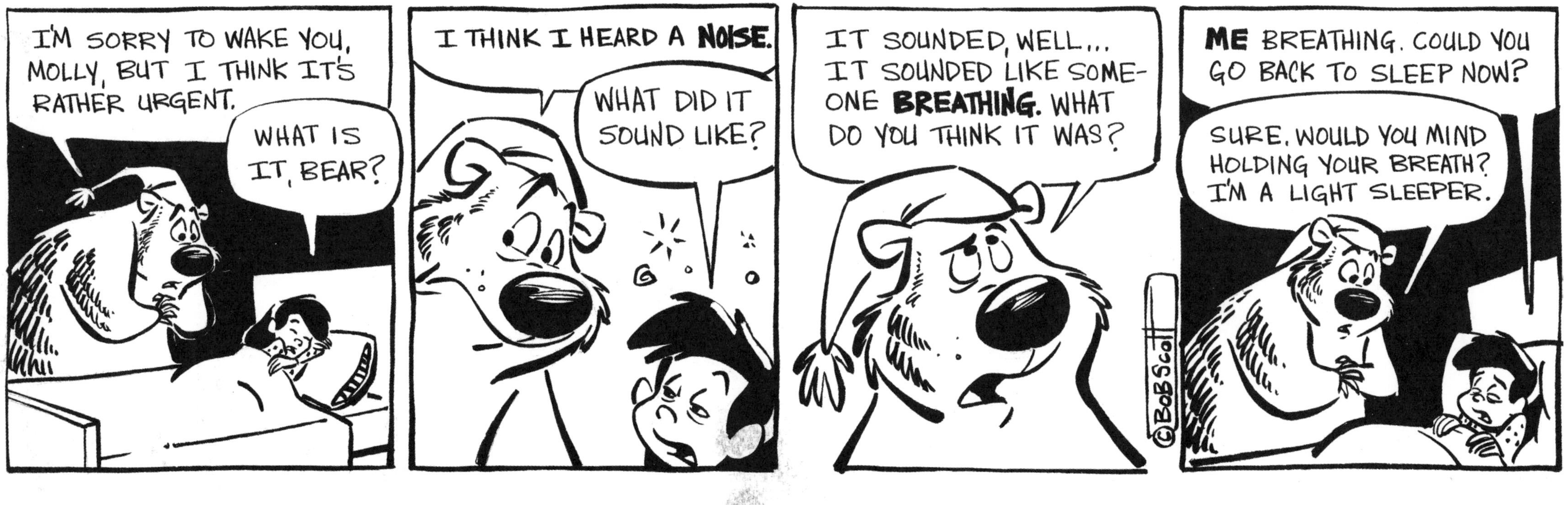
I'M SORRY TO WAKE YOU, MOLLY, BUT I THINK IT'S RATHER URGENT.
WHAT IS IT, BEAR?
I THINK I HEARD A **NOISE**.
WHAT DID IT SOUND LIKE?
IT SOUNDED, WELL... IT SOUNDED LIKE SOME-ONE **BREATHING**. WHAT DO YOU THINK IT WAS?
© BOB SCOTT
ME BREATHING. COULD YOU GO BACK TO SLEEP NOW?
SURE. WOULD YOU MIND HOLDING YOUR BREATH? I'M A LIGHT SLEEPER.

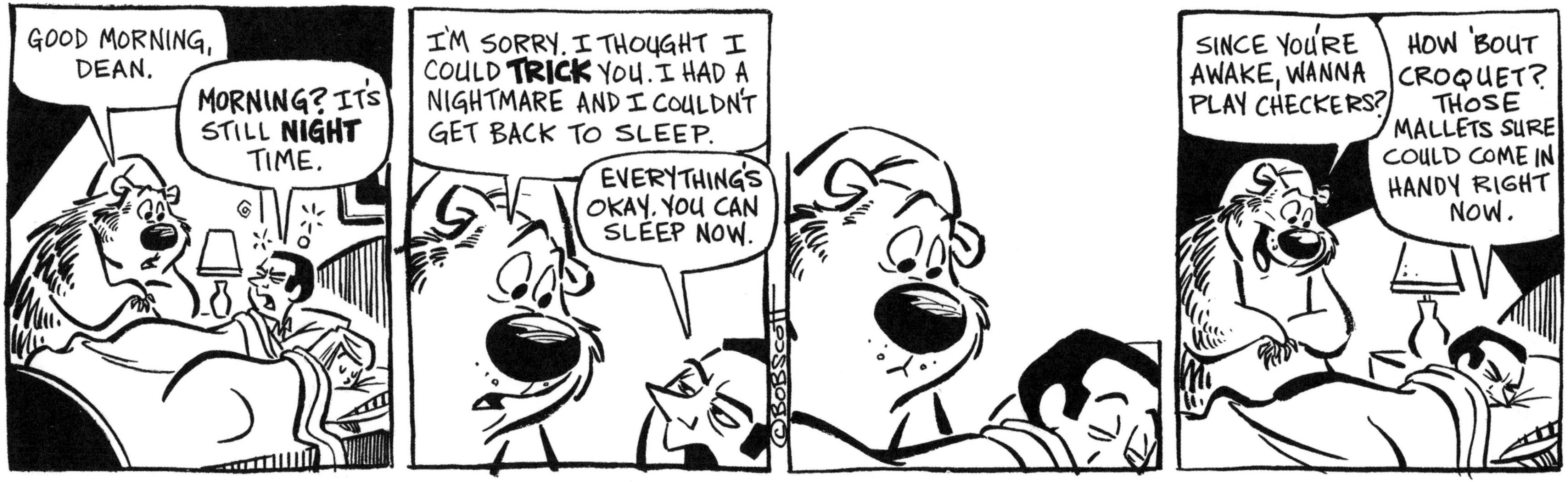
GOOD MORNING, DEAN.
MORNING? IT'S STILL NIGHT TIME.
I'M SORRY. I THOUGHT I COULD TRICK YOU. I HAD A NIGHTMARE AND I COULDN'T GET BACK TO SLEEP.
EVERYTHING'S OKAY. YOU CAN SLEEP NOW.
©BOBSCOTT
SINCE YOU'RE AWAKE, WANNA PLAY CHECKERS?
HOW 'BOUT CROQUET? THOSE MALLETS SURE COULD COME IN HANDY RIGHT NOW.

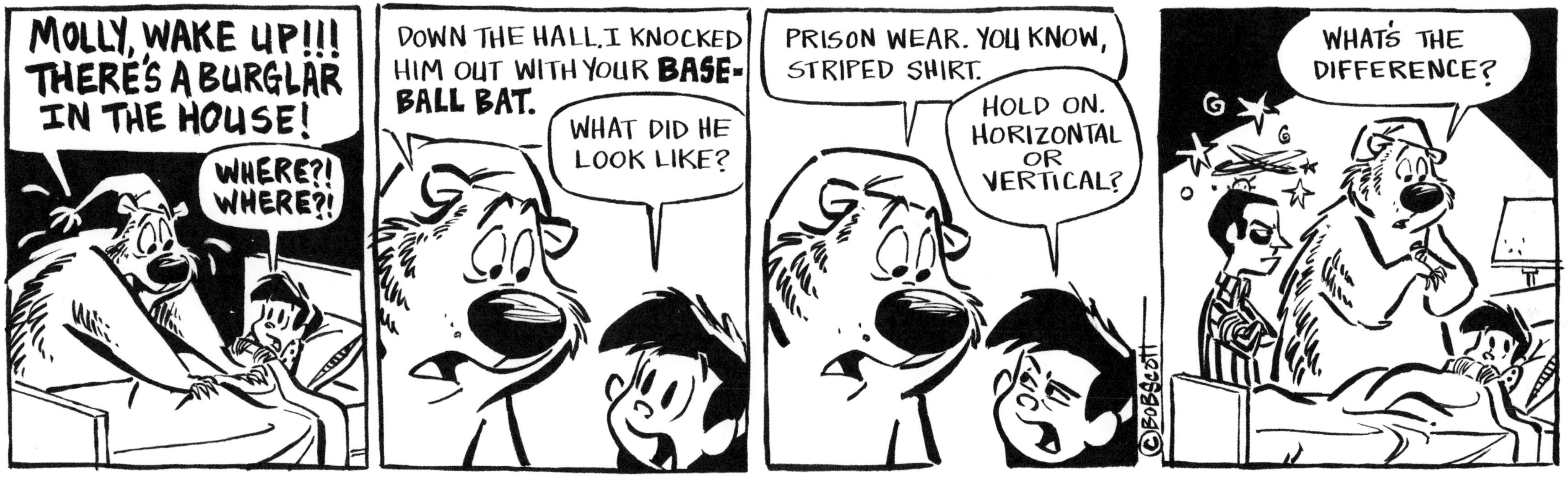
MOLLY, WAKE UP!!! THERE'S A BURGLAR IN THE HOUSE!
WHERE?! WHERE?!
DOWN THE HALL. I KNOCKED HIM OUT WITH YOUR BASE-BALL BAT.
WHAT DID HE LOOK LIKE?
PRISON WEAR. YOU KNOW, STRIPED SHIRT.
HOLD ON. HORIZONTAL OR VERTICAL?
©BOBSCOTT
WHAT'S THE DIFFERENCE?

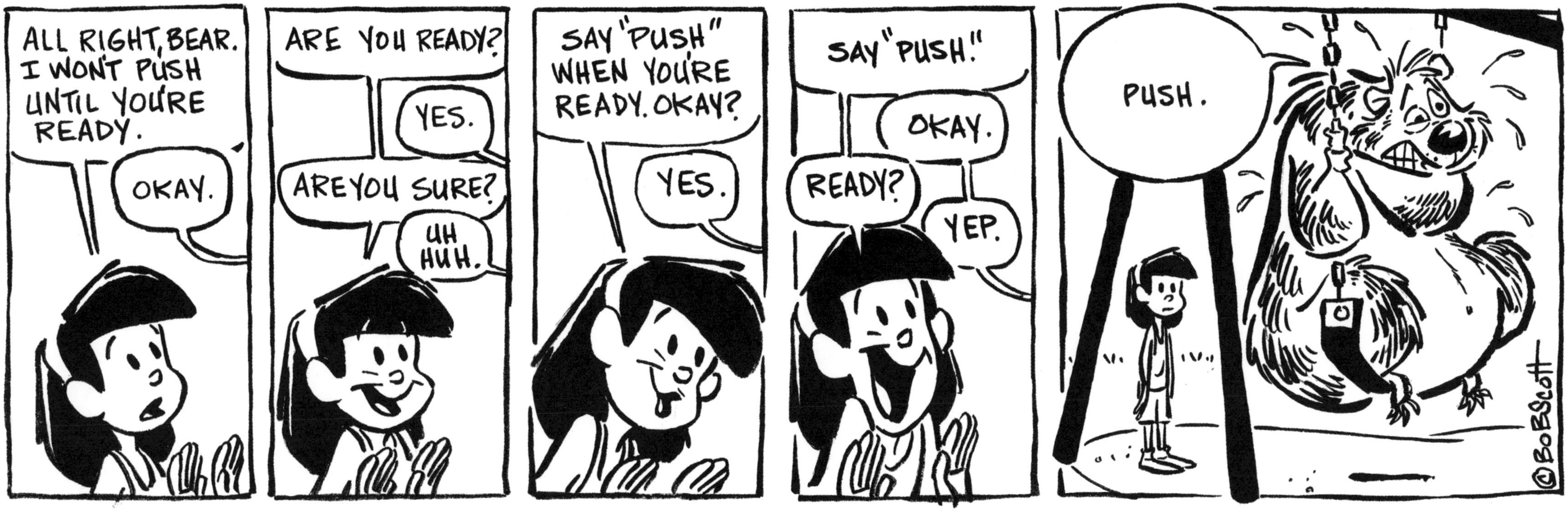
ALL RIGHT, BEAR. I WON'T PUSH UNTIL YOU'RE READY.
OKAY.
ARE YOU READY?
YES.
ARE YOU SURE?
UH HUH.
SAY "PUSH" WHEN YOU'RE READY. OKAY?
YES.
SAY "PUSH!"
OKAY.
READY?
YEP.
PUSH.
©BOBSCOTT

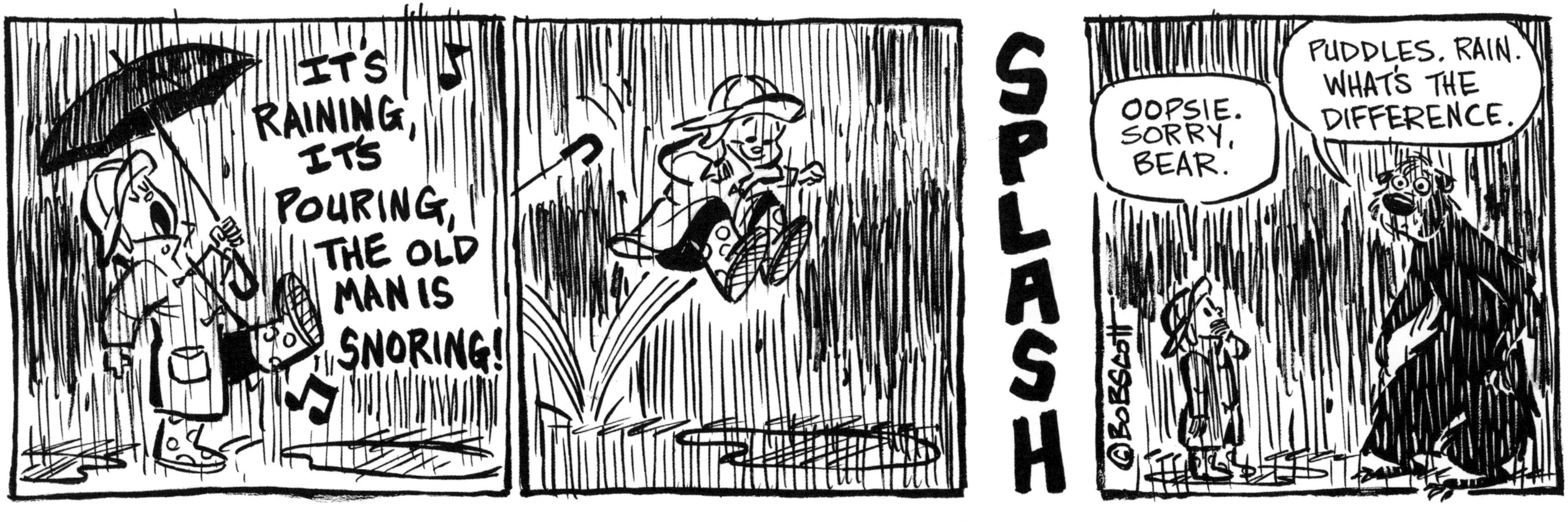
IT'S RAINING, IT'S POURING, THE OLD MAN IS SNORING!
SPLASH
OOPSIE. SORRY, BEAR.
PUDDLES. RAIN. WHAT'S THE DIFFERENCE.
©BOBSCOTT

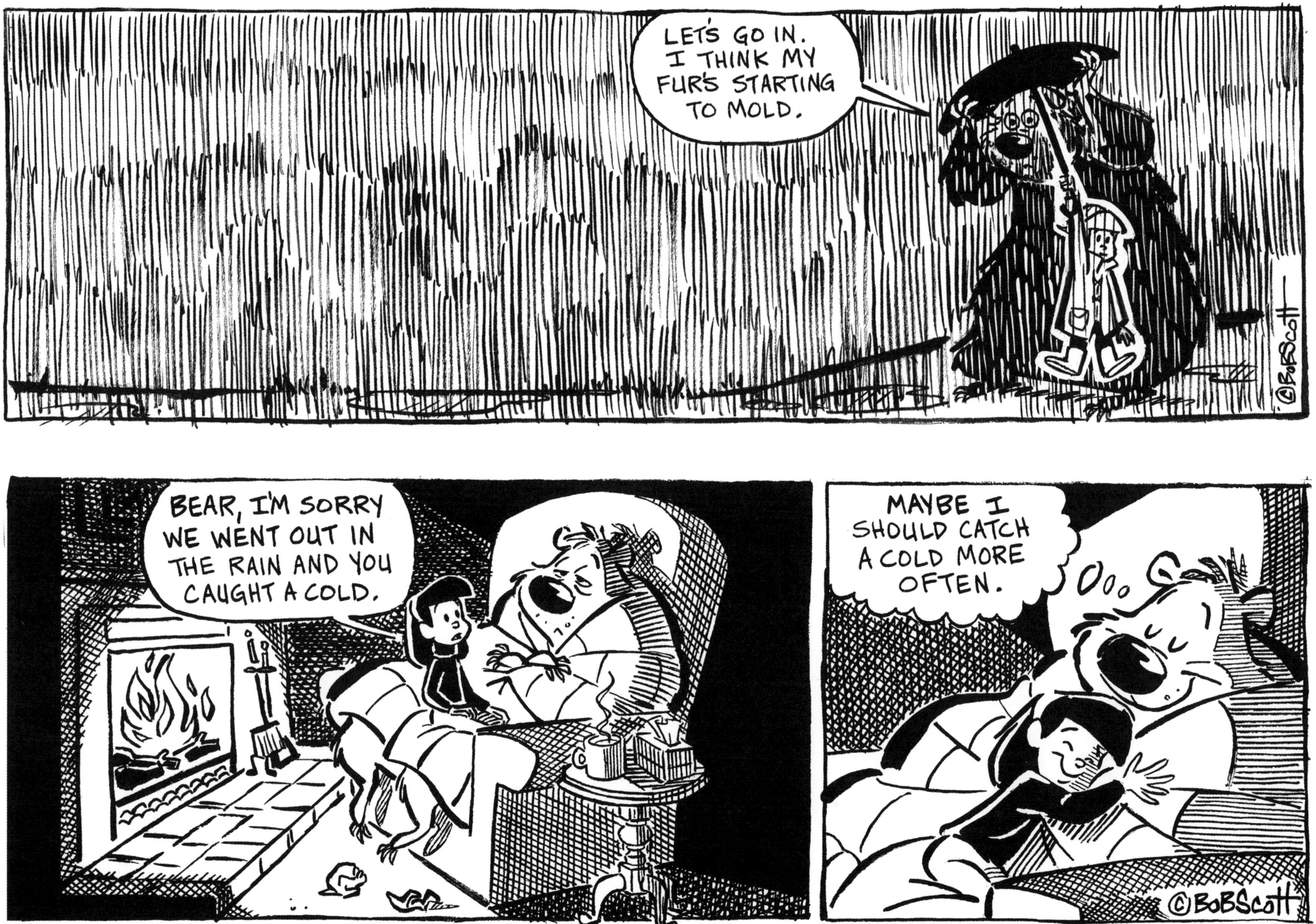
LET'S GO IN. I THINK MY FUR'S STARTING TO MOLD.
©BOBSCOTT
BEAR, I'M SORRY WE WENT OUT IN THE RAIN AND YOU CAUGHT A COLD.
MAYBE I SHOULD CATCH A COLD MORE OFTEN.
©BOBSCOTT

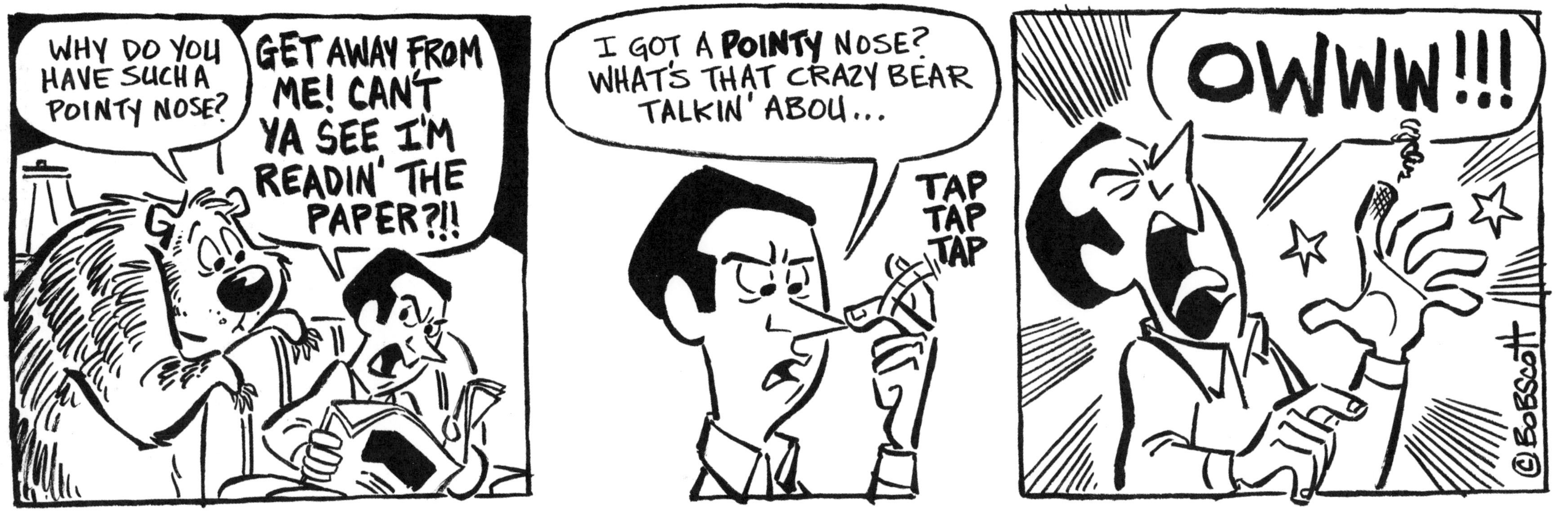
WHY DO YOU HAVE SUCH A POINTY NOSE?
GET AWAY FROM ME! CAN'T YA SEE I'M READIN' THE PAPER?!!
I GOT A **POINTY** NOSE? WHAT'S THAT CRAZY BEAR TALKIN' ABOU...
TAP TAP TAP
OWWW!!!
©BOBSCOTT

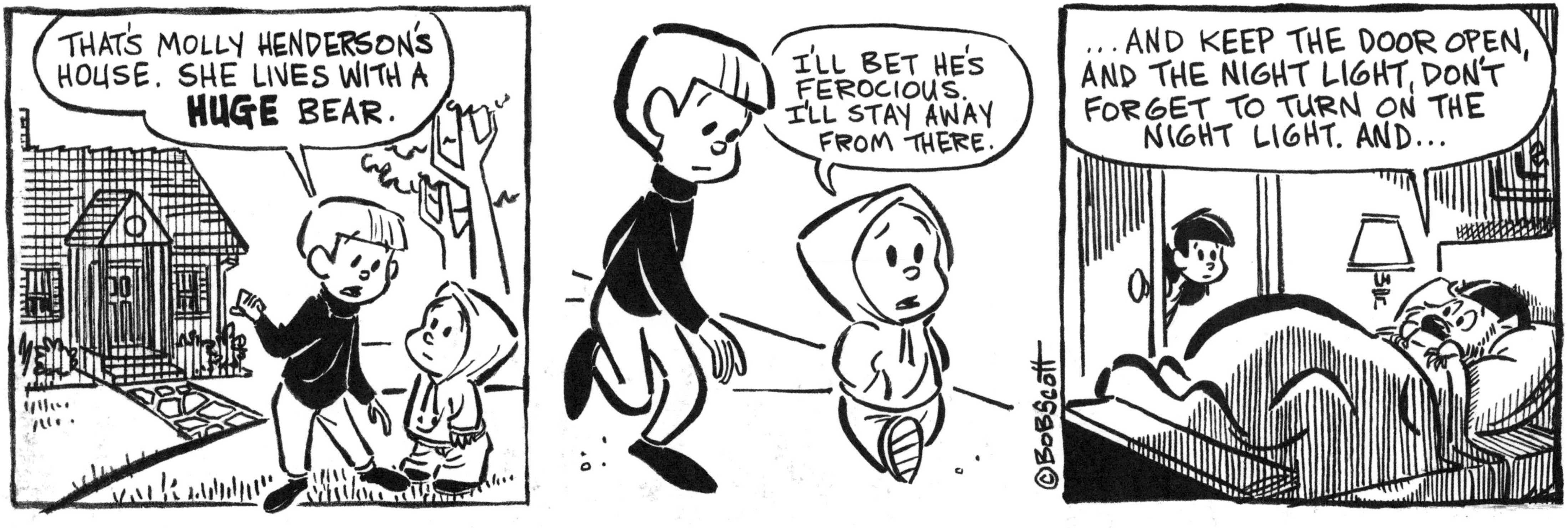
THAT'S MOLLY HENDERSON'S HOUSE. SHE LIVES WITH A **HUGE** BEAR.
I'LL BET HE'S FEROCIOUS. I'LL STAY AWAY FROM THERE.
©BOBSCOTT
...AND KEEP THE DOOR OPEN, AND THE NIGHT LIGHT, DON'T FORGET TO TURN ON THE NIGHT LIGHT. AND...

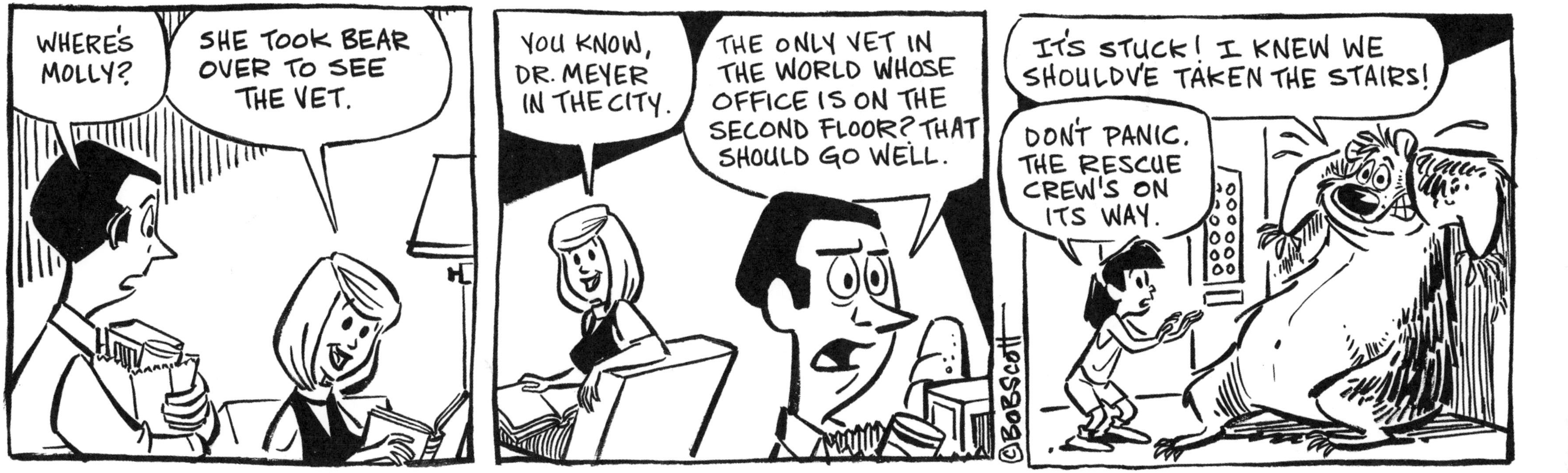
WHERE'S MOLLY?
SHE TOOK BEAR OVER TO SEE THE VET.
YOU KNOW, DR. MEYER IN THE CITY.
THE ONLY VET IN THE WORLD WHOSE OFFICE IS ON THE SECOND FLOOR? THAT SHOULD GO WELL.
©BOBSCOTT
IT'S STUCK! I KNEW WE SHOULD'VE TAKEN THE STAIRS!
DON'T PANIC. THE RESCUE CREW'S ON ITS WAY.

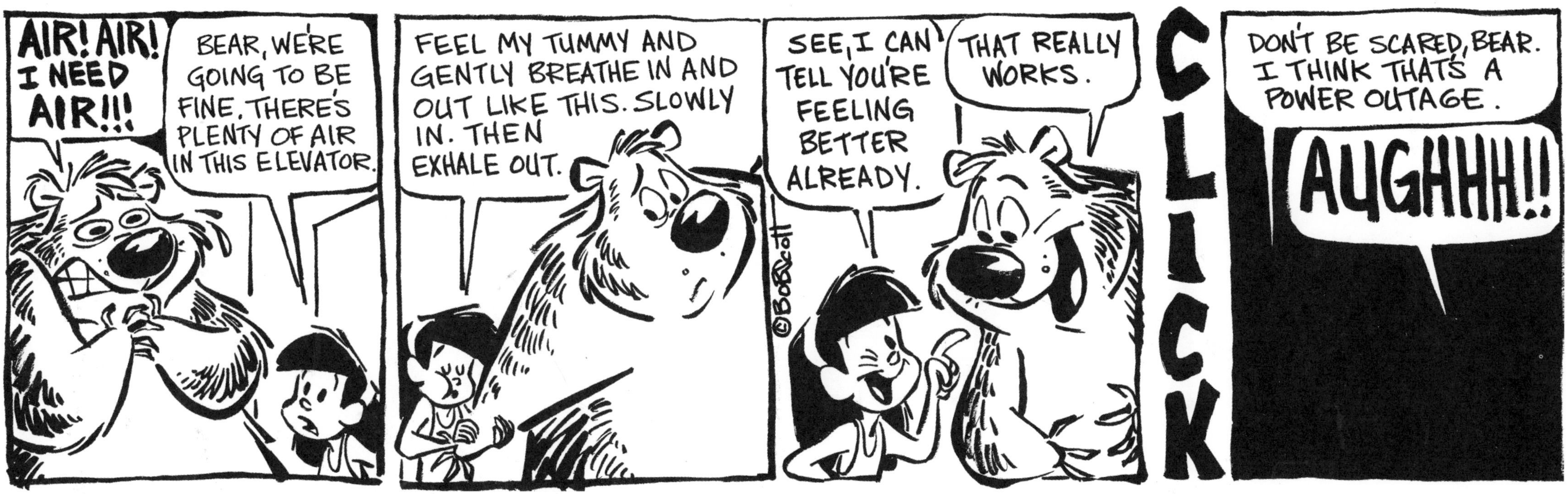
AIR! AIR! I NEED AIR!!!
BEAR, WE'RE GOING TO BE FINE. THERE'S PLENTY OF AIR IN THIS ELEVATOR.
FEEL MY TUMMY AND GENTLY BREATHE IN AND OUT LIKE THIS. SLOWLY IN. THEN EXHALE OUT.
©BOBSCOTT
SEE, I CAN TELL YOU'RE FEELING BETTER ALREADY.
THAT REALLY WORKS.
CLICK
DON'T BE SCARED, BEAR. I THINK THAT'S A POWER OUTAGE.
AUGHHH!!

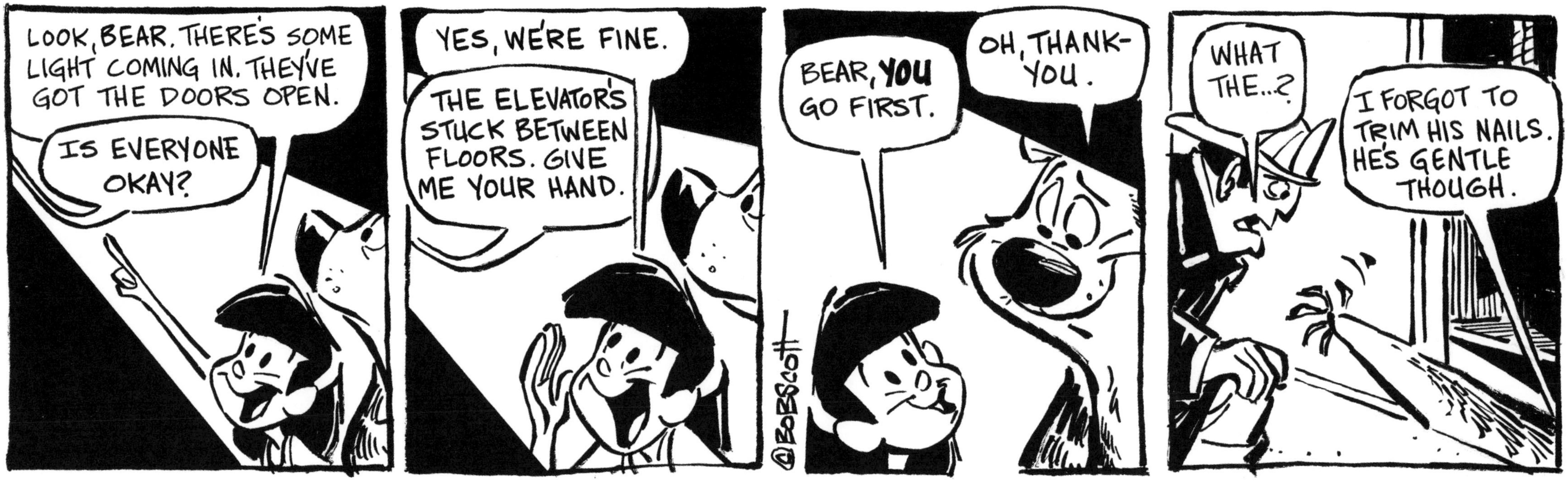
LOOK, BEAR. THERE'S SOME LIGHT COMING IN. THEY'VE GOT THE DOORS OPEN.
IS EVERYONE OKAY?
YES, WE'RE FINE.
THE ELEVATOR'S STUCK BETWEEN FLOORS. GIVE ME YOUR HAND.
©BOBSCOTT
BEAR, **YOU** GO FIRST.
OH, THANK-YOU.
WHAT THE...?
I FORGOT TO TRIM HIS NAILS. HE'S GENTLE THOUGH.

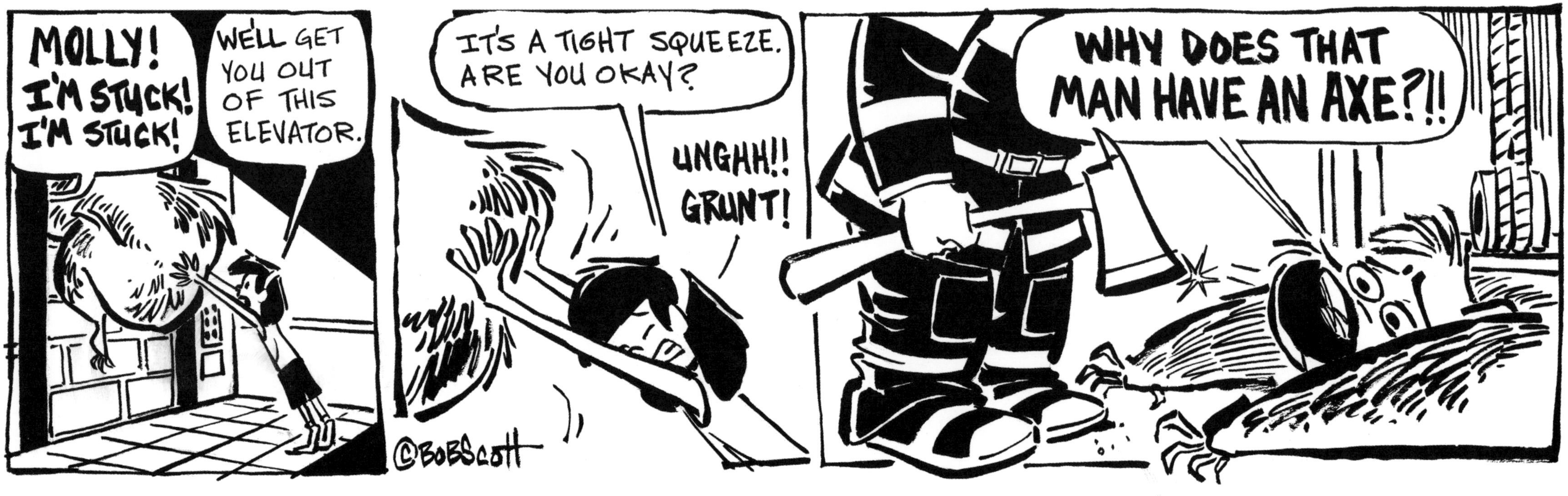
MOLLY! I'M STUCK! I'M STUCK!
WE'LL GET YOU OUT OF THIS ELEVATOR.
IT'S A TIGHT SQUEEZE. ARE YOU OKAY?
UNGHH!! GRUNT!
©BOBSCOTT
WHY DOES THAT MAN HAVE AN AXE?!!

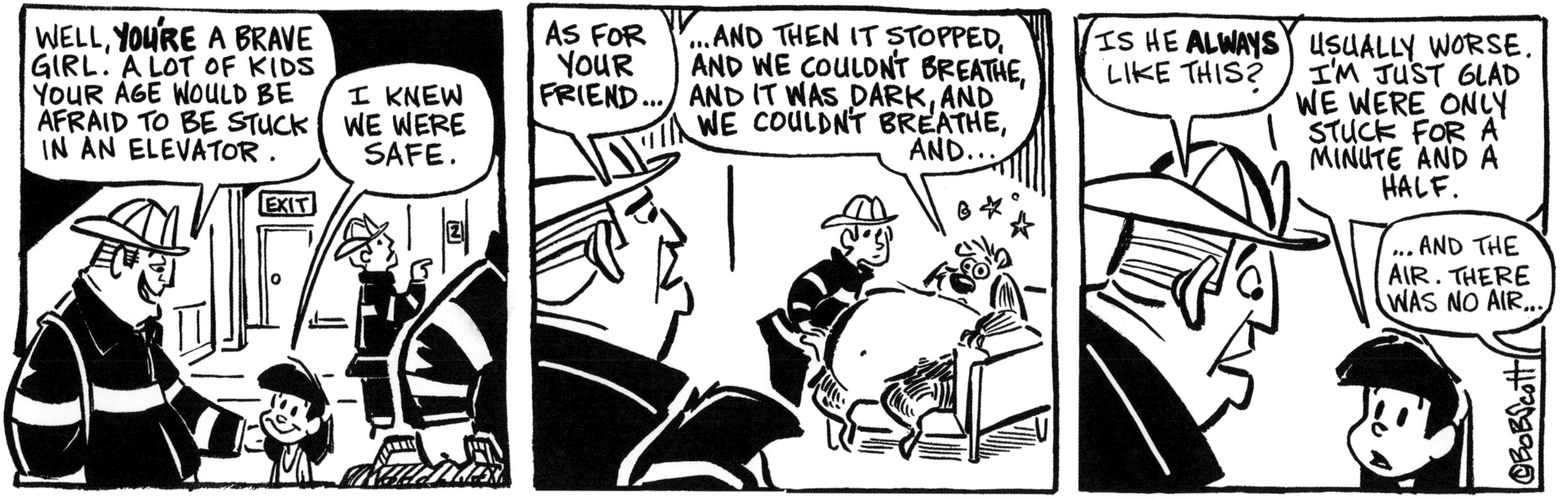
WELL, **YOU'RE** A BRAVE GIRL. A LOT OF KIDS YOUR AGE WOULD BE AFRAID TO BE STUCK IN AN ELEVATOR.
I KNEW WE WERE SAFE.
EXIT
AS FOR YOUR FRIEND...
...AND THEN IT STOPPED, AND WE COULDN'T BREATHE, AND IT WAS DARK, AND WE COULDN'T BREATHE, AND...
IS HE **ALWAYS** LIKE THIS?
USUALLY WORSE. I'M JUST GLAD WE WERE ONLY STUCK FOR A MINUTE AND A HALF.
...AND THE AIR. THERE WAS NO AIR...
©BOBSCOTT

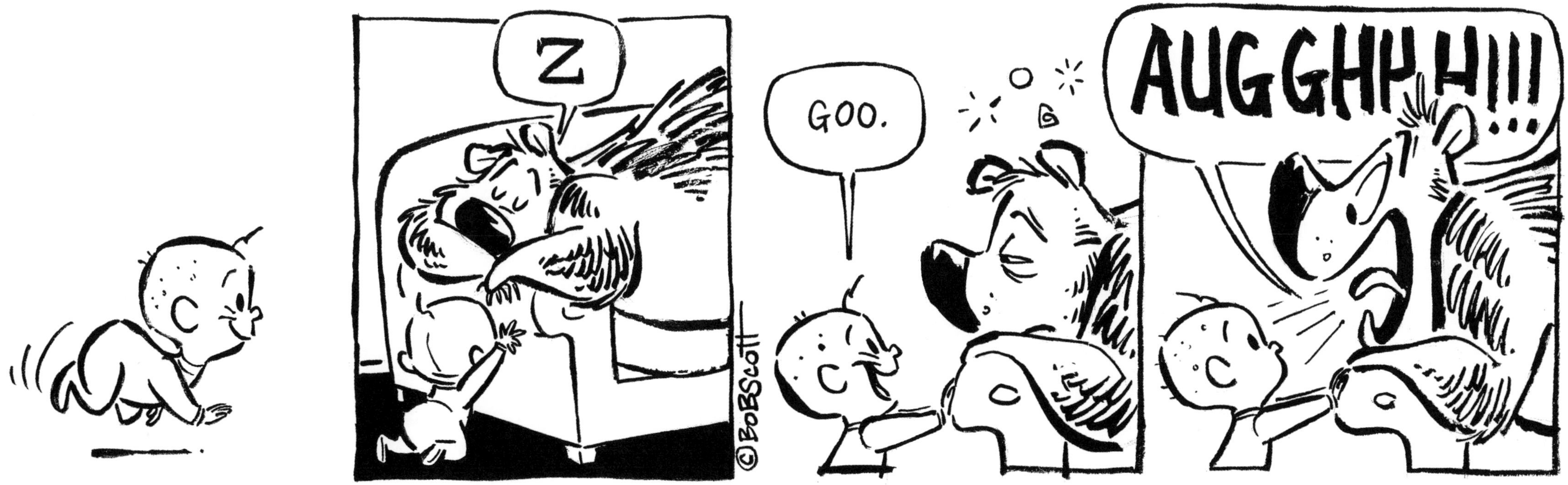
Z
©BOBSCOTT
GOO.
AUGGHHH!!!

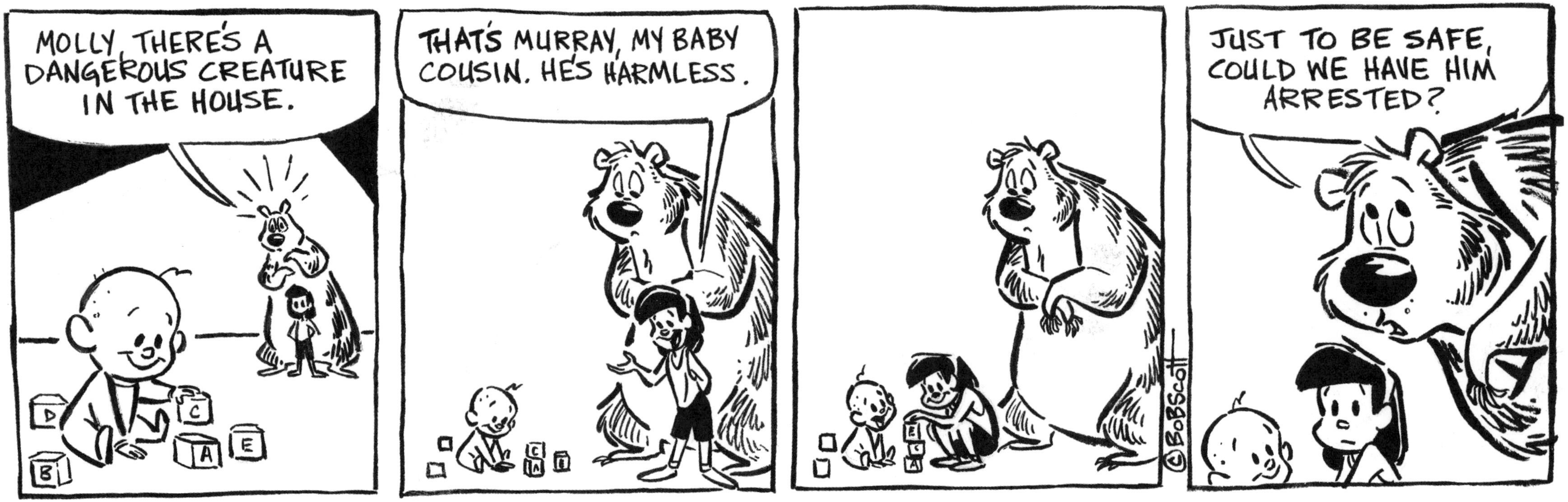
MOLLY, THERE'S A DANGEROUS CREATURE IN THE HOUSE.
THAT'S MURRAY, MY BABY COUSIN. HE'S HARMLESS.
JUST TO BE SAFE, COULD WE HAVE HIM ARRESTED?
©BOBSCOTT

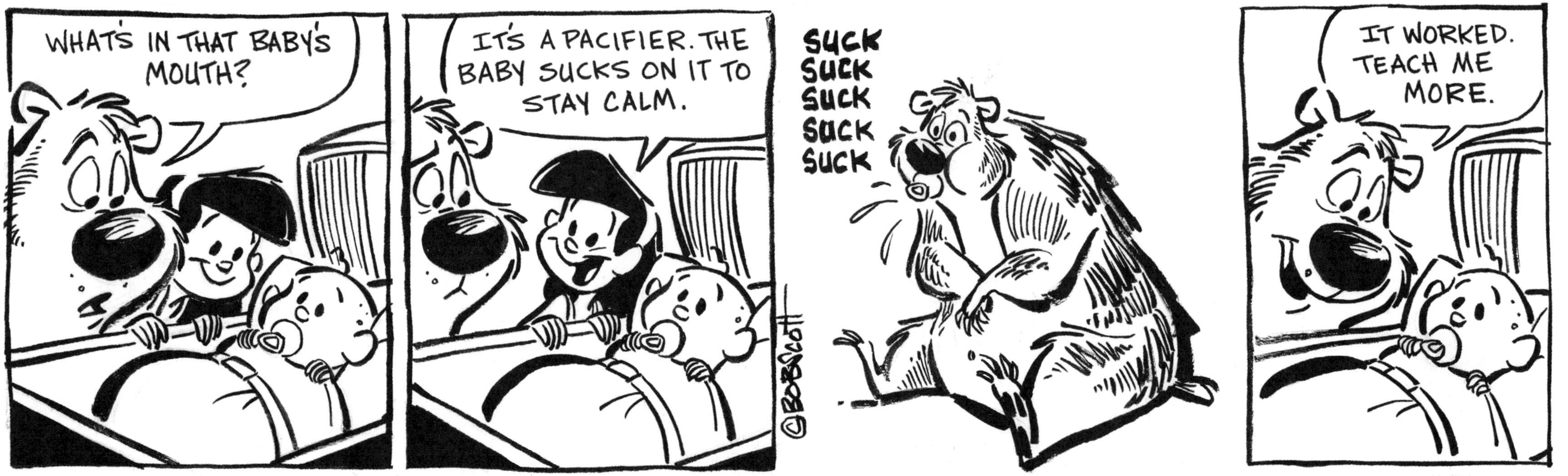
WHAT'S IN THAT BABY'S MOUTH?
IT'S A PACIFIER. THE BABY SUCKS ON IT TO STAY CALM.
©BOBSCOTT
SUCK SUCK SUCK SUCK SUCK
IT WORKED. TEACH ME MORE.

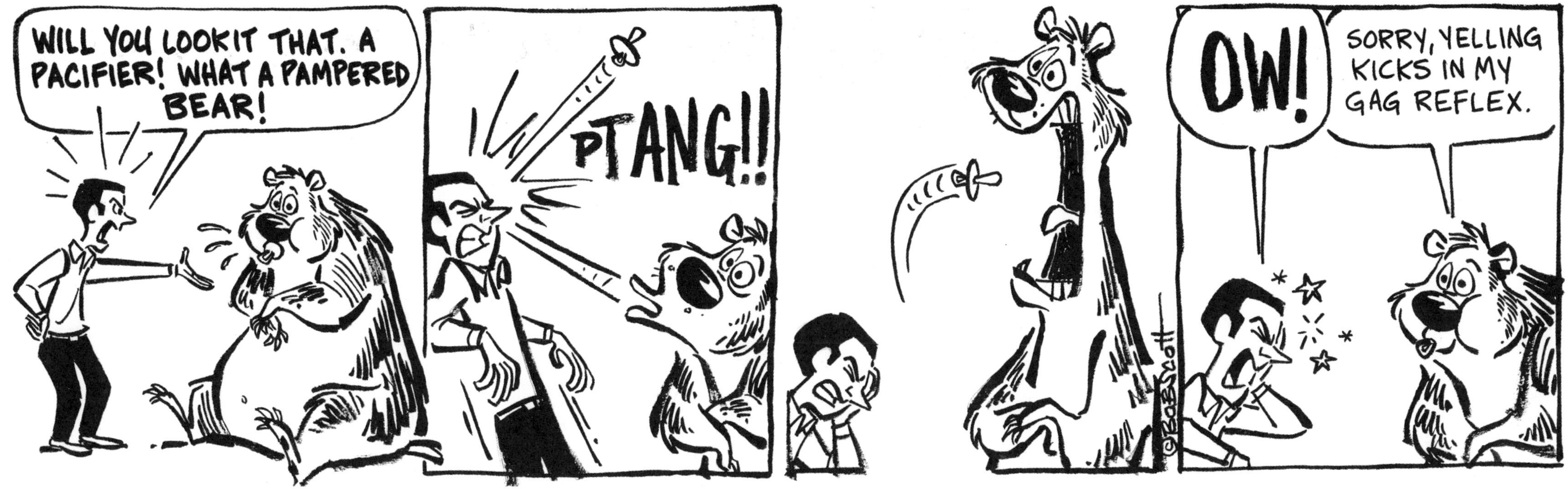
WILL YOU LOOKIT THAT. A PACIFIER! WHAT A PAMPERED BEAR!
PTANG!!
OW!
SORRY, YELLING KICKS IN MY GAG REFLEX.

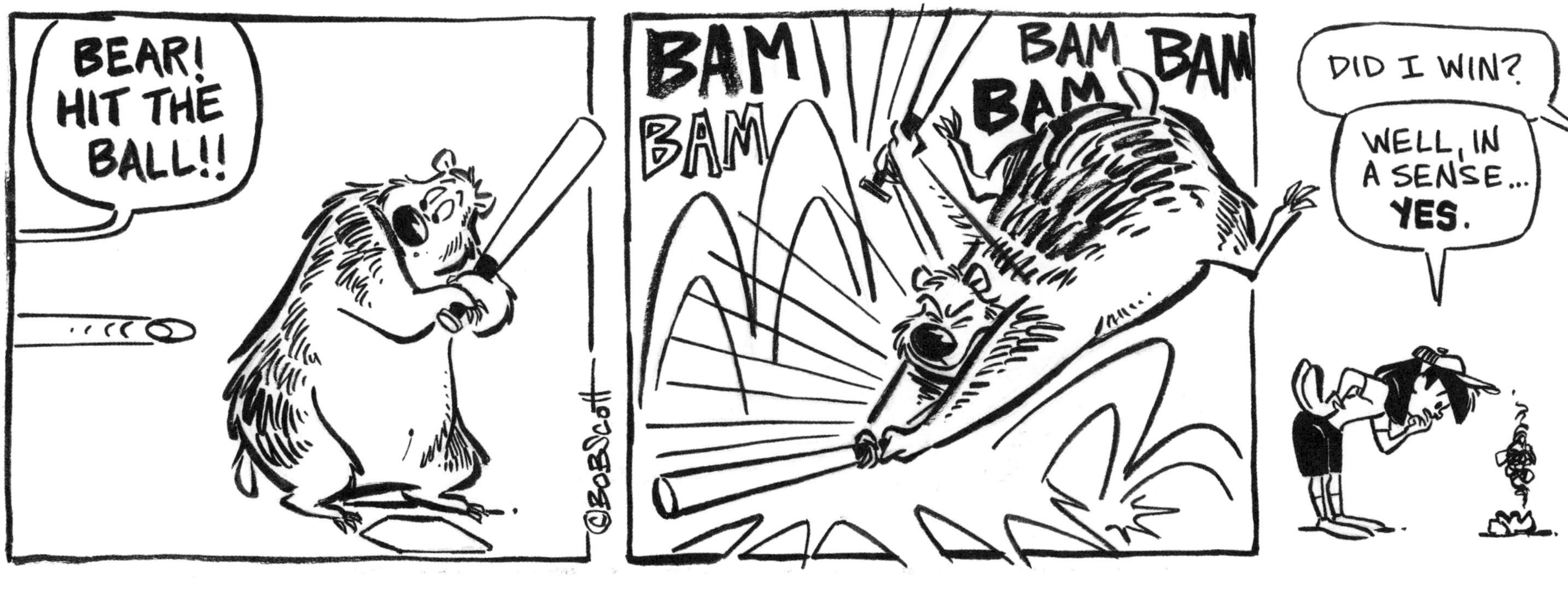
BEAR! HIT THE BALL!!
BAM
BAM
BAM
BAM
BAM
DID I WIN?
WELL, IN A SENSE... YES.

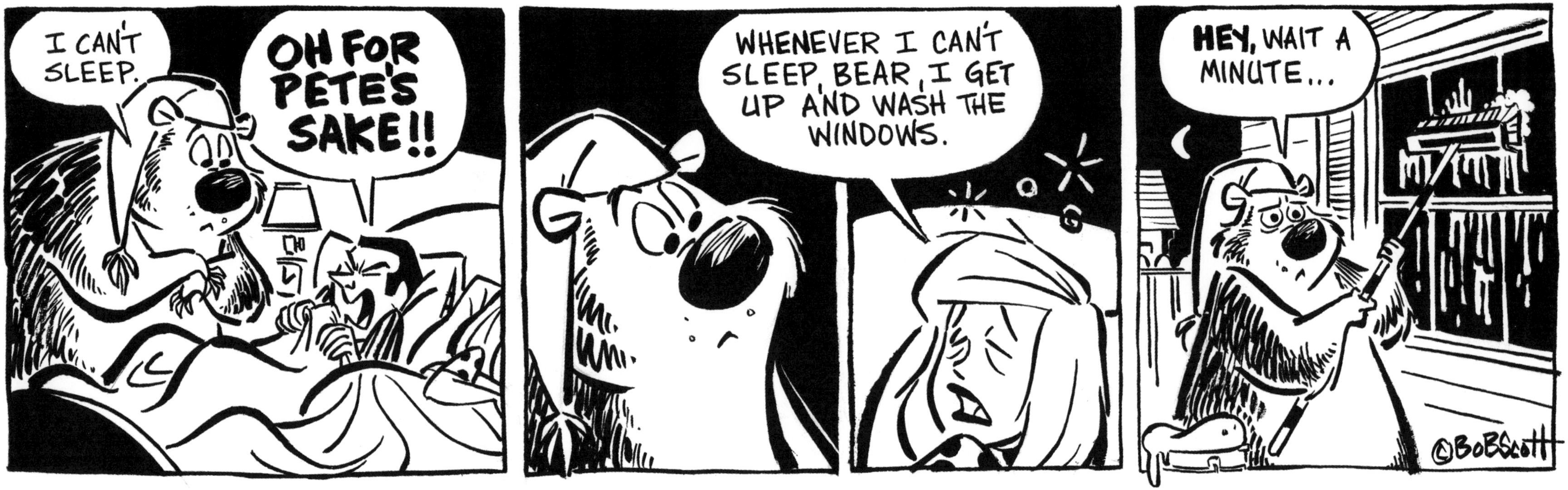
I CAN'T SLEEP.
OH FOR PETE'S SAKE!!
WHENEVER I CAN'T SLEEP, BEAR, I GET UP AND WASH THE WINDOWS.
HEY, WAIT A MINUTE...
©BOBSCOTT

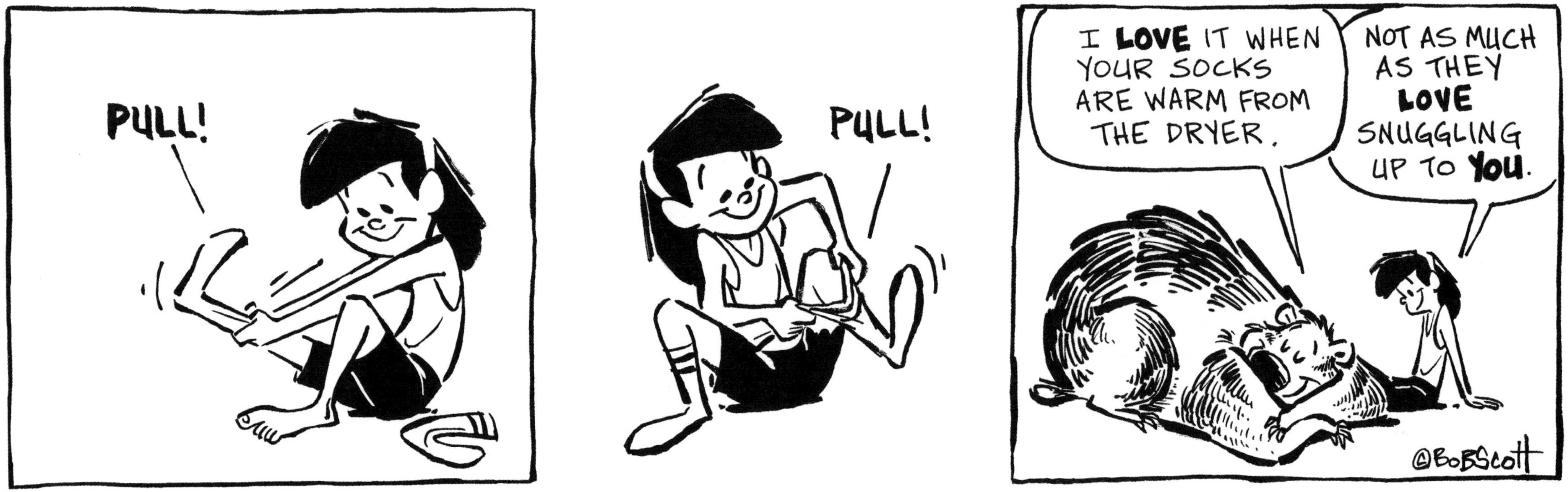
PULL!
PULL!
I LOVE IT WHEN YOUR SOCKS ARE WARM FROM THE DRYER.
NOT AS MUCH AS THEY LOVE SNUGGLING UP TO YOU.
©BOBSCOTT

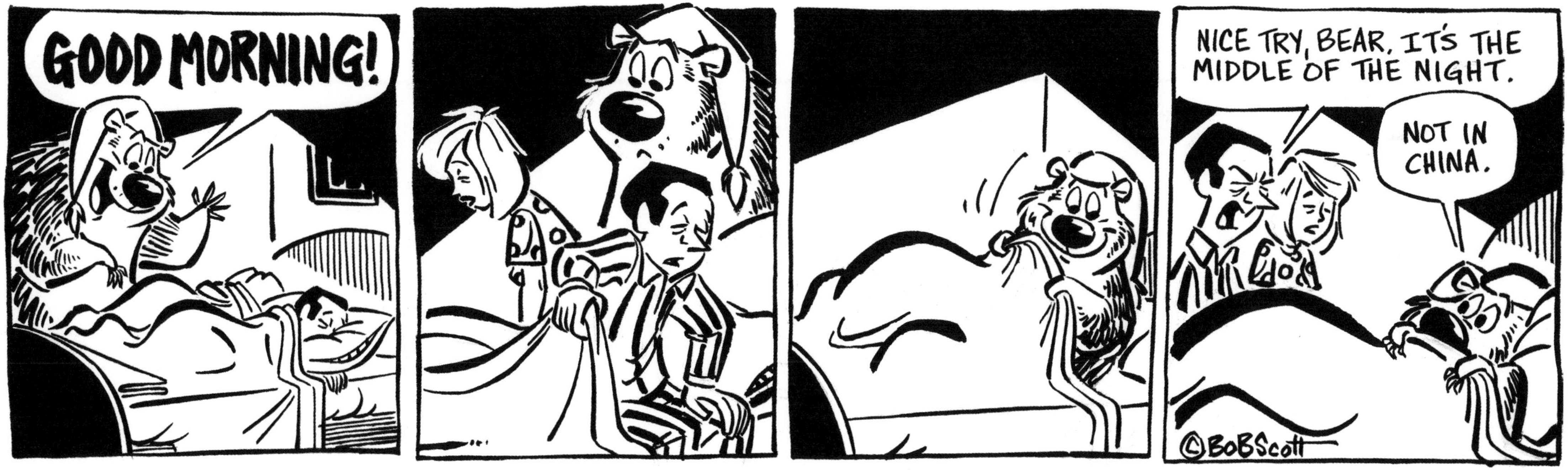
GOOD MORNING!
NICE TRY, BEAR, IT'S THE MIDDLE OF THE NIGHT.
NOT IN CHINA.
©BOBSCOTT

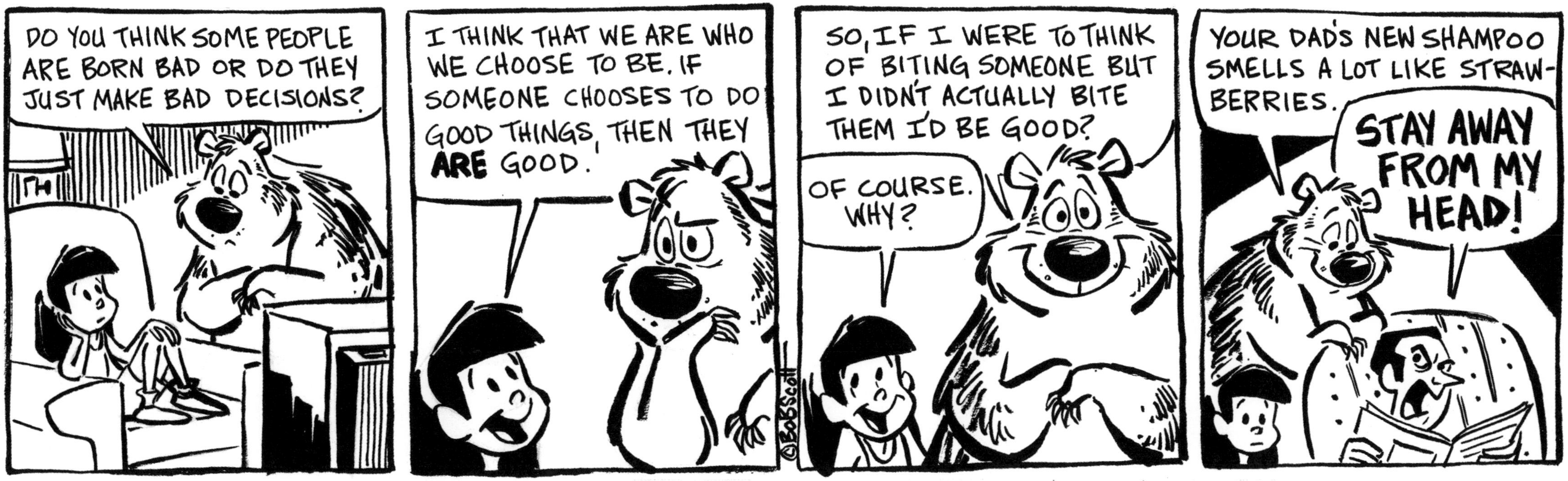
DO YOU THINK SOME PEOPLE ARE BORN BAD OR DO THEY JUST MAKE BAD DECISIONS?
I THINK THAT WE ARE WHO WE CHOOSE TO BE. IF SOMEONE CHOOSES TO DO GOOD THINGS, THEN THEY ARE GOOD.
©BOBSCOTT
SO, IF I WERE TO THINK OF BITING SOMEONE BUT I DIDN'T ACTUALLY BITE THEM I'D BE GOOD?
OF COURSE. WHY?
YOUR DAD'S NEW SHAMPOO SMELLS A LOT LIKE STRAW-BERRIES.
STAY AWAY FROM MY HEAD!

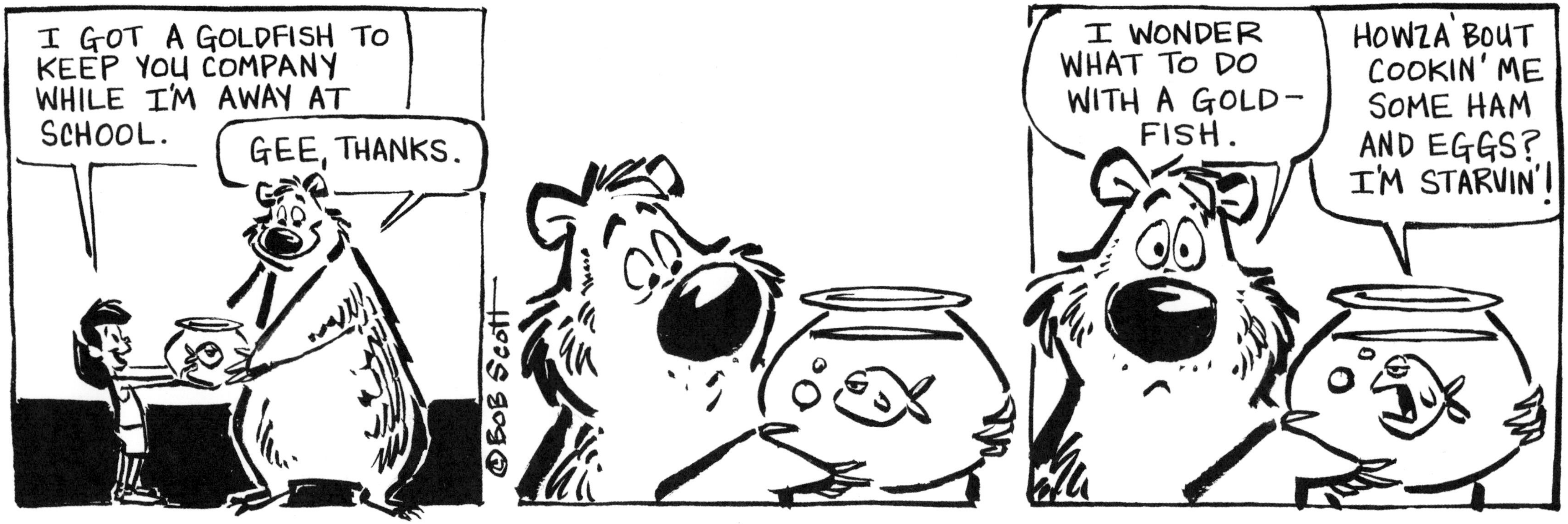
I GOT A GOLDFISH TO KEEP YOU COMPANY WHILE I'M AWAY AT SCHOOL.
GEE, THANKS.
©BOB SCOTT
I WONDER WHAT TO DO WITH A GOLD-FISH.
HOWZA'BOUT COOKIN' ME SOME HAM AND EGGS? I'M STARVIN'!

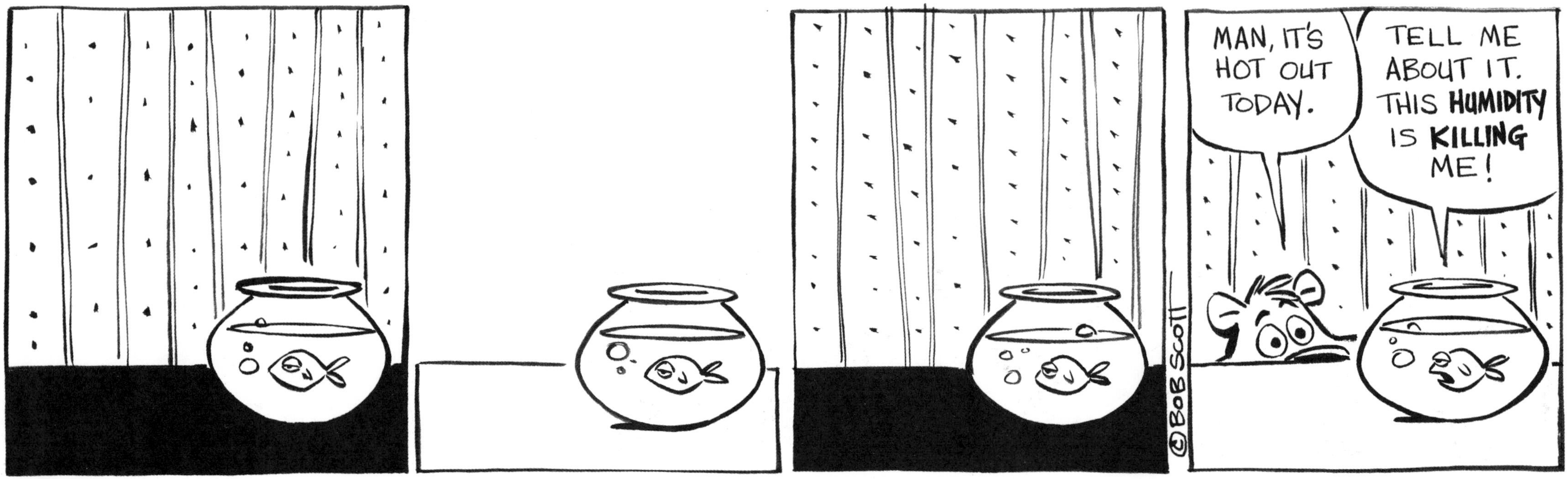
©BOB SCOTT
MAN, IT'S HOT OUT TODAY.
TELL ME ABOUT IT. THIS HUMIDITY IS KILLING ME!

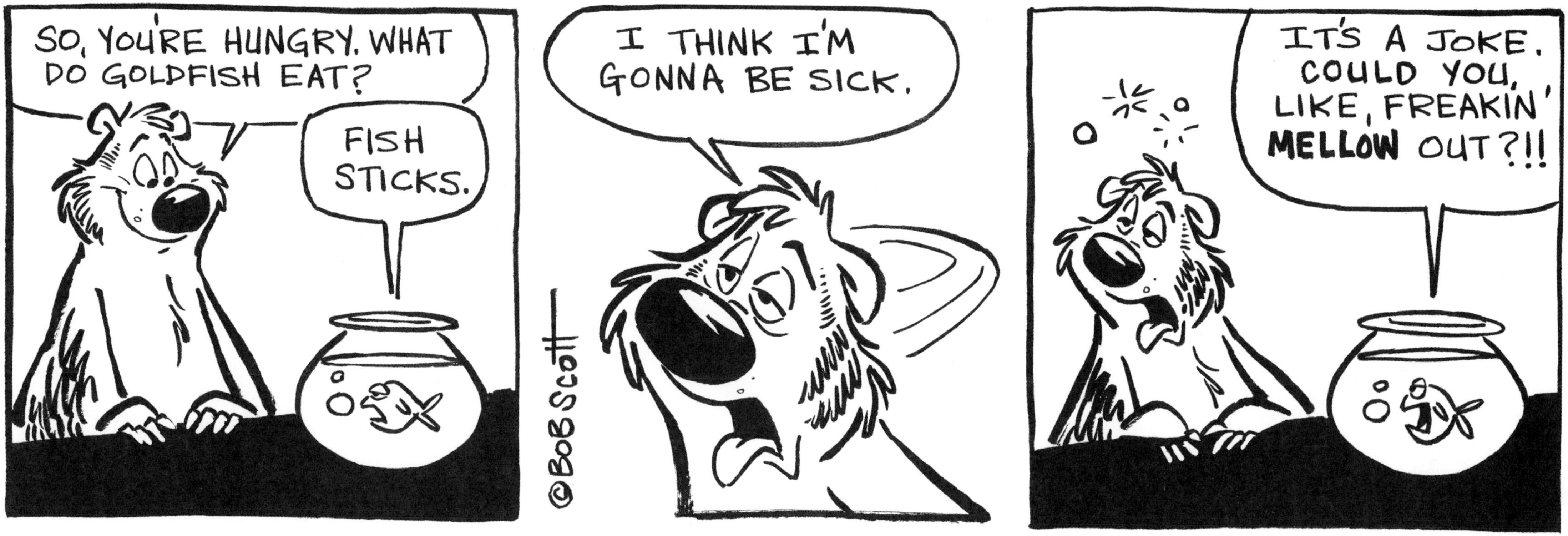
SO, YOU'RE HUNGRY. WHAT DO GOLDFISH EAT?
FISH STICKS.
I THINK I'M GONNA BE SICK.
IT'S A JOKE. COULD YOU, LIKE, FREAKIN' MELLOW OUT?!!
©BOBSCOTT

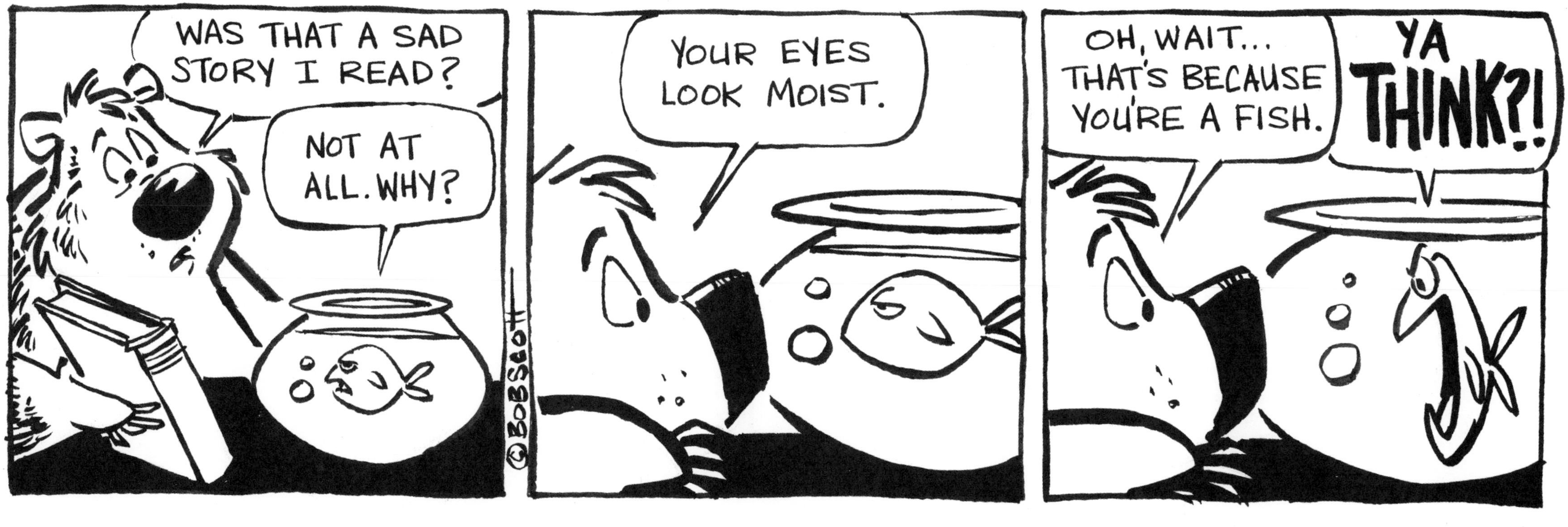
WAS THAT A SAD STORY I READ?
NOT AT ALL. WHY?
YOUR EYES LOOK MOIST.
OH, WAIT... THAT'S BECAUSE YOU'RE A FISH.
YA THINK?!
©BOBSCOTT

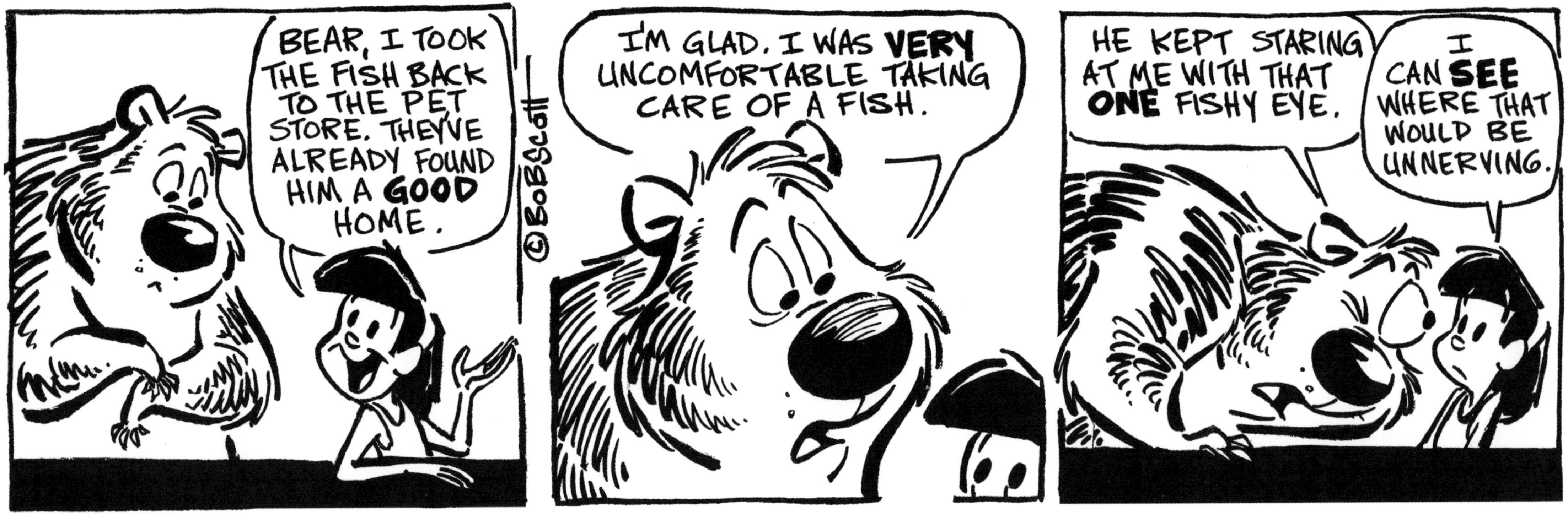
BEAR, I TOOK THE FISH BACK TO THE PET STORE. THEY'VE ALREADY FOUND HIM A **GOOD** HOME.
©BoBScott
I'M GLAD. I WAS **VERY** UNCOMFORTABLE TAKING CARE OF A FISH.
HE KEPT STARING AT ME WITH THAT **ONE** FISHY EYE.
I CAN **SEE** WHERE THAT WOULD BE UNNERVING.

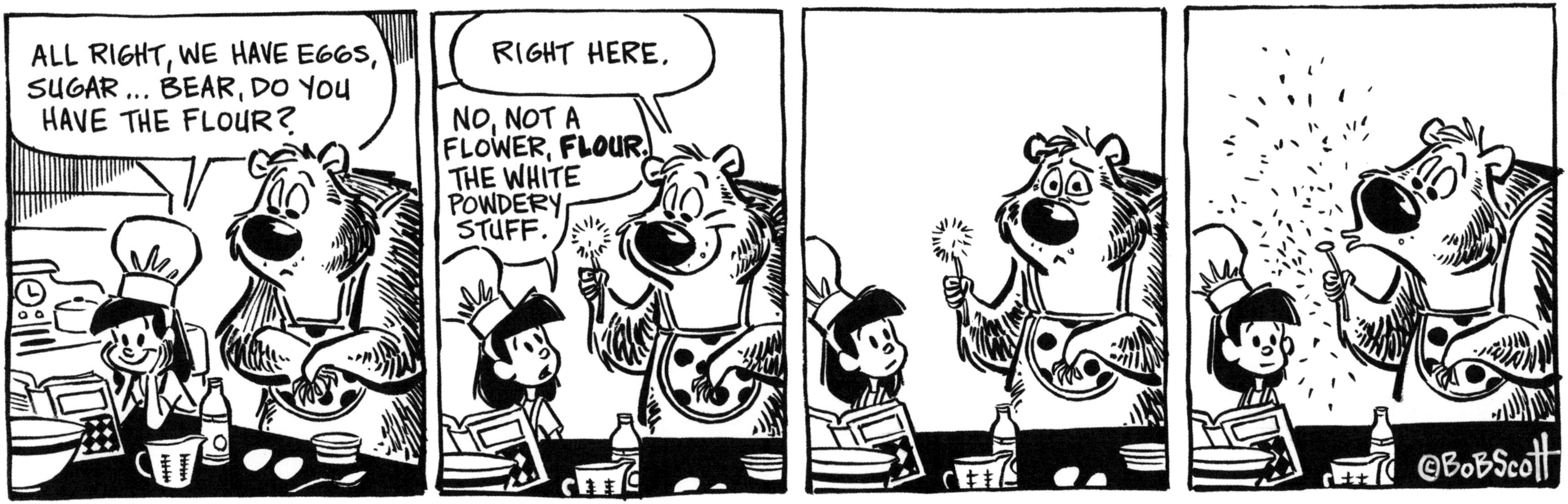
ALL RIGHT, WE HAVE EGGS, SUGAR... BEAR, DO YOU HAVE THE FLOUR?
RIGHT HERE.
NO, NOT A FLOWER, **FLOUR**. THE WHITE POWDERY STUFF.
©BoBScott

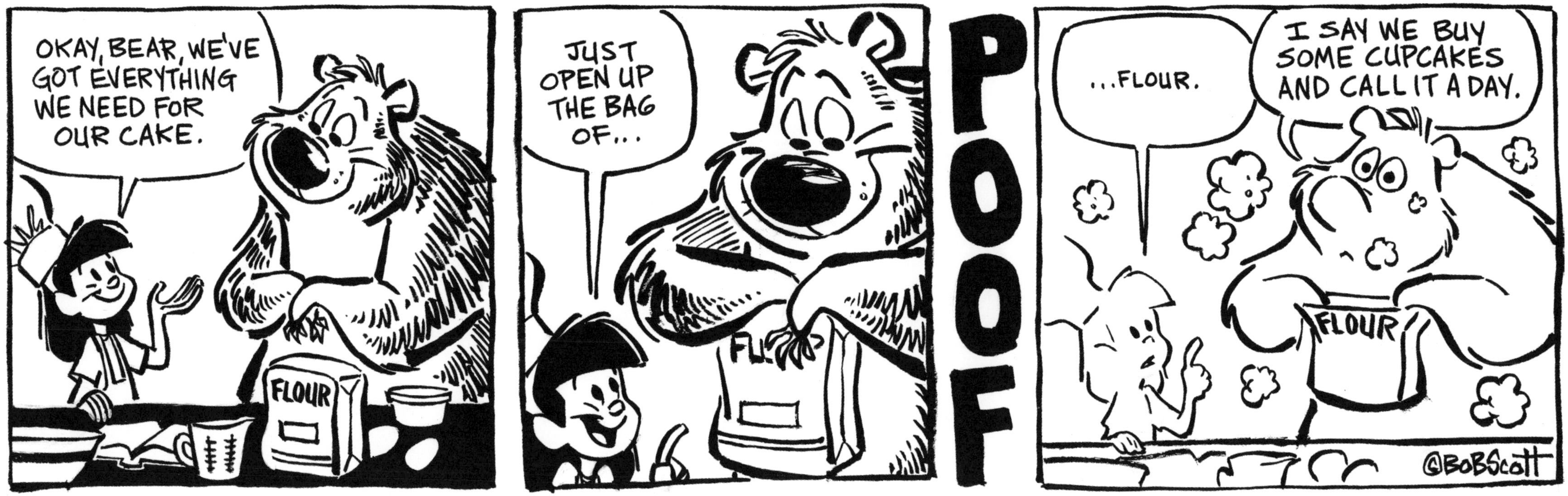
OKAY, BEAR, WE'VE GOT EVERYTHING WE NEED FOR OUR CAKE.
FLOUR
JUST OPEN UP THE BAG OF...
POOF
...FLOUR.
I SAY WE BUY SOME CUPCAKES AND CALL IT A DAY.
FLOUR
©BOBSCOTT

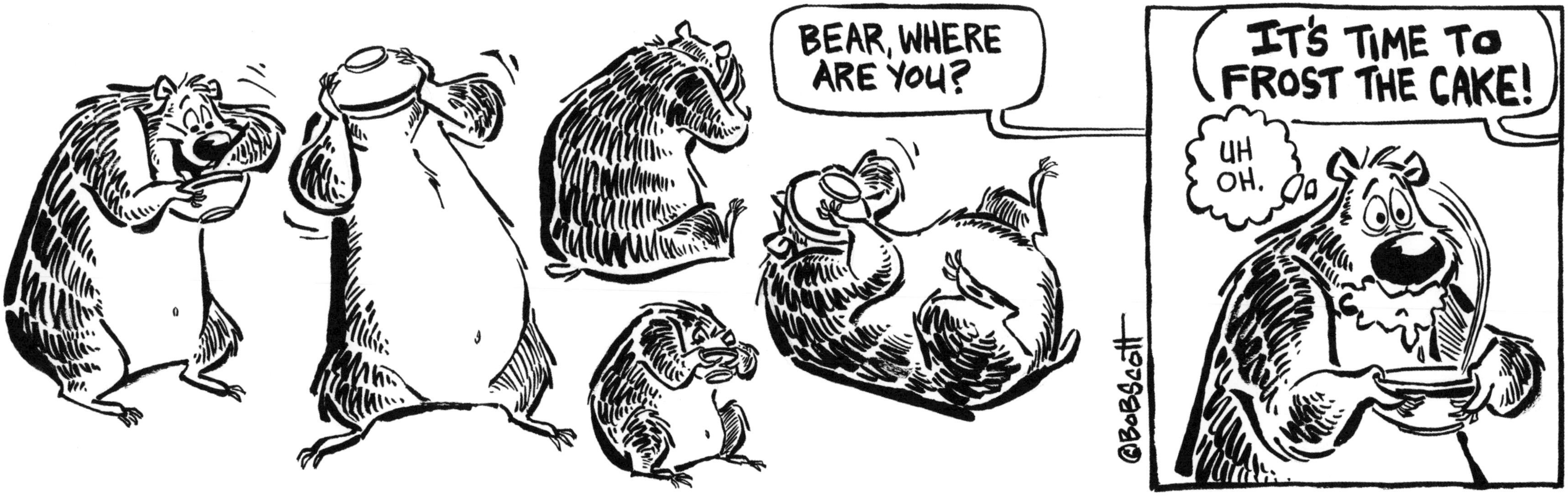
BEAR, WHERE ARE YOU?
©BOBSCOTT
IT'S TIME TO FROST THE CAKE!
UH OH.

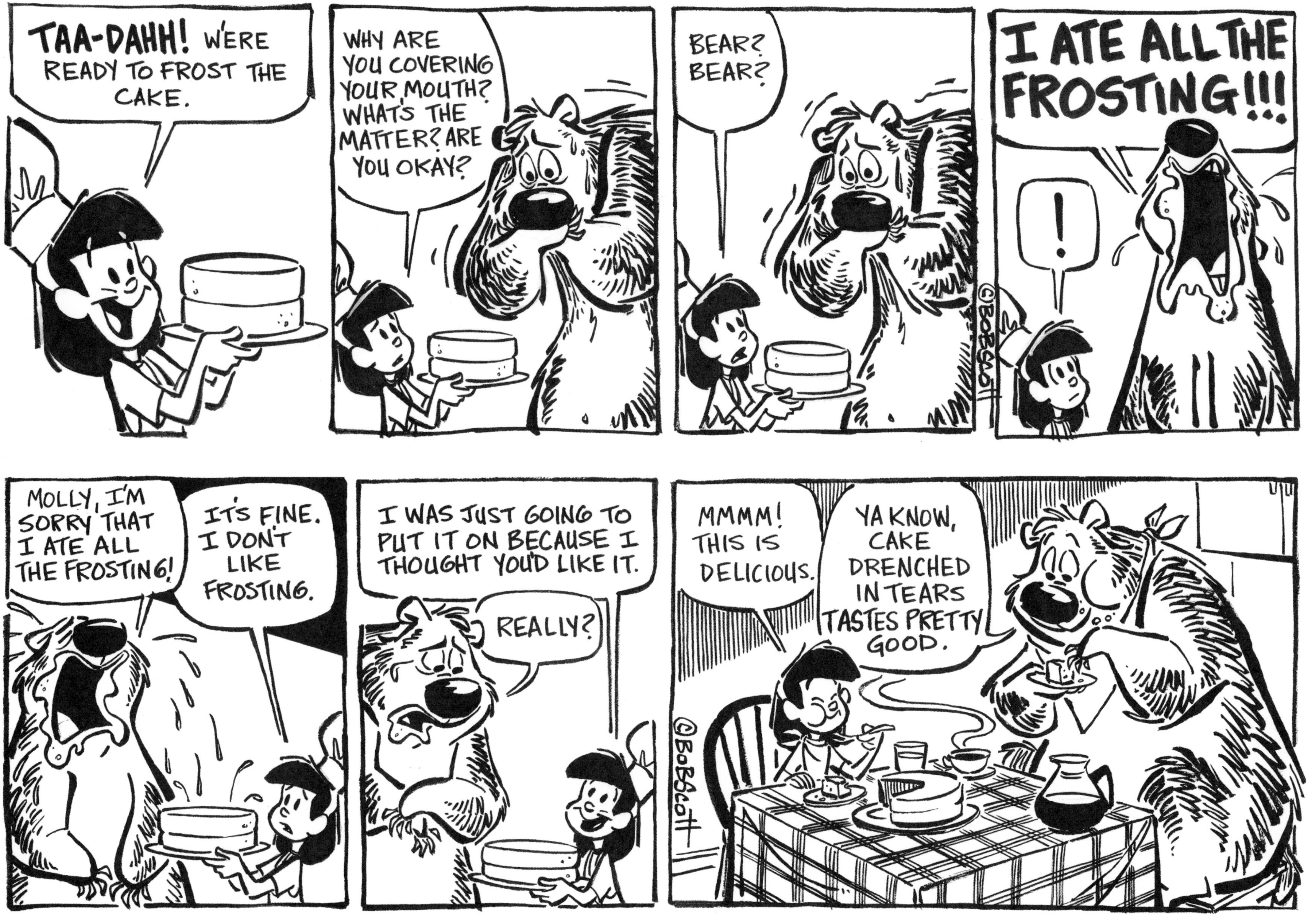
TAA-DAHH! WE'RE READY TO FROST THE CAKE.
WHY ARE YOU COVERING YOUR MOUTH? WHAT'S THE MATTER? ARE YOU OKAY?
BEAR? BEAR?
©BOBSCOTT
I ATE ALL THE FROSTING!!!
!
MOLLY, I'M SORRY THAT I ATE ALL THE FROSTING!
IT'S FINE. I DON'T LIKE FROSTING.
I WAS JUST GOING TO PUT IT ON BECAUSE I THOUGHT YOU'D LIKE IT.
REALLY?
©BOBSCOTT
MMMM! THIS IS DELICIOUS.
YA KNOW, CAKE DRENCHED IN TEARS TASTES PRETTY GOOD.

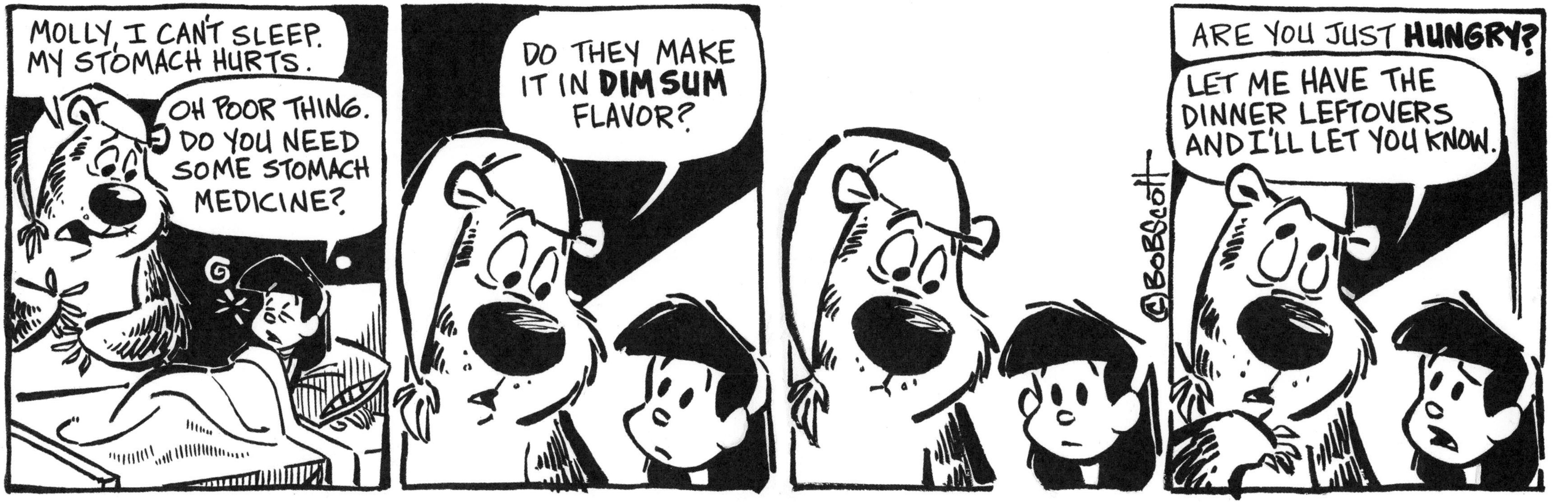
MOLLY, I CAN'T SLEEP. MY STOMACH HURTS.
OH POOR THING. DO YOU NEED SOME STOMACH MEDICINE?
DO THEY MAKE IT IN **DIM SUM** FLAVOR?
ARE YOU JUST **HUNGRY?**
LET ME HAVE THE DINNER LEFTOVERS AND I'LL LET YOU KNOW.
©BOBSCOTT

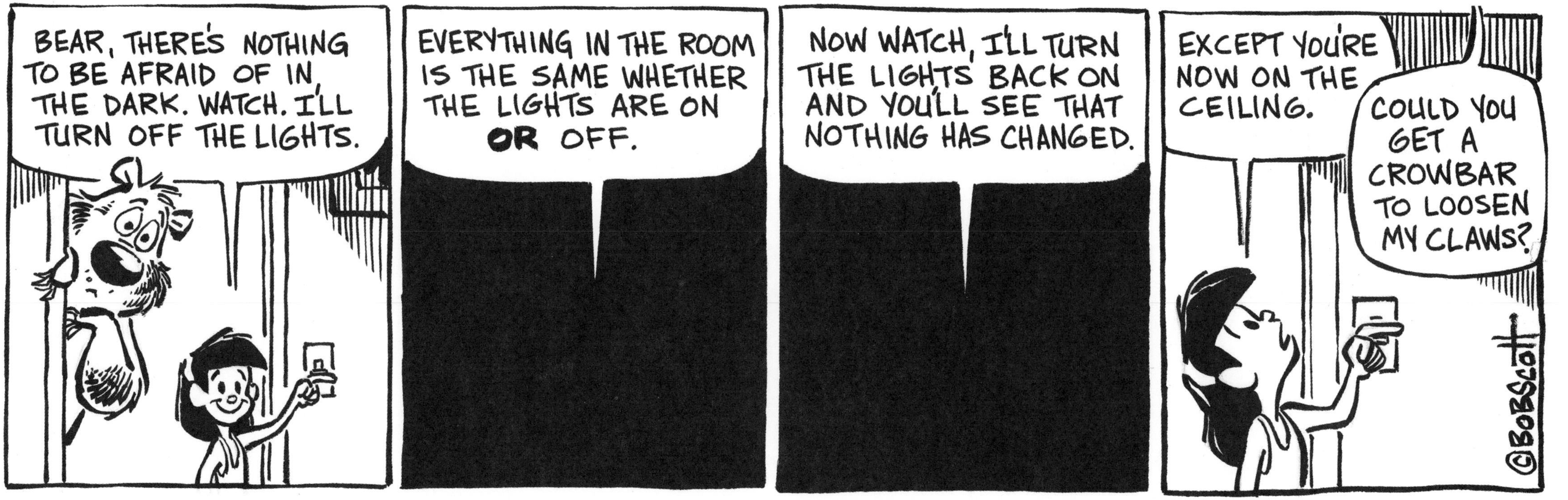
BEAR, THERE'S NOTHING TO BE AFRAID OF IN THE DARK. WATCH. I'LL TURN OFF THE LIGHTS.
EVERYTHING IN THE ROOM IS THE SAME WHETHER THE LIGHTS ARE ON **OR** OFF.
NOW WATCH, I'LL TURN THE LIGHTS BACK ON AND YOU'LL SEE THAT NOTHING HAS CHANGED.
EXCEPT YOU'RE NOW ON THE CEILING.
COULD YOU GET A CROWBAR TO LOOSEN MY CLAWS?
©BOBSCOTT

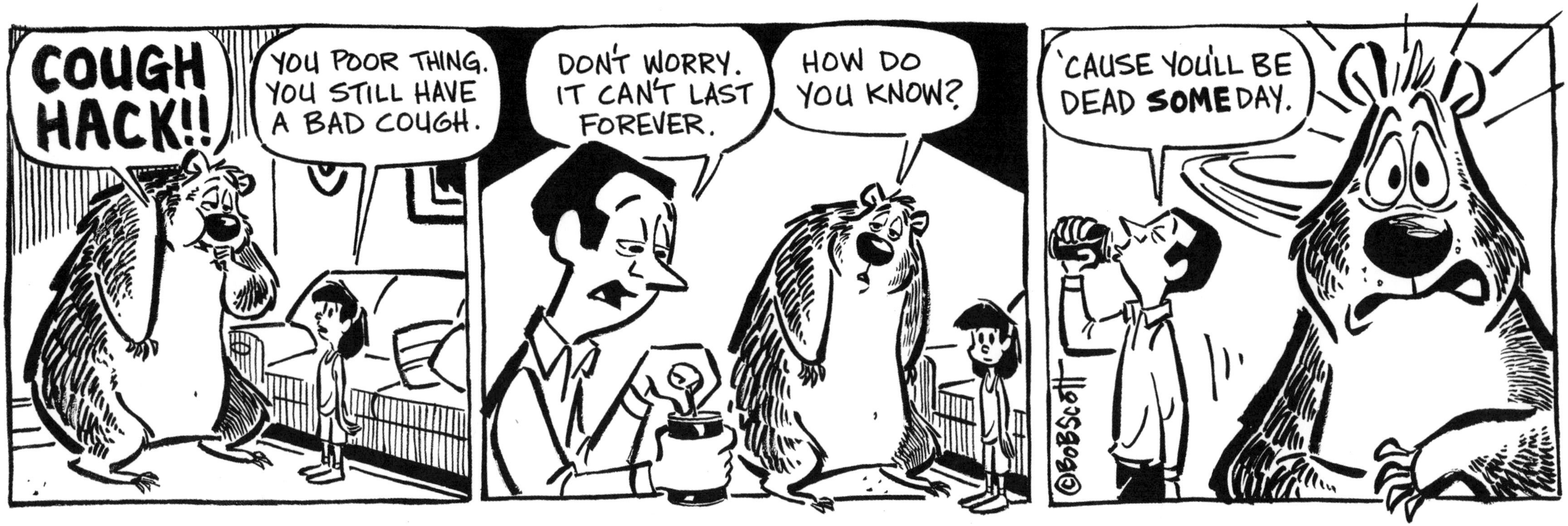
COUGH HACK!!
YOU POOR THING. YOU STILL HAVE A BAD COUGH.
DON'T WORRY. IT CAN'T LAST FOREVER.
HOW DO YOU KNOW?
'CAUSE YOU'LL BE DEAD **SOME**DAY.
©BOBSCOTT

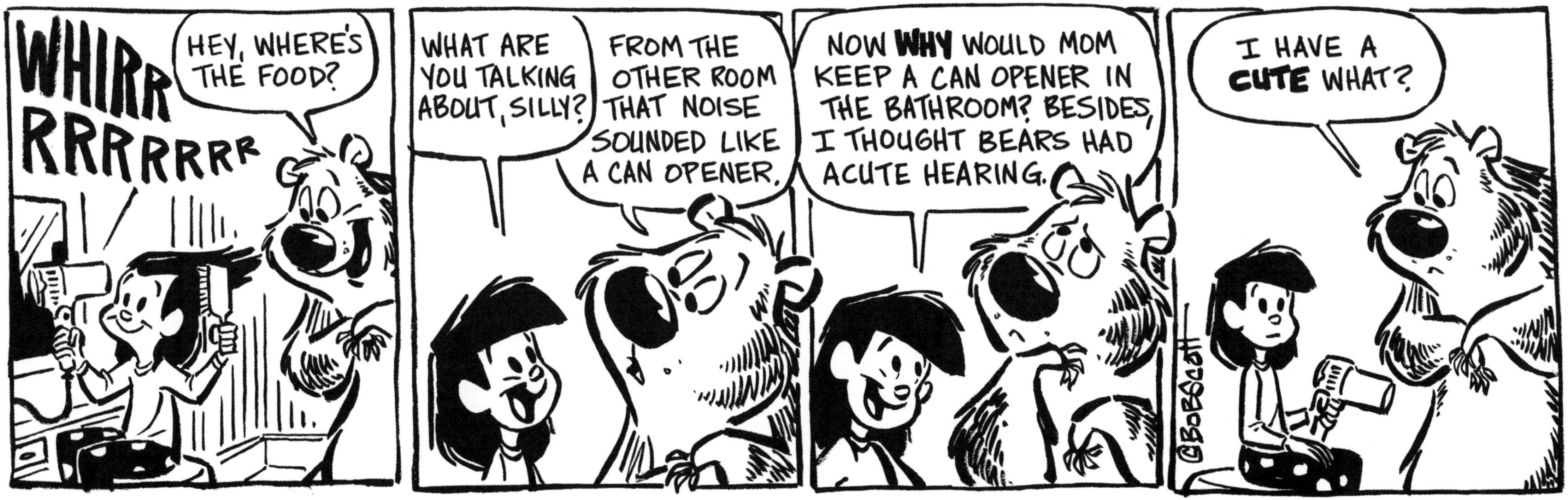
WHIRR RRRRRRR
HEY, WHERE'S THE FOOD?
WHAT ARE YOU TALKING ABOUT, SILLY?
FROM THE OTHER ROOM THAT NOISE SOUNDED LIKE A CAN OPENER.
NOW **WHY** WOULD MOM KEEP A CAN OPENER IN THE BATHROOM? BESIDES, I THOUGHT BEARS HAD ACUTE HEARING.
I HAVE A **CUTE** WHAT?
©BOBSCOTT

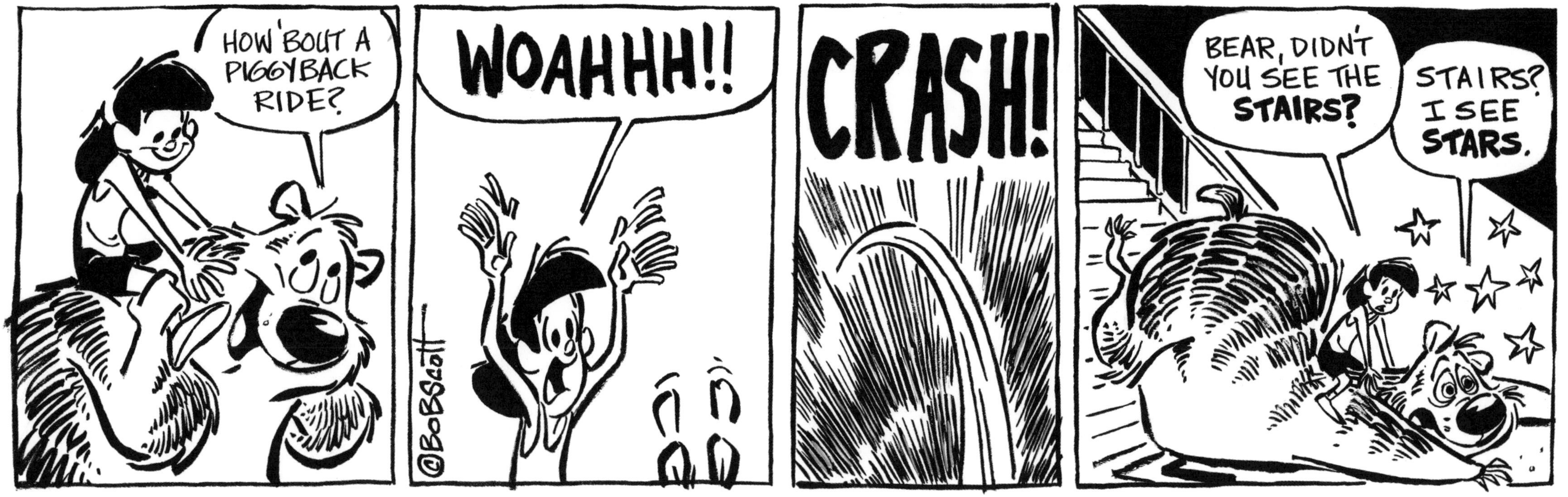
HOW 'BOUT A PIGGYBACK RIDE?
©BOBSCOTT
WOAHHH!!
CRASH!
BEAR, DIDN'T YOU SEE THE **STAIRS?**
STAIRS? I SEE **STARS.**

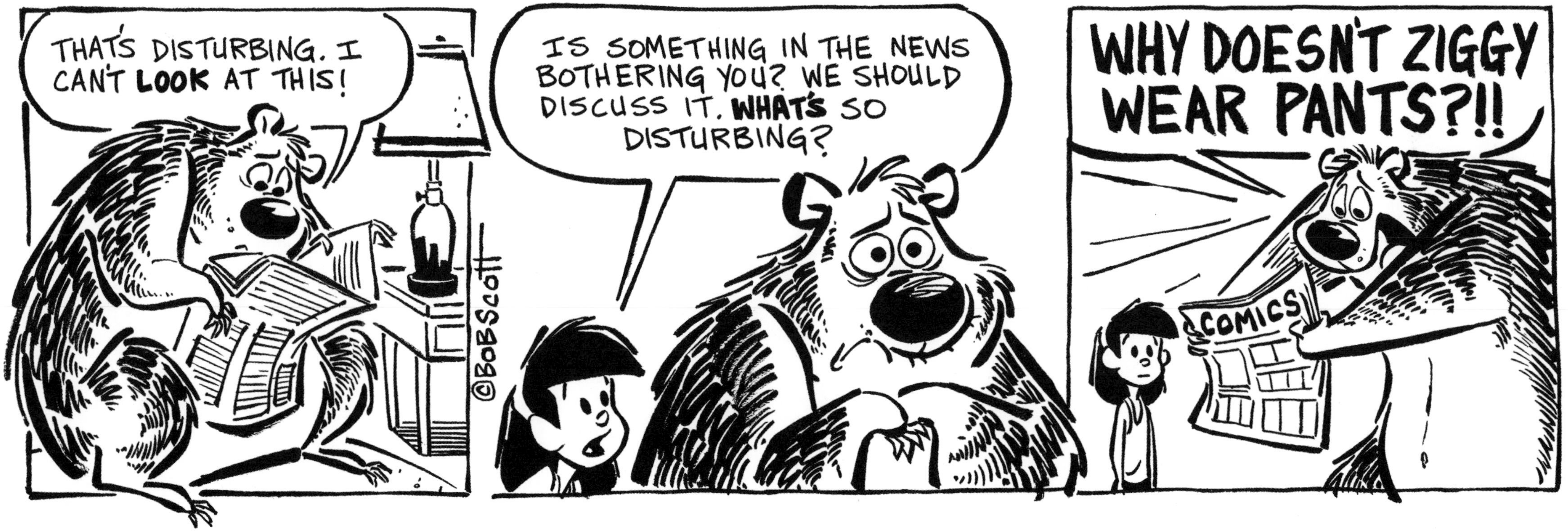
THAT'S DISTURBING. I CAN'T **LOOK** AT THIS!
©BOBSCOTT
IS SOMETHING IN THE NEWS BOTHERING YOU? WE SHOULD DISCUSS IT. **WHAT'S** SO DISTURBING?
WHY DOESN'T ZIGGY WEAR PANTS?!!
COMICS

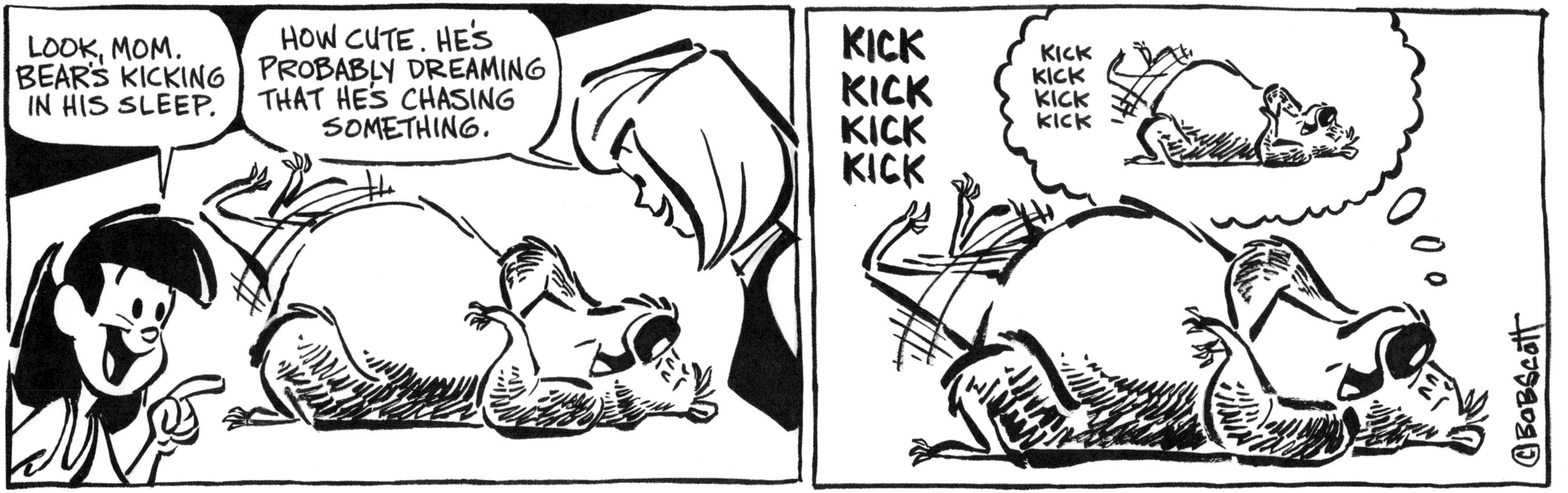
LOOK, MOM. BEAR'S KICKING IN HIS SLEEP.
HOW CUTE. HE'S PROBABLY DREAMING THAT HE'S CHASING SOMETHING.
KICK KICK KICK KICK
KICK KICK KICK KICK
©BOBSCOTT

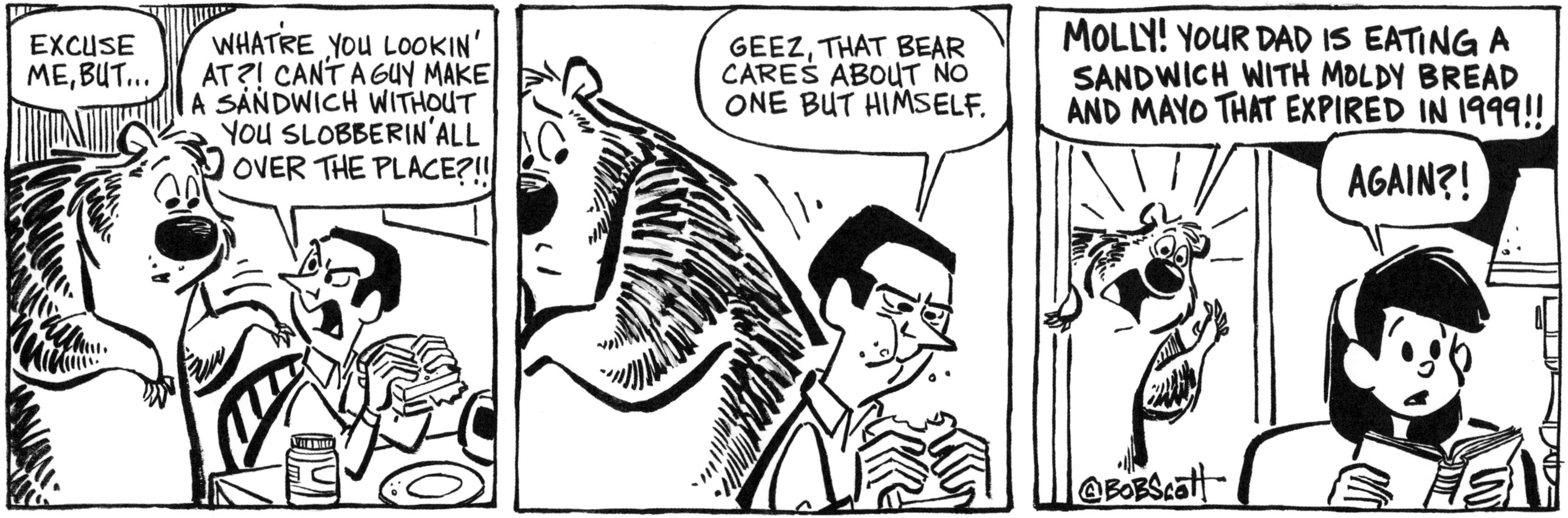
EXCUSE ME, BUT...
WHAT'RE YOU LOOKIN' AT?! CAN'T A GUY MAKE A SANDWICH WITHOUT YOU SLOBBERIN' ALL OVER THE PLACE?!!
GEEZ, THAT BEAR CARES ABOUT NO ONE BUT HIMSELF.
MOLLY! YOUR DAD IS EATING A SANDWICH WITH MOLDY BREAD AND MAYO THAT EXPIRED IN 1999!!
AGAIN?!
©BOBSCOTT

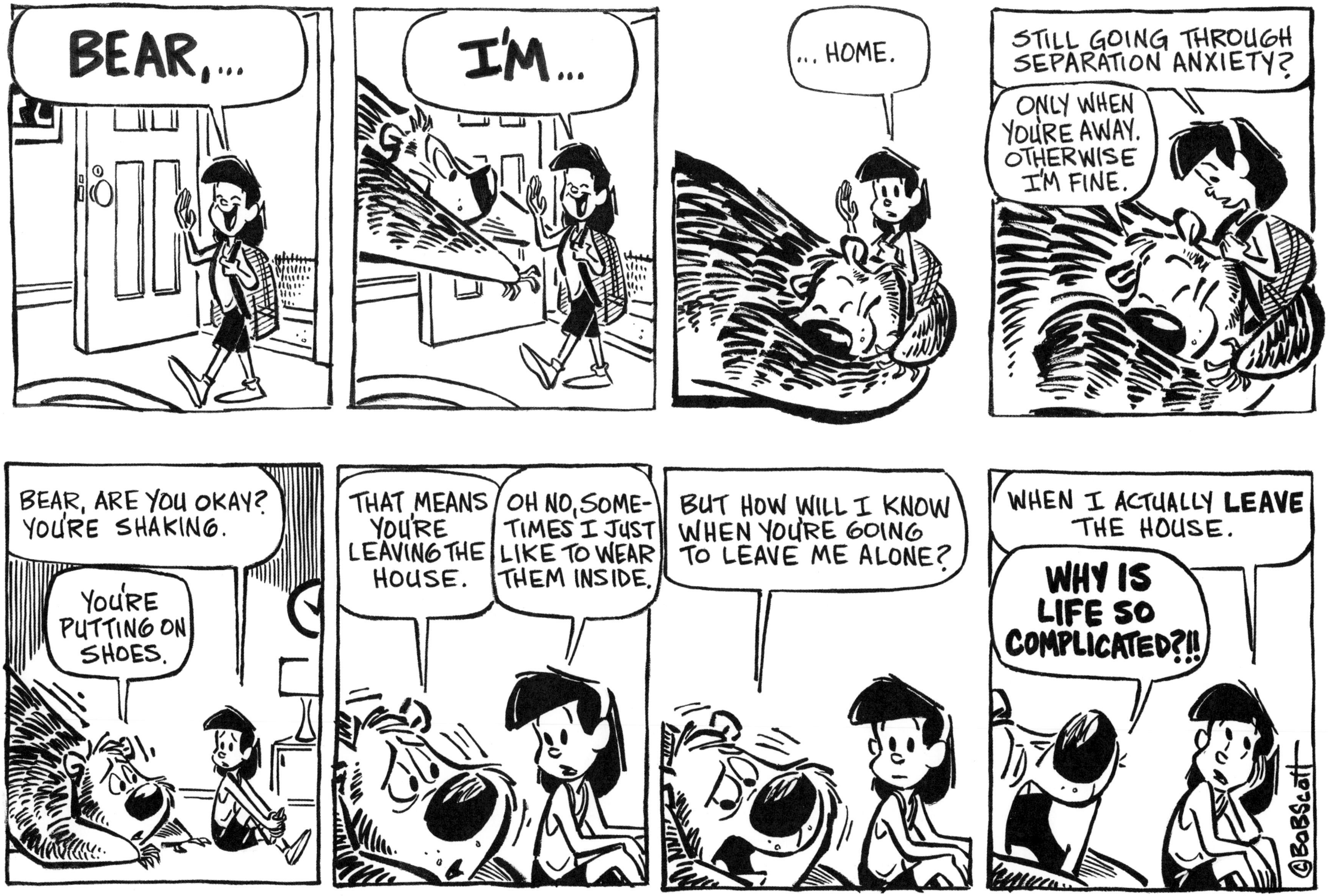
BEAR, ...
I'M...
... HOME.
STILL GOING THROUGH SEPARATION ANXIETY?
ONLY WHEN YOU'RE AWAY. OTHERWISE I'M FINE.
BEAR, ARE YOU OKAY? YOU'RE SHAKING.
YOU'RE PUTTING ON SHOES.
THAT MEANS YOU'RE LEAVING THE HOUSE.
OH NO, SOMETIMES I JUST LIKE TO WEAR THEM INSIDE.
BUT HOW WILL I KNOW WHEN YOU'RE GOING TO LEAVE ME ALONE?
WHEN I ACTUALLY **LEAVE** THE HOUSE.
WHY IS LIFE SO COMPLICATED?!!
©BOBSCOTT

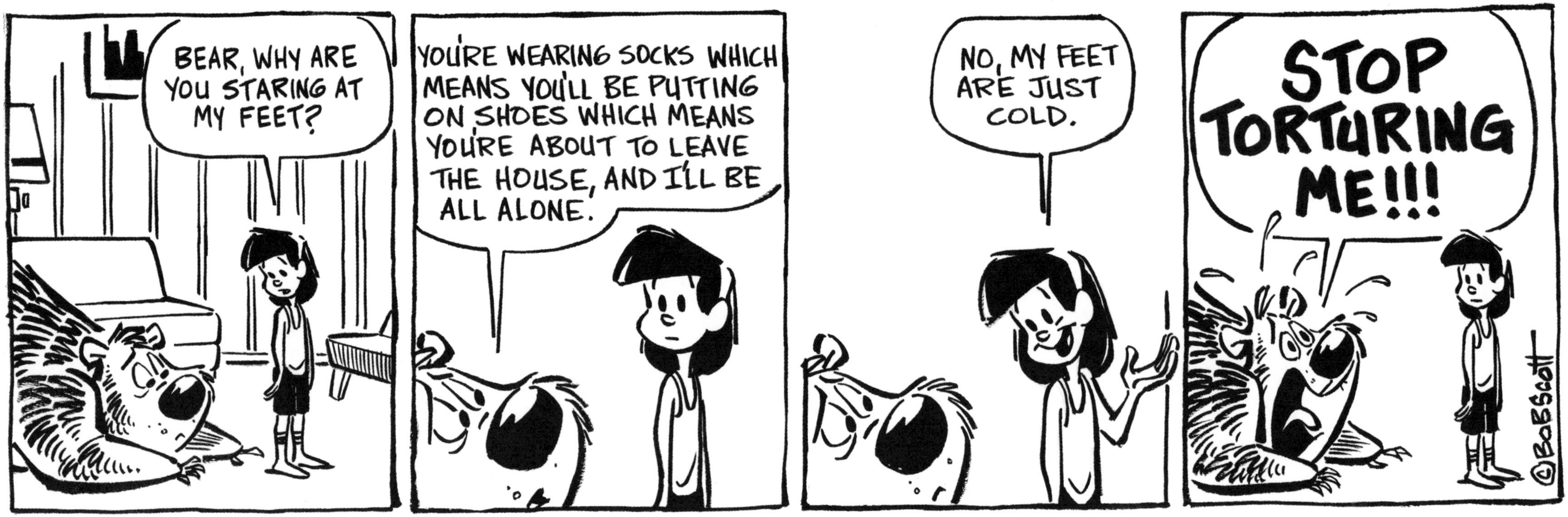
BEAR, WHY ARE YOU STARING AT MY FEET?
YOU'RE WEARING SOCKS WHICH MEANS YOU'LL BE PUTTING ON SHOES WHICH MEANS YOU'RE ABOUT TO LEAVE THE HOUSE, AND I'LL BE ALL ALONE.
NO, MY FEET ARE JUST COLD.
STOP TORTURING ME!!!
©BOBSCOTT

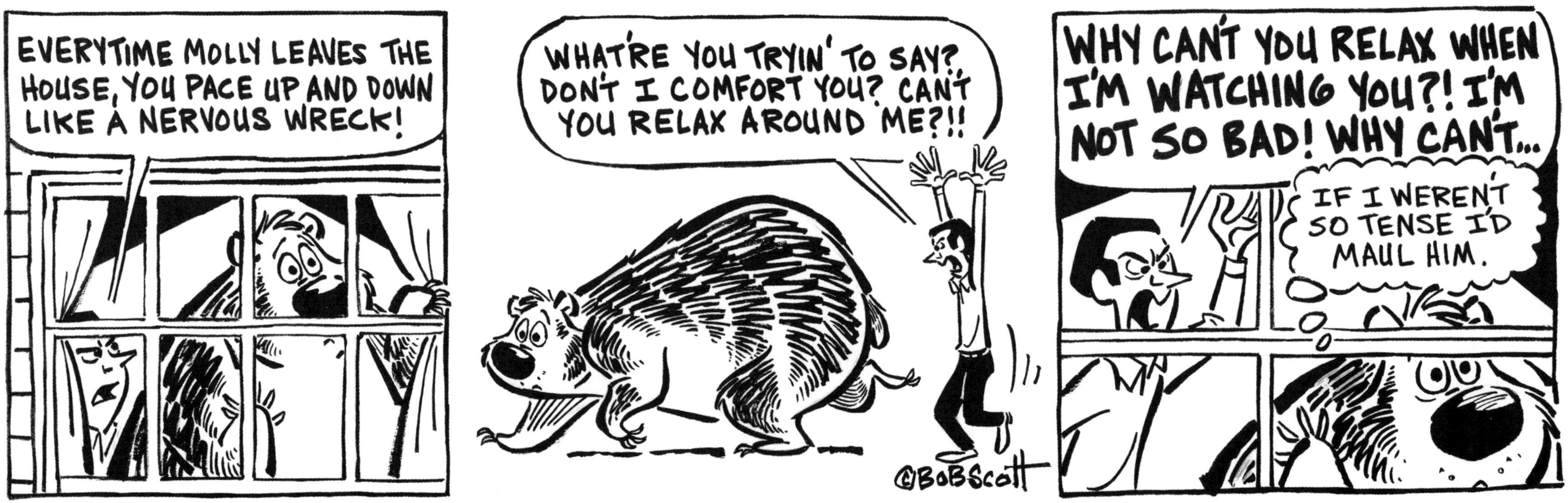
EVERYTIME MOLLY LEAVES THE HOUSE, YOU PACE UP AND DOWN LIKE A NERVOUS WRECK!
WHAT'RE YOU TRYIN' TO SAY? DON'T I COMFORT YOU? CAN'T YOU RELAX AROUND ME?!!
©BOBSCOTT
WHY CAN'T YOU RELAX WHEN I'M WATCHING YOU?! I'M NOT SO BAD! WHY CAN'T...
IF I WEREN'T SO TENSE I'D MAUL HIM.

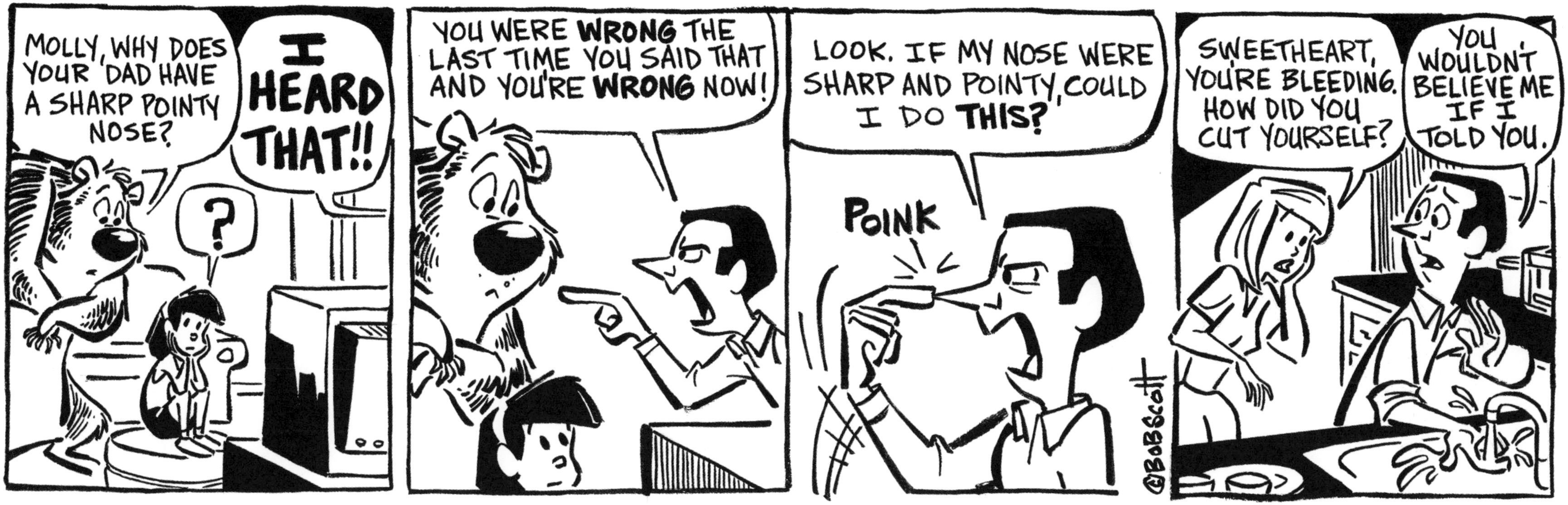
MOLLY, WHY DOES YOUR DAD HAVE A SHARP POINTY NOSE?
?
I HEARD THAT!!
YOU WERE WRONG THE LAST TIME YOU SAID THAT AND YOU'RE WRONG NOW!
LOOK. IF MY NOSE WERE SHARP AND POINTY, COULD I DO THIS?
POINK
©BOBSCOTT
SWEETHEART, YOU'RE BLEEDING. HOW DID YOU CUT YOURSELF?
YOU WOULDN'T BELIEVE ME IF I TOLD YOU.

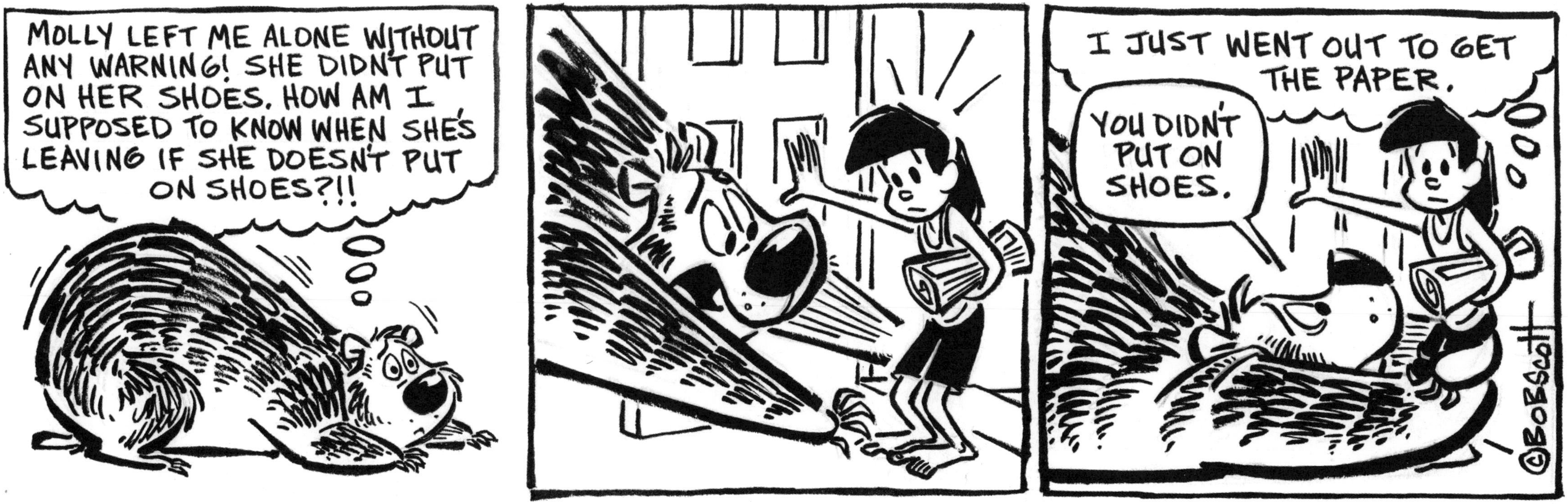
MOLLY LEFT ME ALONE WITHOUT ANY WARNING! SHE DIDN'T PUT ON HER SHOES. HOW AM I SUPPOSED TO KNOW WHEN SHE'S LEAVING IF SHE DOESN'T PUT ON SHOES?!!
I JUST WENT OUT TO GET THE PAPER.
YOU DIDN'T PUT ON SHOES.
©BOBSCOTT

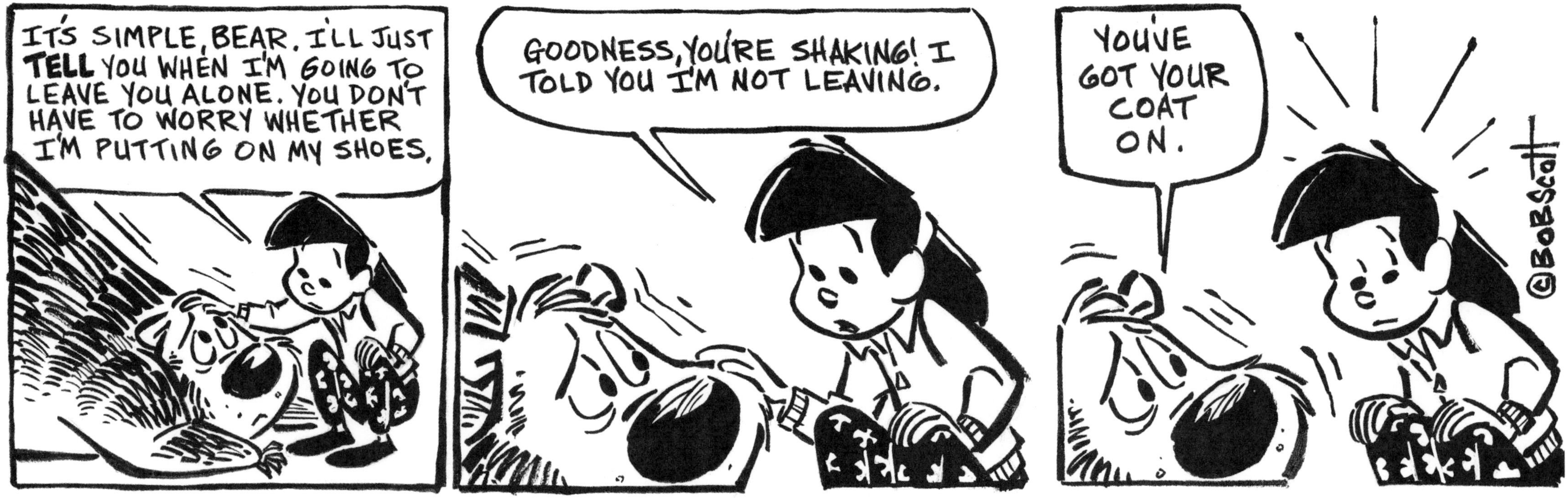
IT'S SIMPLE, BEAR. I'LL JUST TELL YOU WHEN I'M GOING TO LEAVE YOU ALONE. YOU DON'T HAVE TO WORRY WHETHER I'M PUTTING ON MY SHOES.
GOODNESS, YOU'RE SHAKING! I TOLD YOU I'M NOT LEAVING.
YOU'VE GOT YOUR COAT ON.
©BOBSCOTT

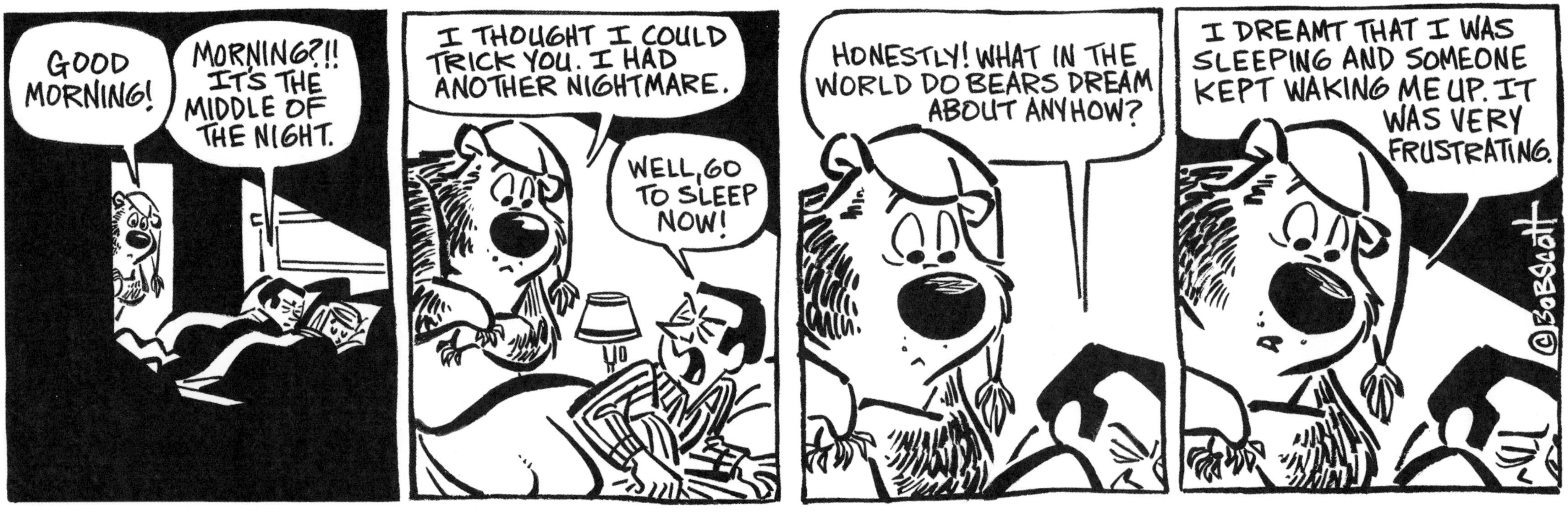
GOOD MORNING!
MORNING?!! IT'S THE MIDDLE OF THE NIGHT.
I THOUGHT I COULD TRICK YOU. I HAD ANOTHER NIGHTMARE.
WELL, GO TO SLEEP NOW!
HONESTLY! WHAT IN THE WORLD DO BEARS DREAM ABOUT ANYHOW?
I DREAMT THAT I WAS SLEEPING AND SOMEONE KEPT WAKING ME UP. IT WAS VERY FRUSTRATING.
©BOBSCOTT

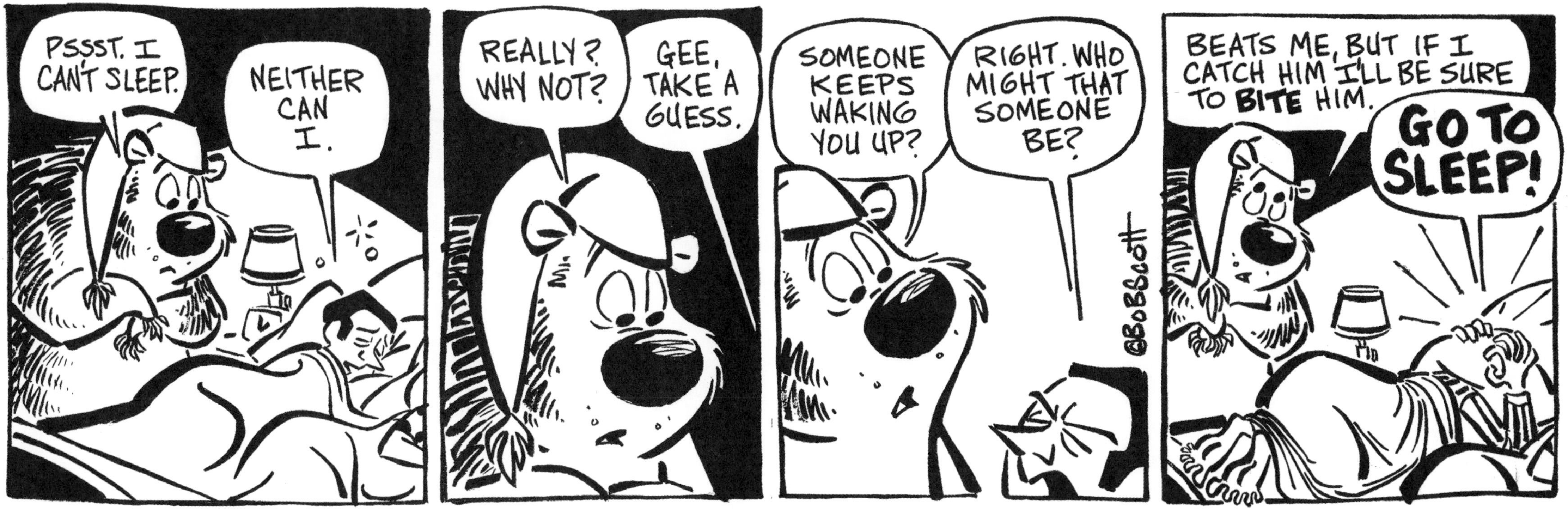
PSSST. I CAN'T SLEEP.
NEITHER CAN I.
REALLY? WHY NOT?
GEE, TAKE A GUESS.
SOMEONE KEEPS WAKING YOU UP?
RIGHT. WHO MIGHT THAT SOMEONE BE?
©BOBSCOTT
BEATS ME, BUT IF I CATCH HIM I'LL BE SURE TO **BITE** HIM.
GO TO SLEEP!

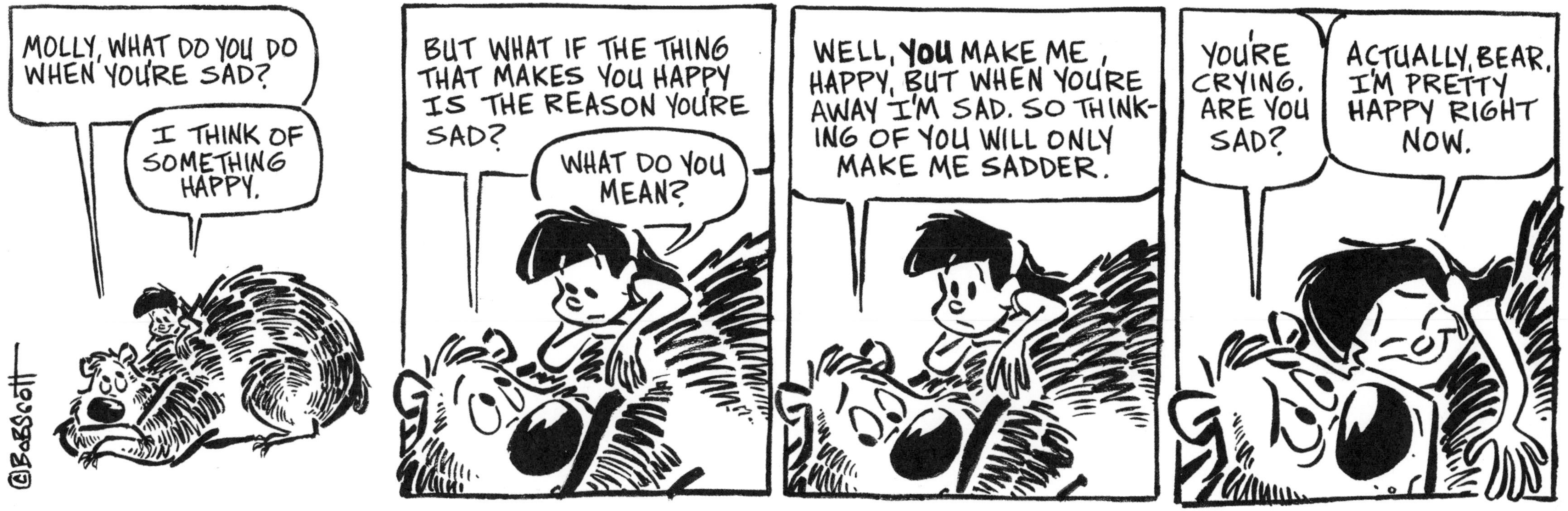
MOLLY, WHAT DO YOU DO WHEN YOU'RE SAD?
I THINK OF SOMETHING HAPPY.
©BOBSCOTT
BUT WHAT IF THE THING THAT MAKES YOU HAPPY IS THE REASON YOU'RE SAD?
WHAT DO YOU MEAN?
WELL, **YOU** MAKE ME, HAPPY, BUT WHEN YOU'RE AWAY I'M SAD. SO THINKING OF YOU WILL ONLY MAKE ME SADDER.
YOU'RE CRYING. ARE YOU SAD?
ACTUALLY, BEAR, I'M PRETTY HAPPY RIGHT NOW.

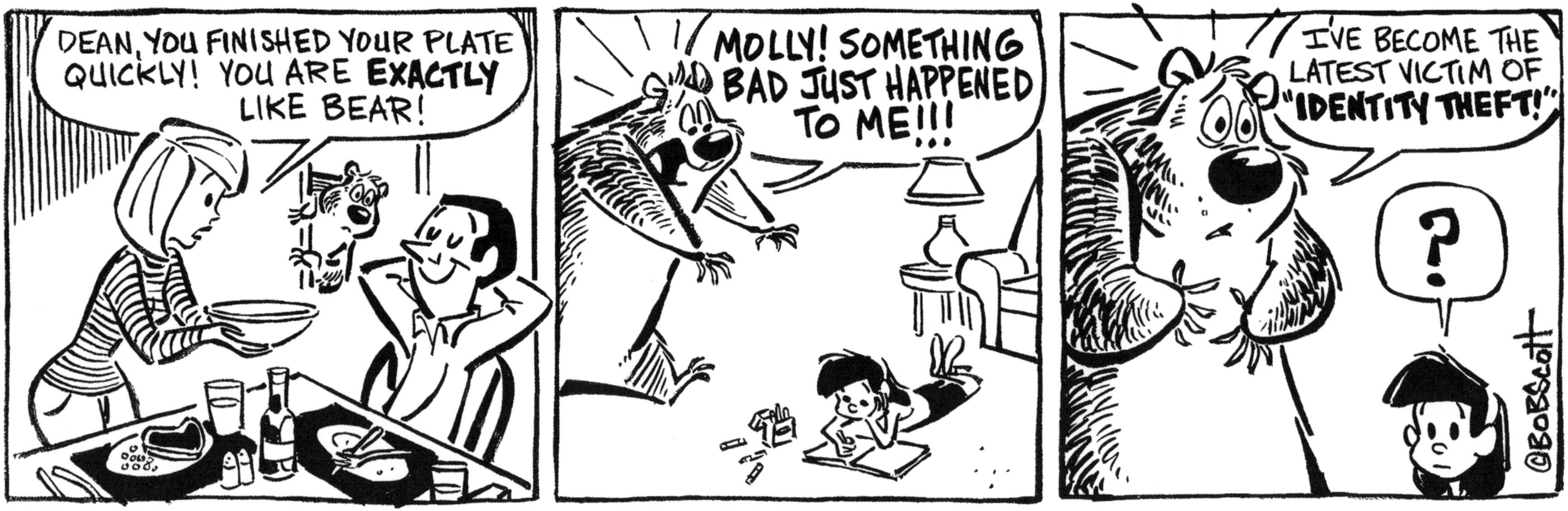
DEAN, YOU FINISHED YOUR PLATE QUICKLY! YOU ARE **EXACTLY** LIKE BEAR!
MOLLY! SOMETHING BAD JUST HAPPENED TO ME!!!
I'VE BECOME THE LATEST VICTIM OF "**IDENTITY THEFT!**"
?
©BOBSCOTT

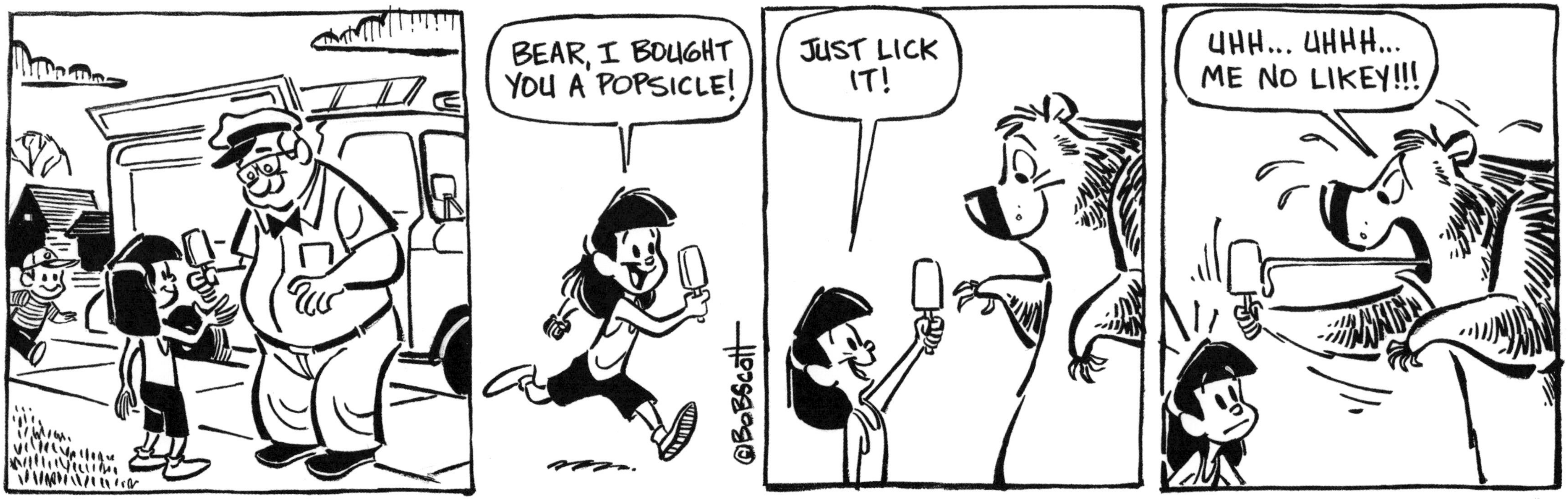
BEAR, I BOUGHT YOU A POPSICLE!
©BOBSCOTT
JUST LICK IT!
UHH... UHHH... ME NO LIKEY!!!

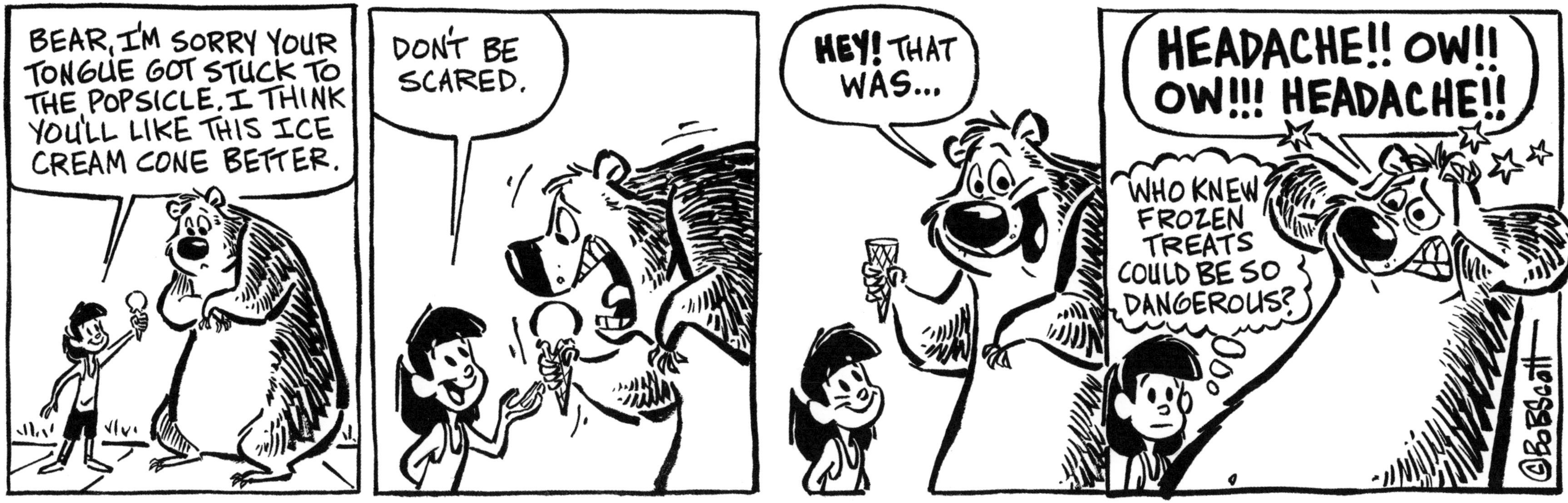
BEAR, I'M SORRY YOUR TONGUE GOT STUCK TO THE POPSICLE. I THINK YOU'LL LIKE THIS ICE CREAM CONE BETTER.
DON'T BE SCARED.
HEY! THAT WAS...
HEADACHE!! OW!! OW!!! HEADACHE!!
WHO KNEW FROZEN TREATS COULD BE SO DANGEROUS?
©BOBSCOTT

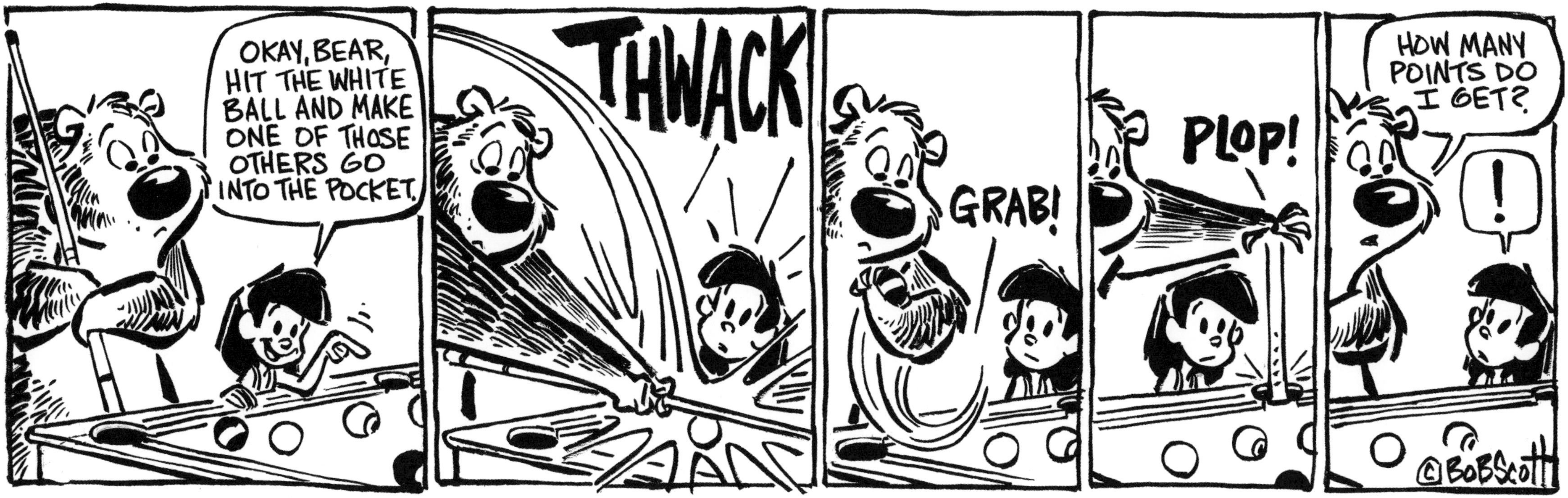
OKAY, BEAR, HIT THE WHITE BALL AND MAKE ONE OF THOSE OTHERS GO INTO THE POCKET.
THWACK
GRAB!
PLOP!
HOW MANY POINTS DO I GET?
!
©BOBSCOTT

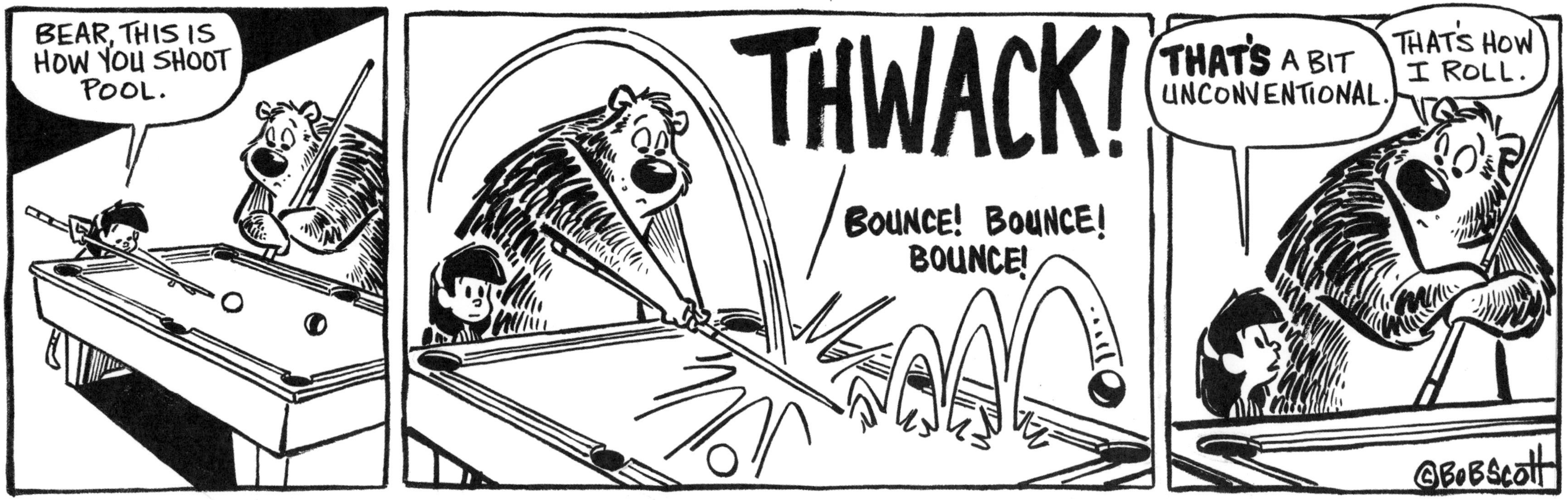
BEAR, THIS IS HOW YOU SHOOT POOL.
THWACK!
BOUNCE! BOUNCE! BOUNCE!
THAT'S A BIT UNCONVENTIONAL.
THAT'S HOW I ROLL.
©BOBSCOTT

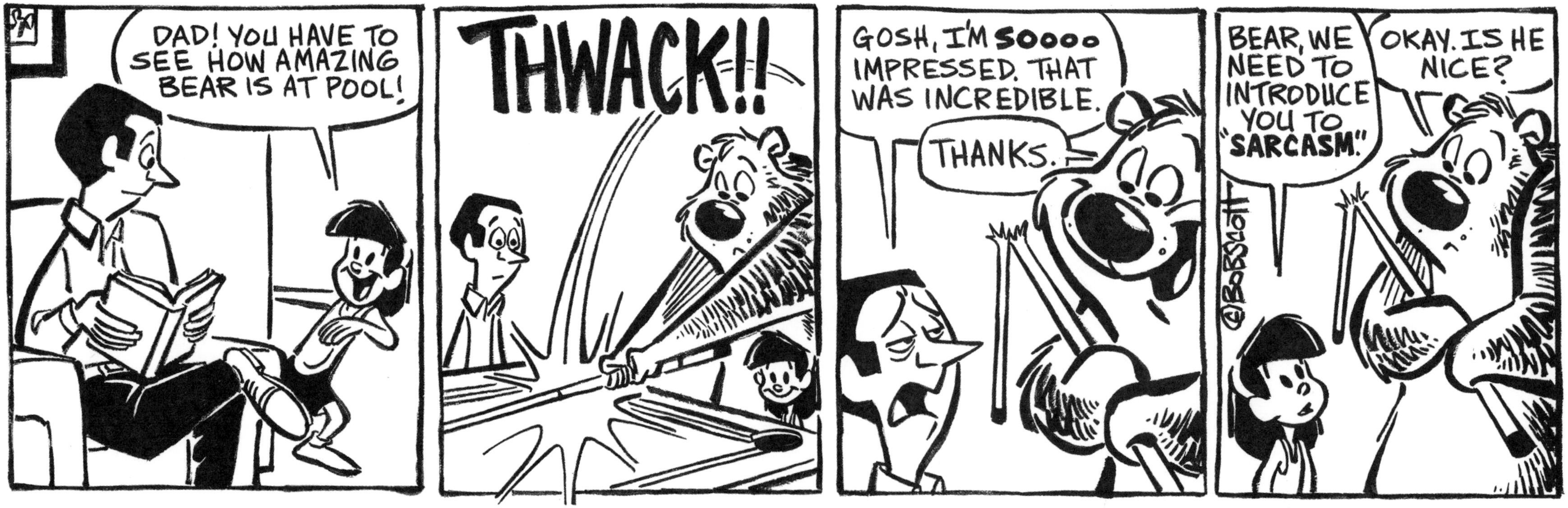
DAD! YOU HAVE TO SEE HOW AMAZING BEAR IS AT POOL!
THWACK!!
GOSH, I'M SOOOOO IMPRESSED. THAT WAS INCREDIBLE.
THANKS.
©BOBSCOTT
BEAR, WE NEED TO INTRODUCE YOU TO "SARCASM."
OKAY. IS HE NICE?

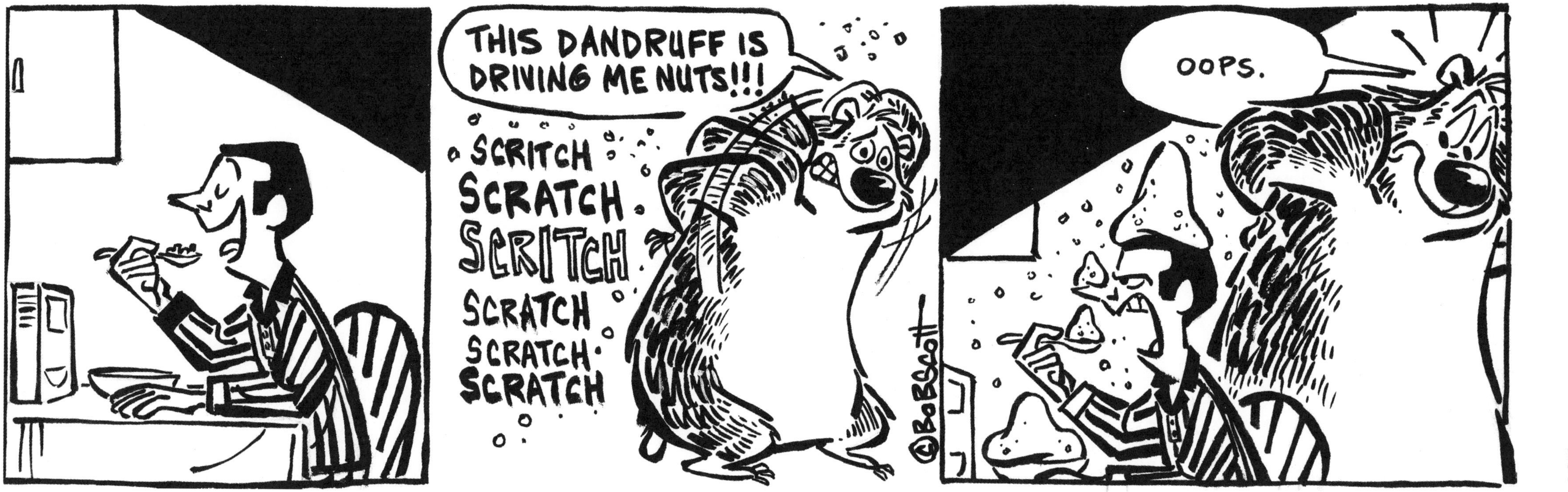
THIS DANDRUFF IS DRIVING ME NUTS!!!
SCRITCH
SCRATCH
SCRITCH
SCRATCH
SCRATCH
SCRATCH
©BOBSCOTT
OOPS.

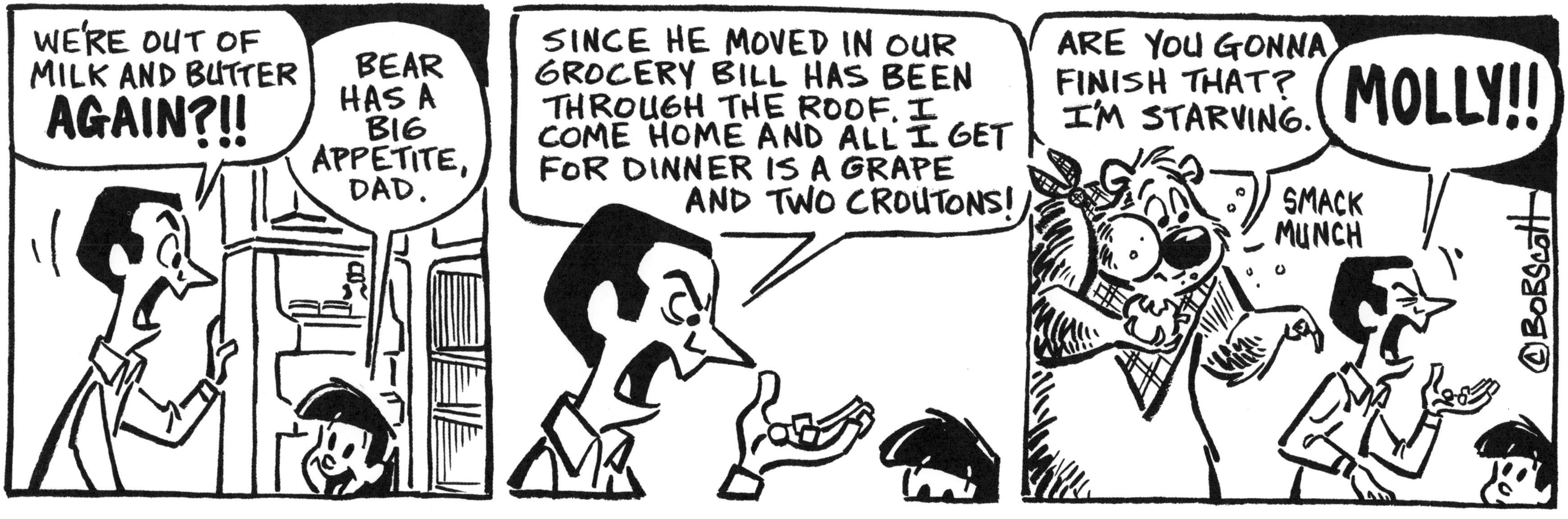
WE'RE OUT OF MILK AND BUTTER AGAIN?!!
BEAR HAS A BIG APPETITE, DAD.
SINCE HE MOVED IN OUR GROCERY BILL HAS BEEN THROUGH THE ROOF. I COME HOME AND ALL I GET FOR DINNER IS A GRAPE AND TWO CROUTONS!
ARE YOU GONNA FINISH THAT? I'M STARVING.
SMACK MUNCH
MOLLY!!
©BOBSCOTT

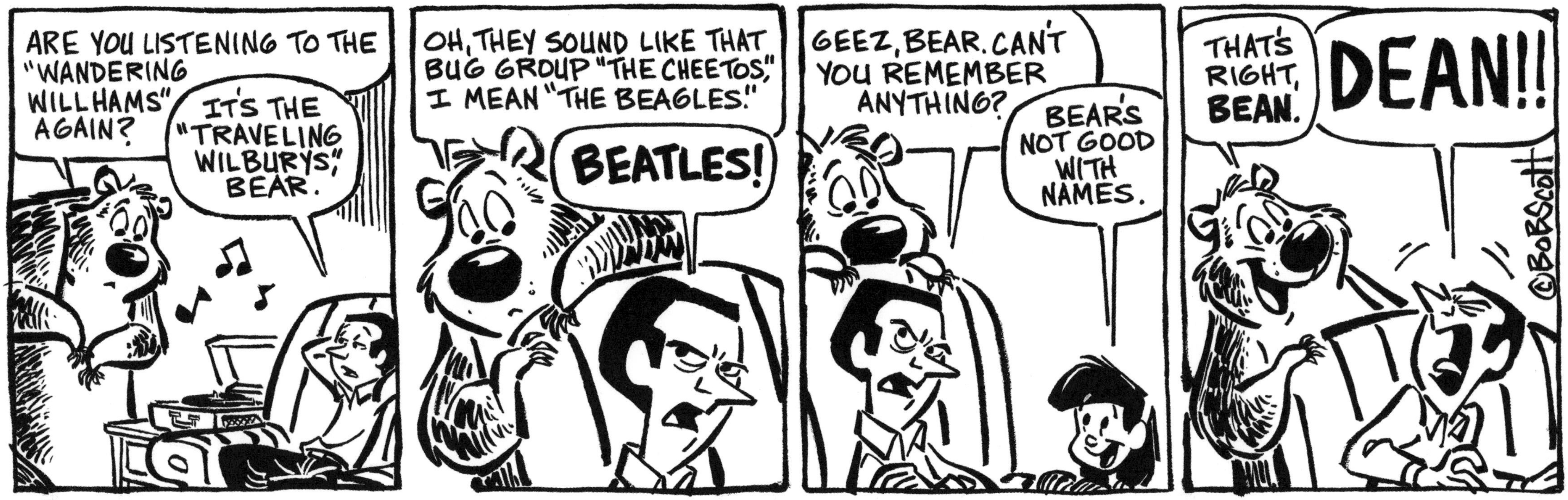
ARE YOU LISTENING TO THE "WANDERING WILLHAMS" AGAIN?
IT'S THE "TRAVELING WILBURYS," BEAR.
OH, THEY SOUND LIKE THAT BUG GROUP "THE CHEETOS," I MEAN "THE BEAGLES."
BEATLES!
GEEZ, BEAR. CAN'T YOU REMEMBER ANYTHING?
BEAR'S NOT GOOD WITH NAMES.
THAT'S RIGHT, BEAN.
DEAN!!
©BOBSCOTT

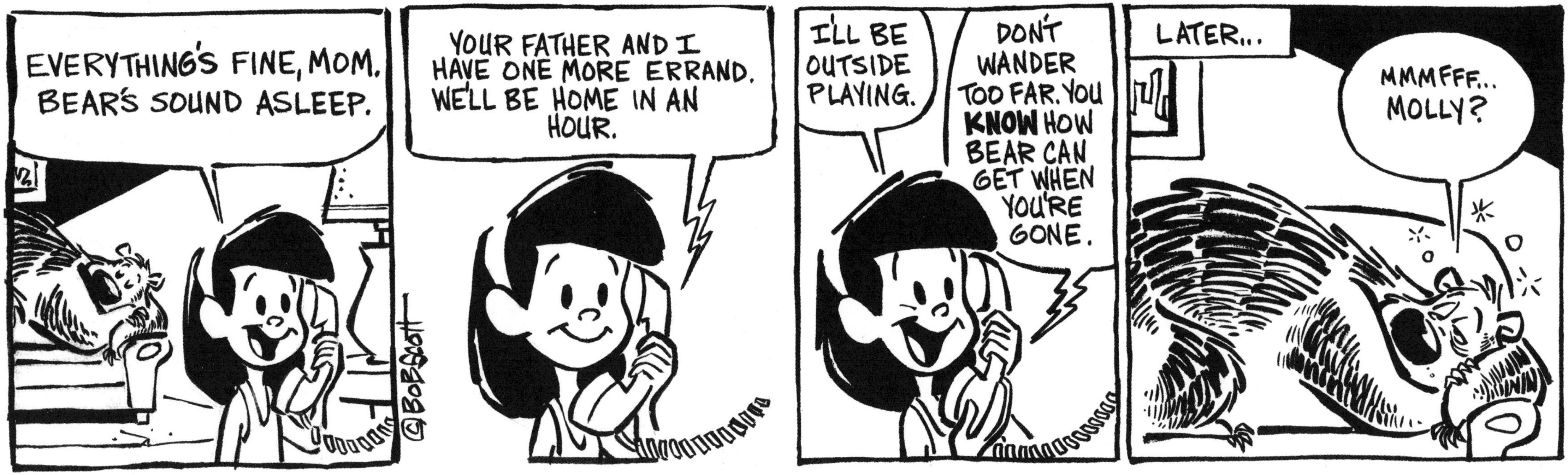
EVERYTHING'S FINE, MOM. BEAR'S SOUND ASLEEP.
©BOBSCOTT
YOUR FATHER AND I HAVE ONE MORE ERRAND. WE'LL BE HOME IN AN HOUR.
I'LL BE OUTSIDE PLAYING.
DON'T WANDER TOO FAR. YOU KNOW HOW BEAR CAN GET WHEN YOU'RE GONE.
LATER...
MMMFFF... MOLLY?

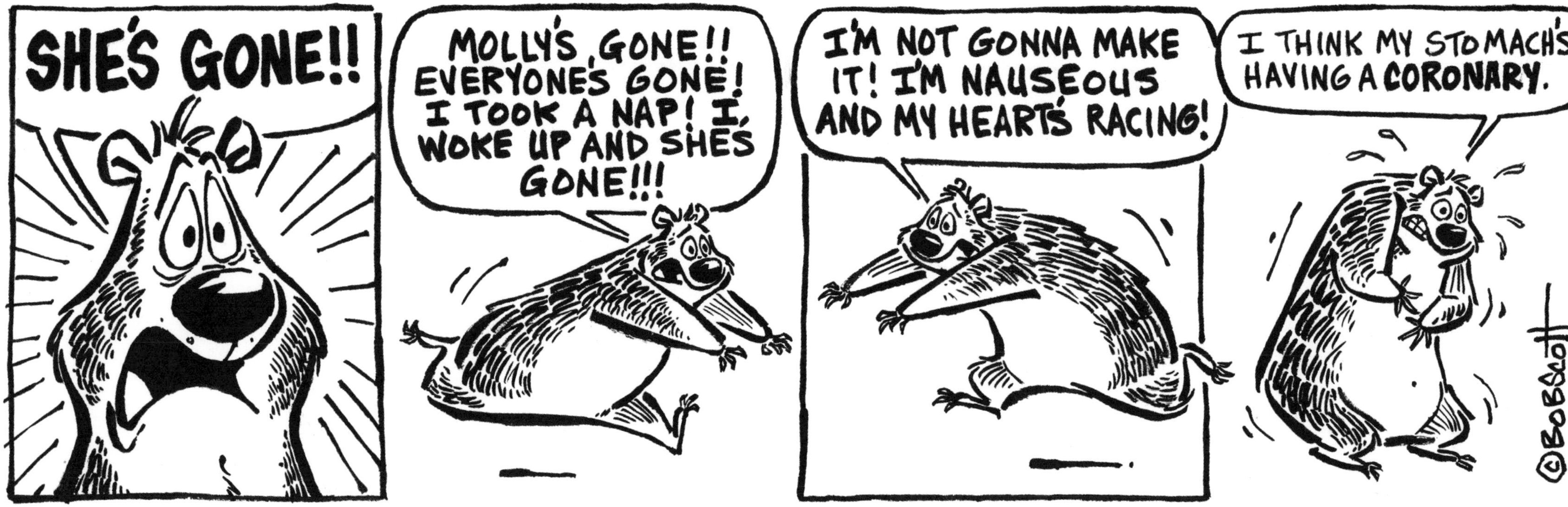
SHE'S GONE!!
MOLLY'S GONE!! EVERYONE'S GONE! I TOOK A NAP! I, WOKE UP AND SHE'S GONE!!!
I'M NOT GONNA MAKE IT! I'M NAUSEOUS AND MY HEART'S RACING!
I THINK MY STOMACH'S HAVING A CORONARY.
©BOBSCOTT

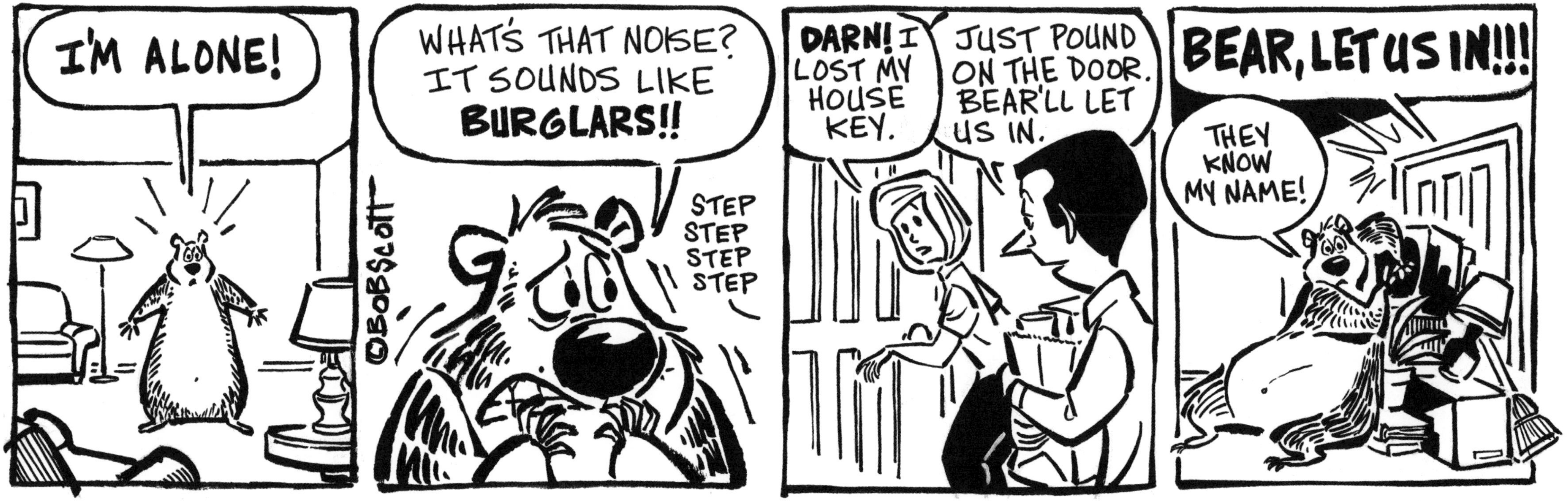
I'M ALONE!
©BOBSCOTT
WHAT'S THAT NOISE? IT SOUNDS LIKE BURGLARS!!
STEP STEP STEP STEP
DARN! I LOST MY HOUSE KEY.
JUST POUND ON THE DOOR. BEAR'LL LET US IN.
BEAR, LET US IN!!!
THEY KNOW MY NAME!

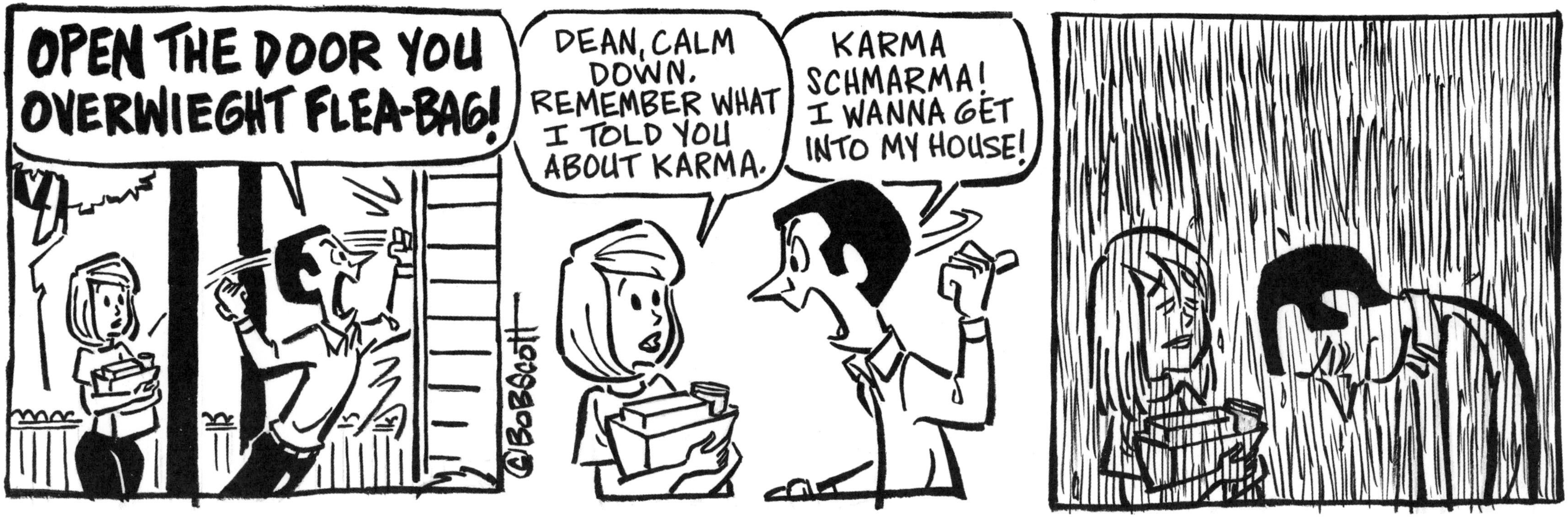

OPEN THE DOOR YOU OVERWIEGHT FLEA-BAG!
©BOBSCOTT
DEAN, CALM DOWN. REMEMBER WHAT I TOLD YOU ABOUT KARMA.
KARMA SCHMARMA! I WANNA GET INTO MY HOUSE!

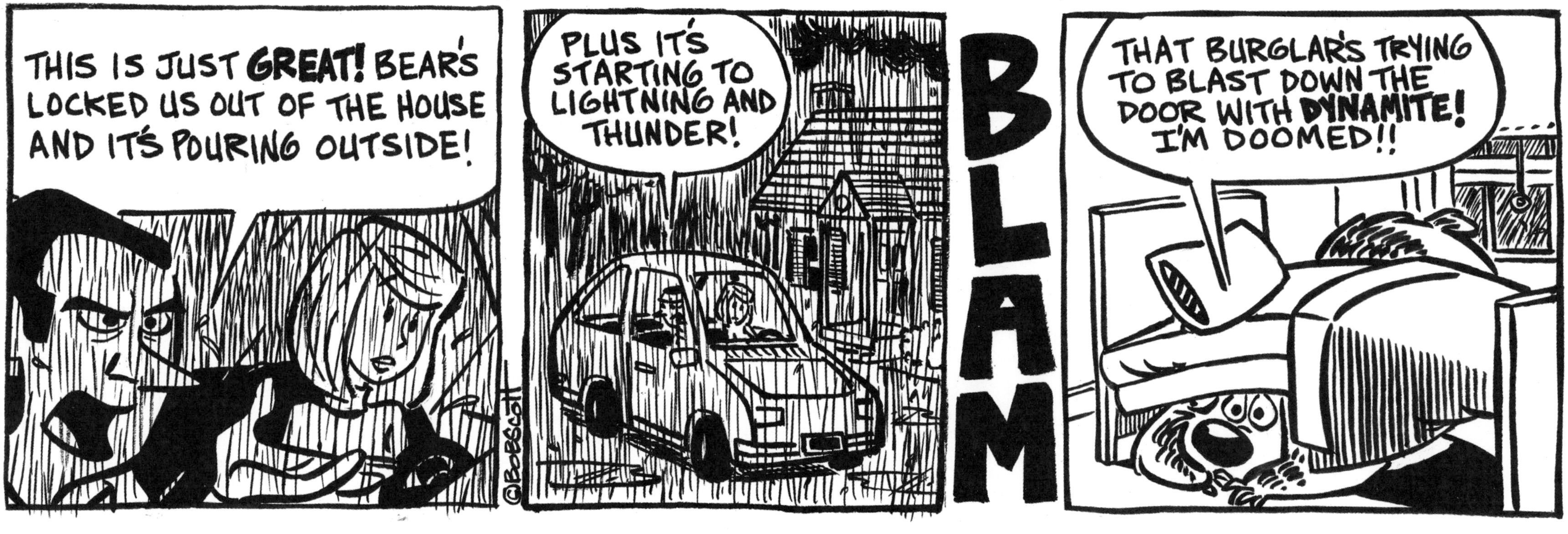

THIS IS JUST GREAT! BEAR'S LOCKED US OUT OF THE HOUSE AND IT'S POURING OUTSIDE!
©BOBSCOTT
PLUS IT'S STARTING TO LIGHTNING AND THUNDER!
BLAM
THAT BURGLAR'S TRYING TO BLAST DOWN THE DOOR WITH DYNAMITE! I'M DOOMED!!

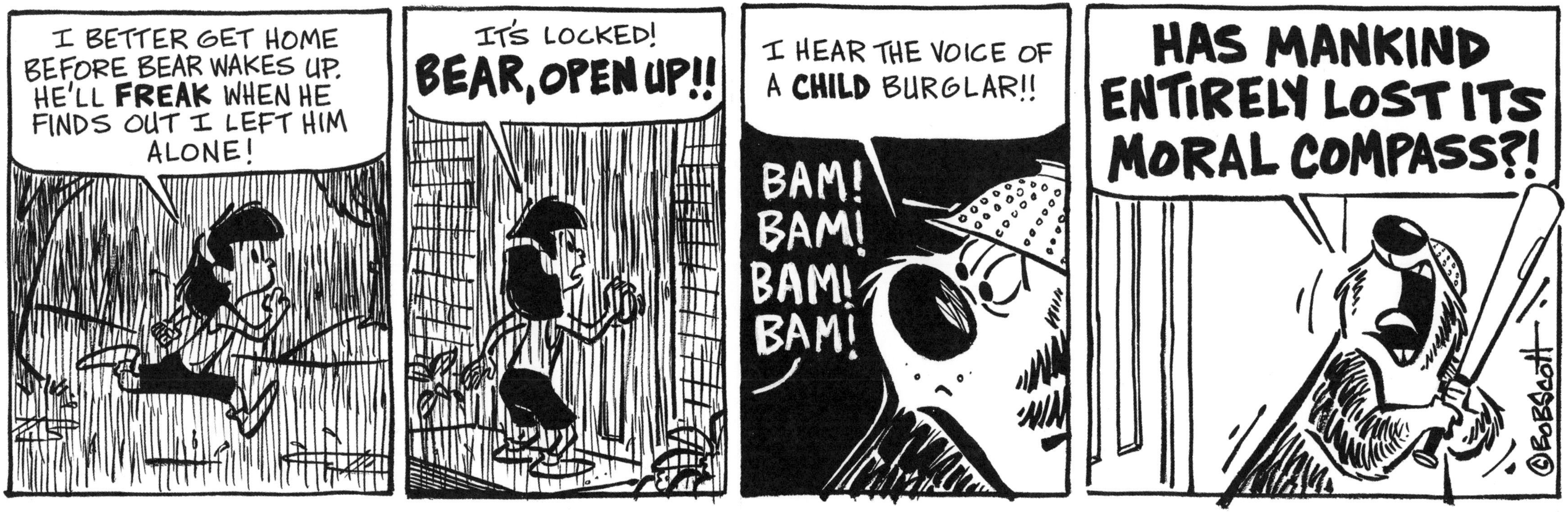
I BETTER GET HOME BEFORE BEAR WAKES UP. HE'LL FREAK WHEN HE FINDS OUT I LEFT HIM ALONE!
IT'S LOCKED! BEAR, OPEN UP!!
BAM! BAM! BAM! BAM!
I HEAR THE VOICE OF A CHILD BURGLAR!!
HAS MANKIND ENTIRELY LOST ITS MORAL COMPASS?!
©BOBSCOTT

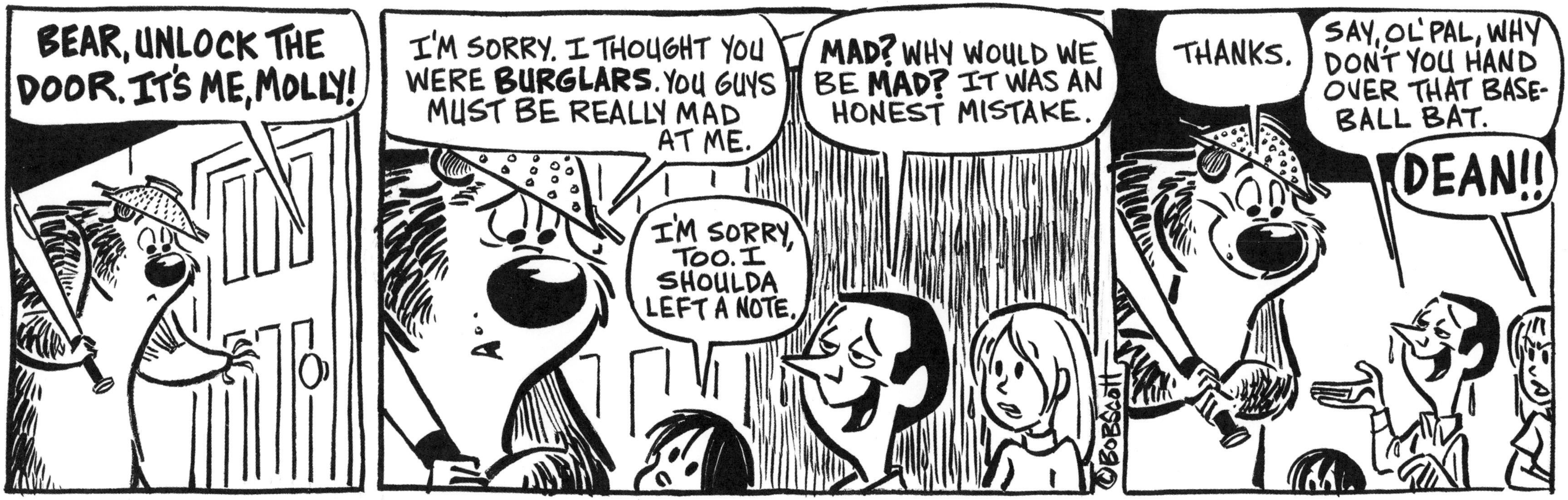
BEAR, UNLOCK THE DOOR. IT'S ME, MOLLY!
I'M SORRY. I THOUGHT YOU WERE BURGLARS. YOU GUYS MUST BE REALLY MAD AT ME.
I'M SORRY, TOO. I SHOULDA LEFT A NOTE.
MAD? WHY WOULD WE BE MAD? IT WAS AN HONEST MISTAKE.
©BOBSCOTT
THANKS.
SAY, OL' PAL, WHY DON'T YOU HAND OVER THAT BASE-BALL BAT.
DEAN!!

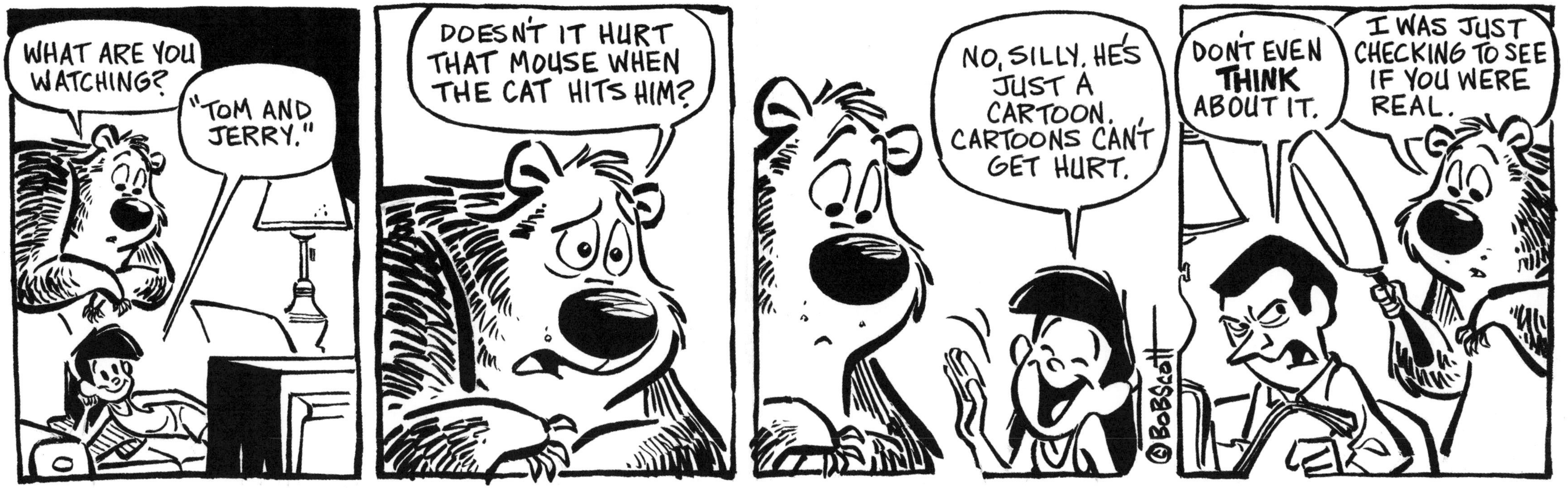
WHAT ARE YOU WATCHING?
"TOM AND JERRY."
DOESN'T IT HURT THAT MOUSE WHEN THE CAT HITS HIM?
NO, SILLY. HE'S JUST A CARTOON. CARTOONS CAN'T GET HURT.
©BOBSCOTT
DON'T EVEN **THINK** ABOUT IT.
I WAS JUST CHECKING TO SEE IF YOU WERE REAL.

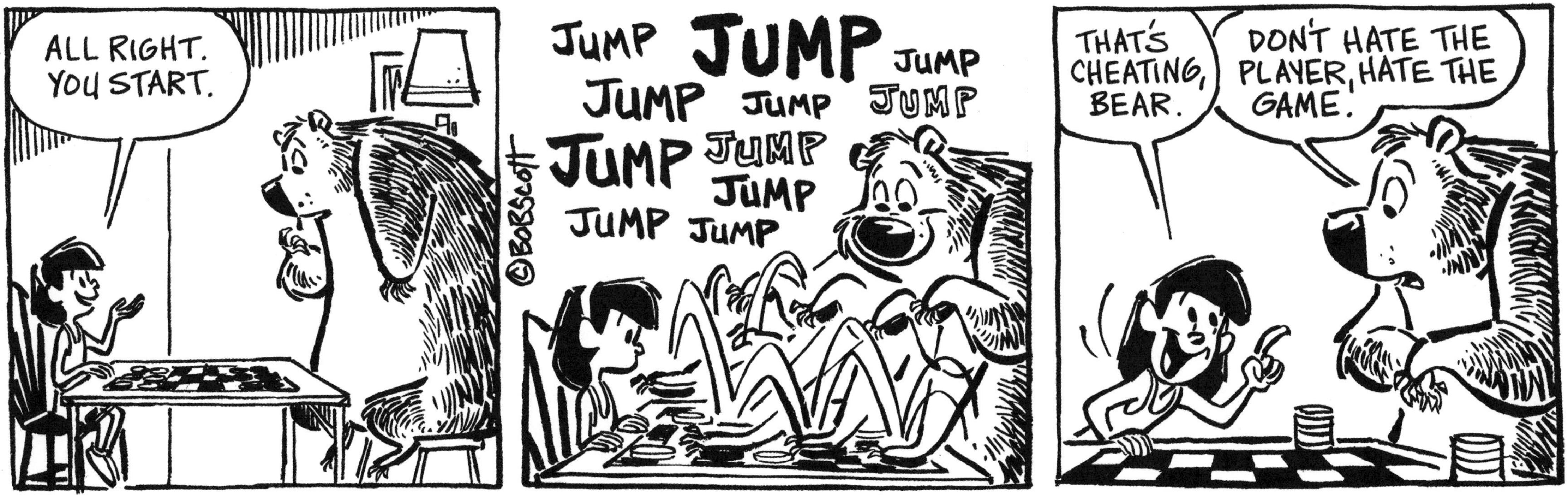
ALL RIGHT. YOU START.
©BOBSCOTT
JUMP JUMP JUMP
JUMP JUMP JUMP
JUMP JUMP
JUMP
JUMP JUMP
THAT'S CHEATING, BEAR.
DON'T HATE THE PLAYER, HATE THE GAME.

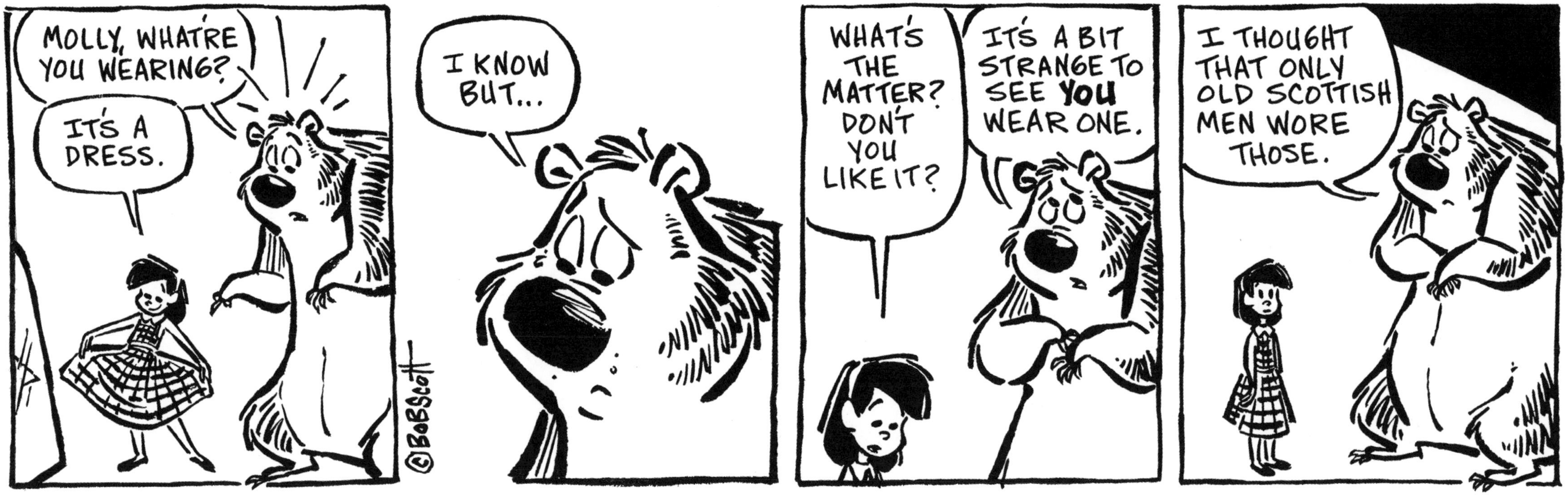
MOLLY, WHAT'RE YOU WEARING?
IT'S A DRESS.
©BOBSCOTT
I KNOW BUT...
WHAT'S THE MATTER? DON'T YOU LIKE IT?
IT'S A BIT STRANGE TO SEE **YOU** WEAR ONE.
I THOUGHT THAT ONLY OLD SCOTTISH MEN WORE THOSE.

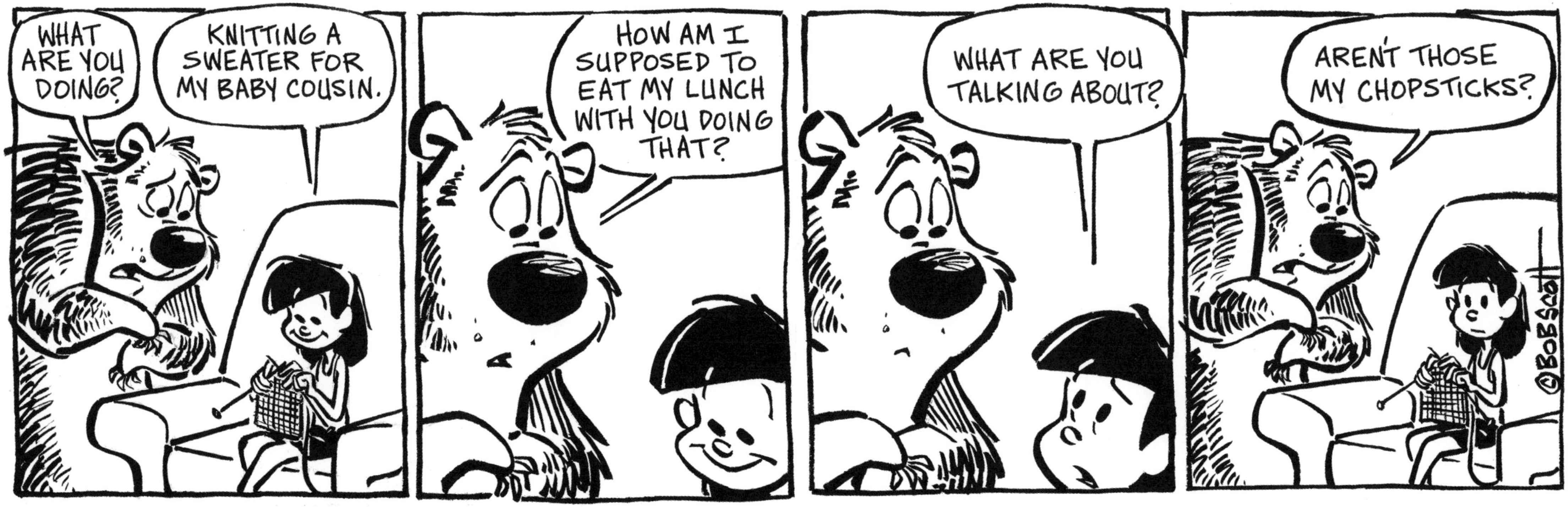
WHAT ARE YOU DOING?
KNITTING A SWEATER FOR MY BABY COUSIN.
HOW AM I SUPPOSED TO EAT MY LUNCH WITH YOU DOING THAT?
WHAT ARE YOU TALKING ABOUT?
AREN'T THOSE MY CHOPSTICKS?
©BOBSCOTT

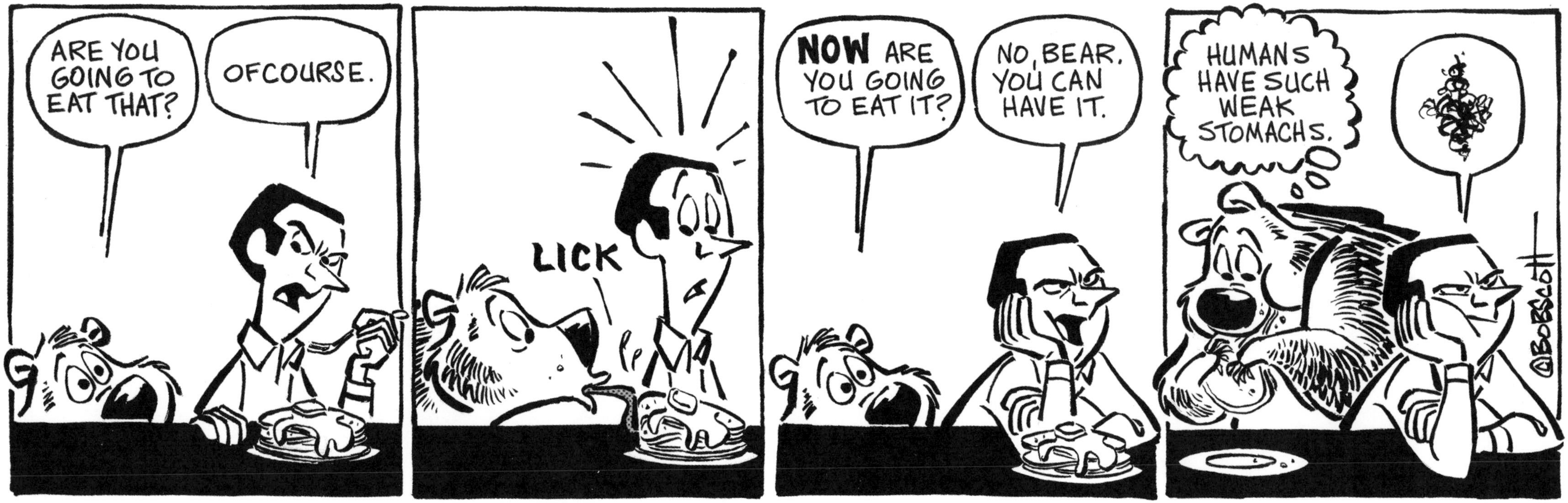
ARE YOU GOING TO EAT THAT?
OFCOURSE.
LICK
NOW ARE YOU GOING TO EAT IT?
NO, BEAR. YOU CAN HAVE IT.
HUMANS HAVE SUCH WEAK STOMACHS.
©BOBSCOTT

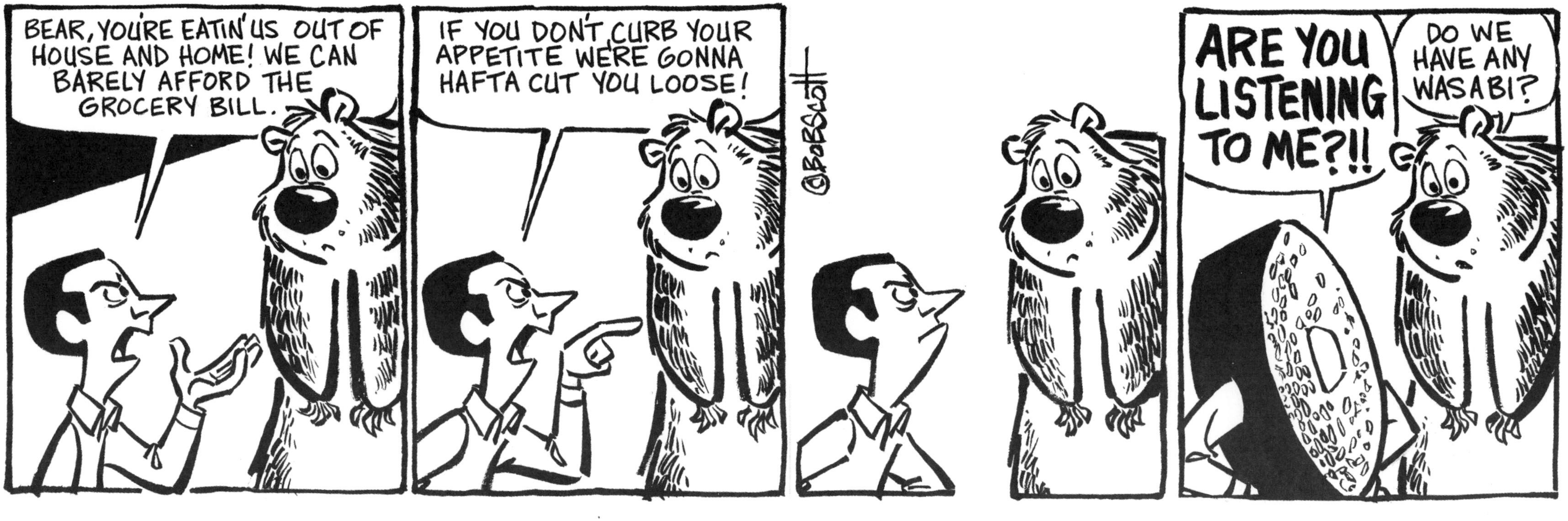
BEAR, YOU'RE EATIN' US OUT OF HOUSE AND HOME! WE CAN BARELY AFFORD THE GROCERY BILL.
IF YOU DON'T CURB YOUR APPETITE WE'RE GONNA HAFTA CUT YOU LOOSE!
©BOBSCOTT
ARE YOU LISTENING TO ME?!!
DO WE HAVE ANY WASABI?

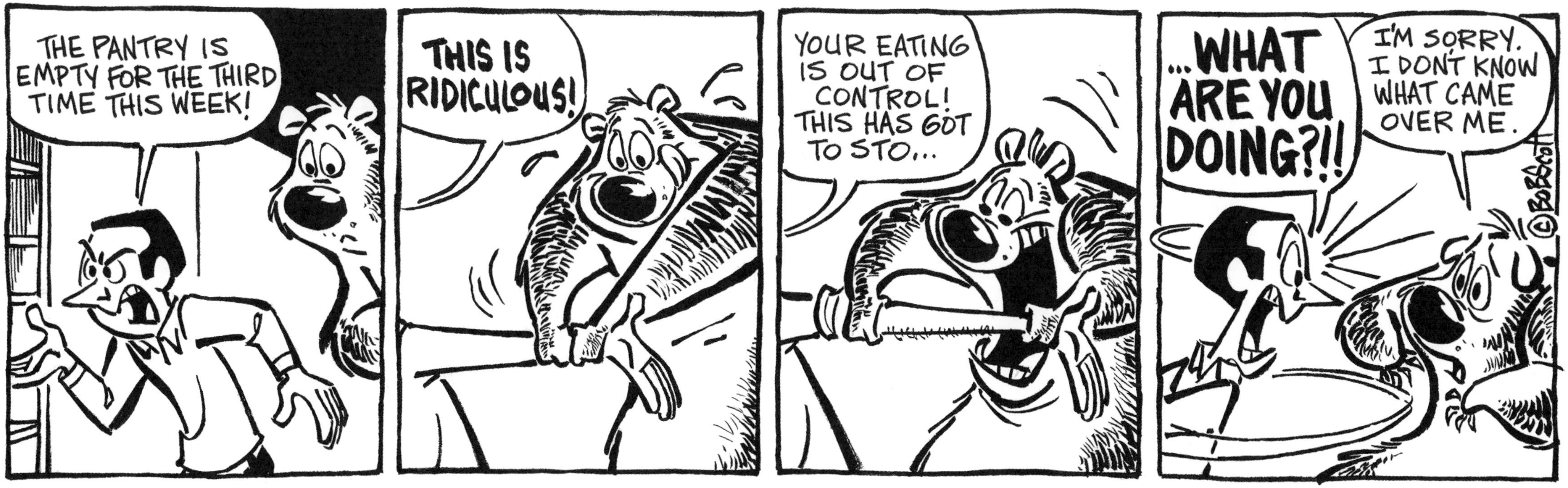
THE PANTRY IS EMPTY FOR THE THIRD TIME THIS WEEK!
THIS IS RIDICULOUS!
YOUR EATING IS OUT OF CONTROL! THIS HAS GOT TO STO...
...WHAT ARE YOU DOING?!!
I'M SORRY. I DON'T KNOW WHAT CAME OVER ME.
©BOBSCOTT

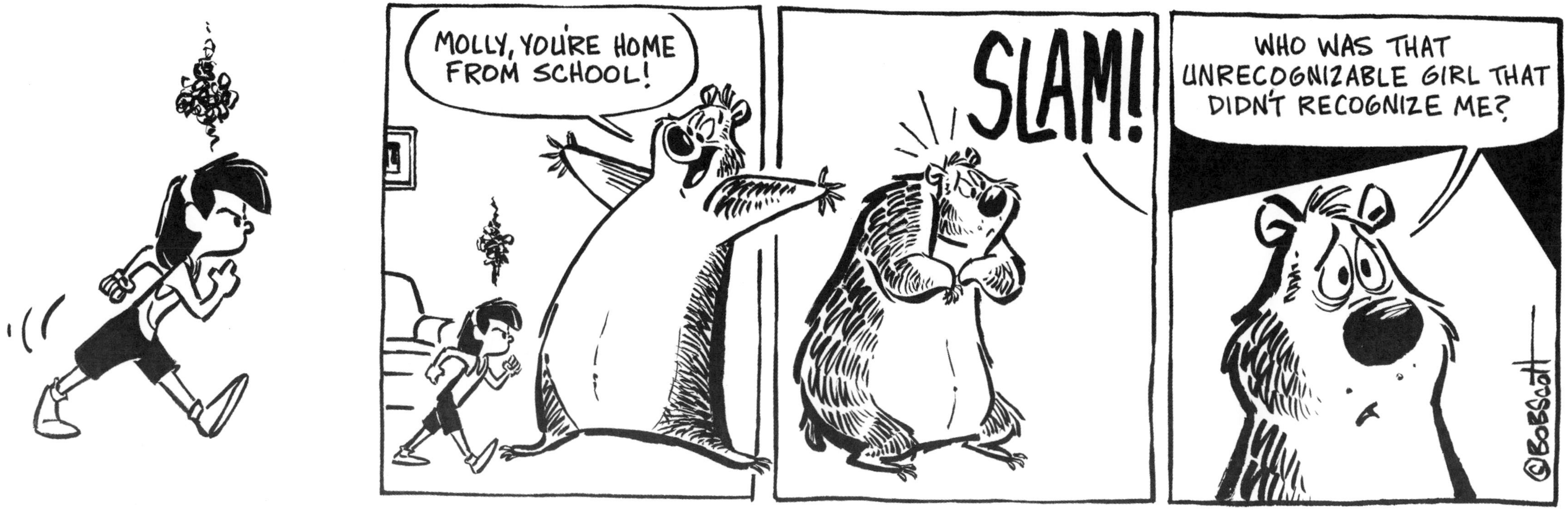
MOLLY, YOU'RE HOME FROM SCHOOL!
SLAM!
WHO WAS THAT UNRECOGNIZABLE GIRL THAT DIDN'T RECOGNIZE ME?
©BOBSCOTT

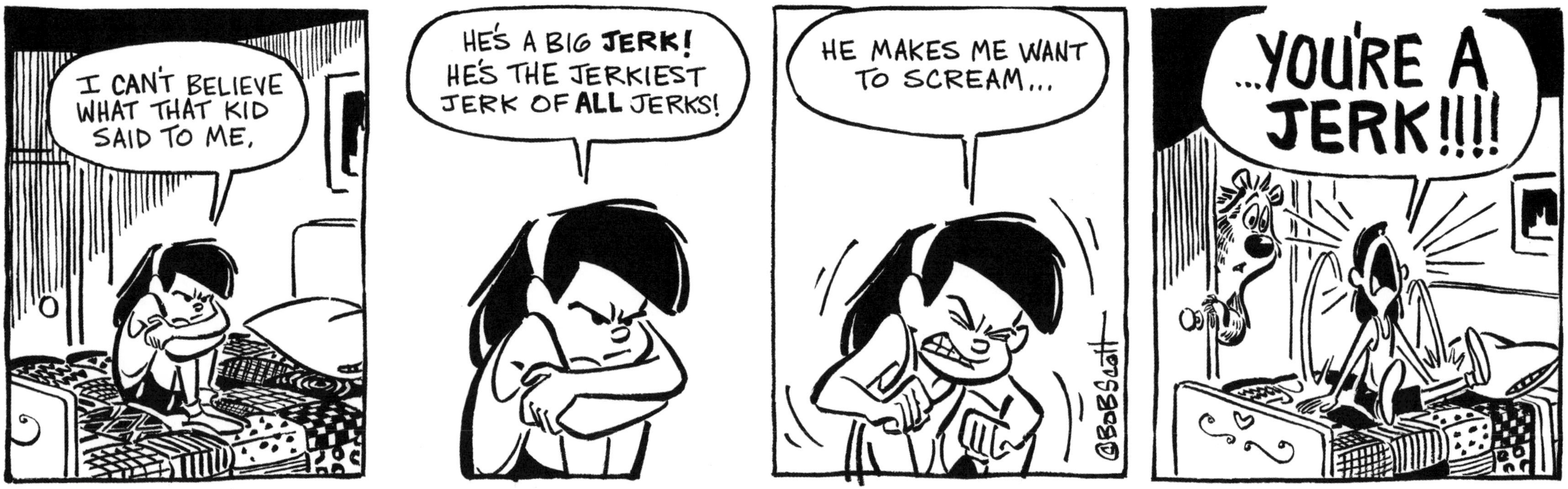
I CAN'T BELIEVE WHAT THAT KID SAID TO ME.
HE'S A BIG **JERK!** HE'S THE JERKIEST JERK OF **ALL** JERKS!
HE MAKES ME WANT TO SCREAM...
...YOU'RE A JERK!!!!
©BOB SCOTT

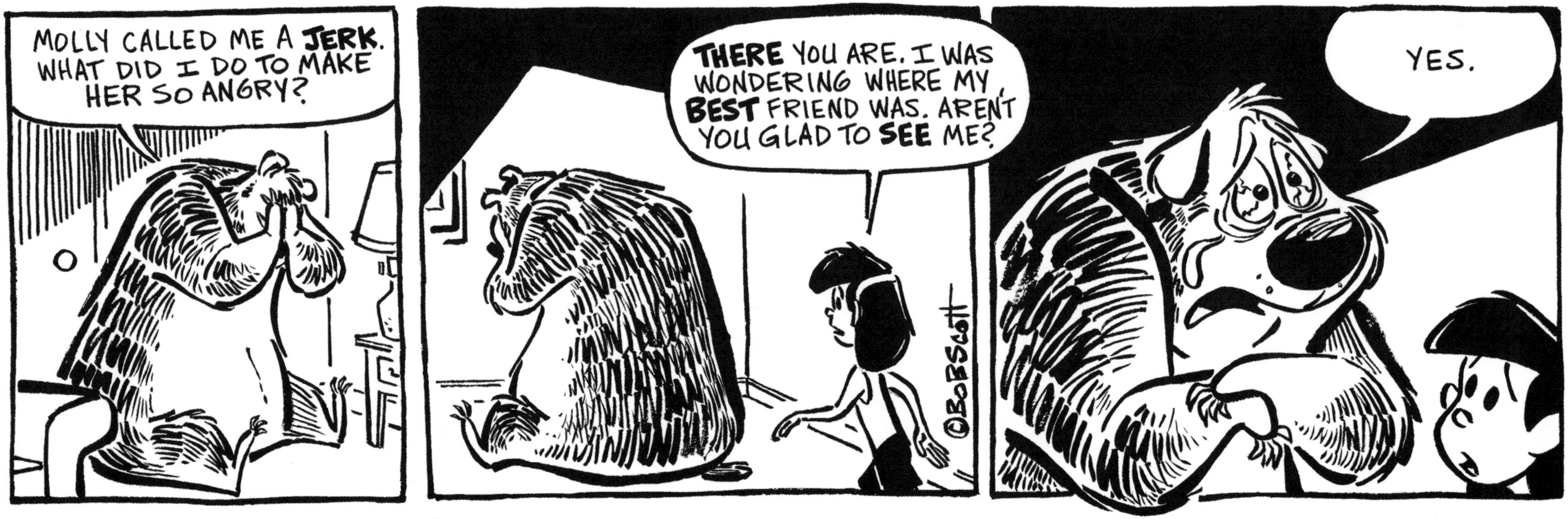
MOLLY CALLED ME A **JERK**. WHAT DID I DO TO MAKE HER SO ANGRY?
THERE YOU ARE. I WAS WONDERING WHERE MY **BEST** FRIEND WAS. AREN'T YOU GLAD TO **SEE** ME?
YES.
©BOB SCOTT

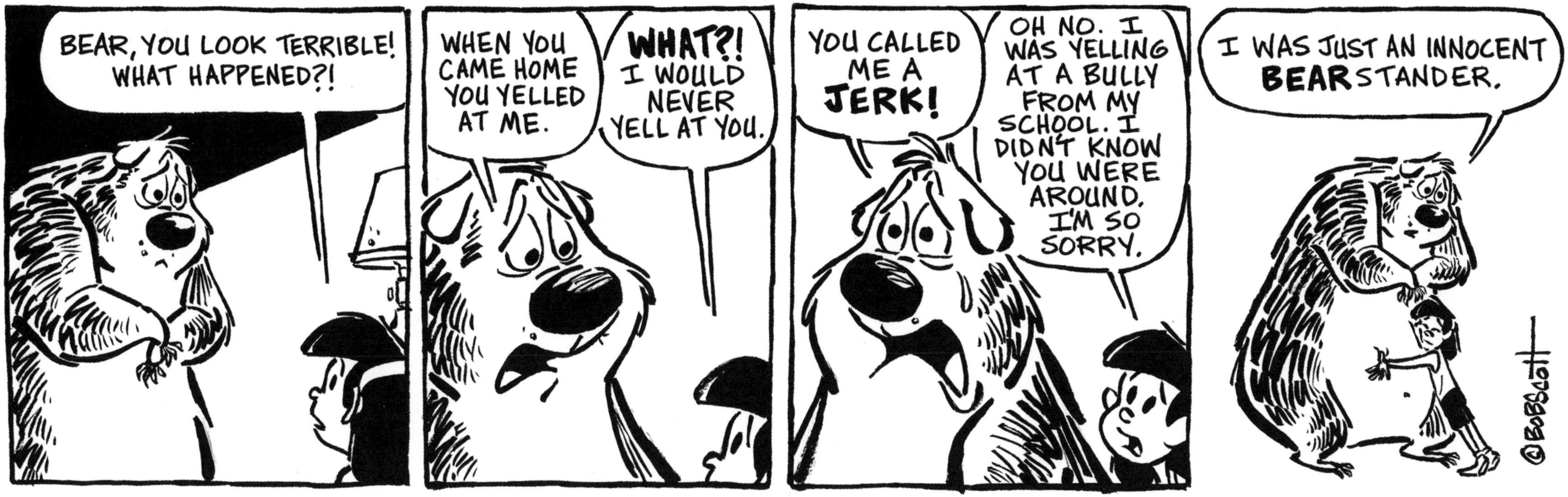
BEAR, YOU LOOK TERRIBLE! WHAT HAPPENED?!
WHEN YOU CAME HOME YOU YELLED AT ME.
WHAT?! I WOULD NEVER YELL AT YOU.
YOU CALLED ME A JERK!
OH NO. I WAS YELLING AT A BULLY FROM MY SCHOOL. I DIDN'T KNOW YOU WERE AROUND. I'M SO SORRY.
I WAS JUST AN INNOCENT BEARSTANDER.
©BOBSCOTT

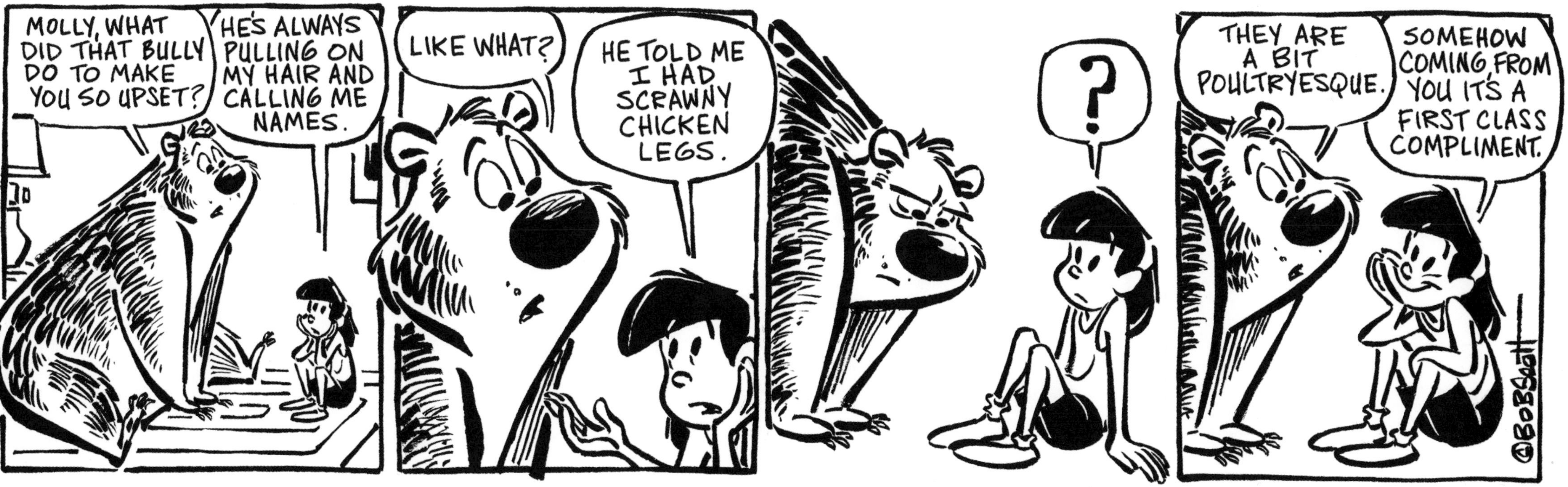
MOLLY, WHAT DID THAT BULLY DO TO MAKE YOU SO UPSET?
HE'S ALWAYS PULLING ON MY HAIR AND CALLING ME NAMES.
LIKE WHAT?
HE TOLD ME I HAD SCRAWNY CHICKEN LEGS.
?
THEY ARE A BIT POULTRYESQUE.
SOMEHOW COMING FROM YOU IT'S A FIRST CLASS COMPLIMENT.
©BOBSCOTT

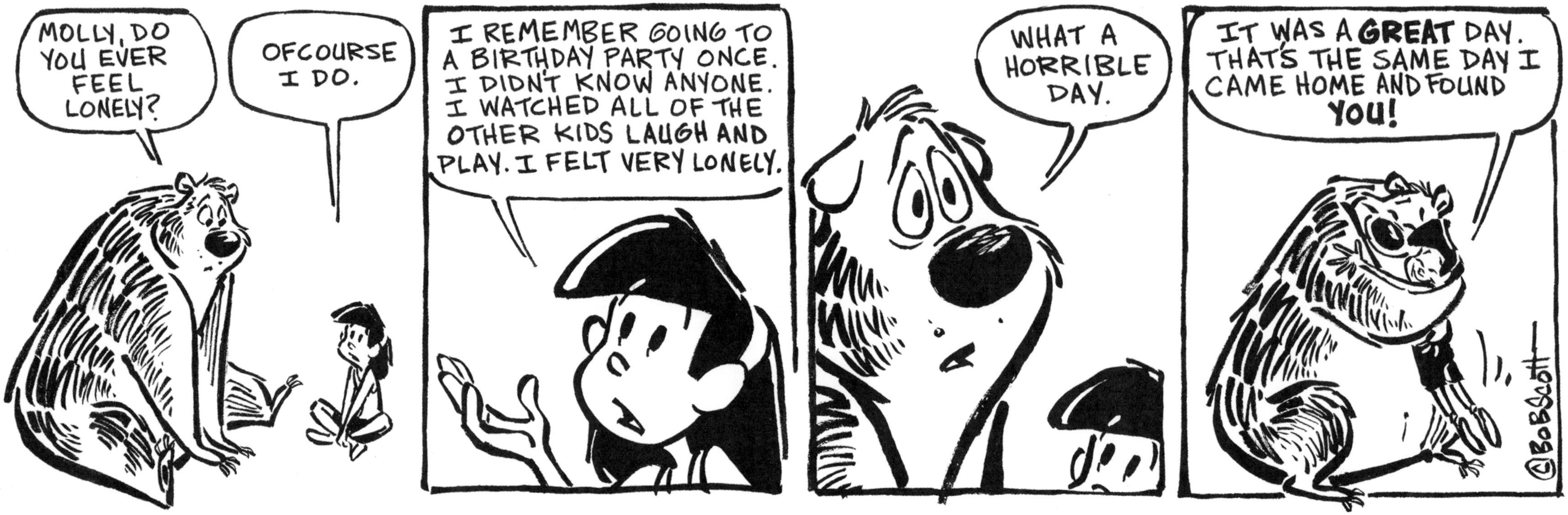
MOLLY, DO YOU EVER FEEL LONELY?
OFCOURSE I DO.
I REMEMBER GOING TO A BIRTHDAY PARTY ONCE. I DIDN'T KNOW ANYONE. I WATCHED ALL OF THE OTHER KIDS LAUGH AND PLAY. I FELT VERY LONELY.
WHAT A HORRIBLE DAY.
IT WAS A **GREAT** DAY. THAT'S THE SAME DAY I CAME HOME AND FOUND **YOU!**
©BOBSCOTT

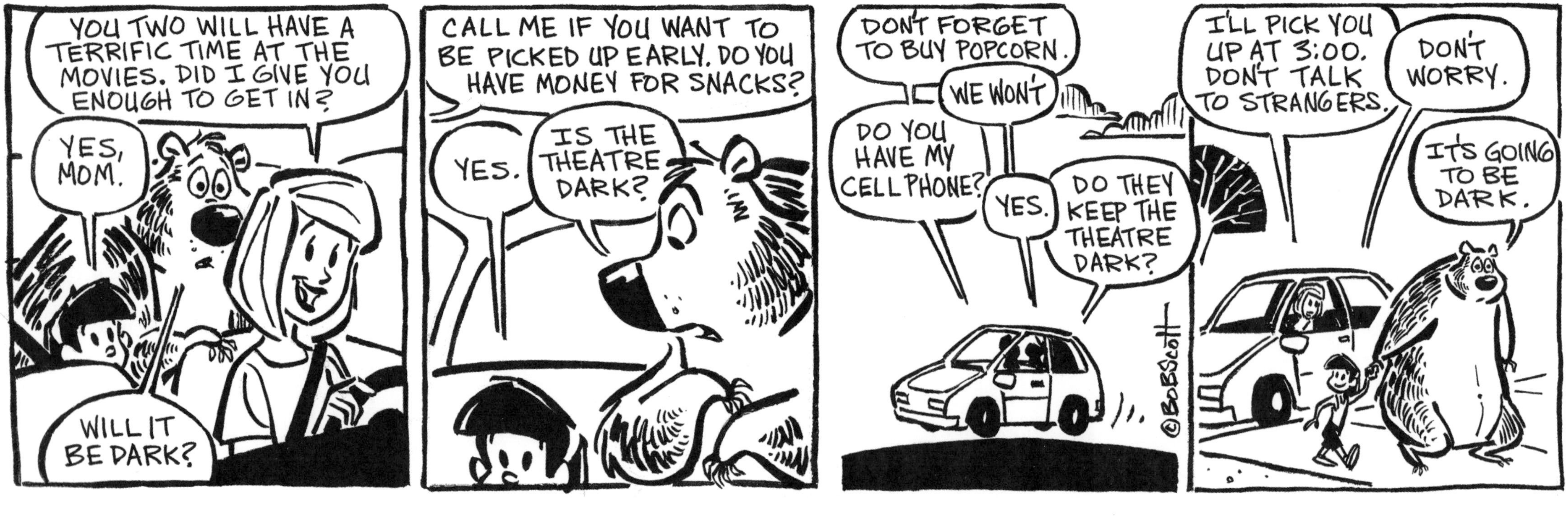
YOU TWO WILL HAVE A TERRIFIC TIME AT THE MOVIES. DID I GIVE YOU ENOUGH TO GET IN?
YES, MOM.
WILL IT BE DARK?
CALL ME IF YOU WANT TO BE PICKED UP EARLY. DO YOU HAVE MONEY FOR SNACKS?
YES.
IS THE THEATRE DARK?
DON'T FORGET TO BUY POPCORN.
WE WON'T
DO YOU HAVE MY CELL PHONE?
YES.
DO THEY KEEP THE THEATRE DARK?
©BOBSCOTT
I'LL PICK YOU UP AT 3:00. DON'T TALK TO STRANGERS.
DON'T WORRY.
IT'S GOING TO BE DARK.

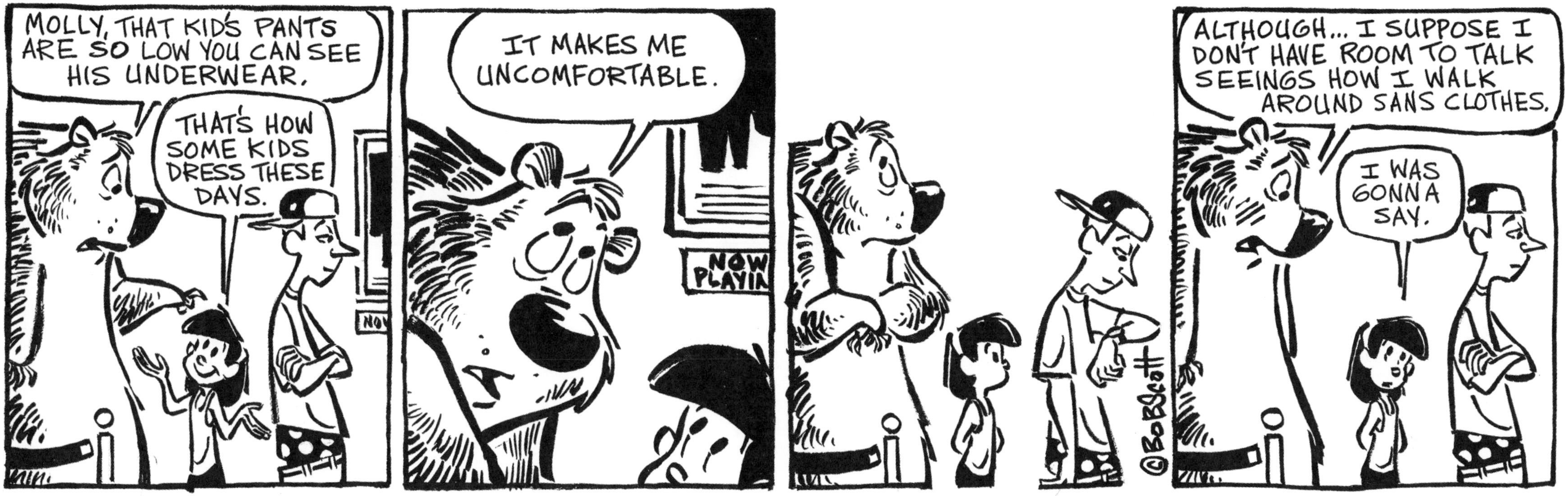
MOLLY, THAT KID'S PANTS ARE SO LOW YOU CAN SEE HIS UNDERWEAR.
THAT'S HOW SOME KIDS DRESS THESE DAYS.
IT MAKES ME UNCOMFORTABLE.
NOW PLAYIN
©BOB SCOTT
ALTHOUGH... I SUPPOSE I DON'T HAVE ROOM TO TALK SEEINGS HOW I WALK AROUND SANS CLOTHES.
I WAS GONNA SAY.

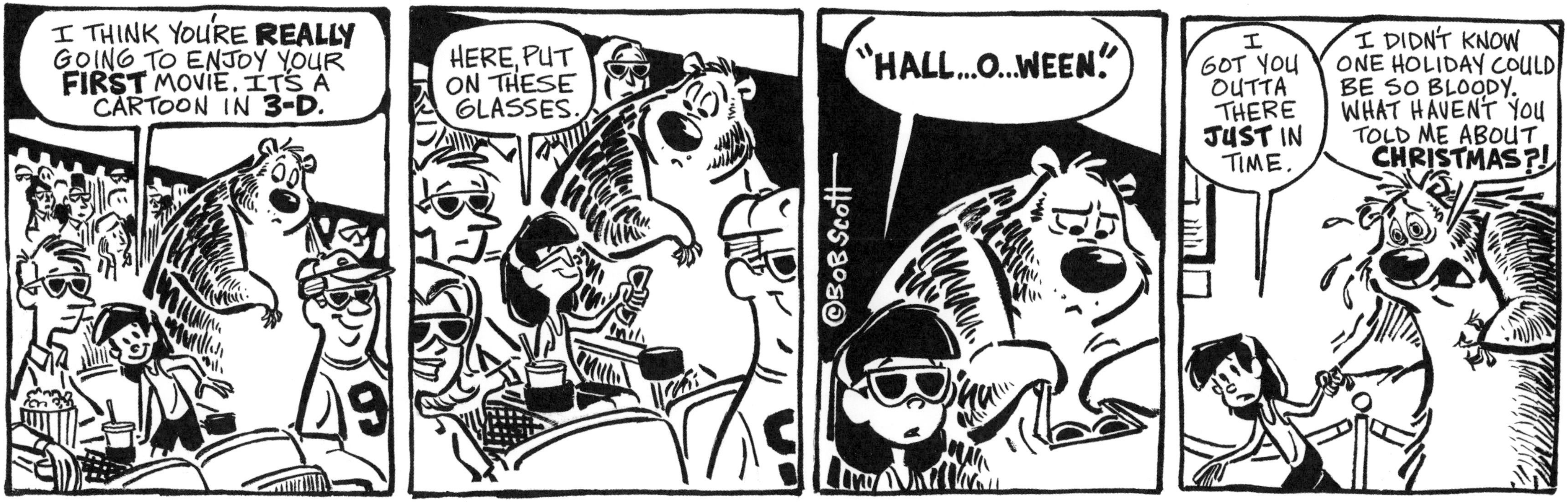
I THINK YOU'RE **REALLY** GOING TO ENJOY YOUR **FIRST** MOVIE. IT'S A CARTOON IN **3-D.**
HERE, PUT ON THESE GLASSES.
©BOB SCOTT
"HALL...O...WEEN."
I GOT YOU OUTTA THERE **JUST** IN TIME.
I DIDN'T KNOW ONE HOLIDAY COULD BE SO BLOODY. WHAT HAVEN'T YOU TOLD ME ABOUT **CHRISTMAS**?!

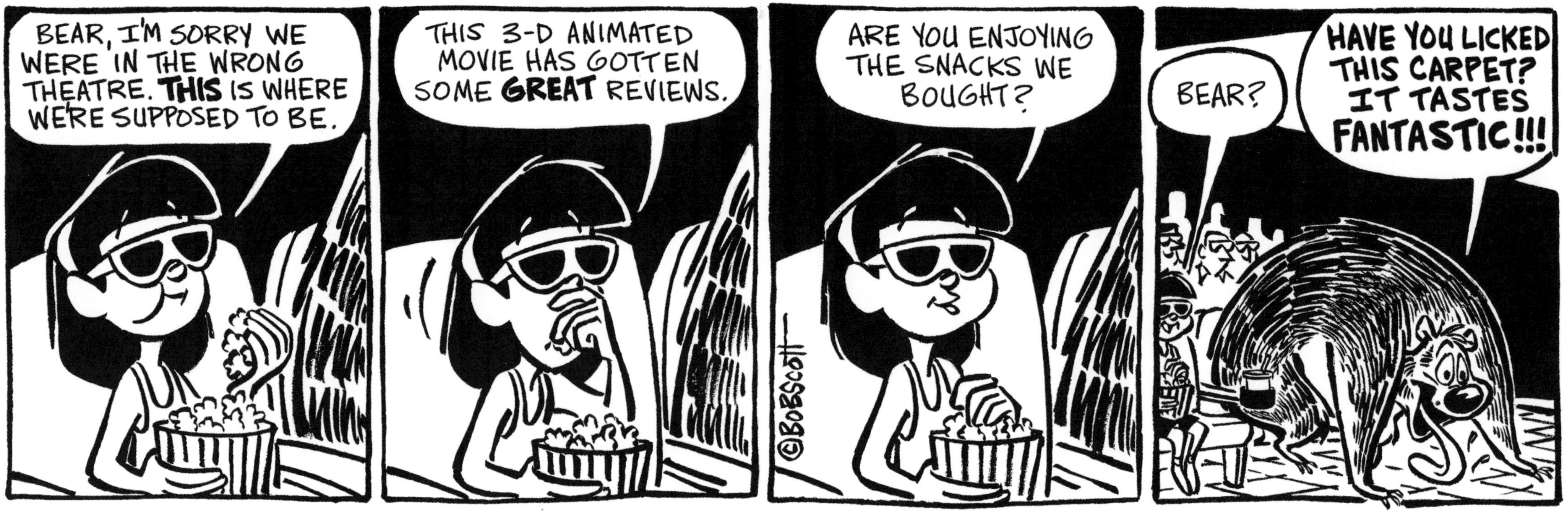
BEAR, I'M SORRY WE WERE IN THE WRONG THEATRE. **THIS** IS WHERE WE'RE SUPPOSED TO BE.
THIS 3-D ANIMATED MOVIE HAS GOTTEN SOME **GREAT** REVIEWS.
ARE YOU ENJOYING THE SNACKS WE BOUGHT?
©BOBSCOTT
BEAR?
HAVE YOU LICKED THIS CARPET? IT TASTES FANTASTIC!!!

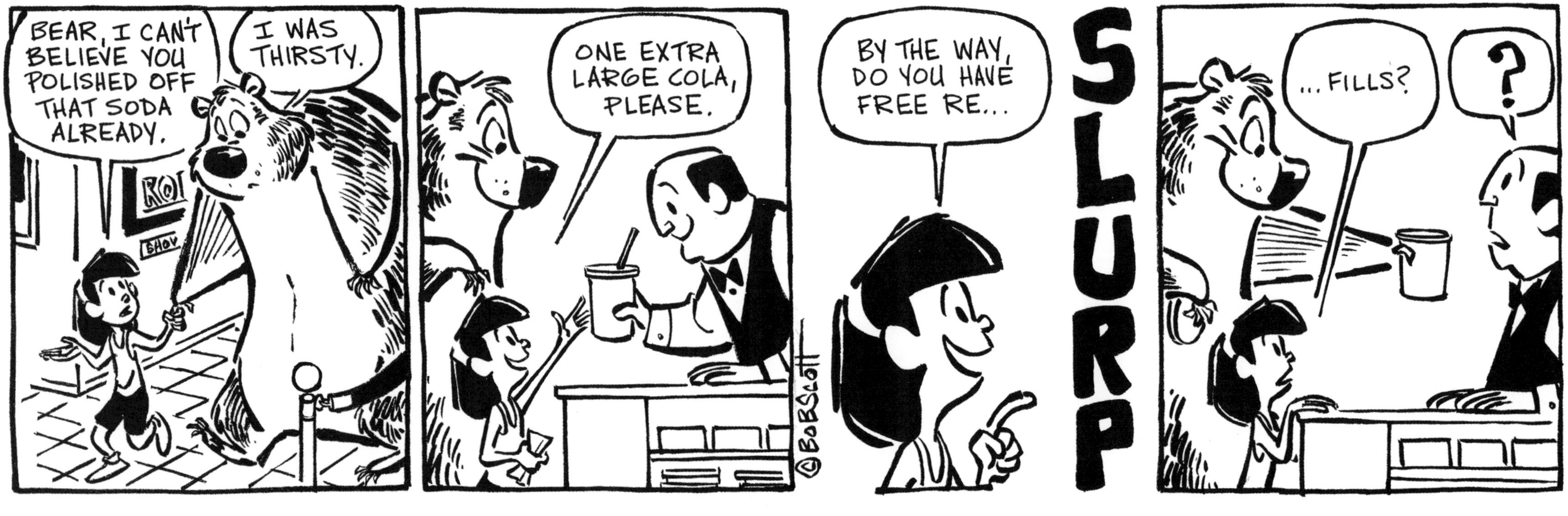
BEAR, I CAN'T BELIEVE YOU POLISHED OFF THAT SODA ALREADY.
I WAS THIRSTY.
ONE EXTRA LARGE COLA, PLEASE.
©BOBSCOTT
BY THE WAY, DO YOU HAVE FREE RE...
SLURP
...FILLS?
?

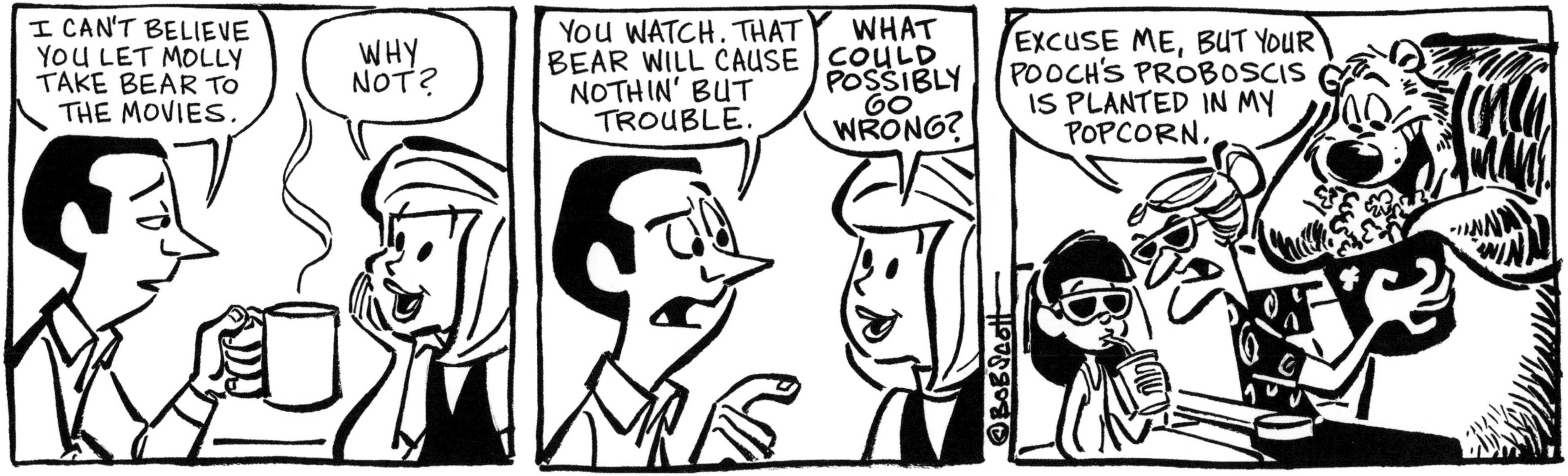
I CAN'T BELIEVE YOU LET MOLLY TAKE BEAR TO THE MOVIES.
WHY NOT?
YOU WATCH. THAT BEAR WILL CAUSE NOTHIN' BUT TROUBLE.
WHAT COULD POSSIBLY GO WRONG?
©BOBSCOTT
EXCUSE ME, BUT YOUR POOCH'S PROBOSCIS IS PLANTED IN MY POPCORN.

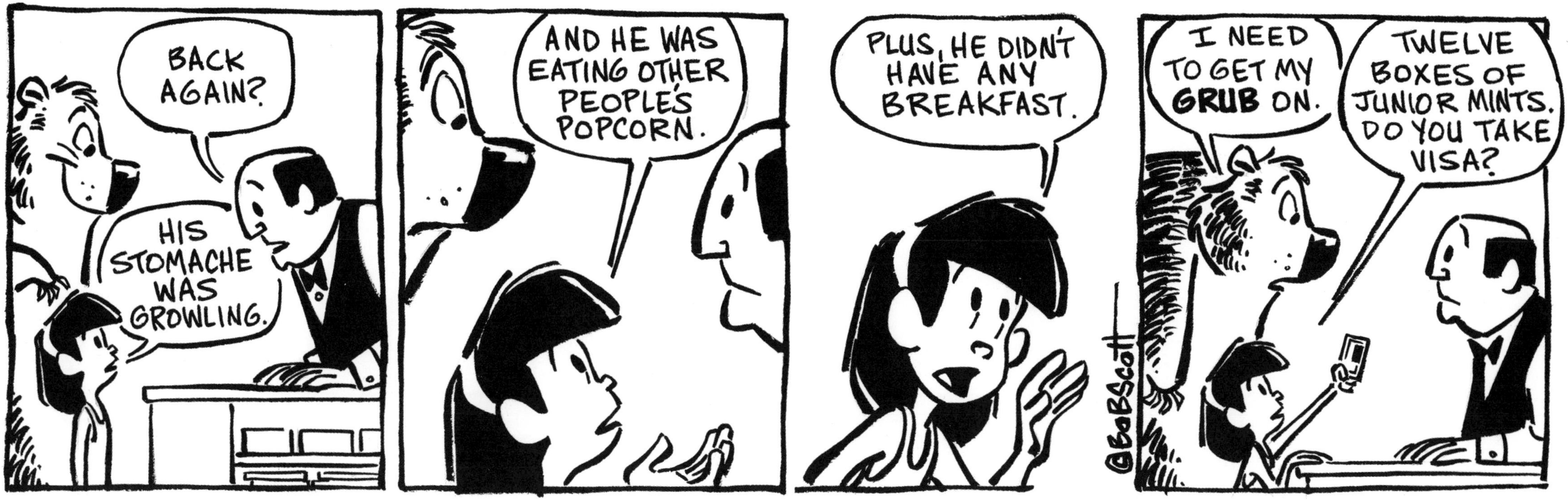
BACK AGAIN?
HIS STOMACHE WAS GROWLING.
AND HE WAS EATING OTHER PEOPLE'S POPCORN.
PLUS, HE DIDN'T HAVE ANY BREAKFAST.
©BOBSCOTT
I NEED TO GET MY **GRUB** ON.
TWELVE BOXES OF JUNIOR MINTS. DO YOU TAKE VISA?

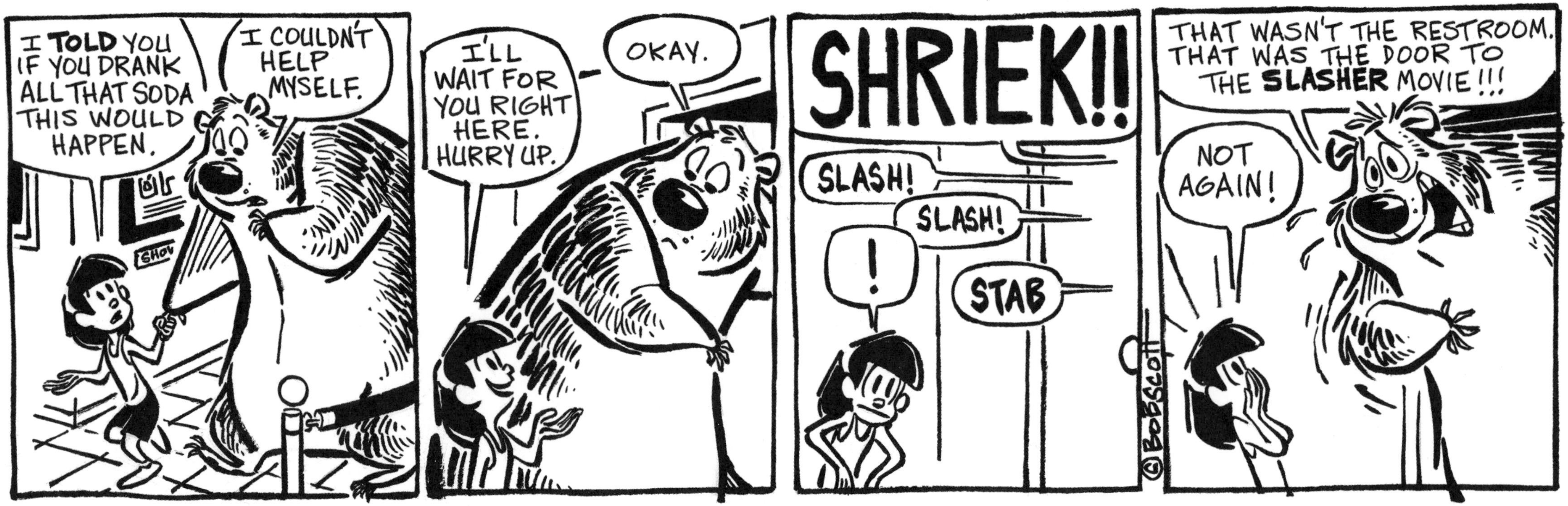
I **TOLD** YOU IF YOU DRANK ALL THAT SODA THIS WOULD HAPPEN.
I COULDN'T HELP MYSELF.
I'LL WAIT FOR YOU RIGHT HERE. HURRY UP.
OKAY.
SHRIEK!!
SLASH!
SLASH!
!
STAB
© BOBSCOTT
THAT WASN'T THE RESTROOM. THAT WAS THE DOOR TO THE **SLASHER** MOVIE!!!
NOT AGAIN!

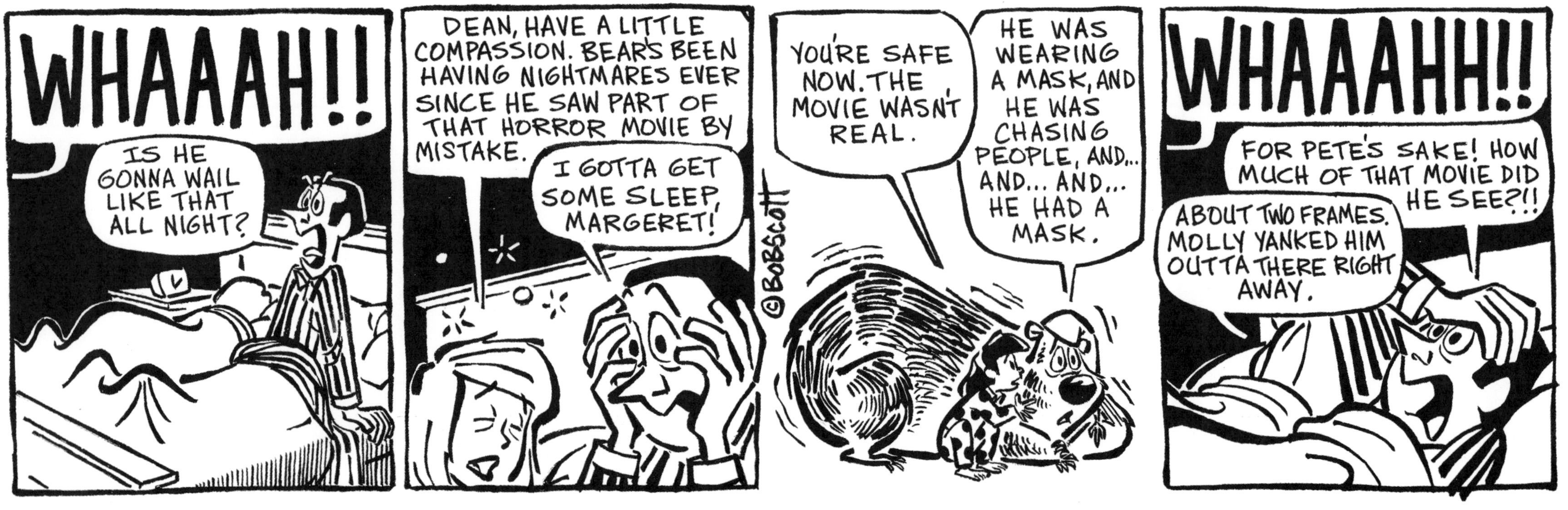
WHAAAH!!
IS HE GONNA WAIL LIKE THAT ALL NIGHT?
DEAN, HAVE A LITTLE COMPASSION. BEAR'S BEEN HAVING NIGHTMARES EVER SINCE HE SAW PART OF THAT HORROR MOVIE BY MISTAKE.
I GOTTA GET SOME SLEEP, MARGERET!
© BOBSCOTT
YOU'RE SAFE NOW. THE MOVIE WASN'T REAL.
HE WAS WEARING A MASK, AND HE WAS CHASING PEOPLE, AND... AND... AND... HE HAD A MASK.
WHAAAHH!!
FOR PETE'S SAKE! HOW MUCH OF THAT MOVIE DID HE SEE?!!
ABOUT TWO FRAMES. MOLLY YANKED HIM OUTTA THERE RIGHT AWAY.

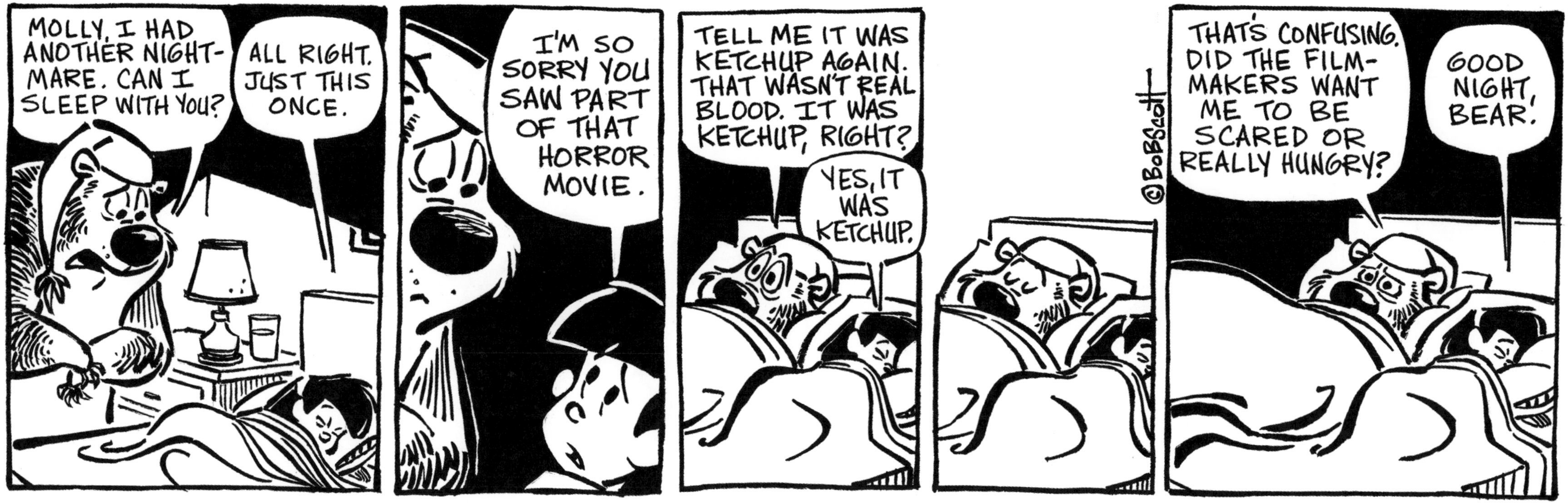
MOLLY, I HAD ANOTHER NIGHT-MARE. CAN I SLEEP WITH YOU?
ALL RIGHT. JUST THIS ONCE.
I'M SO SORRY YOU SAW PART OF THAT HORROR MOVIE.
TELL ME IT WAS KETCHUP AGAIN. THAT WASN'T REAL BLOOD. IT WAS KETCHUP, RIGHT?
YES, IT WAS KETCHUP.
©BOBSCOTT
THAT'S CONFUSING. DID THE FILM-MAKERS WANT ME TO BE SCARED OR REALLY HUNGRY?
GOOD NIGHT, BEAR.

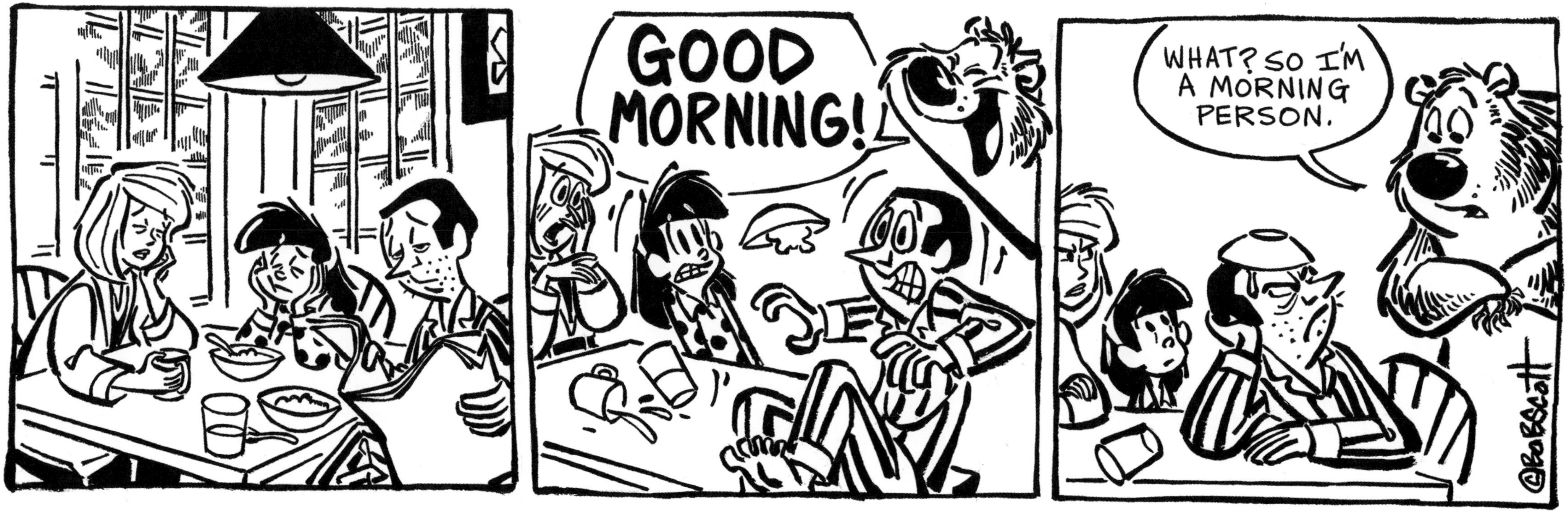
GOOD MORNING!
WHAT? SO I'M A MORNING PERSON.
©BOBSCOTT

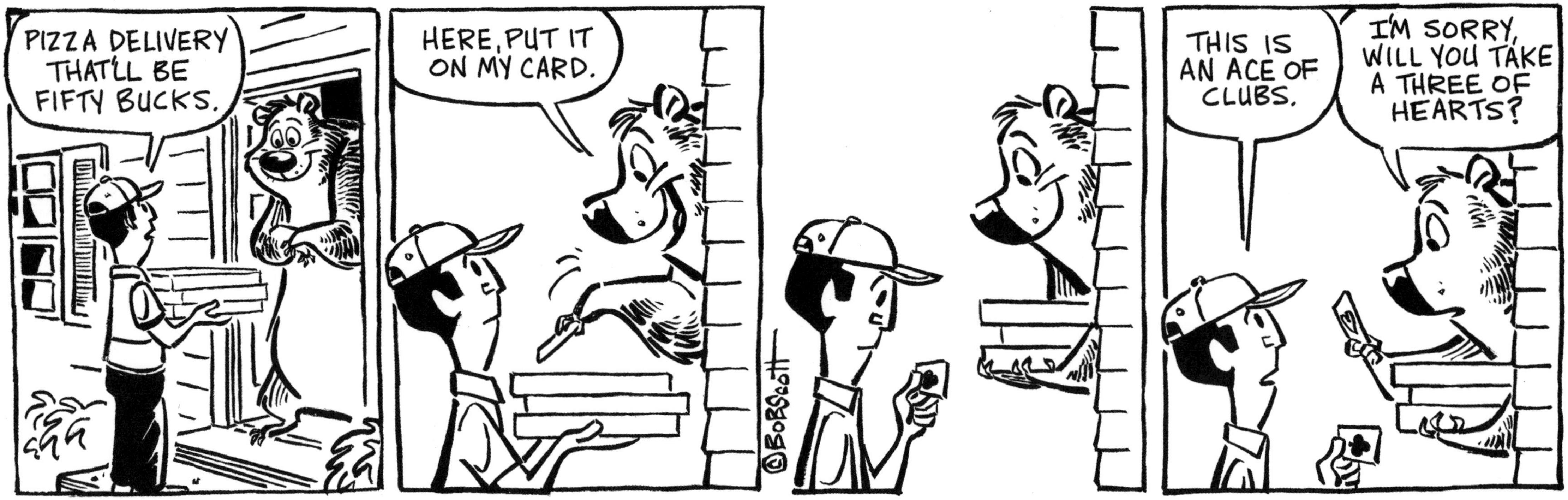
PIZZA DELIVERY THAT'LL BE FIFTY BUCKS.
HERE, PUT IT ON MY CARD.
©BOBSCOTT
THIS IS AN ACE OF CLUBS.
I'M SORRY, WILL YOU TAKE A THREE OF HEARTS?

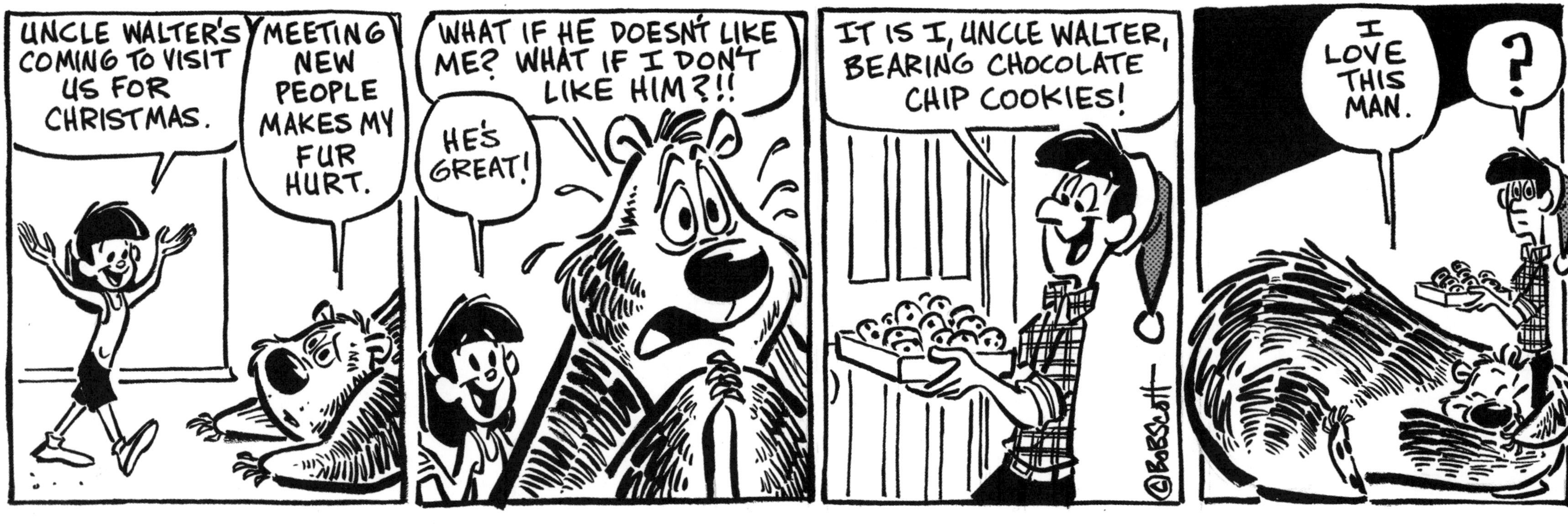
UNCLE WALTER'S COMING TO VISIT US FOR CHRISTMAS.
MEETING NEW PEOPLE MAKES MY FUR HURT.
WHAT IF HE DOESN'T LIKE ME? WHAT IF I DON'T LIKE HIM?!!
HE'S GREAT!
IT IS I, UNCLE WALTER, BEARING CHOCOLATE CHIP COOKIES!
©BOBSCOTT
I LOVE THIS MAN.
?

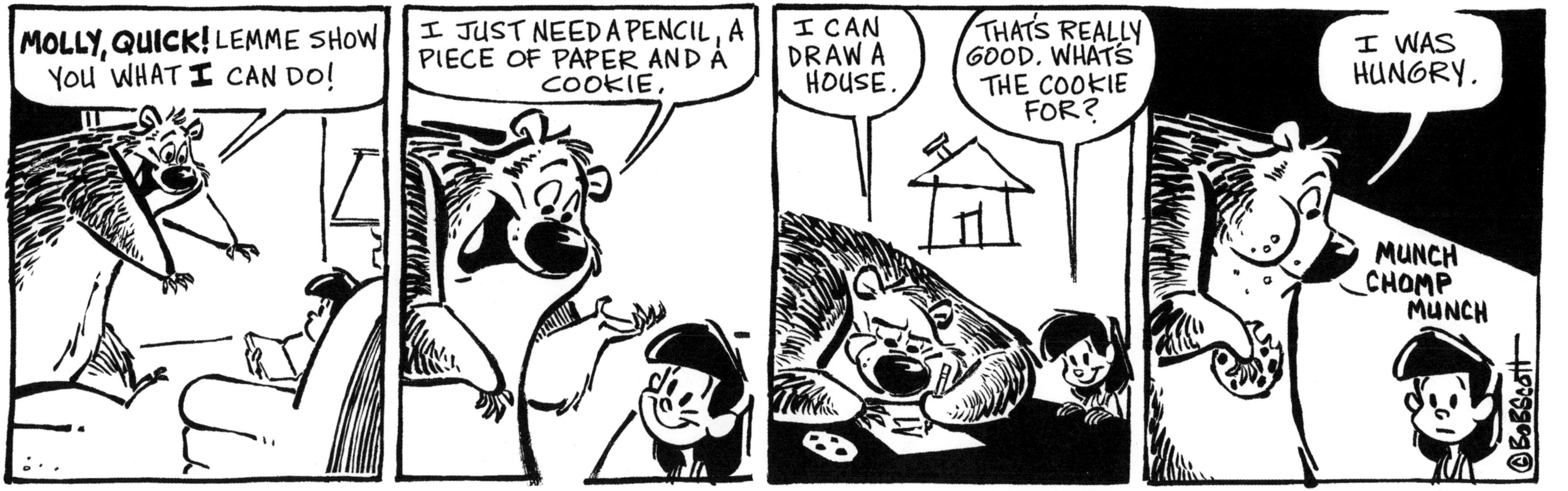
MOLLY, QUICK! LEMME SHOW YOU WHAT I CAN DO!
I JUST NEED A PENCIL, A PIECE OF PAPER AND A COOKIE.
I CAN DRAW A HOUSE.
THAT'S REALLY GOOD. WHAT'S THE COOKIE FOR?
I WAS HUNGRY.
MUNCH CHOMP MUNCH
©BOBSCOTT

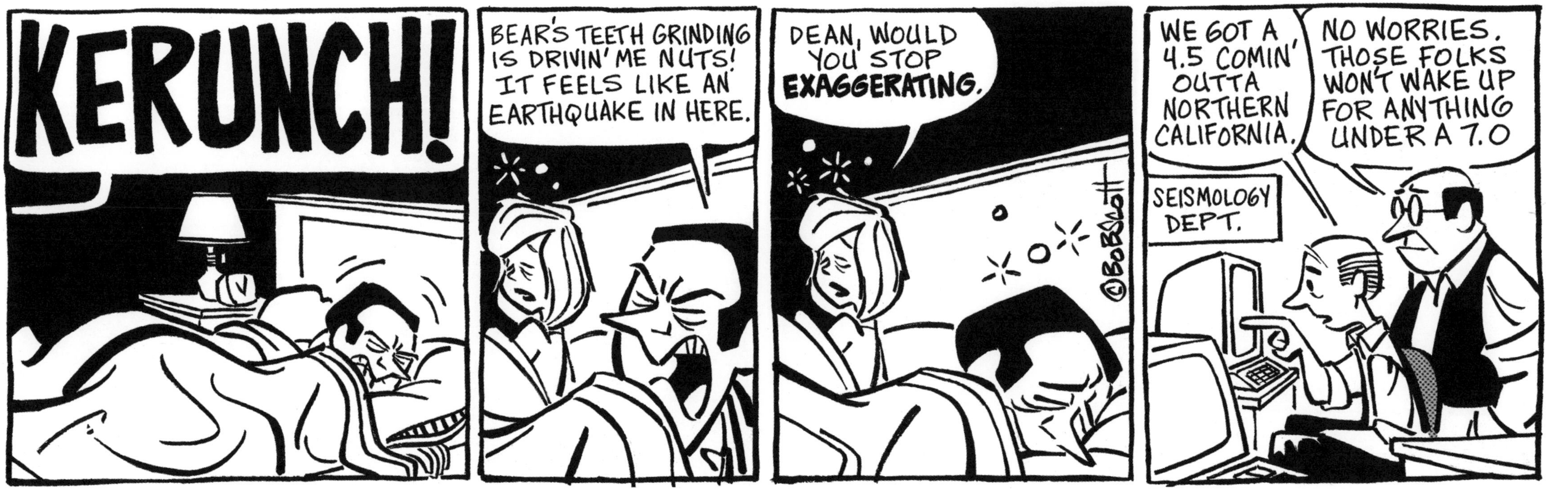
KERUNCH!
BEAR'S TEETH GRINDING IS DRIVIN' ME NUTS! IT FEELS LIKE AN EARTHQUAKE IN HERE.
DEAN, WOULD YOU STOP EXAGGERATING.
©BOBSCOTT
WE GOT A 4.5 COMIN' OUTTA NORTHERN CALIFORNIA.
NO WORRIES. THOSE FOLKS WON'T WAKE UP FOR ANYTHING UNDER A 7.0
SEISMOLOGY DEPT.

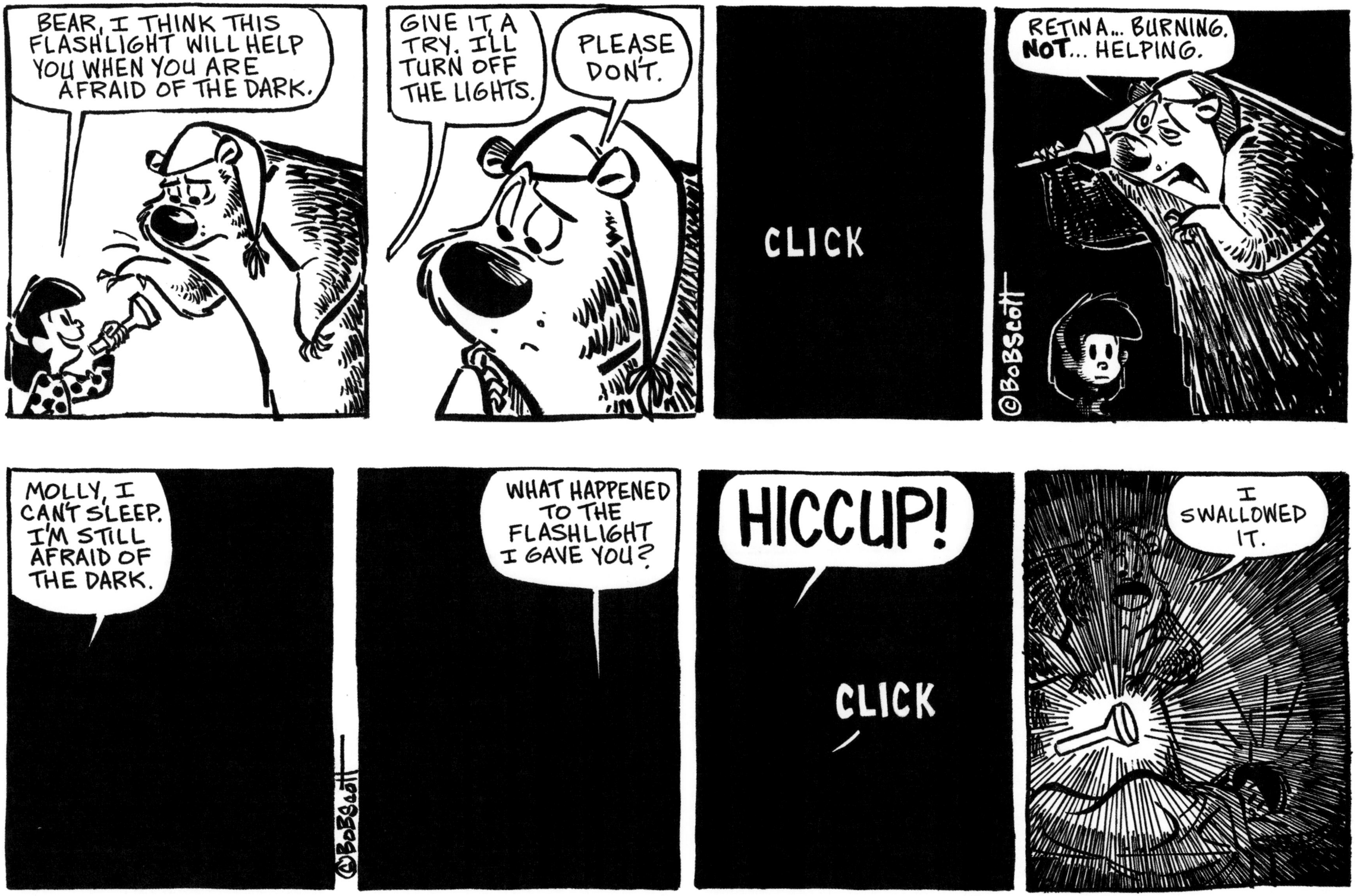
BEAR, I THINK THIS FLASHLIGHT WILL HELP YOU WHEN YOU ARE AFRAID OF THE DARK.
GIVE IT A TRY. I'LL TURN OFF THE LIGHTS.
PLEASE DON'T.
CLICK
RETINA... BURNING. NOT... HELPING.
©BOBSCOTT
MOLLY, I CAN'T SLEEP. I'M STILL AFRAID OF THE DARK.
©BOBSCOTT
WHAT HAPPENED TO THE FLASHLIGHT I GAVE YOU?
HICCUP!
CLICK
I SWALLOWED IT.

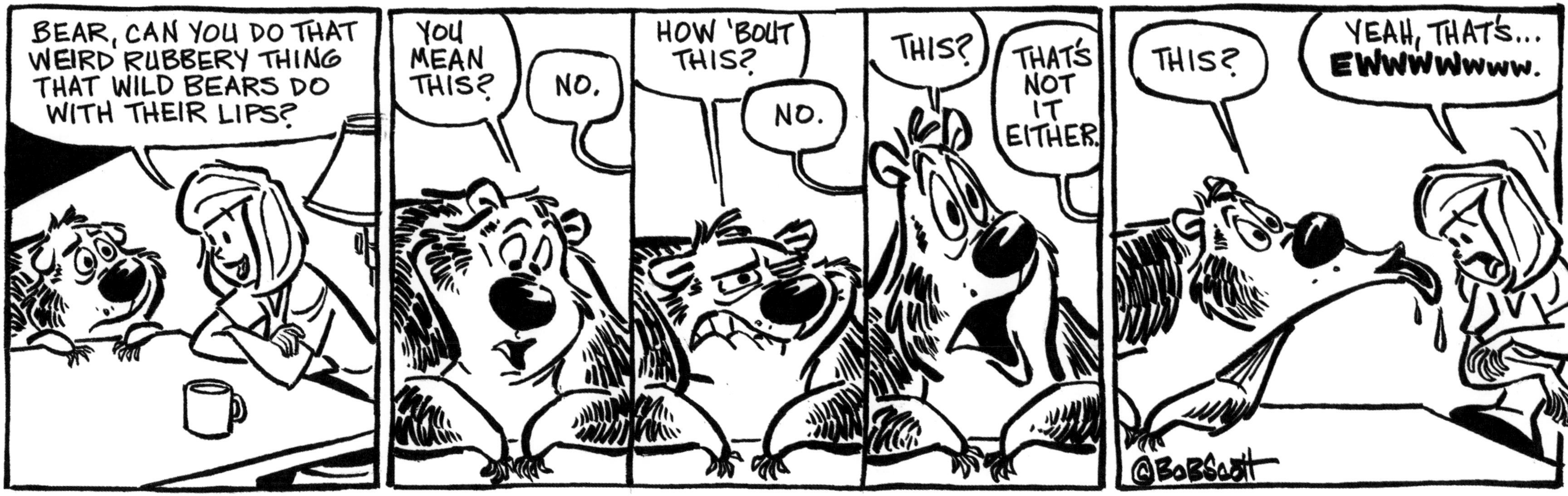
BEAR, CAN YOU DO THAT WEIRD RUBBERY THING THAT WILD BEARS DO WITH THEIR LIPS?
YOU MEAN THIS?
NO.
HOW 'BOUT THIS?
NO.
THIS?
THAT'S NOT IT EITHER.
THIS?
YEAH, THAT'S... EWWWWWWW.
©BOBSCOTT

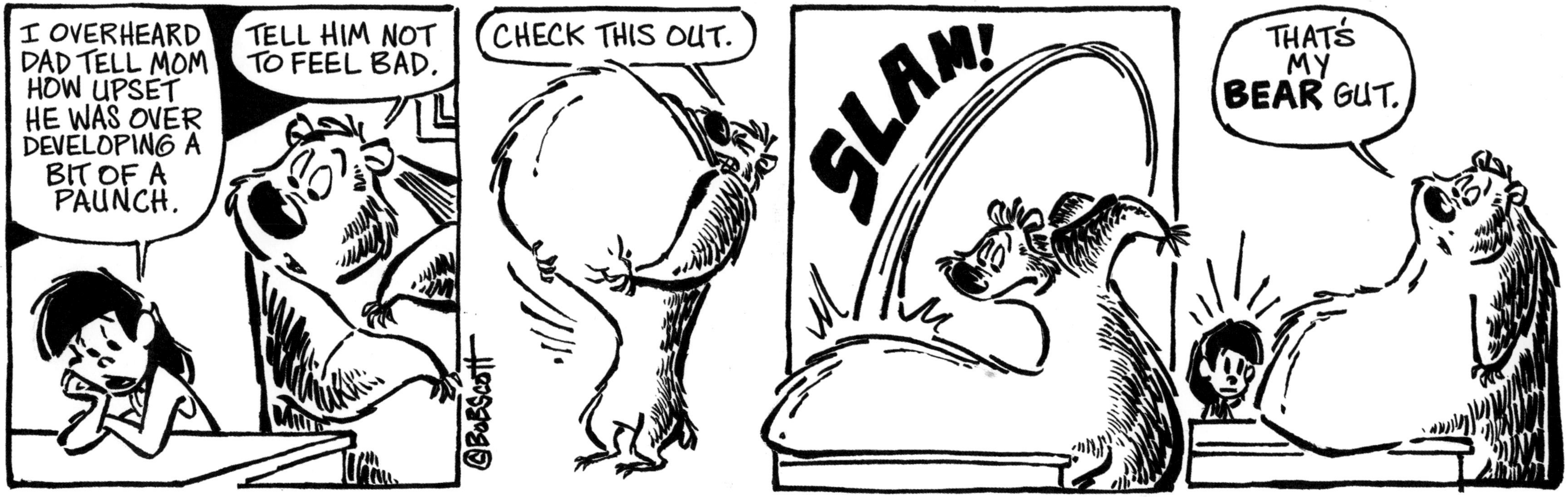
I OVERHEARD DAD TELL MOM HOW UPSET HE WAS OVER DEVELOPING A BIT OF A PAUNCH.
TELL HIM NOT TO FEEL BAD.
©BOBSCOTT
CHECK THIS OUT.
SLAM!
THAT'S MY **BEAR** GUT.

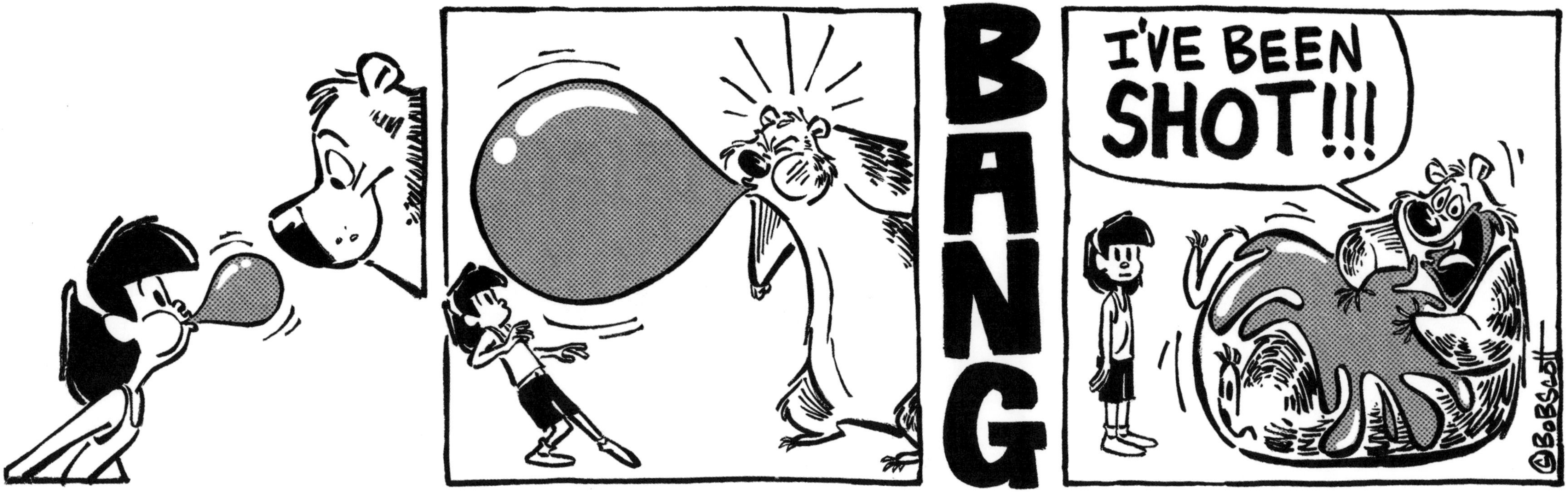
BANG
I'VE BEEN SHOT!!!
©BOBSCOTT

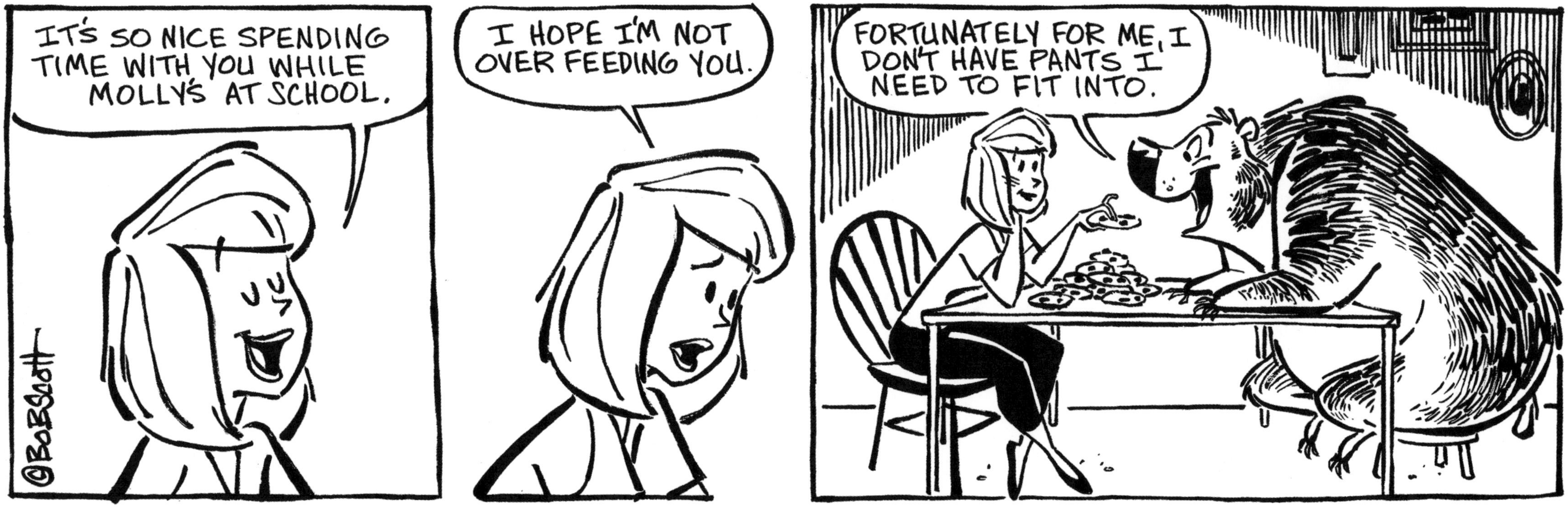
IT'S SO NICE SPENDING TIME WITH YOU WHILE MOLLY'S AT SCHOOL.
©BOBSCOTT
I HOPE I'M NOT OVER FEEDING YOU.
FORTUNATELY FOR ME, I DON'T HAVE PANTS I NEED TO FIT INTO.

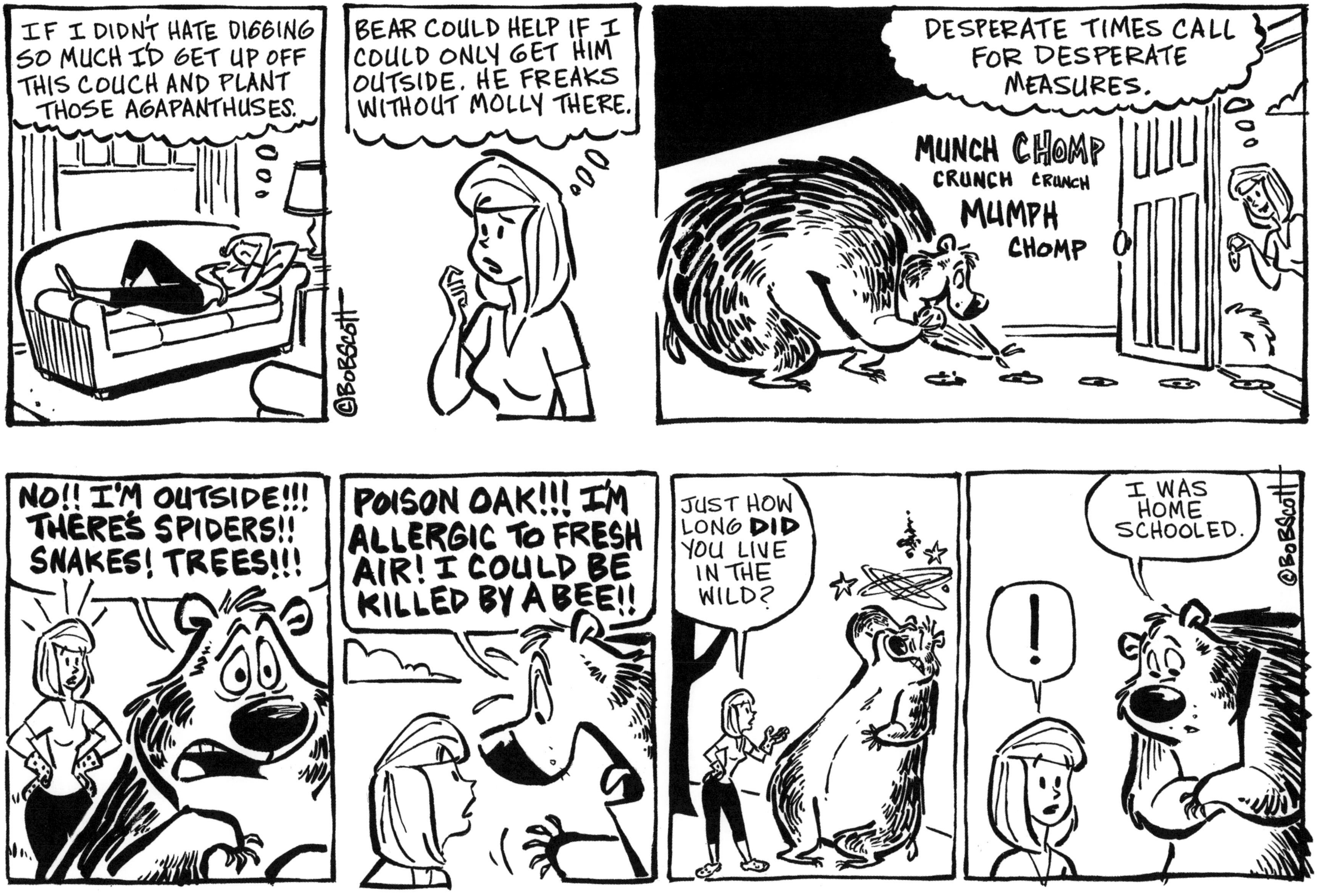
IF I DIDN'T HATE DIGGING SO MUCH I'D GET UP OFF THIS COUCH AND PLANT THOSE AGAPANTHUSES.
©BOBSCOTT
BEAR COULD HELP IF I COULD ONLY GET HIM OUTSIDE. HE FREAKS WITHOUT MOLLY THERE.
DESPERATE TIMES CALL FOR DESPERATE MEASURES.
MUNCH CHOMP
CRUNCH CRUNCH
MUMPH
CHOMP
NO!! I'M OUTSIDE!!! THERE'S SPIDERS!! SNAKES! TREES!!!
POISON OAK!!! I'M ALLERGIC TO FRESH AIR! I COULD BE KILLED BY A BEE!!
JUST HOW LONG DID YOU LIVE IN THE WILD?
!
I WAS HOME SCHOOLED.
©BOBSCOTT

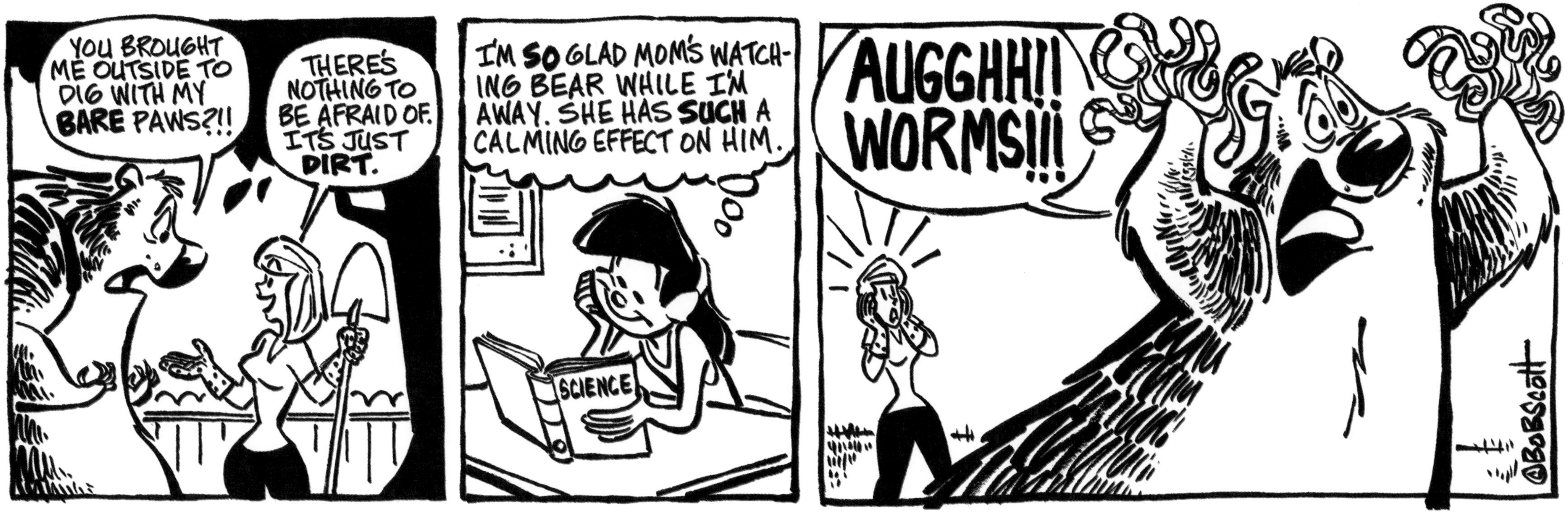
YOU BROUGHT ME OUTSIDE TO DIG WITH MY BARE PAWS?!!
THERE'S NOTHING TO BE AFRAID OF. IT'S JUST DIRT.
I'M SO GLAD MOM'S WATCHING BEAR WHILE I'M AWAY. SHE HAS SUCH A CALMING EFFECT ON HIM.
SCIENCE
AUGGHH!! WORMS!!!!
©BOBSCOTT

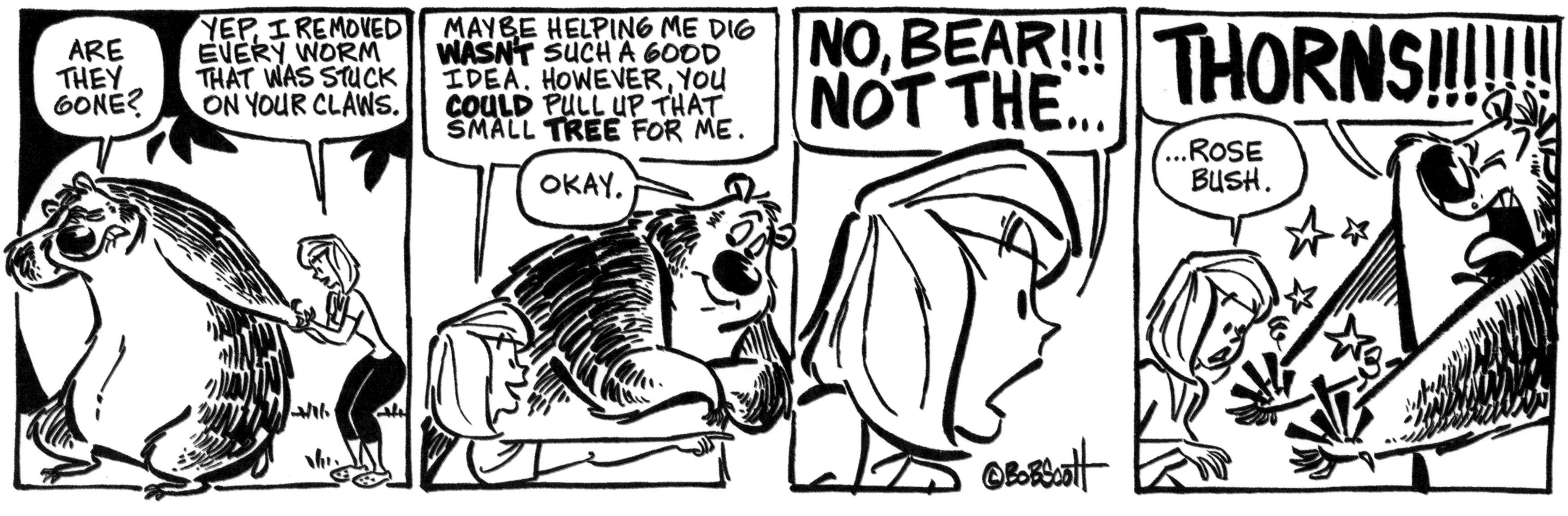
ARE THEY GONE?
YEP, I REMOVED EVERY WORM THAT WAS STUCK ON YOUR CLAWS.
MAYBE HELPING ME DIG WASN'T SUCH A GOOD IDEA. HOWEVER, YOU COULD PULL UP THAT SMALL TREE FOR ME.
OKAY.
NO, BEAR!!! NOT THE...
©BOBSCOTT
THORNS!!!!!!!
...ROSE BUSH.

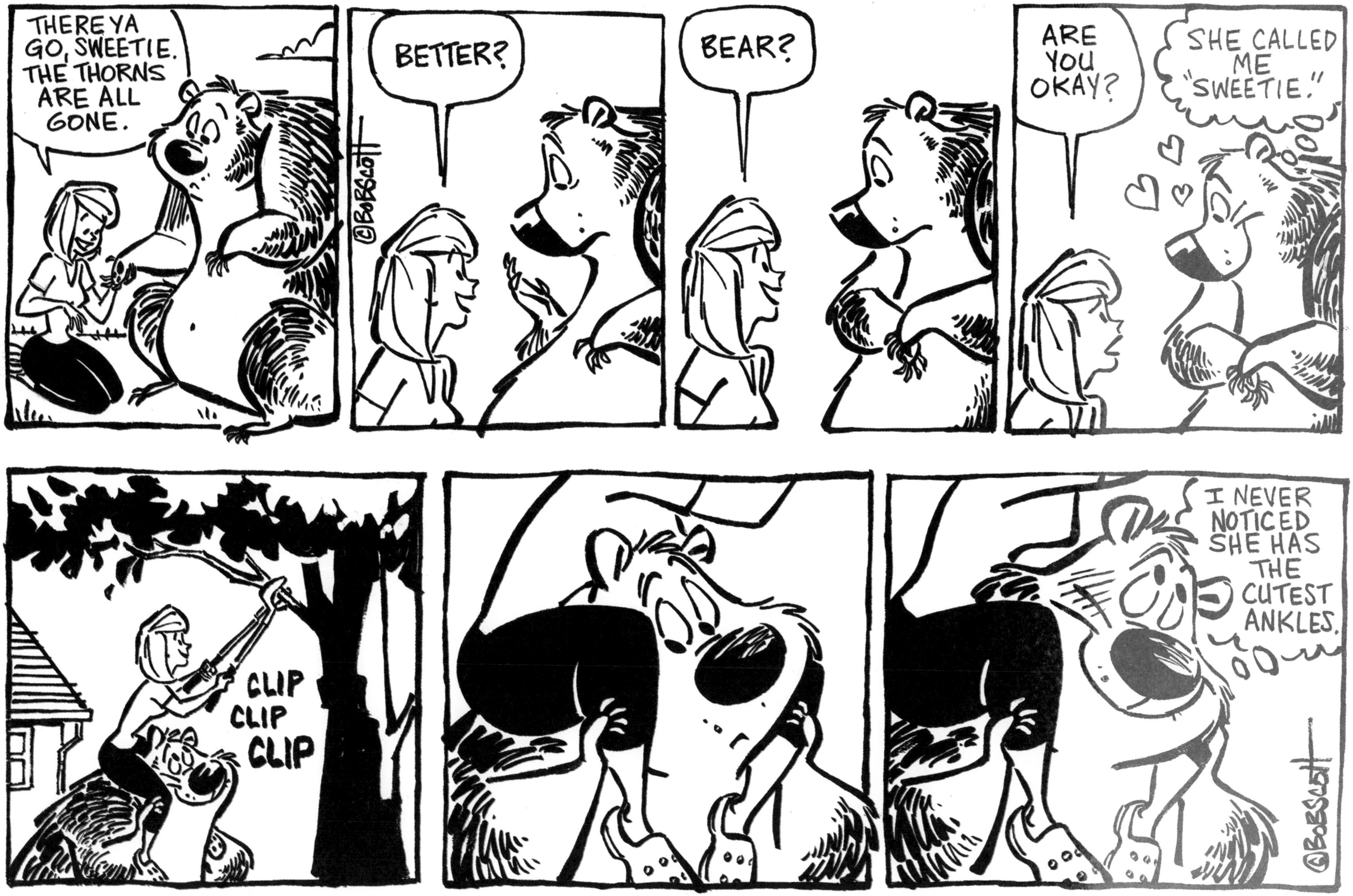
THERE YA GO, SWEETIE. THE THORNS ARE ALL GONE.
©BOBSCOTT
BETTER?
BEAR?
ARE YOU OKAY?
SHE CALLED ME "SWEETIE."
CLIP CLIP CLIP
I NEVER NOTICED SHE HAS THE CUTEST ANKLES.
©BOBSCOTT

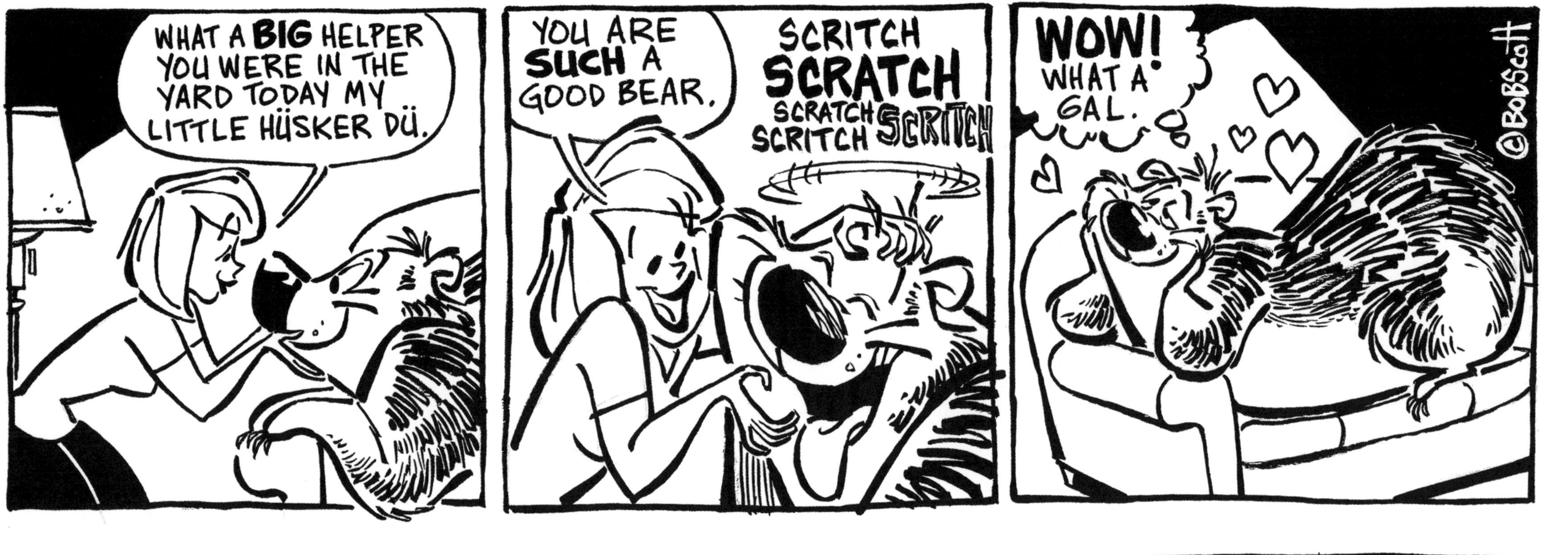
WHAT A BIG HELPER YOU WERE IN THE YARD TODAY MY LITTLE HÜSKER DÜ.
YOU ARE SUCH A GOOD BEAR.
SCRITCH SCRATCH SCRATCH SCRITCH SCRITCH
WOW! WHAT A GAL.
©BOBSCOTT

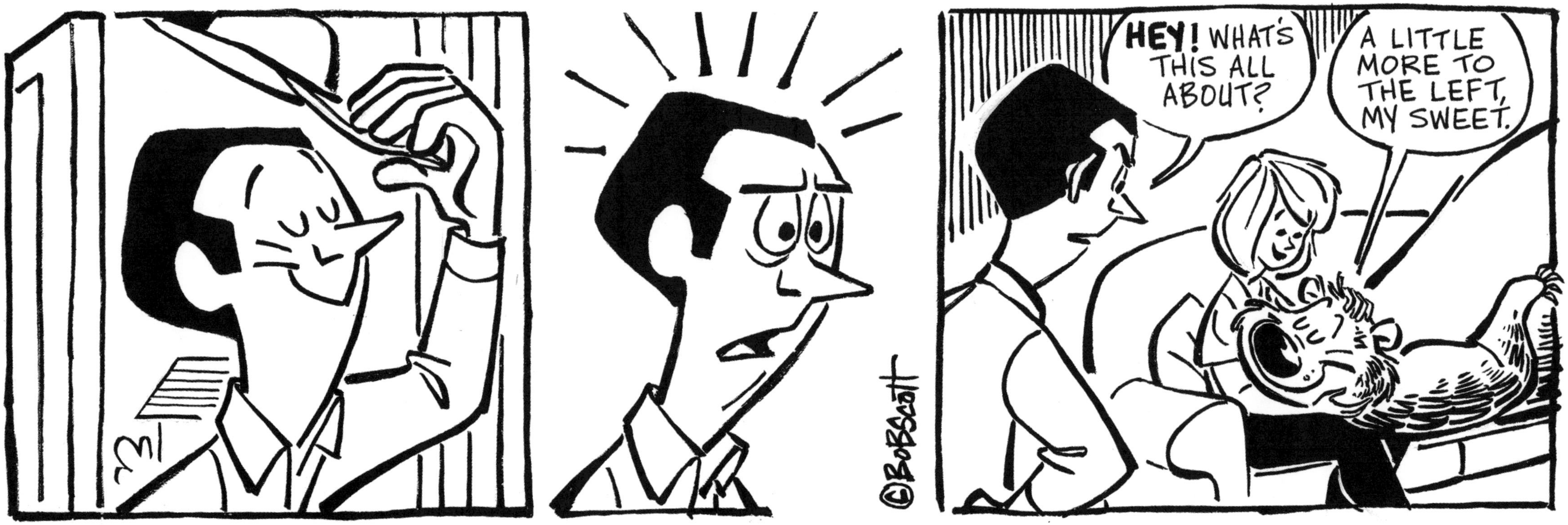
©BOBSCOTT
HEY! WHAT'S THIS ALL ABOUT?
A LITTLE MORE TO THE LEFT, MY SWEET.

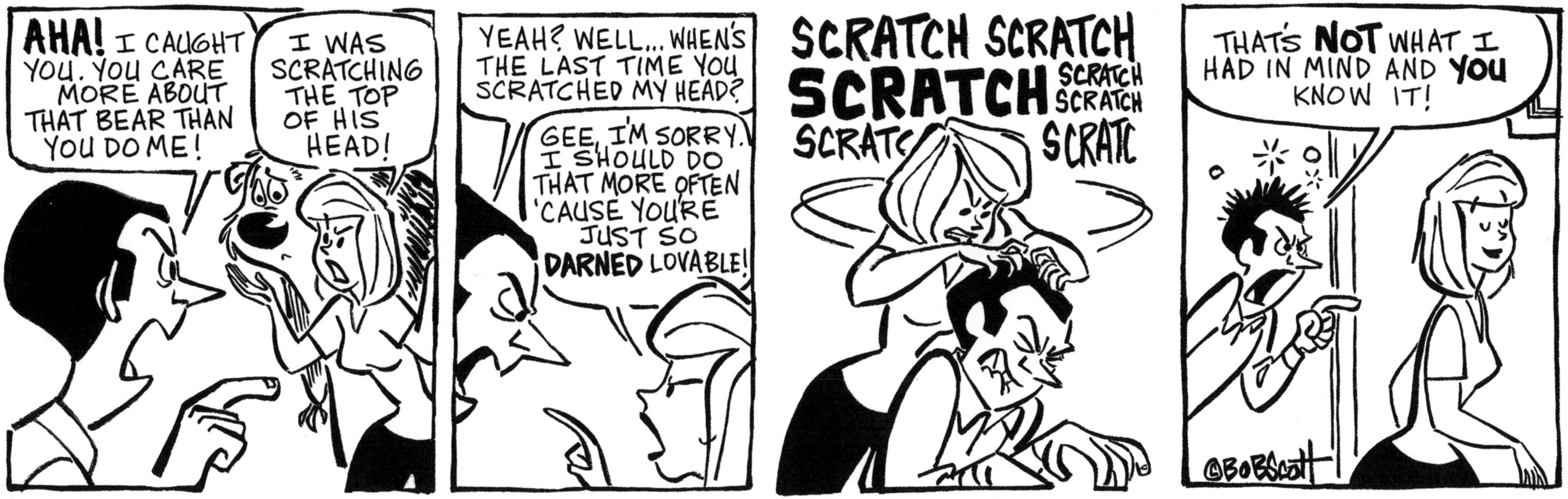
AHA! I CAUGHT YOU. YOU CARE MORE ABOUT THAT BEAR THAN YOU DO ME!
I WAS SCRATCHING THE TOP OF HIS HEAD!
YEAH? WELL... WHEN'S THE LAST TIME YOU SCRATCHED MY HEAD?
GEE, I'M SORRY. I SHOULD DO THAT MORE OFTEN 'CAUSE YOU'RE JUST SO DARNED LOVABLE!
SCRATCH SCRATCH SCRATCH SCRATCH SCRATCH SCRATC SCRATC
THAT'S NOT WHAT I HAD IN MIND AND YOU KNOW IT!
©BOBSCOTT

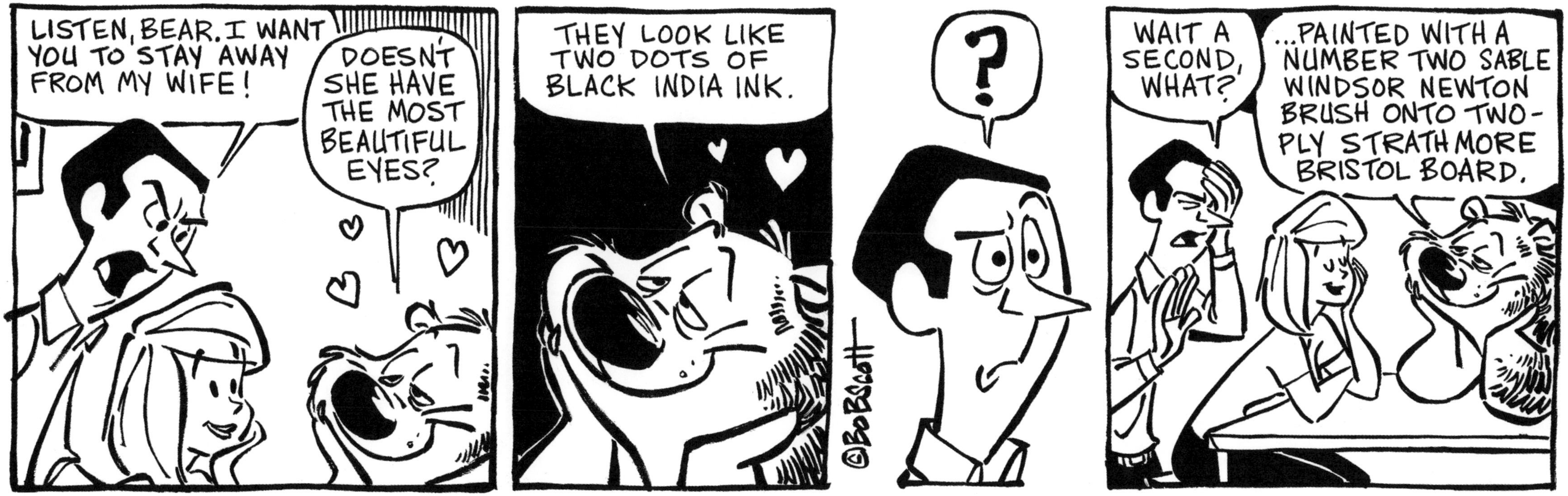
LISTEN, BEAR. I WANT YOU TO STAY AWAY FROM MY WIFE!
DOESN'T SHE HAVE THE MOST BEAUTIFUL EYES?
THEY LOOK LIKE TWO DOTS OF BLACK INDIA INK.
©BOBSCOTT
?
WAIT A SECOND, WHAT?
...PAINTED WITH A NUMBER TWO SABLE WINDSOR NEWTON BRUSH ONTO TWO-PLY STRATHMORE BRISTOL BOARD.

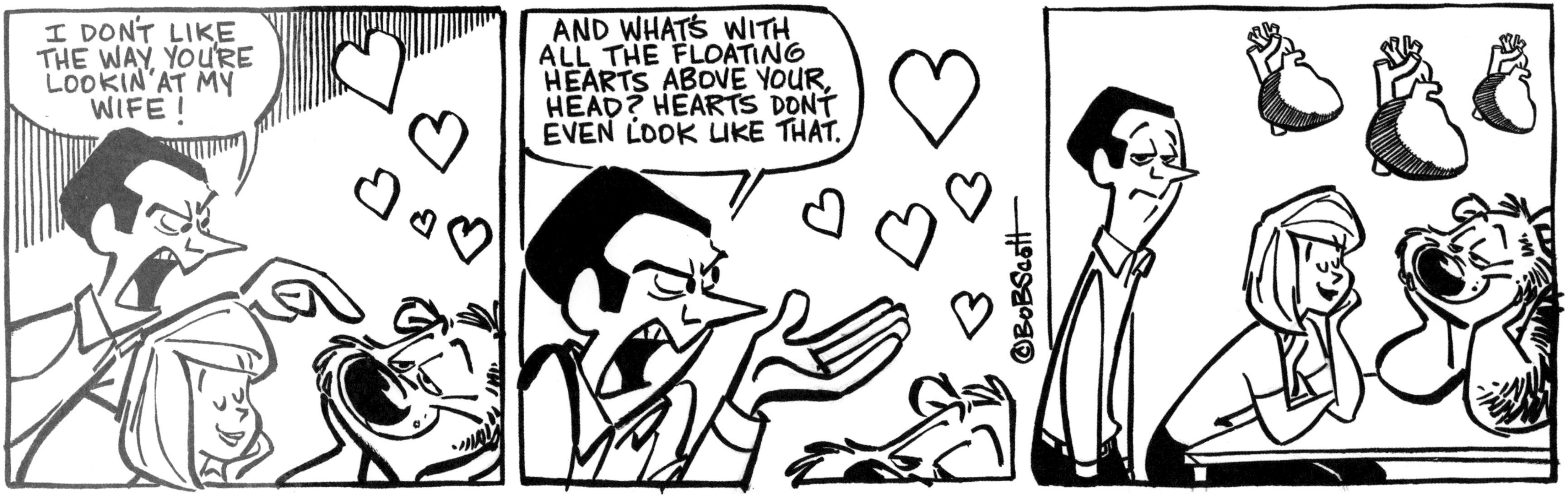
I DON'T LIKE THE WAY YOU'RE LOOKIN' AT MY WIFE!
AND WHAT'S WITH ALL THE FLOATING HEARTS ABOVE YOUR HEAD? HEARTS DON'T EVEN LOOK LIKE THAT.
©BOBSCOTT

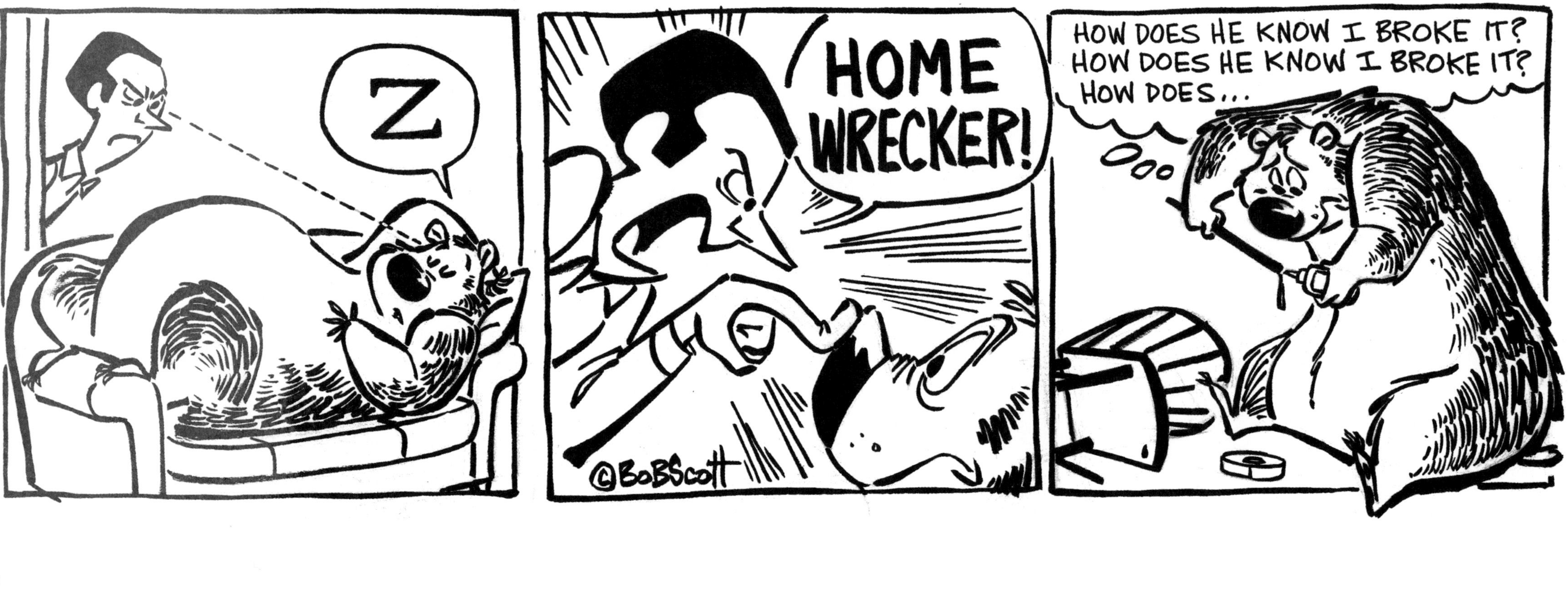
Z
HOME WRECKER!
©BOBSCOTT
HOW DOES HE KNOW I BROKE IT? HOW DOES HE KNOW I BROKE IT? HOW DOES...

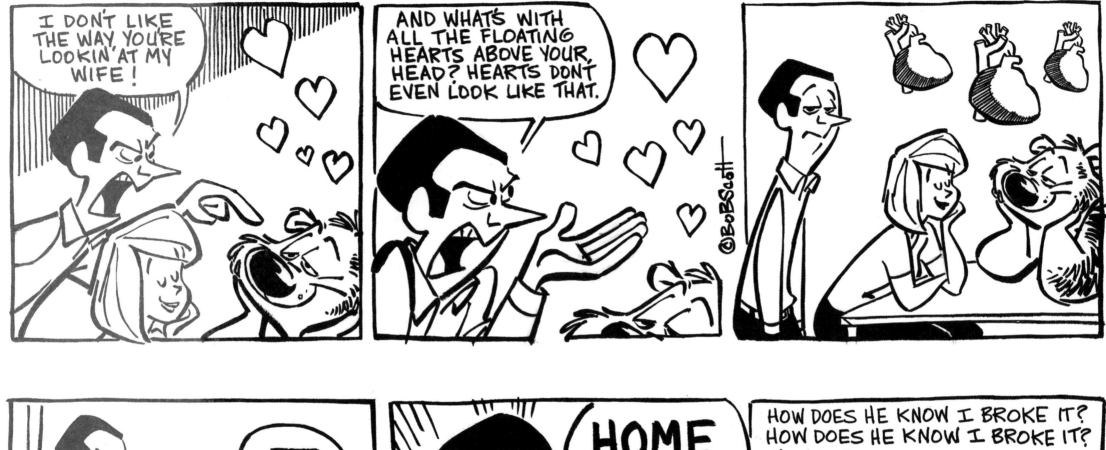

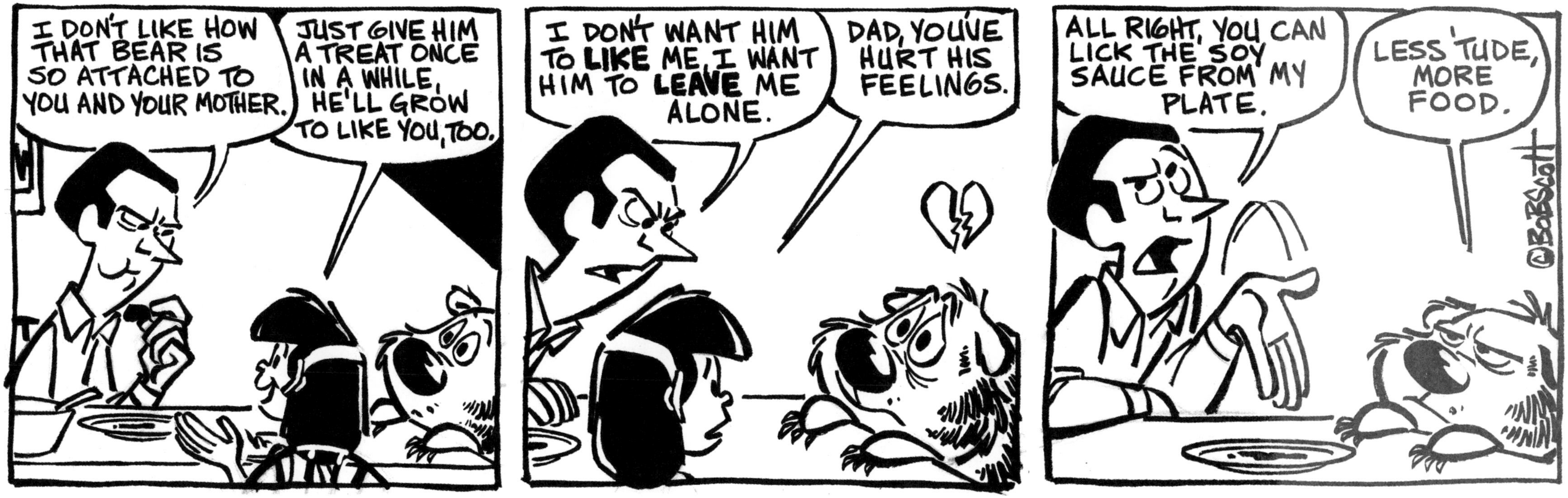
I DON'T LIKE HOW THAT BEAR IS SO ATTACHED TO YOU AND YOUR MOTHER.
JUST GIVE HIM A TREAT ONCE IN A WHILE, HE'LL GROW TO LIKE YOU, TOO.
I DON'T WANT HIM TO **LIKE** ME. I WANT HIM TO **LEAVE** ME ALONE.
DAD, YOU'VE HURT HIS FEELINGS.
ALL RIGHT, YOU CAN LICK THE SOY SAUCE FROM MY PLATE.
LESS 'TUDE, MORE FOOD.
©BOBSCOTT

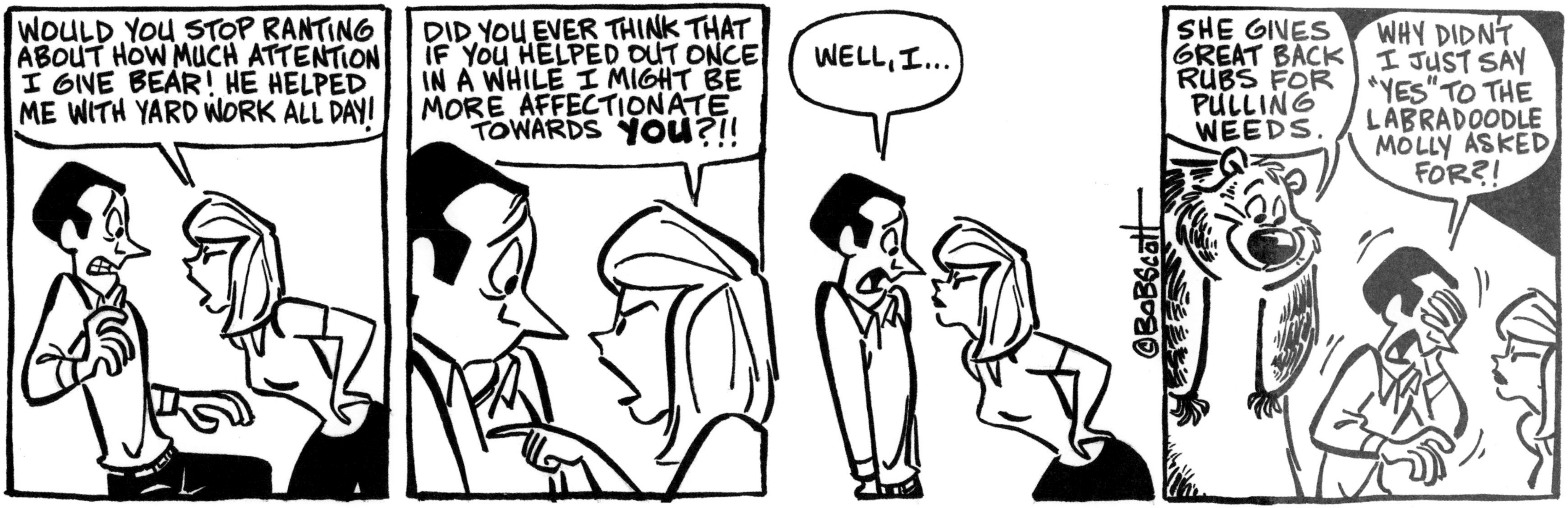
WOULD YOU STOP RANTING ABOUT HOW MUCH ATTENTION I GIVE BEAR! HE HELPED ME WITH YARD WORK ALL DAY!
DID YOU EVER THINK THAT IF YOU HELPED OUT ONCE IN A WHILE I MIGHT BE MORE AFFECTIONATE TOWARDS **YOU**?!!
WELL, I...
©BOBSCOTT
SHE GIVES GREAT BACK RUBS FOR PULLING WEEDS.
WHY DIDN'T I JUST SAY "YES" TO THE LABRADOODLE MOLLY ASKED FOR?!

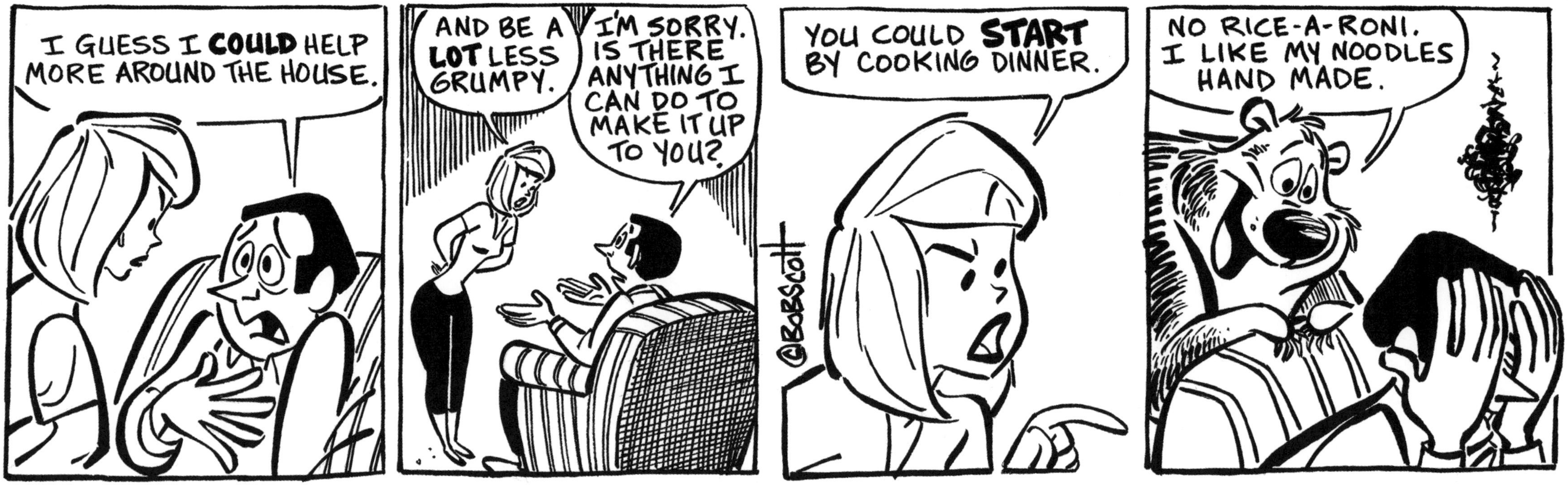
I GUESS I **COULD** HELP MORE AROUND THE HOUSE.
AND BE A **LOT** LESS GRUMPY.
I'M SORRY. IS THERE ANYTHING I CAN DO TO MAKE IT UP TO YOU?
©BOBSCOTT
YOU COULD **START** BY COOKING DINNER.
NO RICE-A-RONI. I LIKE MY NOODLES HAND MADE.

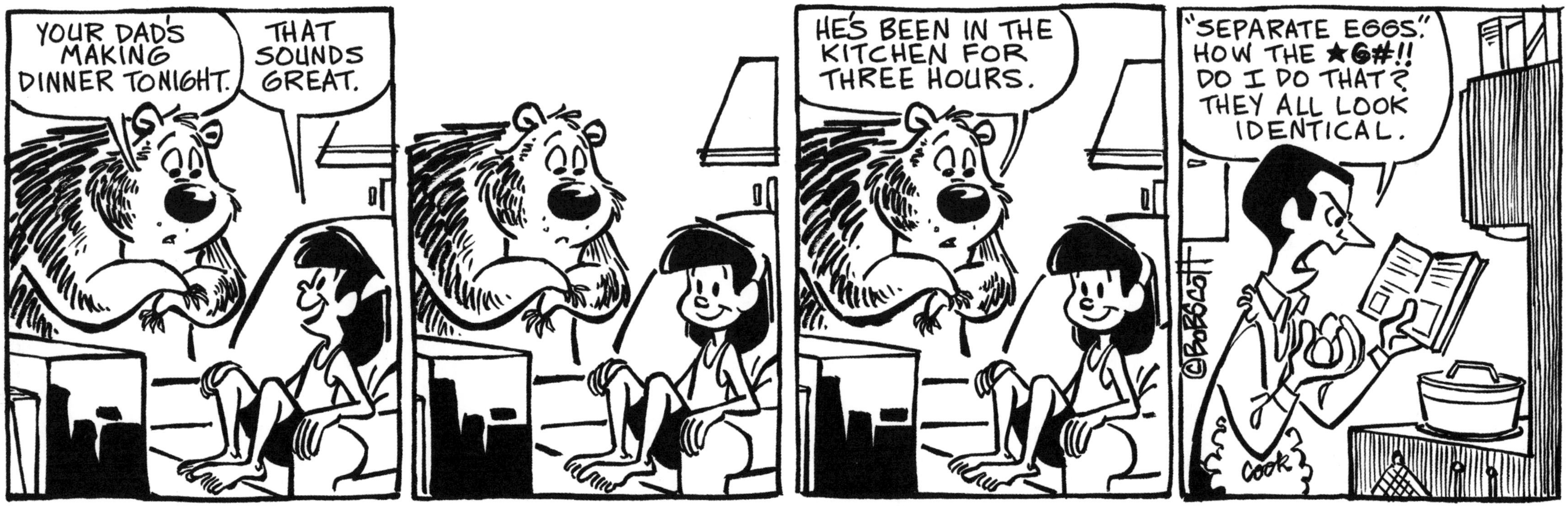
YOUR DAD'S MAKING DINNER TONIGHT.
THAT SOUNDS GREAT.
HE'S BEEN IN THE KITCHEN FOR THREE HOURS.
©BOBSCOTT
"SEPARATE EGGS." HOW THE ★@#!! DO I DO THAT? THEY ALL LOOK IDENTICAL.
COOK

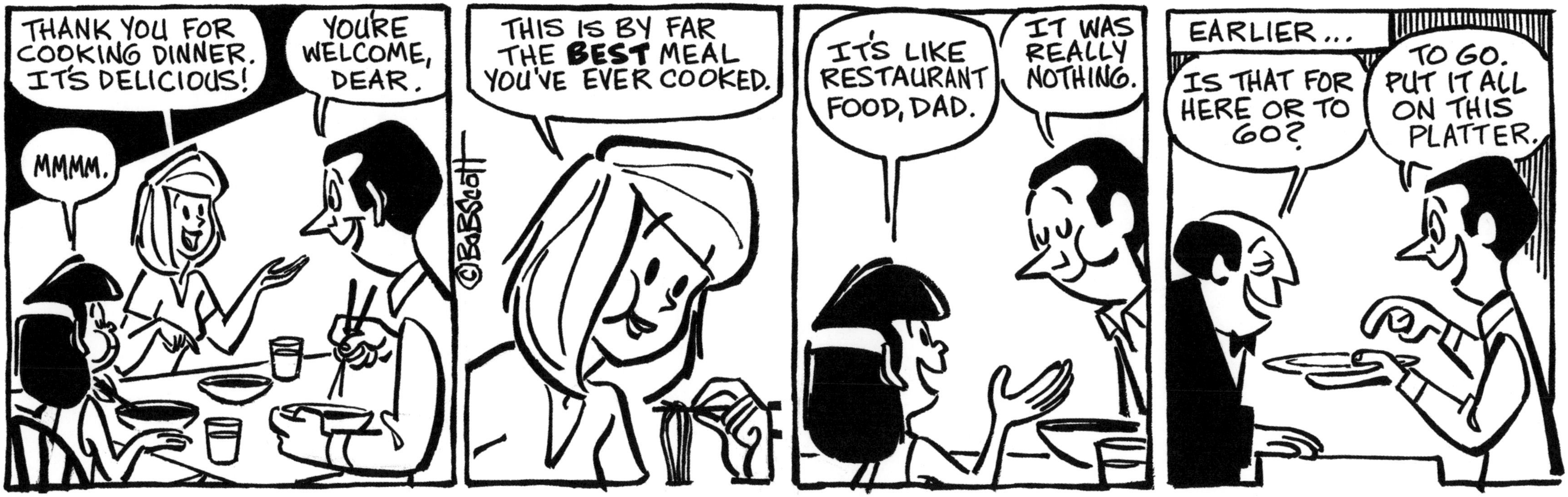
THANK YOU FOR COOKING DINNER. IT'S DELICIOUS!
MMMM.
YOU'RE WELCOME, DEAR.
THIS IS BY FAR THE **BEST** MEAL YOU'VE EVER COOKED.
IT'S LIKE RESTAURANT FOOD, DAD.
IT WAS REALLY NOTHING.
EARLIER...
IS THAT FOR HERE OR TO GO?
TO GO. PUT IT ALL ON THIS PLATTER.

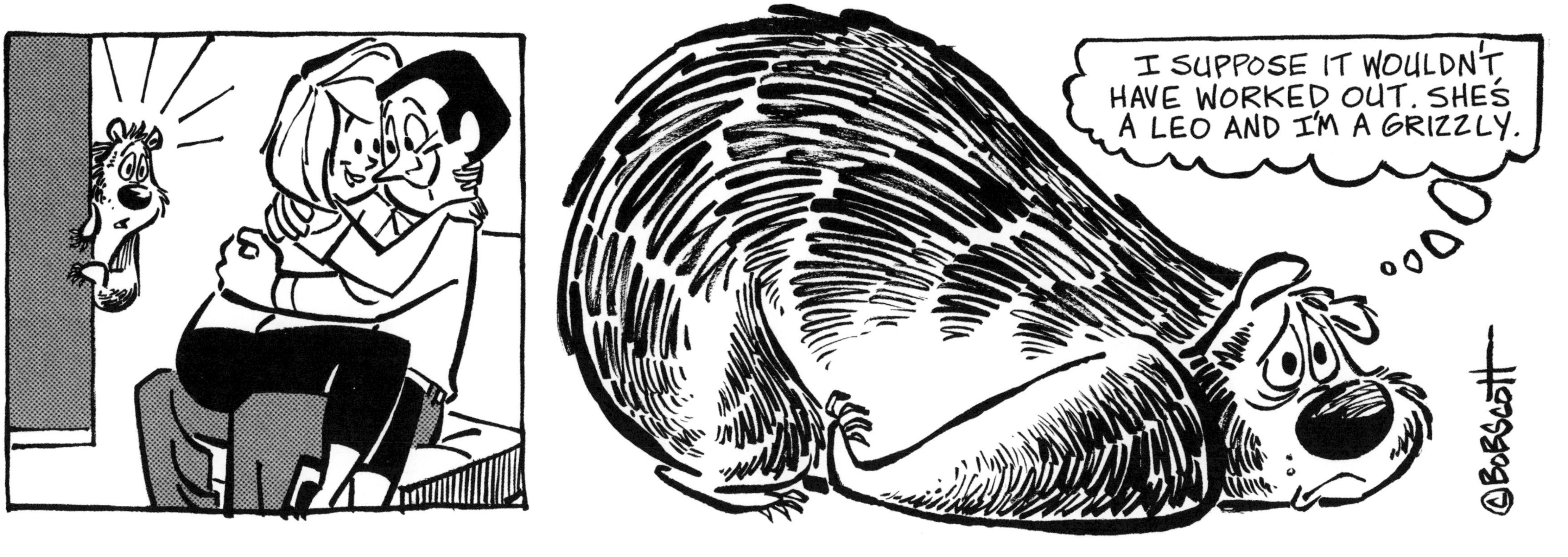
I SUPPOSE IT WOULDN'T HAVE WORKED OUT. SHE'S A LEO AND I'M A GRIZZLY.

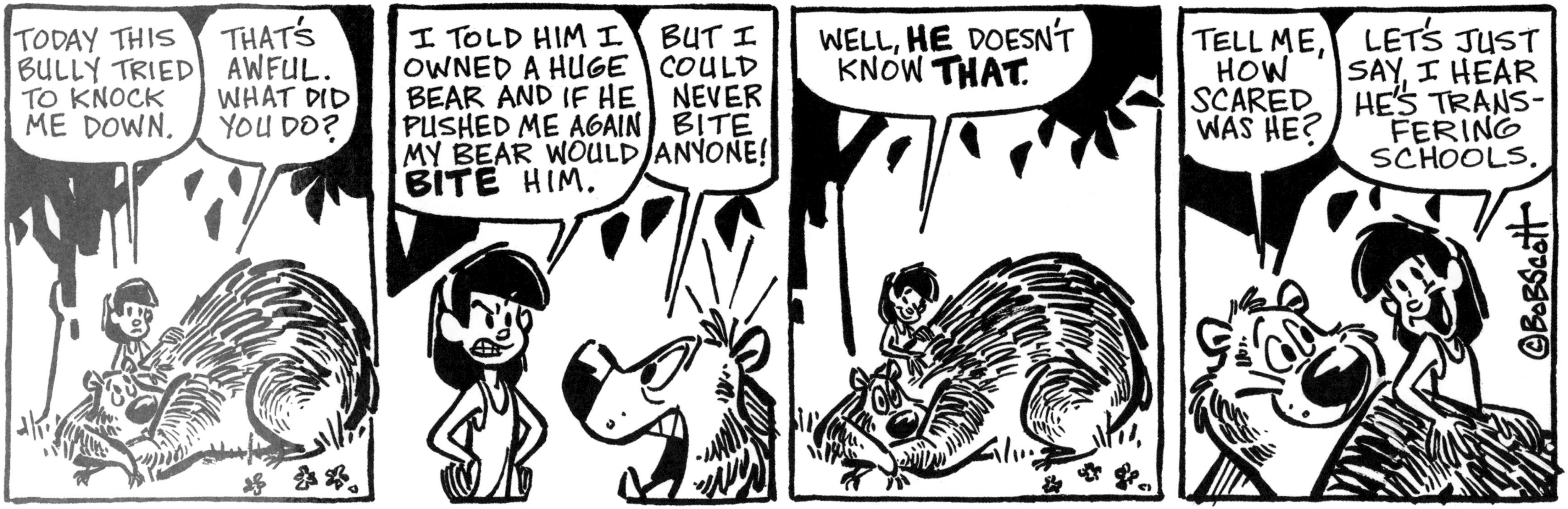
TODAY THIS BULLY TRIED TO KNOCK ME DOWN.
THAT'S AWFUL. WHAT DID YOU DO?
I TOLD HIM I OWNED A HUGE BEAR AND IF HE PUSHED ME AGAIN MY BEAR WOULD **BITE** HIM.
BUT I COULD NEVER BITE ANYONE!
WELL, **HE** DOESN'T KNOW **THAT**.
TELL ME, HOW SCARED WAS HE?
LET'S JUST SAY, I HEAR HE'S TRANS-FERING SCHOOLS.
©BoBScott

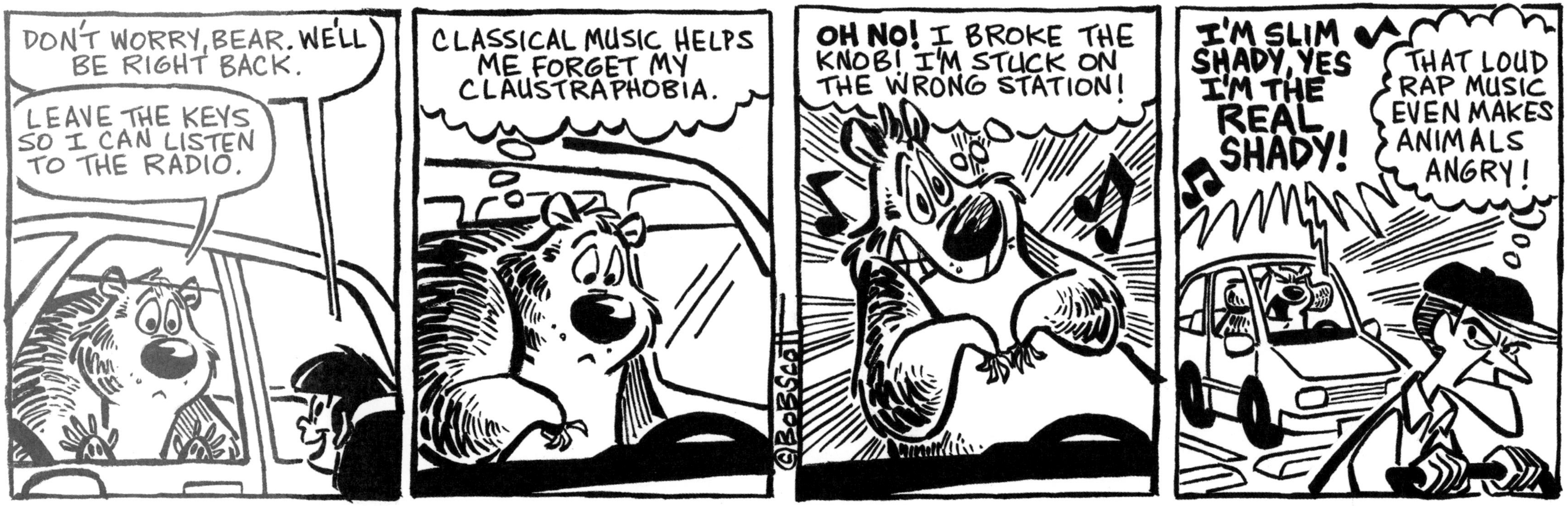
DON'T WORRY, BEAR. WE'LL BE RIGHT BACK.
LEAVE THE KEYS SO I CAN LISTEN TO THE RADIO.
CLASSICAL MUSIC HELPS ME FORGET MY CLAUSTRAPHOBIA.
©BoBScott
OH NO! I BROKE THE KNOB! I'M STUCK ON THE WRONG STATION!
I'M SLIM SHADY, YES I'M THE REAL SHADY!
THAT LOUD RAP MUSIC EVEN MAKES ANIMALS ANGRY!

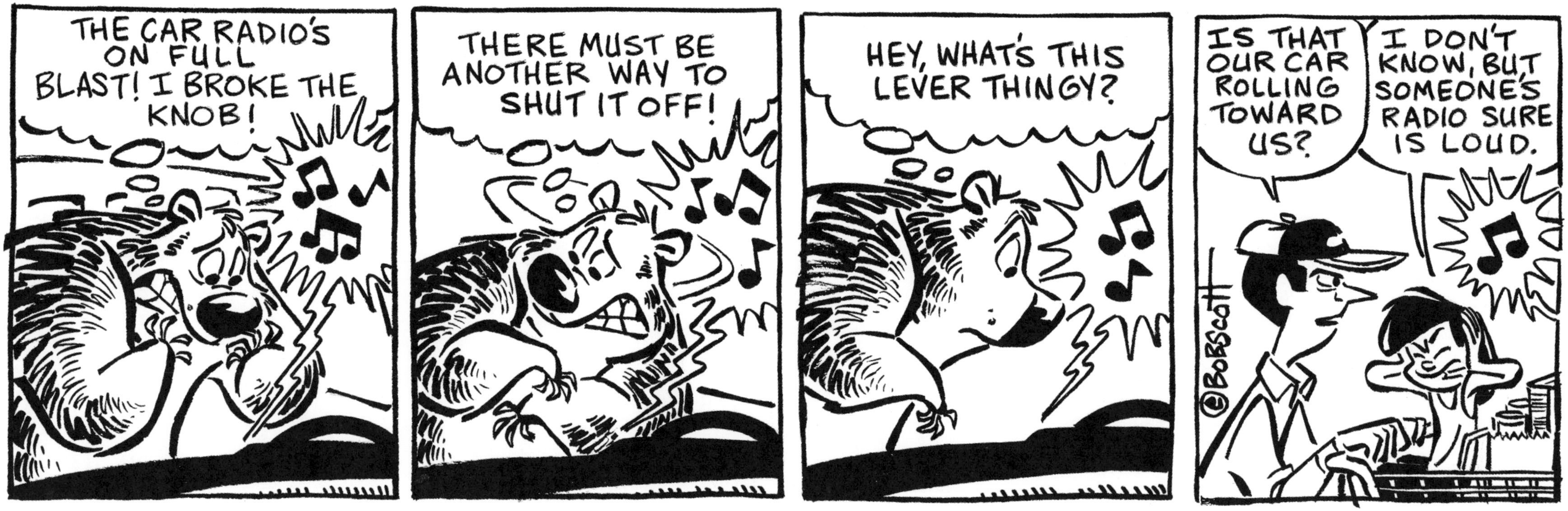
THE CAR RADIO'S ON FULL BLAST! I BROKE THE KNOB!
THERE MUST BE ANOTHER WAY TO SHUT IT OFF!
HEY, WHAT'S THIS LEVER THINGY?
IS THAT OUR CAR ROLLING TOWARD US?
I DON'T KNOW, BUT SOMEONE'S RADIO SURE IS LOUD.
©BOBSCOTT

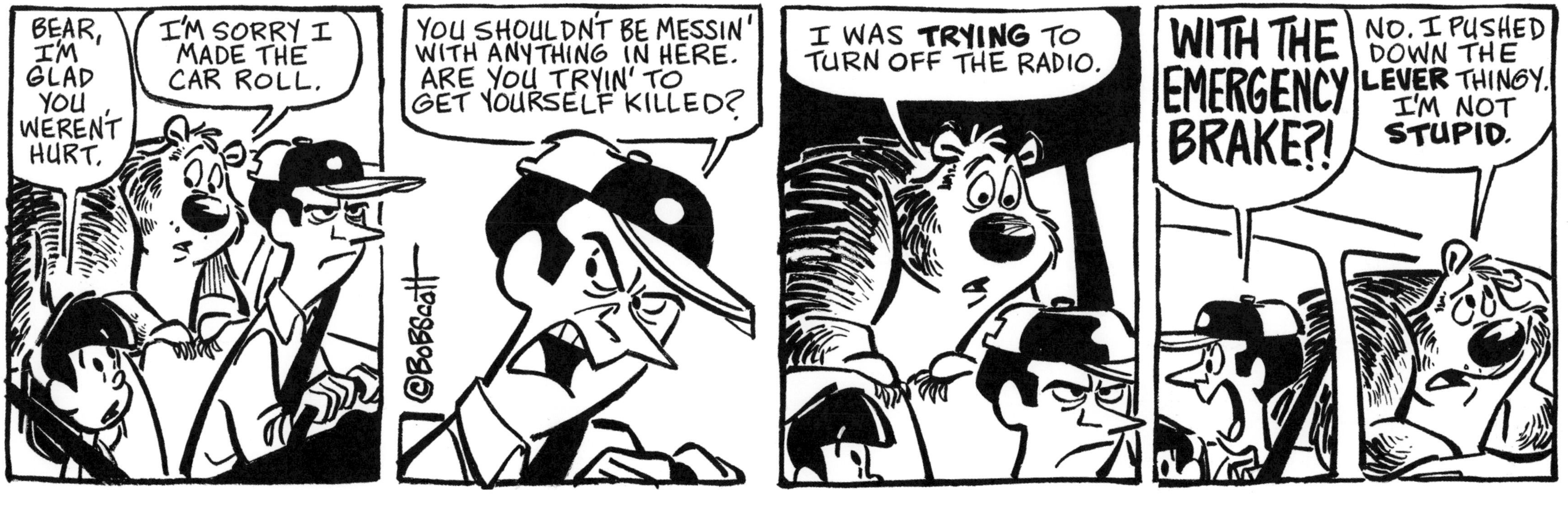
BEAR, I'M GLAD YOU WEREN'T HURT.
I'M SORRY I MADE THE CAR ROLL.
©BOBSCOTT
YOU SHOULDN'T BE MESSIN' WITH ANYTHING IN HERE. ARE YOU TRYIN' TO GET YOURSELF KILLED?
I WAS TRYING TO TURN OFF THE RADIO.
WITH THE EMERGENCY BRAKE?!
NO. I PUSHED DOWN THE LEVER THINGY. I'M NOT STUPID.

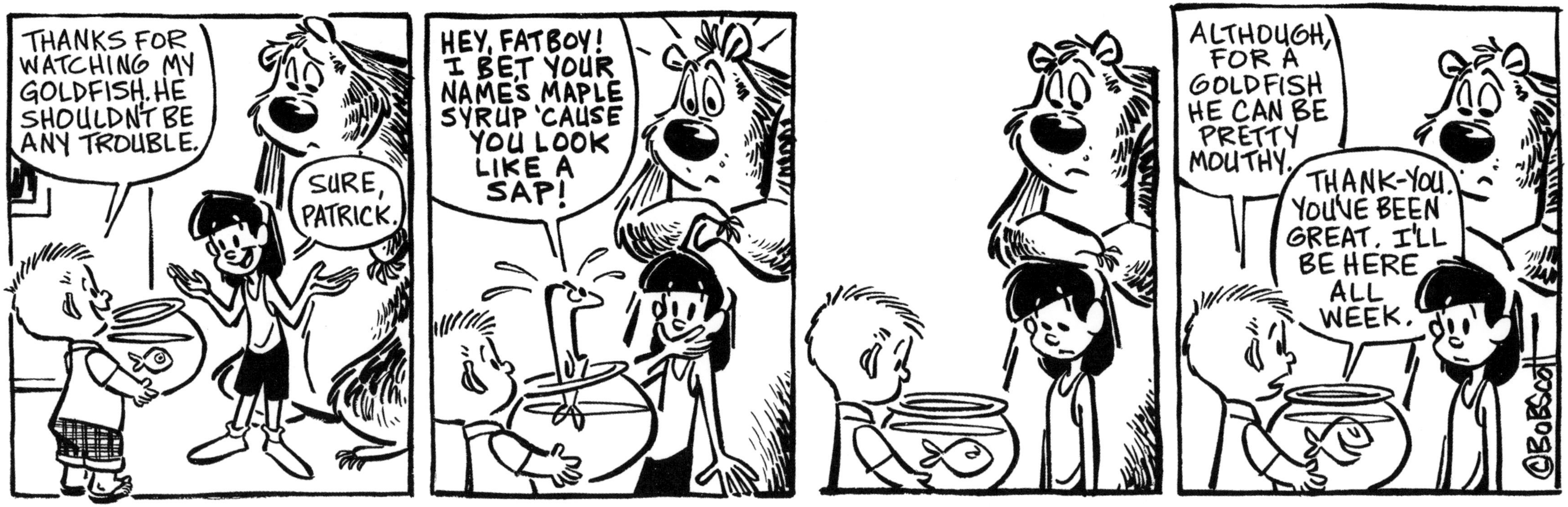
THANKS FOR WATCHING MY GOLDFISH. HE SHOULDN'T BE ANY TROUBLE.
SURE, PATRICK.
HEY, FATBOY! I BET YOUR NAME'S MAPLE SYRUP 'CAUSE YOU LOOK LIKE A SAP!
ALTHOUGH, FOR A GOLDFISH HE CAN BE PRETTY MOUTHY.
THANK-YOU. YOU'VE BEEN GREAT. I'LL BE HERE ALL WEEK.
©BOBSCOTT

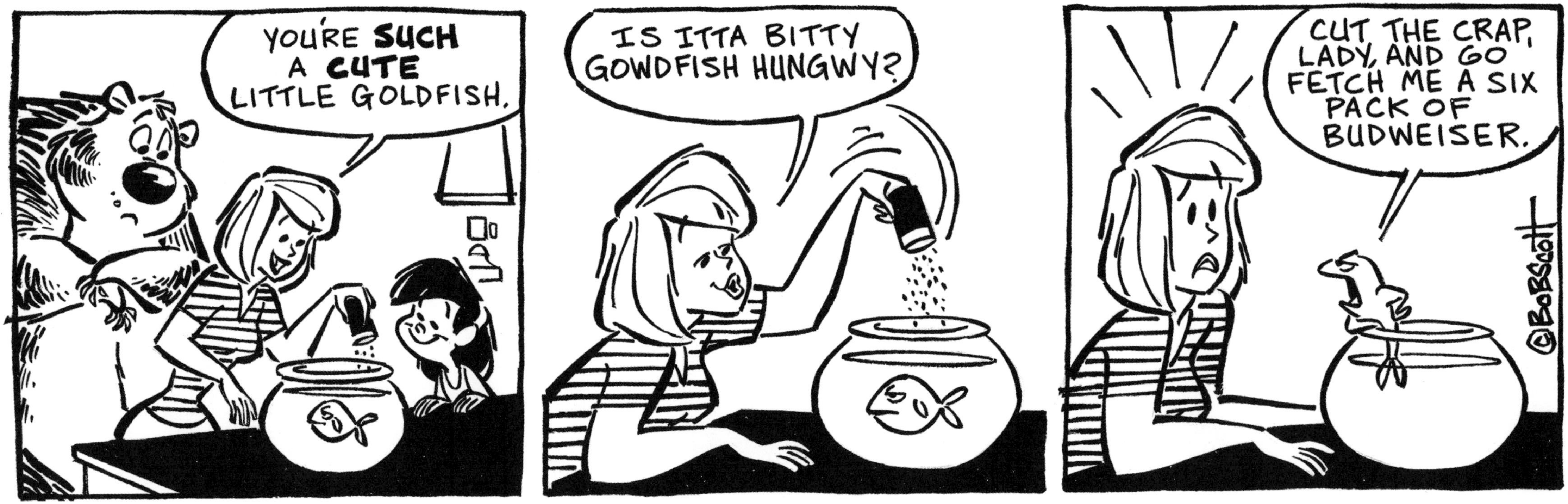
YOU'RE **SUCH** A **CUTE** LITTLE GOLDFISH.
IS ITTA BITTY GOWDFISH HUNGWY?
CUT THE CRAP, LADY, AND GO FETCH ME A SIX PACK OF BUDWEISER.
©BOBSCOTT

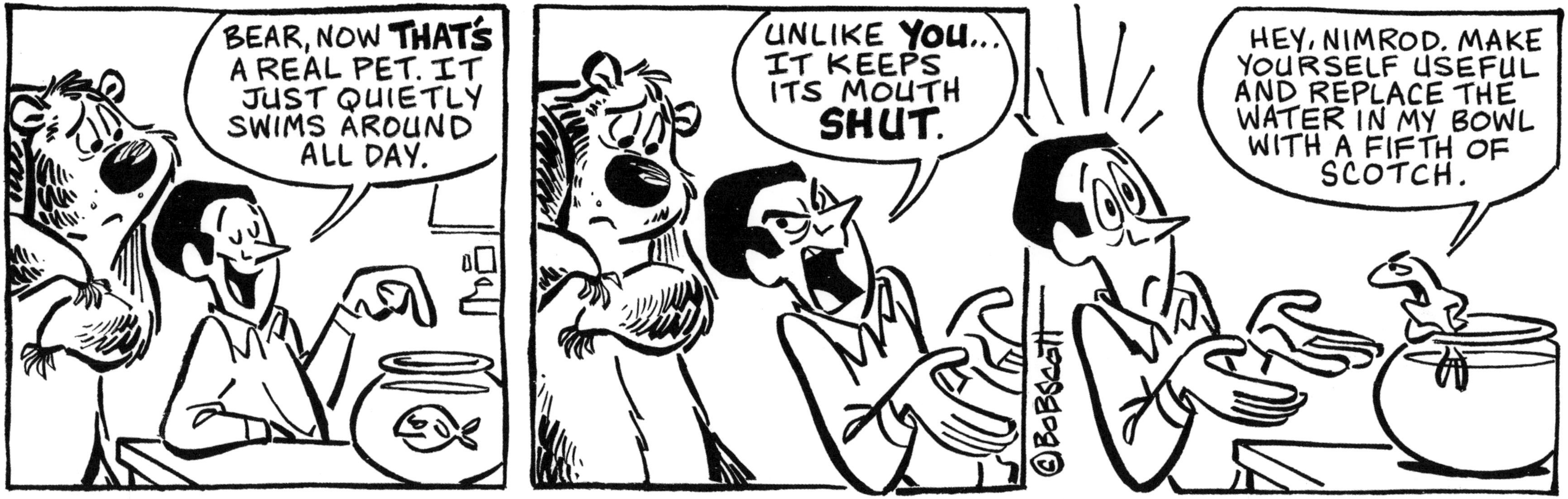
BEAR, NOW THAT'S A REAL PET. IT JUST QUIETLY SWIMS AROUND ALL DAY.
UNLIKE YOU... IT KEEPS ITS MOUTH SHUT.
©BOBSCOTT
HEY, NIMROD. MAKE YOURSELF USEFUL AND REPLACE THE WATER IN MY BOWL WITH A FIFTH OF SCOTCH.

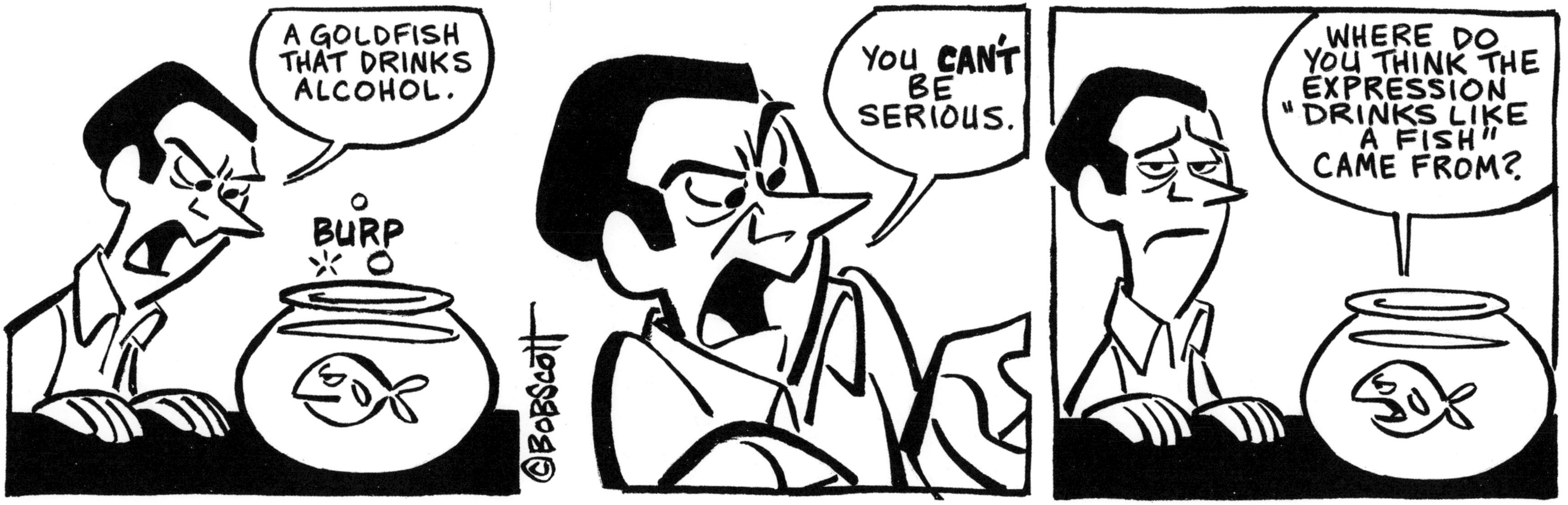
A GOLDFISH THAT DRINKS ALCOHOL.
BURP
©BOBSCOTT
YOU CAN'T BE SERIOUS.
WHERE DO YOU THINK THE EXPRESSION "DRINKS LIKE A FISH" CAME FROM?

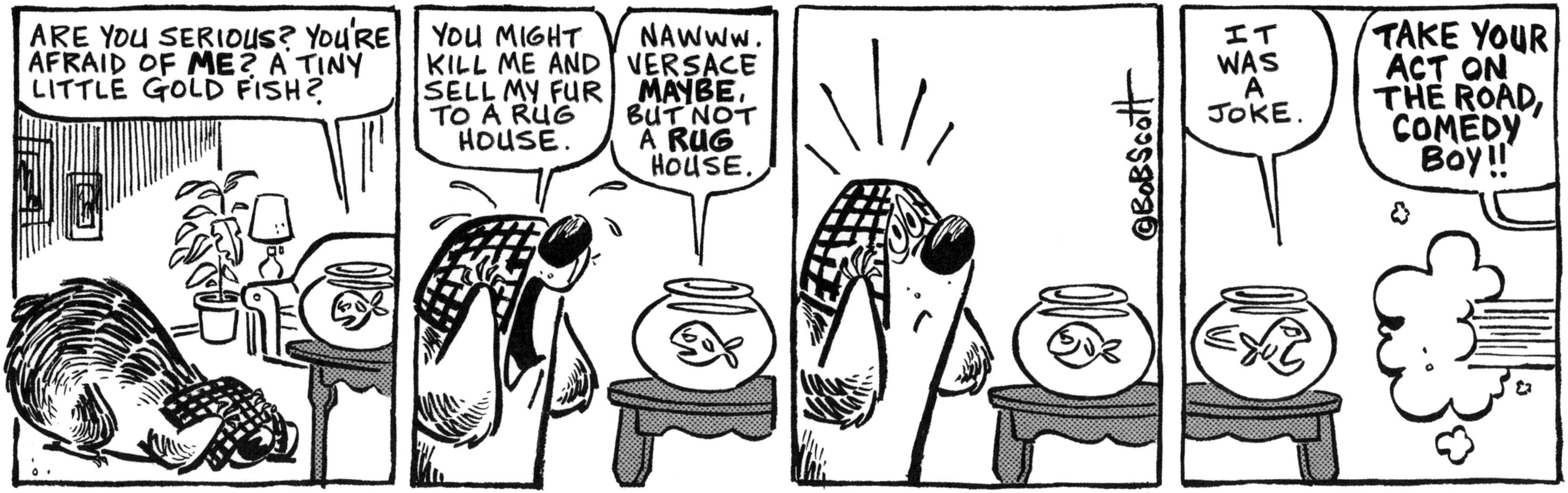
ARE YOU SERIOUS? YOU'RE AFRAID OF **ME**? A TINY LITTLE GOLD FISH?
YOU MIGHT KILL ME AND SELL MY FUR TO A RUG HOUSE.
NAWWW. VERSACE **MAYBE**, BUT NOT A **RUG** HOUSE.
©BoBScott
IT WAS A JOKE.
TAKE YOUR ACT ON THE ROAD, COMEDY BOY!!

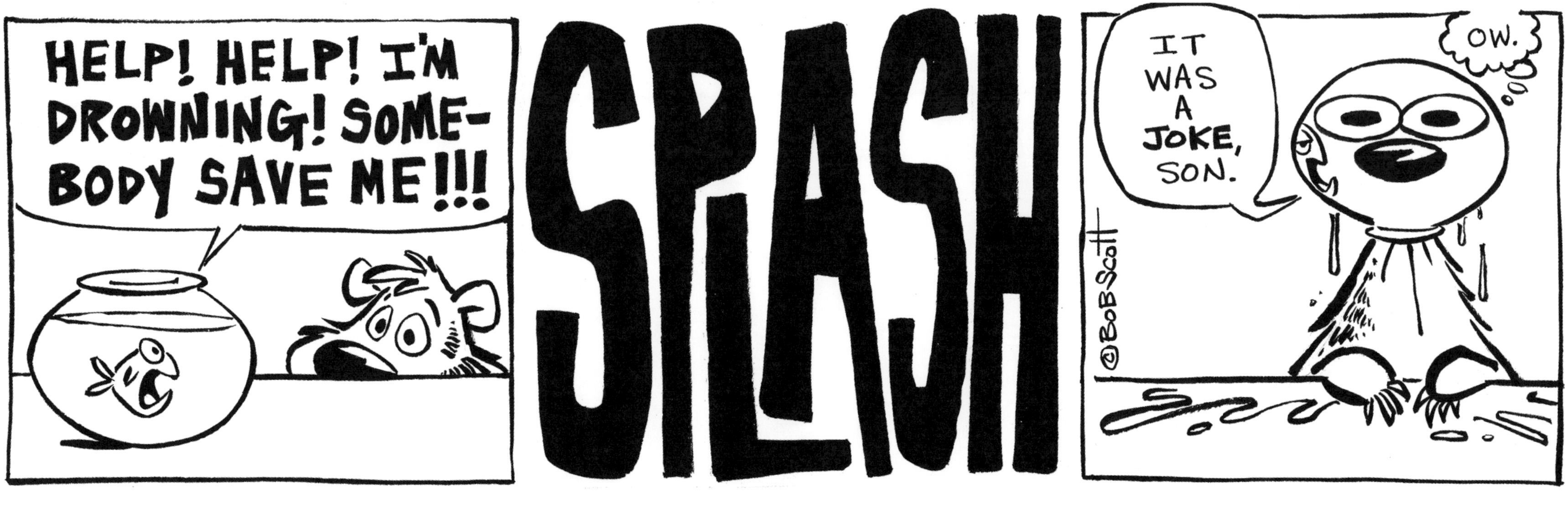
HELP! HELP! I'M DROWNING! SOMEBODY SAVE ME!!!
SPLASH
©BoBScott
IT WAS A **JOKE**, SON.
OW.

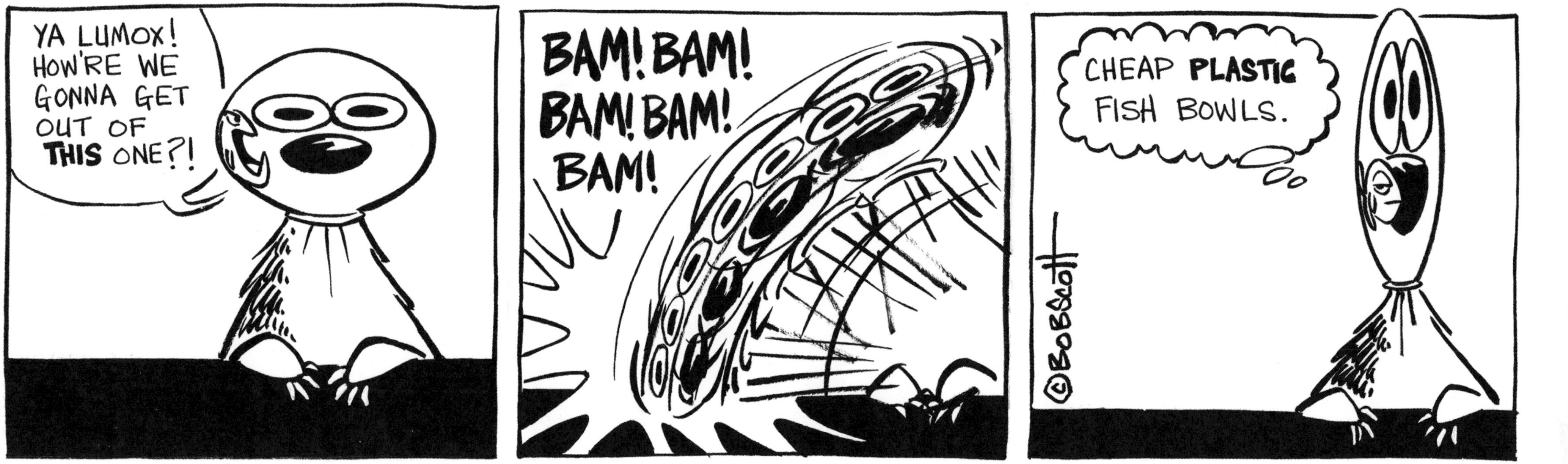
YA LUMOX! HOW'RE WE GONNA GET OUT OF **THIS** ONE?!
BAM! BAM! BAM! BAM! BAM!
CHEAP **PLASTIC** FISH BOWLS.
©BOBSCOTT

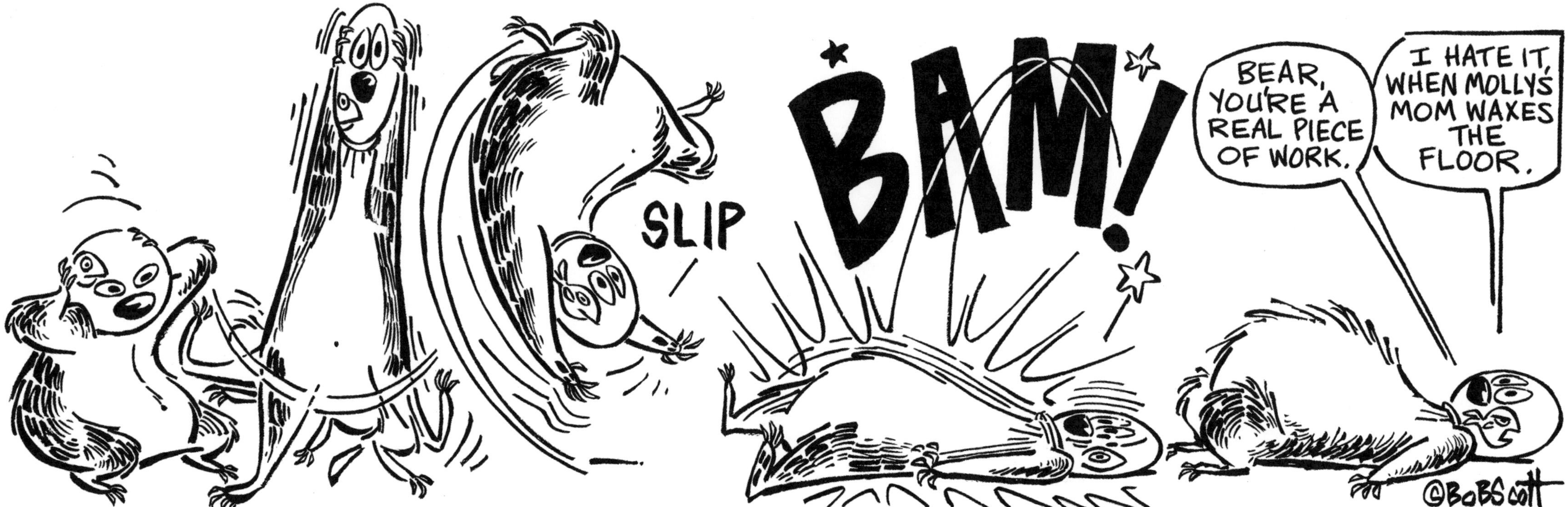
SLIP
BAM!
BEAR, YOU'RE A REAL PIECE OF WORK.
I HATE IT WHEN MOLLY'S MOM WAXES THE FLOOR.
©BOBSCOTT

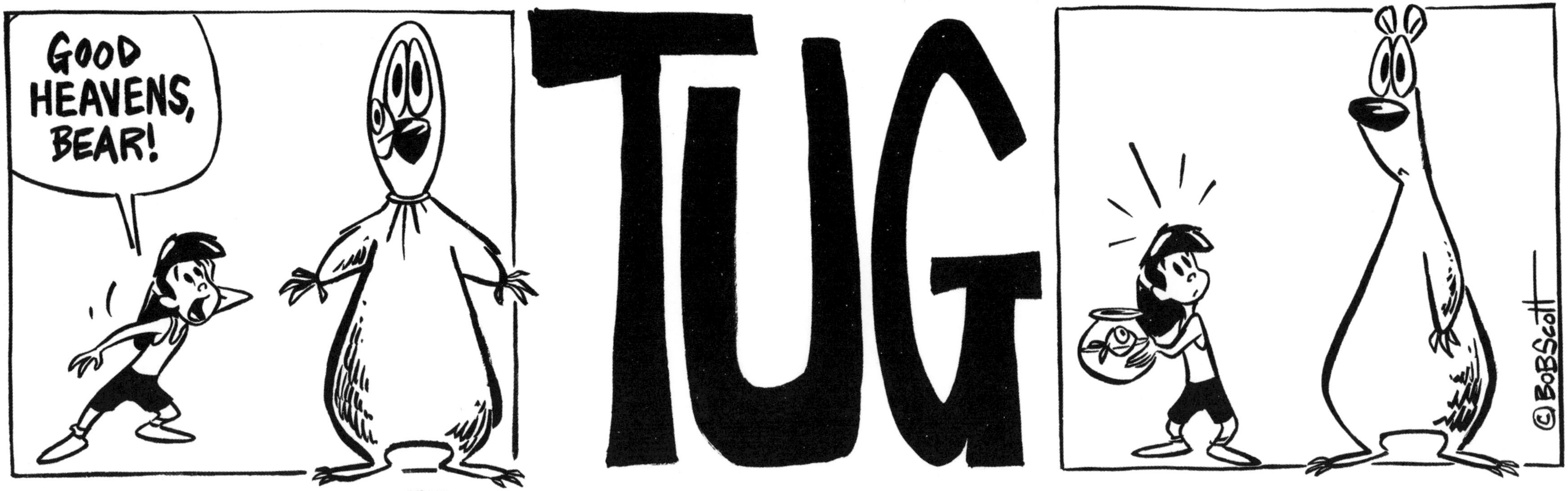
GOOD HEAVENS, BEAR!
TUG
©BOBScott

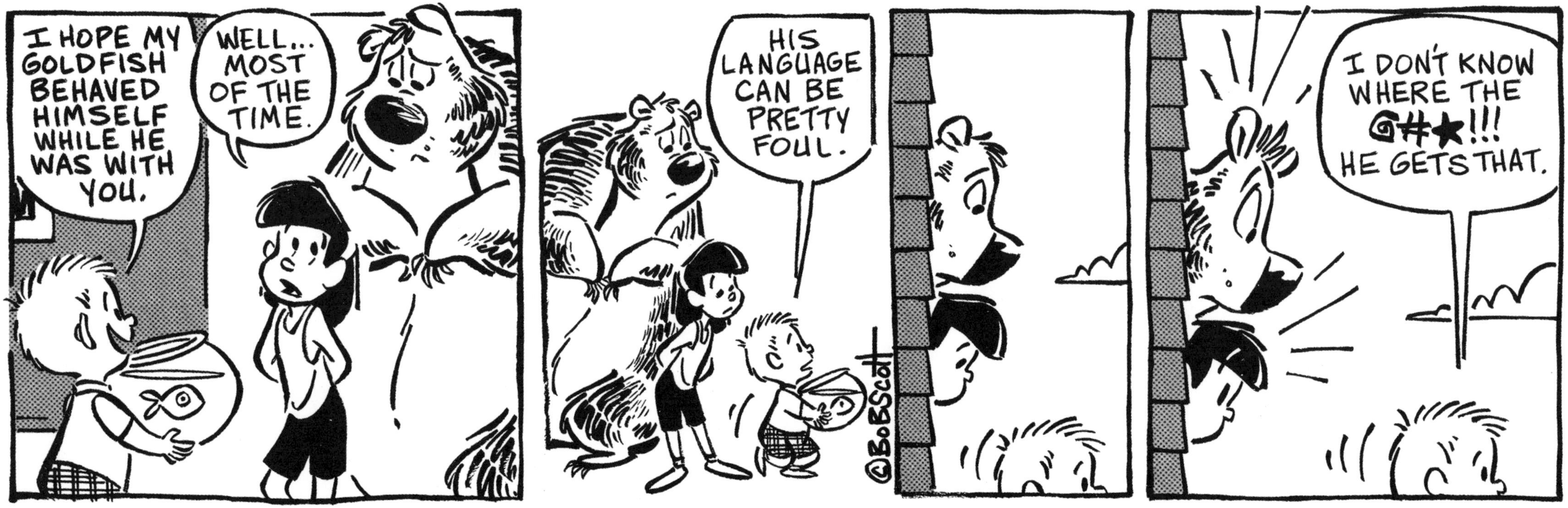
I HOPE MY GOLDFISH BEHAVED HIMSELF WHILE HE WAS WITH YOU.
WELL... MOST OF THE TIME.
HIS LANGUAGE CAN BE PRETTY FOUL.
©BOBScott
I DON'T KNOW WHERE THE @#★!!! HE GETS THAT.

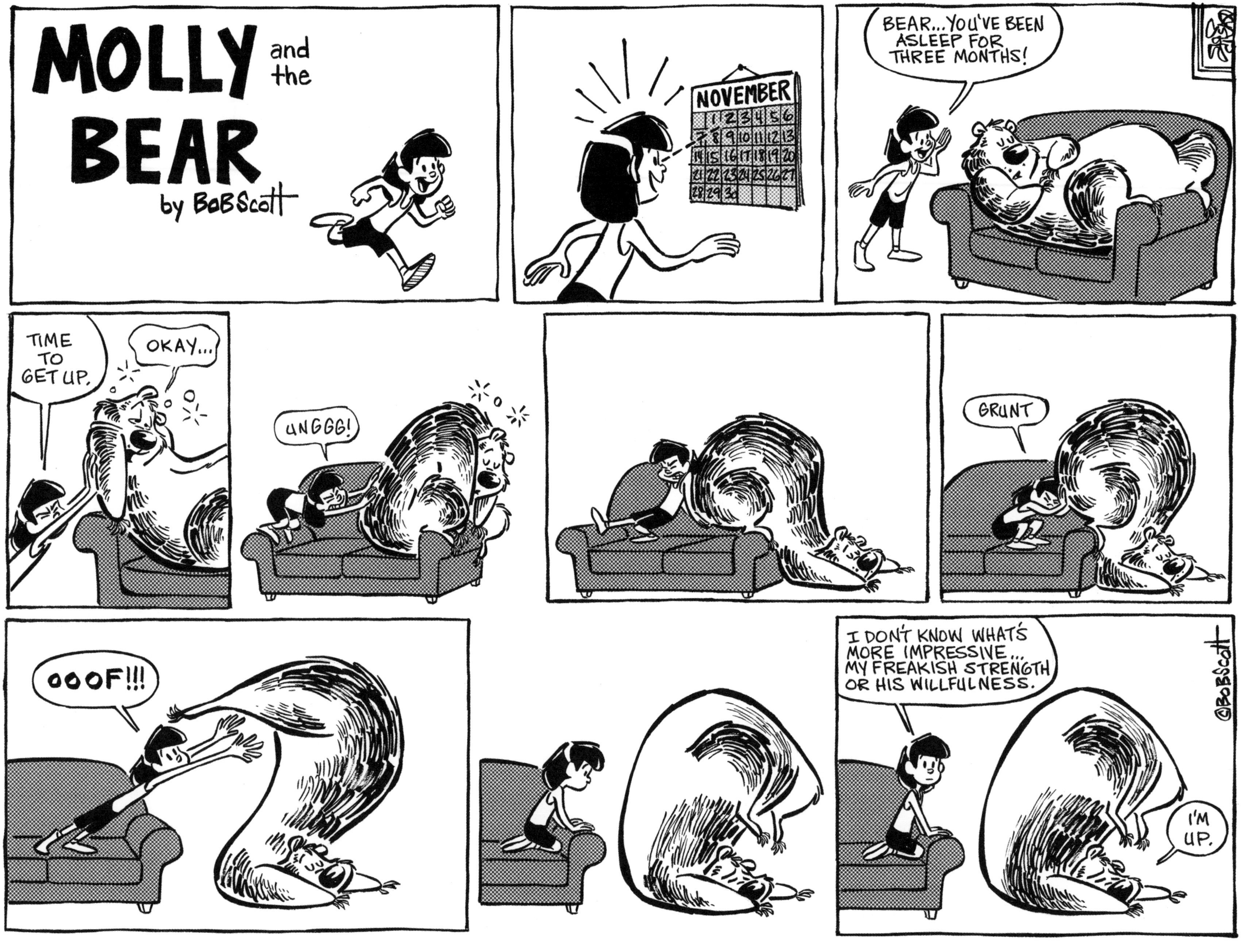

MOLLY and the BEAR
by BOB SCOTT
NOVEMBER
BEAR... YOU'VE BEEN ASLEEP FOR THREE MONTHS!
TIME TO GET UP.
OKAY...
UNGGG!
GRUNT
OOOF!!!
I DON'T KNOW WHAT'S MORE IMPRESSIVE... MY FREAKISH STRENGTH OR HIS WILLFULNESS.
I'M UP.
©BOB SCOTT

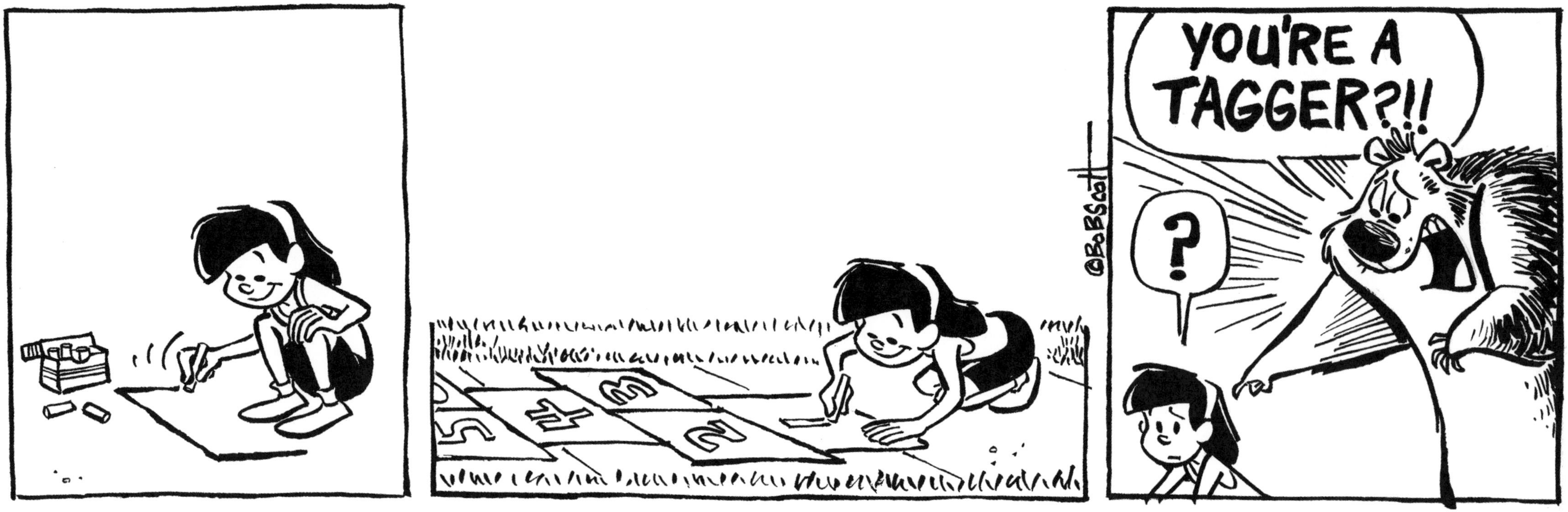
©BoBScott
?
YOU'RE A TAGGER?!!

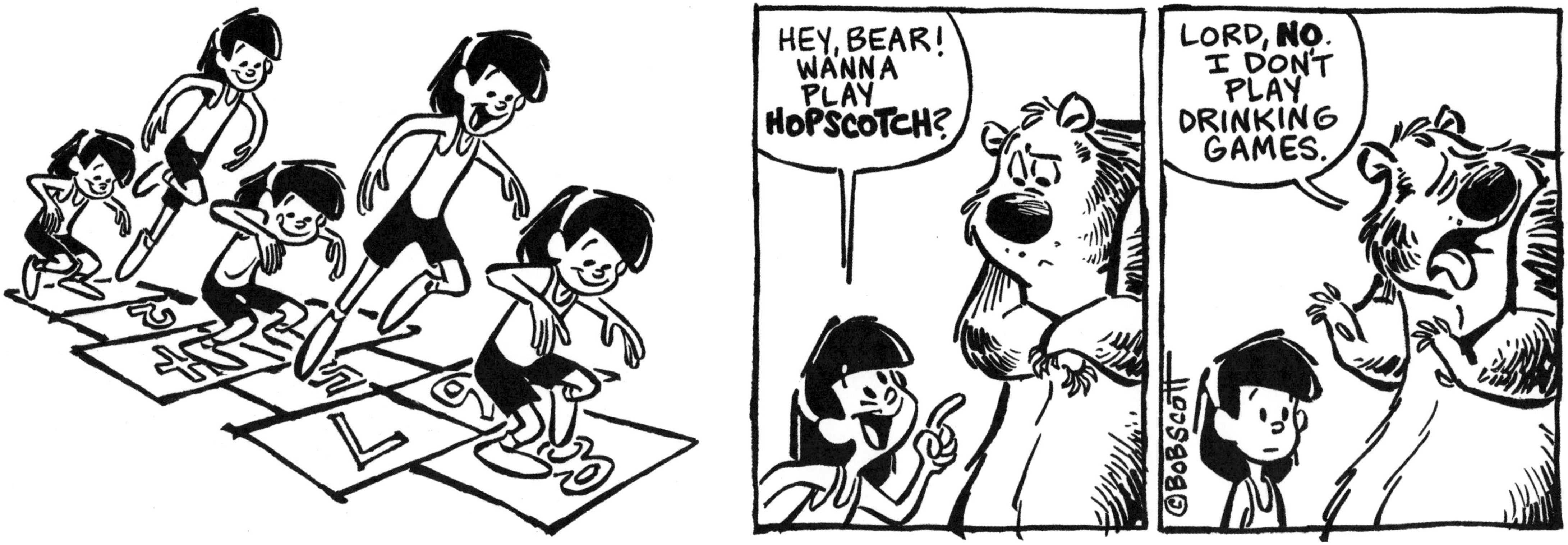
HEY, BEAR! WANNA PLAY **HOPSCOTCH**?
LORD, **NO**. I DON'T PLAY DRINKING GAMES.
©BoBScott

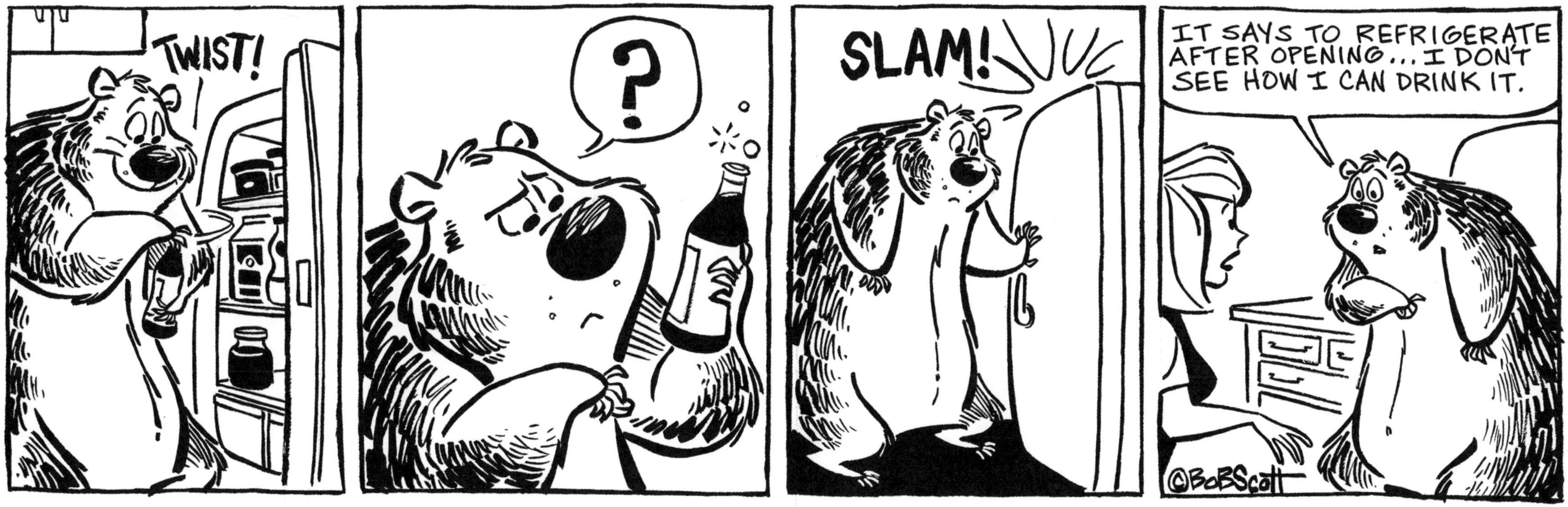
TWIST!
?
SLAM!
IT SAYS TO REFRIGERATE AFTER OPENING... I DON'T SEE HOW I CAN DRINK IT.
©BoBScott

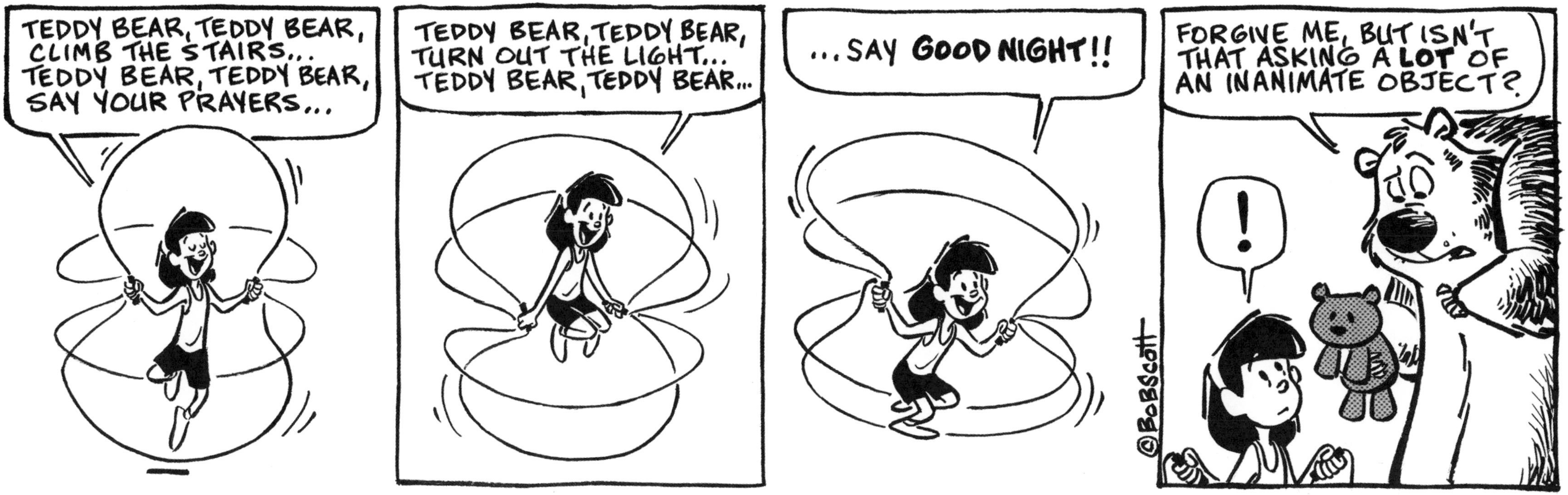
TEDDY BEAR, TEDDY BEAR, CLIMB THE STAIRS... TEDDY BEAR, TEDDY BEAR, SAY YOUR PRAYERS...
TEDDY BEAR, TEDDY BEAR, TURN OUT THE LIGHT... TEDDY BEAR, TEDDY BEAR...
...SAY GOOD NIGHT!!
FORGIVE ME, BUT ISN'T THAT ASKING A LOT OF AN INANIMATE OBJECT?
!
©BoBScott

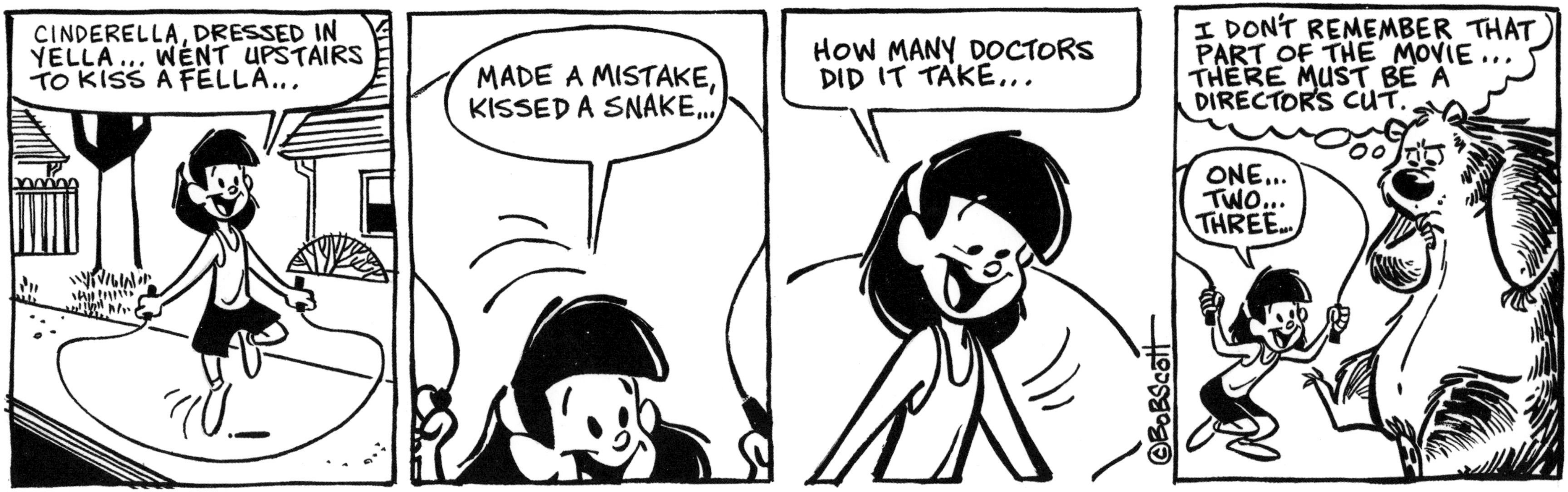
CINDERELLA, DRESSED IN YELLA... WENT UPSTAIRS TO KISS A FELLA...
MADE A MISTAKE, KISSED A SNAKE...
HOW MANY DOCTORS DID IT TAKE...
I DON'T REMEMBER THAT PART OF THE MOVIE... THERE MUST BE A DIRECTOR'S CUT.
ONE... TWO... THREE...
©BOBSCOTT

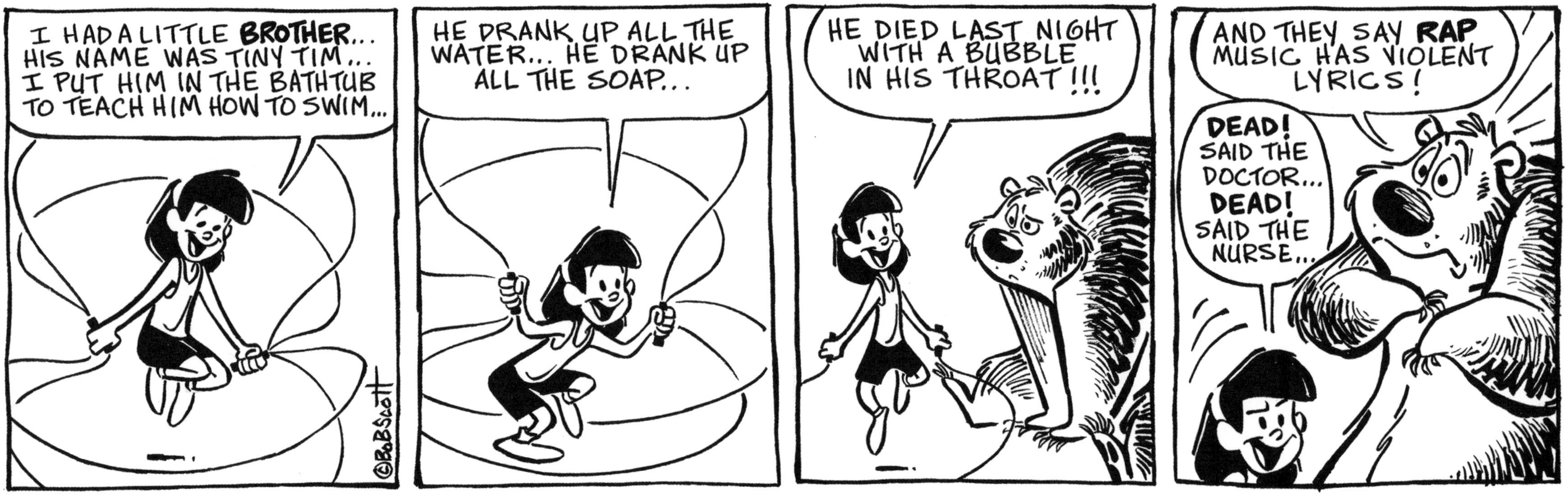
I HAD A LITTLE **BROTHER**... HIS NAME WAS TINY TIM... I PUT HIM IN THE BATHTUB TO TEACH HIM HOW TO SWIM...
©BOBSCOTT
HE DRANK UP ALL THE WATER... HE DRANK UP ALL THE SOAP...
HE DIED LAST NIGHT WITH A BUBBLE IN HIS THROAT!!!
DEAD! SAID THE DOCTOR... **DEAD!** SAID THE NURSE...
AND THEY SAY **RAP** MUSIC HAS VIOLENT LYRICS!

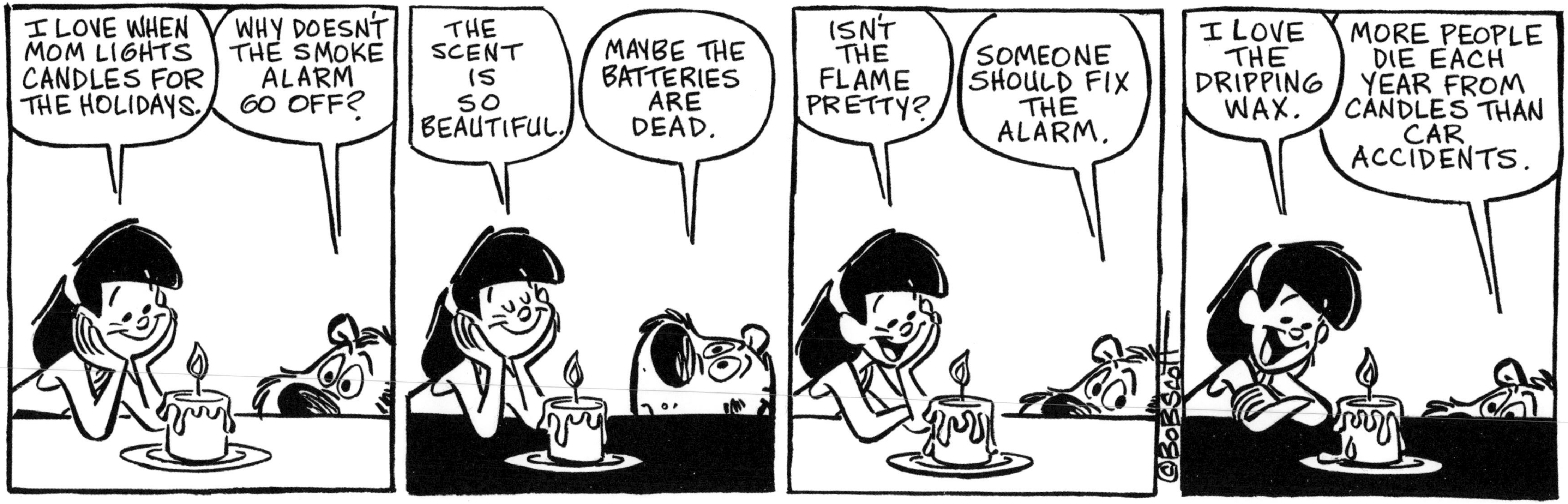
I LOVE WHEN MOM LIGHTS CANDLES FOR THE HOLIDAYS.
WHY DOESN'T THE SMOKE ALARM GO OFF?
THE SCENT IS SO BEAUTIFUL.
MAYBE THE BATTERIES ARE DEAD.
ISN'T THE FLAME PRETTY?
SOMEONE SHOULD FIX THE ALARM.
I LOVE THE DRIPPING WAX.
MORE PEOPLE DIE EACH YEAR FROM CANDLES THAN CAR ACCIDENTS.
©BoBScott

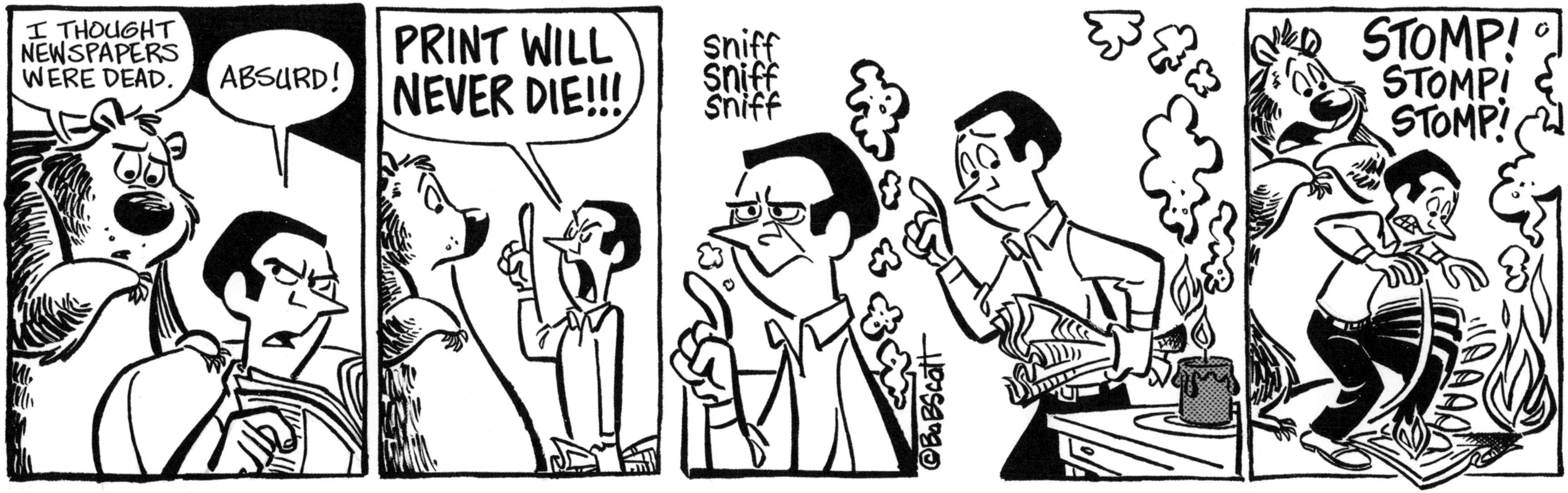
I THOUGHT NEWSPAPERS WERE DEAD.
ABSURD!
PRINT WILL NEVER DIE!!!
sniff sniff sniff
STOMP! STOMP! STOMP!
©BoBScott

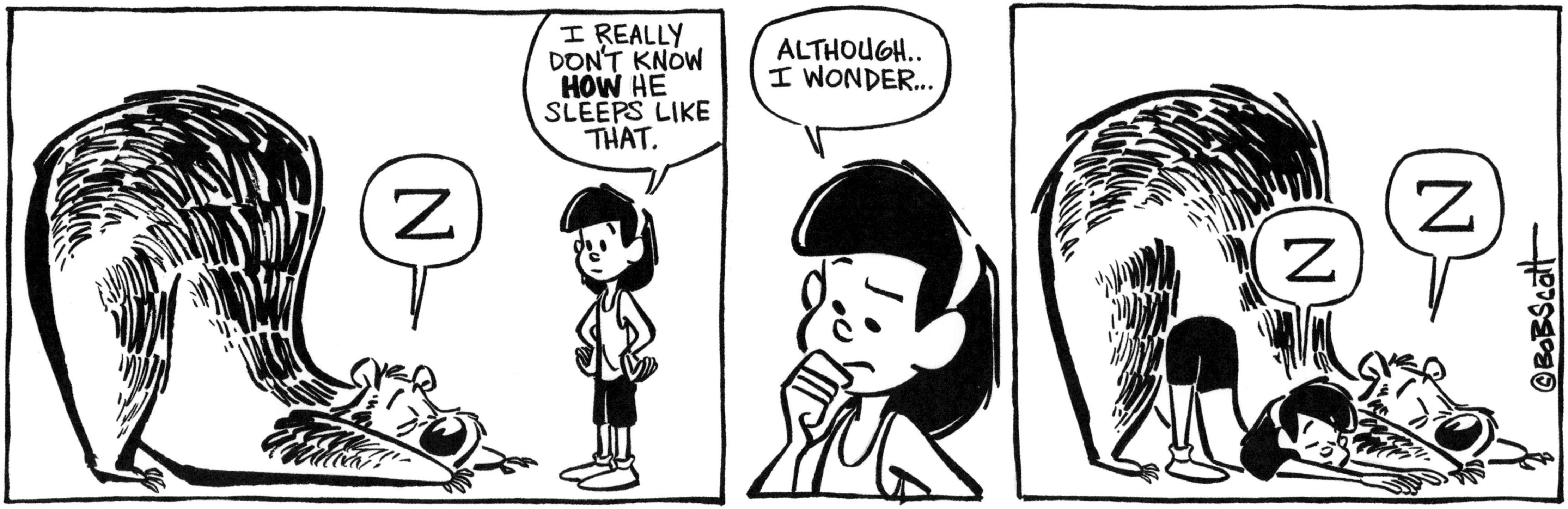
Z
I REALLY DON'T KNOW **HOW** HE SLEEPS LIKE THAT.
ALTHOUGH.. I WONDER...
Z
Z
©BoBScott

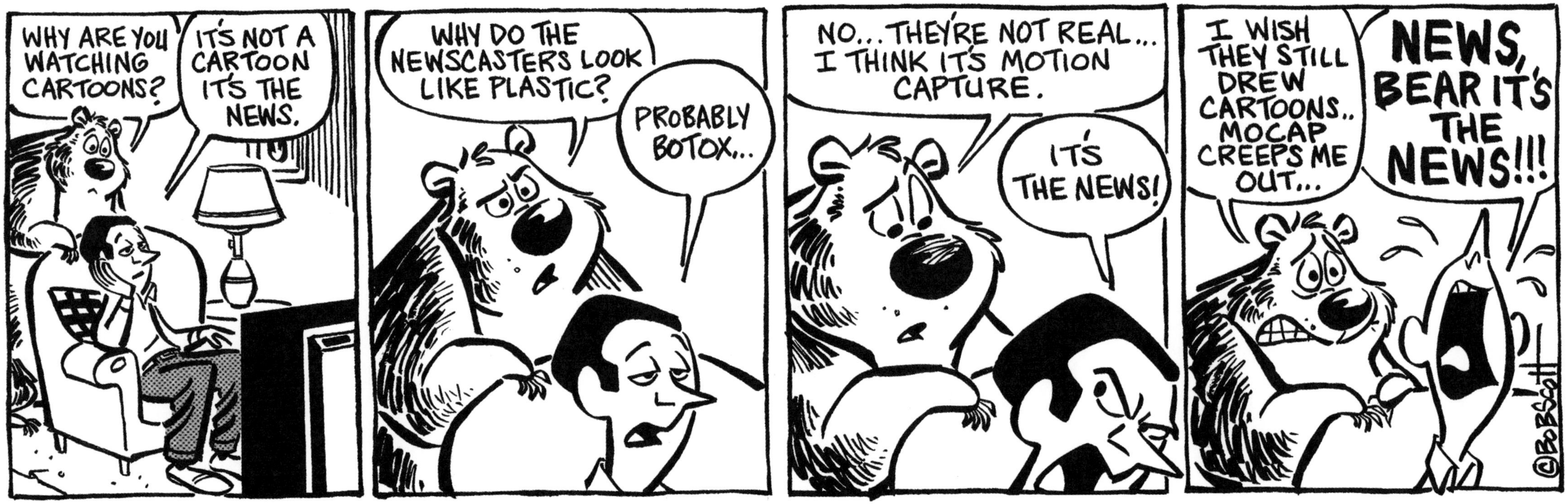
WHY ARE YOU WATCHING CARTOONS?
IT'S NOT A CARTOON IT'S THE NEWS.
WHY DO THE NEWSCASTERS LOOK LIKE PLASTIC?
PROBABLY BOTOX...
NO... THEY'RE NOT REAL... I THINK IT'S MOTION CAPTURE.
IT'S THE NEWS!
I WISH THEY STILL DREW CARTOONS.. MOCAP CREEPS ME OUT...
NEWS, BEAR IT'S THE NEWS!!!
©BoBScott

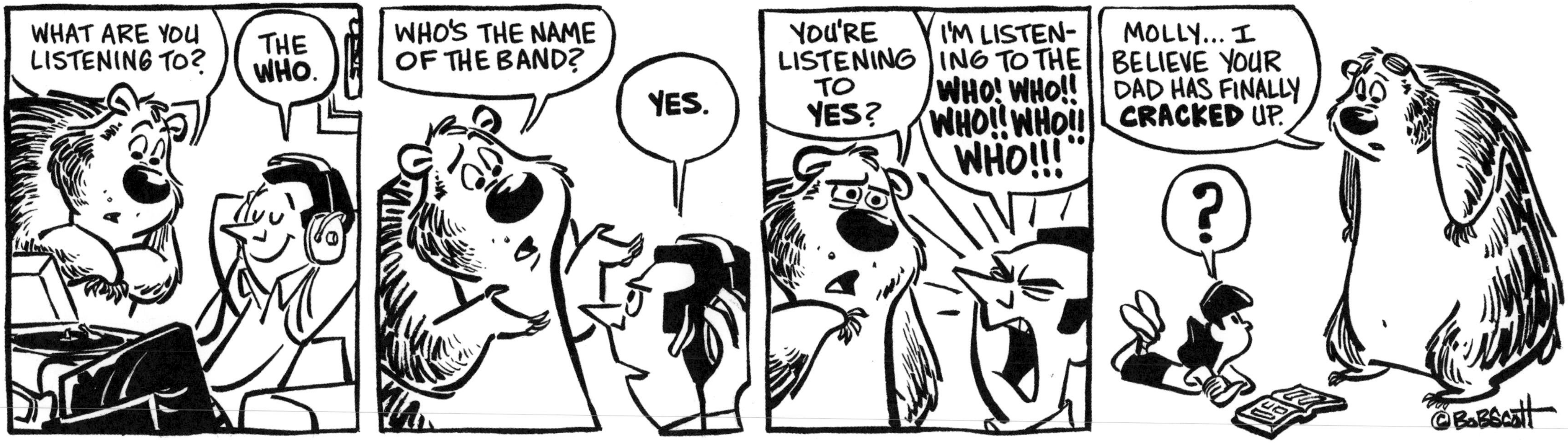
WHAT ARE YOU LISTENING TO?
THE **WHO**.
WHO'S THE NAME OF THE BAND?
YES.
YOU'RE LISTENING TO **YES**?
I'M LISTEN-ING TO THE **WHO! WHO!! WHO!! WHO!! WHO!!!**
?
MOLLY... I BELIEVE YOUR DAD HAS FINALLY **CRACKED** UP.
©BOBSCOTT

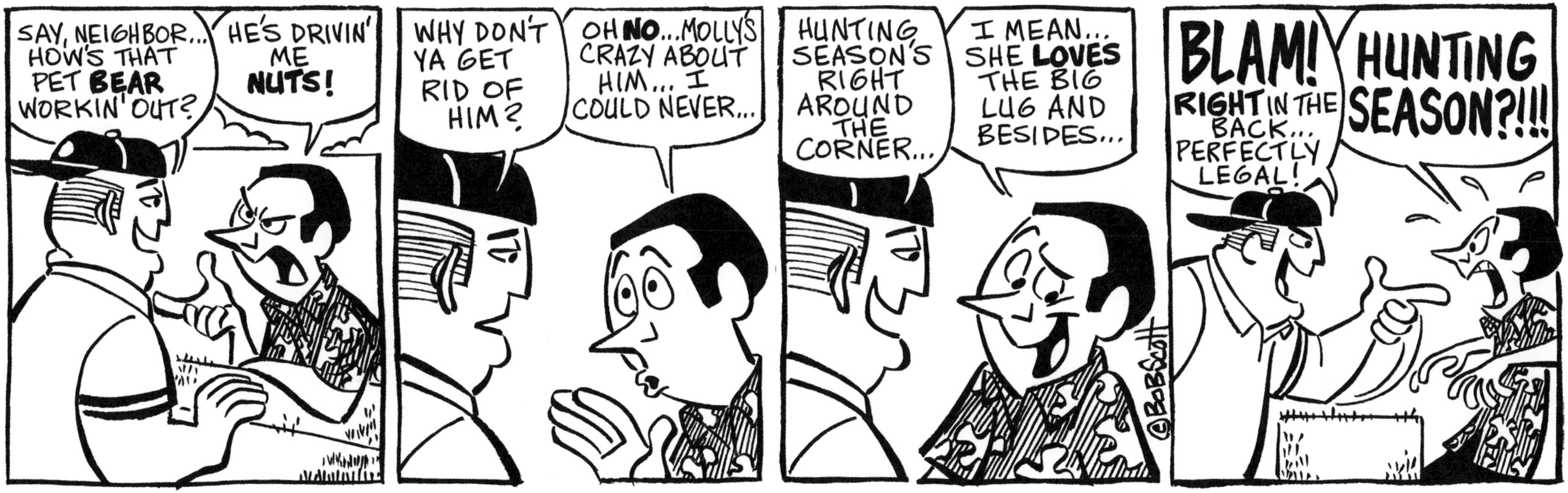
SAY, NEIGHBOR... HOW'S THAT PET **BEAR** WORKIN' OUT?
HE'S DRIVIN' ME **NUTS**!
WHY DON'T YA GET RID OF HIM?
OH **NO**...MOLLY'S CRAZY ABOUT HIM... I COULD NEVER...
HUNTING SEASON'S RIGHT AROUND THE CORNER...
I MEAN... SHE **LOVES** THE BIG LUG AND BESIDES...
©BOBSCOTT
BLAM! **RIGHT** IN THE BACK... PERFECTLY LEGAL!
HUNTING SEASON?!!!

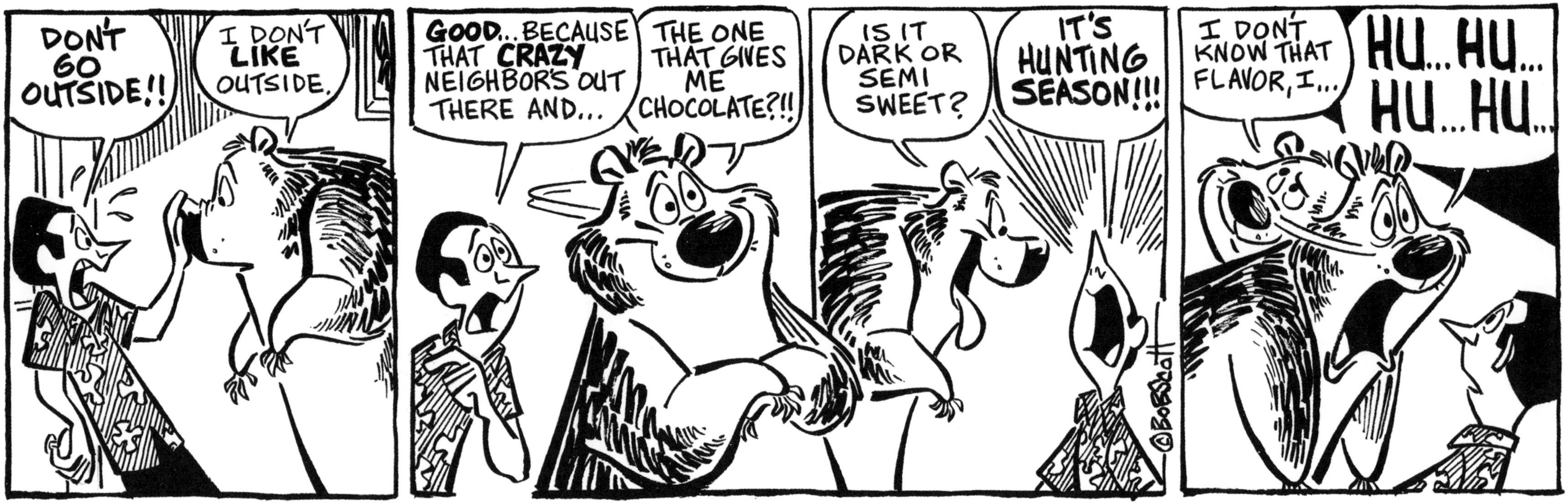
DON'T GO OUTSIDE!!
I DON'T **LIKE** OUTSIDE.
GOOD... BECAUSE THAT **CRAZY** NEIGHBOR'S OUT THERE AND...
THE ONE THAT GIVES ME CHOCOLATE?!!
IS IT DARK OR SEMI SWEET?
IT'S HUNTING SEASON!!!
©BOBSCOTT
I DON'T KNOW THAT FLAVOR, I...
HU... HU... HU... HU...

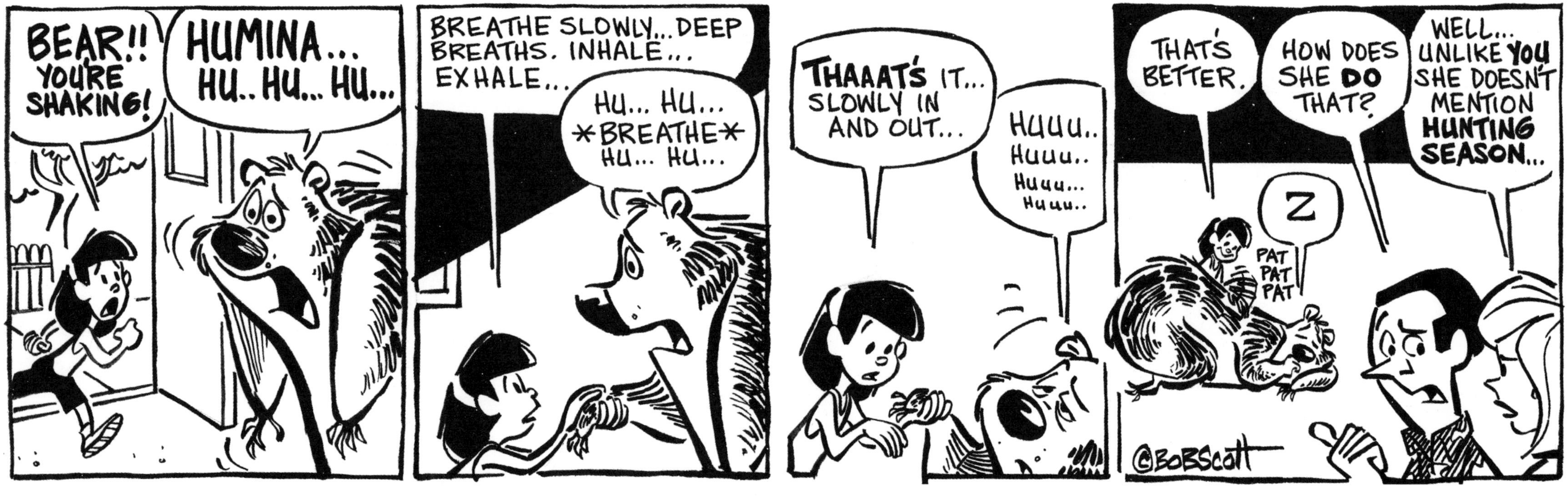
BEAR!! YOU'RE SHAKING!
HUMINA... HU.. HU... HU...
BREATHE SLOWLY... DEEP BREATHS. INHALE... EXHALE...
HU... HU... *BREATHE* HU... HU...
THAAAT'S IT... SLOWLY IN AND OUT...
Huuu.. Huuu.. Huuu... Huuu..
THAT'S BETTER.
Z
PAT PAT PAT
HOW DOES SHE **DO** THAT?
WELL... UNLIKE **YOU** SHE DOESN'T MENTION **HUNTING SEASON**...
©BOBSCOTT

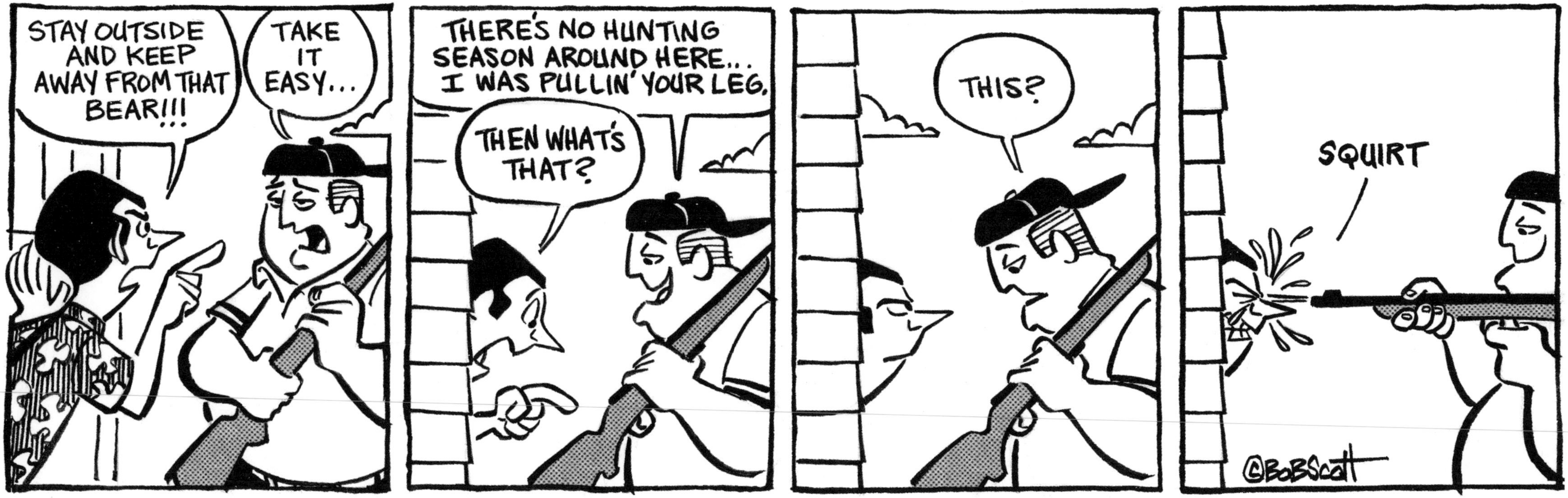
STAY OUTSIDE AND KEEP AWAY FROM THAT BEAR!!!
TAKE IT EASY...
THERE'S NO HUNTING SEASON AROUND HERE... I WAS PULLIN' YOUR LEG.
THEN WHAT'S THAT?
THIS?
SQUIRT
©BOBSCOTT

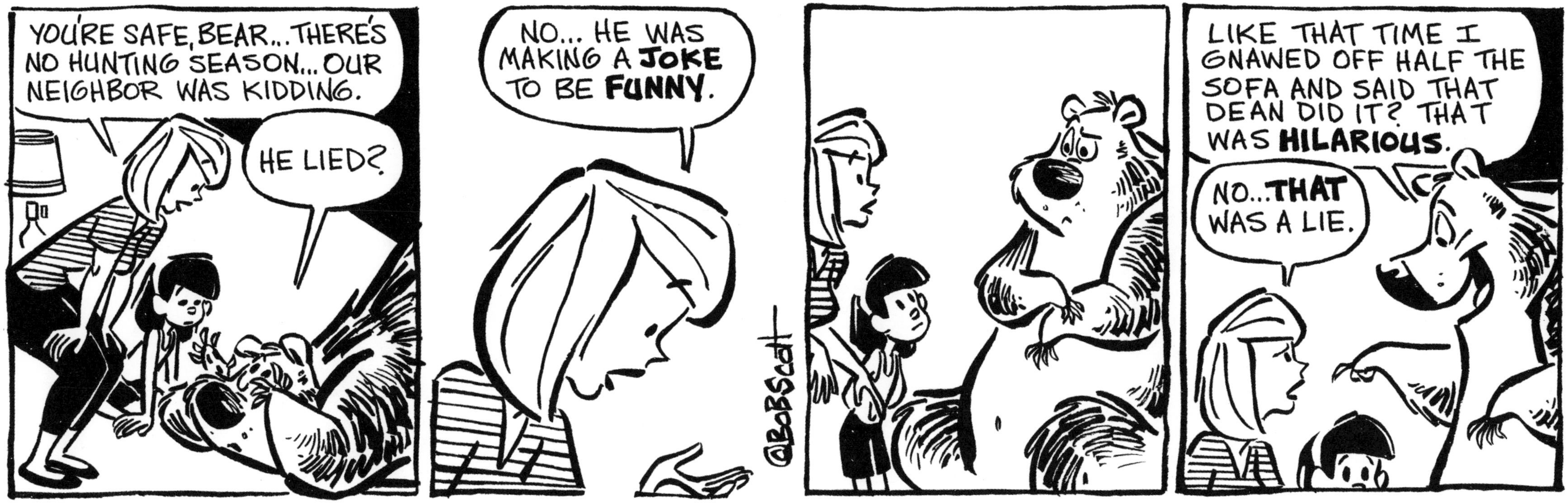
YOU'RE SAFE, BEAR... THERE'S NO HUNTING SEASON... OUR NEIGHBOR WAS KIDDING.
HE LIED?
NO... HE WAS MAKING A **JOKE** TO BE **FUNNY**.
©BOBSCOTT
LIKE THAT TIME I GNAWED OFF HALF THE SOFA AND SAID THAT DEAN DID IT? THAT WAS **HILARIOUS**.
NO... **THAT** WAS A LIE.

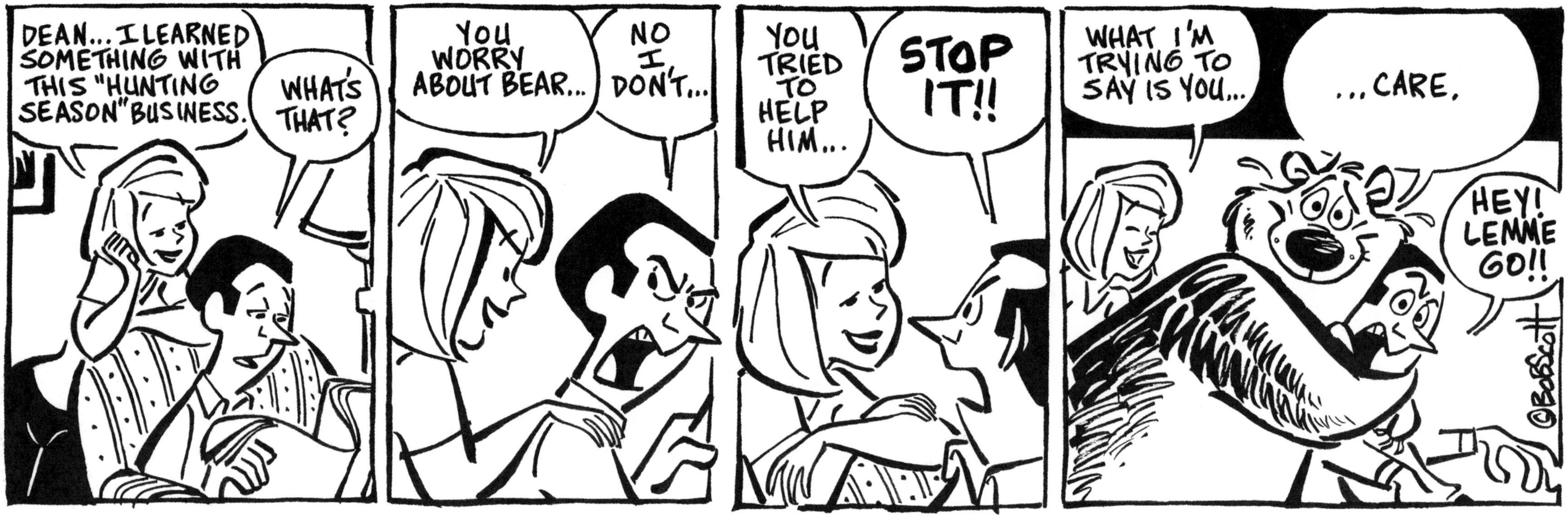
DEAN... I LEARNED SOMETHING WITH THIS "HUNTING SEASON" BUSINESS.
WHAT'S THAT?
YOU WORRY ABOUT BEAR...
NO I DON'T...
YOU TRIED TO HELP HIM...
STOP IT!!
WHAT I'M TRYING TO SAY IS YOU...
...CARE.
HEY! LEMME GO!!
©BOBSCOTT

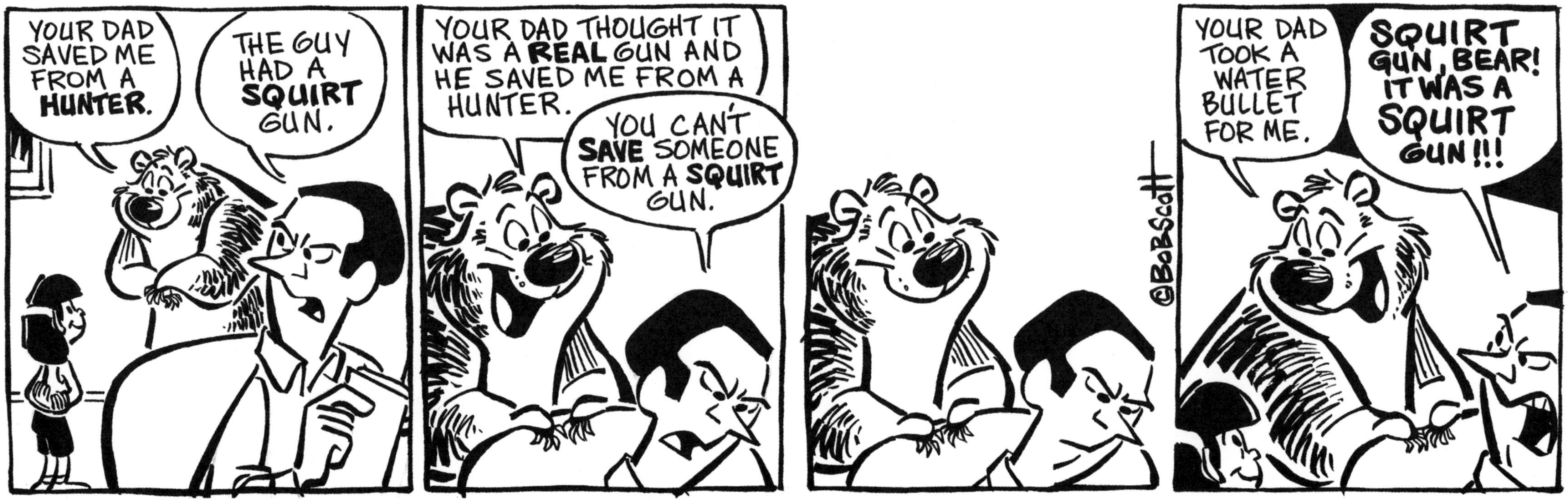
YOUR DAD SAVED ME FROM A **HUNTER**.
THE GUY HAD A **SQUIRT** GUN.
YOUR DAD THOUGHT IT WAS A **REAL** GUN AND HE SAVED ME FROM A HUNTER.
YOU CAN'T **SAVE** SOMEONE FROM A **SQUIRT** GUN.
©BOBSCOTT
YOUR DAD TOOK A WATER BULLET FOR ME.
SQUIRT GUN, BEAR! IT WAS A SQUIRT GUN!!!

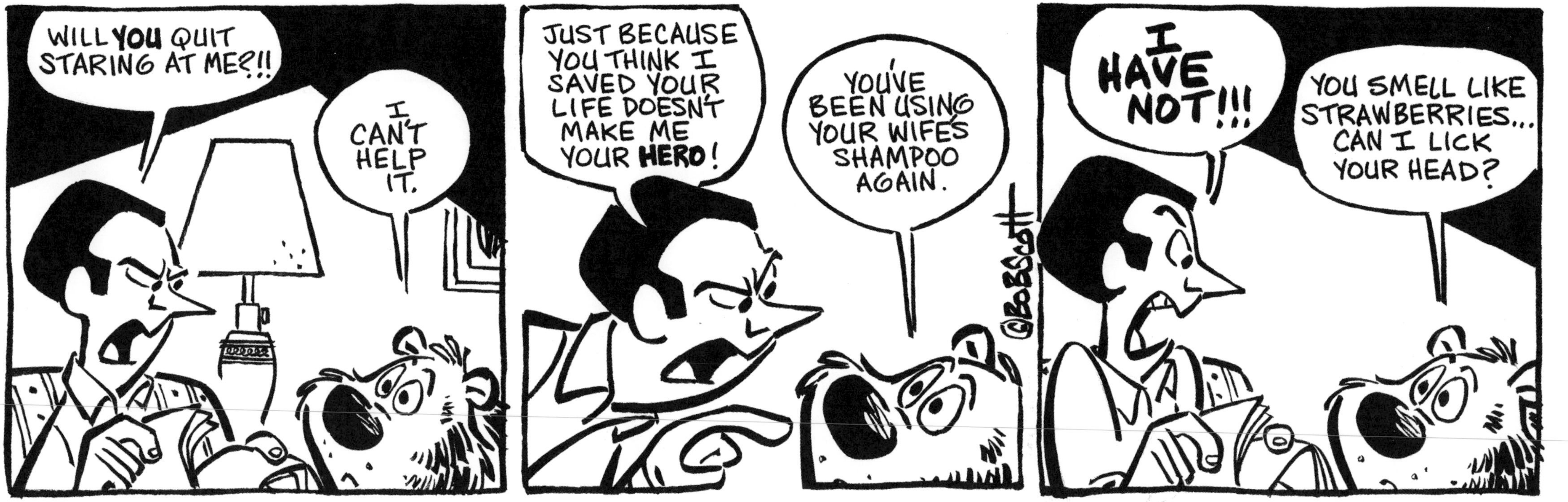
WILL YOU QUIT STARING AT ME?!!
I CAN'T HELP IT.
JUST BECAUSE YOU THINK I SAVED YOUR LIFE DOESN'T MAKE ME YOUR HERO!
YOU'VE BEEN USING YOUR WIFE'S SHAMPOO AGAIN.
©BOBSCOTT
I HAVE NOT!!!
YOU SMELL LIKE STRAWBERRIES... CAN I LICK YOUR HEAD?

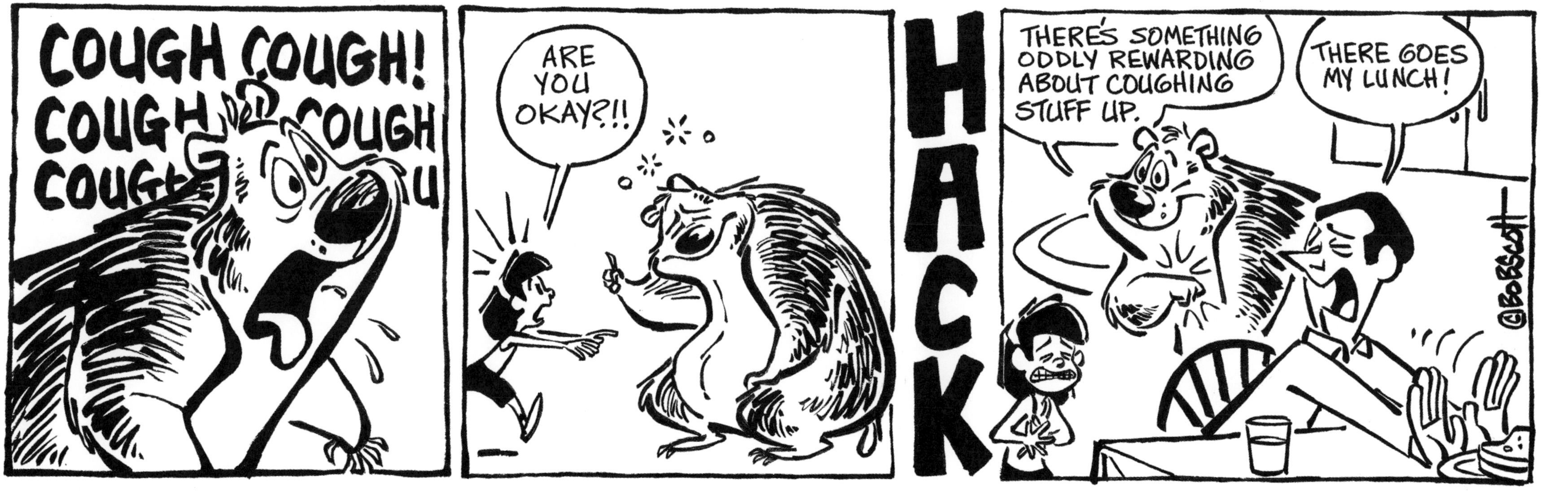
COUGH COUGH!
COUGH COUGH
ARE YOU OKAY?!!
HACK
THERE'S SOMETHING ODDLY REWARDING ABOUT COUGHING STUFF UP.
THERE GOES MY LUNCH!
©BOBSCOTT

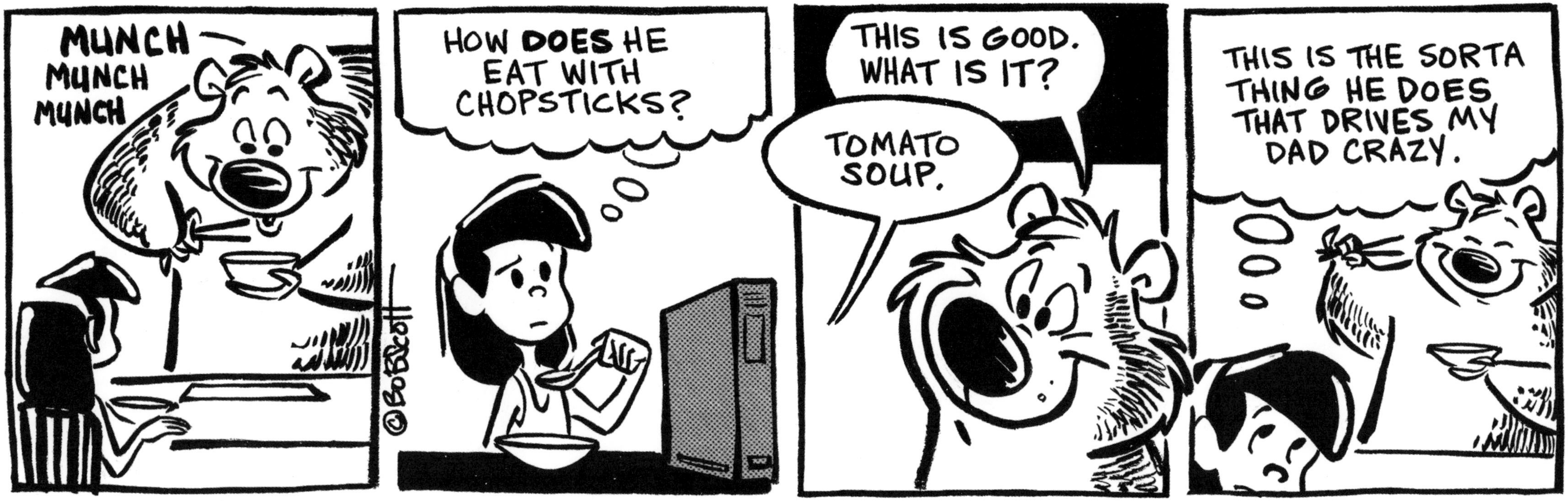
MUNCH MUNCH MUNCH MUNCH
HOW DOES HE EAT WITH CHOPSTICKS?
©BoBScott
THIS IS GOOD. WHAT IS IT?
TOMATO SOUP.
THIS IS THE SORTA THING HE DOES THAT DRIVES MY DAD CRAZY.

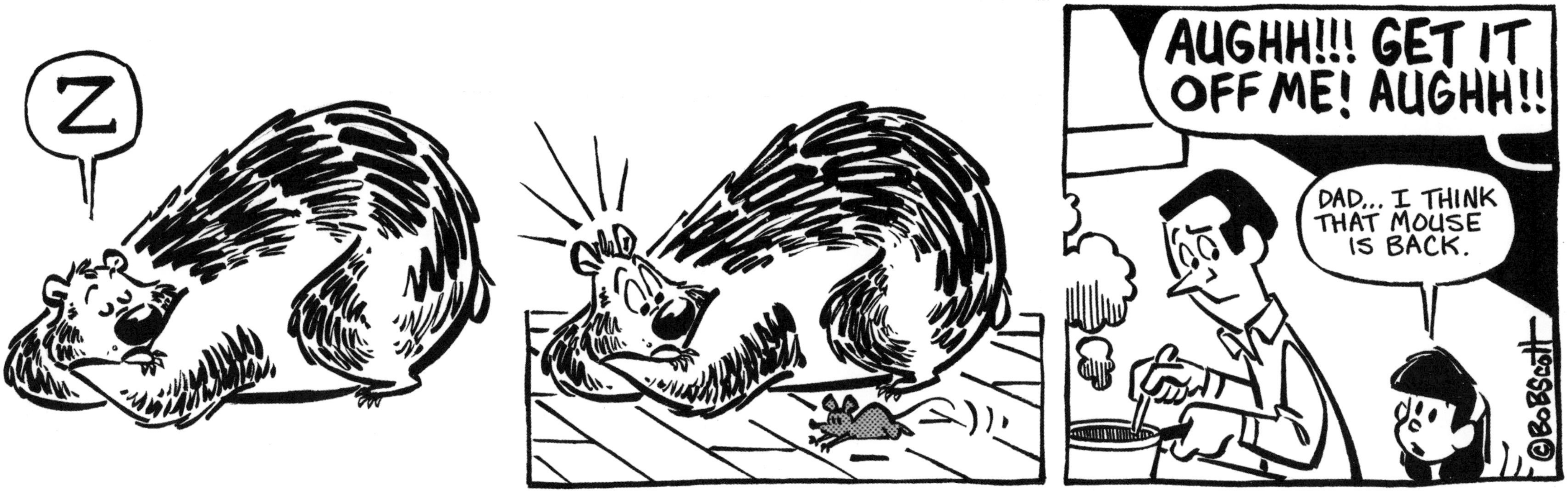
Z
AUGHH!!! GET IT OFF ME! AUGHH!!
DAD... I THINK THAT MOUSE IS BACK.
©BoBScott

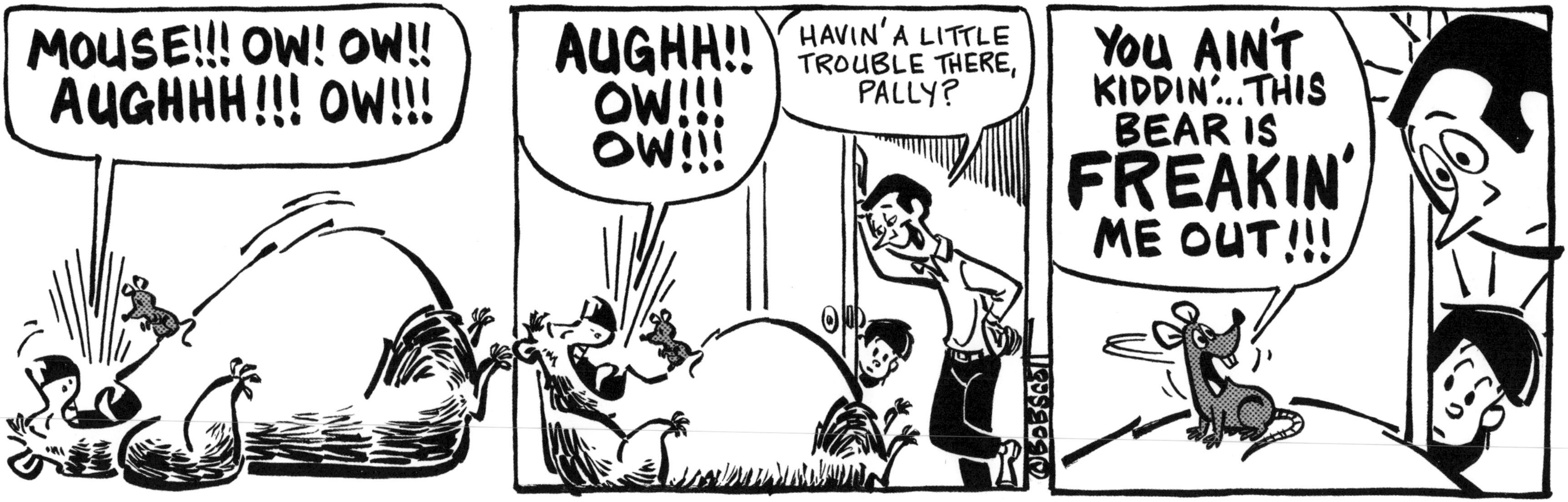
MOUSE!!! OW! OW!! AUGHHH!!! OW!!!
AUGHH!! OW!!! OW!!!
HAVIN' A LITTLE TROUBLE THERE, PALLY?
©BOBSCOTT
YOU AIN'T KIDDIN'... THIS BEAR IS FREAKIN' ME OUT!!!

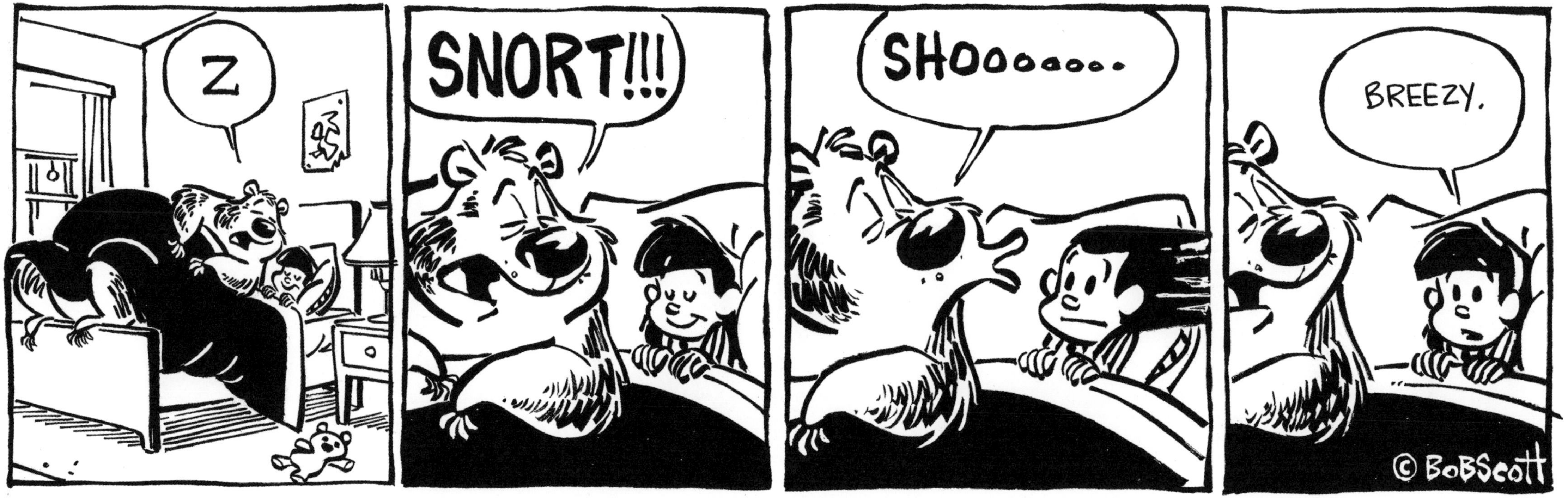
Z
SNORT!!!
SHOOoooo.
BREEZY.
© BOBSCOTT

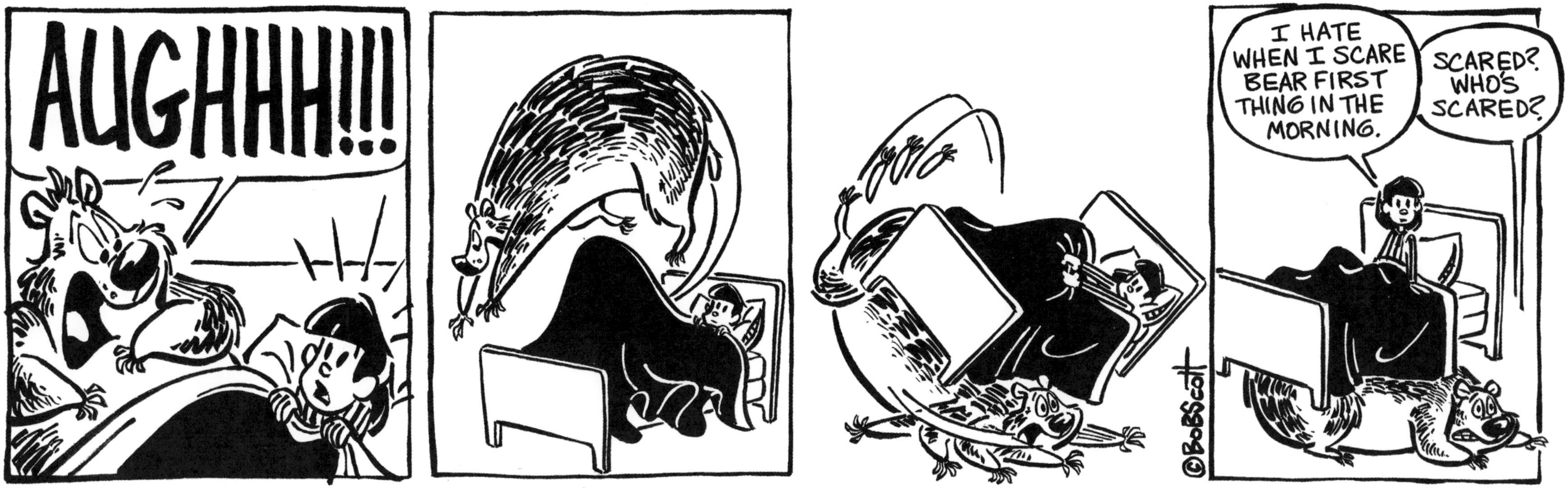
AUGHHH!!!
I HATE WHEN I SCARE BEAR FIRST THING IN THE MORNING.
SCARED? WHO'S SCARED?
©BoBScott

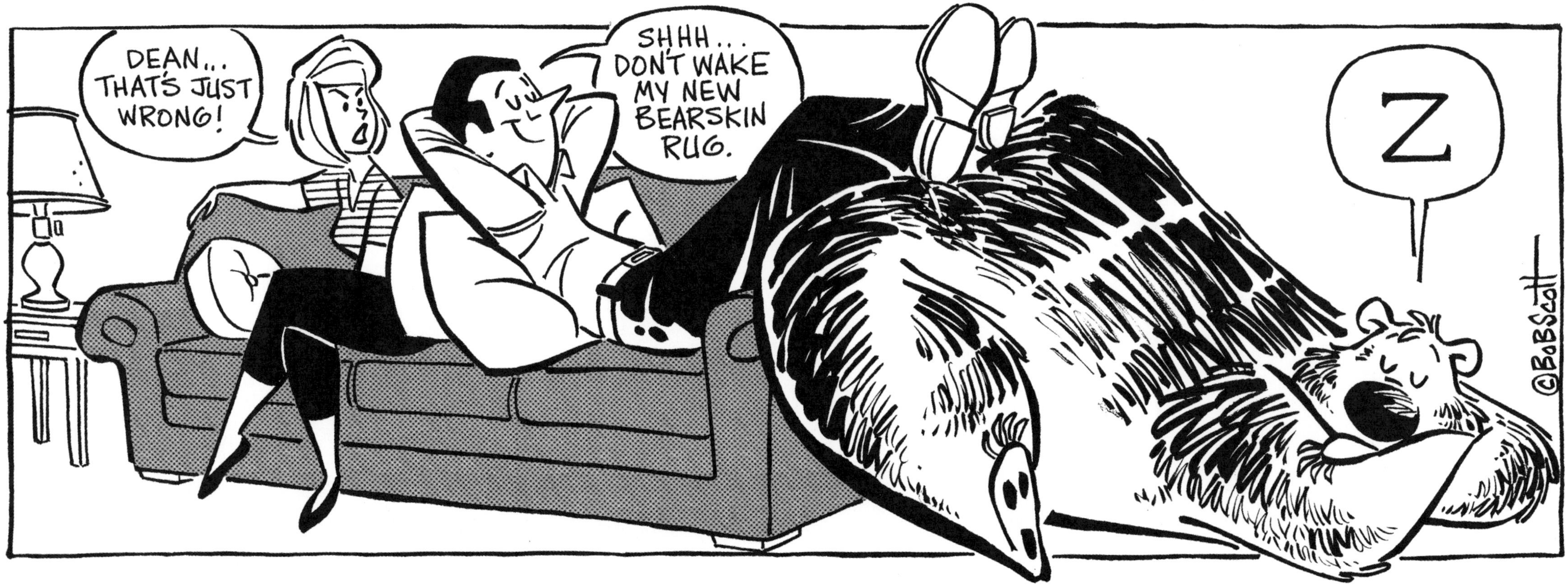
DEAN... THAT'S JUST WRONG!
SHHH... DON'T WAKE MY NEW BEARSKIN RUG.
Z
©BoBScott

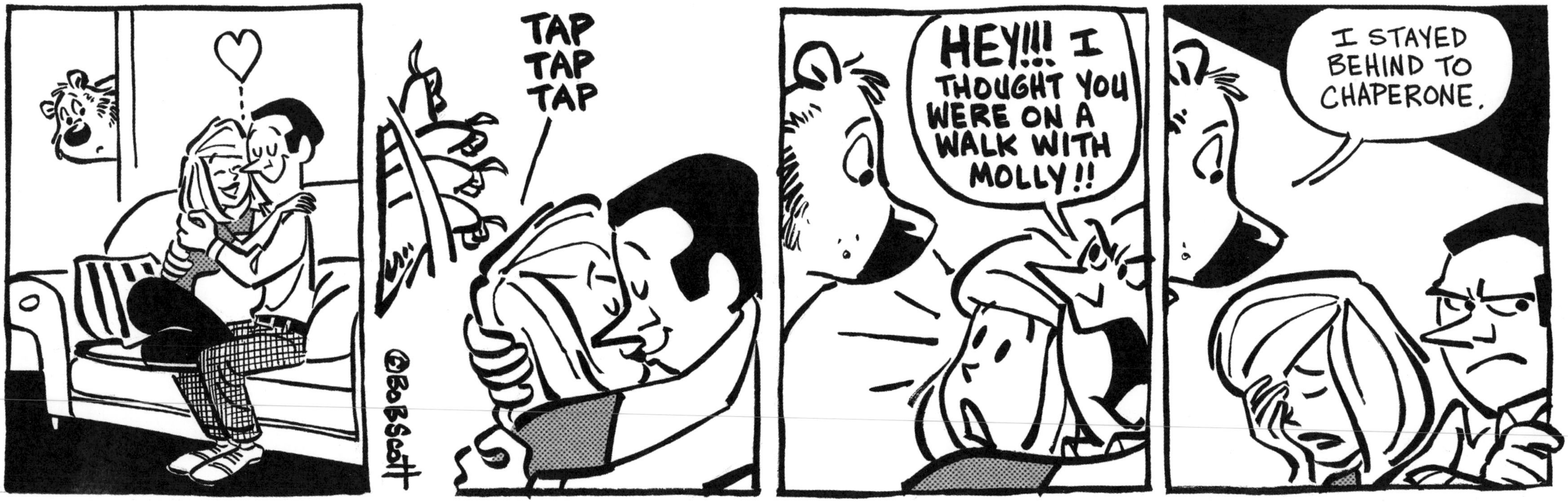
TAP
TAP
TAP
©BoBScott
HEY!!! I THOUGHT YOU WERE ON A WALK WITH MOLLY!!
I STAYED BEHIND TO CHAPERONE.

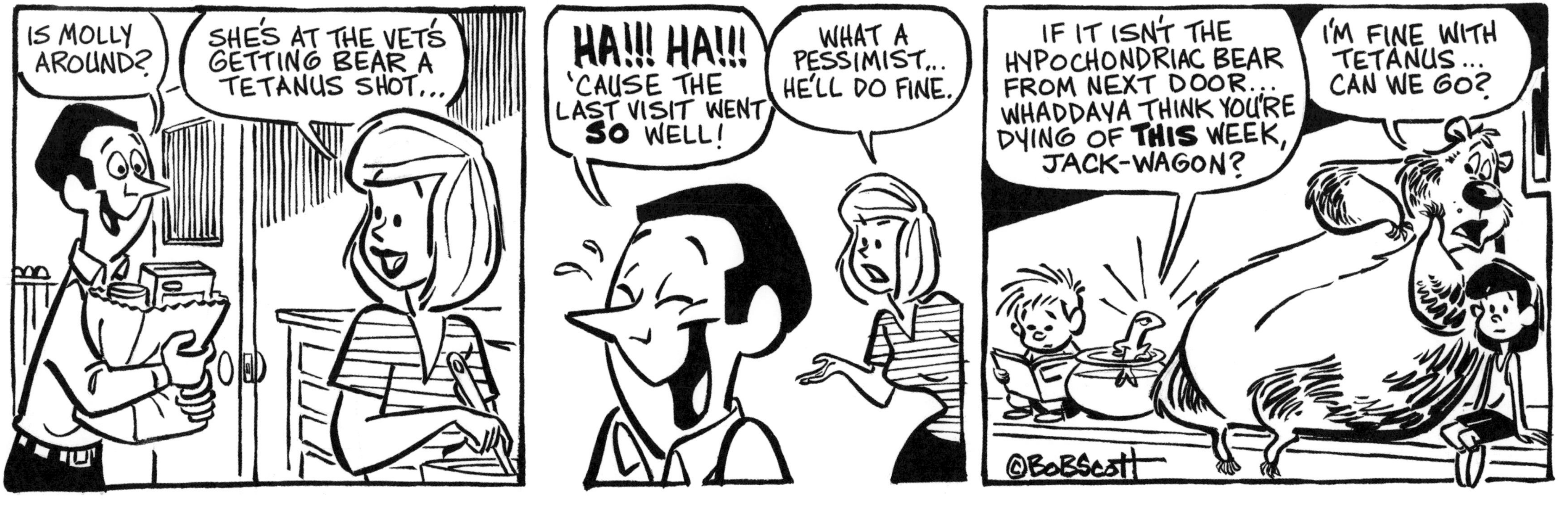
IS MOLLY AROUND?
SHE'S AT THE VET'S GETTING BEAR A TETANUS SHOT...
HA!!! HA!!! 'CAUSE THE LAST VISIT WENT SO WELL!
WHAT A PESSIMIST... HE'LL DO FINE.
IF IT ISN'T THE HYPOCHONDRIAC BEAR FROM NEXT DOOR... WHADDAYA THINK YOU'RE DYING OF THIS WEEK, JACK-WAGON?
I'M FINE WITH TETANUS... CAN WE GO?
©BoBScott

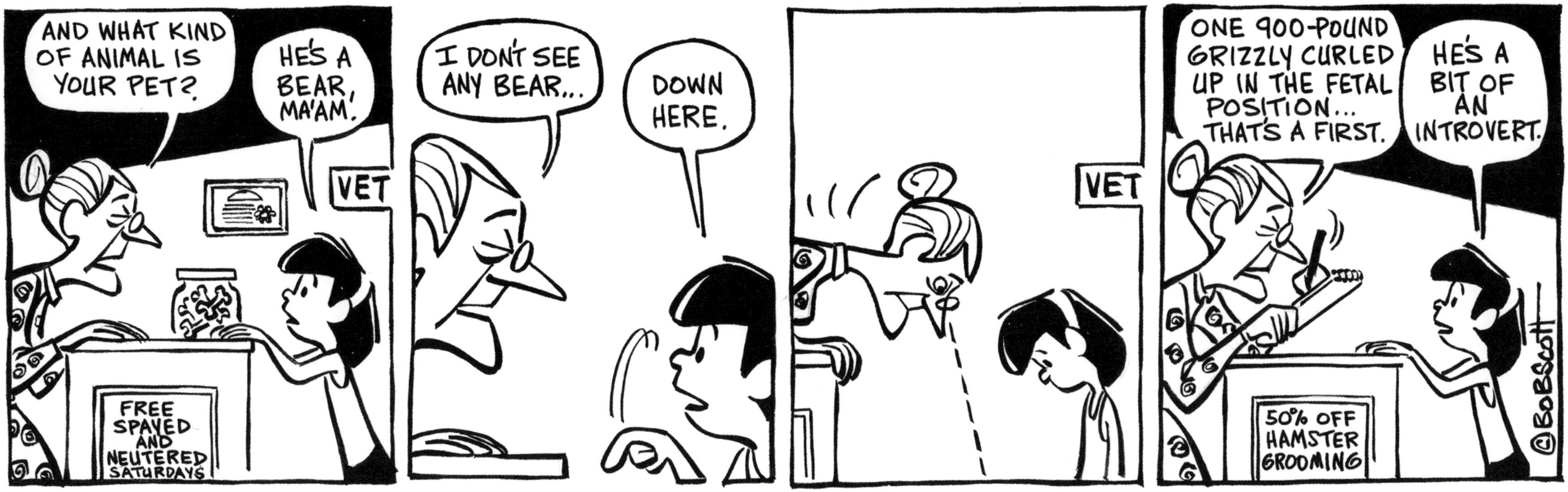
AND WHAT KIND OF ANIMAL IS YOUR PET?
HE'S A BEAR, MA'AM.
VET
FREE SPAYED AND NEUTERED SATURDAYS
I DON'T SEE ANY BEAR...
DOWN HERE.
VET
ONE 900-POUND GRIZZLY CURLED UP IN THE FETAL POSITION... THAT'S A FIRST.
HE'S A BIT OF AN INTROVERT.
50% OFF HAMSTER GROOMING
©BOBSCOTT

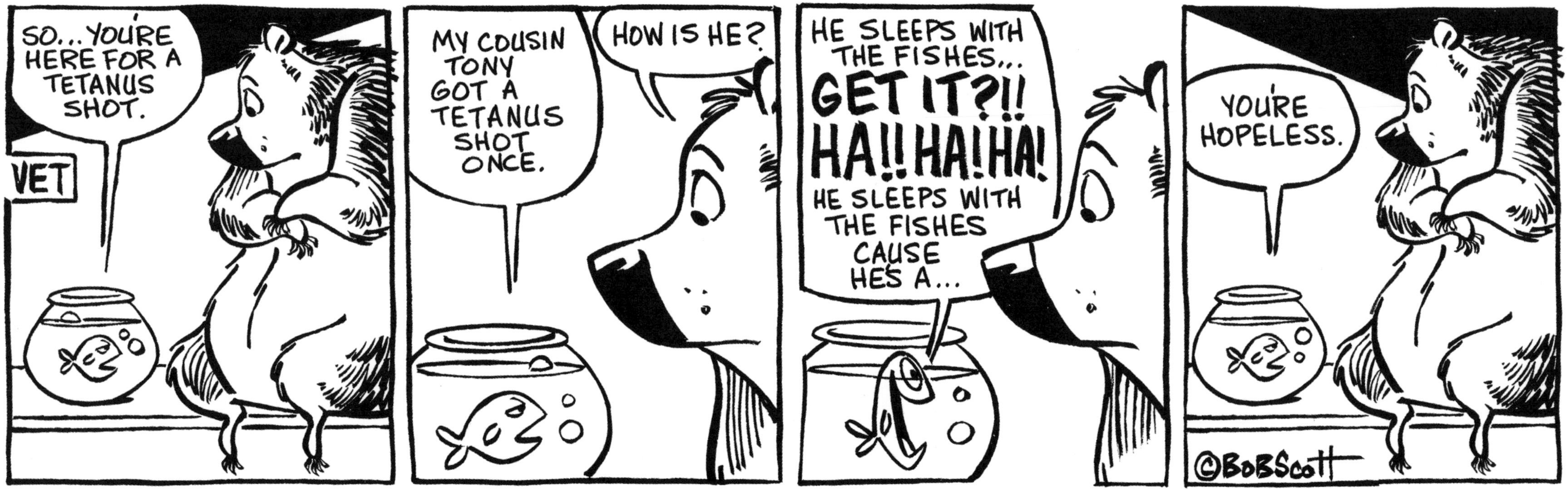
SO... YOU'RE HERE FOR A TETANUS SHOT.
VET
MY COUSIN TONY GOT A TETANUS SHOT ONCE.
HOW IS HE?
HE SLEEPS WITH THE FISHES... GET IT?!! HA!! HA! HA!
HE SLEEPS WITH THE FISHES CAUSE HE'S A...
YOU'RE HOPELESS.
©BOBSCOTT

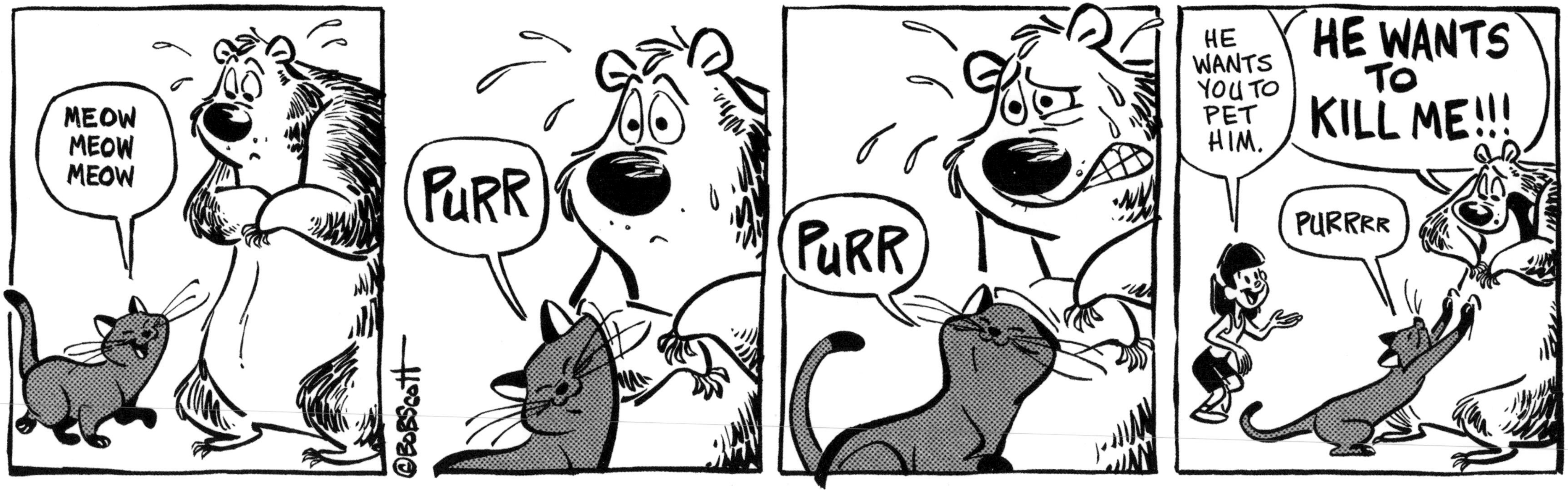
MEOW MEOW MEOW
©BOBSCOTT
PURR
PURR
HE WANTS YOU TO PET HIM.
HE WANTS TO KILL ME!!!
PURRRRR

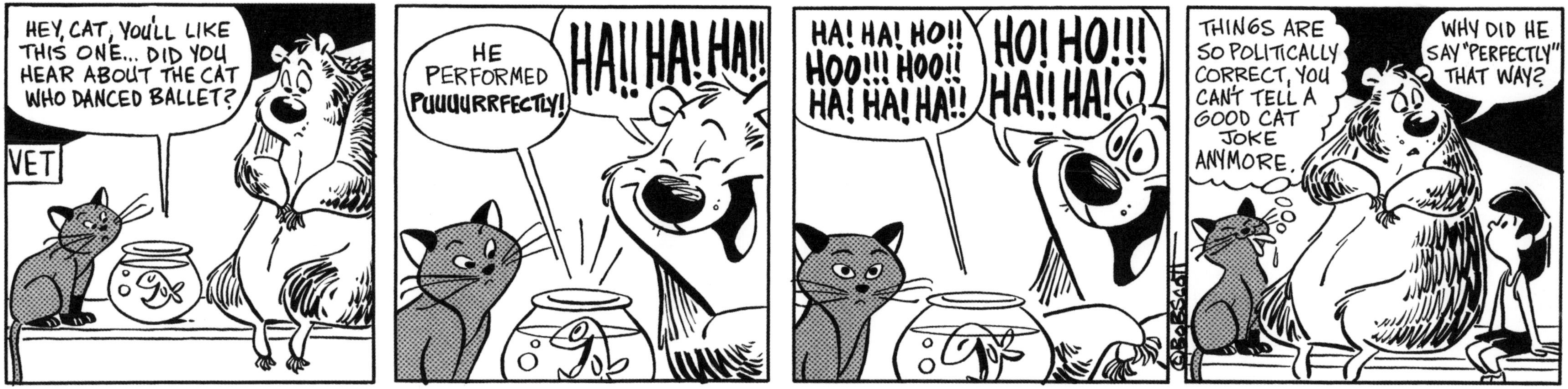
HEY, CAT, YOU'LL LIKE THIS ONE... DID YOU HEAR ABOUT THE CAT WHO DANCED BALLET?
VET
HE PERFORMED PUUUURRFECTLY!
HA!! HA! HA!!
HA! HA! HO!! HOO!!! HOO!! HA! HA! HA!!
HO! HO!!! HA!! HA!
THINGS ARE SO POLITICALLY CORRECT, YOU CAN'T TELL A GOOD CAT JOKE ANYMORE.
WHY DID HE SAY "PERFECTLY" THAT WAY?
©BOBSCOTT

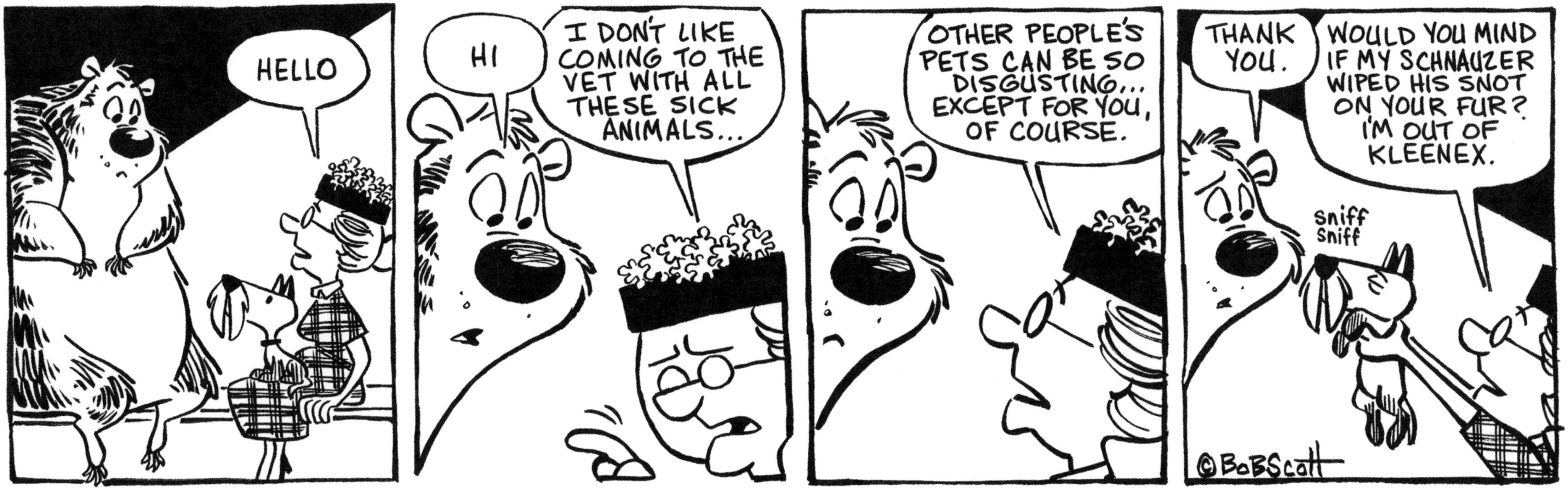
HELLO
HI
I DON'T LIKE COMING TO THE VET WITH ALL THESE SICK ANIMALS...
OTHER PEOPLE'S PETS CAN BE SO DISGUSTING... EXCEPT FOR YOU, OF COURSE.
THANK YOU.
WOULD YOU MIND IF MY SCHNAUZER WIPED HIS SNOT ON YOUR FUR? I'M OUT OF KLEENEX.
sniff sniff
© BoBScott

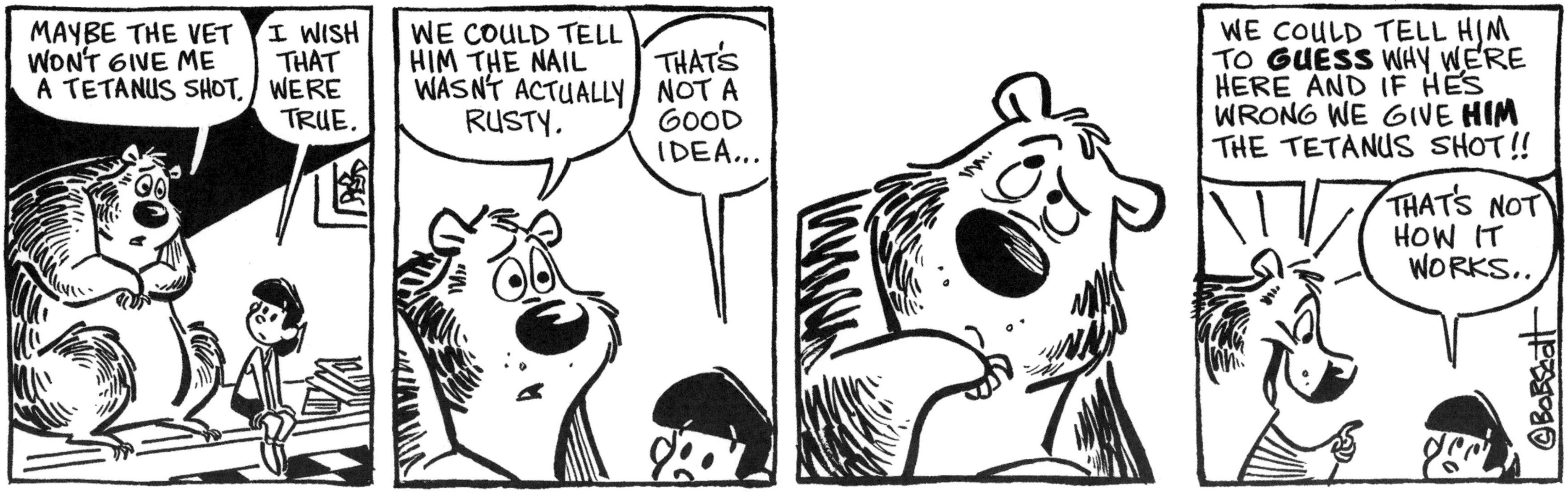
MAYBE THE VET WON'T GIVE ME A TETANUS SHOT.
I WISH THAT WERE TRUE.
WE COULD TELL HIM THE NAIL WASN'T ACTUALLY RUSTY.
THAT'S NOT A GOOD IDEA...
WE COULD TELL HIM TO GUESS WHY WE'RE HERE AND IF HE'S WRONG WE GIVE HIM THE TETANUS SHOT!!
THAT'S NOT HOW IT WORKS..
© BoBScott

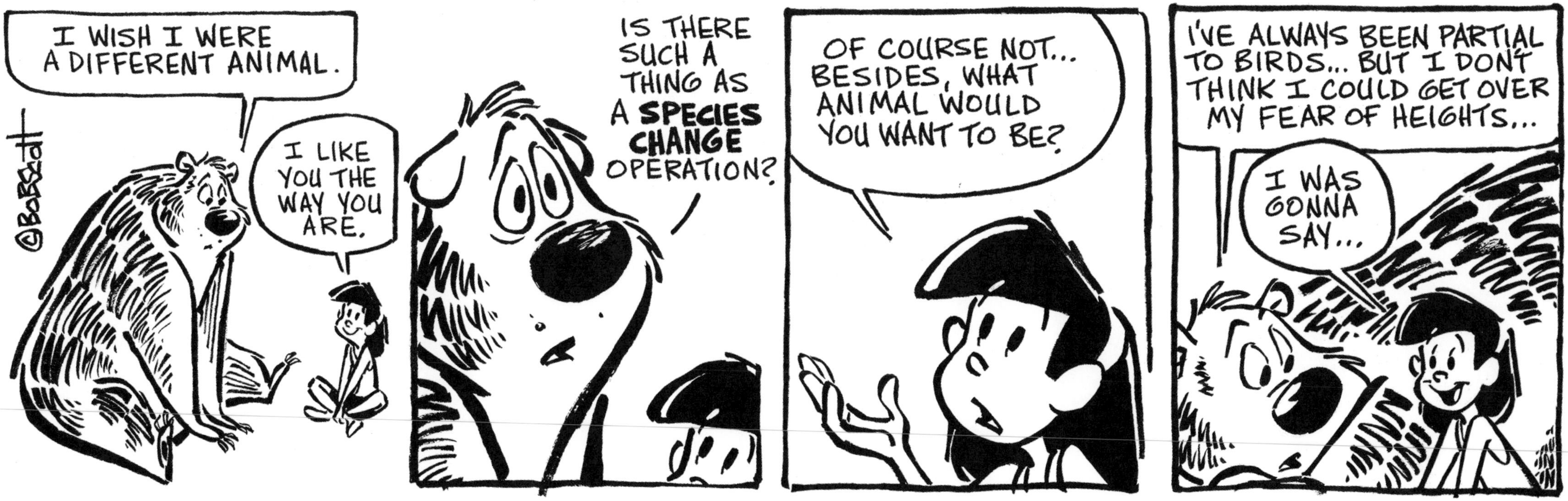
©BoBScott
I WISH I WERE A DIFFERENT ANIMAL.
I LIKE YOU THE WAY YOU ARE.
IS THERE SUCH A THING AS A **SPECIES CHANGE** OPERATION?
OF COURSE NOT... BESIDES, WHAT ANIMAL WOULD YOU WANT TO BE?
I'VE ALWAYS BEEN PARTIAL TO BIRDS... BUT I DON'T THINK I COULD GET OVER MY FEAR OF HEIGHTS...
I WAS GONNA SAY...

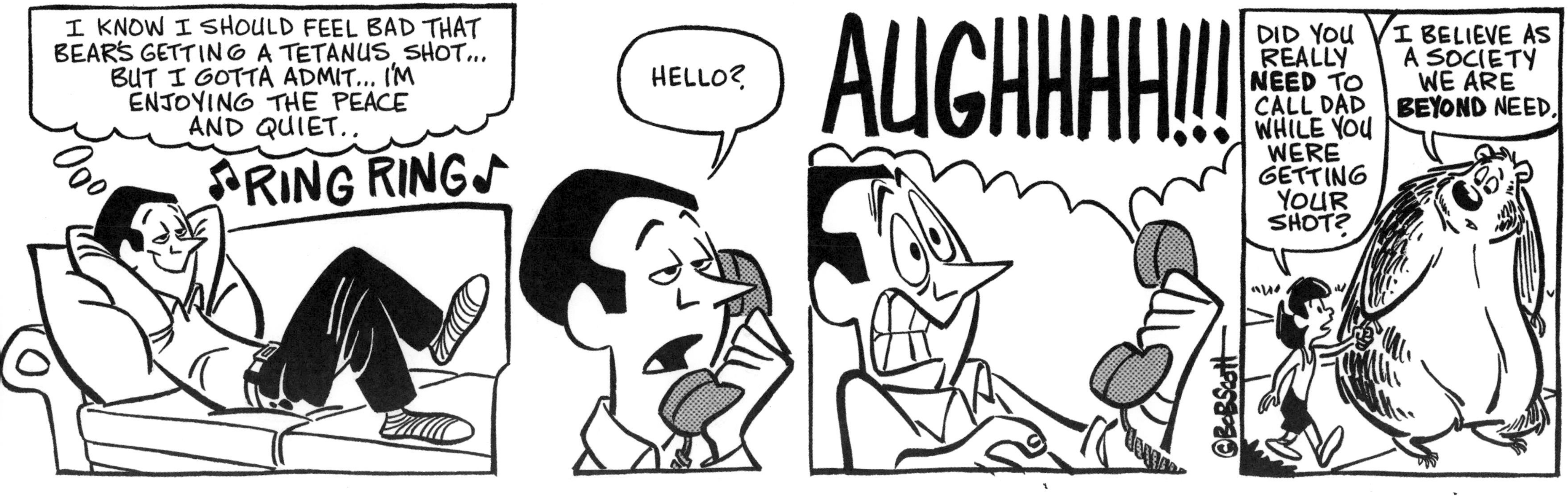
I KNOW I SHOULD FEEL BAD THAT BEAR'S GETTING A TETANUS SHOT... BUT I GOTTA ADMIT... I'M ENJOYING THE PEACE AND QUIET..
RING RING
HELLO?
AUGHHHH!!!
©BoBScott
DID YOU REALLY **NEED** TO CALL DAD WHILE YOU WERE GETTING YOUR SHOT?
I BELIEVE AS A SOCIETY WE ARE **BEYOND** NEED.

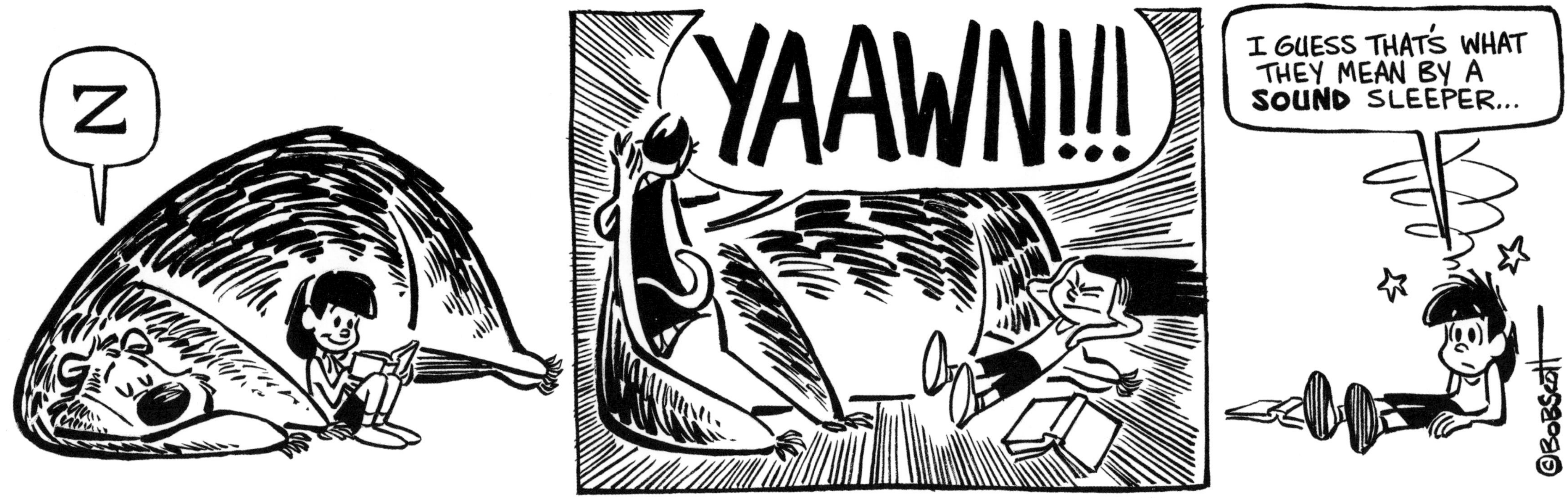
Z
YAAWN!!!
I GUESS THAT'S WHAT THEY MEAN BY A **SOUND** SLEEPER...
©BOBSCOTT

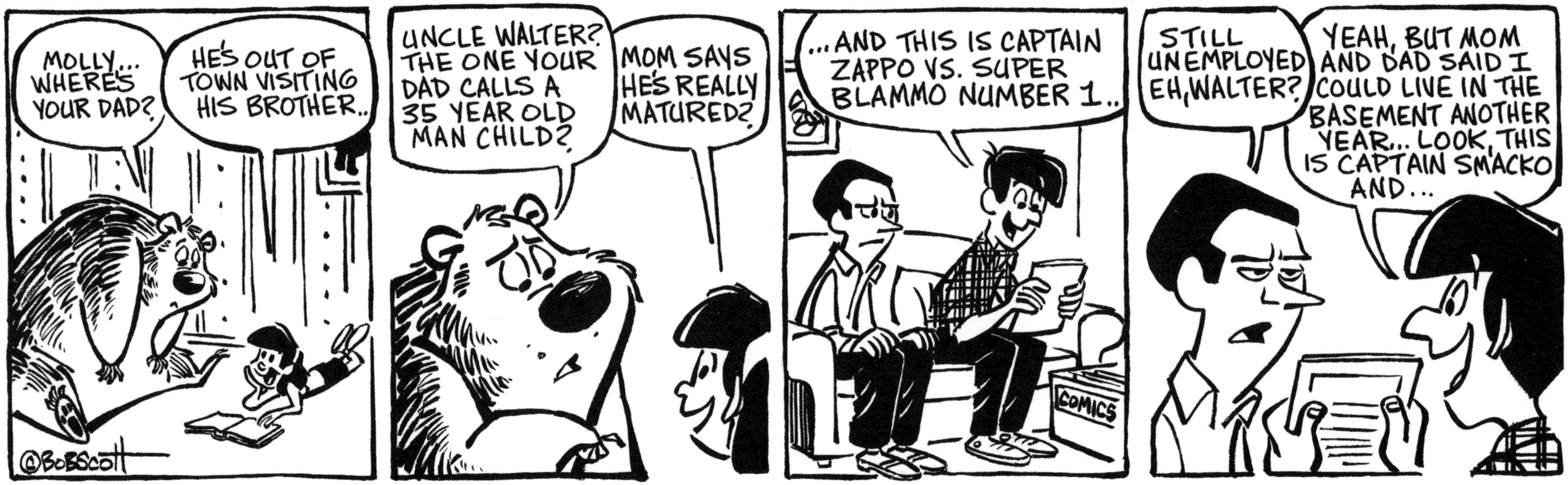
MOLLY... WHERE'S YOUR DAD?
HE'S OUT OF TOWN VISITING HIS BROTHER..
UNCLE WALTER? THE ONE YOUR DAD CALLS A 35 YEAR OLD MAN CHILD?
MOM SAYS HE'S REALLY MATURED?
...AND THIS IS CAPTAIN ZAPPO VS. SUPER BLAMMO NUMBER 1..
COMICS
STILL UNEMPLOYED EH, WALTER?
YEAH, BUT MOM AND DAD SAID I COULD LIVE IN THE BASEMENT ANOTHER YEAR... LOOK, THIS IS CAPTAIN SMACKO AND...
©BOBSCOTT

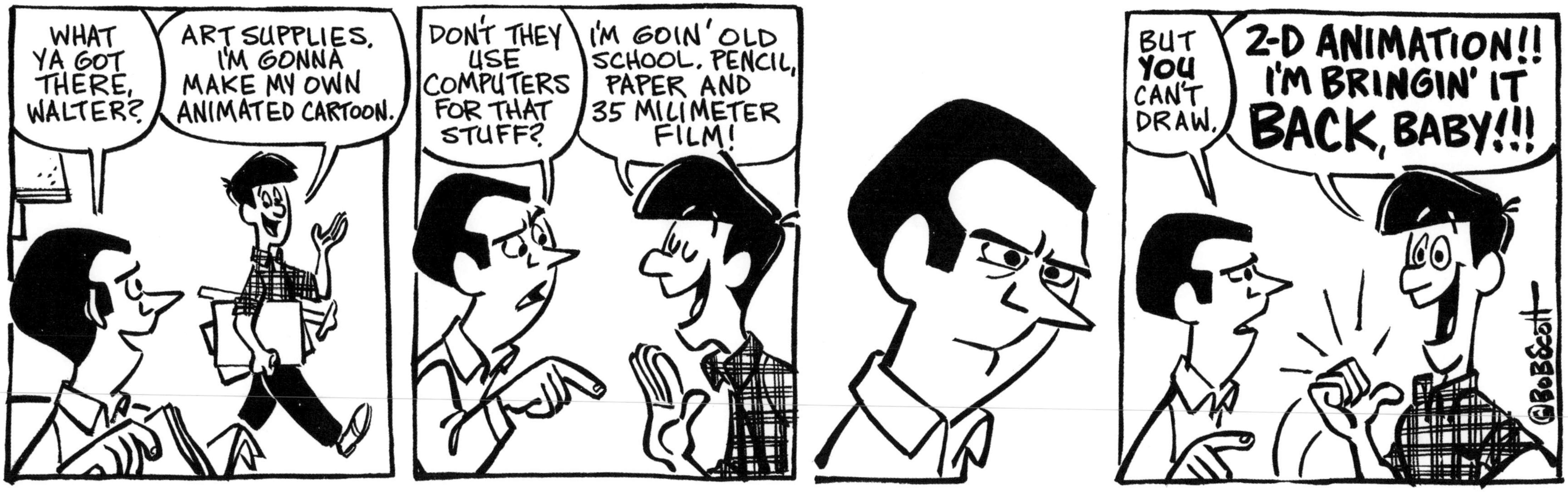
WHAT YA GOT THERE, WALTER?
ART SUPPLIES. I'M GONNA MAKE MY OWN ANIMATED CARTOON.
DON'T THEY USE COMPUTERS FOR THAT STUFF?
I'M GOIN' OLD SCHOOL. PENCIL, PAPER AND 35 MILIMETER FILM!
BUT YOU CAN'T DRAW.
2-D ANIMATION!! I'M BRINGIN' IT BACK, BABY!!!
©BOBSCOTT

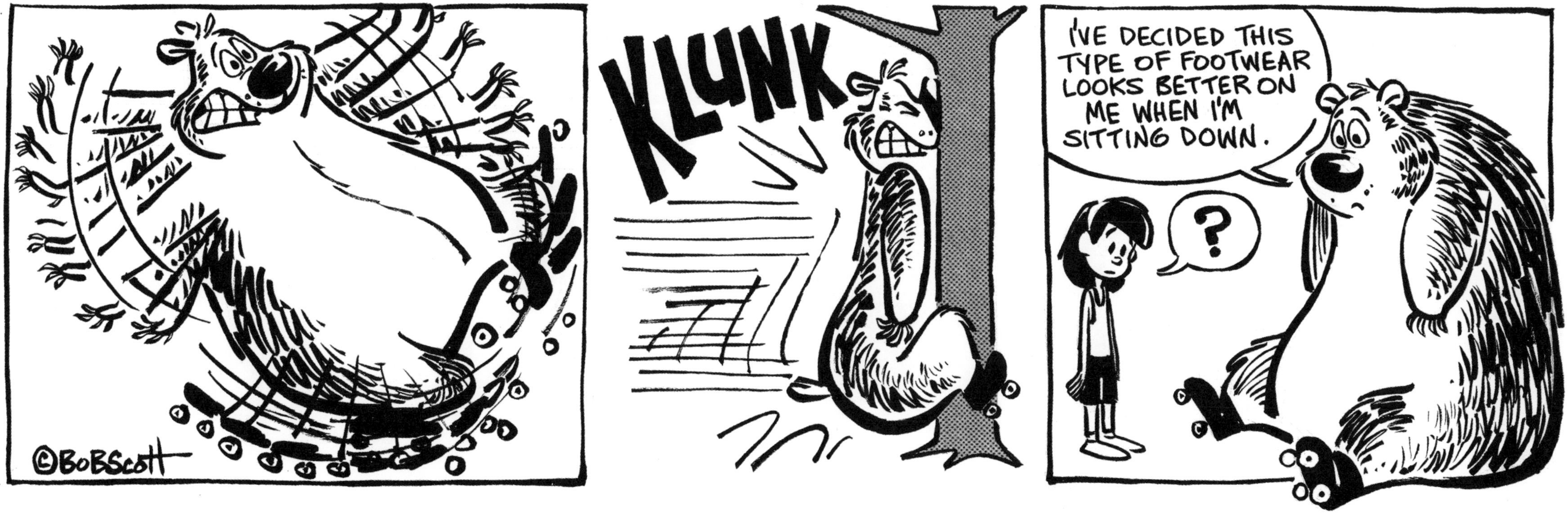
©BOBSCOTT
KLUNK
I'VE DECIDED THIS TYPE OF FOOTWEAR LOOKS BETTER ON ME WHEN I'M SITTING DOWN.
?

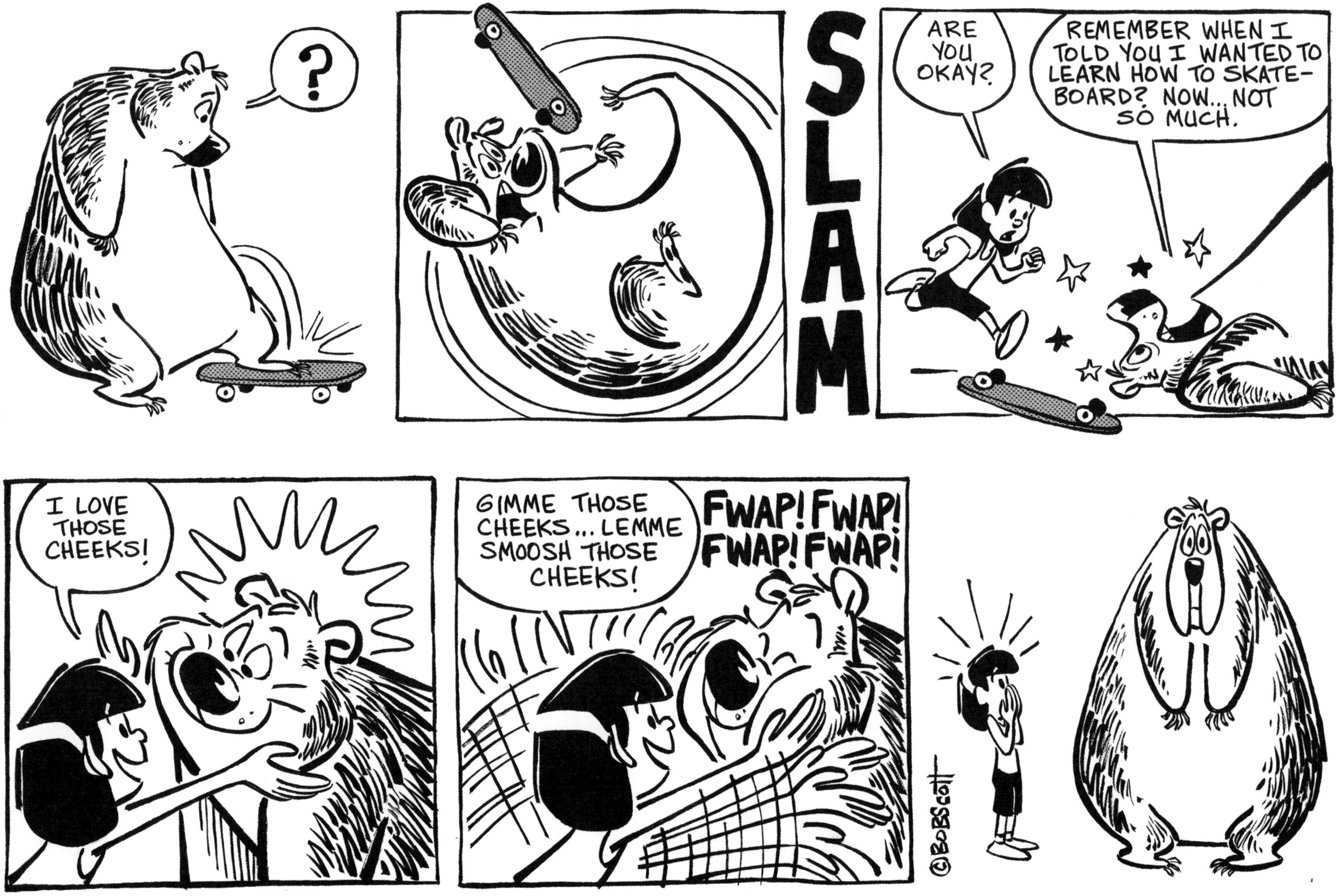
?
SLAM
ARE YOU OKAY?
REMEMBER WHEN I TOLD YOU I WANTED TO LEARN HOW TO SKATE-BOARD? NOW... NOT SO MUCH.
I LOVE THOSE CHEEKS!
GIMME THOSE CHEEKS... LEMME SMOOSH THOSE CHEEKS!
FWAP! FWAP! FWAP! FWAP!
©BOBSCOTT

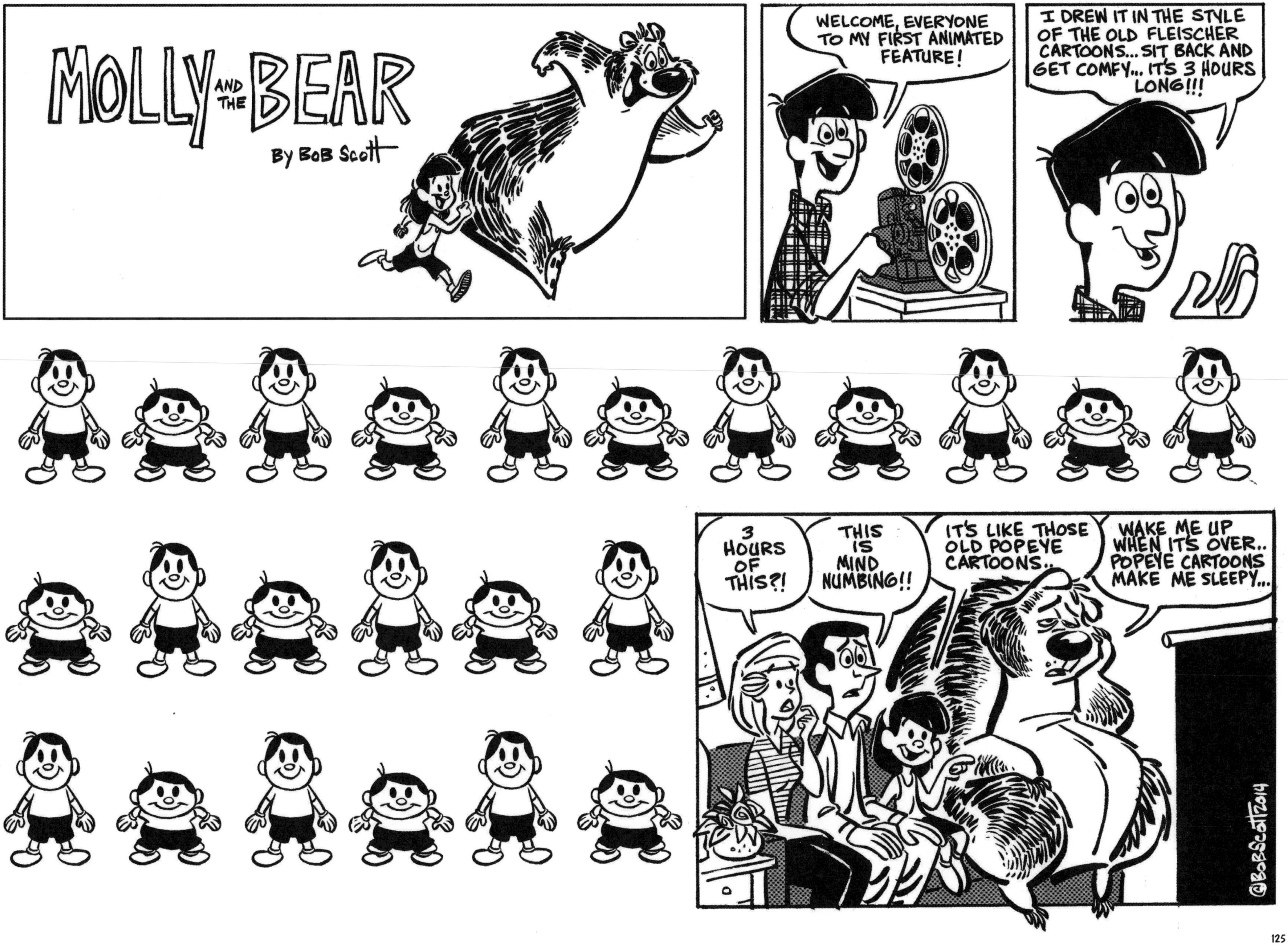
MOLLY AND THE BEAR
BY BOB SCOTT
WELCOME, EVERYONE TO MY FIRST ANIMATED FEATURE!
I DREW IT IN THE STYLE OF THE OLD FLEISCHER CARTOONS... SIT BACK AND GET COMFY... IT'S 3 HOURS LONG!!!
3 HOURS OF THIS?!
THIS IS MIND NUMBING!!
IT'S LIKE THOSE OLD POPEYE CARTOONS..
WAKE ME UP WHEN IT'S OVER.. POPEYE CARTOONS MAKE ME SLEEPY...
©BoBScott2014

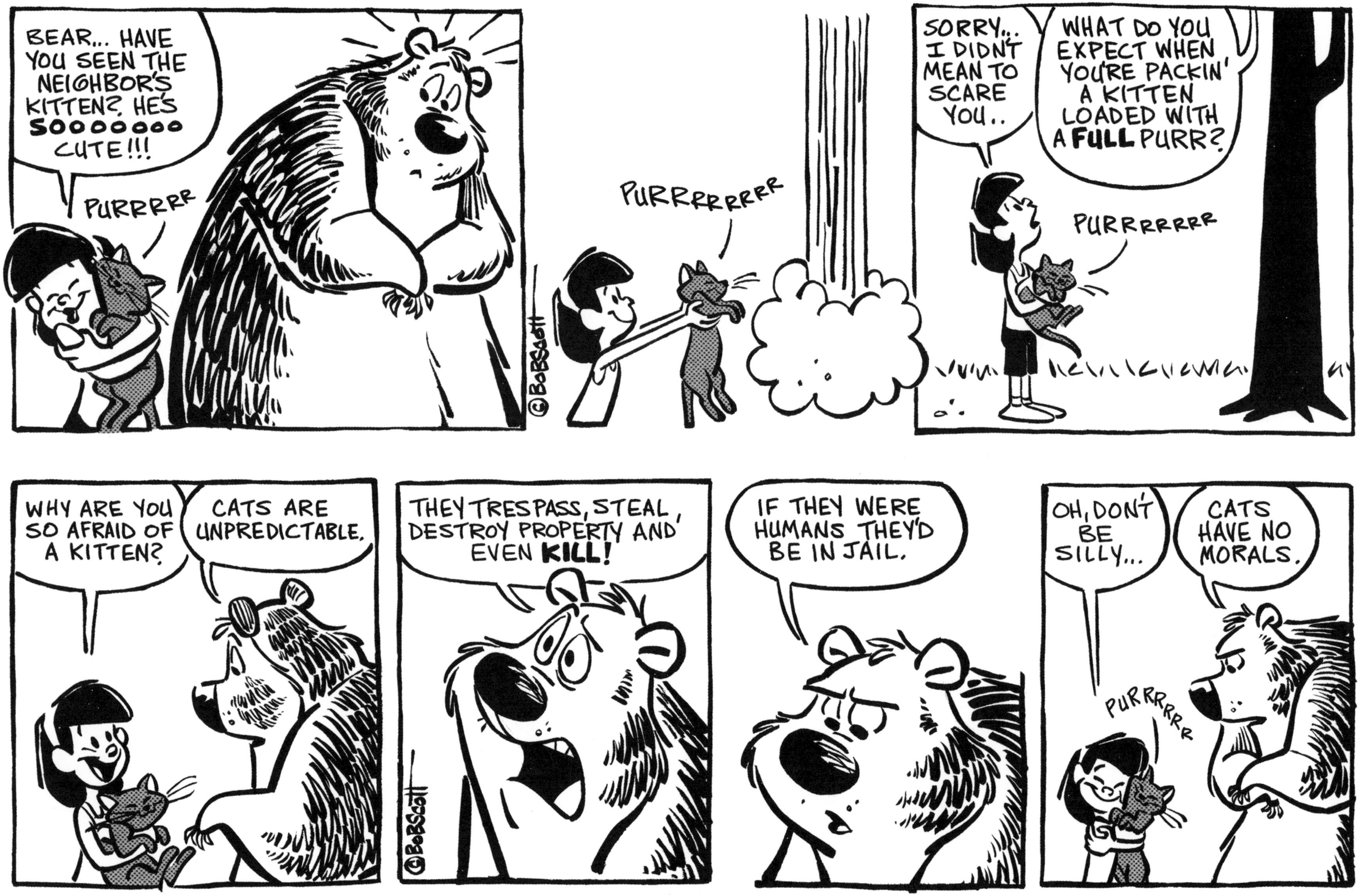
BEAR... HAVE YOU SEEN THE NEIGHBOR'S KITTEN? HE'S SOOOOOOO CUTE!!!
PURRRRR
©BoBScott
PURRRRRRRR
SORRY... I DIDN'T MEAN TO SCARE YOU..
WHAT DO YOU EXPECT WHEN YOU'RE PACKIN' A KITTEN LOADED WITH A FULL PURR?
PURRRRRRR
WHY ARE YOU SO AFRAID OF A KITTEN?
CATS ARE UNPREDICTABLE.
©BoBScott
THEY TRESPASS, STEAL, DESTROY PROPERTY AND EVEN KILL!
IF THEY WERE HUMANS THEY'D BE IN JAIL.
OH, DON'T BE SILLY...
CATS HAVE NO MORALS.
PURRRRRRR

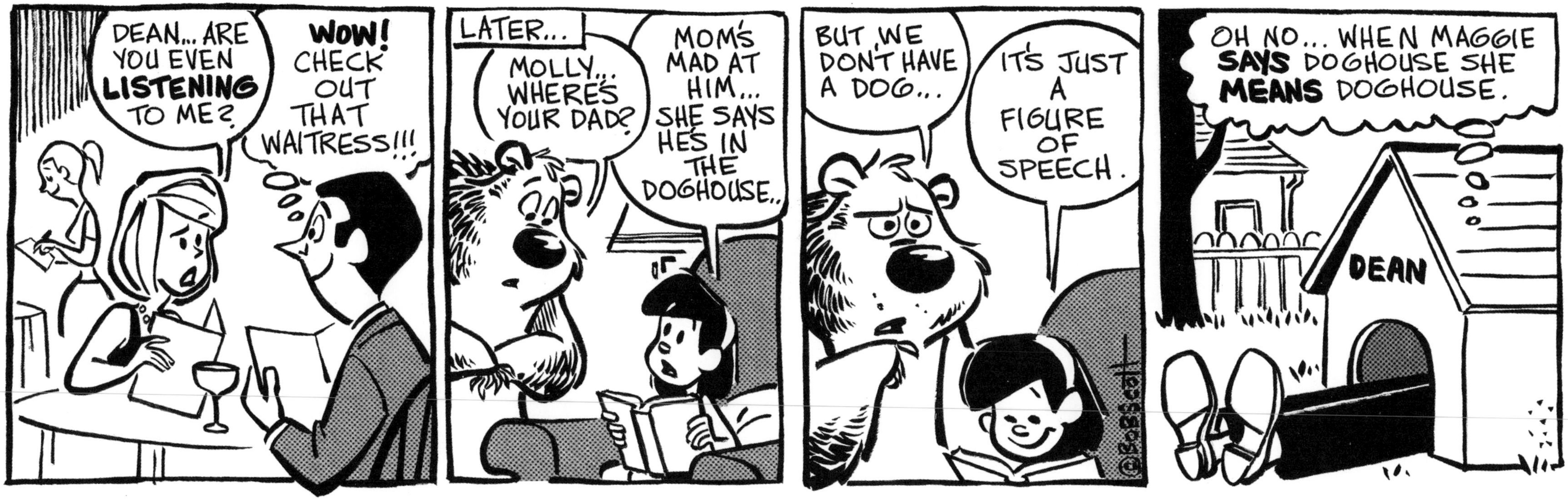
DEAN... ARE YOU EVEN LISTENING TO ME?
WOW! CHECK OUT THAT WAITRESS!!!
LATER...
MOLLY... WHERE'S YOUR DAD?
MOM'S MAD AT HIM... SHE SAYS HE'S IN THE DOGHOUSE..
BUT WE DON'T HAVE A DOG...
IT'S JUST A FIGURE OF SPEECH.
OH NO... WHEN MAGGIE SAYS DOGHOUSE SHE MEANS DOGHOUSE.
DEAN
© BOB SCOTT

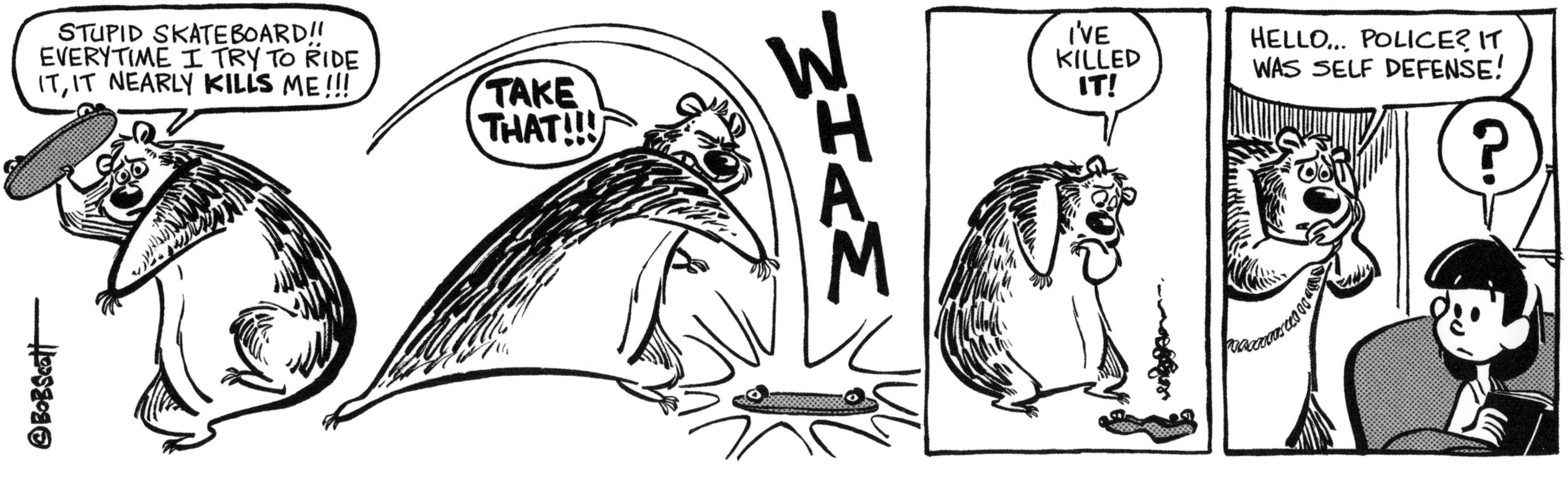
STUPID SKATEBOARD!! EVERYTIME I TRY TO RIDE IT, IT NEARLY KILLS ME!!!
TAKE THAT!!!
WHAM
I'VE KILLED IT!
HELLO... POLICE? IT WAS SELF DEFENSE!
?
© BOB SCOTT

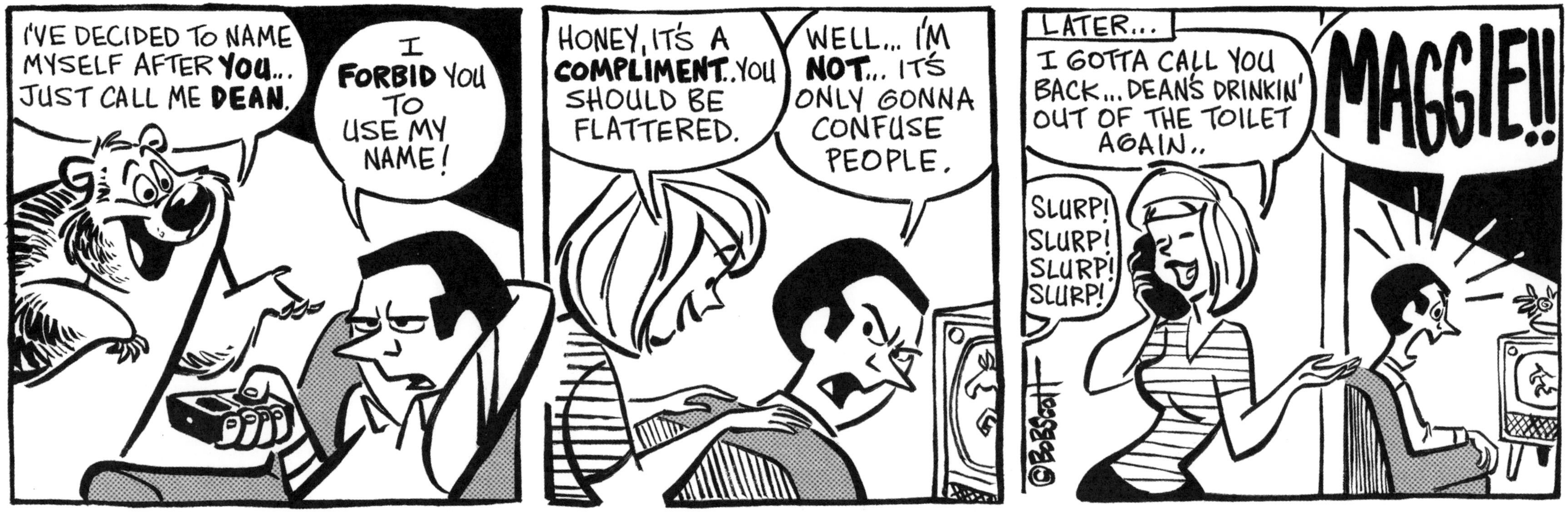
I'VE DECIDED TO NAME MYSELF AFTER YOU... JUST CALL ME DEAN.
I FORBID YOU TO USE MY NAME!
HONEY, IT'S A COMPLIMENT..YOU SHOULD BE FLATTERED.
WELL... I'M NOT... IT'S ONLY GONNA CONFUSE PEOPLE.
LATER...
I GOTTA CALL YOU BACK... DEAN'S DRINKIN' OUT OF THE TOILET AGAIN..
SLURP! SLURP! SLURP! SLURP!
MAGGIE!!
©BOBSCOTT

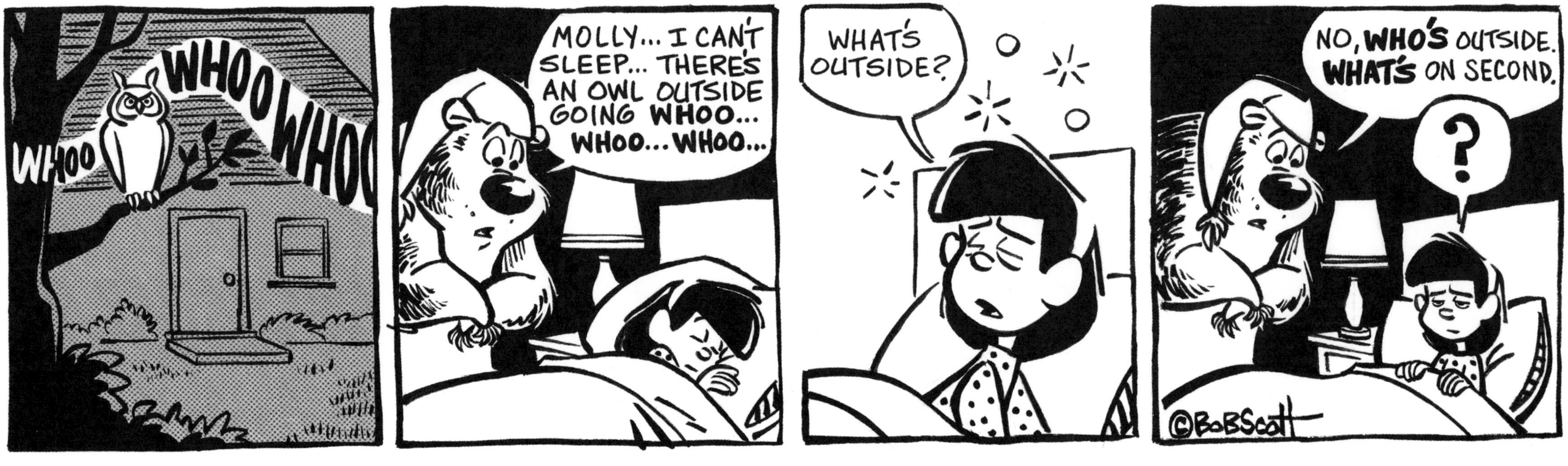
WHOO WHOO WHOO
MOLLY... I CAN'T SLEEP... THERE'S AN OWL OUTSIDE GOING WHOO... WHOO... WHOO...
WHAT'S OUTSIDE?
NO, WHO'S OUTSIDE. WHAT'S ON SECOND.
?
©BOBSCOTT

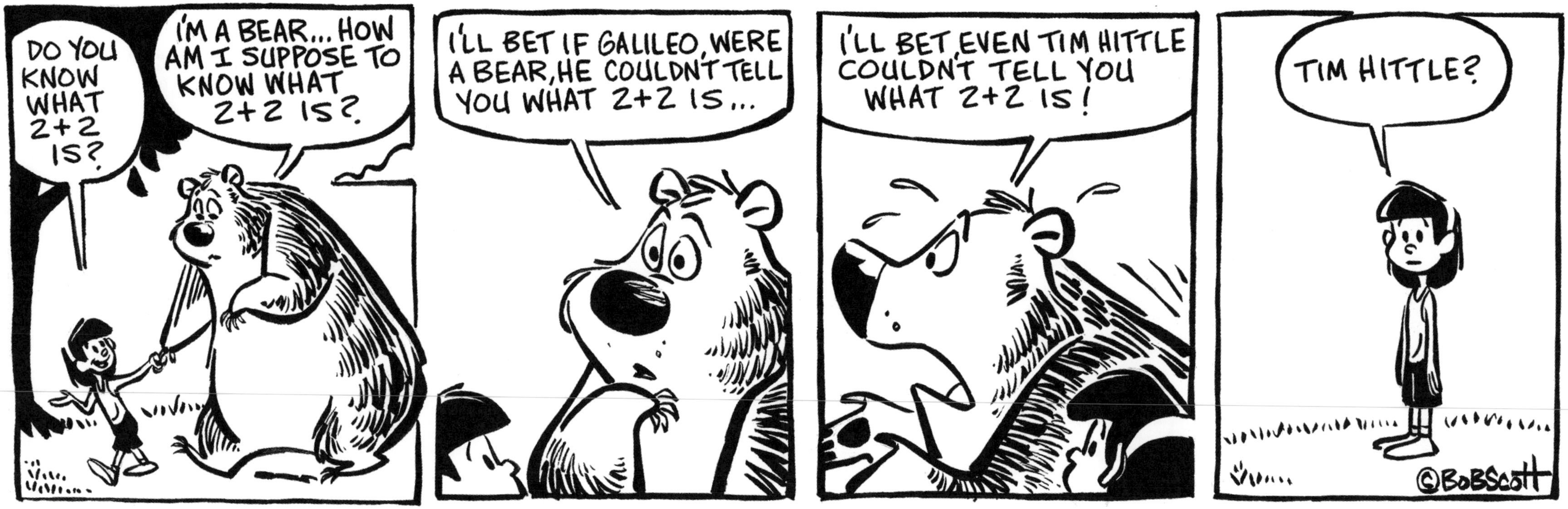
DO YOU KNOW WHAT 2+2 IS?
I'M A BEAR... HOW AM I SUPPOSE TO KNOW WHAT 2+2 IS?
I'LL BET IF GALILEO, WERE A BEAR, HE COULDN'T TELL YOU WHAT 2+2 IS...
I'LL BET, EVEN TIM HITTLE COULDN'T TELL YOU WHAT 2+2 IS!
TIM HITTLE?
©BOBSCOTT

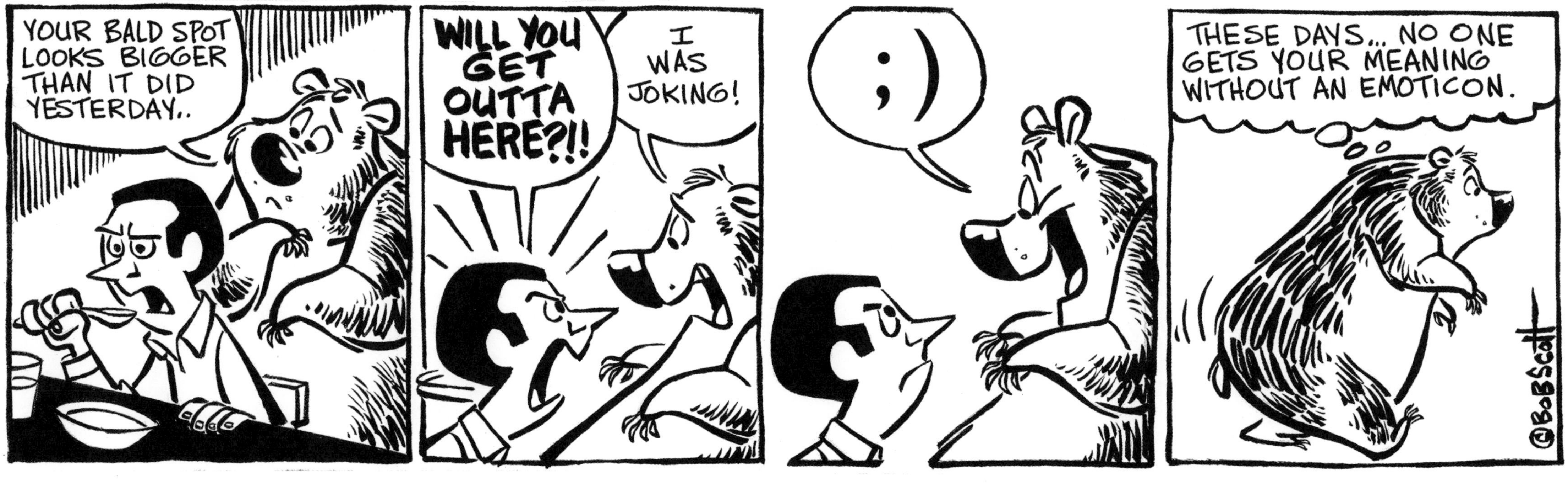
YOUR BALD SPOT LOOKS BIGGER THAN IT DID YESTERDAY..
WILL YOU GET OUTTA HERE?!!
I WAS JOKING!
;)
THESE DAYS... NO ONE GETS YOUR MEANING WITHOUT AN EMOTICON.
©BOBSCOTT

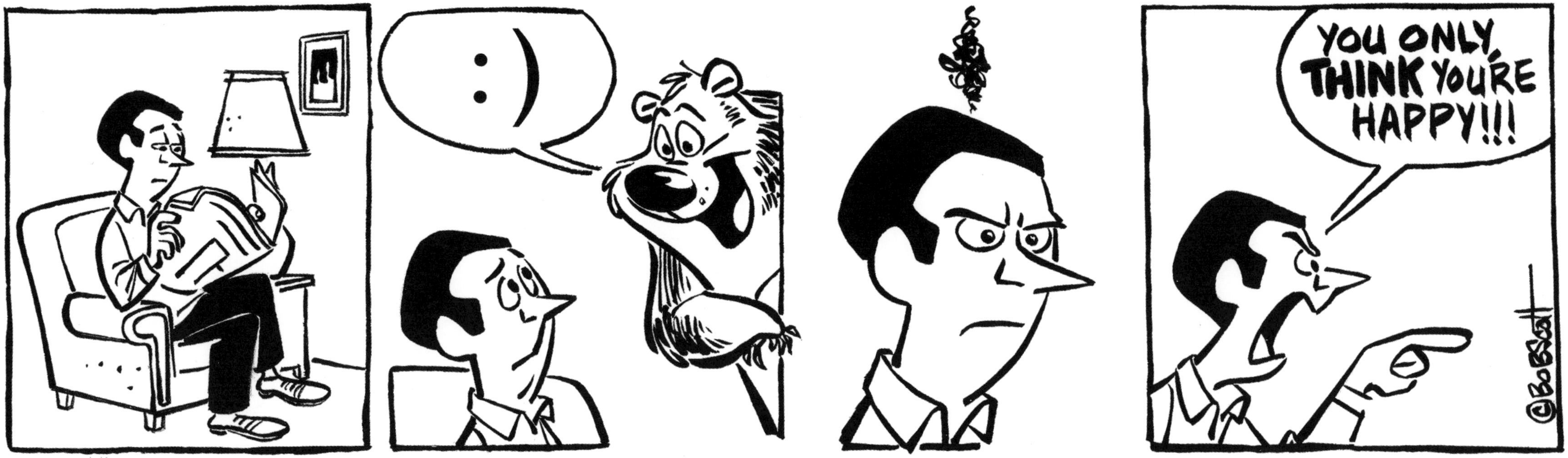
:)
YOU ONLY THINK YOU'RE HAPPY!!!
©BOBSCOTT

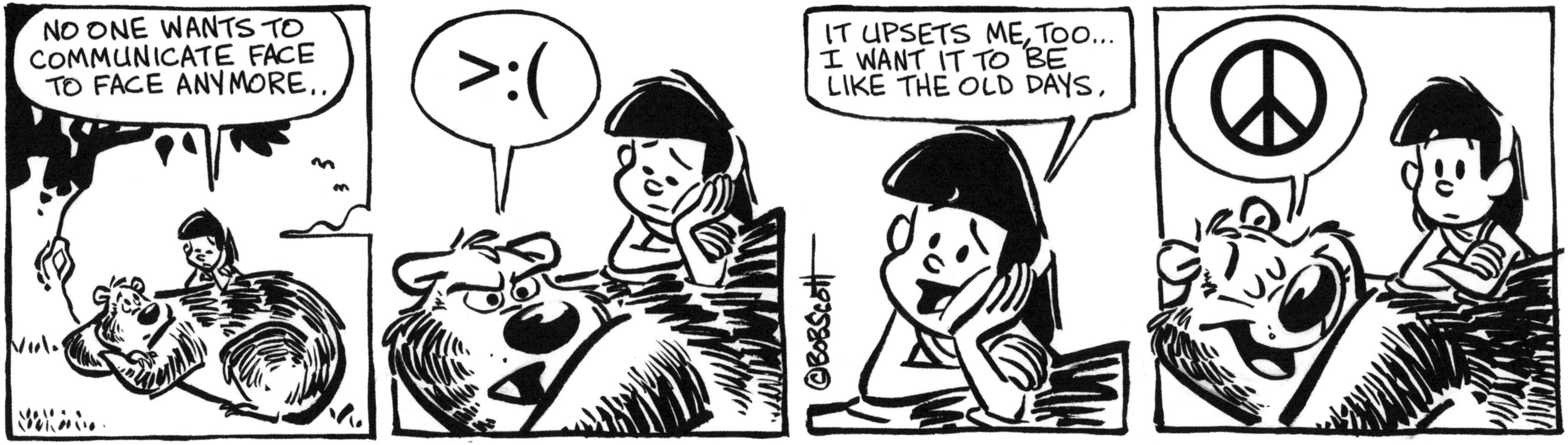
NO ONE WANTS TO COMMUNICATE FACE TO FACE ANYMORE..
>:(
IT UPSETS ME, TOO... I WANT IT TO BE LIKE THE OLD DAYS.
©BOBSCOTT

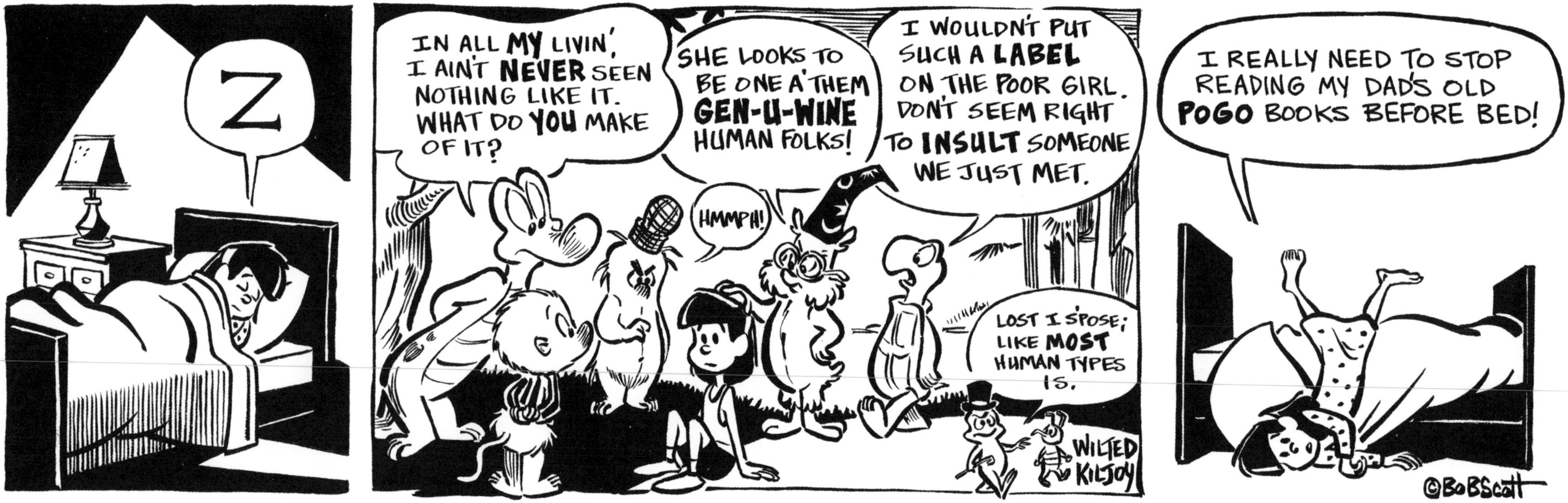
Z
IN ALL MY LIVIN', I AIN'T NEVER SEEN NOTHING LIKE IT. WHAT DO YOU MAKE OF IT?
SHE LOOKS TO BE ONE A' THEM GEN-U-WINE HUMAN FOLKS!
HMMPH!
I WOULDN'T PUT SUCH A LABEL ON THE POOR GIRL. DON'T SEEM RIGHT TO INSULT SOMEONE WE JUST MET.
LOST I S'POSE; LIKE MOST HUMAN TYPES IS.
WILTED KILJOY
I REALLY NEED TO STOP READING MY DAD'S OLD POGO BOOKS BEFORE BED!
©BoBScott

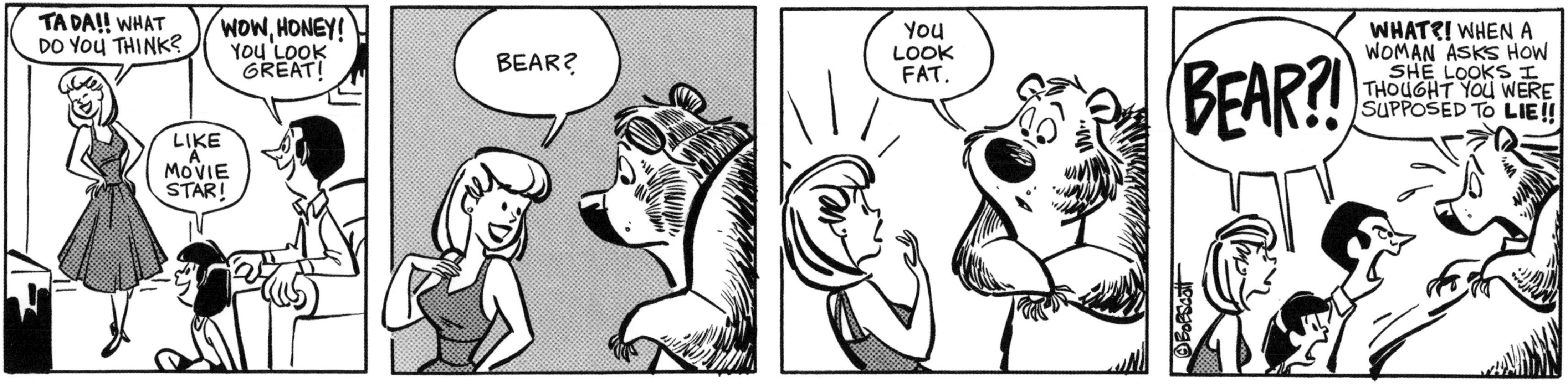
TA DA!! WHAT DO YOU THINK?
WOW, HONEY! YOU LOOK GREAT!
LIKE A MOVIE STAR!
BEAR?
YOU LOOK FAT.
BEAR?!
WHAT?! WHEN A WOMAN ASKS HOW SHE LOOKS I THOUGHT YOU WERE SUPPOSED TO LIE!!
©BoBScott

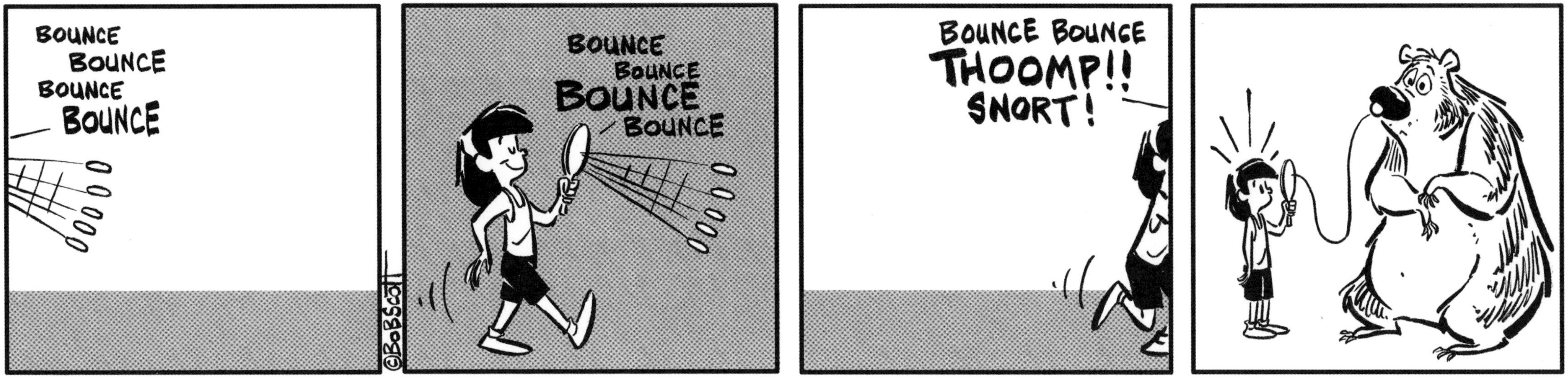
BOUNCE
BOUNCE
BOUNCE
BOUNCE
©BOBSCOTT
BOUNCE
BOUNCE
BOUNCE
BOUNCE
BOUNCE BOUNCE
THOOMP!!
SNORT!

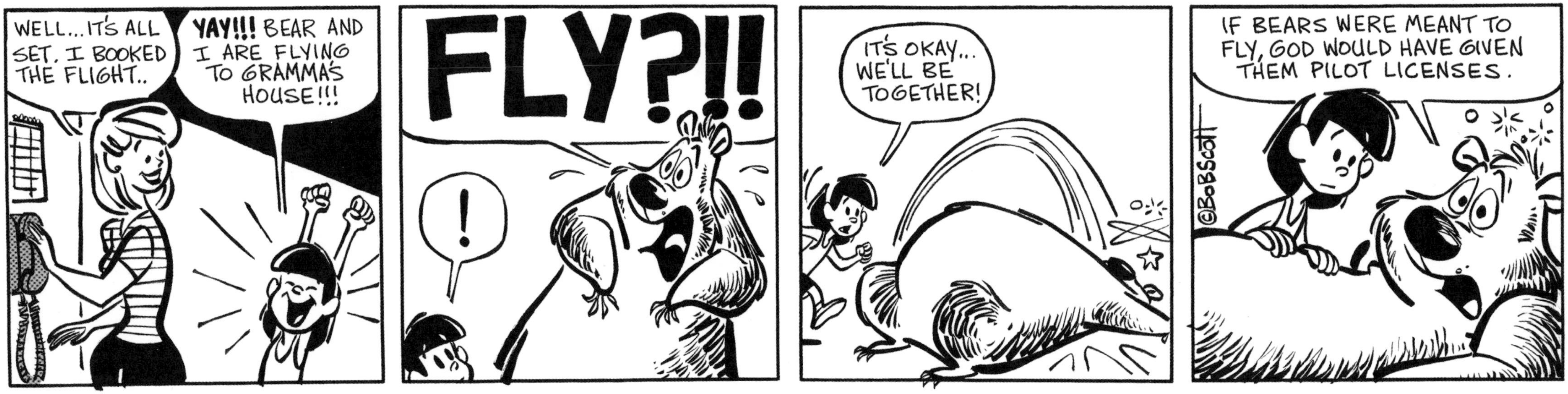
WELL... IT'S ALL SET. I BOOKED THE FLIGHT..
YAY!!! BEAR AND I ARE FLYING TO GRAMMA'S HOUSE!!!
FLY?!!
!
IT'S OKAY... WE'LL BE TOGETHER!
©BOBSCOTT
IF BEARS WERE MEANT TO FLY, GOD WOULD HAVE GIVEN THEM PILOT LICENSES.

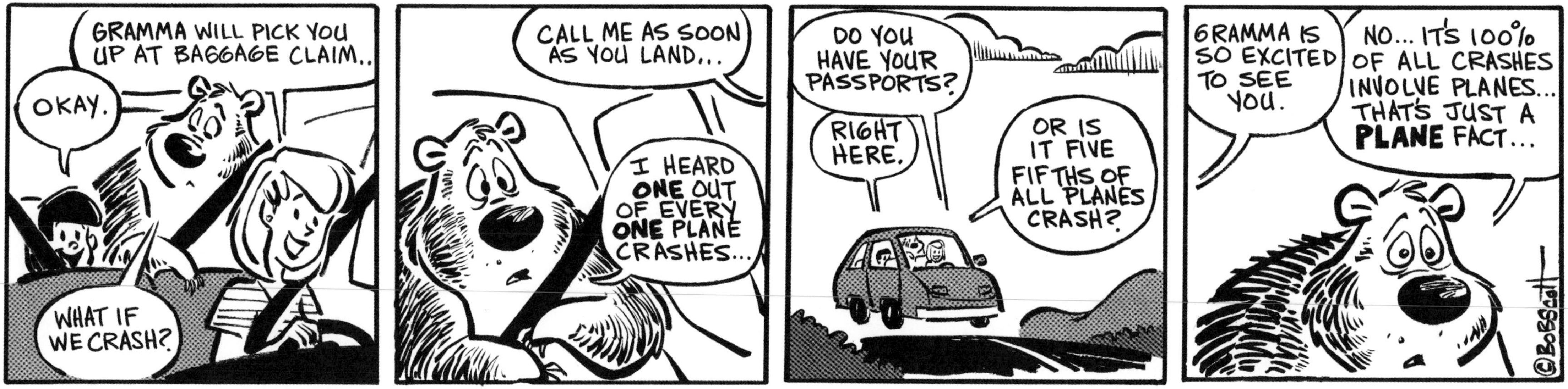
GRAMMA WILL PICK YOU UP AT BAGGAGE CLAIM..
OKAY.
WHAT IF WE CRASH?
CALL ME AS SOON AS YOU LAND...
I HEARD ONE OUT OF EVERY ONE PLANE CRASHES...
DO YOU HAVE YOUR PASSPORTS?
RIGHT HERE.
OR IS IT FIVE FIFTHS OF ALL PLANES CRASH?
GRAMMA IS SO EXCITED TO SEE YOU.
NO... IT'S 100% OF ALL CRASHES INVOLVE PLANES... THAT'S JUST A PLANE FACT...
©BoBScott

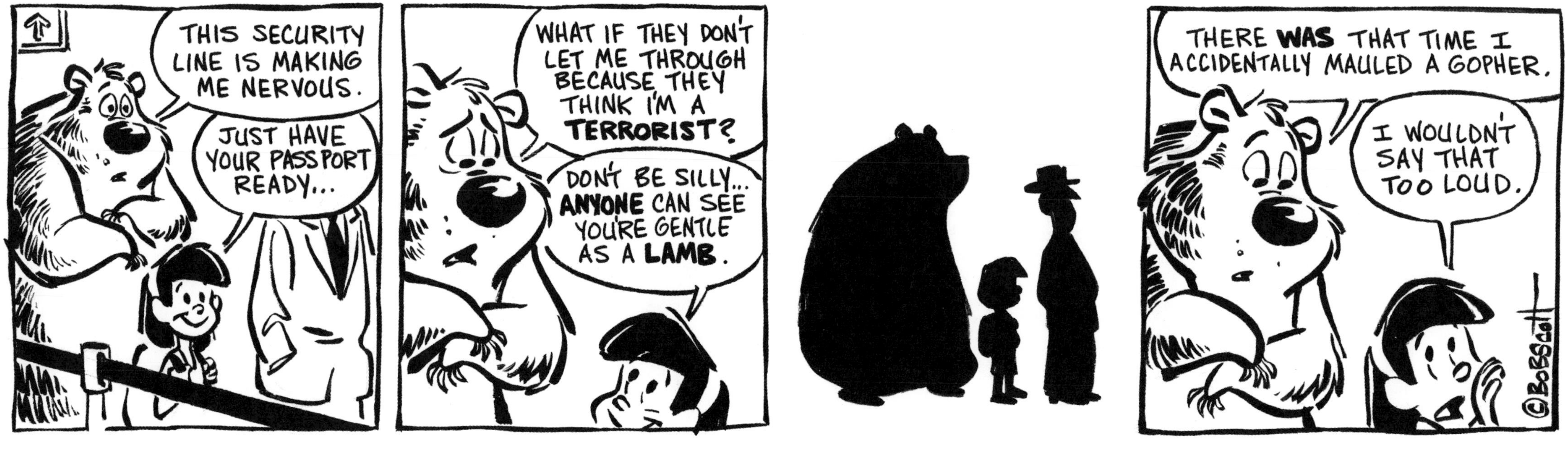
THIS SECURITY LINE IS MAKING ME NERVOUS.
JUST HAVE YOUR PASSPORT READY...
WHAT IF THEY DON'T LET ME THROUGH BECAUSE THEY THINK I'M A TERRORIST?
DON'T BE SILLY... ANYONE CAN SEE YOU'RE GENTLE AS A LAMB.
THERE WAS THAT TIME I ACCIDENTALLY MAULED A GOPHER.
I WOULDN'T SAY THAT TOO LOUD.
©BoBScott

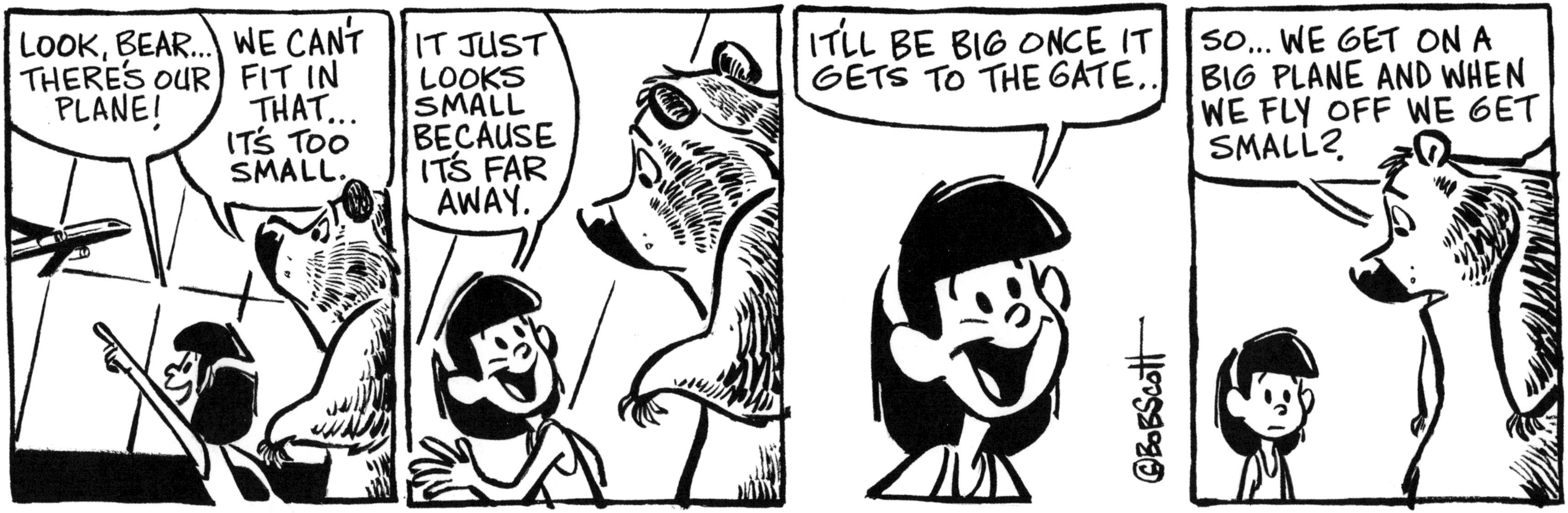
LOOK, BEAR... THERE'S OUR PLANE!
WE CAN'T FIT IN THAT... IT'S TOO SMALL.
IT JUST LOOKS SMALL BECAUSE IT'S FAR AWAY.
IT'LL BE BIG ONCE IT GETS TO THE GATE..
SO... WE GET ON A BIG PLANE AND WHEN WE FLY OFF WE GET SMALL?
©BOBSCOTT

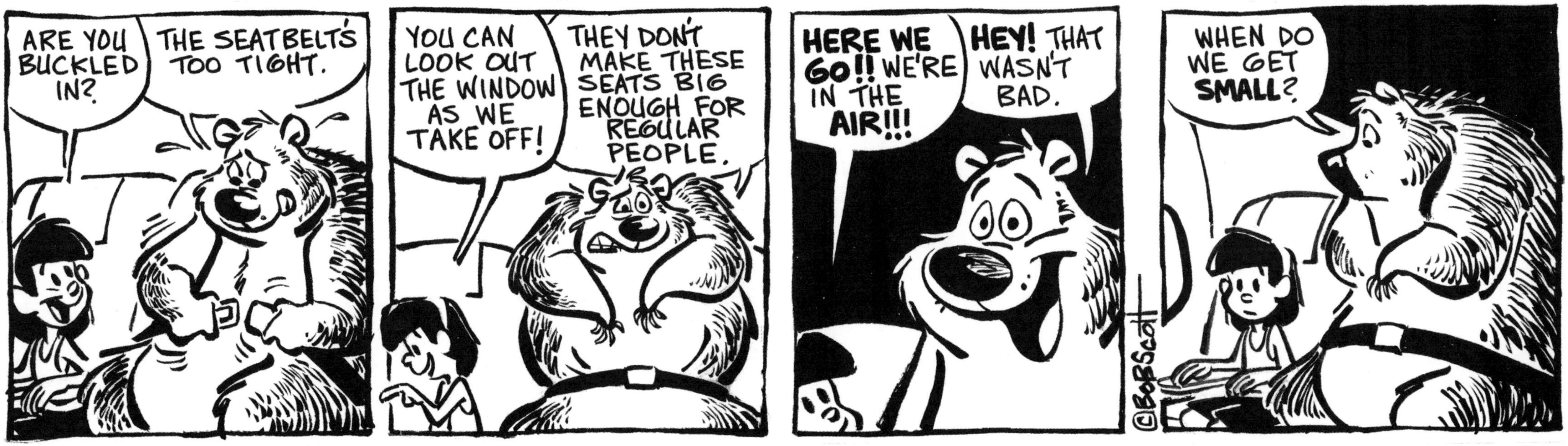
ARE YOU BUCKLED IN?
THE SEATBELT'S TOO TIGHT.
YOU CAN LOOK OUT THE WINDOW AS WE TAKE OFF!
THEY DON'T MAKE THESE SEATS BIG ENOUGH FOR REGULAR PEOPLE.
HERE WE GO!! WE'RE IN THE AIR!!!
HEY! THAT WASN'T BAD.
WHEN DO WE GET SMALL?
©BOBSCOTT

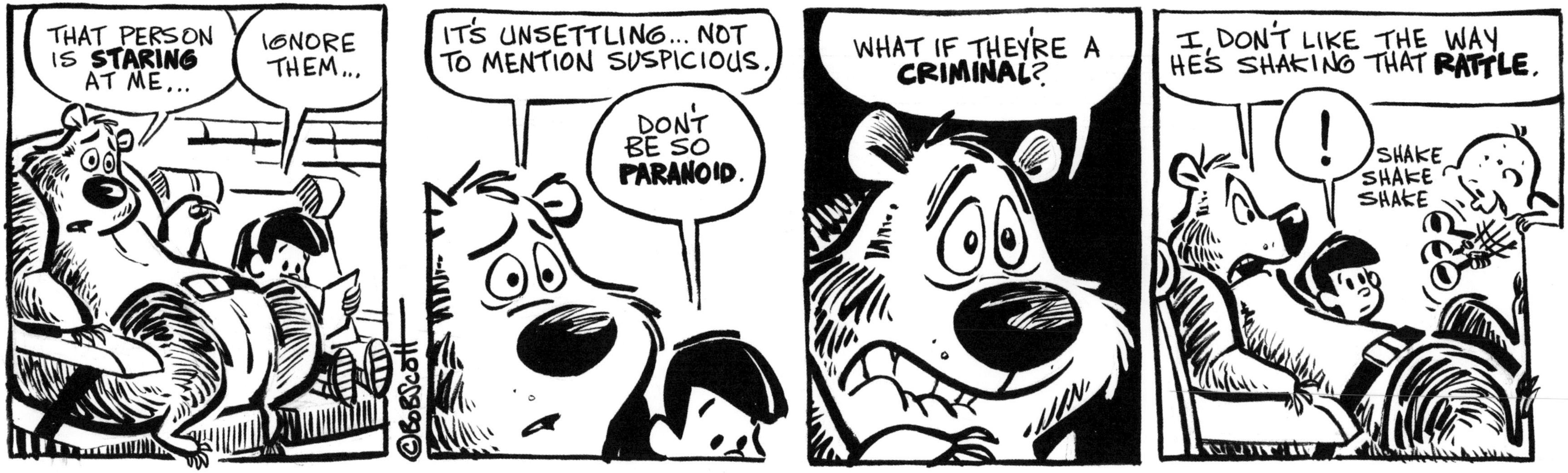
THAT PERSON IS STARING AT ME...
IGNORE THEM...
©BOBSCOTT
IT'S UNSETTLING... NOT TO MENTION SUSPICIOUS.
DON'T BE SO PARANOID.
WHAT IF THEY'RE A CRIMINAL?
I DON'T LIKE THE WAY HE'S SHAKING THAT RATTLE.
!
SHAKE SHAKE SHAKE

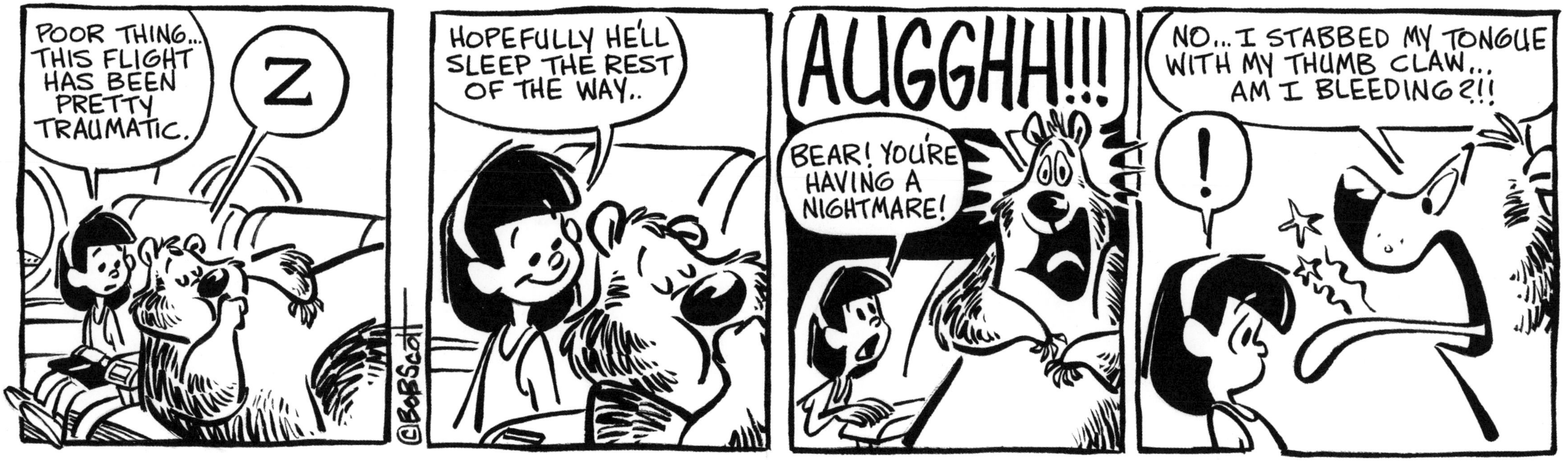
POOR THING... THIS FLIGHT HAS BEEN PRETTY TRAUMATIC.
Z
©BOBSCOTT
HOPEFULLY HE'LL SLEEP THE REST OF THE WAY..
AUGGHH!!!
BEAR! YOU'RE HAVING A NIGHTMARE!
NO... I STABBED MY TONGUE WITH MY THUMB CLAW... AM I BLEEDING?!!
!

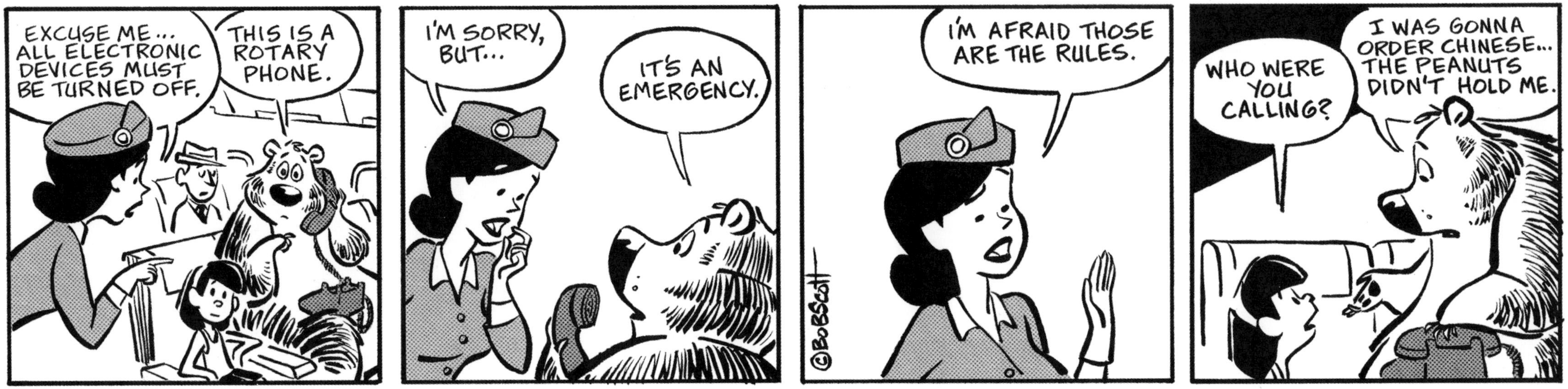
EXCUSE ME... ALL ELECTRONIC DEVICES MUST BE TURNED OFF.
THIS IS A ROTARY PHONE.
I'M SORRY, BUT...
IT'S AN EMERGENCY.
©BOBSCOTT
I'M AFRAID THOSE ARE THE RULES.
WHO WERE YOU CALLING?
I WAS GONNA ORDER CHINESE... THE PEANUTS DIDN'T HOLD ME.

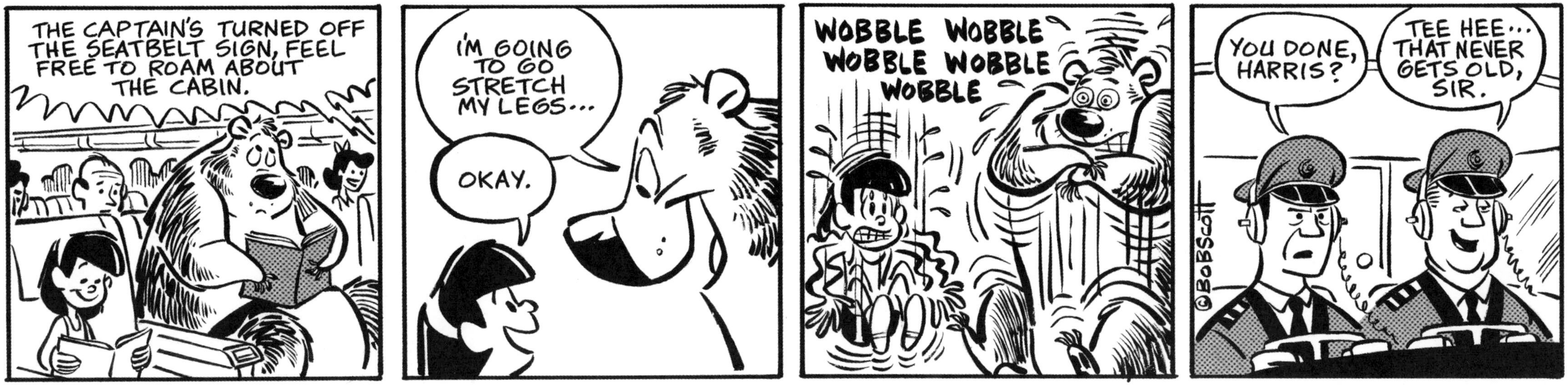
THE CAPTAIN'S TURNED OFF THE SEATBELT SIGN, FEEL FREE TO ROAM ABOUT THE CABIN.
I'M GOING TO GO STRETCH MY LEGS...
OKAY.
WOBBLE WOBBLE WOBBLE WOBBLE WOBBLE
©BOBSCOTT
YOU DONE, HARRIS?
TEE HEE... THAT NEVER GETS OLD, SIR.

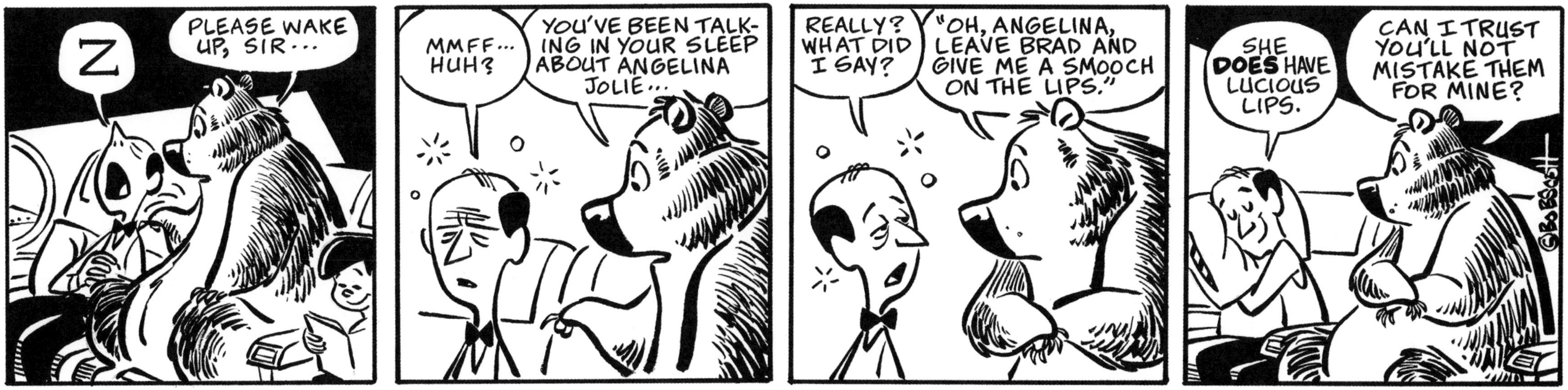
Z
PLEASE WAKE UP, SIR...
MMFF... HUH?
YOU'VE BEEN TALKING IN YOUR SLEEP ABOUT ANGELINA JOLIE...
REALLY? WHAT DID I SAY?
"OH, ANGELINA, LEAVE BRAD AND GIVE ME A SMOOCH ON THE LIPS."
SHE **DOES** HAVE LUCIOUS LIPS.
CAN I TRUST YOU'LL NOT MISTAKE THEM FOR MINE?
©BOBSCOTT

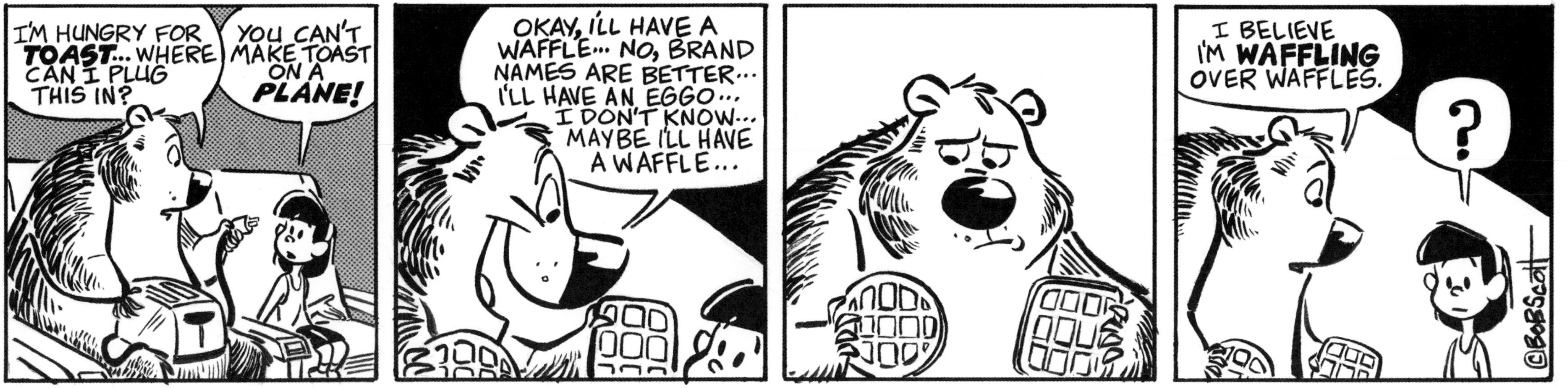
I'M HUNGRY FOR **TOAST**... WHERE CAN I PLUG THIS IN?
YOU CAN'T MAKE TOAST ON A ***PLANE!***
OKAY, I'LL HAVE A WAFFLE... NO, BRAND NAMES ARE BETTER... I'LL HAVE AN EGGO... I DON'T KNOW... MAYBE I'LL HAVE A WAFFLE...
I BELIEVE I'M **WAFFLING** OVER WAFFLES.
?
©BOBSCOTT

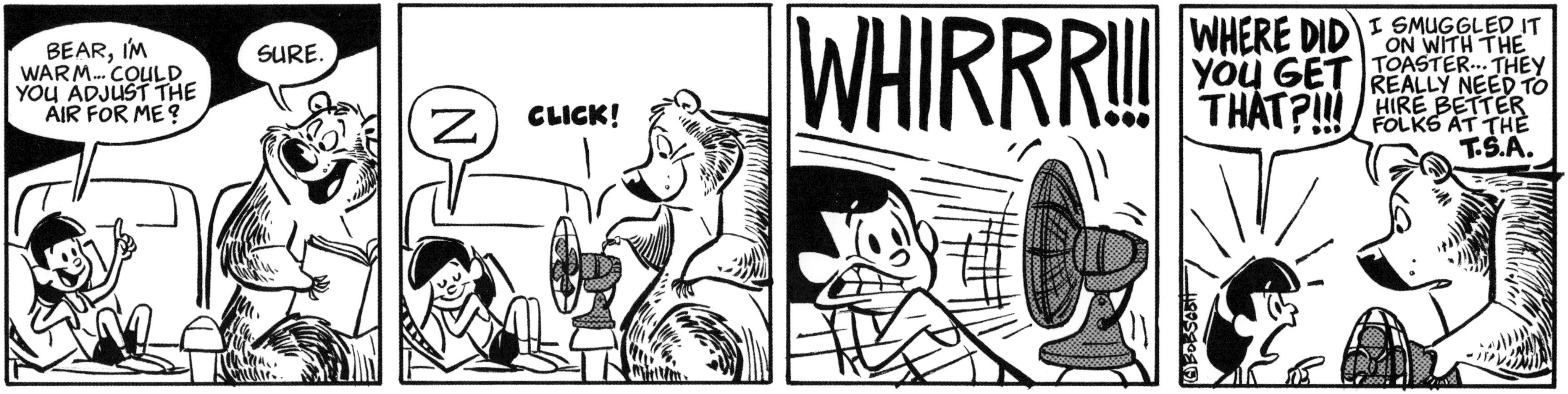
BEAR, I'M WARM... COULD YOU ADJUST THE AIR FOR ME?
SURE.
Z
CLICK!
WHIRRR!!!...
WHERE DID YOU GET THAT?!!!
I SMUGGLED IT ON WITH THE TOASTER... THEY REALLY NEED TO HIRE BETTER FOLKS AT THE T.S.A.

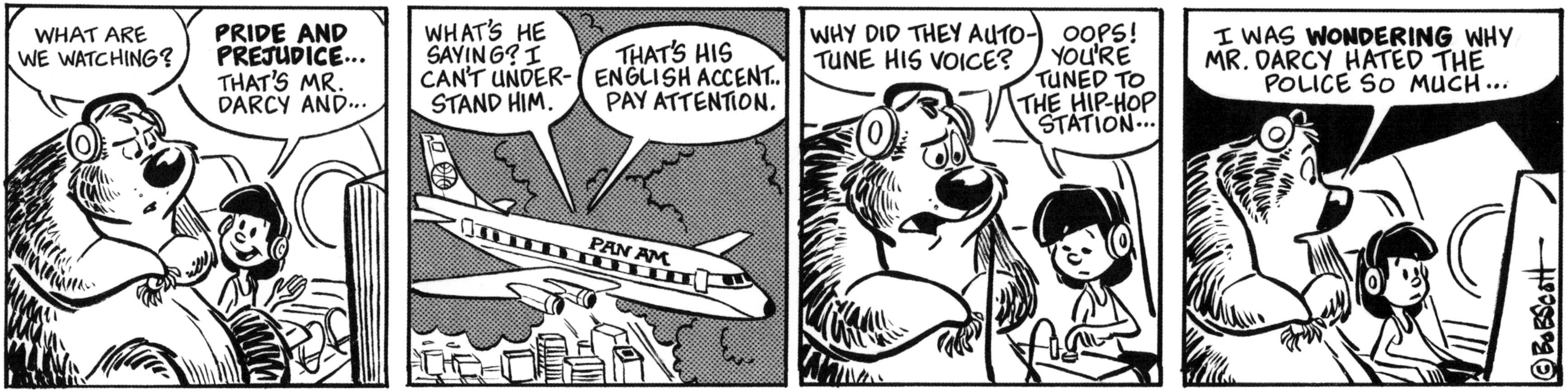
WHAT ARE WE WATCHING?
PRIDE AND PREJUDICE... THAT'S MR. DARCY AND...
WHAT'S HE SAYING? I CAN'T UNDERSTAND HIM.
THAT'S HIS ENGLISH ACCENT.. PAY ATTENTION.
PAN AM
WHY DID THEY AUTO-TUNE HIS VOICE?
OOPS! YOU'RE TUNED TO THE HIP-HOP STATION...
I WAS WONDERING WHY MR. DARCY HATED THE POLICE SO MUCH...

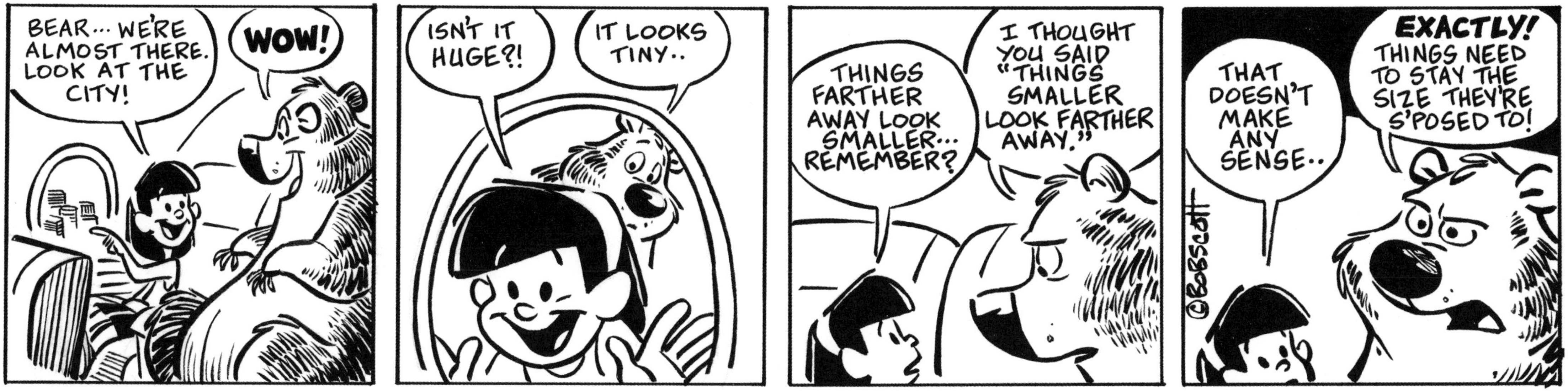
BEAR... WE'RE ALMOST THERE. LOOK AT THE CITY!
WOW!
ISN'T IT HUGE?!
IT LOOKS TINY..
THINGS FARTHER AWAY LOOK SMALLER... REMEMBER?
I THOUGHT YOU SAID "THINGS SMALLER LOOK FARTHER AWAY."
THAT DOESN'T MAKE ANY SENSE..
EXACTLY! THINGS NEED TO STAY THE SIZE THEY'RE S'POSED TO!
©BOBSCOTT

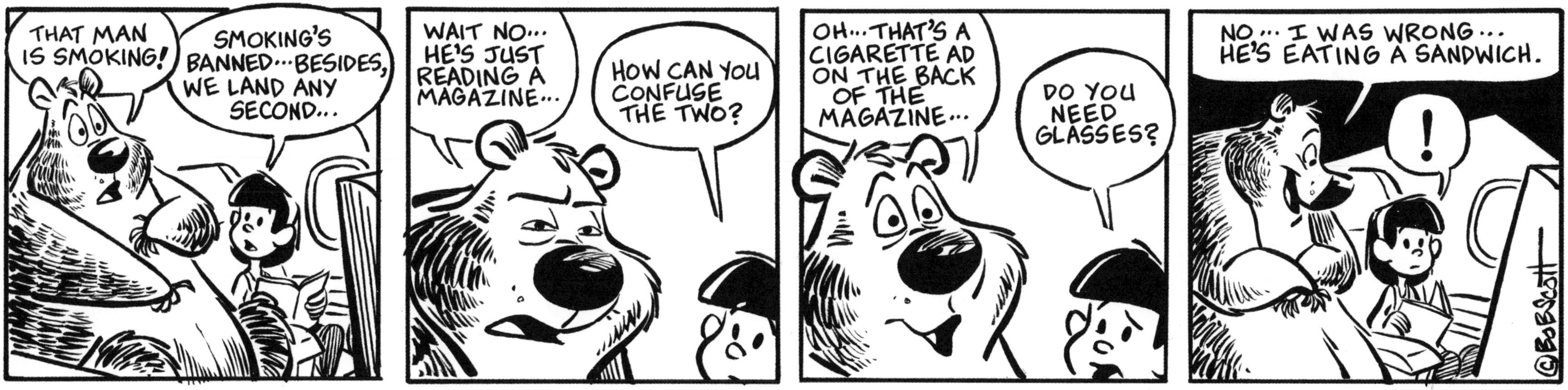
THAT MAN IS SMOKING!
SMOKING'S BANNED...BESIDES, WE LAND ANY SECOND...
WAIT NO... HE'S JUST READING A MAGAZINE...
HOW CAN YOU CONFUSE THE TWO?
OH...THAT'S A CIGARETTE AD ON THE BACK OF THE MAGAZINE...
DO YOU NEED GLASSES?
NO... I WAS WRONG... HE'S EATING A SANDWICH.
!
©BOBSCOTT

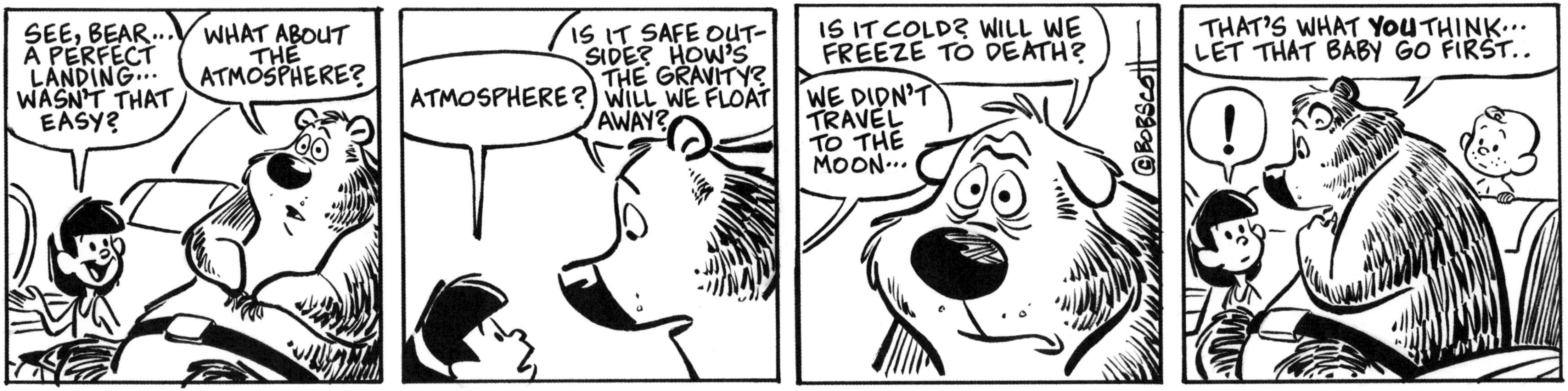
SEE, BEAR... A PERFECT LANDING... WASN'T THAT EASY?
WHAT ABOUT THE ATMOSPHERE?
ATMOSPHERE?
IS IT SAFE OUTSIDE? HOW'S THE GRAVITY? WILL WE FLOAT AWAY?
IS IT COLD? WILL WE FREEZE TO DEATH?
WE DIDN'T TRAVEL TO THE MOON...
©BOBSCOTT
THAT'S WHAT **YOU** THINK... LET THAT BABY GO FIRST..
!

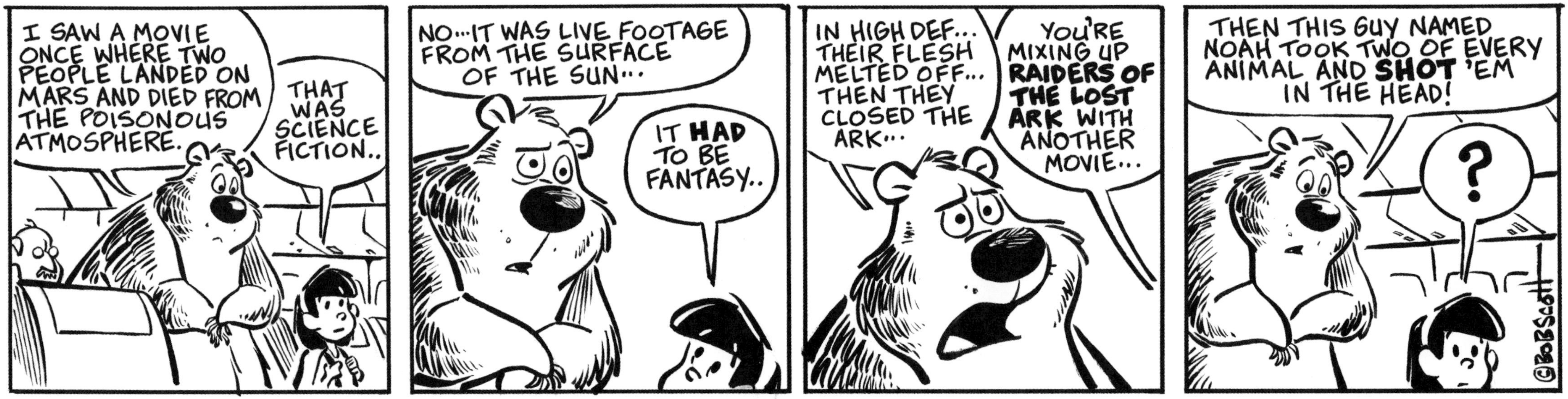
I SAW A MOVIE ONCE WHERE TWO PEOPLE LANDED ON MARS AND DIED FROM THE POISONOUS ATMOSPHERE.
THAT WAS SCIENCE FICTION..
NO...IT WAS LIVE FOOTAGE FROM THE SURFACE OF THE SUN...
IT **HAD** TO BE FANTASY..
IN HIGH DEF... THEIR FLESH MELTED OFF... THEN THEY CLOSED THE ARK...
YOU'RE MIXING UP **RAIDERS OF THE LOST ARK** WITH ANOTHER MOVIE...
THEN THIS GUY NAMED NOAH TOOK TWO OF EVERY ANIMAL AND **SHOT** 'EM IN THE HEAD!
?
©BOBSCOTT

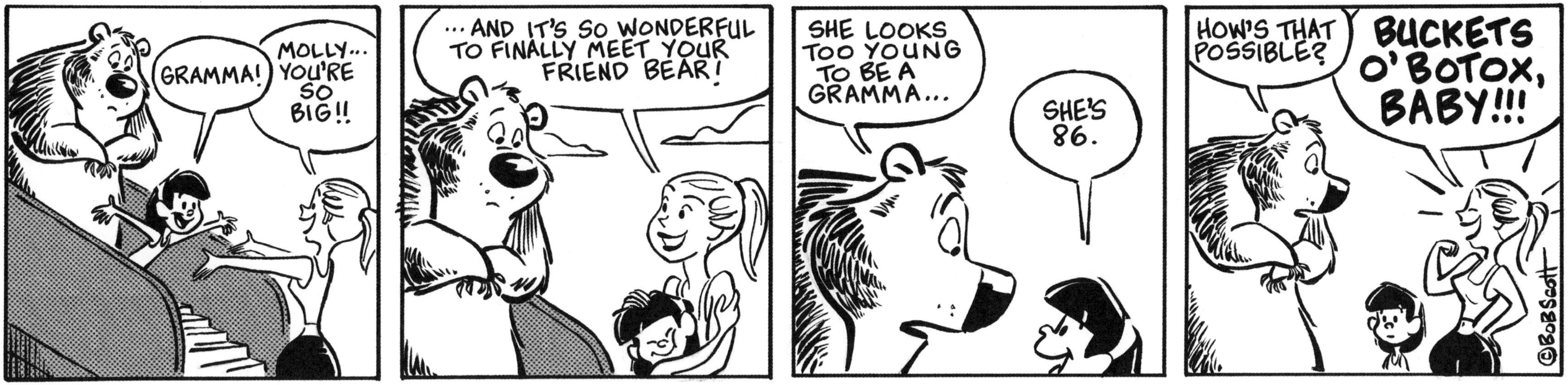
GRAMMA!
MOLLY... YOU'RE SO BIG!!
...AND IT'S SO WONDERFUL TO FINALLY MEET YOUR FRIEND BEAR!
SHE LOOKS TOO YOUNG TO BE A GRAMMA...
SHE'S 86.
HOW'S THAT POSSIBLE?
BUCKETS O'BOTOX, BABY!!!
©BOBSCOTT

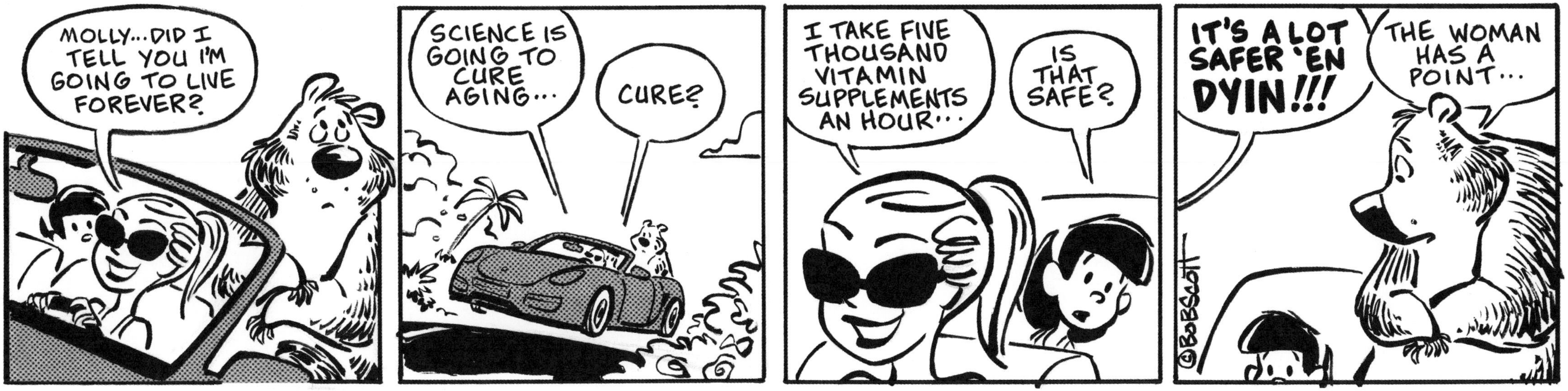
MOLLY...DID I TELL YOU I'M GOING TO LIVE FOREVER?
SCIENCE IS GOING TO CURE AGING...
CURE?
I TAKE FIVE THOUSAND VITAMIN SUPPLEMENTS AN HOUR...
IS THAT SAFE?
©BOBSCOTT
IT'S A LOT SAFER 'EN DYIN!!!
THE WOMAN HAS A POINT...

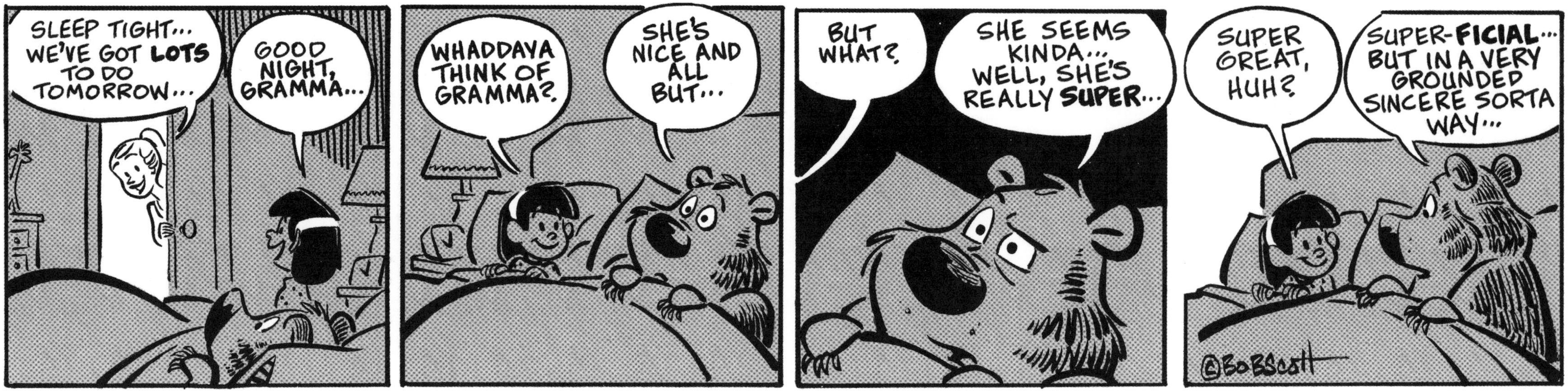

SLEEP TIGHT... WE'VE GOT LOTS TO DO TOMORROW...
GOOD NIGHT, GRAMMA...
WHADDAYA THINK OF GRAMMA?
SHE'S NICE AND ALL BUT...
BUT WHAT?
SHE SEEMS KINDA... WELL, SHE'S REALLY SUPER...
SUPER GREAT, HUH?
SUPER-FICIAL... BUT IN A VERY GROUNDED SINCERE SORTA WAY...
©BOBSCOTT

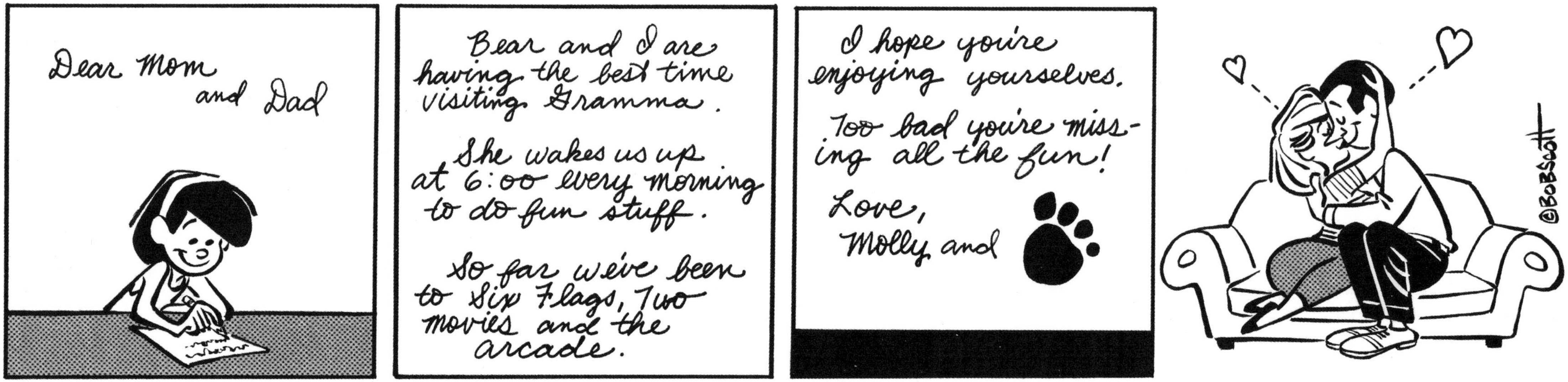

Dear Mom and Dad
Bear and I are having the best time visiting Gramma.
She wakes us up at 6:00 every morning to do fun stuff.
So far we've been to Six Flags, Two movies and the arcade.
I hope you're enjoying yourselves.
Too bad you're missing all the fun!
Love, Molly and
©BOBSCOTT

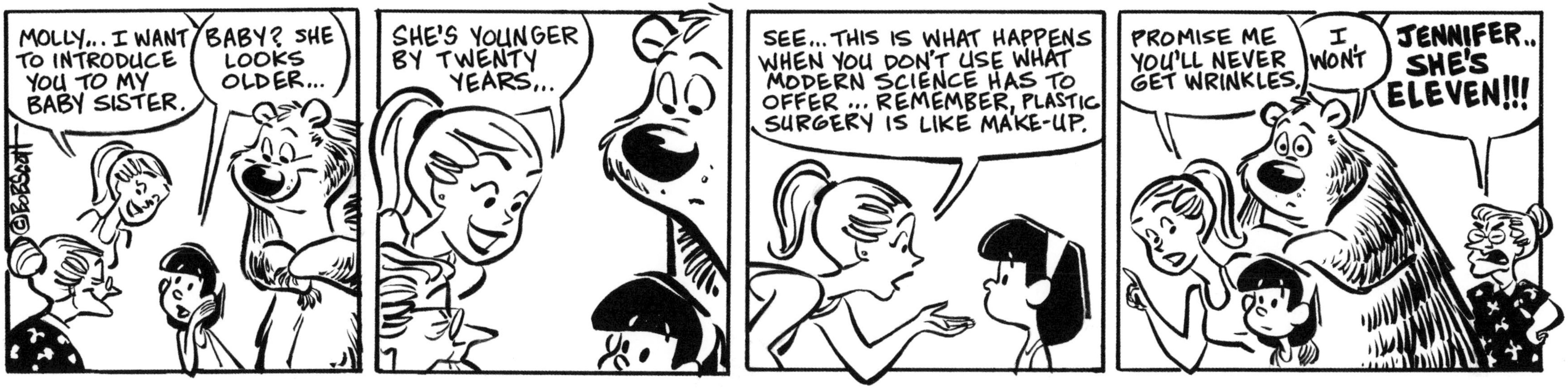
MOLLY... I WANT TO INTRODUCE YOU TO MY BABY SISTER.
BABY? SHE LOOKS OLDER...
SHE'S YOUNGER BY TWENTY YEARS...
SEE... THIS IS WHAT HAPPENS WHEN YOU DON'T USE WHAT MODERN SCIENCE HAS TO OFFER ... REMEMBER, PLASTIC SURGERY IS LIKE MAKE-UP.
PROMISE ME YOU'LL NEVER GET WRINKLES.
I WON'T
JENNIFER.. SHE'S ELEVEN!!!
©BOBSCOTT

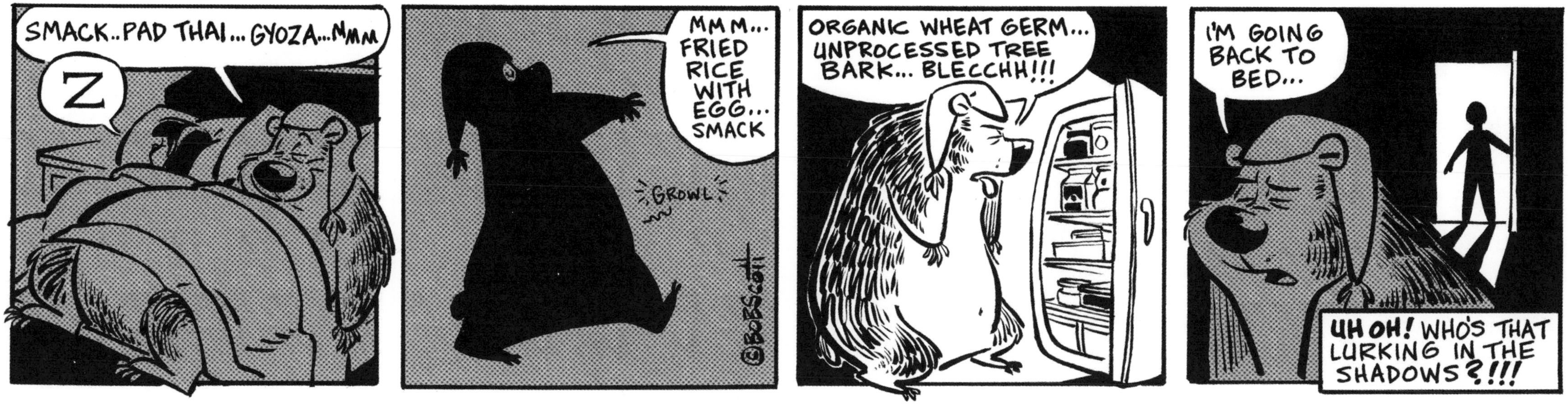
SMACK..PAD THAI... GYOZA...NMM
Z
MMM... FRIED RICE WITH EGG... SMACK
GROWL
©BOBSCOTT
ORGANIC WHEAT GERM... UNPROCESSED TREE BARK... BLECCHH!!!
I'M GOING BACK TO BED...
UH OH! WHO'S THAT LURKING IN THE SHADOWS?!!!

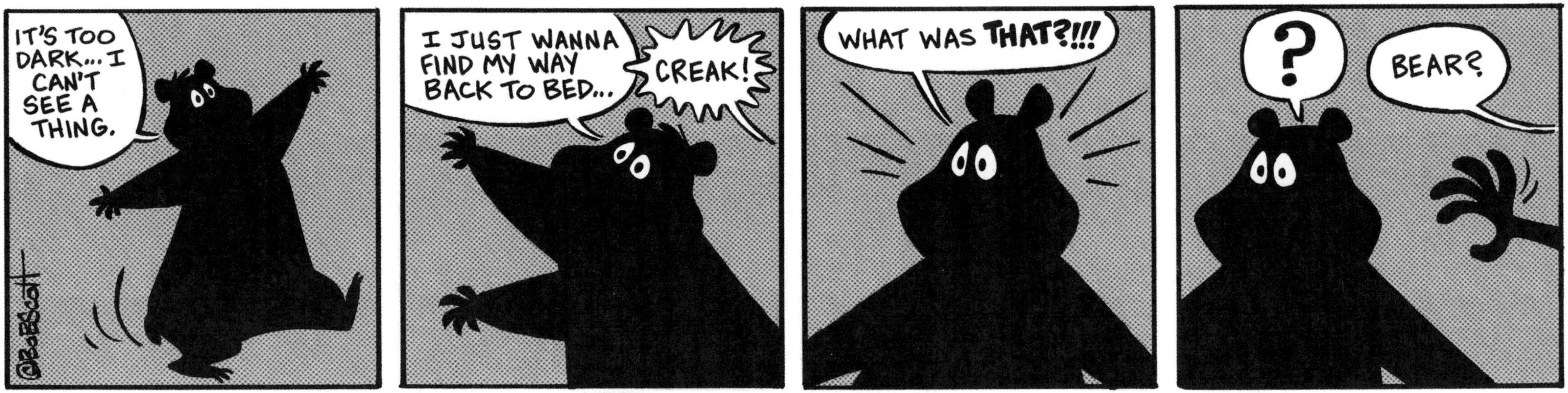
IT'S TOO DARK... I CAN'T SEE A THING.
©BOBSCOTT
I JUST WANNA FIND MY WAY BACK TO BED...
CREAK!
WHAT WAS THAT?!!!
?
BEAR?

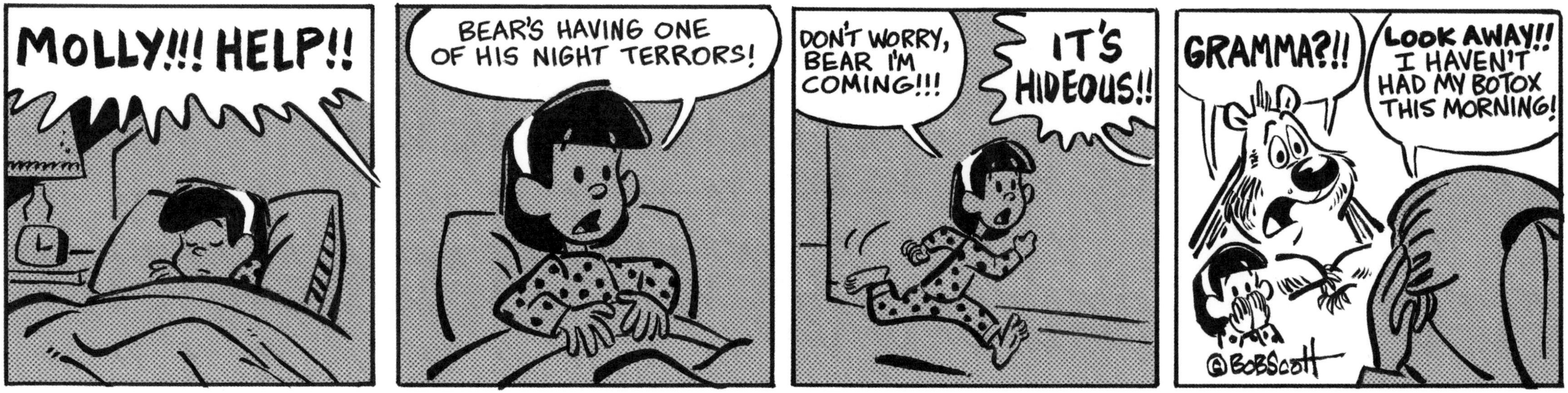
MOLLY!!! HELP!!
BEAR'S HAVING ONE OF HIS NIGHT TERRORS!
DON'T WORRY, BEAR I'M COMING!!!
IT'S HIDEOUS!!
GRAMMA?!!
LOOK AWAY!! I HAVEN'T HAD MY BOTOX THIS MORNING!
©BOBSCOTT

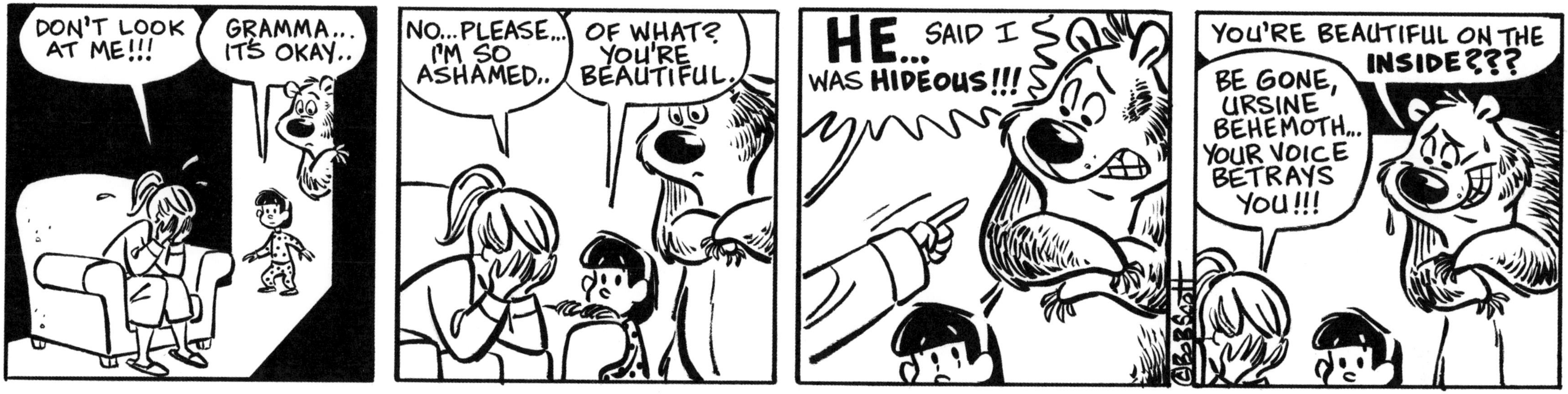
DON'T LOOK AT ME!!!
GRAMMA... IT'S OKAY..
NO...PLEASE... I'M SO ASHAMED..
OF WHAT? YOU'RE BEAUTIFUL.
HE... SAID I WAS HIDEOUS!!!
YOU'RE BEAUTIFUL ON THE INSIDE???
BE GONE, URSINE BEHEMOTH... YOUR VOICE BETRAYS YOU!!!
©BoBScott

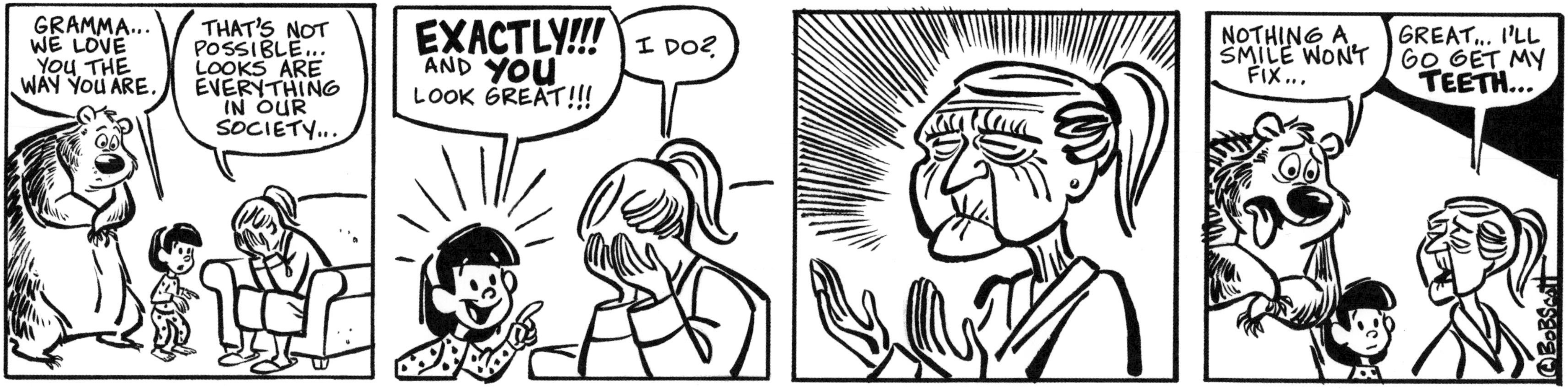
GRAMMA... WE LOVE YOU THE WAY YOU ARE.
THAT'S NOT POSSIBLE... LOOKS ARE EVERYTHING IN OUR SOCIETY...
EXACTLY!!! AND YOU LOOK GREAT!!!
I DO?
NOTHING A SMILE WON'T FIX...
GREAT... I'LL GO GET MY TEETH...
©BoBScott

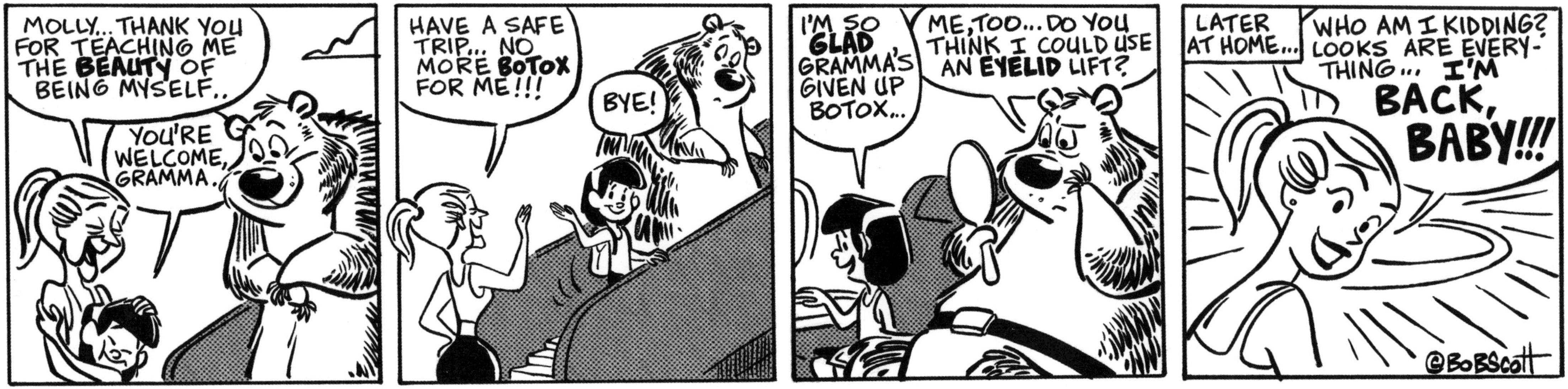
MOLLY... THANK YOU FOR TEACHING ME THE BEAUTY OF BEING MYSELF..
YOU'RE WELCOME, GRAMMA.
HAVE A SAFE TRIP... NO MORE BOTOX FOR ME!!!
BYE!
I'M SO GLAD GRAMMA'S GIVEN UP BOTOX...
ME, TOO... DO YOU THINK I COULD USE AN EYELID LIFT?
LATER AT HOME...
WHO AM I KIDDING? LOOKS ARE EVERYTHING... I'M BACK, BABY!!!
©BOBSCOTT

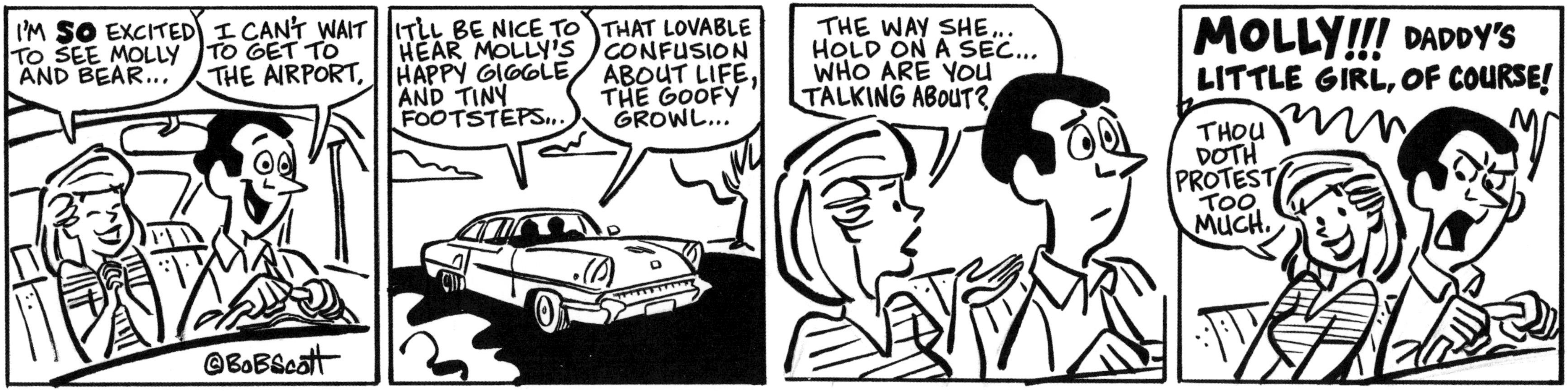
I'M SO EXCITED TO SEE MOLLY AND BEAR...
I CAN'T WAIT TO GET TO THE AIRPORT.
©BOBSCOTT
IT'LL BE NICE TO HEAR MOLLY'S HAPPY GIGGLE AND TINY FOOTSTEPS...
THAT LOVABLE CONFUSION ABOUT LIFE, THE GOOFY GROWL...
THE WAY SHE... HOLD ON A SEC... WHO ARE YOU TALKING ABOUT?
MOLLY!!! DADDY'S LITTLE GIRL, OF COURSE!
THOU DOTH PROTEST TOO MUCH.

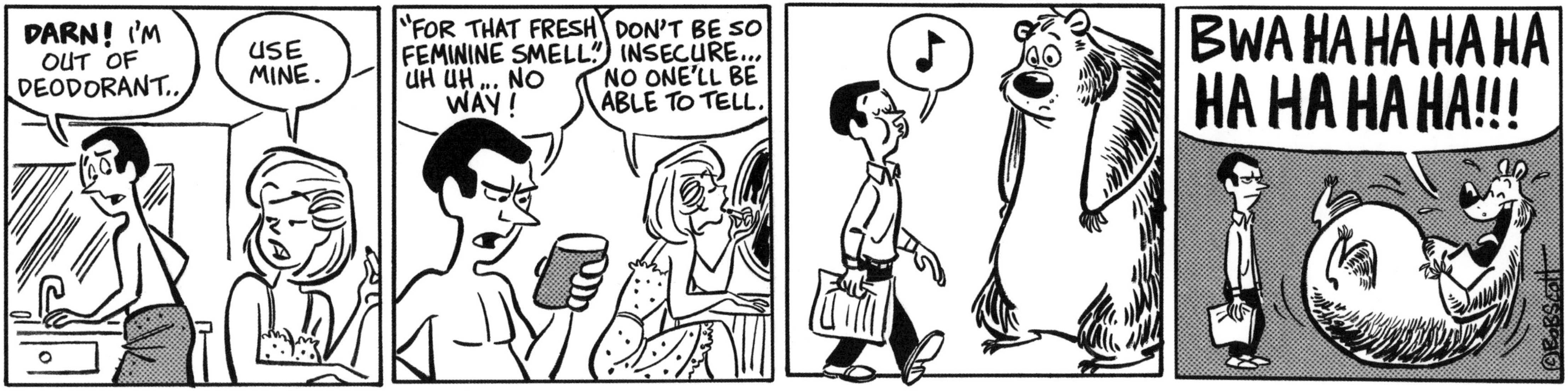
DARN! I'M OUT OF DEODORANT..
USE MINE.
"FOR THAT FRESH FEMININE SMELL." UH UH... NO WAY!
DON'T BE SO INSECURE... NO ONE'LL BE ABLE TO TELL.
♪
BWA HA HA HA HA HA HA HA HA HA!!!
©BOBSCOTT

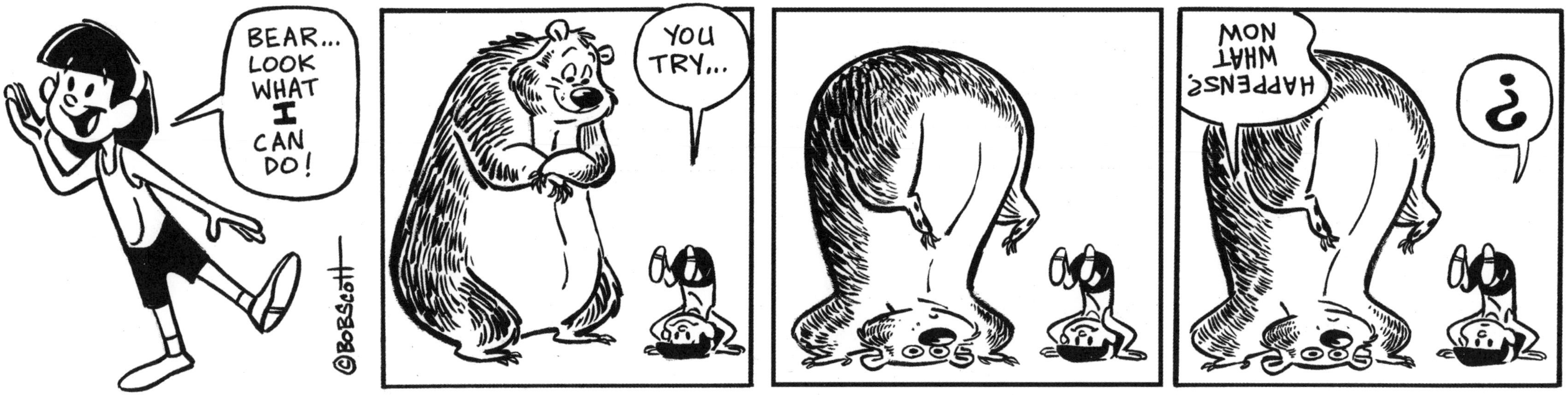
BEAR... LOOK WHAT I CAN DO!
©BOBSCOTT
YOU TRY...
NOW WHAT HAPPENS?
¿

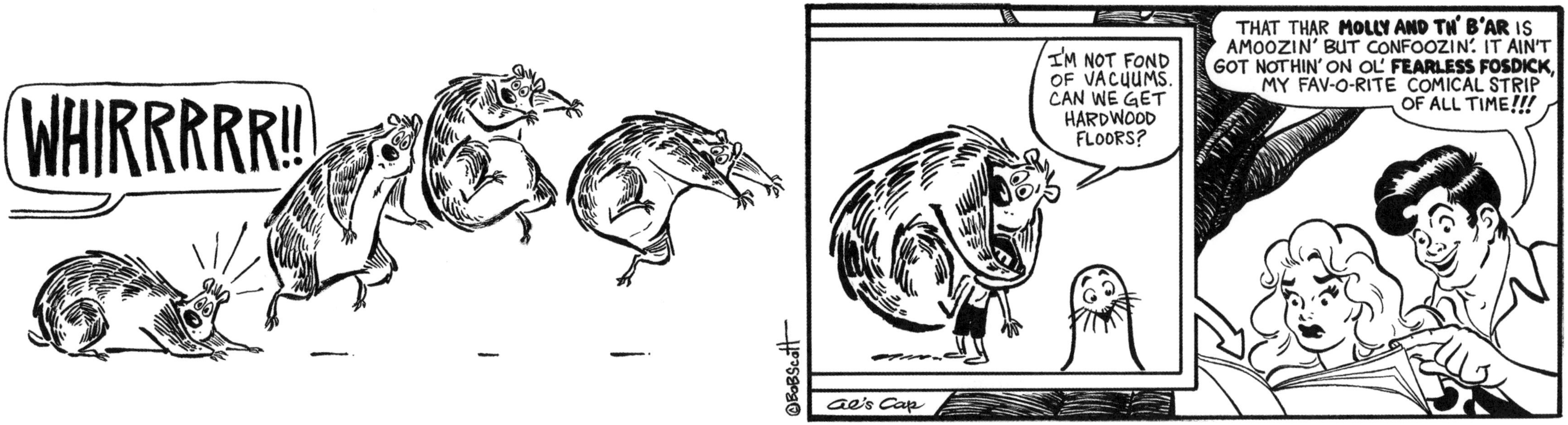
WHIRRRRR!!
©BOBScott
I'M NOT FOND OF VACUUMS. CAN WE GET HARDWOOD FLOORS?
Al's Cap
THAT THAR **MOLLY AND TH' B'AR** IS AMOOZIN' BUT CONFOOZIN'. IT AIN'T GOT NOTHIN' ON OL' **FEARLESS FOSDICK**, MY FAV-O-RITE COMICAL STRIP OF ALL TIME!!!

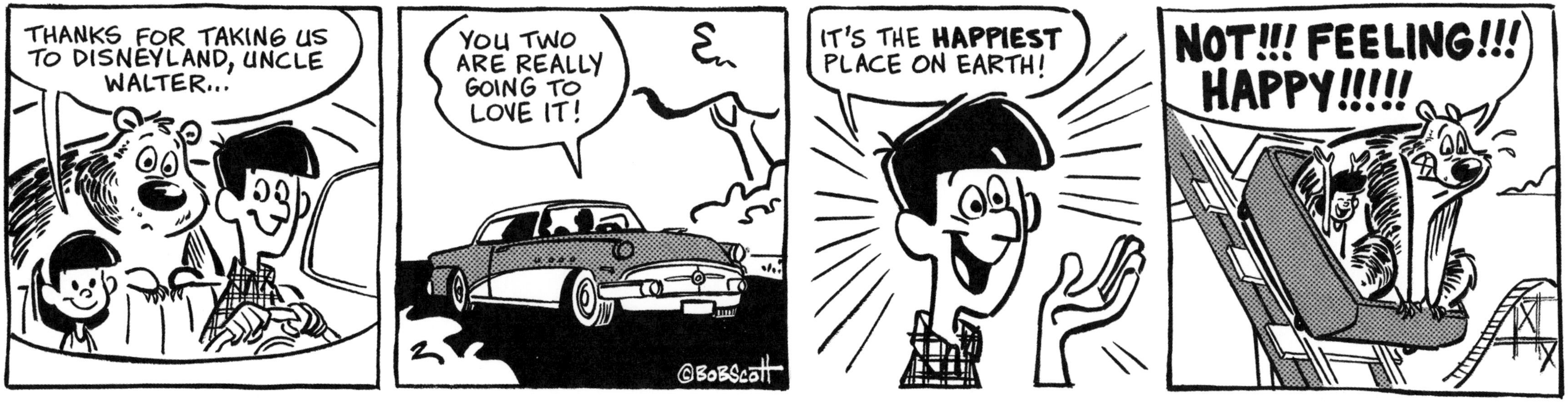
THANKS FOR TAKING US TO DISNEYLAND, UNCLE WALTER...
YOU TWO ARE REALLY GOING TO LOVE IT!
©BOBScott
IT'S THE **HAPPIEST** PLACE ON EARTH!
NOT!!! FEELING!!! HAPPY!!!!!

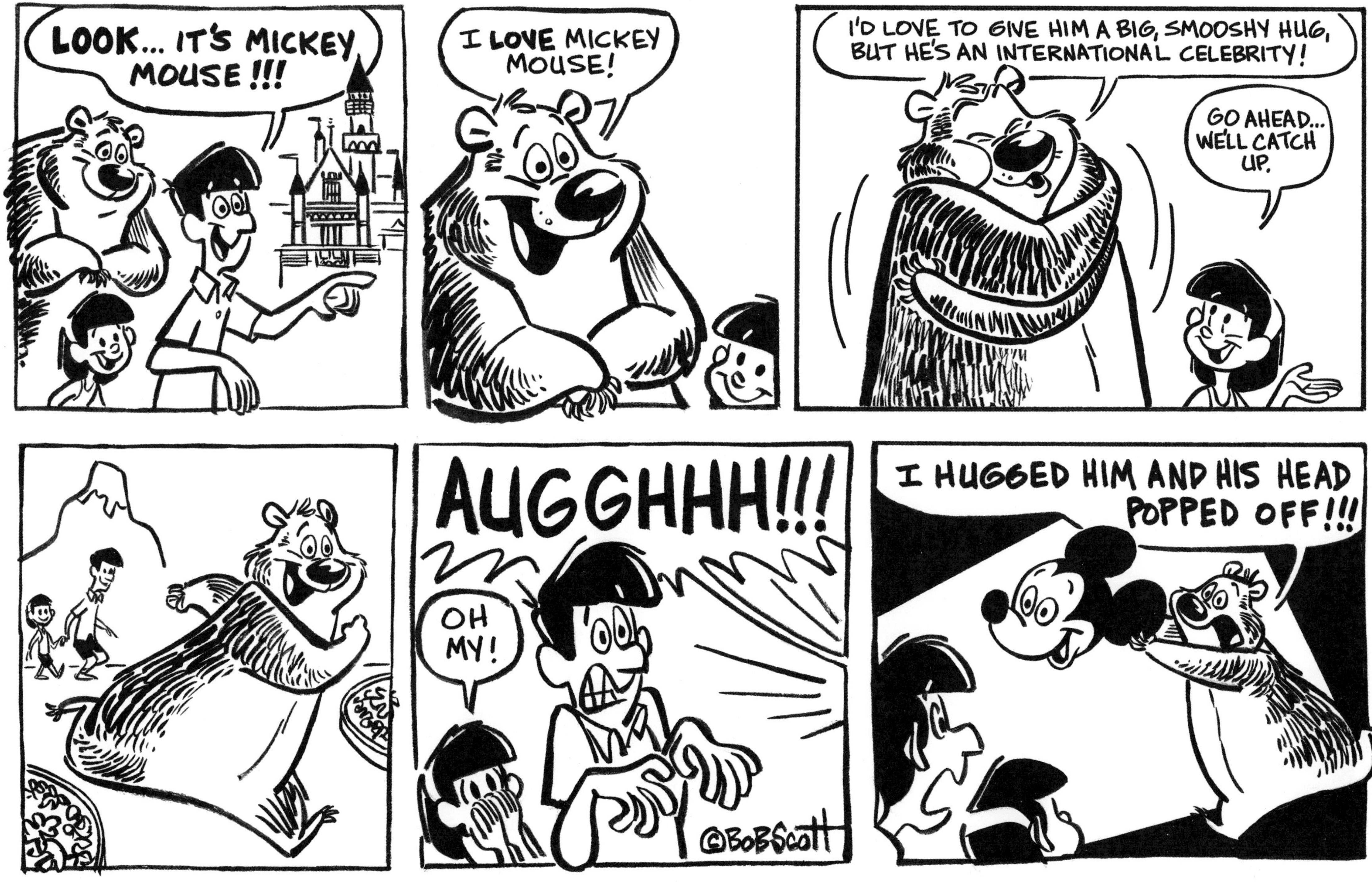
LOOK... IT'S MICKEY MOUSE!!!
I LOVE MICKEY MOUSE!
I'D LOVE TO GIVE HIM A BIG, SMOOSHY HUG, BUT HE'S AN INTERNATIONAL CELEBRITY!
GO AHEAD... WE'LL CATCH UP.
AUGGHHH!!!
OH MY!
©BOB SCOTT
I HUGGED HIM AND HIS HEAD POPPED OFF!!!

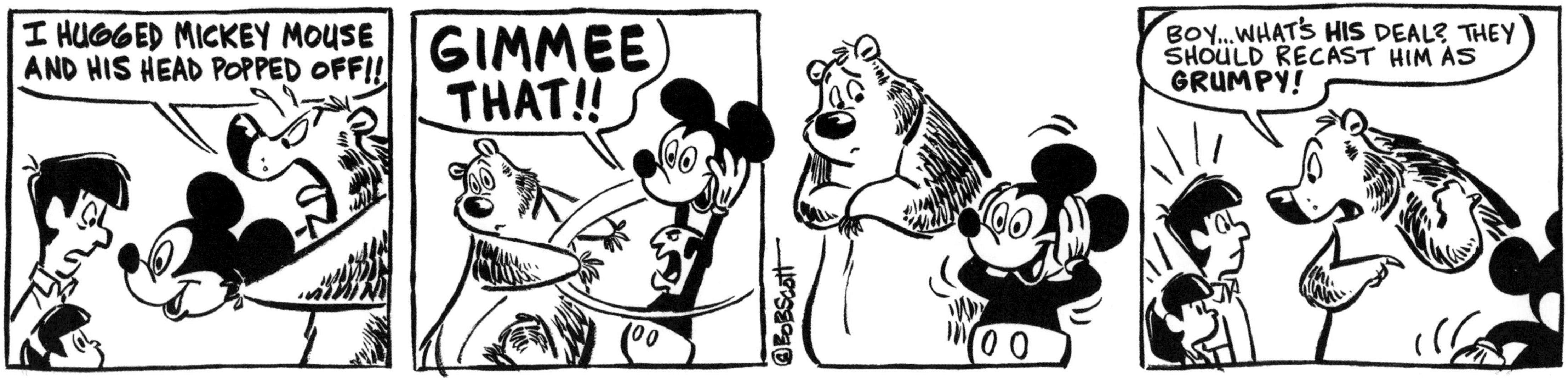
I HUGGED MICKEY MOUSE AND HIS HEAD POPPED OFF!!
GIMMEE THAT!!
©BOBSCOTT
BOY...WHAT'S HIS DEAL? THEY SHOULD RECAST HIM AS GRUMPY!

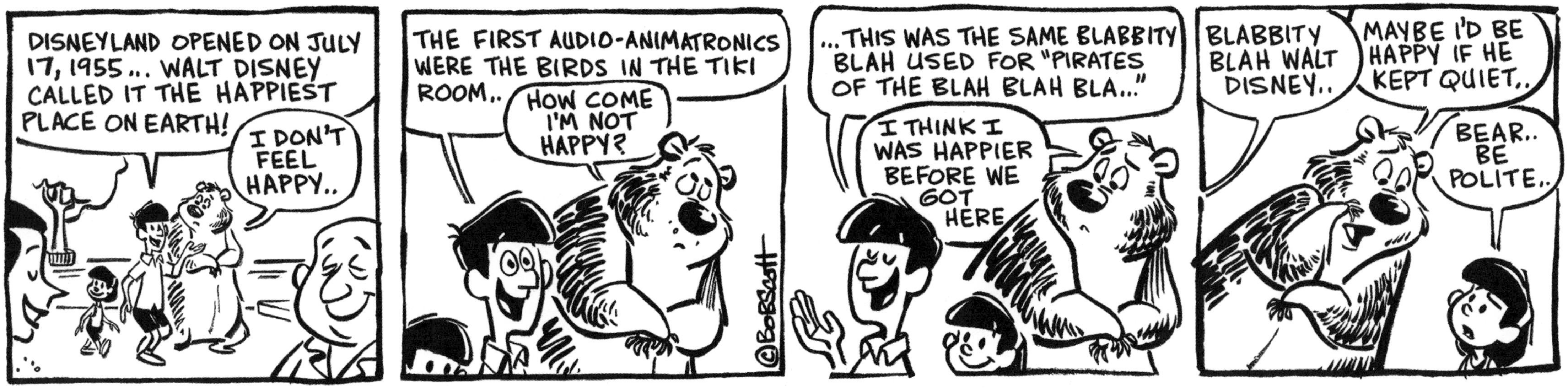
DISNEYLAND OPENED ON JULY 17, 1955... WALT DISNEY CALLED IT THE HAPPIEST PLACE ON EARTH!
I DON'T FEEL HAPPY..
THE FIRST AUDIO-ANIMATRONICS WERE THE BIRDS IN THE TIKI ROOM..
HOW COME I'M NOT HAPPY?
©BOBSCOTT
...THIS WAS THE SAME BLABBITY BLAH USED FOR "PIRATES OF THE BLAH BLAH BLA..."
I THINK I WAS HAPPIER BEFORE WE GOT HERE
BLABBITY BLAH WALT DISNEY..
MAYBE I'D BE HAPPY IF HE KEPT QUIET..
BEAR.. BE POLITE..

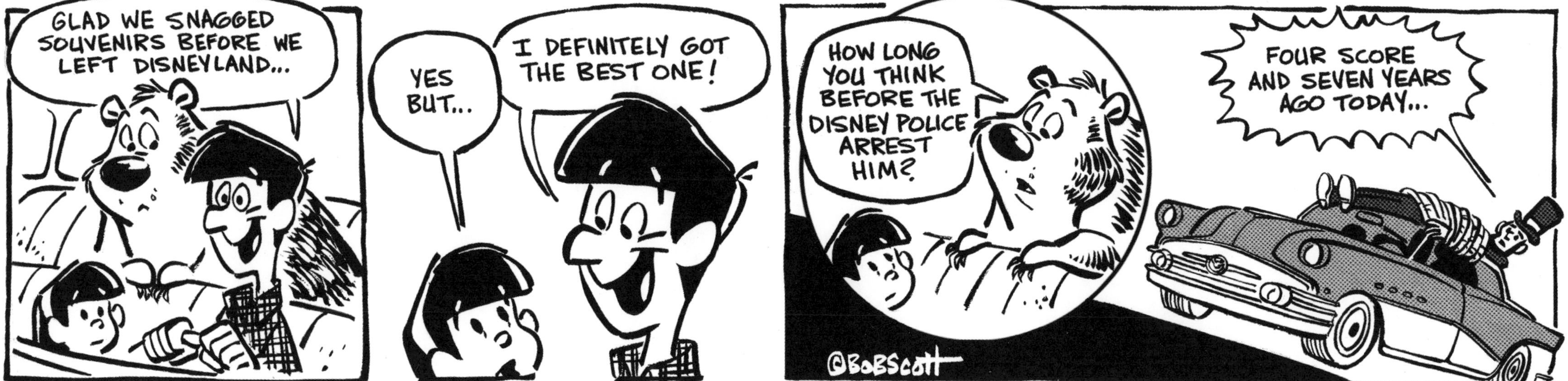
GLAD WE SNAGGED SOUVENIRS BEFORE WE LEFT DISNEYLAND...
YES BUT...
I DEFINITELY GOT THE BEST ONE!
HOW LONG YOU THINK BEFORE THE DISNEY POLICE ARREST HIM?
FOUR SCORE AND SEVEN YEARS AGO TODAY...
©BOBSCOTT

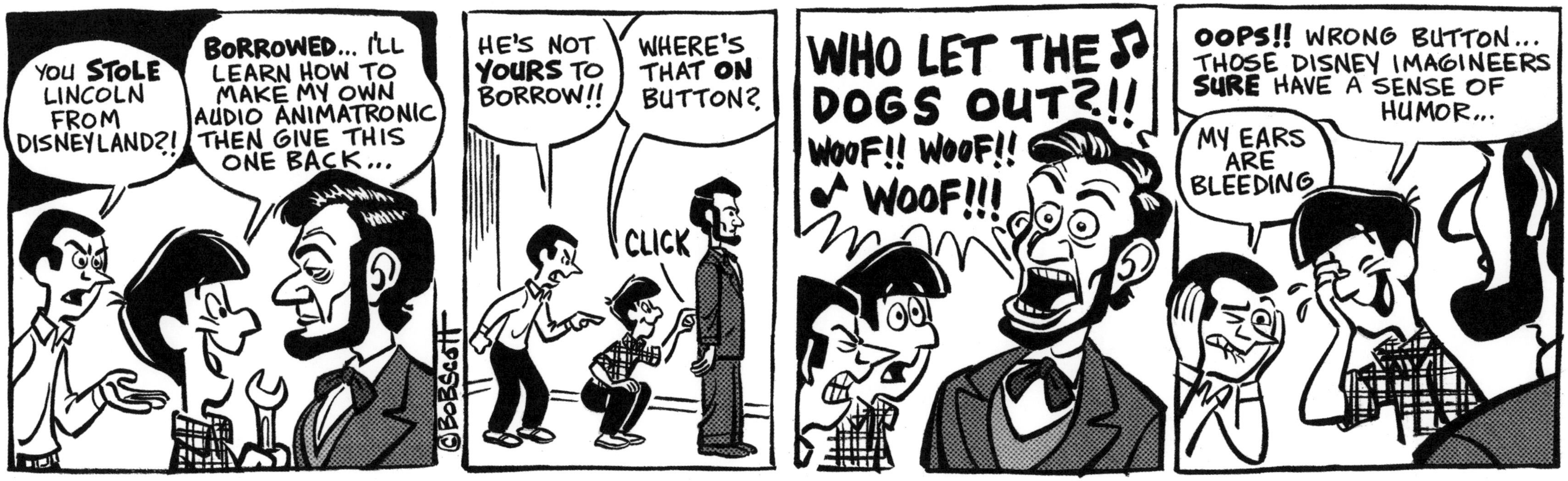
YOU **STOLE** LINCOLN FROM DISNEYLAND?!
BORROWED... I'LL LEARN HOW TO MAKE MY OWN AUDIO ANIMATRONIC THEN GIVE THIS ONE BACK...
©BOBSCOTT
HE'S NOT **YOURS** TO BORROW!!
WHERE'S THAT **ON** BUTTON?
CLICK
WHO LET THE DOGS OUT?!!
WOOF!! WOOF!! WOOF!!!
OOPS!! WRONG BUTTON... THOSE DISNEY IMAGINEERS **SURE** HAVE A SENSE OF HUMOR...
MY EARS ARE BLEEDING

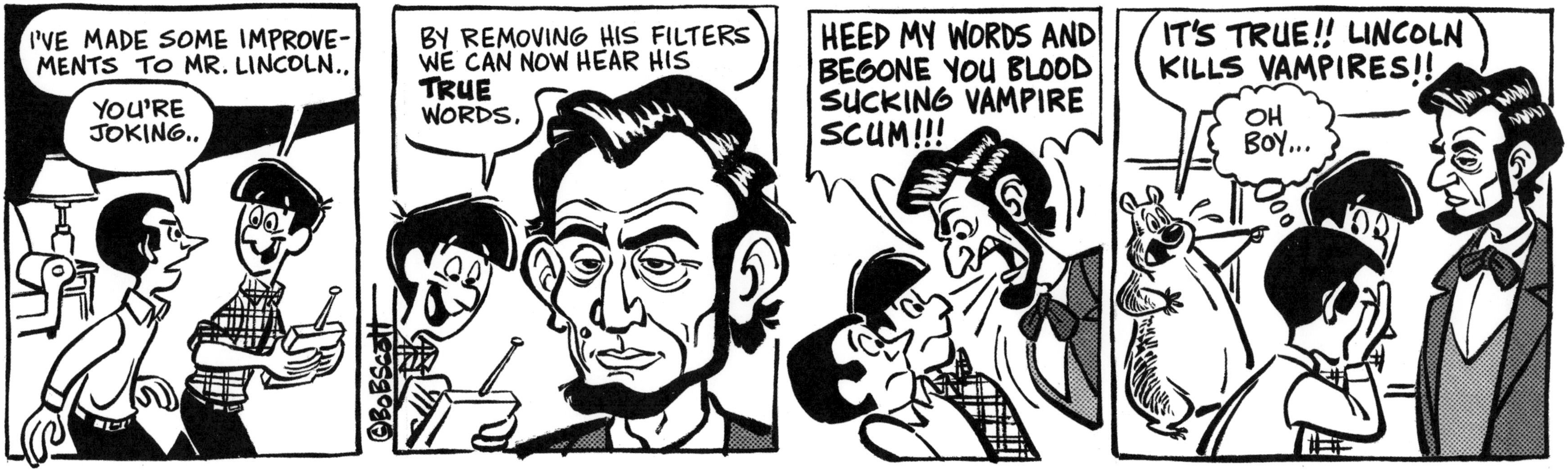
I'VE MADE SOME IMPROVEMENTS TO MR. LINCOLN..
YOU'RE JOKING..
BY REMOVING HIS FILTERS WE CAN NOW HEAR HIS **TRUE** WORDS.
©BOBSCOTT
HEED MY WORDS AND BEGONE YOU BLOOD SUCKING VAMPIRE SCUM!!!
IT'S TRUE!! LINCOLN KILLS VAMPIRES!!
OH BOY...

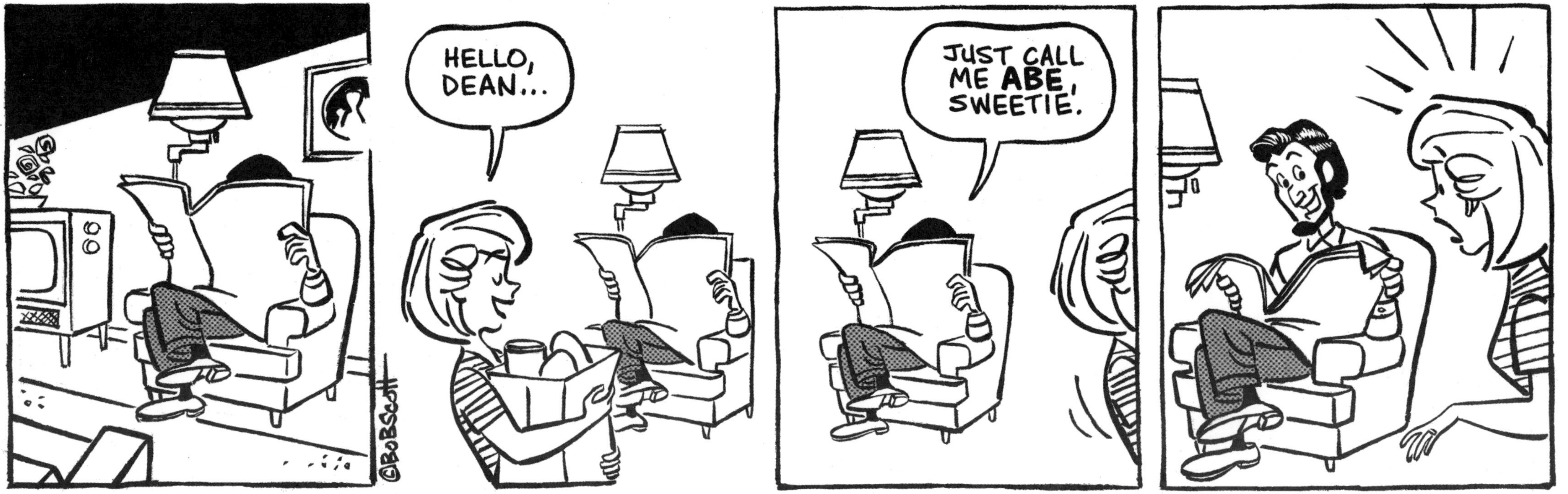
©BOBSCOTT
HELLO, DEAN...
JUST CALL ME **ABE**, SWEETIE.

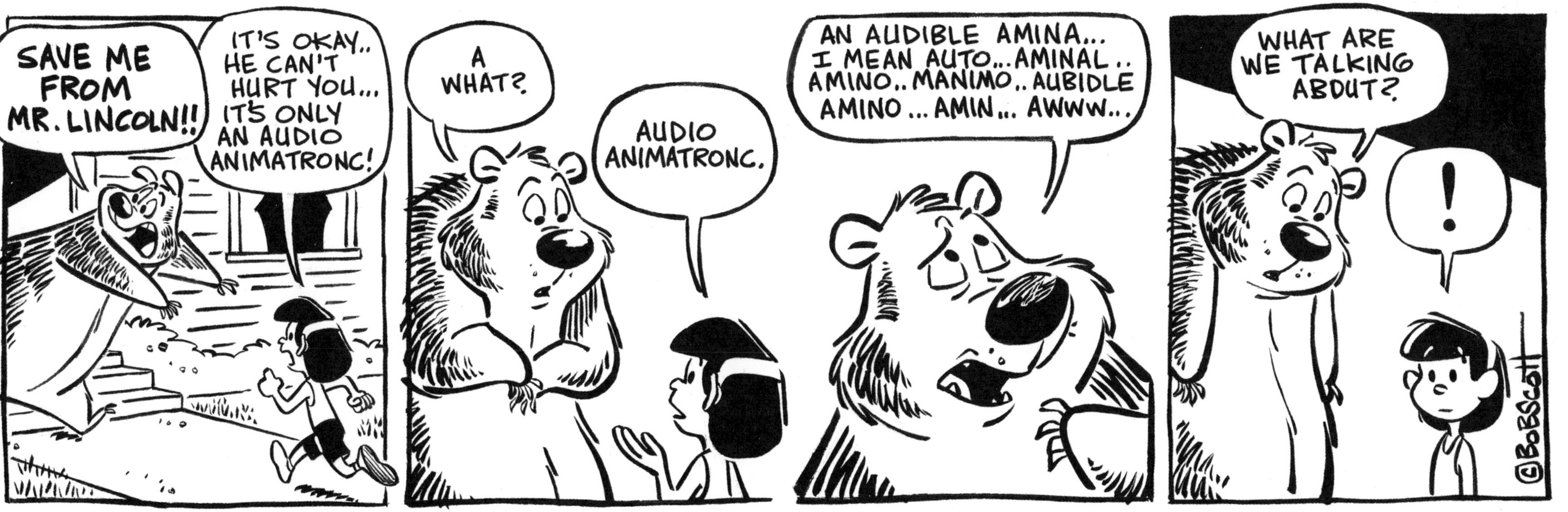
SAVE ME FROM MR. LINCOLN!!
IT'S OKAY.. HE CAN'T HURT YOU... IT'S ONLY AN AUDIO ANIMATRONC!
A WHAT?
AUDIO ANIMATRONC.
AN AUDIBLE AMINA... I MEAN AUTO... AMINAL.. AMINO.. MANIMO.. AUBIDLE AMINO ... AMIN... AWWW...
WHAT ARE WE TALKING ABOUT?
!
©BOBSCOTT

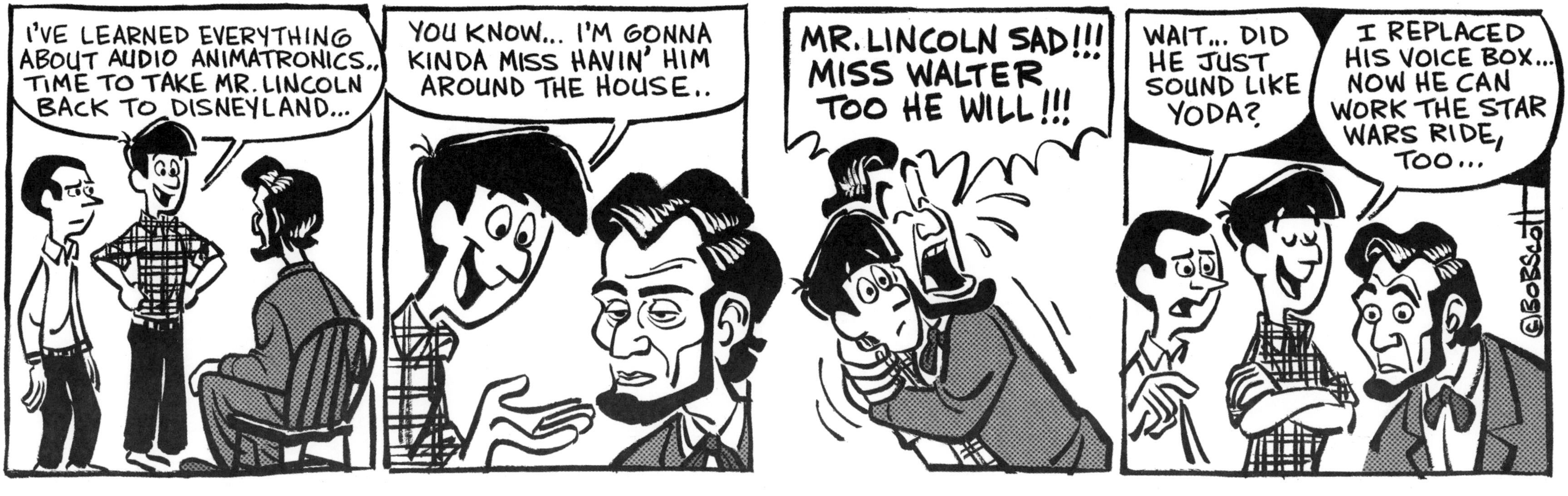
I'VE LEARNED EVERYTHING ABOUT AUDIO ANIMATRONICS.. TIME TO TAKE MR. LINCOLN BACK TO DISNEYLAND...
YOU KNOW... I'M GONNA KINDA MISS HAVIN' HIM AROUND THE HOUSE..
MR. LINCOLN SAD!!! MISS WALTER TOO HE WILL!!!
WAIT... DID HE JUST SOUND LIKE YODA?
I REPLACED HIS VOICE BOX... NOW HE CAN WORK THE STAR WARS RIDE, TOO...
©BOBSCOTT

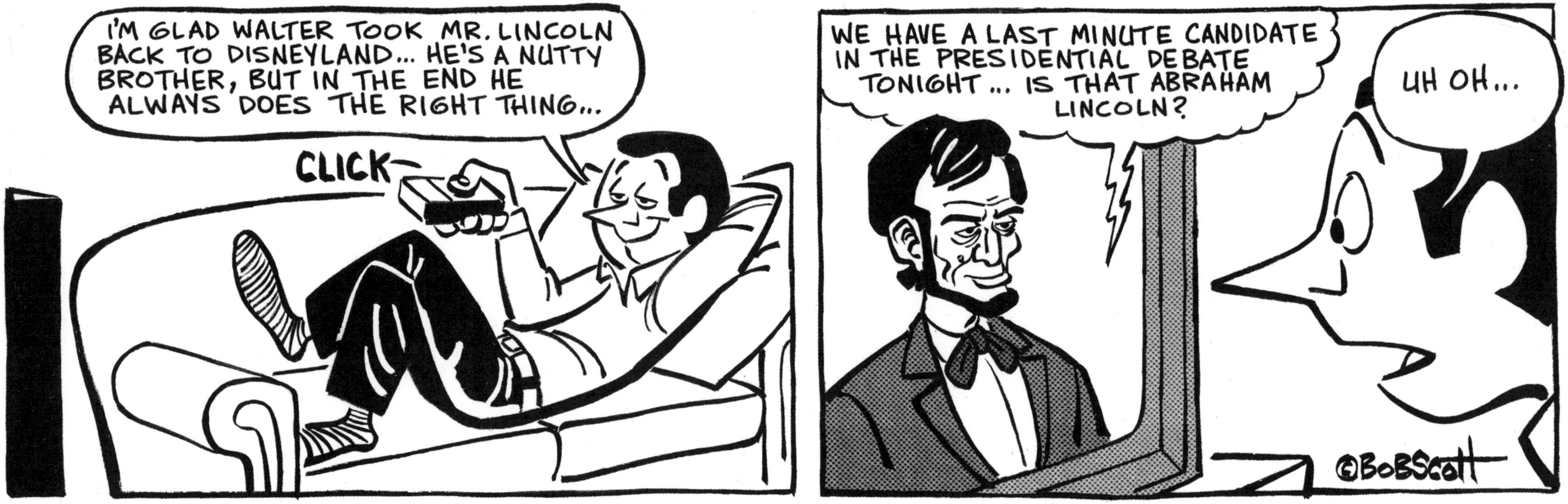
I'M GLAD WALTER TOOK MR. LINCOLN BACK TO DISNEYLAND... HE'S A NUTTY BROTHER, BUT IN THE END HE ALWAYS DOES THE RIGHT THING...
CLICK
WE HAVE A LAST MINUTE CANDIDATE IN THE PRESIDENTIAL DEBATE TONIGHT... IS THAT ABRAHAM LINCOLN?
UH OH...
©BOBSCOTT

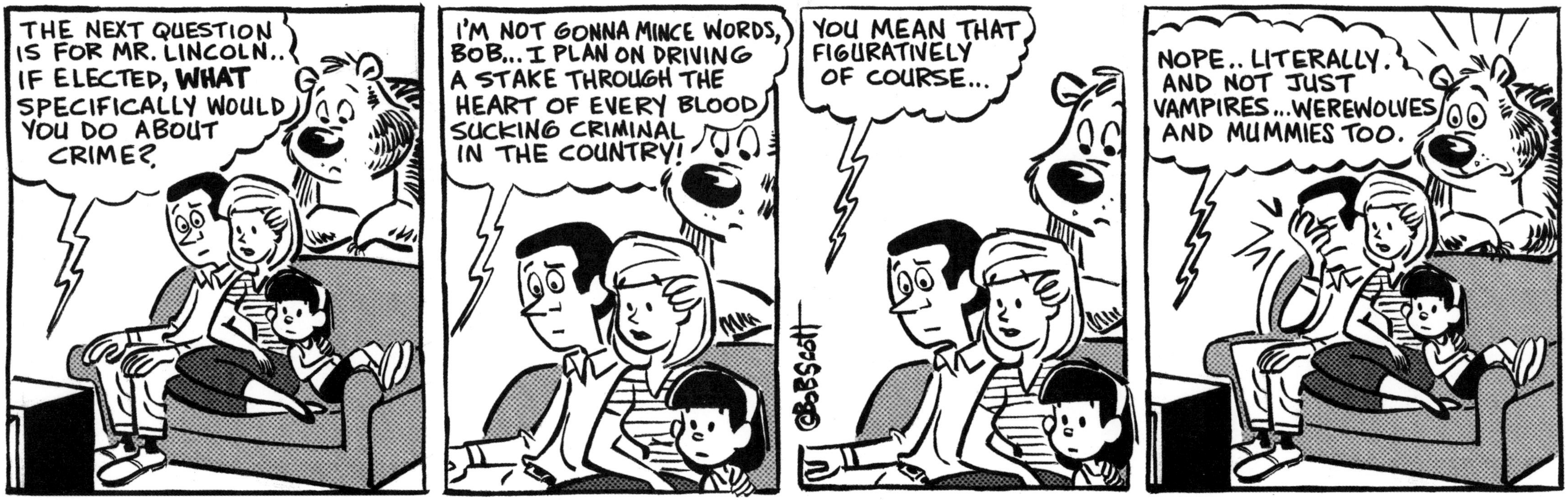
THE NEXT QUESTION IS FOR MR. LINCOLN.. IF ELECTED, WHAT SPECIFICALLY WOULD YOU DO ABOUT CRIME?
I'M NOT GONNA MINCE WORDS, BOB... I PLAN ON DRIVING A STAKE THROUGH THE HEART OF EVERY BLOOD SUCKING CRIMINAL IN THE COUNTRY!
©BOBSCOTT
YOU MEAN THAT FIGURATIVELY OF COURSE...
NOPE.. LITERALLY. AND NOT JUST VAMPIRES...WEREWOLVES AND MUMMIES TOO.

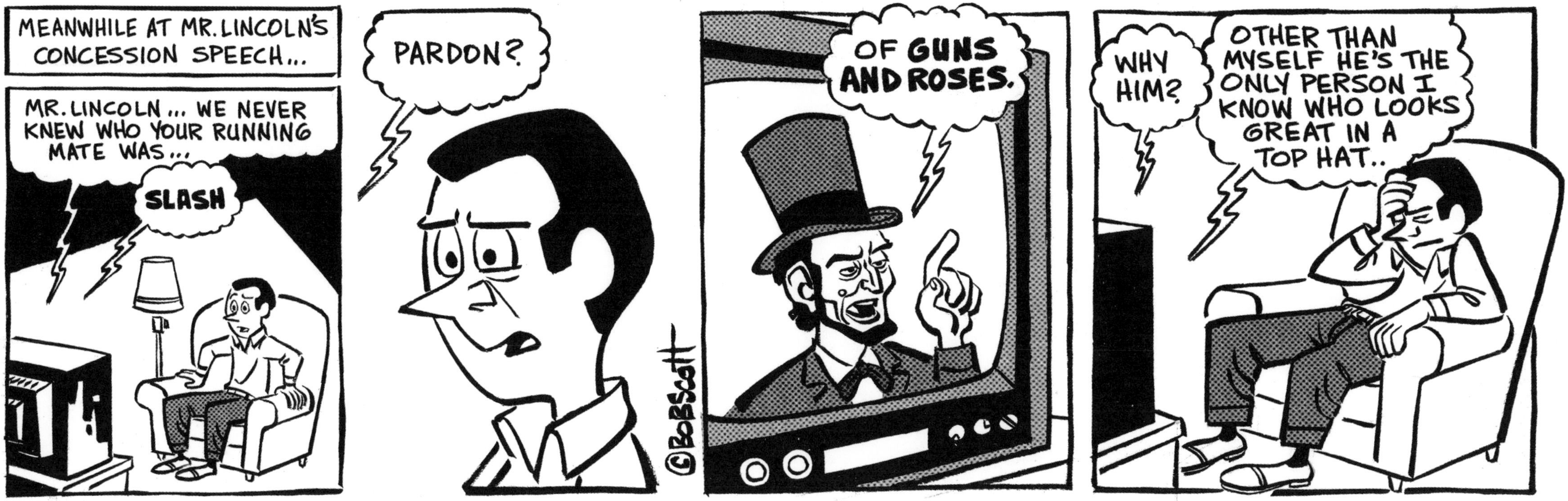
MEANWHILE AT MR. LINCOLN'S CONCESSION SPEECH...
MR. LINCOLN... WE NEVER KNEW WHO YOUR RUNNING MATE WAS...
SLASH
PARDON?
©BOBSCOTT
OF GUNS AND ROSES.
WHY HIM?
OTHER THAN MYSELF HE'S THE ONLY PERSON I KNOW WHO LOOKS GREAT IN A TOP HAT..

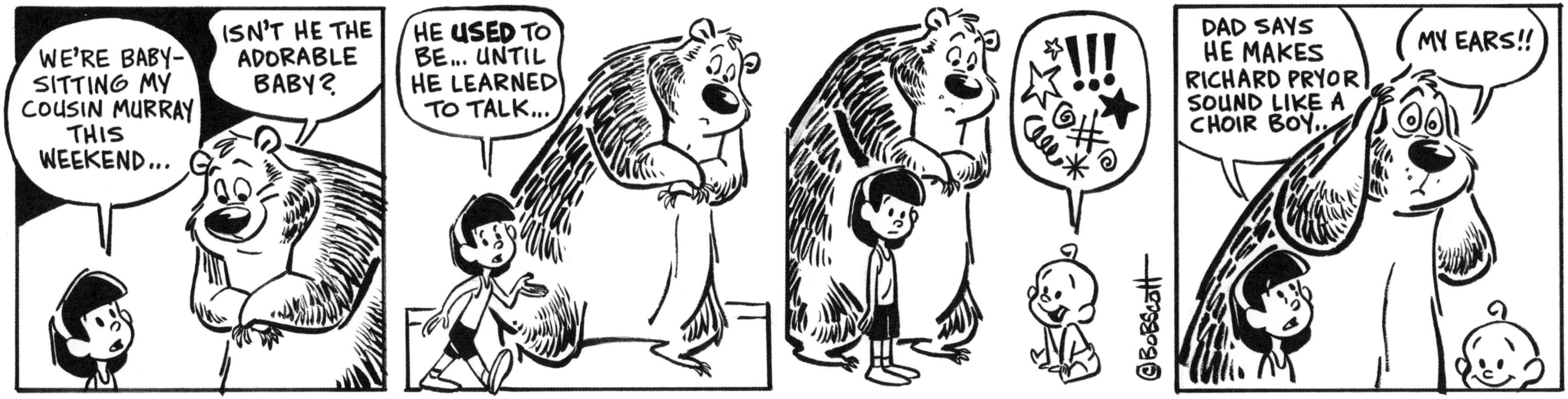
WE'RE BABY-SITTING MY COUSIN MURRAY THIS WEEKEND...
ISN'T HE THE ADORABLE BABY?
HE USED TO BE... UNTIL HE LEARNED TO TALK...
!!!
©BOBSCOTT
DAD SAYS HE MAKES RICHARD PRYOR SOUND LIKE A CHOIR BOY..
MY EARS!!

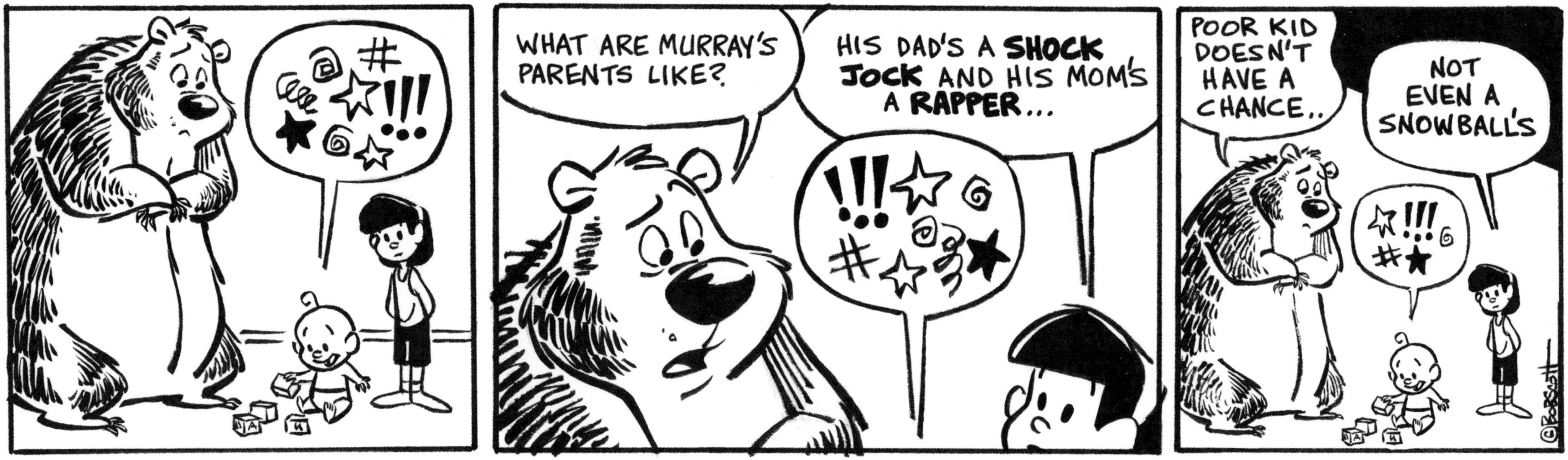
WHAT ARE MURRAY'S PARENTS LIKE?
HIS DAD'S A **SHOCK JOCK** AND HIS MOM'S A **RAPPER**...
POOR KID DOESN'T HAVE A CHANCE..
NOT EVEN A SNOWBALL'S
©BOBSCOTT

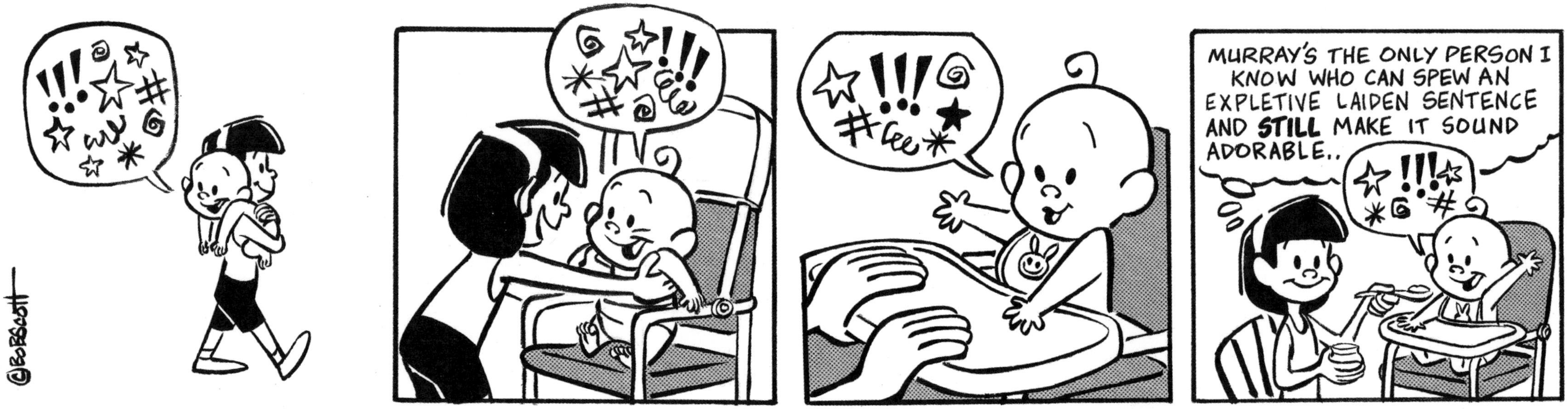
©BOBSCOTT
MURRAY'S THE ONLY PERSON I KNOW WHO CAN SPEW AN EXPLETIVE LAIDEN SENTENCE AND **STILL** MAKE IT SOUND ADORABLE..

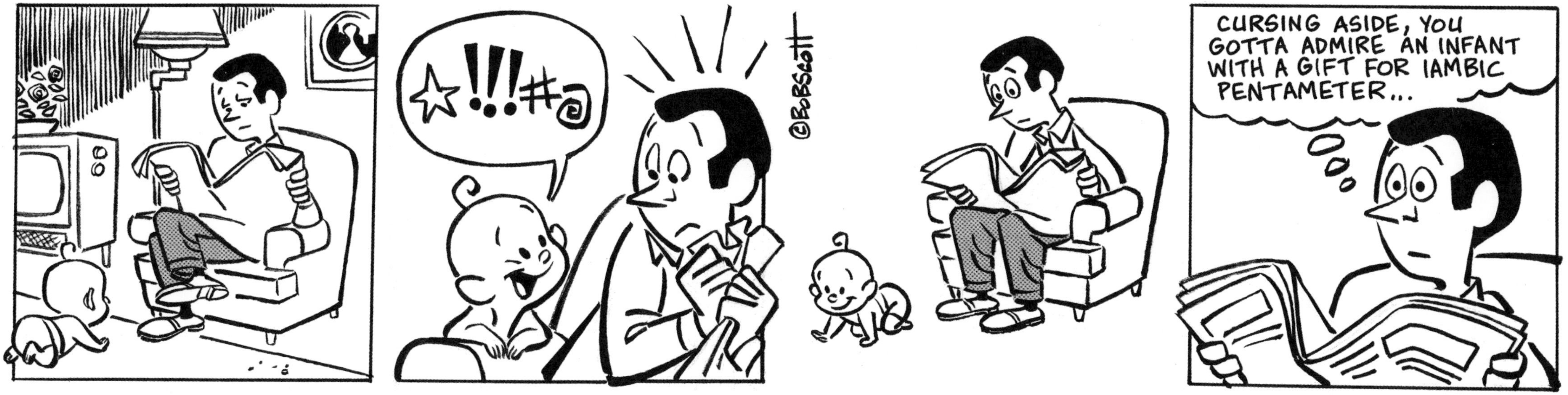
©BOBSCOTT
CURSING ASIDE, YOU GOTTA ADMIRE AN INFANT WITH A GIFT FOR IAMBIC PENTAMETER...

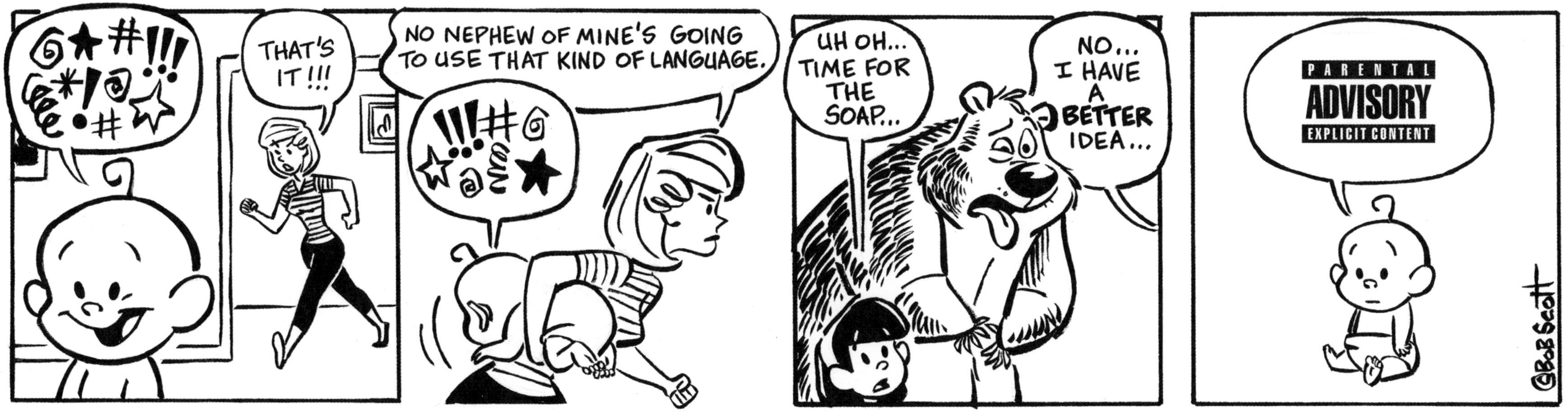
THAT'S IT!!!
NO NEPHEW OF MINE'S GOING TO USE THAT KIND OF LANGUAGE.
UH OH... TIME FOR THE SOAP...
NO... I HAVE A BETTER IDEA...
PARENTAL ADVISORY EXPLICIT CONTENT
©BOBSCOTT

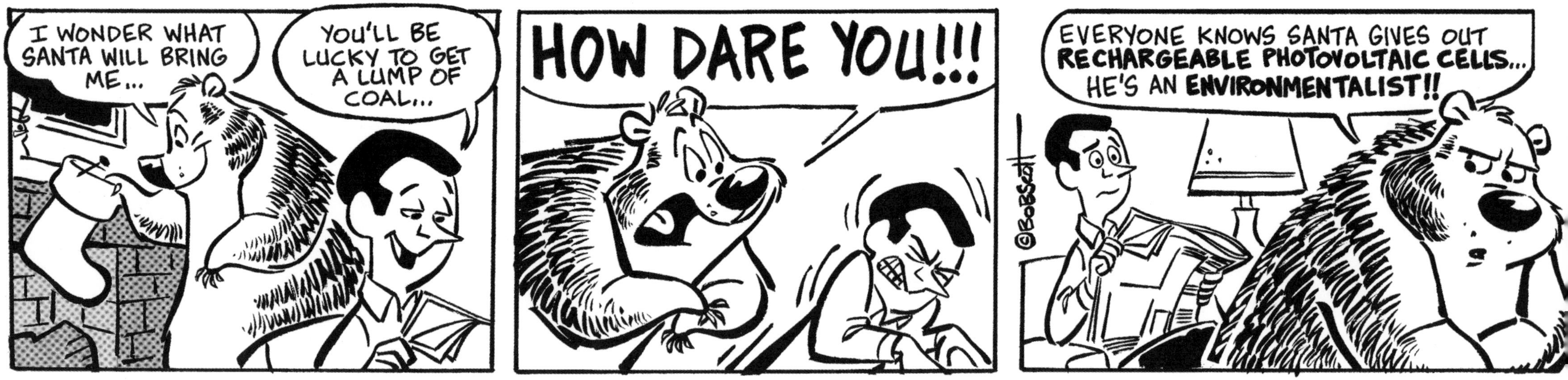
I WONDER WHAT SANTA WILL BRING ME...
YOU'LL BE LUCKY TO GET A LUMP OF COAL...
HOW DARE YOU!!!
EVERYONE KNOWS SANTA GIVES OUT RECHARGEABLE PHOTOVOLTAIC CELLS... HE'S AN ENVIRONMENTALIST!!
©BOBSCOTT

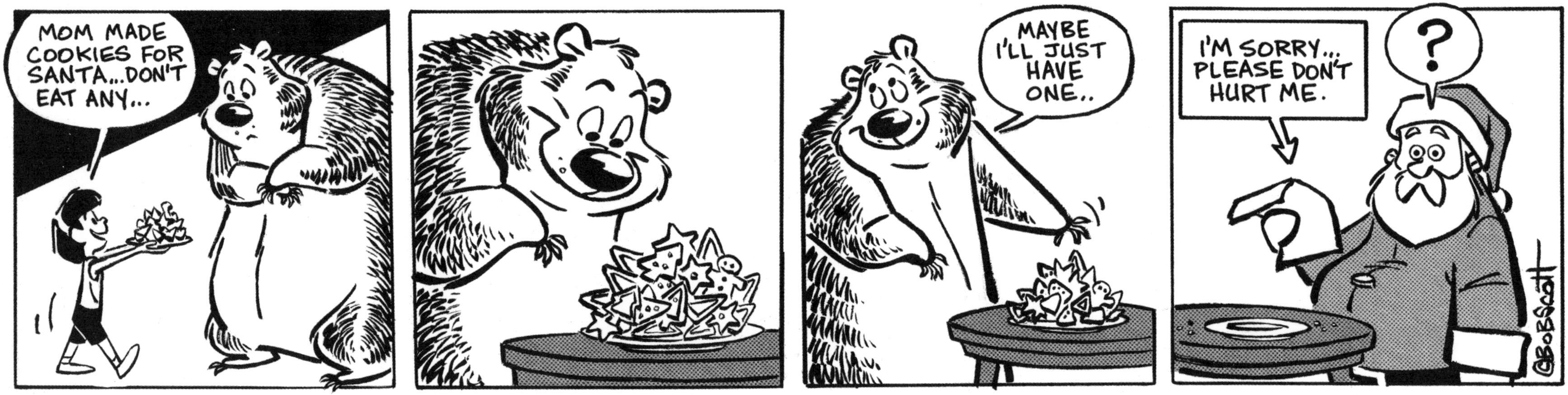
MOM MADE COOKIES FOR SANTA...DON'T EAT ANY...
MAYBE I'LL JUST HAVE ONE..
I'M SORRY... PLEASE DON'T HURT ME.
?
©BOBSCOTT

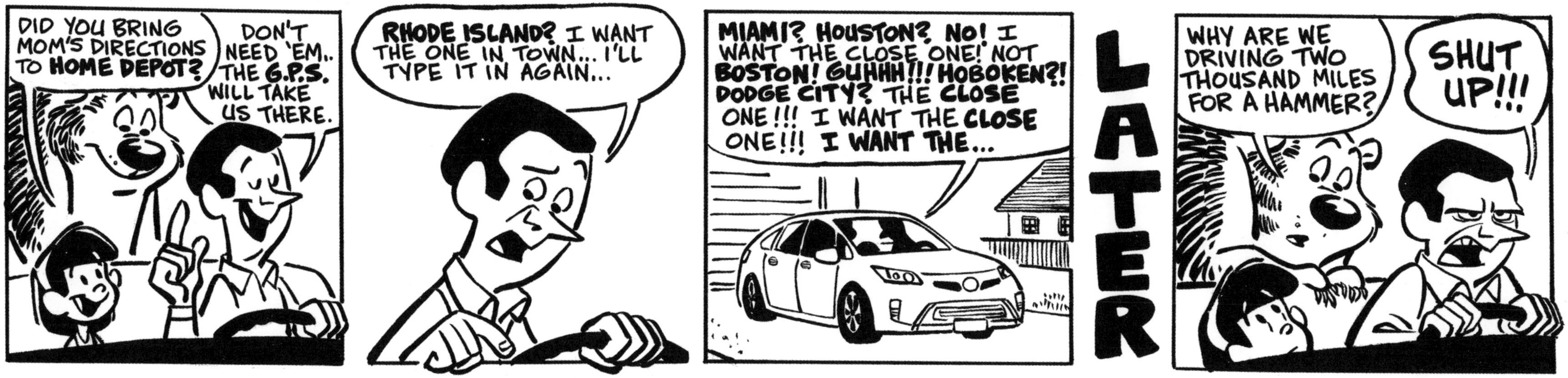
DID YOU BRING MOM'S DIRECTIONS TO HOME DEPOT?
DON'T NEED 'EM.. THE G.P.S. WILL TAKE US THERE.
RHODE ISLAND? I WANT THE ONE IN TOWN... I'LL TYPE IT IN AGAIN...
MIAMI? HOUSTON? NO! I WANT THE CLOSE ONE! NOT BOSTON! GUHHH!!! HOBOKEN?! DODGE CITY? THE CLOSE ONE!!! I WANT THE CLOSE ONE!!! I WANT THE...
LATER
WHY ARE WE DRIVING TWO THOUSAND MILES FOR A HAMMER?
SHUT UP!!!

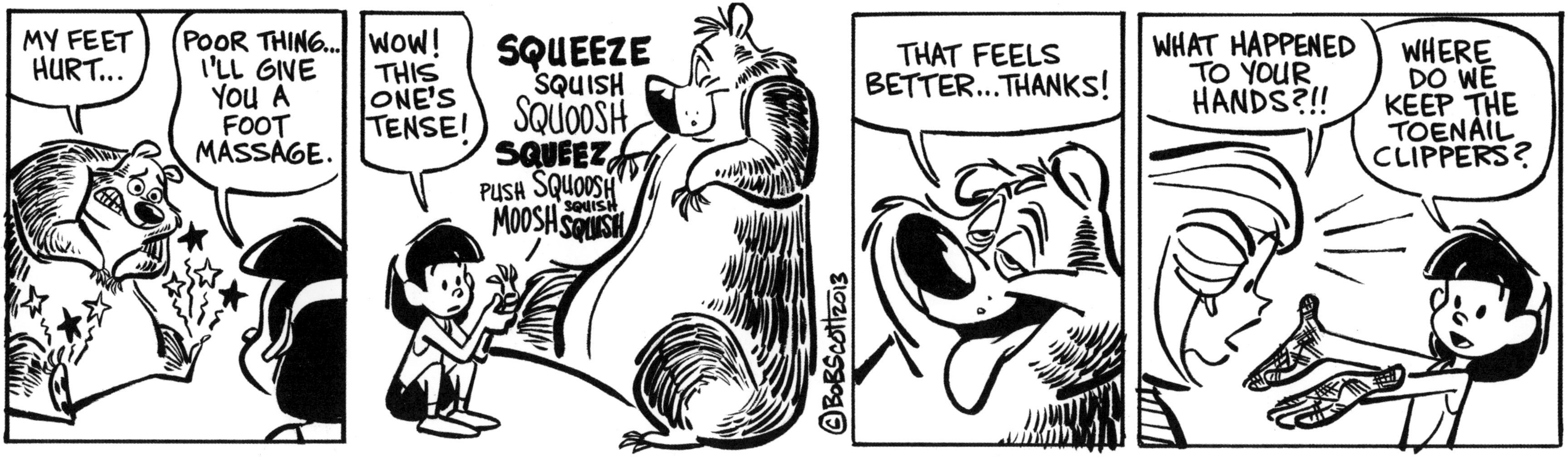
MY FEET HURT...
POOR THING... I'LL GIVE YOU A FOOT MASSAGE.
WOW! THIS ONE'S TENSE!
SQUEEZE
SQUISH
SQUOOSH
SQUEEZ
PUSH SQUOOSH
SQUISH
MOOSH SQUISH
©BOBSCOTT2013
THAT FEELS BETTER...THANKS!
WHAT HAPPENED TO YOUR HANDS?!!
WHERE DO WE KEEP THE TOENAIL CLIPPERS?

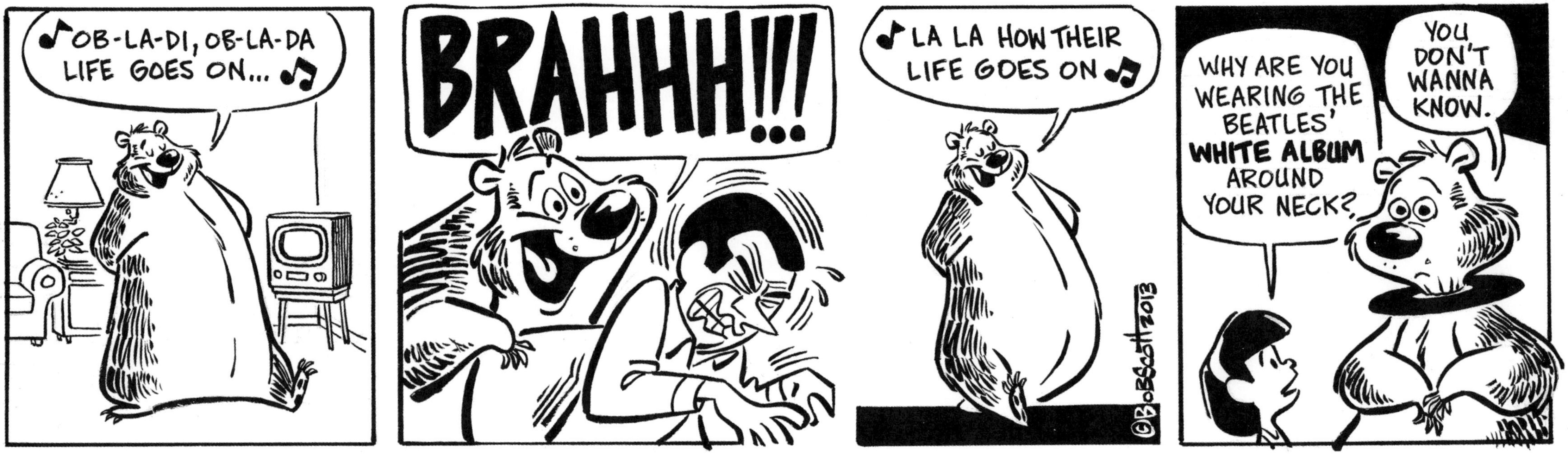
OB-LA-DI, OB-LA-DA LIFE GOES ON...
BRAHHH!!!...
LA LA HOW THEIR LIFE GOES ON
©BOBSCOTT2013
WHY ARE YOU WEARING THE BEATLES' **WHITE ALBUM** AROUND YOUR NECK?
YOU DON'T WANNA KNOW.

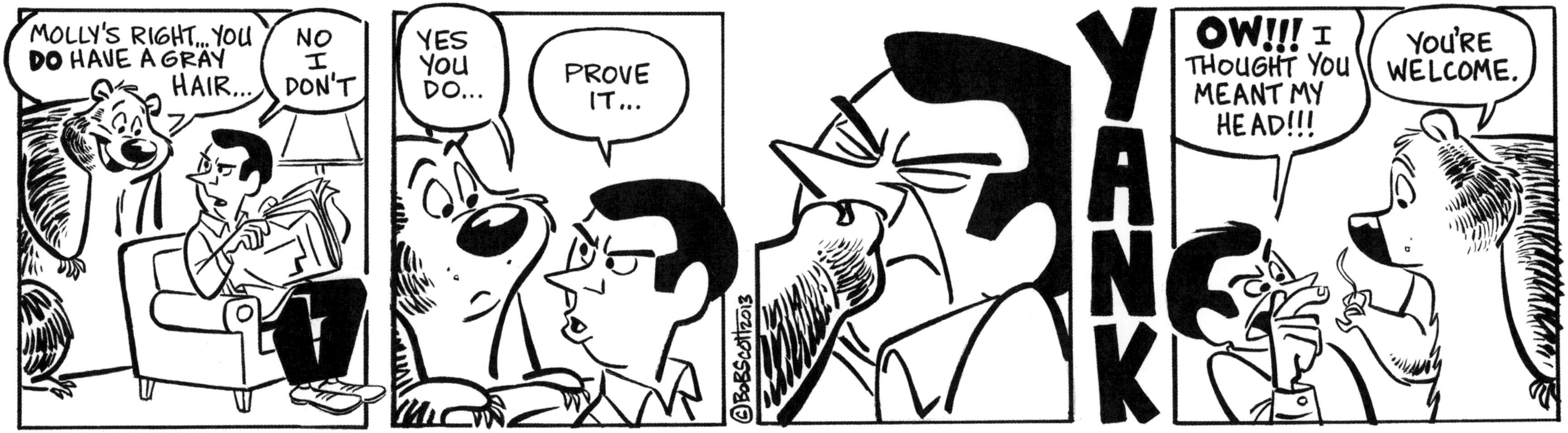
MOLLY'S RIGHT... YOU **DO** HAVE A GRAY HAIR...
NO I DON'T
YES YOU DO...
PROVE IT...
©BOBSCOTT2013
YANK
OW!!! I THOUGHT YOU MEANT MY HEAD!!!
YOU'RE WELCOME.

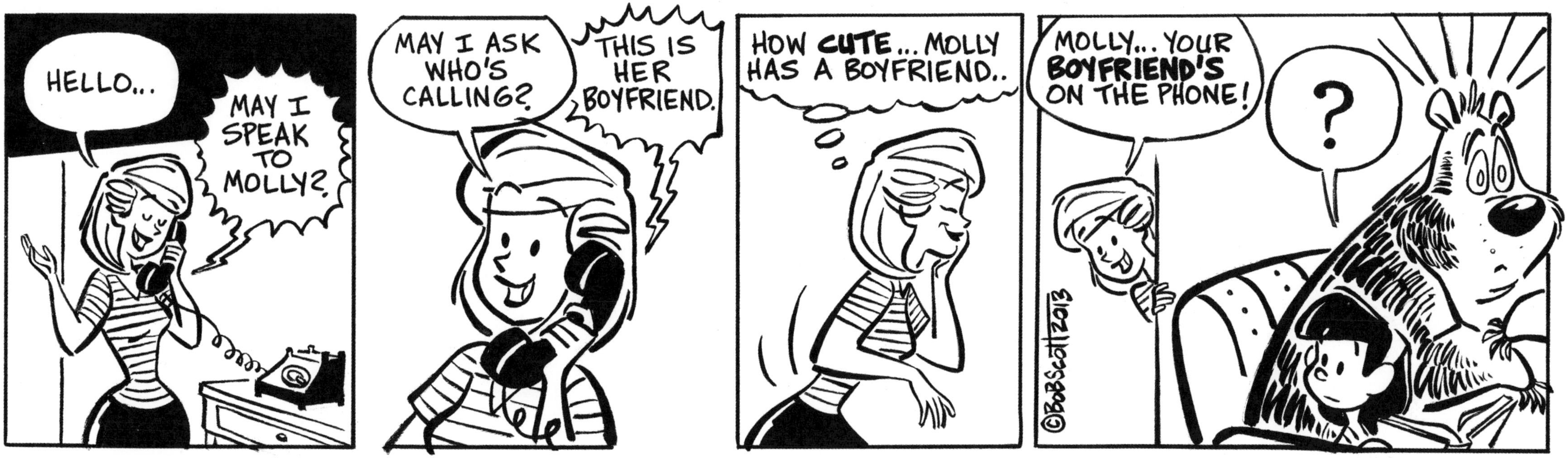
HELLO...
MAY I SPEAK TO MOLLY?
MAY I ASK WHO'S CALLING?
THIS IS HER BOYFRIEND.
HOW CUTE... MOLLY HAS A BOYFRIEND..
MOLLY... YOUR BOYFRIEND'S ON THE PHONE!
?
©BOBSCOTT2013

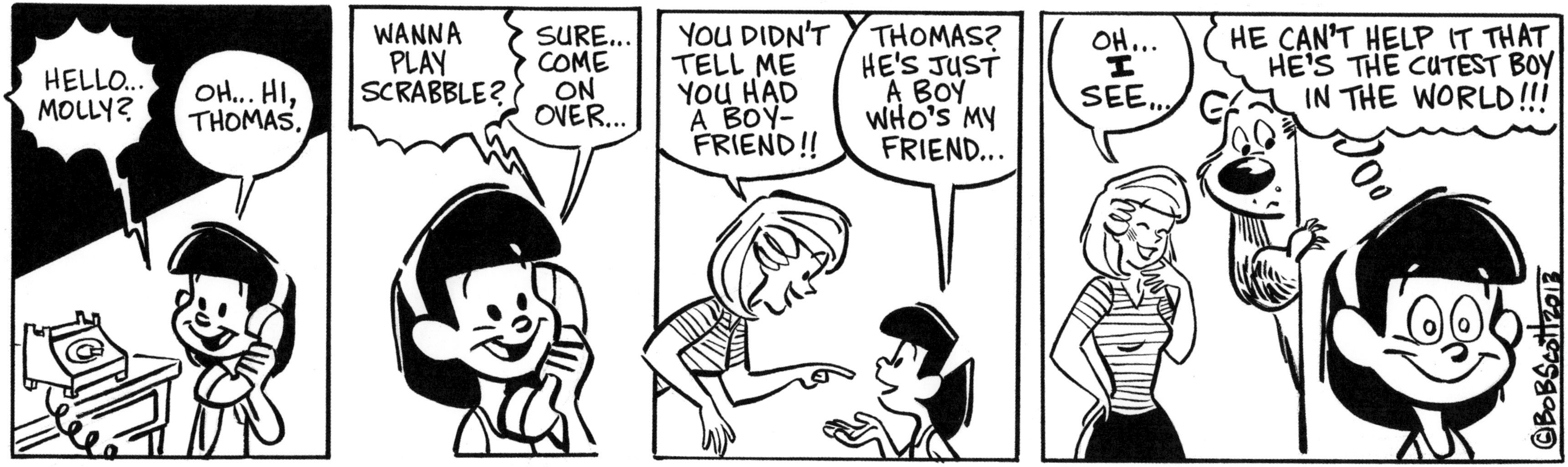
HELLO... MOLLY?
OH... HI, THOMAS.
WANNA PLAY SCRABBLE?
SURE... COME ON OVER...
YOU DIDN'T TELL ME YOU HAD A BOY-FRIEND!!
THOMAS? HE'S JUST A BOY WHO'S MY FRIEND...
OH... I SEE...
HE CAN'T HELP IT THAT HE'S THE CUTEST BOY IN THE WORLD!!!
©BOBSCOTT2013

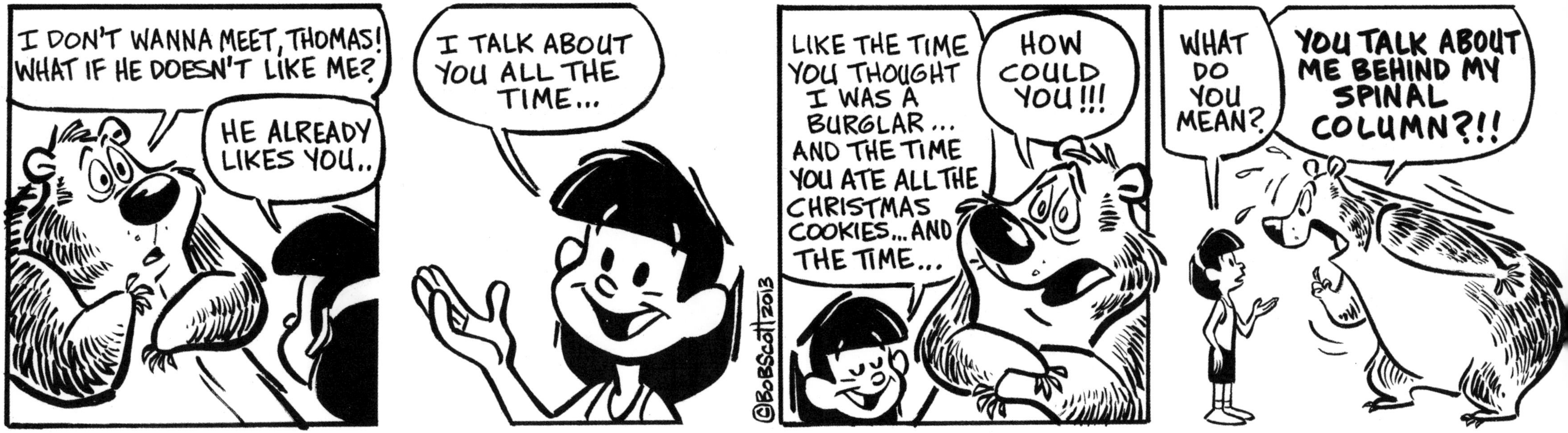
I DON'T WANNA MEET, THOMAS! WHAT IF HE DOESN'T LIKE ME?
HE ALREADY LIKES YOU..
I TALK ABOUT YOU ALL THE TIME...
©BoBSCott2013
LIKE THE TIME YOU THOUGHT I WAS A BURGLAR... AND THE TIME YOU ATE ALL THE CHRISTMAS COOKIES... AND THE TIME...
HOW COULD YOU!!!
WHAT DO YOU MEAN?
YOU TALK ABOUT ME BEHIND MY SPINAL COLUMN?!!

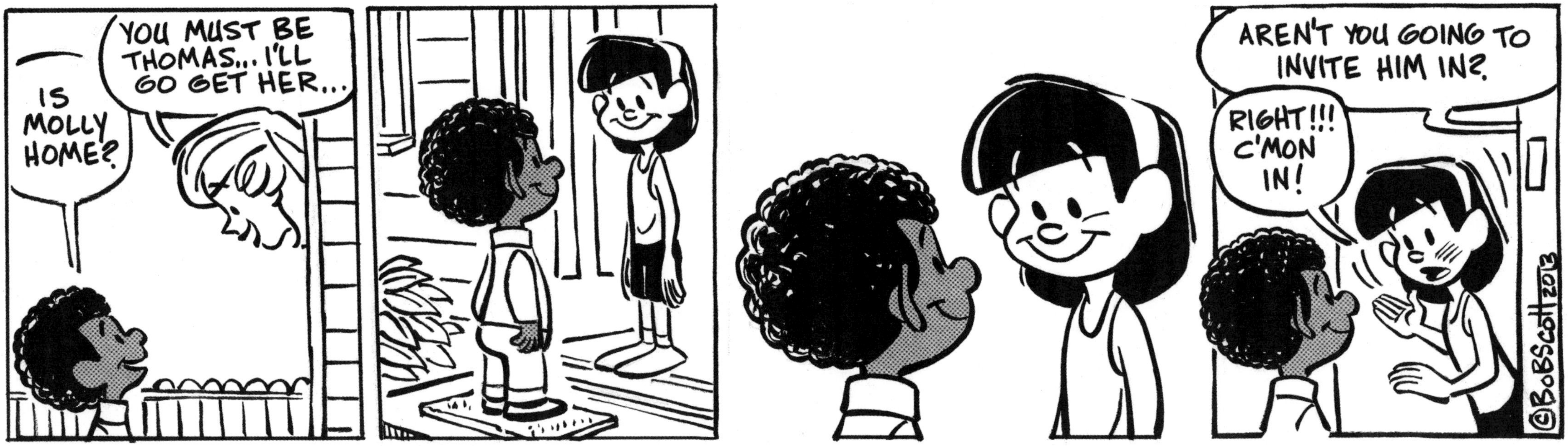
IS MOLLY HOME?
YOU MUST BE THOMAS... I'LL GO GET HER...
AREN'T YOU GOING TO INVITE HIM IN?
RIGHT!!! C'MON IN!
©BoBSCott2013

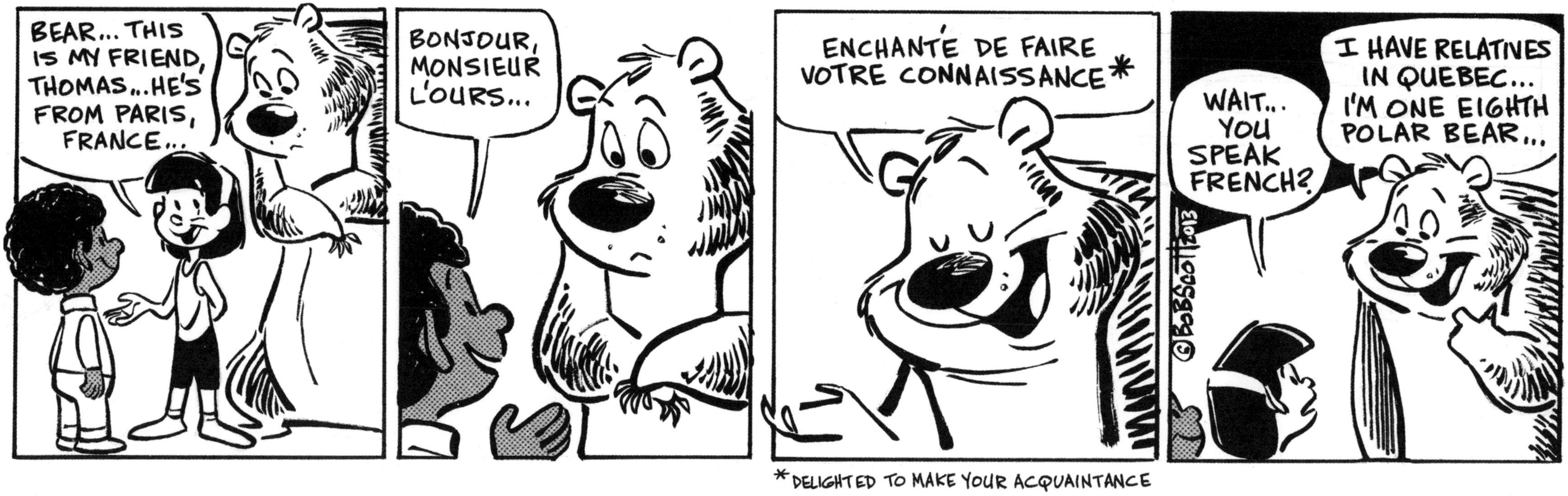
BEAR... THIS IS MY FRIEND, THOMAS... HE'S FROM PARIS, FRANCE...
BONJOUR, MONSIEUR L'OURS...
ENCHANTÉ DE FAIRE VOTRE CONNAISSANCE*
WAIT... YOU SPEAK FRENCH?
I HAVE RELATIVES IN QUEBEC... I'M ONE EIGHTH POLAR BEAR...
©BOBSCOTT2013
*DELIGHTED TO MAKE YOUR ACQUAINTANCE

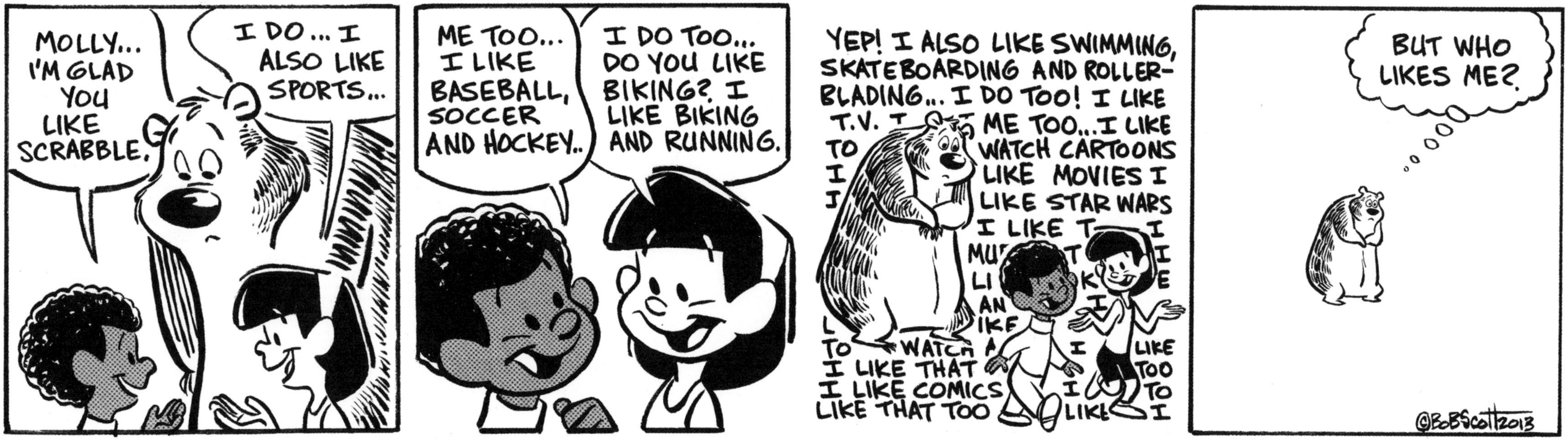
MOLLY... I'M GLAD YOU LIKE SCRABBLE.
I DO... I ALSO LIKE SPORTS...
ME TOO... I LIKE BASEBALL, SOCCER AND HOCKEY..
I DO TOO... DO YOU LIKE BIKING? I LIKE BIKING AND RUNNING.
YEP! I ALSO LIKE SWIMMING, SKATEBOARDING AND ROLLER-BLADING... I DO TOO! I LIKE
ME TOO... I LIKE WATCH CARTOONS LIKE MOVIES I LIKE STAR WARS
I LIKE THAT
I LIKE COMICS
LIKE THAT TOO
BUT WHO LIKES ME?
©BOBSCOTT2013

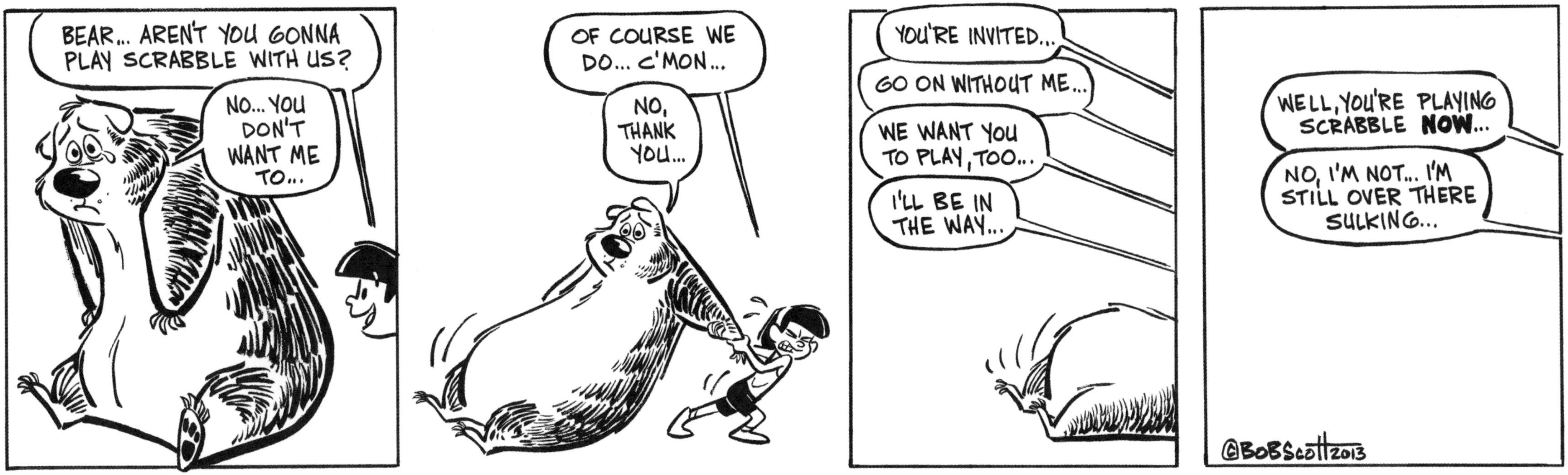
BEAR... AREN'T YOU GONNA PLAY SCRABBLE WITH US?
NO... YOU DON'T WANT ME TO...
OF COURSE WE DO... C'MON...
NO, THANK YOU...
YOU'RE INVITED...
GO ON WITHOUT ME...
WE WANT YOU TO PLAY, TOO...
I'LL BE IN THE WAY...
WELL, YOU'RE PLAYING SCRABBLE **NOW**...
NO, I'M NOT... I'M STILL OVER THERE SULKING...
©BOBSCOTT 2013

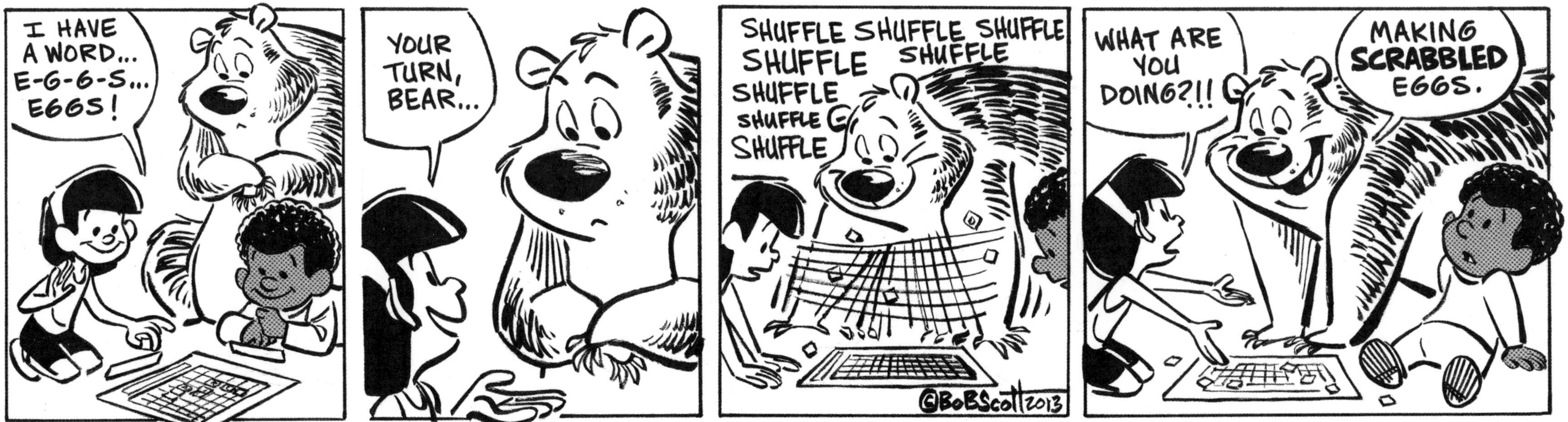
I HAVE A WORD... E-G-G-S... EGGS!
YOUR TURN, BEAR...
SHUFFLE SHUFFLE SHUFFLE
SHUFFLE SHUFFLE
SHUFFLE
SHUFFLE
SHUFFLE
©BOBSCOTT 2013
WHAT ARE YOU DOING?!!
MAKING **SCRABBLED** EGGS.

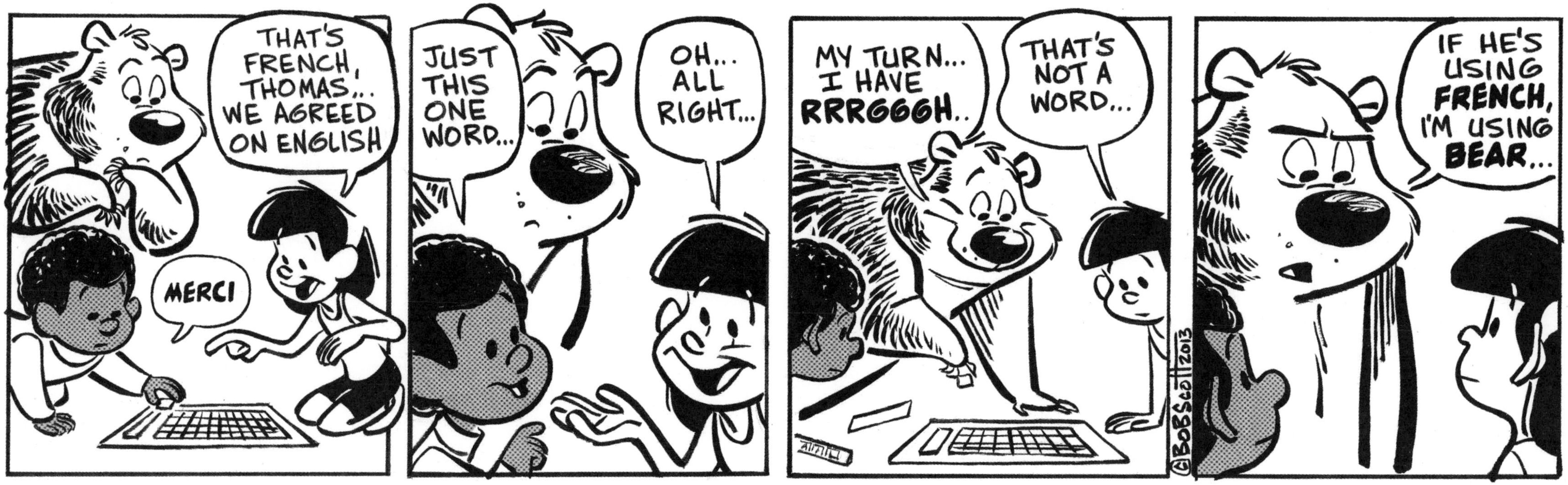
THAT'S FRENCH, THOMAS... WE AGREED ON ENGLISH
MERCI
JUST THIS ONE WORD...
OH... ALL RIGHT...
MY TURN... I HAVE **RRRGGGH**...
THAT'S NOT A WORD...
IF HE'S USING **FRENCH**, I'M USING **BEAR**...
©BOBSCOTT2013

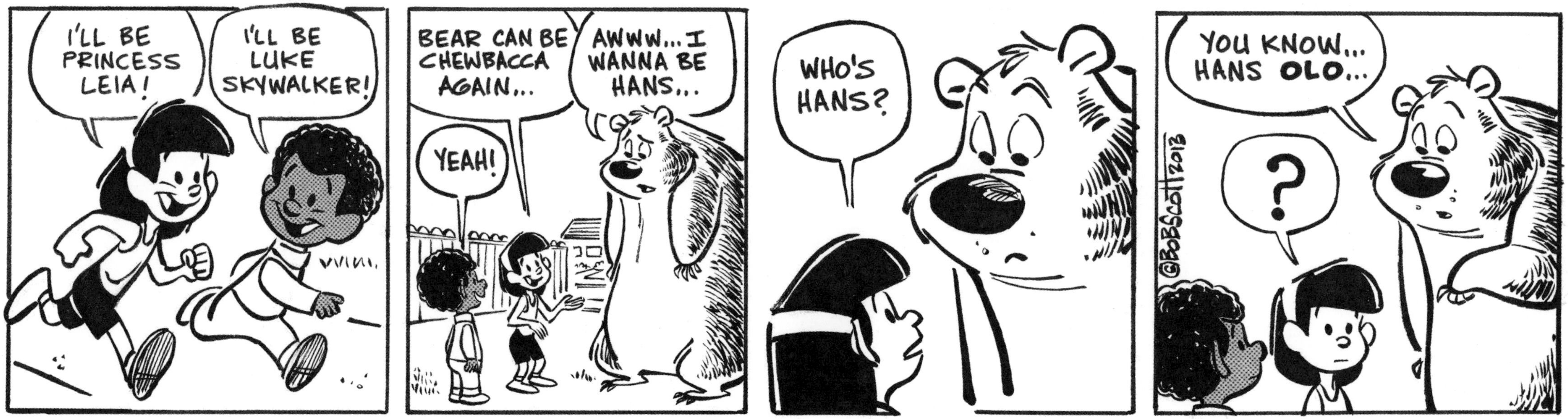
I'LL BE PRINCESS LEIA!
I'LL BE LUKE SKYWALKER!
BEAR CAN BE CHEWBACCA AGAIN...
YEAH!
AWWW... I WANNA BE HANS...
WHO'S HANS?
YOU KNOW... HANS **OLO**...
?
©BOBSCOTT2013

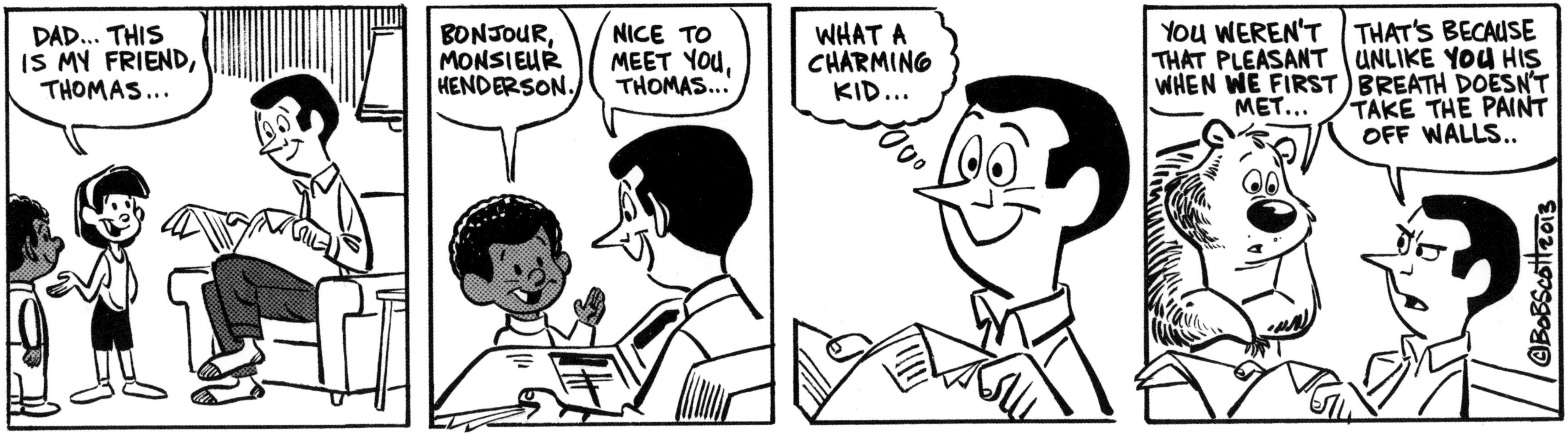
DAD... THIS IS MY FRIEND, THOMAS...
BONJOUR, MONSIEUR HENDERSON.
NICE TO MEET YOU, THOMAS...
WHAT A CHARMING KID...
YOU WEREN'T THAT PLEASANT WHEN WE FIRST MET...
THAT'S BECAUSE UNLIKE YOU HIS BREATH DOESN'T TAKE THE PAINT OFF WALLS..
©BoBScott2013

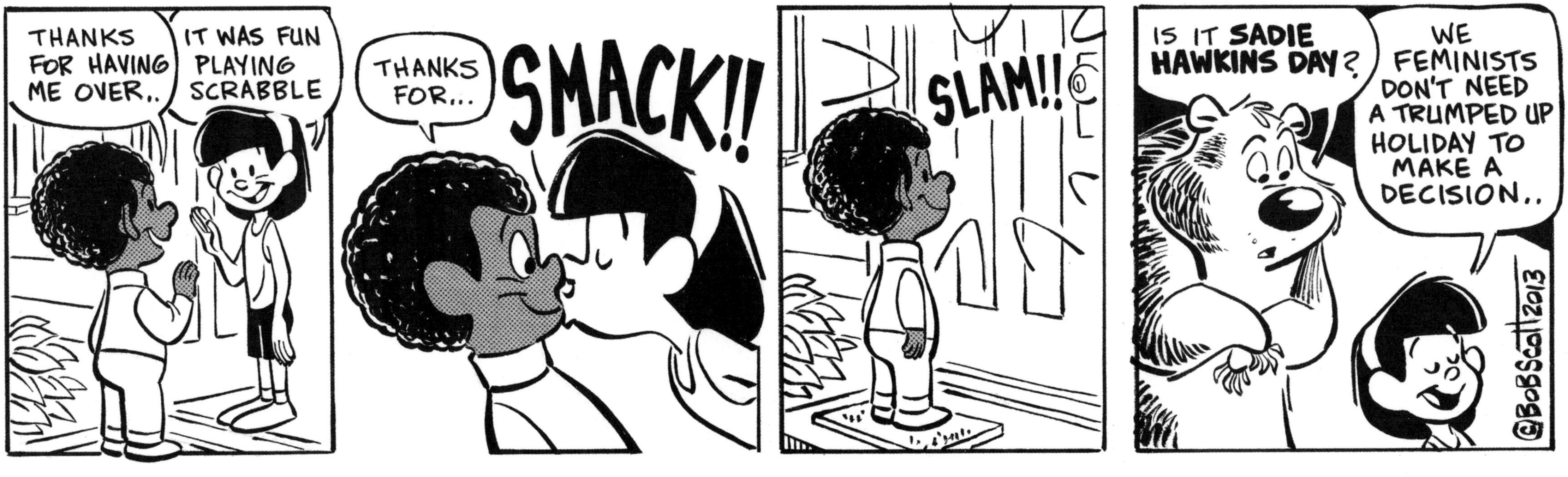
THANKS FOR HAVING ME OVER..
IT WAS FUN PLAYING SCRABBLE
THANKS FOR...
SMACK!!
SLAM!!
IS IT SADIE HAWKINS DAY?
WE FEMINISTS DON'T NEED A TRUMPED UP HOLIDAY TO MAKE A DECISION..
©BoBScott2013

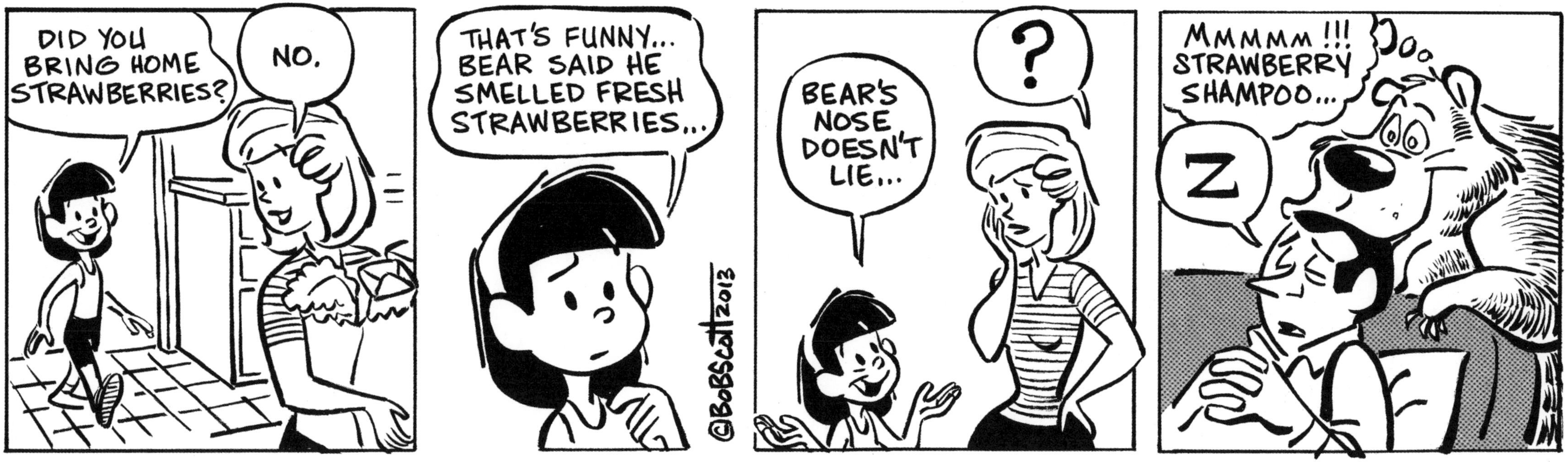
DID YOU BRING HOME STRAWBERRIES?
NO.
THAT'S FUNNY... BEAR SAID HE SMELLED FRESH STRAWBERRIES...
©BOBSCOTT2013
BEAR'S NOSE DOESN'T LIE...
?
MMMMM!!! STRAWBERRY SHAMPOO...
Z

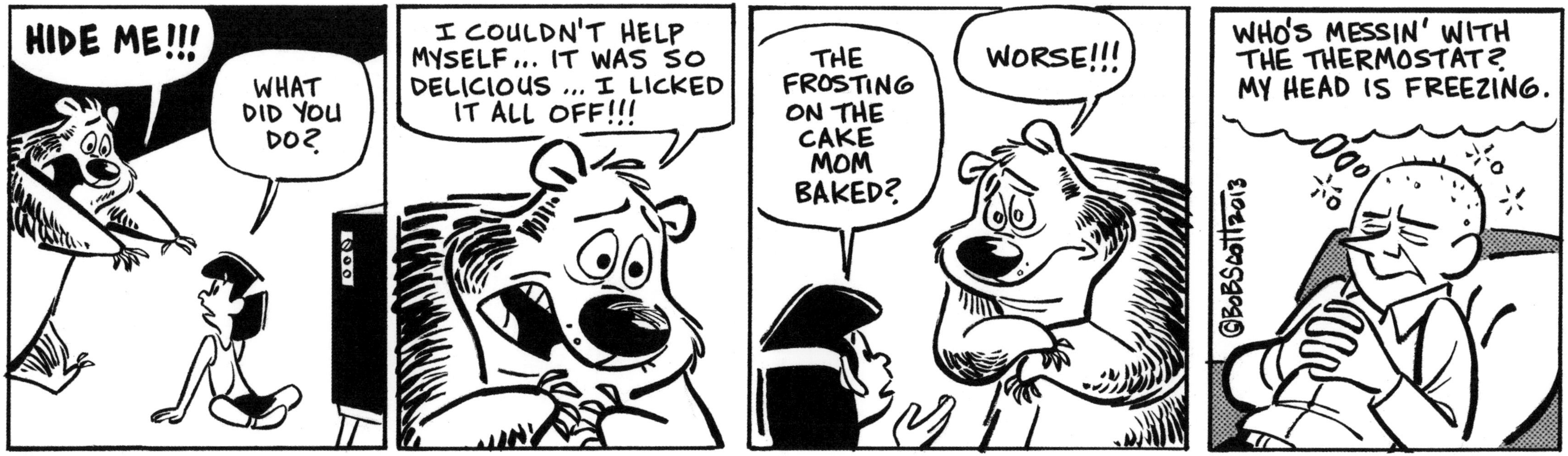
HIDE ME!!!
WHAT DID YOU DO?
I COULDN'T HELP MYSELF... IT WAS SO DELICIOUS ... I LICKED IT ALL OFF!!!
THE FROSTING ON THE CAKE MOM BAKED?
WORSE!!!
WHO'S MESSIN' WITH THE THERMOSTAT? MY HEAD IS FREEZING.
©BOBSCOTT2013

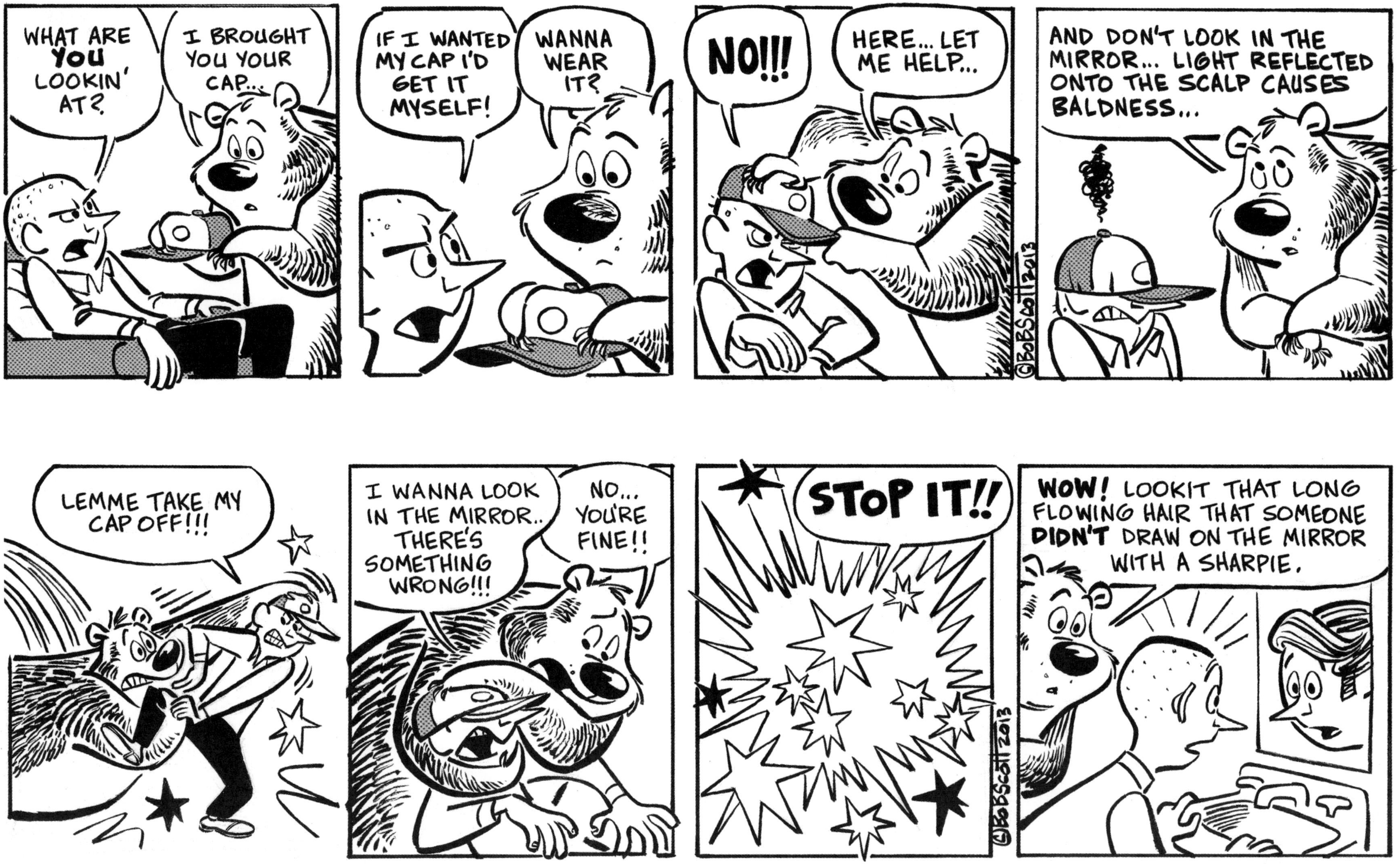
WHAT ARE **YOU** LOOKIN' AT?
I BROUGHT YOU YOUR CAP...
IF I WANTED MY CAP I'D GET IT MYSELF!
WANNA WEAR IT?
NO!!!
HERE... LET ME HELP...
©BOBSCOTT 2013
AND DON'T LOOK IN THE MIRROR... LIGHT REFLECTED ONTO THE SCALP CAUSES BALDNESS...
LEMME TAKE MY CAP OFF!!!
I WANNA LOOK IN THE MIRROR.. THERE'S SOMETHING WRONG!!!
NO... YOU'RE FINE!!
STOP IT!!
©BOBSCOTT 2013
WOW! LOOKIT THAT LONG FLOWING HAIR THAT SOMEONE **DIDN'T** DRAW ON THE MIRROR WITH A SHARPIE.

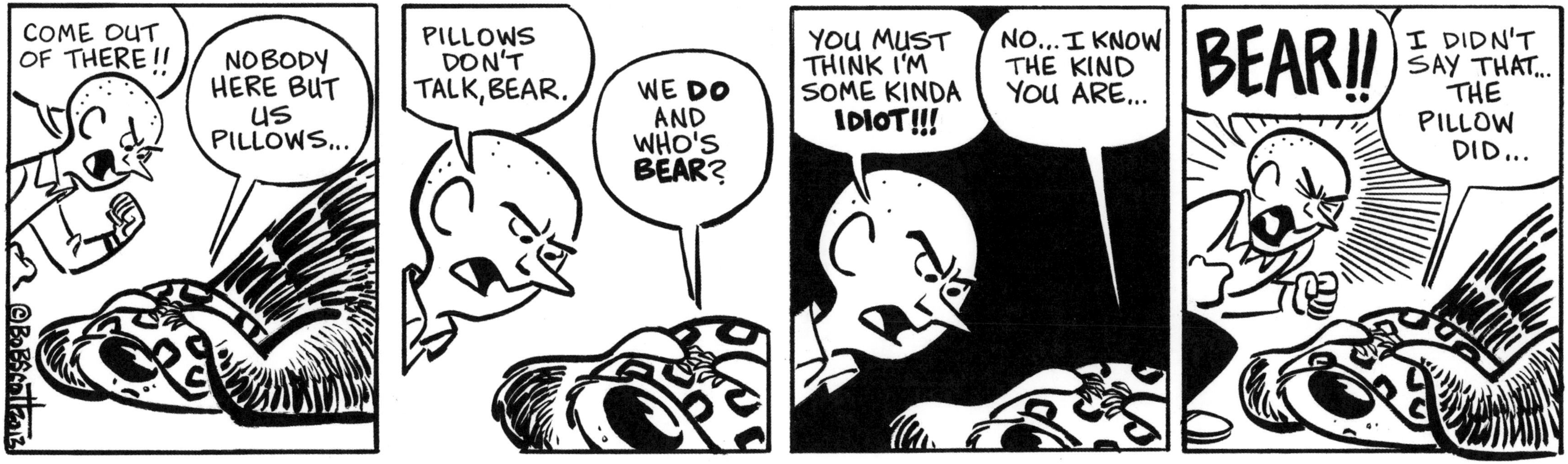
COME OUT OF THERE!!
NOBODY HERE BUT US PILLOWS...
PILLOWS DON'T TALK, BEAR.
WE **DO** AND WHO'S **BEAR**?
YOU MUST THINK I'M SOME KINDA **IDIOT!!!**
NO... I KNOW THE KIND YOU ARE...
BEAR!!
I DIDN'T SAY THAT... THE PILLOW DID...
©BOBSCOTT2012

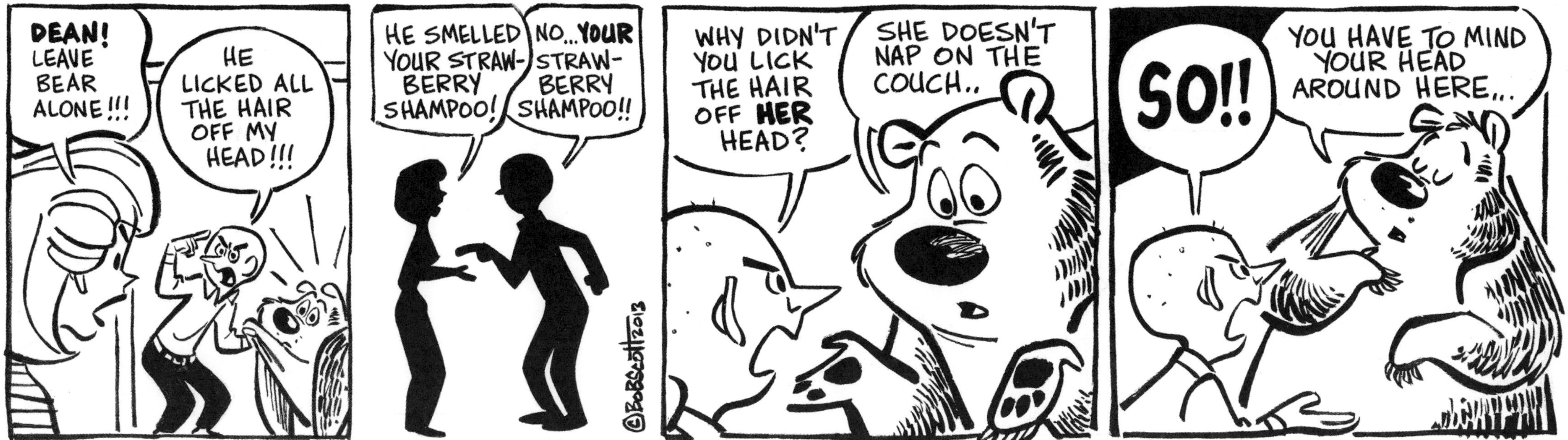
DEAN! LEAVE BEAR ALONE!!!
HE LICKED ALL THE HAIR OFF MY HEAD!!!
HE SMELLED YOUR STRAW-BERRY SHAMPOO!
NO... **YOUR** STRAW-BERRY SHAMPOO!!
©BOBSCOTT2013
WHY DIDN'T YOU LICK THE HAIR OFF **HER** HEAD?
SHE DOESN'T NAP ON THE COUCH..
SO!!
YOU HAVE TO MIND YOUR HEAD AROUND HERE...

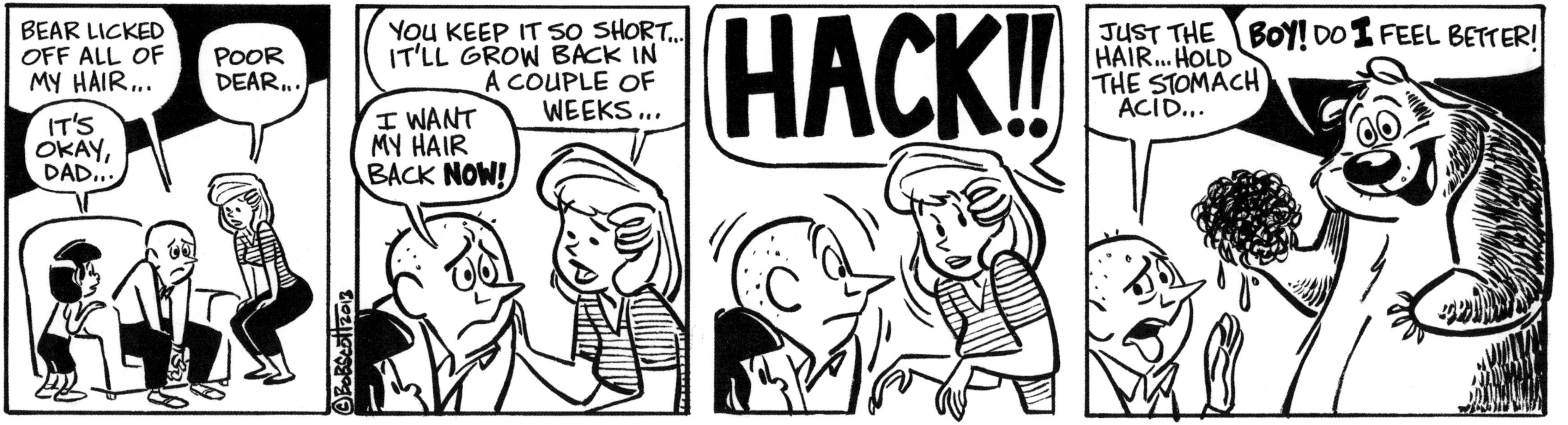
BEAR LICKED OFF ALL OF MY HAIR...
IT'S OKAY, DAD...
POOR DEAR...
©BOBSCOTT2013
YOU KEEP IT SO SHORT... IT'LL GROW BACK IN A COUPLE OF WEEKS...
I WANT MY HAIR BACK NOW!
HACK!!
JUST THE HAIR... HOLD THE STOMACH ACID...
BOY! DO I FEEL BETTER!

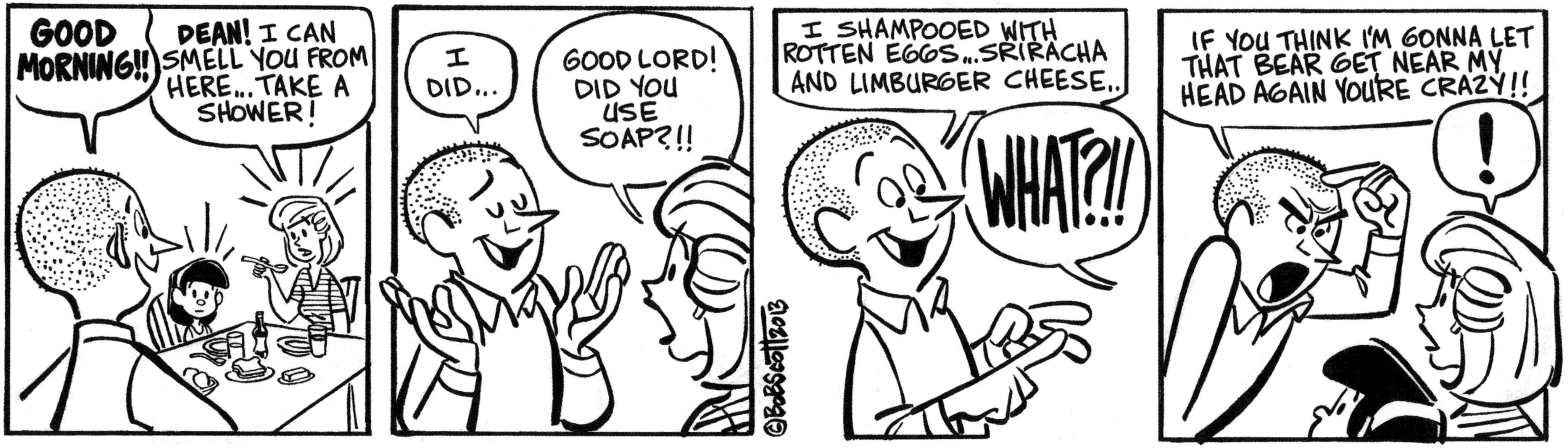
GOOD MORNING!!
DEAN! I CAN SMELL YOU FROM HERE... TAKE A SHOWER!
I DID...
GOOD LORD! DID YOU USE SOAP?!!
©BOBSCOTT2013
I SHAMPOOED WITH ROTTEN EGGS... SRIRACHA AND LIMBURGER CHEESE..
WHAT?!!
IF YOU THINK I'M GONNA LET THAT BEAR GET NEAR MY HEAD AGAIN YOU'RE CRAZY!!
!

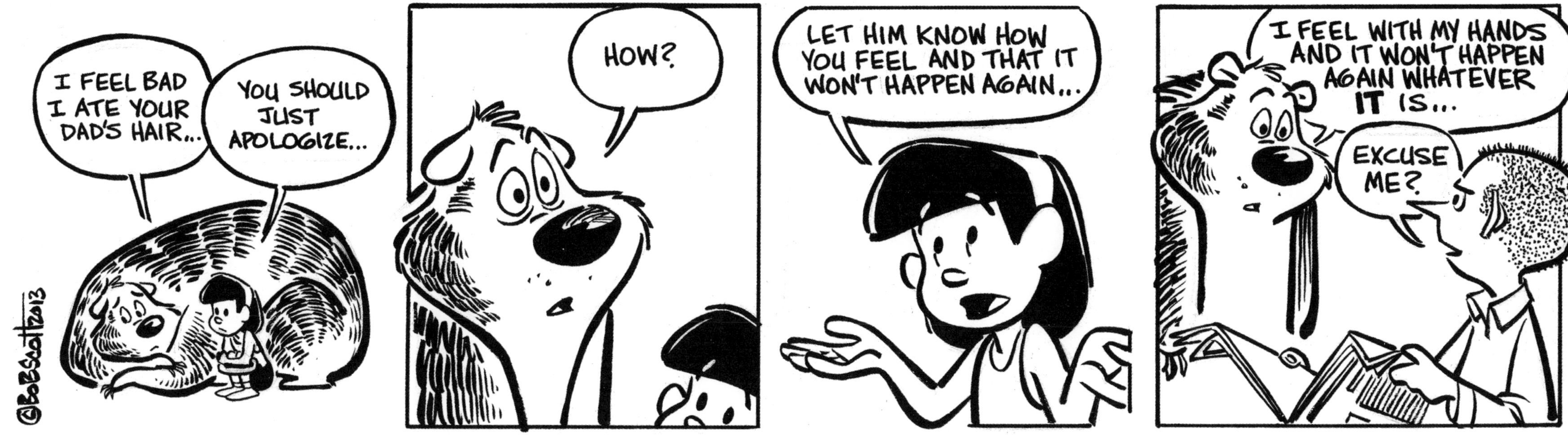
©BOBSCOTT2013
I FEEL BAD I ATE YOUR DAD'S HAIR...
YOU SHOULD JUST APOLOGIZE...
HOW?
LET HIM KNOW HOW YOU FEEL AND THAT IT WON'T HAPPEN AGAIN...
I FEEL WITH MY HANDS AND IT WON'T HAPPEN AGAIN WHATEVER **IT** IS...
EXCUSE ME?

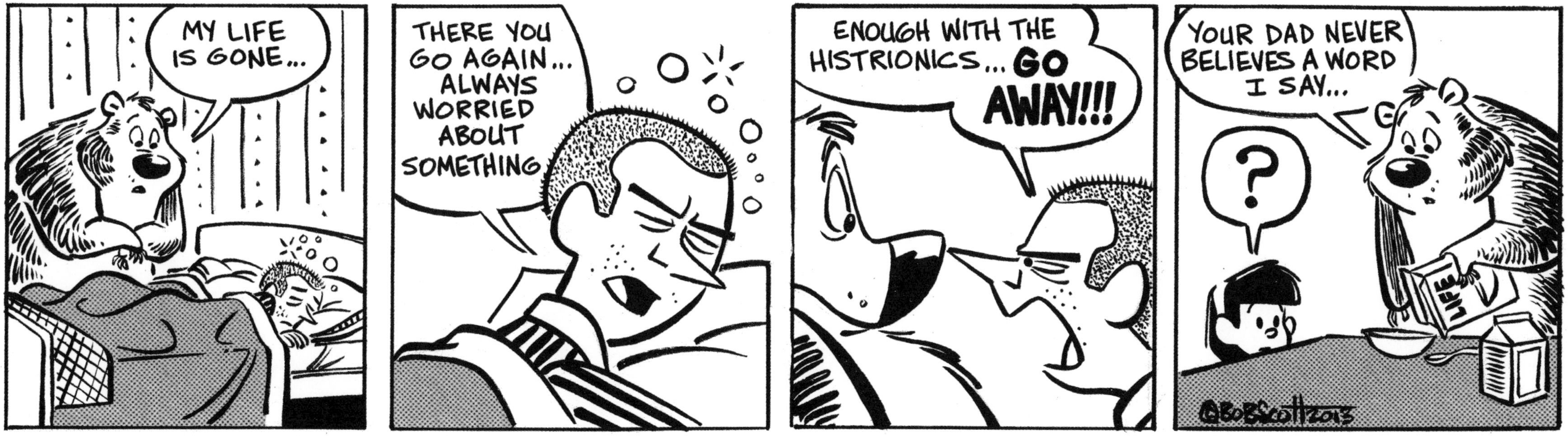
MY LIFE IS GONE...
THERE YOU GO AGAIN... ALWAYS WORRIED ABOUT SOMETHING
ENOUGH WITH THE HISTRIONICS... **GO AWAY!!!**
YOUR DAD NEVER BELIEVES A WORD I SAY...
?
LIFE
©BOBSCOTT2013

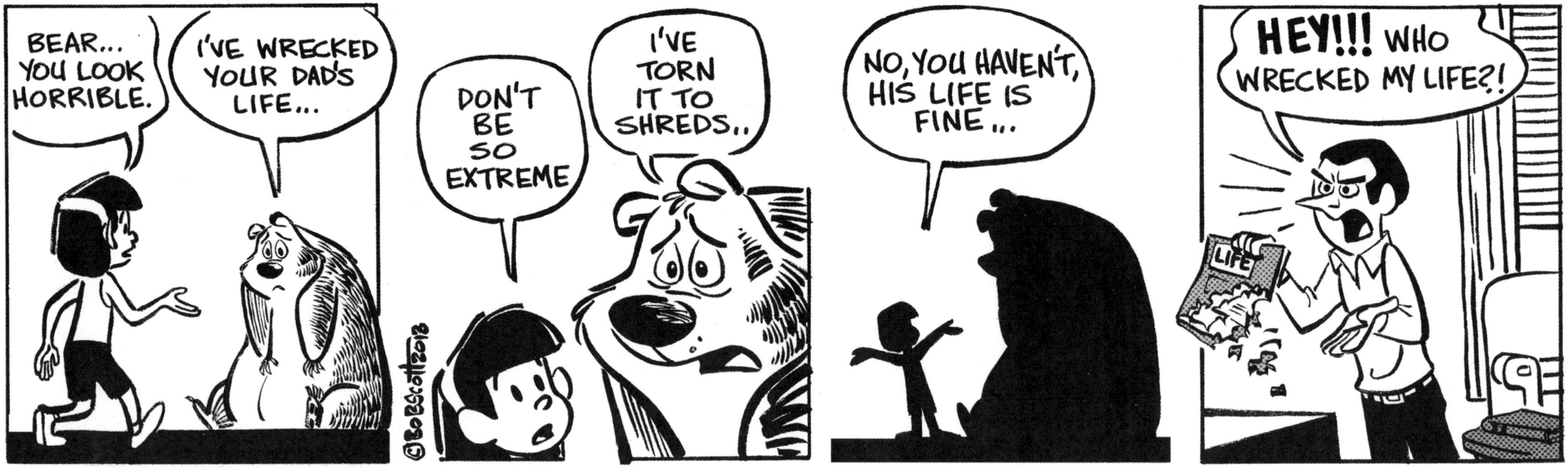
BEAR... YOU LOOK HORRIBLE.
I'VE WRECKED YOUR DAD'S LIFE...
©BOBSCOTT2013
DON'T BE SO EXTREME
I'VE TORN IT TO SHREDS..
NO, YOU HAVEN'T, HIS LIFE IS FINE...
HEY!!! WHO WRECKED MY LIFE?!
LIFE

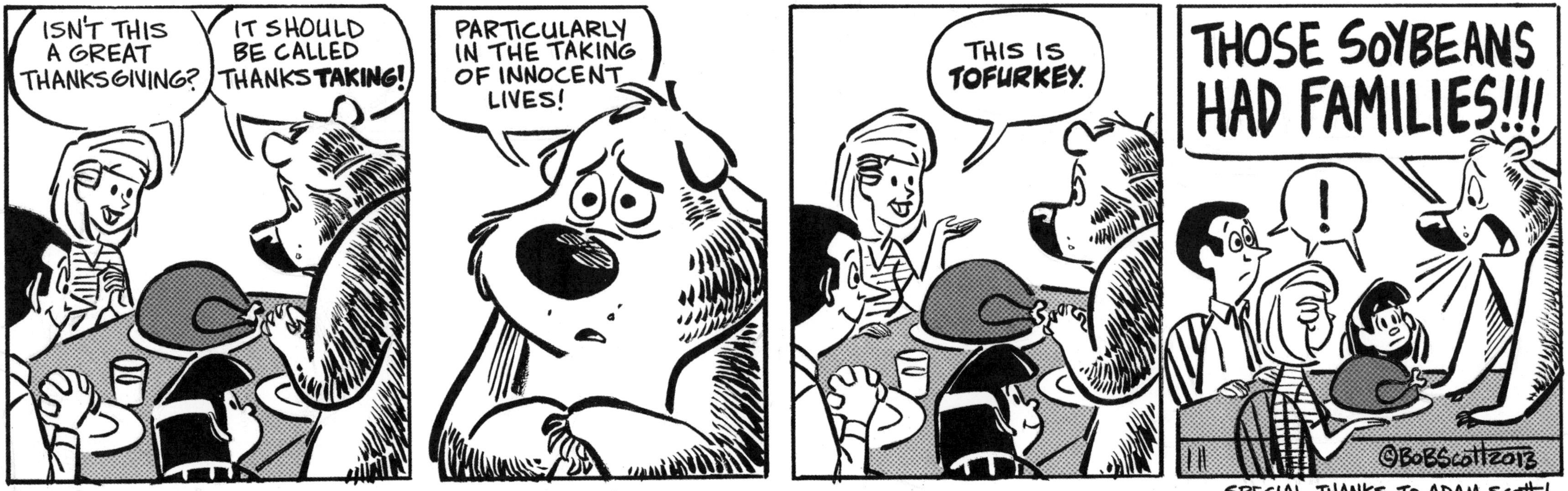
ISN'T THIS A GREAT THANKSGIVING?
IT SHOULD BE CALLED THANKS**TAKING!**
PARTICULARLY IN THE TAKING OF INNOCENT LIVES!
THIS IS **TOFURKEY**.
THOSE SOYBEANS HAD FAMILIES!!!
!
©BOBSCOTT2013

SPECIAL THANKS TO ADAM SCOTT!

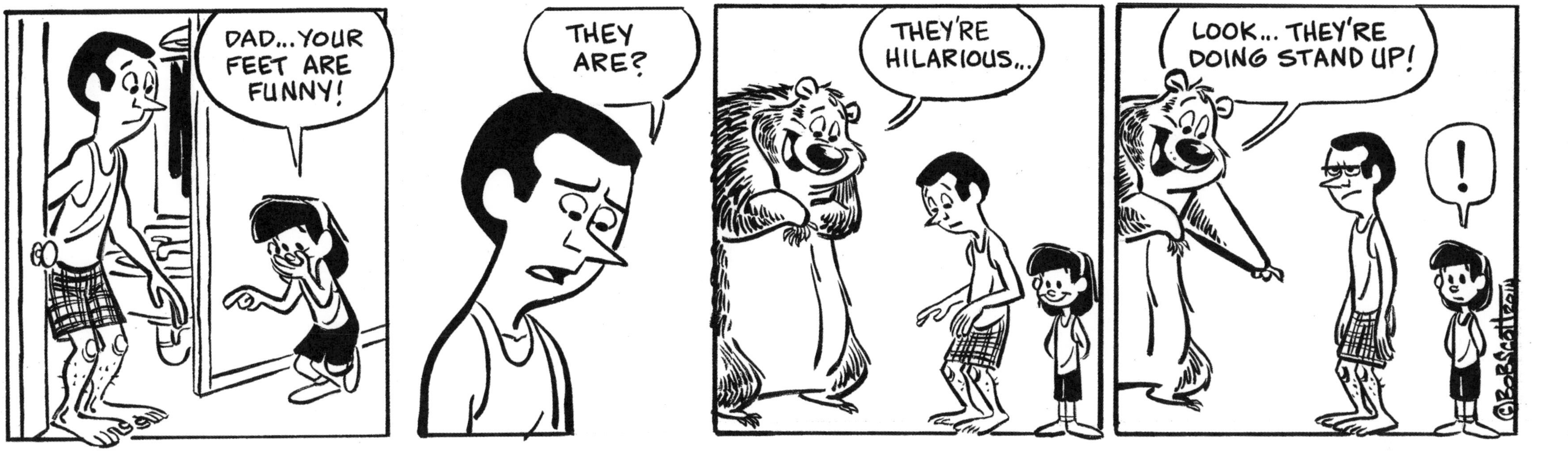
DAD... YOUR FEET ARE FUNNY!
THEY ARE?
THEY'RE HILARIOUS...
LOOK... THEY'RE DOING STAND UP!
!
©BOBSCOTT2011

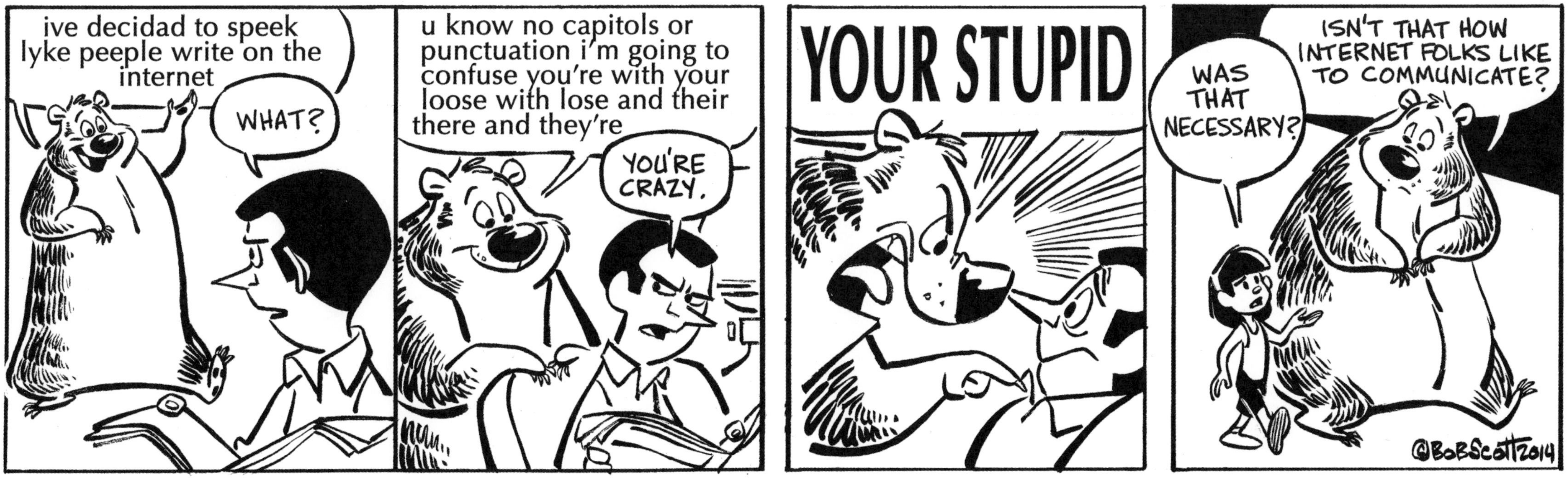
ive decidad to speek lyke peeple write on the internet
WHAT?
u know no capitols or punctuation i'm going to confuse you're with your loose with lose and their there and they're
YOU'RE CRAZY.
YOUR STUPID
ISN'T THAT HOW INTERNET FOLKS LIKE TO COMMUNICATE?
WAS THAT NECESSARY?
©BOBSCOTT2014

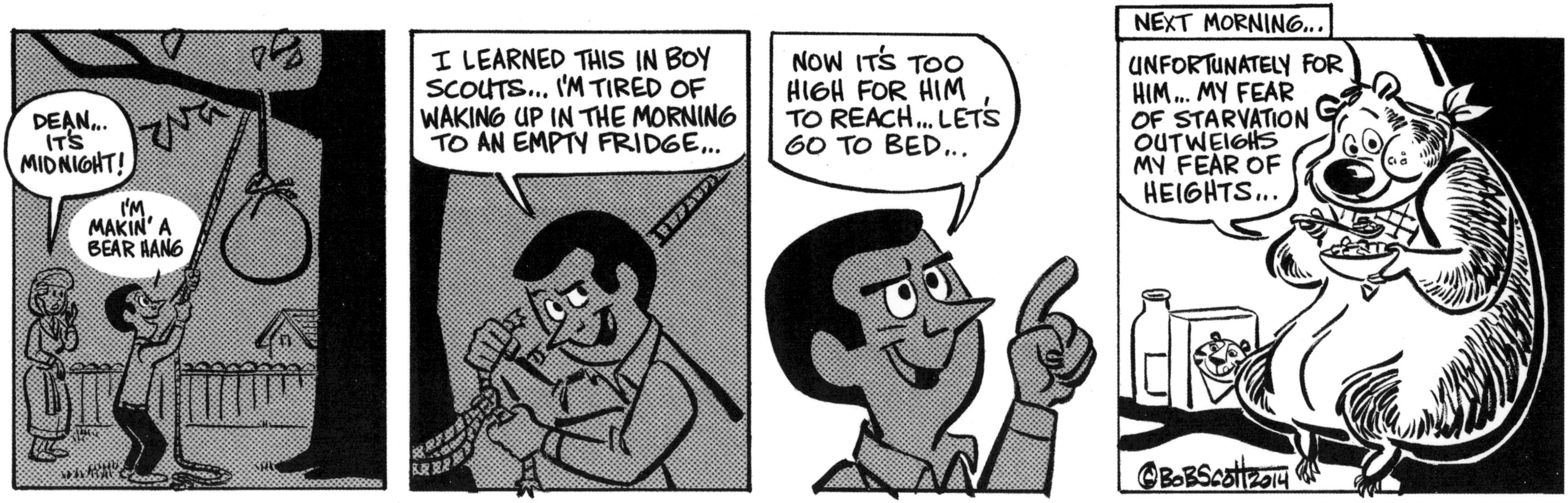
DEAN... IT'S MIDNIGHT!
I'M MAKIN' A BEAR HANG
I LEARNED THIS IN BOY SCOUTS... I'M TIRED OF WAKING UP IN THE MORNING TO AN EMPTY FRIDGE...
NOW IT'S TOO HIGH FOR HIM, TO REACH... LET'S GO TO BED...
NEXT MORNING...
UNFORTUNATELY FOR HIM... MY FEAR OF STARVATION OUTWEIGHS MY FEAR OF HEIGHTS...
©BOBSCOTT2014

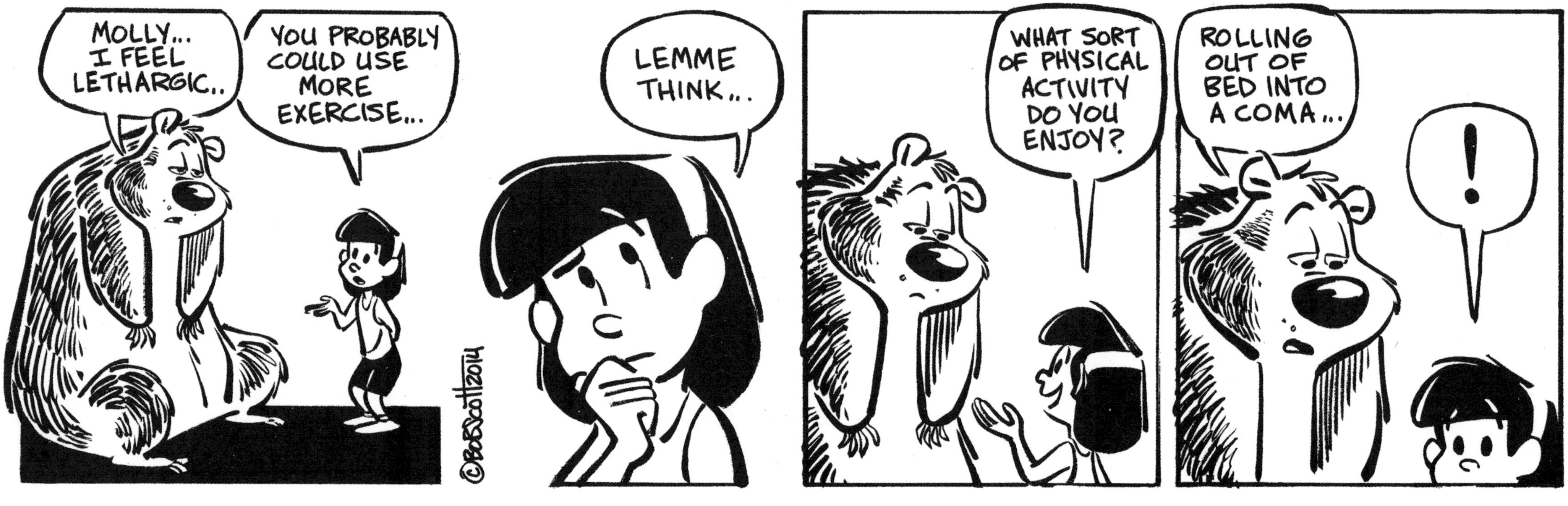
MOLLY... I FEEL LETHARGIC..
YOU PROBABLY COULD USE MORE EXERCISE...
©BOBSCOTT2014
LEMME THINK...
WHAT SORT OF PHYSICAL ACTIVITY DO YOU ENJOY?
ROLLING OUT OF BED INTO A COMA...
!

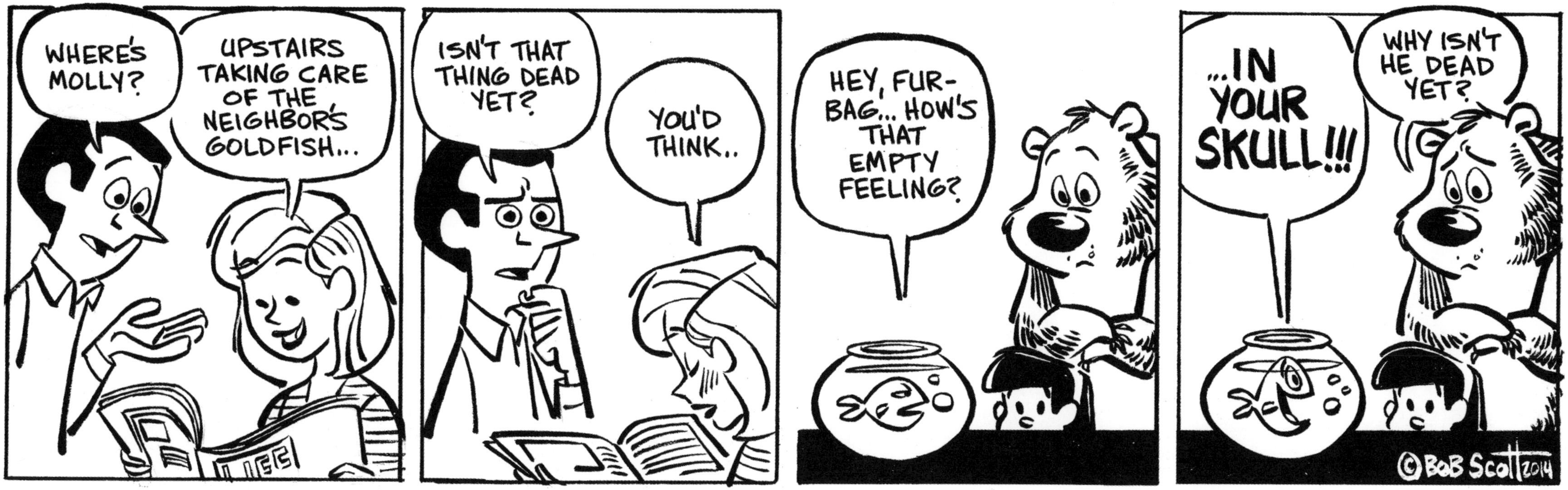
WHERE'S MOLLY?
UPSTAIRS TAKING CARE OF THE NEIGHBOR'S GOLDFISH...
ISN'T THAT THING DEAD YET?
YOU'D THINK..
HEY, FUR-BAG... HOW'S THAT EMPTY FEELING?
...IN YOUR SKULL!!!
WHY ISN'T HE DEAD YET?
©BOB SCOTT 2014

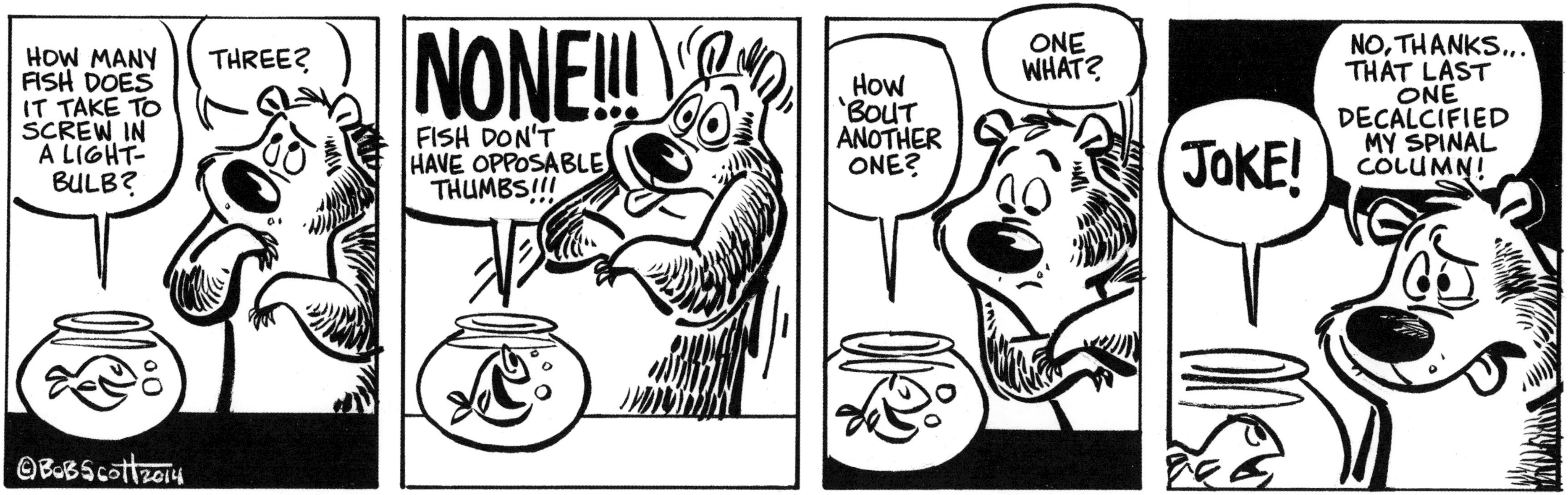
HOW MANY FISH DOES IT TAKE TO SCREW IN A LIGHT-BULB?
THREE?
NONE!!!
FISH DON'T HAVE OPPOSABLE THUMBS!!!
HOW 'BOUT ANOTHER ONE?
ONE WHAT?
JOKE!
NO, THANKS... THAT LAST ONE DECALCIFIED MY SPINAL COLUMN!
©BOB SCOTT 2014

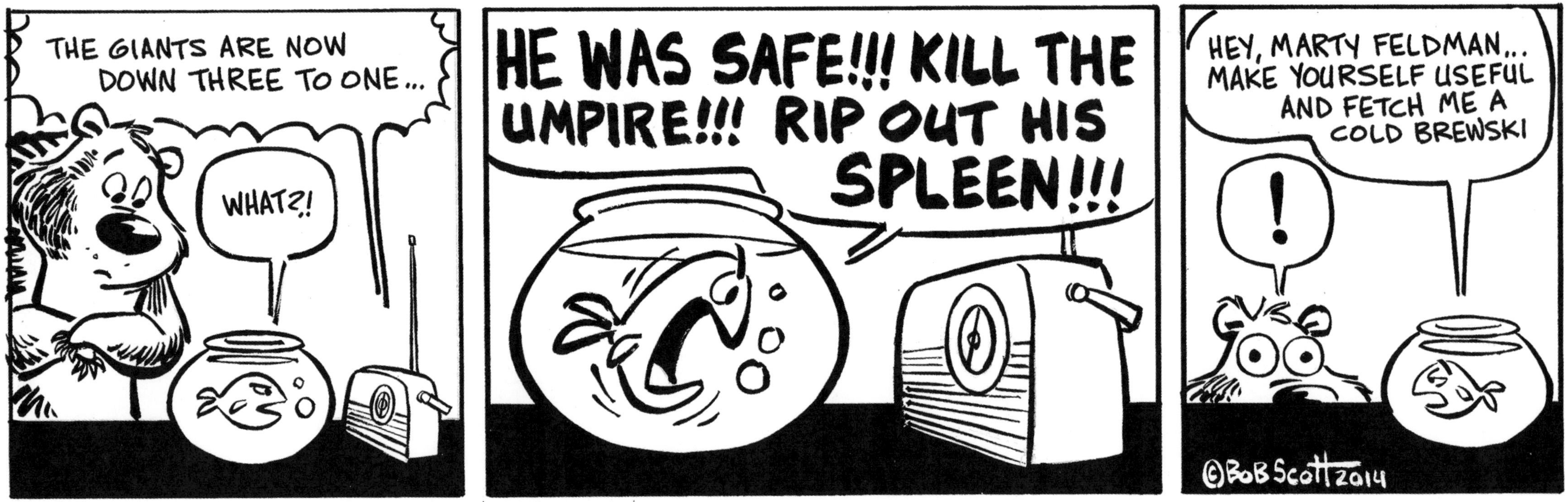
THE GIANTS ARE NOW DOWN THREE TO ONE...
WHAT?!
HE WAS SAFE!!! KILL THE UMPIRE!!! RIP OUT HIS SPLEEN!!!
!
HEY, MARTY FELDMAN... MAKE YOURSELF USEFUL AND FETCH ME A COLD BREWSKI
©BOB SCOTT 2014

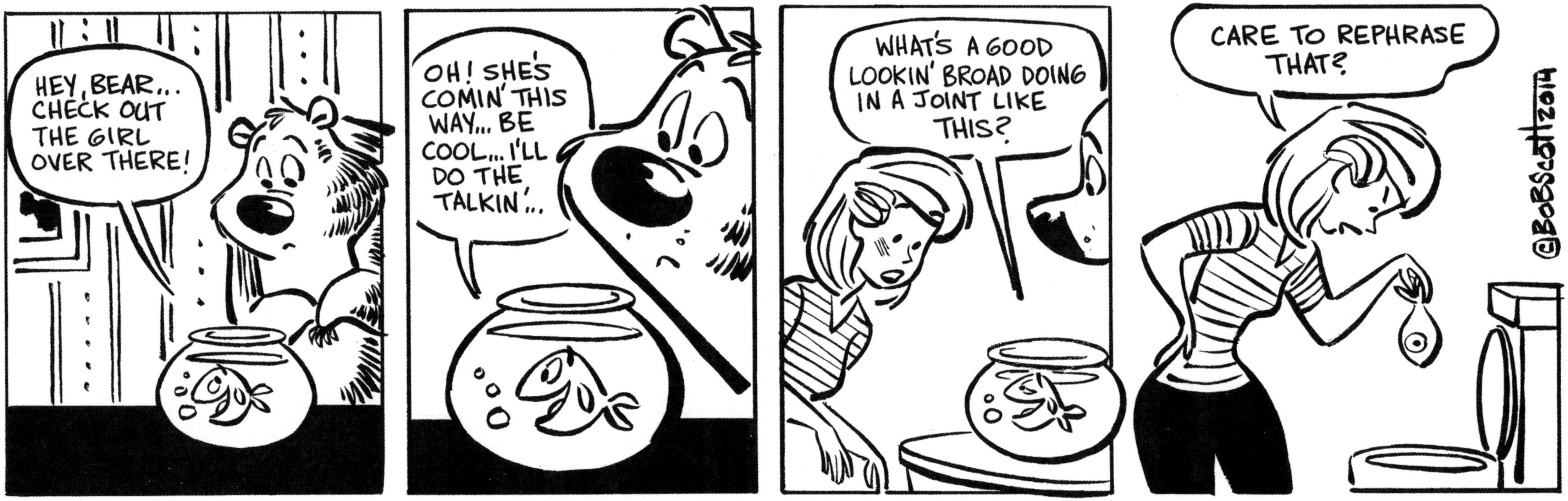
HEY, BEAR... CHECK OUT THE GIRL OVER THERE!
OH! SHE'S COMIN' THIS WAY... BE COOL... I'LL DO THE TALKIN'...
WHAT'S A GOOD LOOKIN' BROAD DOING IN A JOINT LIKE THIS?
CARE TO REPHRASE THAT?
©BOBSCOTT 2014

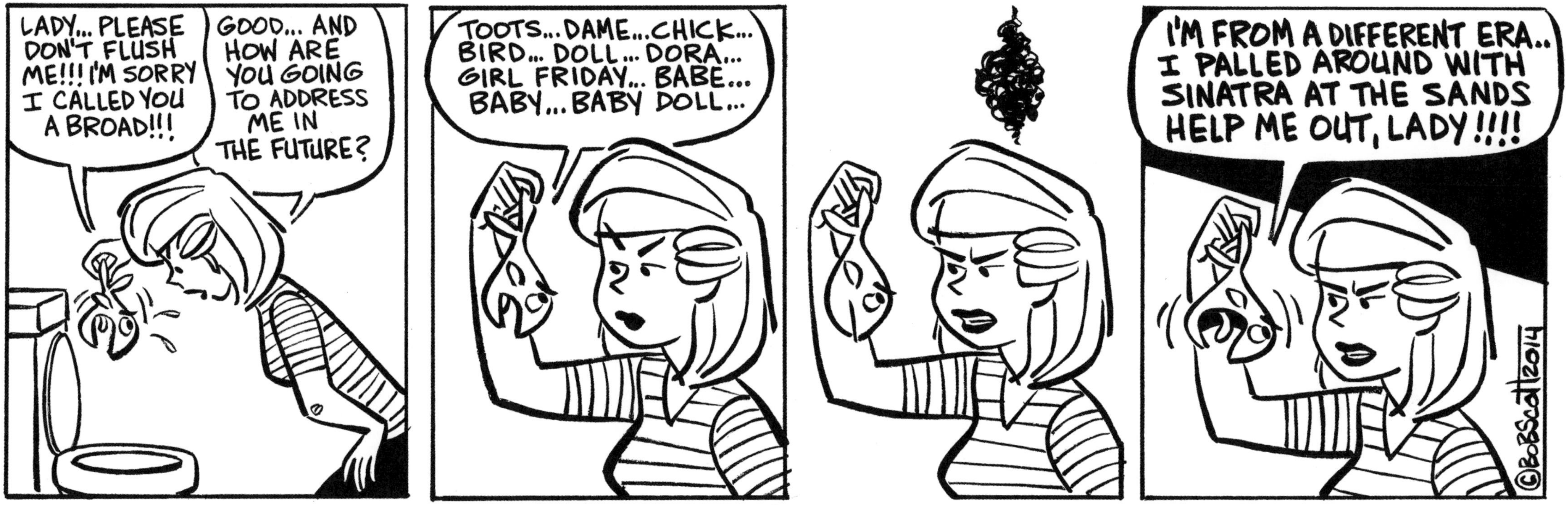
LADY... PLEASE DON'T FLUSH ME!!! I'M SORRY I CALLED YOU A BROAD!!!
GOOD... AND HOW ARE YOU GOING TO ADDRESS ME IN THE FUTURE?
TOOTS... DAME... CHICK... BIRD... DOLL... DORA... GIRL FRIDAY... BABE... BABY... BABY DOLL...
I'M FROM A DIFFERENT ERA.. I PALLED AROUND WITH SINATRA AT THE SANDS HELP ME OUT, LADY!!!!
©BOBSCOTT2014

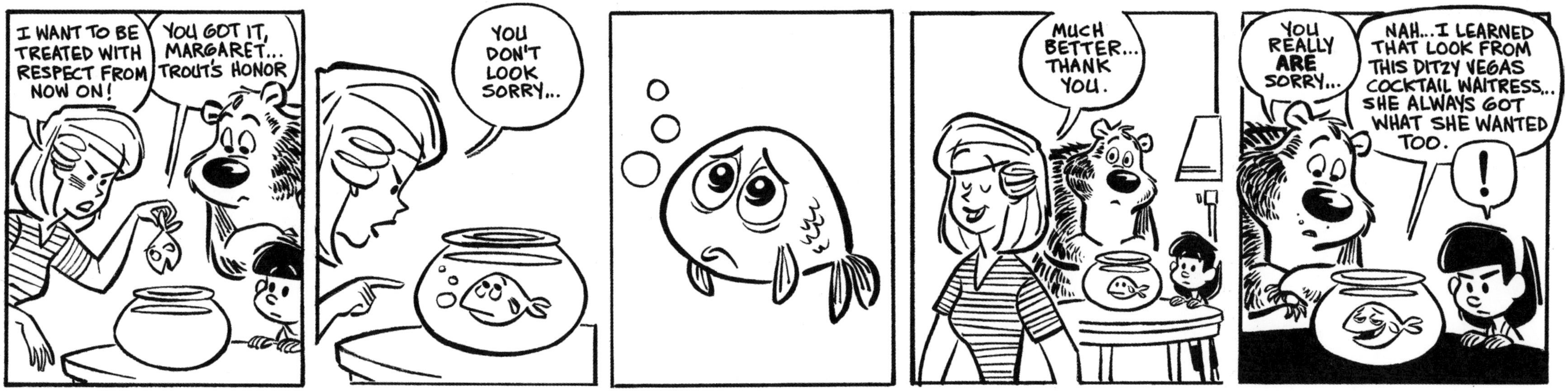
I WANT TO BE TREATED WITH RESPECT FROM NOW ON!
YOU GOT IT, MARGARET... TROUT'S HONOR
YOU DON'T LOOK SORRY...
MUCH BETTER... THANK YOU.
YOU REALLY **ARE** SORRY...
NAH... I LEARNED THAT LOOK FROM THIS DITZY VEGAS COCKTAIL WAITRESS... SHE ALWAYS GOT WHAT SHE WANTED TOO.
!

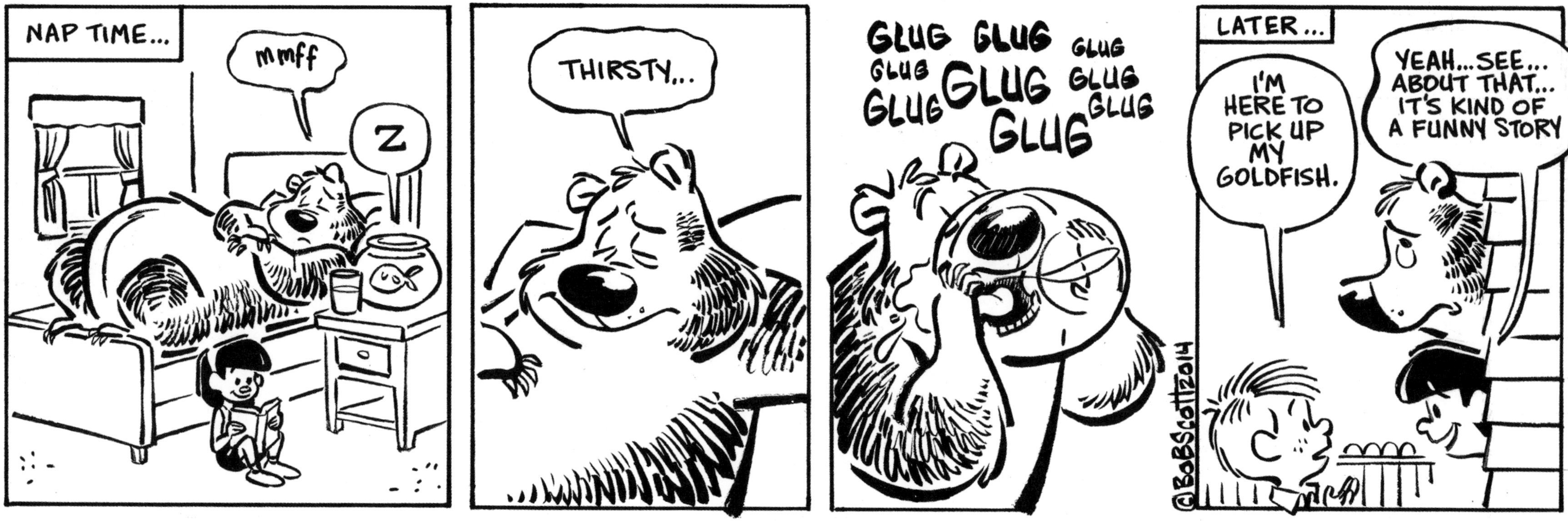
NAP TIME...
mmff
Z
THIRSTY...
GLUG GLUG GLUG GLUG GLUG GLUG GLUG GLUG GLUG GLUG
LATER...
I'M HERE TO PICK UP MY GOLDFISH.
YEAH...SEE... ABOUT THAT... IT'S KIND OF A FUNNY STORY
©BoBScott2014

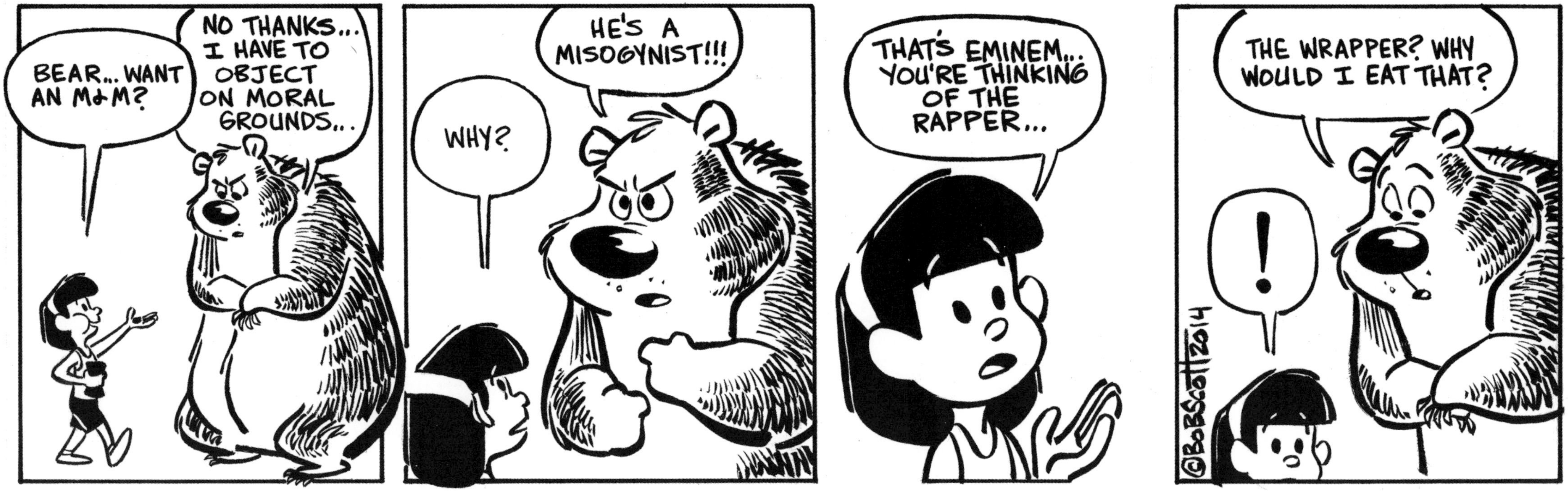
BEAR... WANT AN M&M?
NO THANKS... I HAVE TO OBJECT ON MORAL GROUNDS...
WHY?
HE'S A MISOGYNIST!!!
THAT'S EMINEM... YOU'RE THINKING OF THE RAPPER...
!
THE WRAPPER? WHY WOULD I EAT THAT?
©BoBScott2014

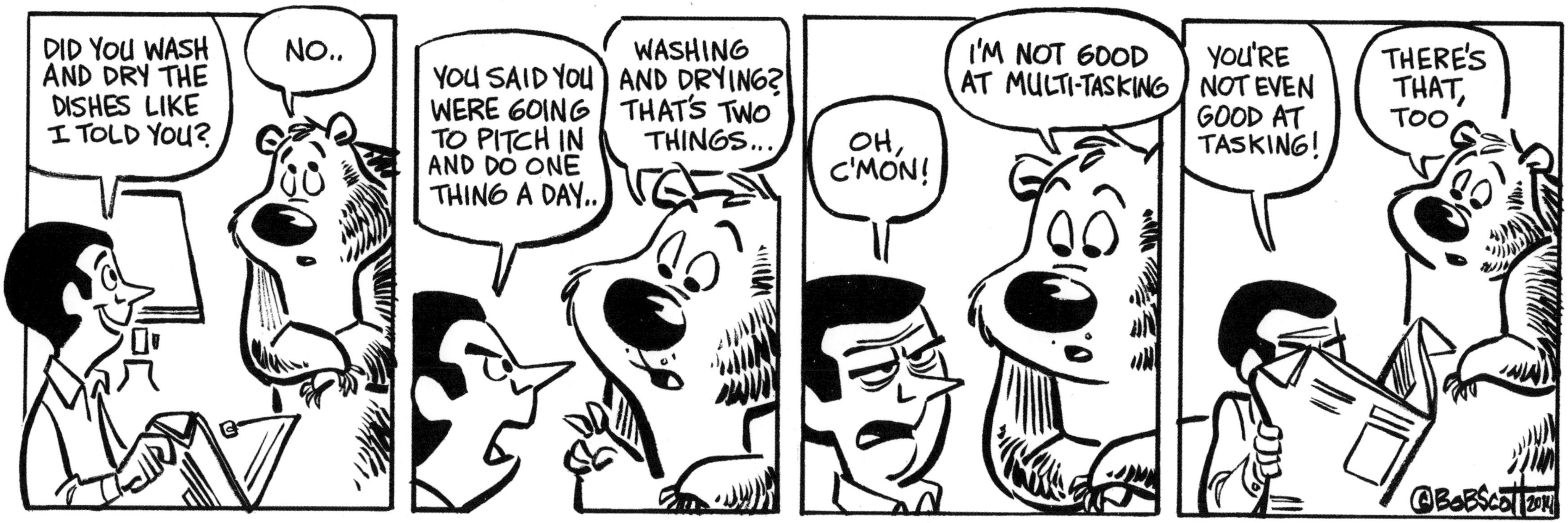
DID YOU WASH AND DRY THE DISHES LIKE I TOLD YOU?
NO..
YOU SAID YOU WERE GOING TO PITCH IN AND DO ONE THING A DAY..
WASHING AND DRYING? THAT'S TWO THINGS...
OH, C'MON!
I'M NOT GOOD AT MULTI-TASKING
YOU'RE NOT EVEN GOOD AT TASKING!
THERE'S THAT, TOO
©BOBSCOTT 2014

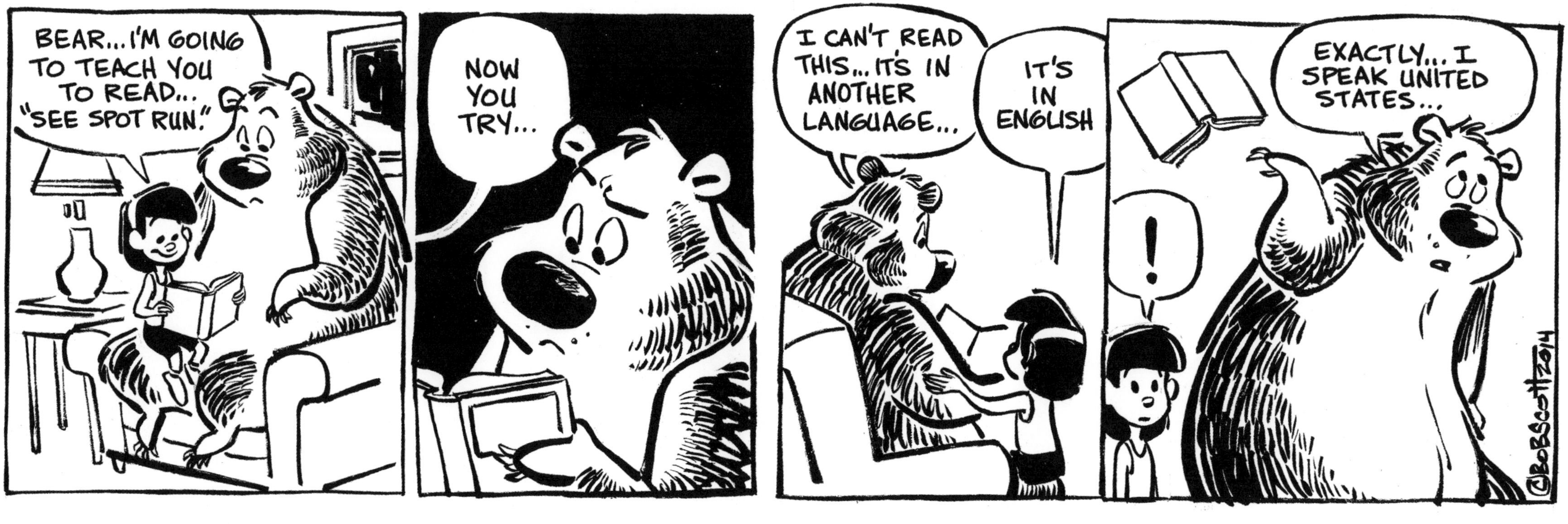
BEAR... I'M GOING TO TEACH YOU TO READ... "SEE SPOT RUN."
NOW YOU TRY...
I CAN'T READ THIS... IT'S IN ANOTHER LANGUAGE...
IT'S IN ENGLISH
EXACTLY... I SPEAK UNITED STATES...
!
©BOBSCOTT 2014

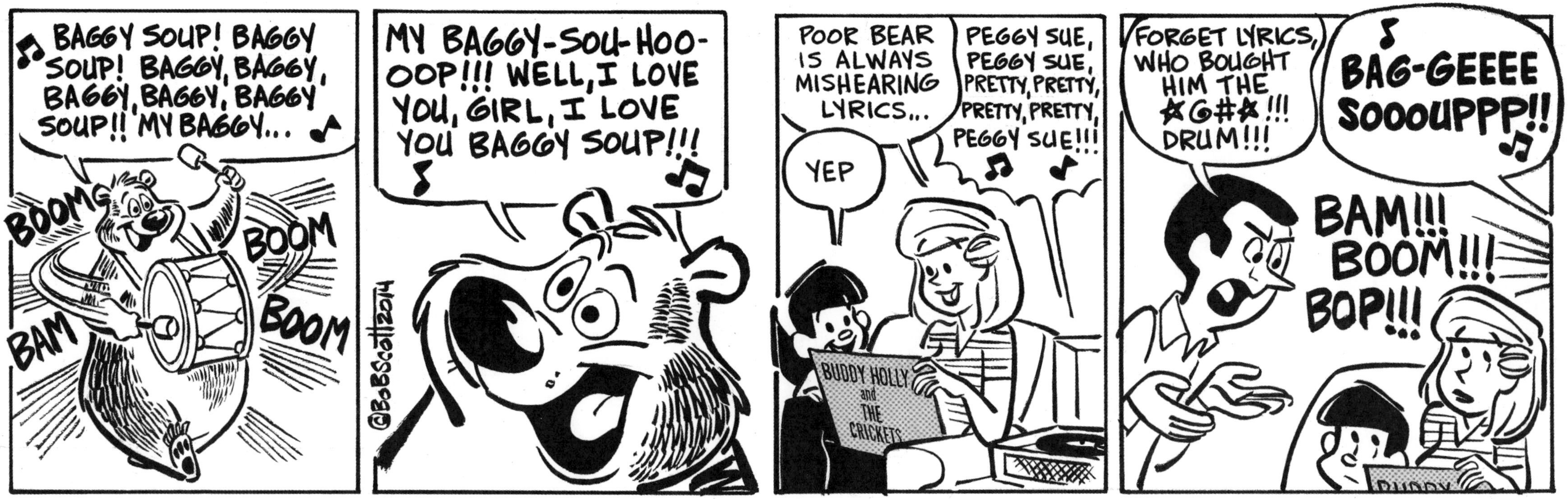
BAGGY SOUP! BAGGY SOUP! BAGGY, BAGGY, BAGGY, BAGGY, BAGGY SOUP!! MY BAGGY...
BOOM
BOOM
BAM
BOOM
©BoBScott2014
MY BAGGY-SOU-HOO-OOP!!! WELL, I LOVE YOU, GIRL, I LOVE YOU BAGGY SOUP!!!
POOR BEAR IS ALWAYS MISHEARING LYRICS...
PEGGY SUE, PEGGY SUE, PRETTY, PRETTY, PRETTY, PRETTY, PEGGY SUE!!!
YEP
BUDDY HOLLY and THE CRICKETS
FORGET LYRICS, WHO BOUGHT HIM THE ☆@#☆!!! DRUM!!!
BAG-GEEEE SOOOUPPP!!
BAM!!! BOOM!!! BOP!!!

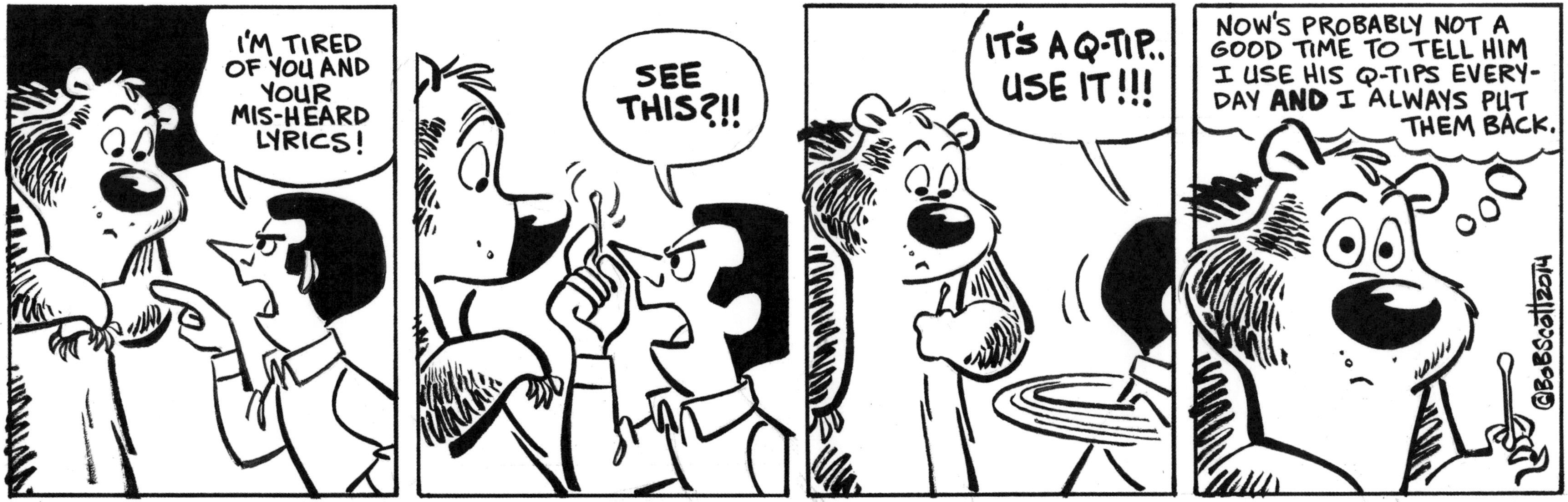
I'M TIRED OF YOU AND YOUR MIS-HEARD LYRICS!
SEE THIS?!!
IT'S A Q-TIP.. USE IT!!!
NOW'S PROBABLY NOT A GOOD TIME TO TELL HIM I USE HIS Q-TIPS EVERY-DAY AND I ALWAYS PUT THEM BACK.
©BoBScott2014

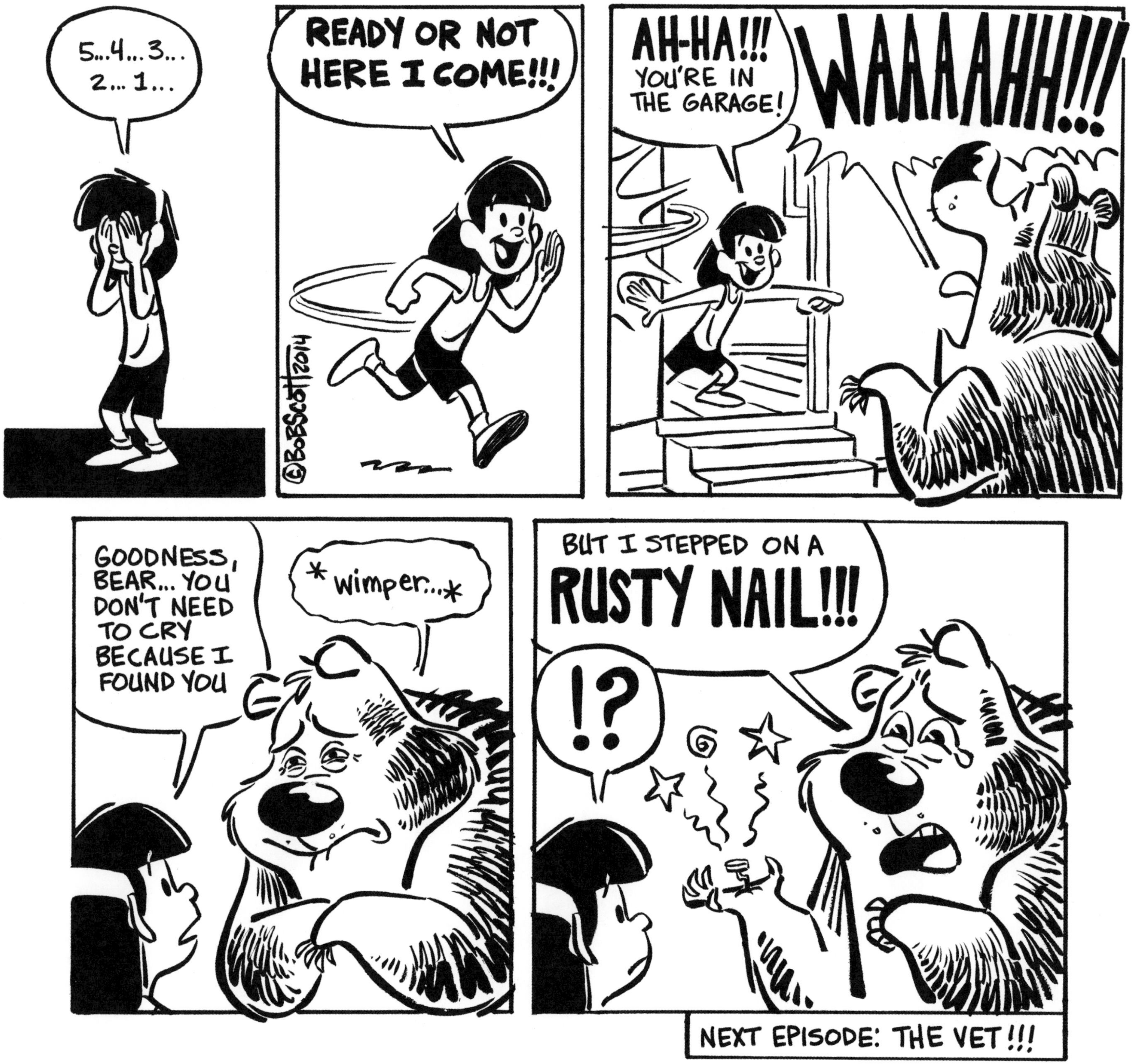
5...4...3...
2...1...
READY OR NOT
HERE I COME!!!
©BOBSCOTT 2014
AH-HA!!!
YOU'RE IN
THE GARAGE!
WAAAAHH!!!...
GOODNESS,
BEAR... YOU
DON'T NEED
TO CRY
BECAUSE I
FOUND YOU
wimper...
BUT I STEPPED ON A
RUSTY NAIL!!!
!?
NEXT EPISODE: THE VET!!!

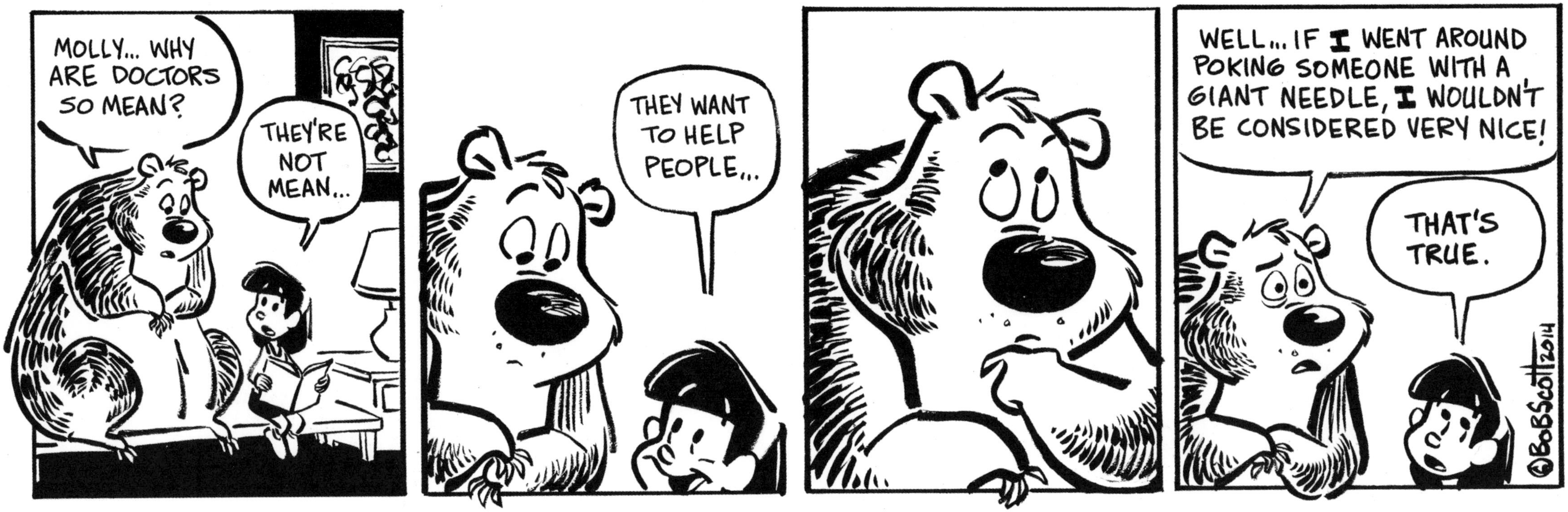
MOLLY... WHY ARE DOCTORS SO MEAN?
THEY'RE NOT MEAN...
THEY WANT TO HELP PEOPLE...
WELL... IF I WENT AROUND POKING SOMEONE WITH A GIANT NEEDLE, I WOULDN'T BE CONSIDERED VERY NICE!
THAT'S TRUE.
©BOBSCOTT2014

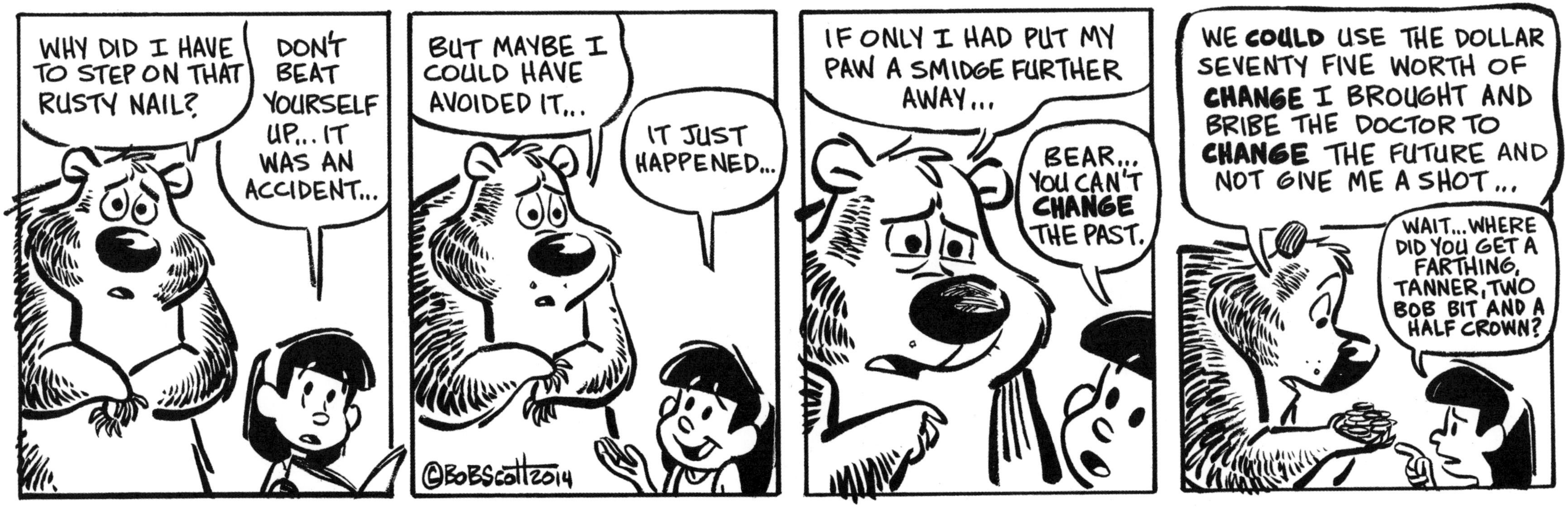
WHY DID I HAVE TO STEP ON THAT RUSTY NAIL?
DON'T BEAT YOURSELF UP... IT WAS AN ACCIDENT...
BUT MAYBE I COULD HAVE AVOIDED IT...
IT JUST HAPPENED...
©BOBSCOTT2014
IF ONLY I HAD PUT MY PAW A SMIDGE FURTHER AWAY...
BEAR... YOU CAN'T CHANGE THE PAST.
WE COULD USE THE DOLLAR SEVENTY FIVE WORTH OF CHANGE I BROUGHT AND BRIBE THE DOCTOR TO CHANGE THE FUTURE AND NOT GIVE ME A SHOT...
WAIT... WHERE DID YOU GET A FARTHING, TANNER, TWO BOB BIT AND A HALF CROWN?

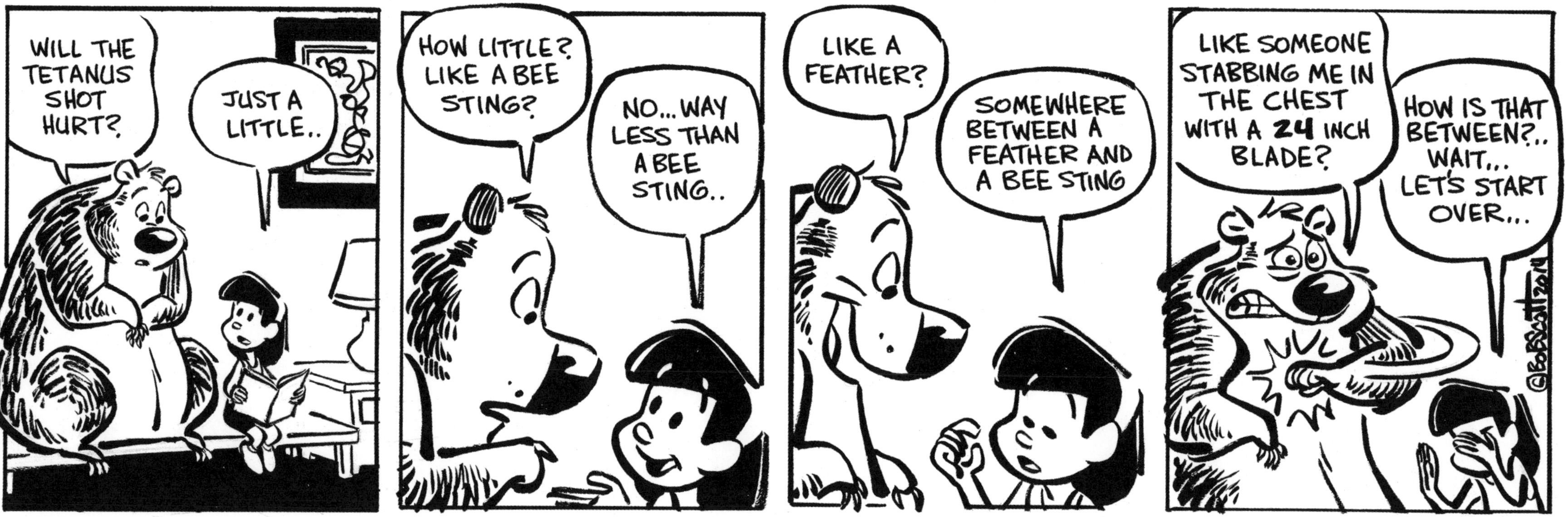
WILL THE TETANUS SHOT HURT?
JUST A LITTLE..
HOW LITTLE? LIKE A BEE STING?
NO... WAY LESS THAN A BEE STING..
LIKE A FEATHER?
SOMEWHERE BETWEEN A FEATHER AND A BEE STING
LIKE SOMEONE STABBING ME IN THE CHEST WITH A 24 INCH BLADE?
HOW IS THAT BETWEEN?.. WAIT,.. LET'S START OVER...
©BOBSCOTT2014

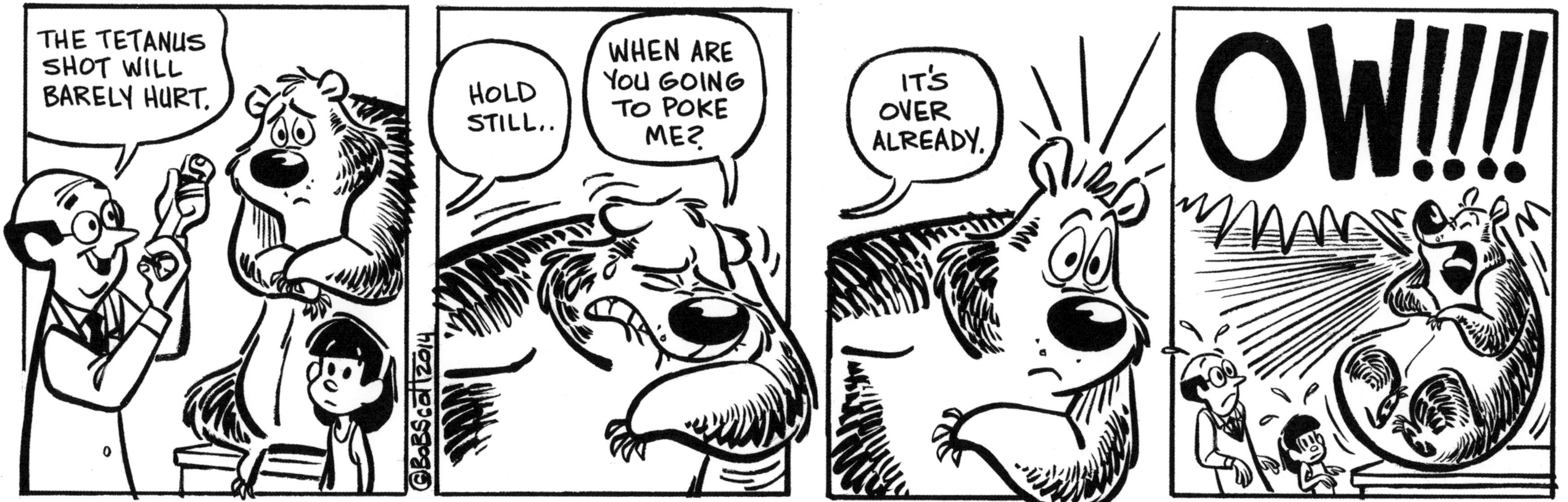
THE TETANUS SHOT WILL BARELY HURT.
©BOBSCOTT2014
HOLD STILL..
WHEN ARE YOU GOING TO POKE ME?
IT'S OVER ALREADY.
OW!!!!

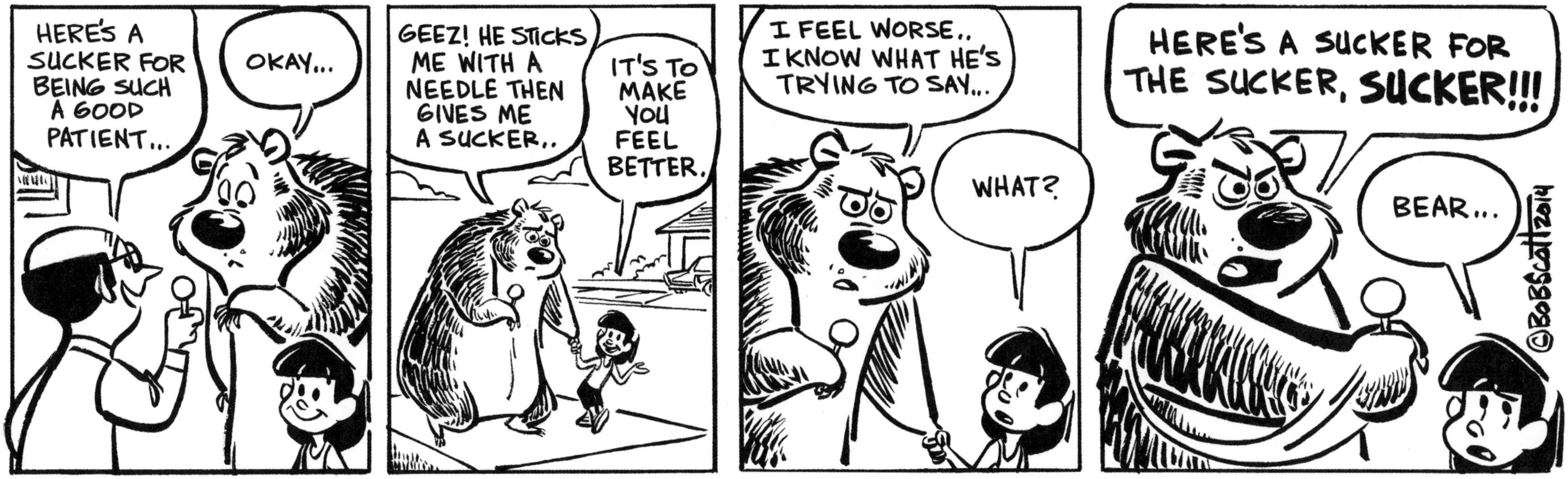
HERE'S A SUCKER FOR BEING SUCH A GOOD PATIENT...
OKAY...
GEEZ! HE STICKS ME WITH A NEEDLE THEN GIVES ME A SUCKER..
IT'S TO MAKE YOU FEEL BETTER.
I FEEL WORSE.. I KNOW WHAT HE'S TRYING TO SAY...
WHAT?
HERE'S A SUCKER FOR THE SUCKER, SUCKER!!!
BEAR...
©BOBSCOTT2014

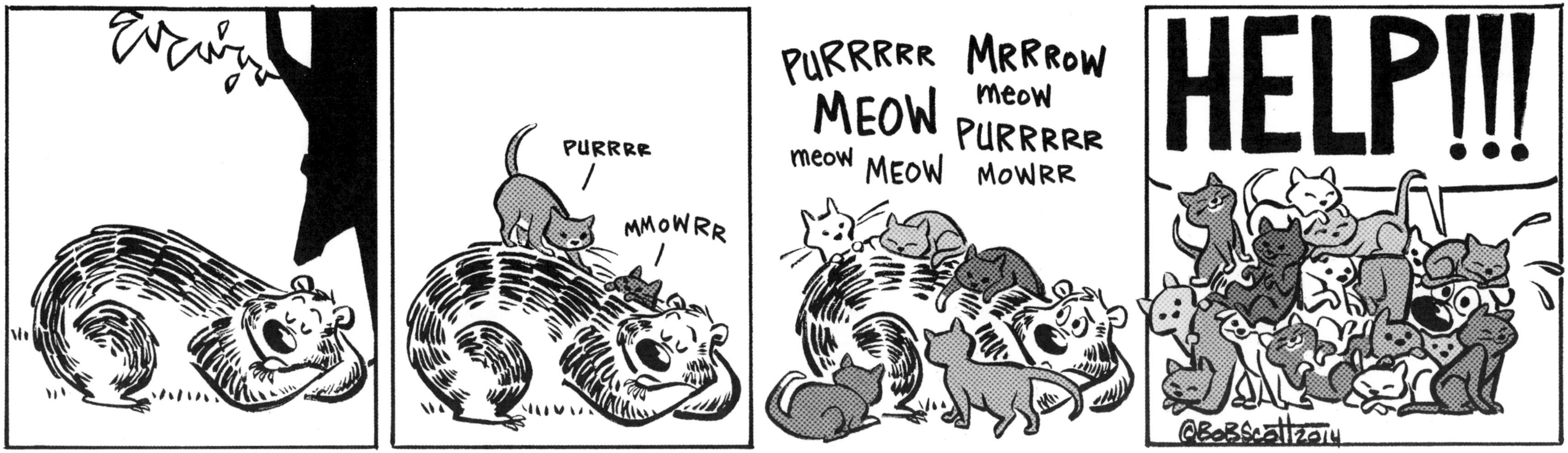
PURRRR
MMOWRR
PURRRRR
MEOW
meow
MEOW
MRRROW
meow
PURRRRR
MOWRR
HELP!!!
©BOBSCOTT2014

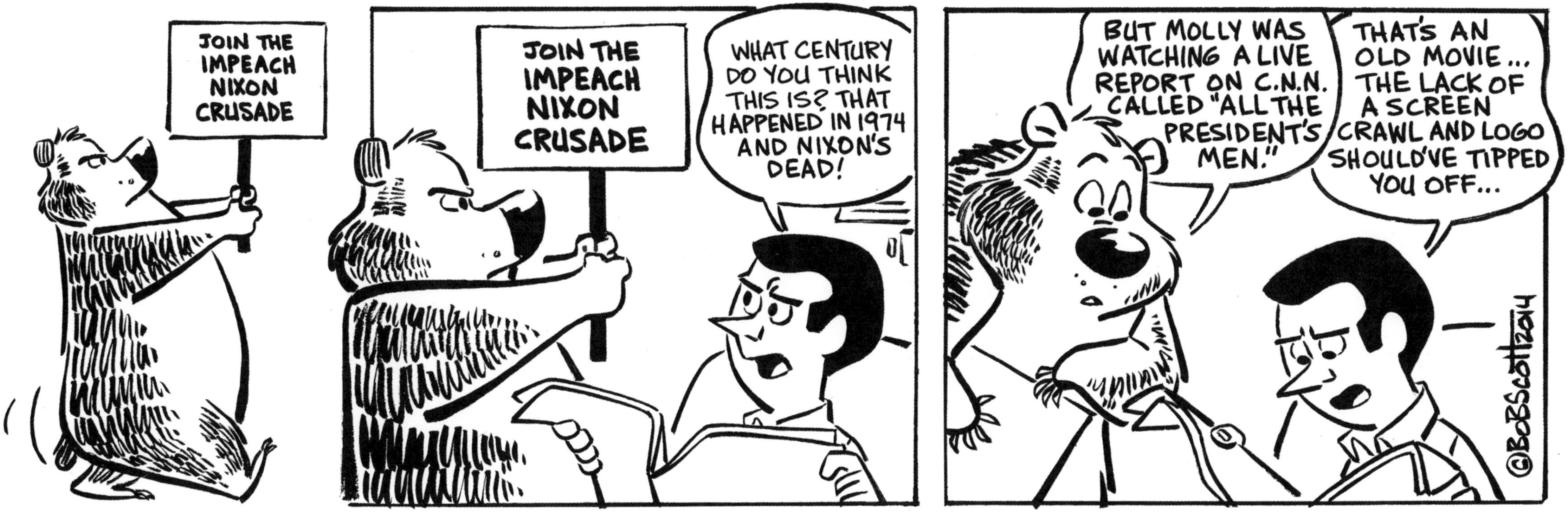
JOIN THE IMPEACH NIXON CRUSADE
JOIN THE IMPEACH NIXON CRUSADE
WHAT CENTURY DO YOU THINK THIS IS? THAT HAPPENED IN 1974 AND NIXON'S DEAD!
BUT MOLLY WAS WATCHING A LIVE REPORT ON C.N.N. CALLED "ALL THE PRESIDENT'S MEN."
THAT'S AN OLD MOVIE... THE LACK OF A SCREEN CRAWL AND LOGO SHOULD'VE TIPPED YOU OFF...
©BOBSCOTT 2014

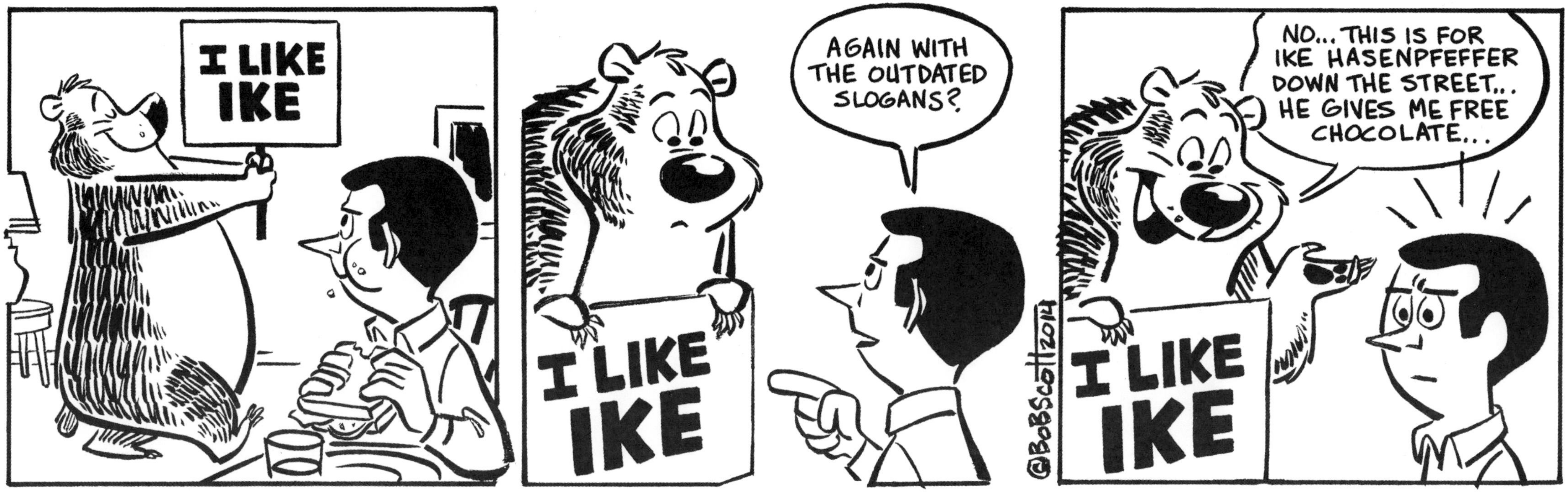
I LIKE IKE
I LIKE IKE
AGAIN WITH THE OUTDATED SLOGANS?
©BOBSCOTT 2014
NO... THIS IS FOR IKE HASENPFEFFER DOWN THE STREET... HE GIVES ME FREE CHOCOLATE...
I LIKE IKE

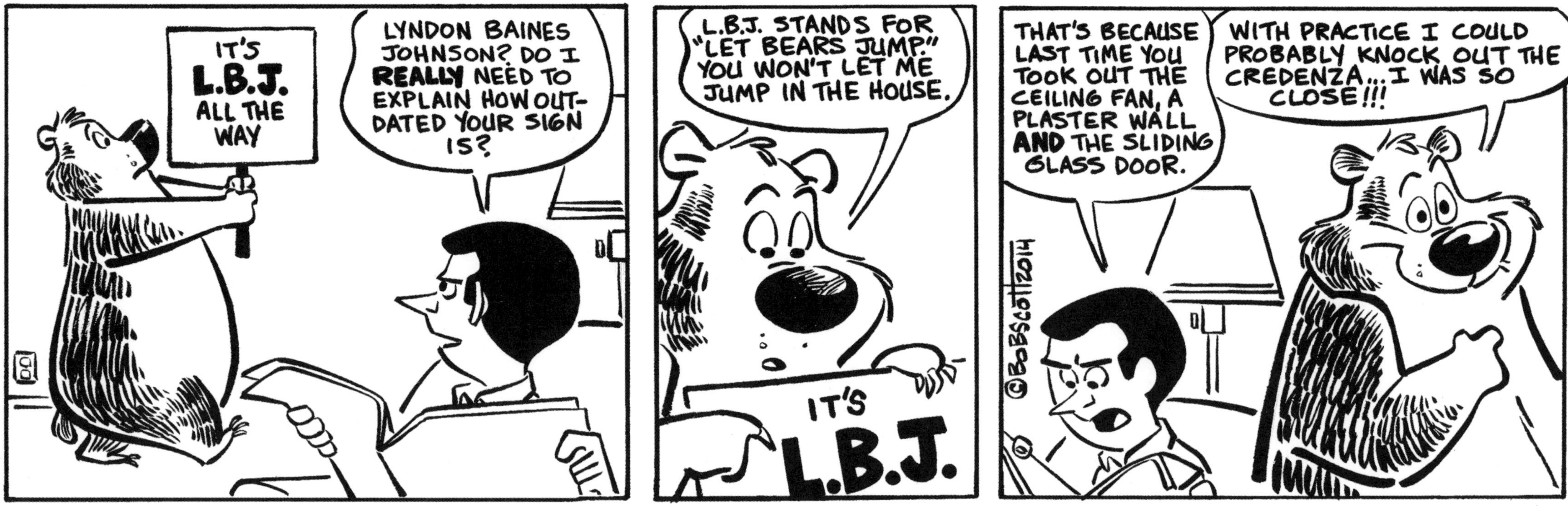
IT'S L.B.J. ALL THE WAY
LYNDON BAINES JOHNSON? DO I REALLY NEED TO EXPLAIN HOW OUT-DATED YOUR SIGN IS?
L.B.J. STANDS FOR "LET BEARS JUMP." YOU WON'T LET ME JUMP IN THE HOUSE.
IT'S L.B.J.
THAT'S BECAUSE LAST TIME YOU TOOK OUT THE CEILING FAN, A PLASTER WALL AND THE SLIDING GLASS DOOR.
WITH PRACTICE I COULD PROBABLY KNOCK OUT THE CREDENZA... I WAS SO CLOSE!!!
©BOBSCOTT2014

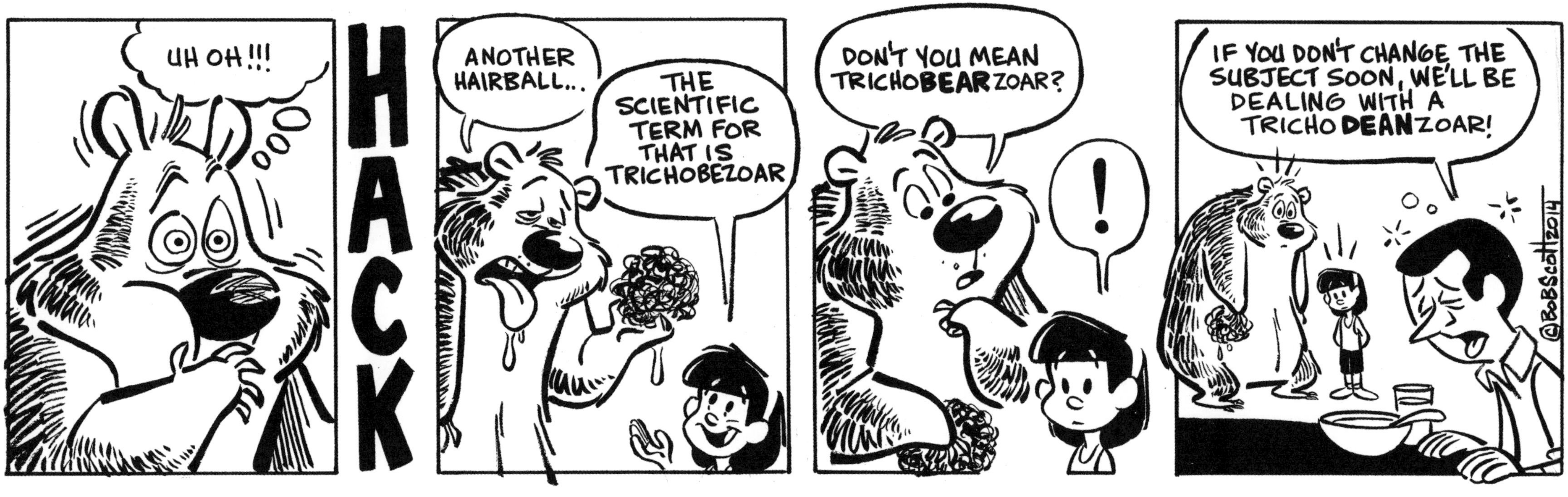
UH OH!!!
HACK
ANOTHER HAIRBALL...
THE SCIENTIFIC TERM FOR THAT IS TRICHOBEZOAR
DON'T YOU MEAN TRICHOBEARZOAR?
!
IF YOU DON'T CHANGE THE SUBJECT SOON, WE'LL BE DEALING WITH A TRICHODEANZOAR!
©BOBSCOTT2014

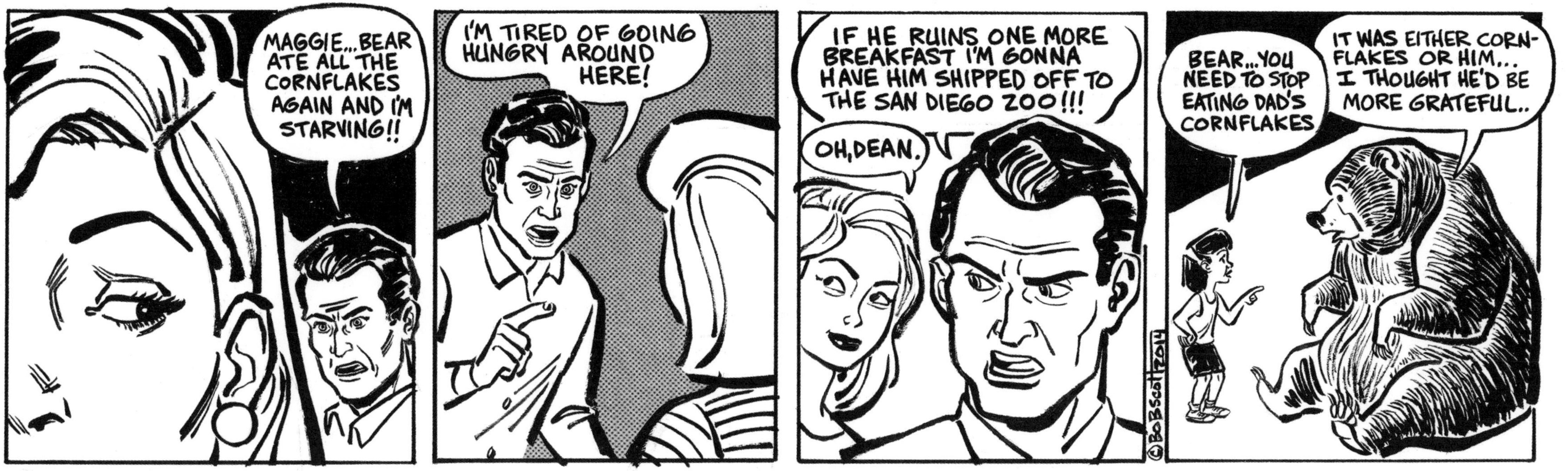
MAGGIE... BEAR ATE ALL THE CORNFLAKES AGAIN AND I'M STARVING!!
I'M TIRED OF GOING HUNGRY AROUND HERE!
IF HE RUINS ONE MORE BREAKFAST I'M GONNA HAVE HIM SHIPPED OFF TO THE SAN DIEGO ZOO!!!
OH, DEAN.
BEAR... YOU NEED TO STOP EATING DAD'S CORNFLAKES
IT WAS EITHER CORNFLAKES OR HIM... I THOUGHT HE'D BE MORE GRATEFUL..
©BoBScott2014

*April Fool's strip, published April 1, 2014

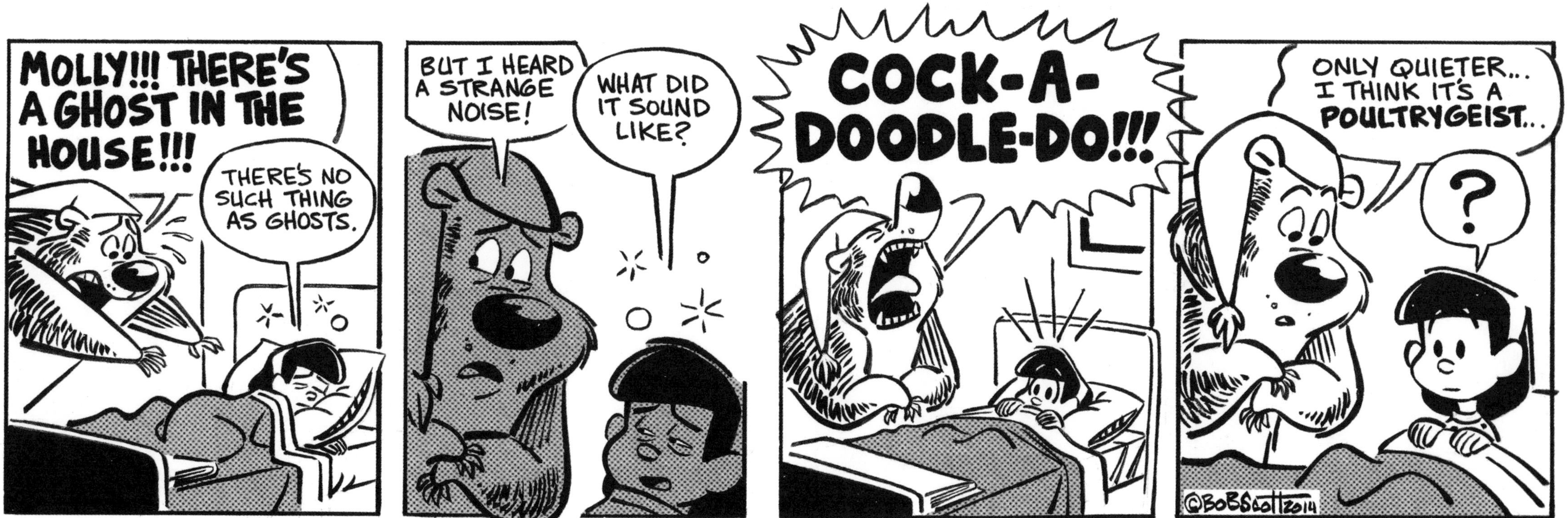
MOLLY!!! THERE'S A GHOST IN THE HOUSE!!!
THERE'S NO SUCH THING AS GHOSTS.
BUT I HEARD A STRANGE NOISE!
WHAT DID IT SOUND LIKE?
COCK-A-DOODLE-DO!!!
ONLY QUIETER... I THINK IT'S A POULTRYGEIST...
?
©BoBScott2014

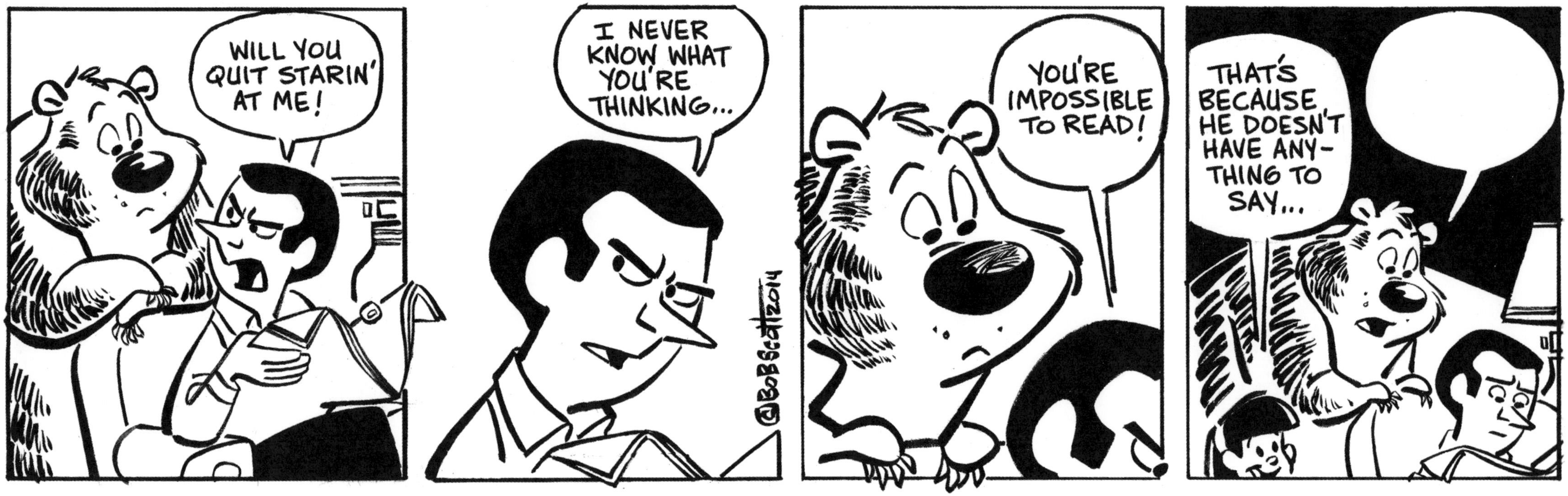
WILL YOU QUIT STARIN' AT ME!
I NEVER KNOW WHAT YOU'RE THINKING...
©BoBScott2014
YOU'RE IMPOSSIBLE TO READ!
THAT'S BECAUSE HE DOESN'T HAVE ANY-THING TO SAY...

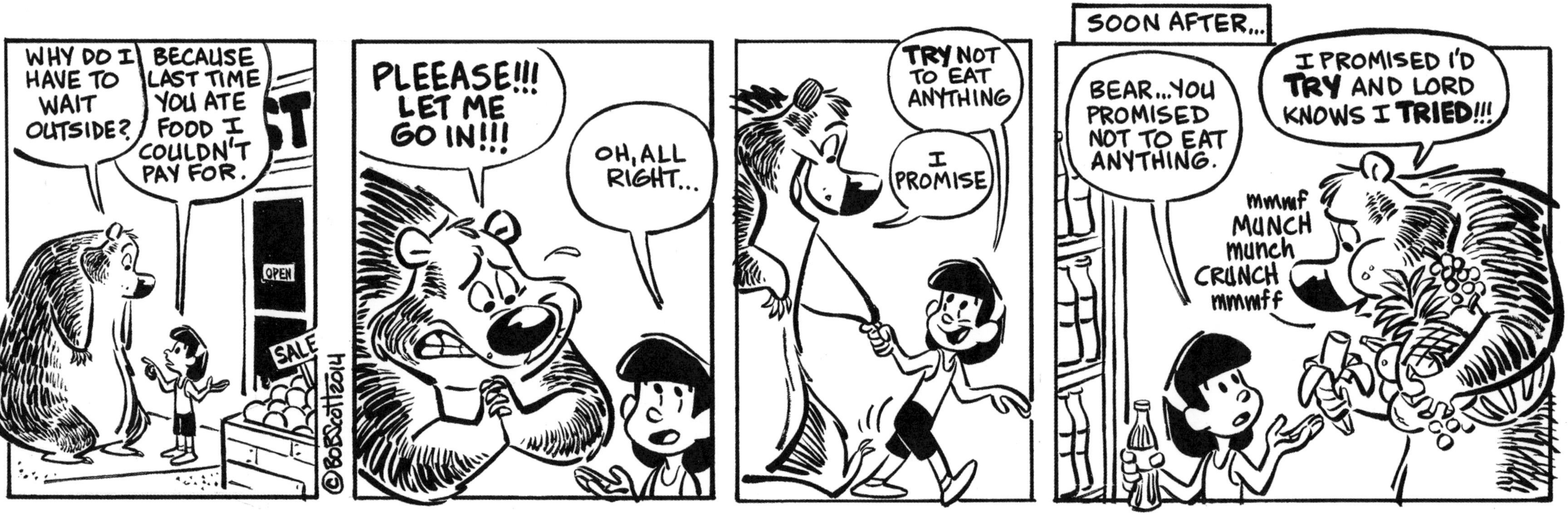
WHY DO I HAVE TO WAIT OUTSIDE?
BECAUSE LAST TIME YOU ATE FOOD I COULDN'T PAY FOR.
OPEN
SALE
©BoBScott2014
PLEEASE!!! LET ME GO IN!!!
OH, ALL RIGHT...
TRY NOT TO EAT ANYTHING
I PROMISE
SOON AFTER...
BEAR...YOU PROMISED NOT TO EAT ANYTHING.
I PROMISED I'D TRY AND LORD KNOWS I TRIED!!!
mmmf MUNCH munch CRUNCH mmmff

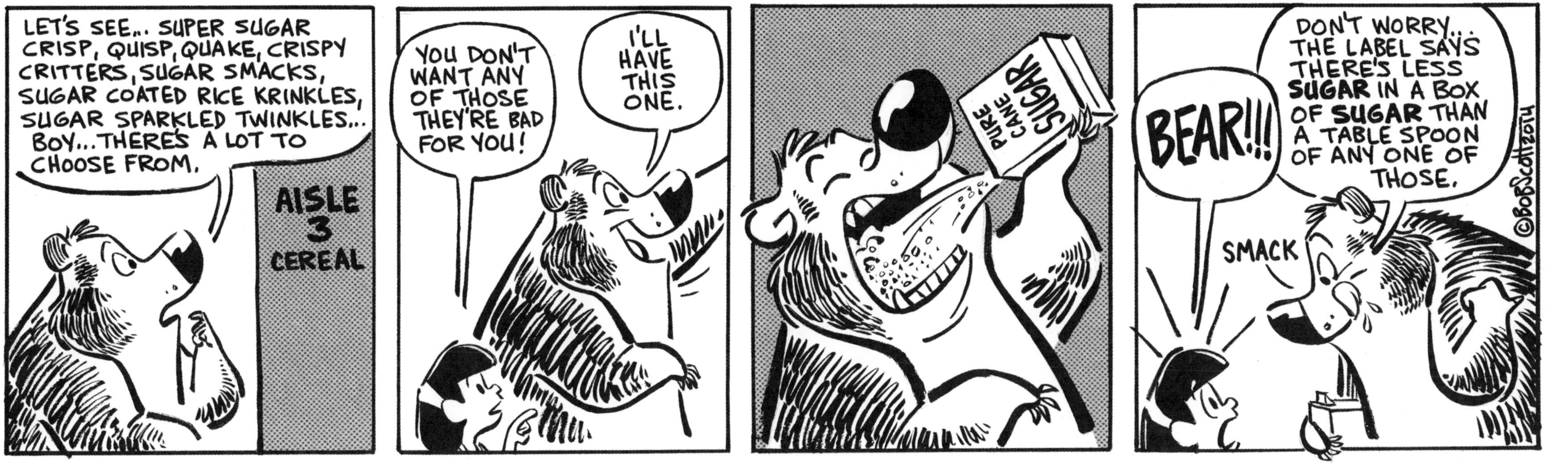
LET'S SEE... SUPER SUGAR CRISP, QUISP, QUAKE, CRISPY CRITTERS, SUGAR SMACKS, SUGAR COATED RICE KRINKLES, SUGAR SPARKLED TWINKLES... BOY... THERE'S A LOT TO CHOOSE FROM.
AISLE 3 CEREAL
YOU DON'T WANT ANY OF THOSE THEY'RE BAD FOR YOU!
I'LL HAVE THIS ONE.
PURE CANE SUGAR
BEAR!!!
SMACK
DON'T WORRY... THE LABEL SAYS THERE'S LESS **SUGAR** IN A BOX OF **SUGAR** THAN A TABLE SPOON OF ANY ONE OF THOSE.
©BOBSCOTT2014

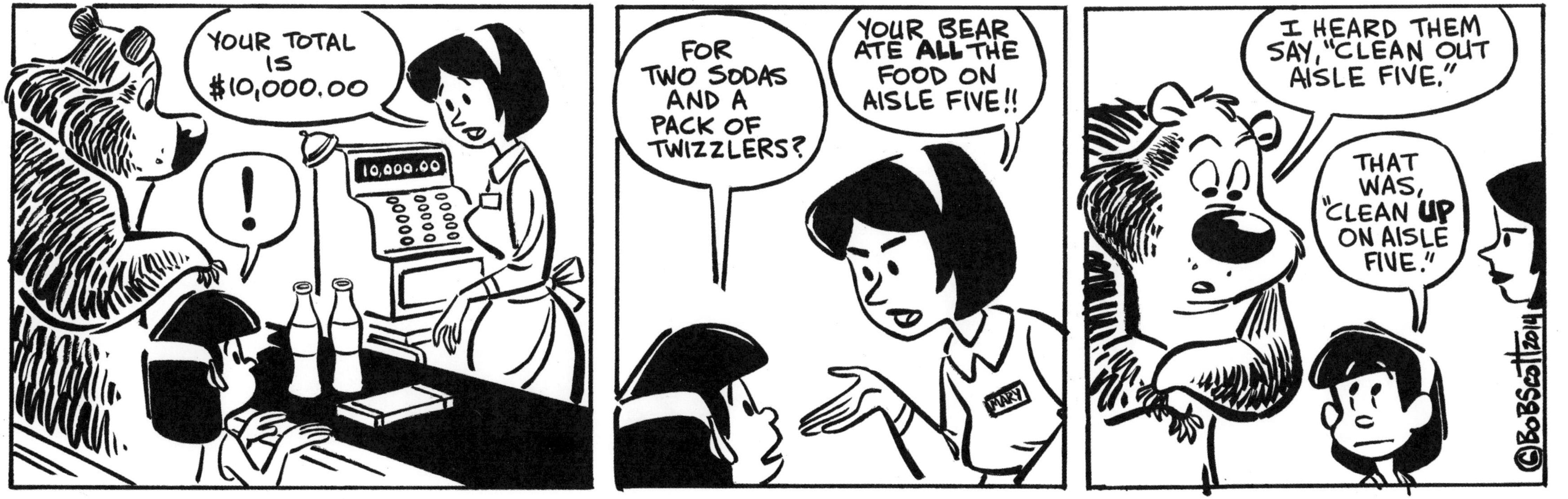
YOUR TOTAL IS $10,000.00
!
10,000.00
FOR TWO SODAS AND A PACK OF TWIZZLERS?
YOUR BEAR ATE **ALL** THE FOOD ON AISLE FIVE!!
MARY
I HEARD THEM SAY, "CLEAN OUT AISLE FIVE."
THAT WAS, "CLEAN **UP** ON AISLE FIVE."
©BOBSCOTT2014

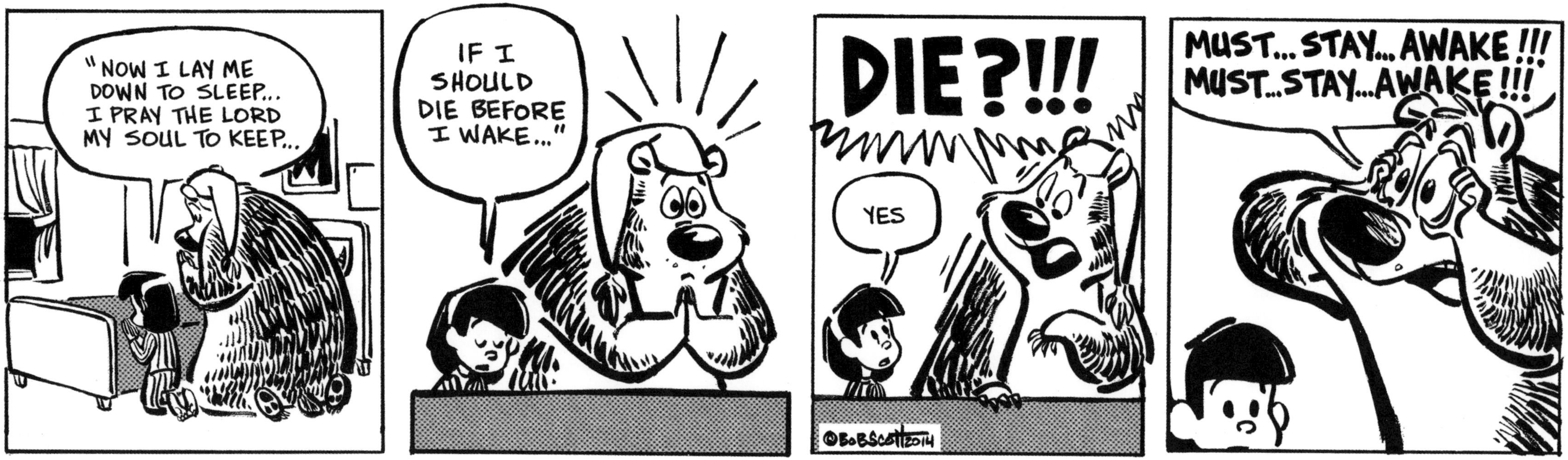
"NOW I LAY ME DOWN TO SLEEP... I PRAY THE LORD MY SOUL TO KEEP...
IF I SHOULD DIE BEFORE I WAKE..."
DIE?!!!
YES
©BOBSCOTT2014
MUST... STAY... AWAKE!!!
MUST...STAY...AWAKE!!!

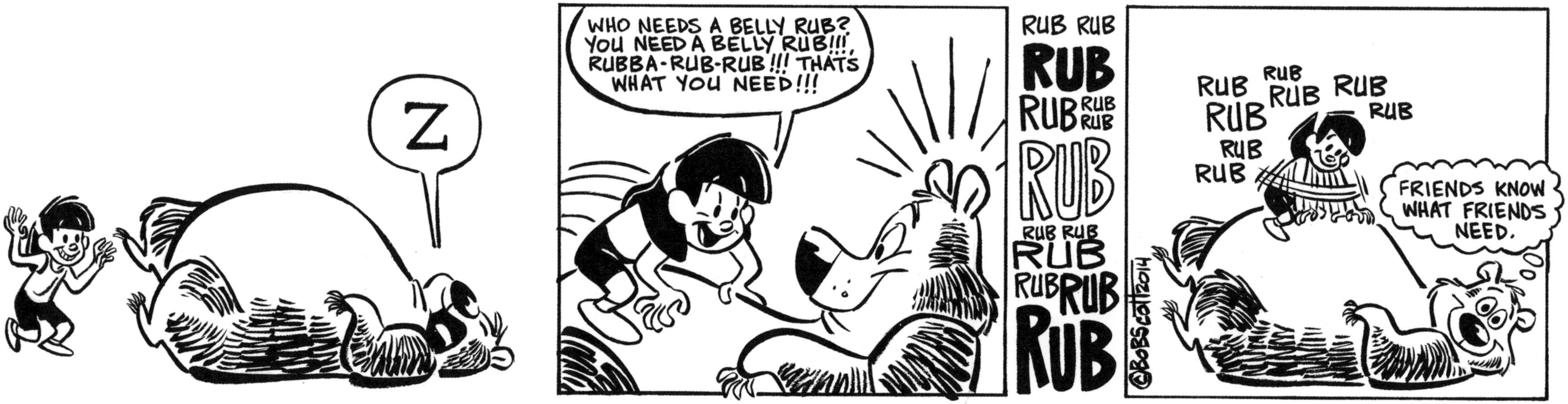
Z
WHO NEEDS A BELLY RUB? YOU NEED A BELLY RUB!!! RUBBA-RUB-RUB!!! THAT'S WHAT YOU NEED!!!
RUB RUB
RUB
RUB RUB RUB
RUB
RUB RUB
RUB
RUB RUB
RUB
©BOBSCOTT2014
RUB RUB RUB RUB RUB RUB RUB RUB
FRIENDS KNOW WHAT FRIENDS NEED.

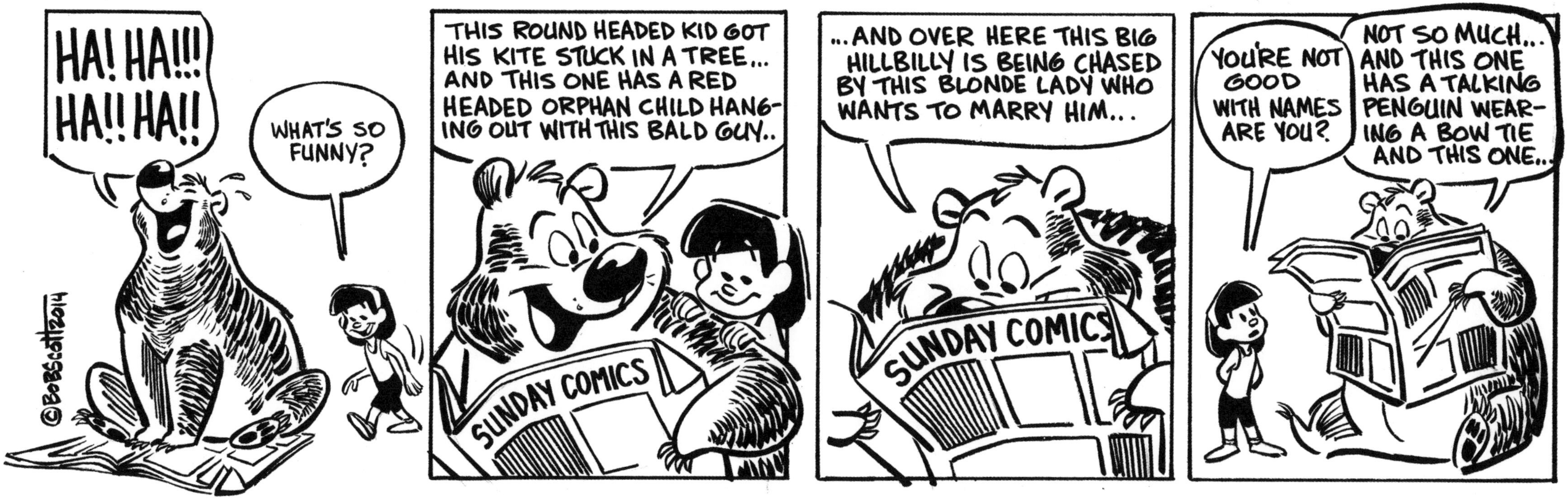
HA! HA!!! HA!! HA!!
WHAT'S SO FUNNY?
©BOBSCOTT2014
THIS ROUND HEADED KID GOT HIS KITE STUCK IN A TREE... AND THIS ONE HAS A RED HEADED ORPHAN CHILD HANGING OUT WITH THIS BALD GUY..
SUNDAY COMICS
...AND OVER HERE THIS BIG HILLBILLY IS BEING CHASED BY THIS BLONDE LADY WHO WANTS TO MARRY HIM...
SUNDAY COMICS
YOU'RE NOT GOOD WITH NAMES ARE YOU?
NOT SO MUCH... AND THIS ONE HAS A TALKING PENGUIN WEARING A BOW TIE AND THIS ONE..

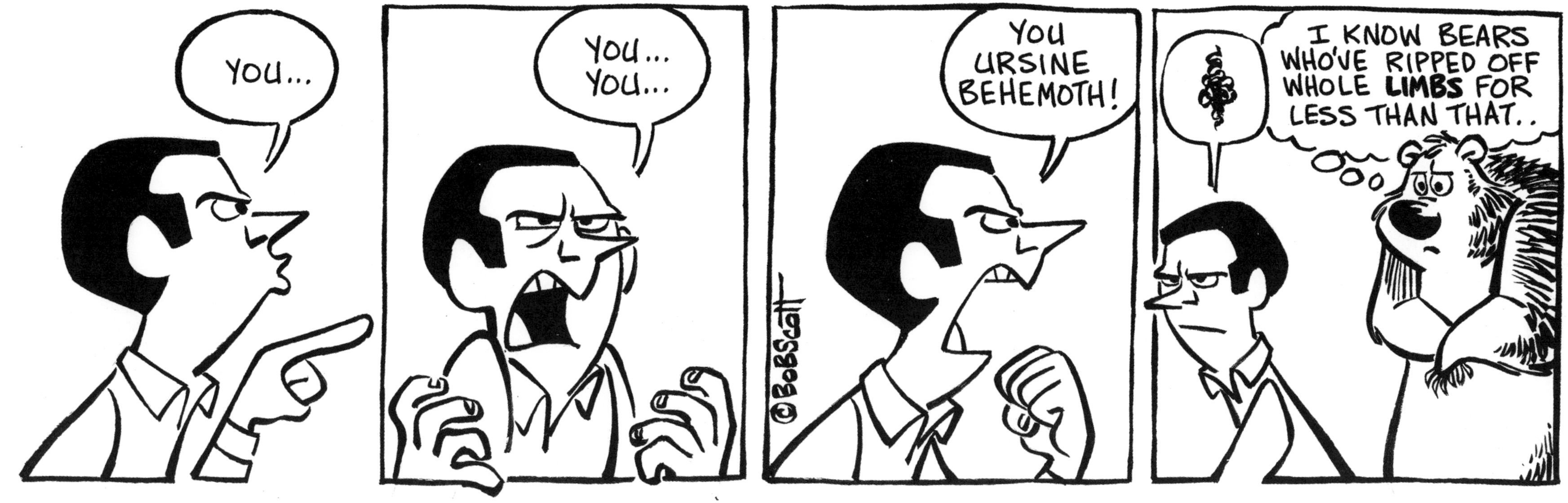
YOU...
YOU... YOU...
YOU URSINE BEHEMOTH!
©BOBSCOTT
I KNOW BEARS WHO'VE RIPPED OFF WHOLE **LIMBS** FOR LESS THAN THAT..

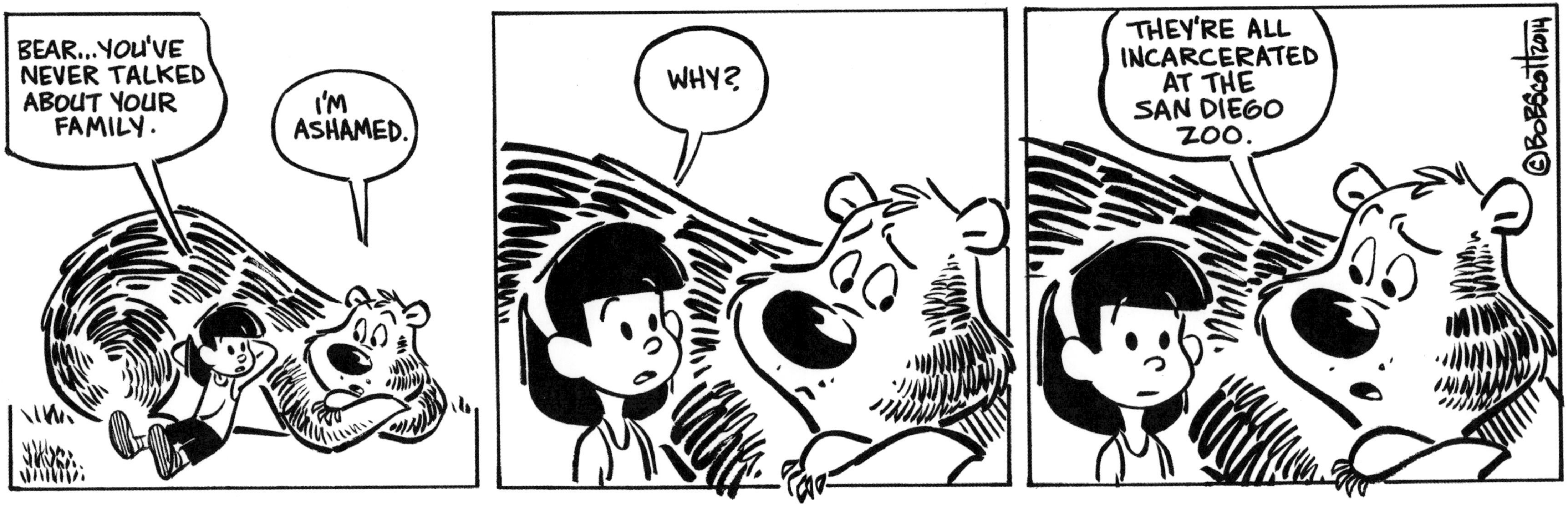
BEAR...YOU'VE NEVER TALKED ABOUT YOUR FAMILY.
I'M ASHAMED.
WHY?
THEY'RE ALL INCARCERATED AT THE SAN DIEGO ZOO.
©BOBSCOTT 2014

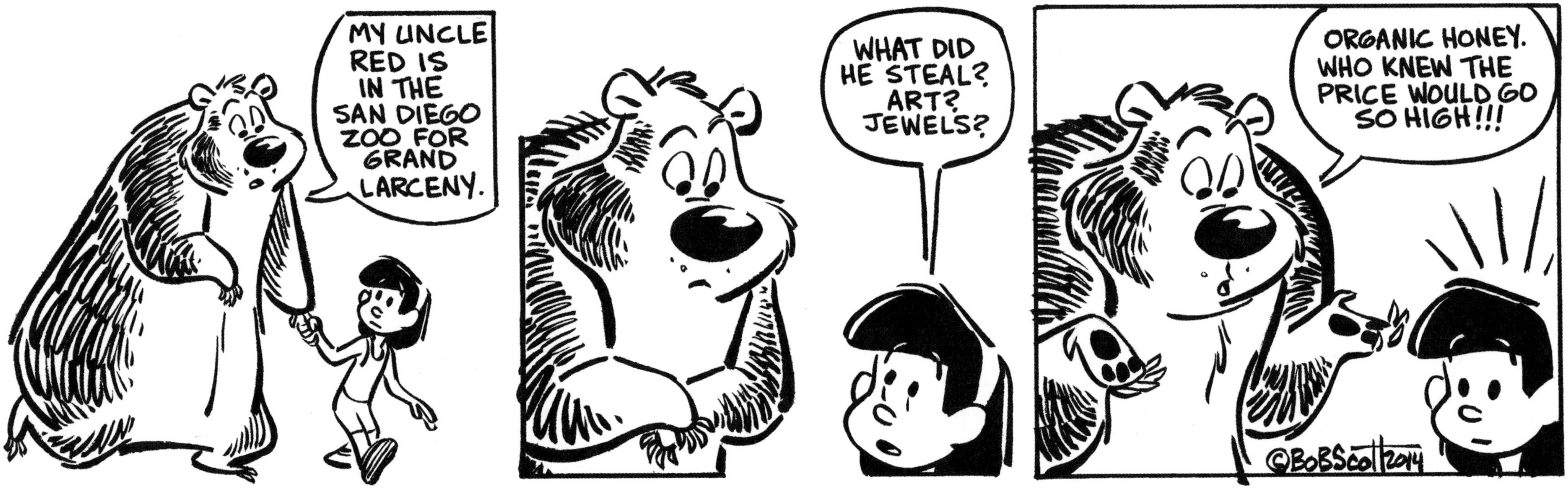
MY UNCLE RED IS IN THE SAN DIEGO ZOO FOR GRAND LARCENY.
WHAT DID HE STEAL? ART? JEWELS?
ORGANIC HONEY. WHO KNEW THE PRICE WOULD GO SO HIGH!!!
©BOBSCOTT 2014

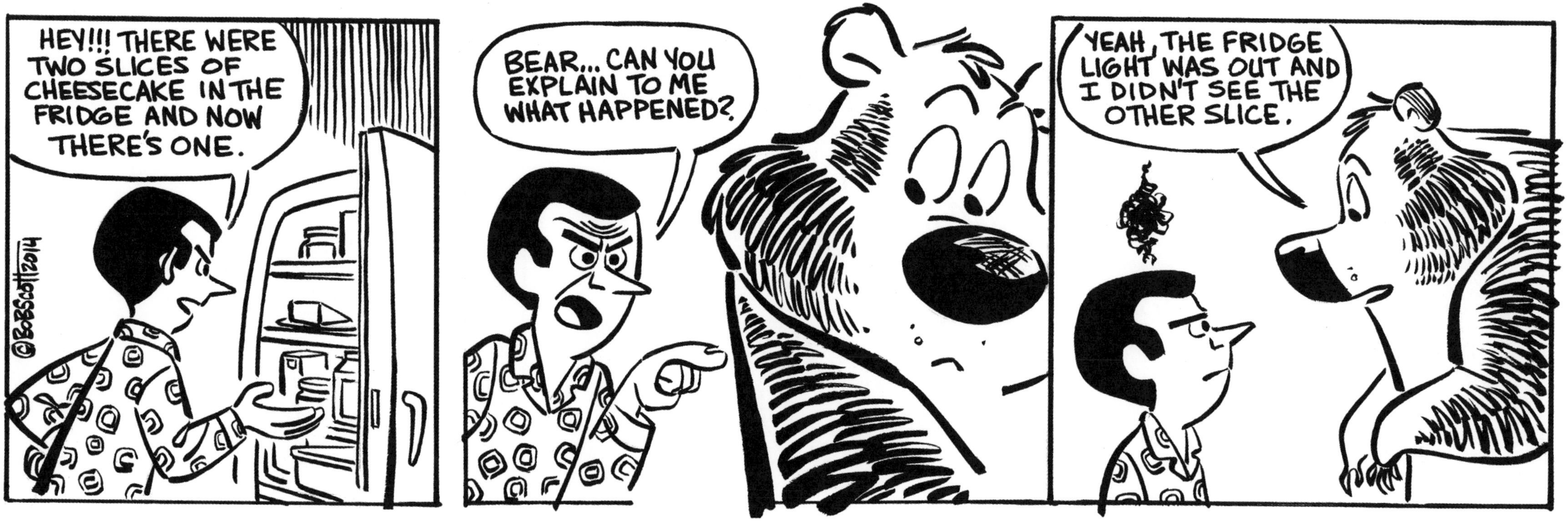
©BOBSCOTT2014
HEY!!! THERE WERE TWO SLICES OF CHEESECAKE IN THE FRIDGE AND NOW THERE'S ONE.
BEAR... CAN YOU EXPLAIN TO ME WHAT HAPPENED?
YEAH, THE FRIDGE LIGHT WAS OUT AND I DIDN'T SEE THE OTHER SLICE.

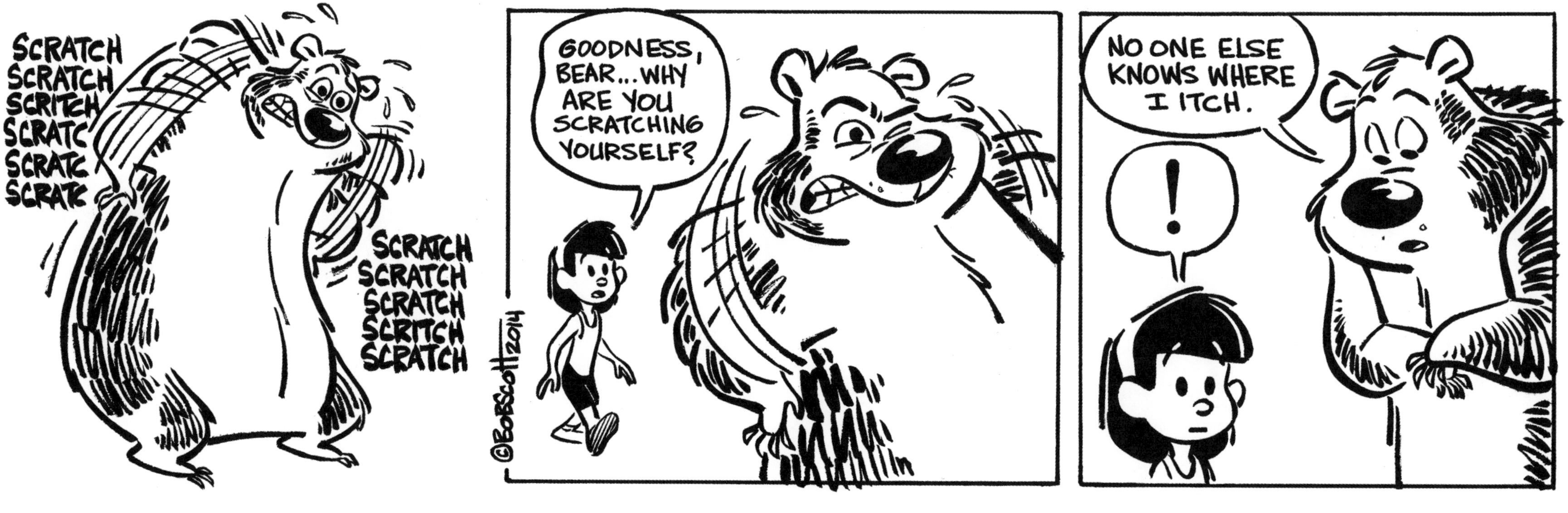
SCRATCH SCRATCH SCRITCH SCRATC SCRATC SCRATC
SCRATCH SCRATCH SCRATCH SCRITCH SCRATCH
©BOBSCOTT2014
GOODNESS, BEAR... WHY ARE YOU SCRATCHING YOURSELF?
NO ONE ELSE KNOWS WHERE I ITCH.
!

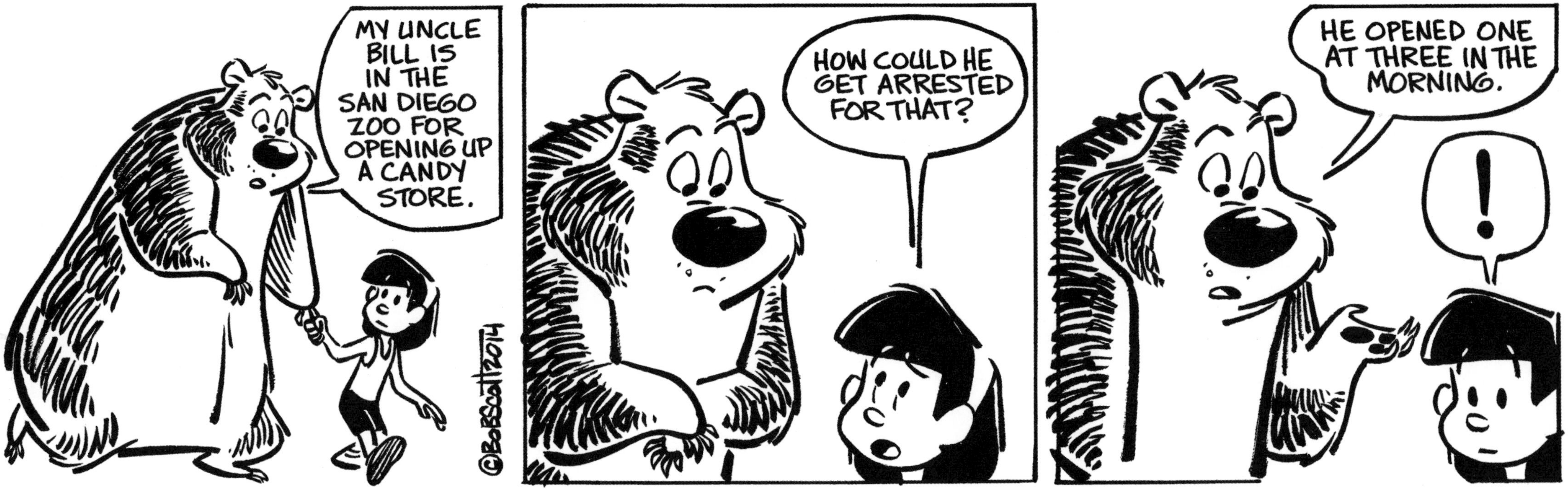
MY UNCLE BILL IS IN THE SAN DIEGO ZOO FOR OPENING UP A CANDY STORE.
©BOBSCOTT2014
HOW COULD HE GET ARRESTED FOR THAT?
HE OPENED ONE AT THREE IN THE MORNING.
!

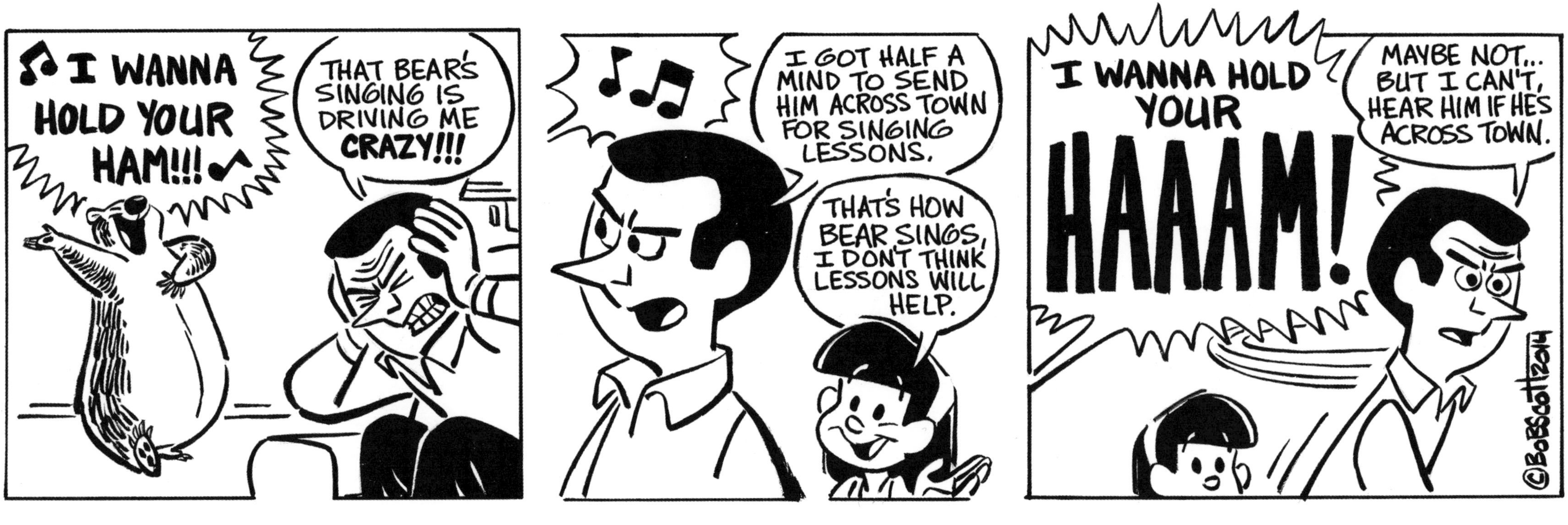
♫ I WANNA HOLD YOUR HAM!!! ♪
THAT BEAR'S SINGING IS DRIVING ME CRAZY!!!
♪♫
I GOT HALF A MIND TO SEND HIM ACROSS TOWN FOR SINGING LESSONS.
THAT'S HOW BEAR SINGS, I DON'T THINK LESSONS WILL HELP.
I WANNA HOLD YOUR HAAAM!
MAYBE NOT... BUT I CAN'T HEAR HIM IF HE'S ACROSS TOWN.
©BOBSCOTT2014

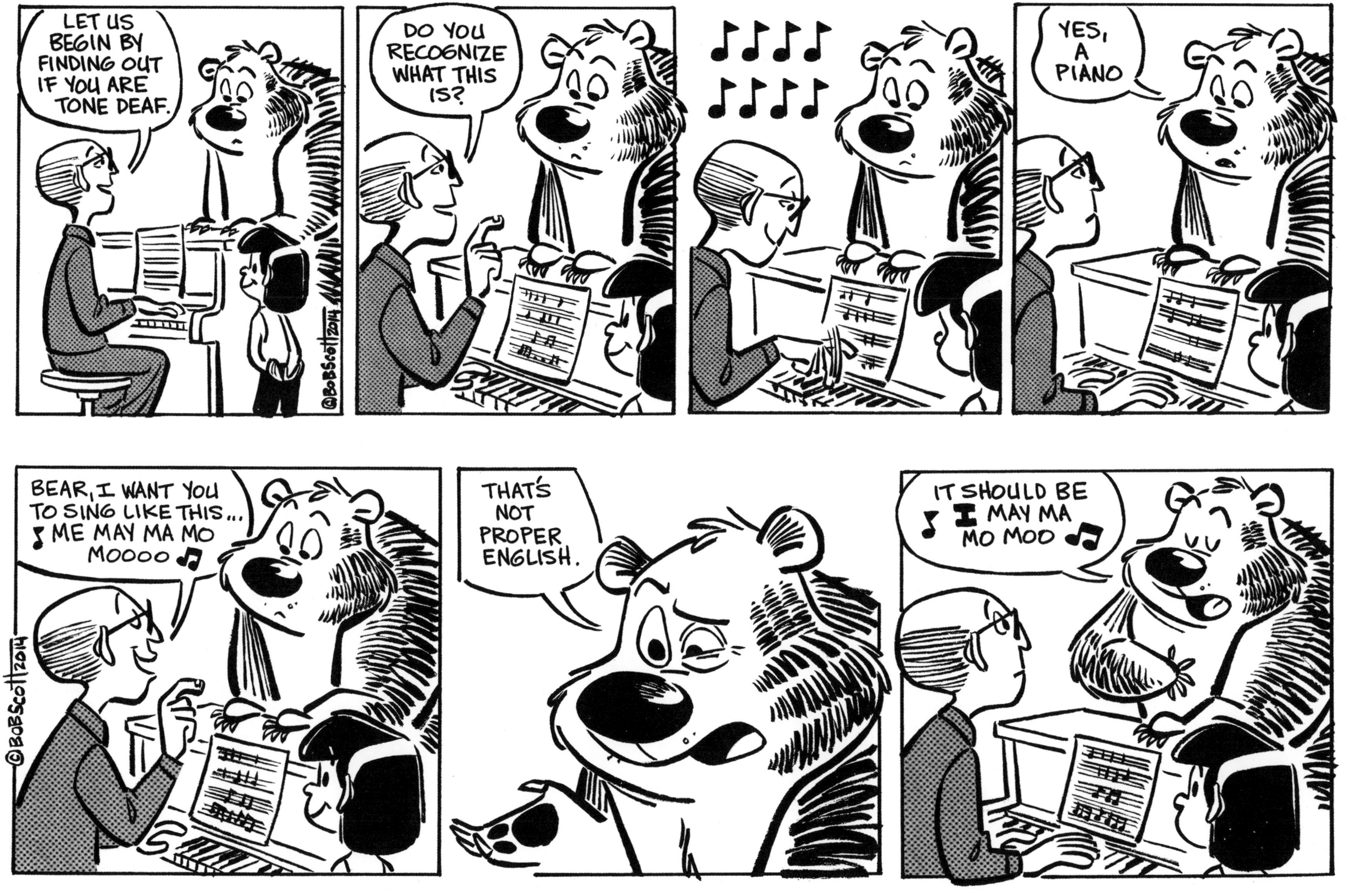
LET US BEGIN BY FINDING OUT IF YOU ARE TONE DEAF.
©BOBSCOTT2014
DO YOU RECOGNIZE WHAT THIS IS?
YES, A PIANO
BEAR, I WANT YOU TO SING LIKE THIS... ME MAY MA MO MOOOO
©BOBSCOTT2014
THAT'S NOT PROPER ENGLISH.
IT SHOULD BE I MAY MA MO MOO

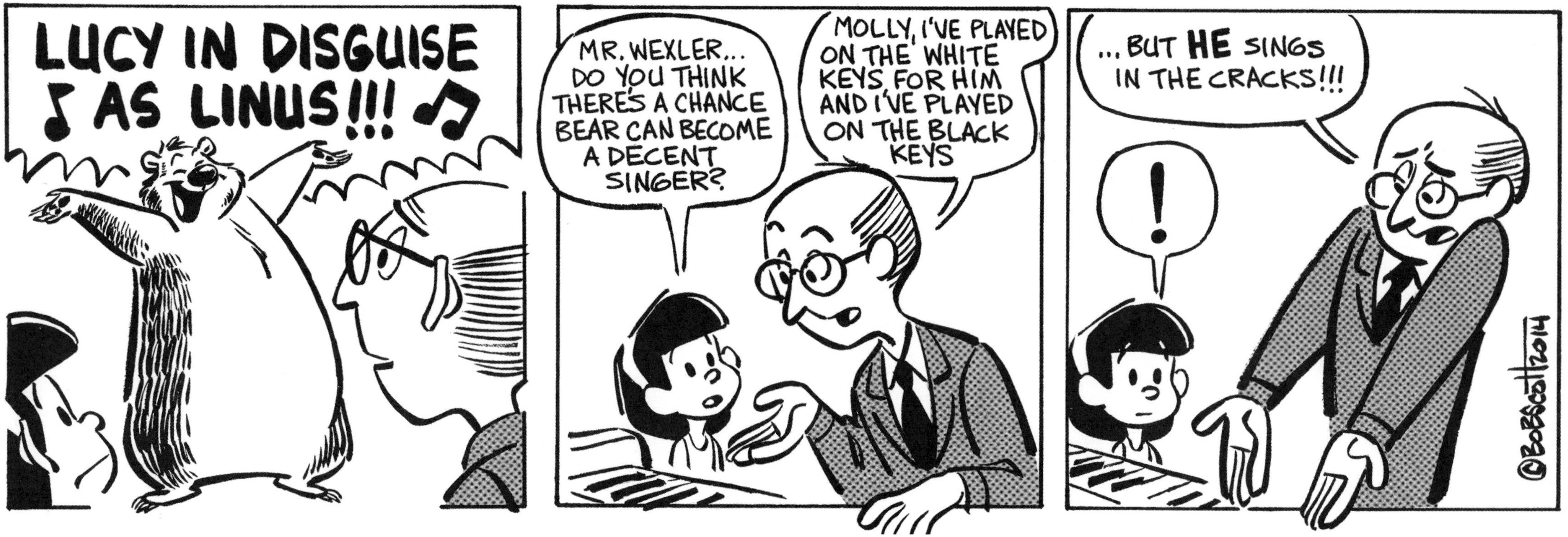
LUCY IN DISGUISE AS LINUS!!!
MR. WEXLER... DO YOU THINK THERE'S A CHANCE BEAR CAN BECOME A DECENT SINGER?
MOLLY, I'VE PLAYED ON THE WHITE KEYS FOR HIM AND I'VE PLAYED ON THE BLACK KEYS
... BUT HE SINGS IN THE CRACKS!!!
!
©BOBSCOTT2014

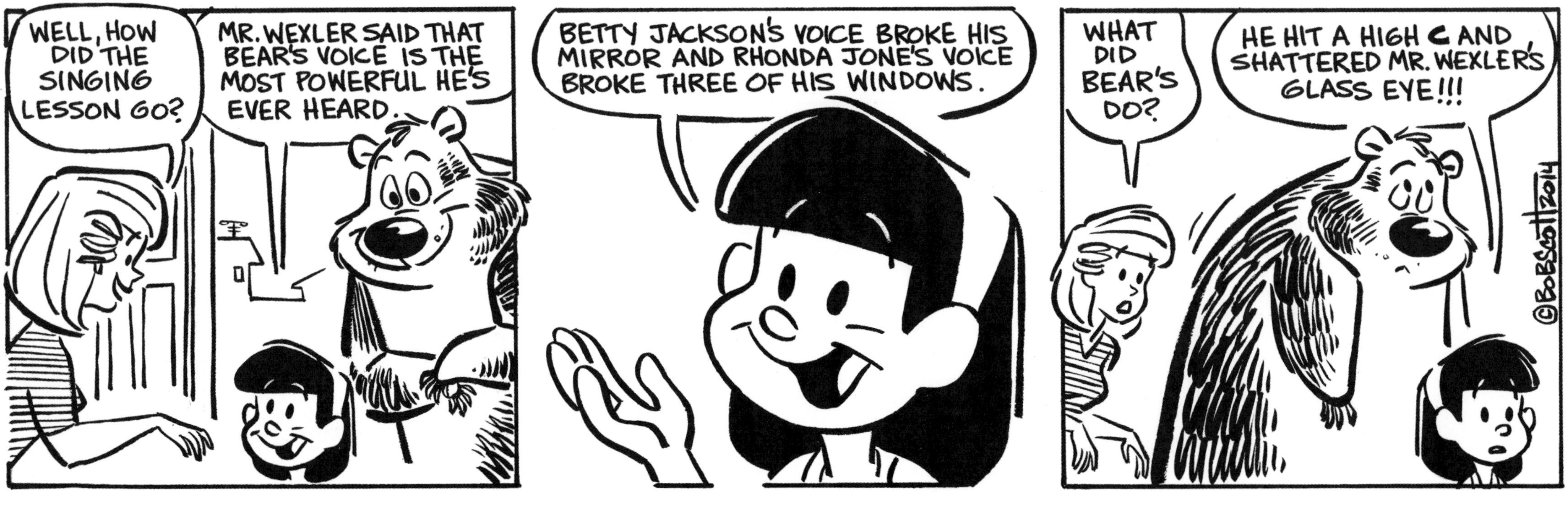
WELL, HOW DID THE SINGING LESSON GO?
MR. WEXLER SAID THAT BEAR'S VOICE IS THE MOST POWERFUL HE'S EVER HEARD.
BETTY JACKSON'S VOICE BROKE HIS MIRROR AND RHONDA JONE'S VOICE BROKE THREE OF HIS WINDOWS.
WHAT DID BEAR'S DO?
HE HIT A HIGH C AND SHATTERED MR. WEXLER'S GLASS EYE!!!
©BOBSCOTT2014

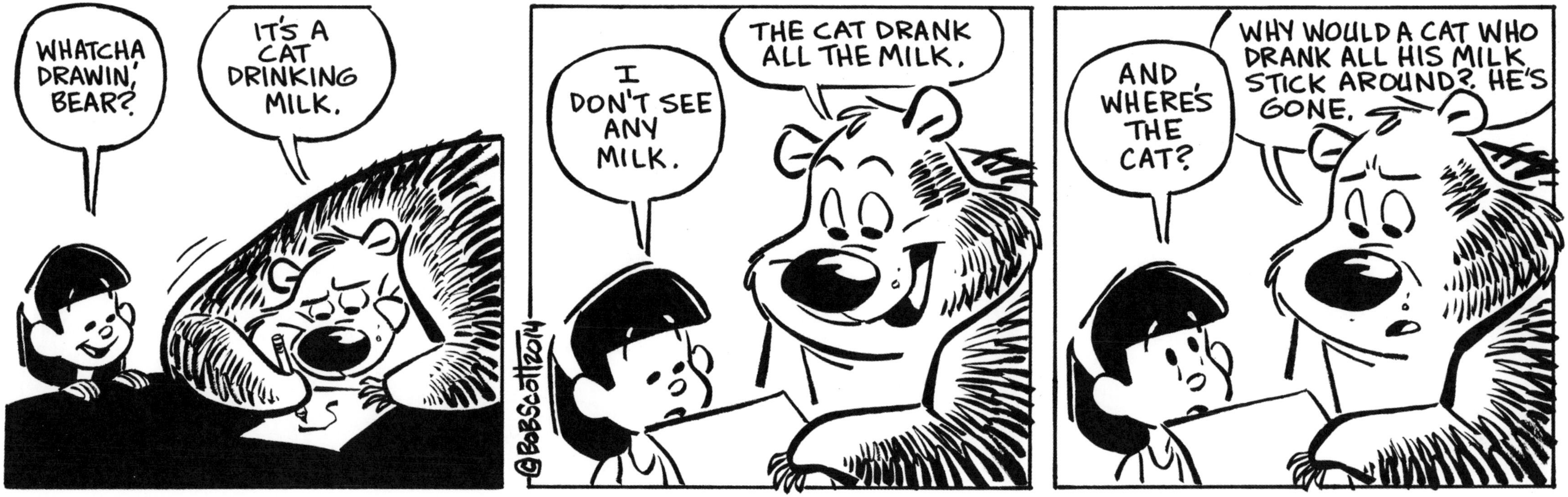
WHATCHA DRAWIN' BEAR?
IT'S A CAT DRINKING MILK.
©BOBSCOTT2014
THE CAT DRANK ALL THE MILK.
I DON'T SEE ANY MILK.
AND WHERE'S THE CAT?
WHY WOULD A CAT WHO DRANK ALL HIS MILK STICK AROUND? HE'S GONE.

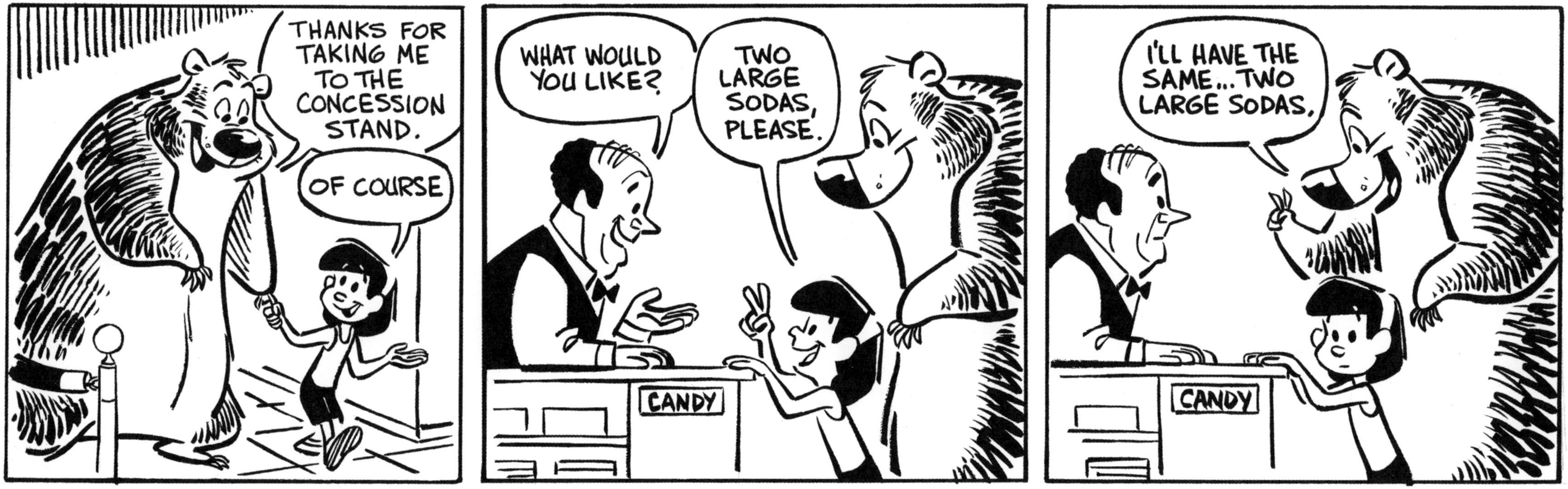
THANKS FOR TAKING ME TO THE CONCESSION STAND.
OF COURSE
WHAT WOULD YOU LIKE?
TWO LARGE SODAS, PLEASE.
CANDY
I'LL HAVE THE SAME... TWO LARGE SODAS.
CANDY

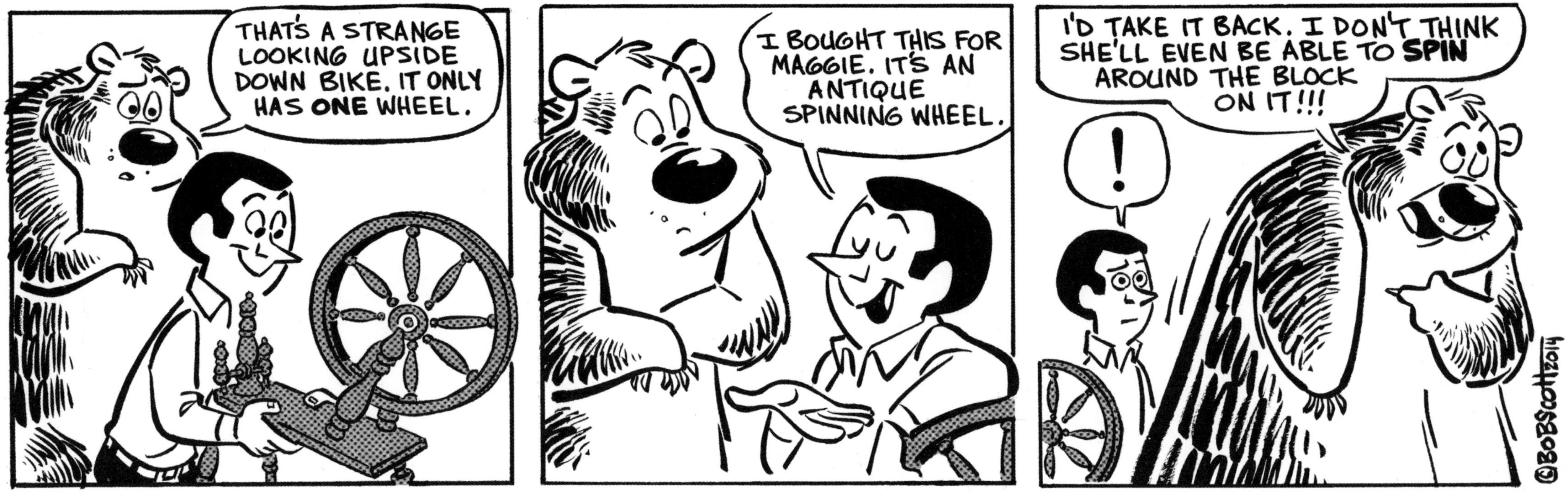
THAT'S A STRANGE LOOKING UPSIDE DOWN BIKE. IT ONLY HAS **ONE** WHEEL.
I BOUGHT THIS FOR MAGGIE. IT'S AN ANTIQUE SPINNING WHEEL.
!
I'D TAKE IT BACK. I DON'T THINK SHE'LL EVEN BE ABLE TO **SPIN** AROUND THE BLOCK ON IT!!!
©BOBSCOTT2014

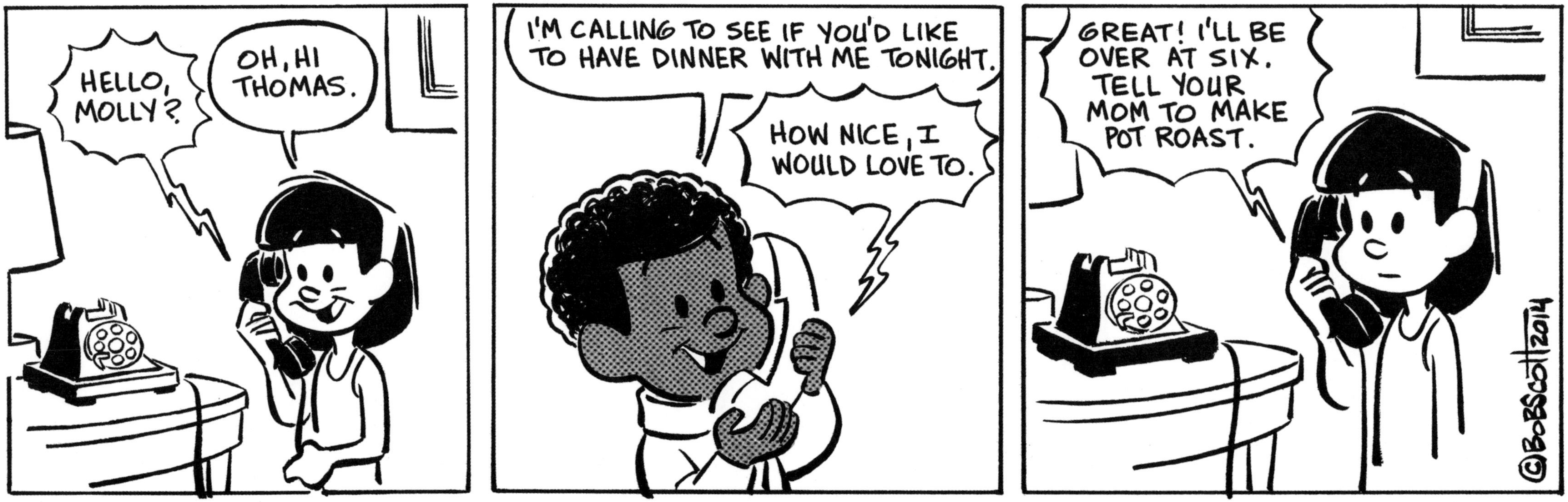
HELLO, MOLLY?
OH, HI THOMAS.
I'M CALLING TO SEE IF YOU'D LIKE TO HAVE DINNER WITH ME TONIGHT.
HOW NICE, I WOULD LOVE TO.
GREAT! I'LL BE OVER AT SIX. TELL YOUR MOM TO MAKE POT ROAST.
©BOBSCOTT2014

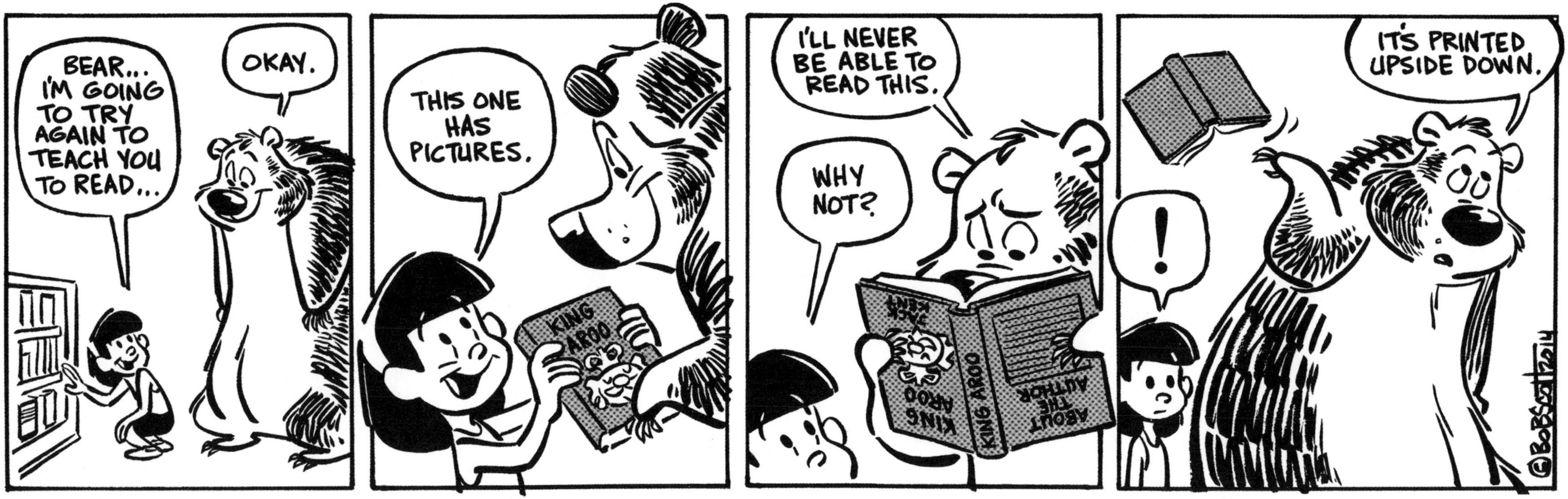
BEAR... I'M GOING TO TRY AGAIN TO TEACH YOU TO READ...
OKAY.
THIS ONE HAS PICTURES.
KING AROO
I'LL NEVER BE ABLE TO READ THIS.
WHY NOT?
KING AROO
!
IT'S PRINTED UPSIDE DOWN.
©BOBSCOTT2014

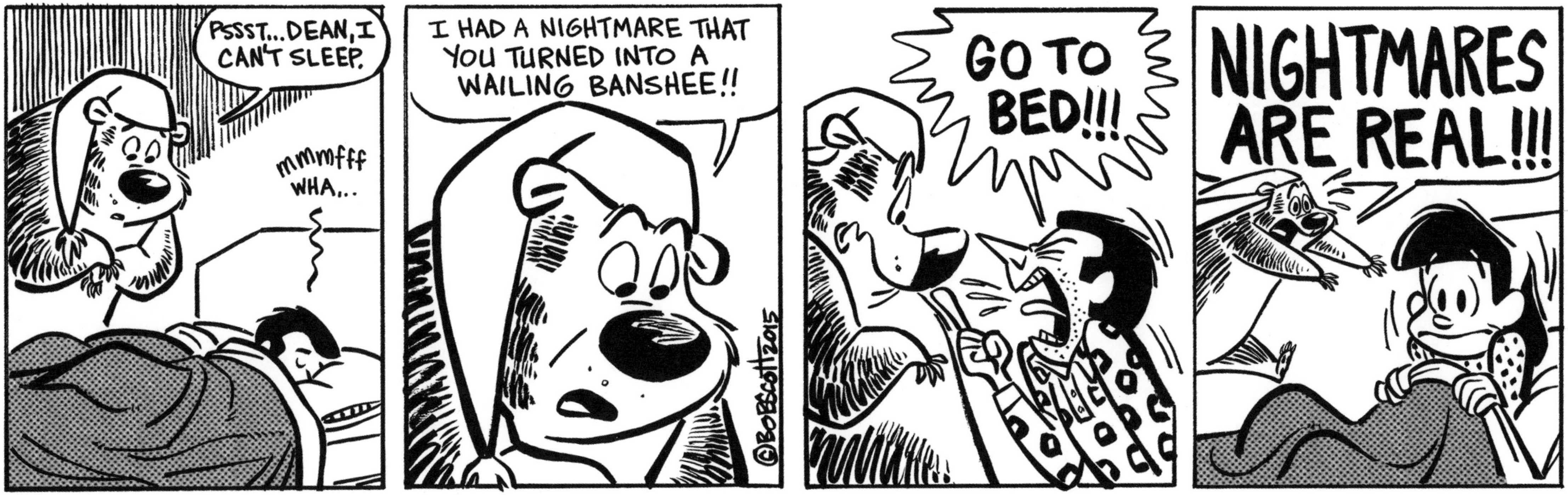
PSSST...DEAN, I CAN'T SLEEP.
mmmfff WHA...
I HAD A NIGHTMARE THAT YOU TURNED INTO A WAILING BANSHEE!!
©BOBSCOTT2015
GO TO BED!!!
NIGHTMARES ARE REAL!!!

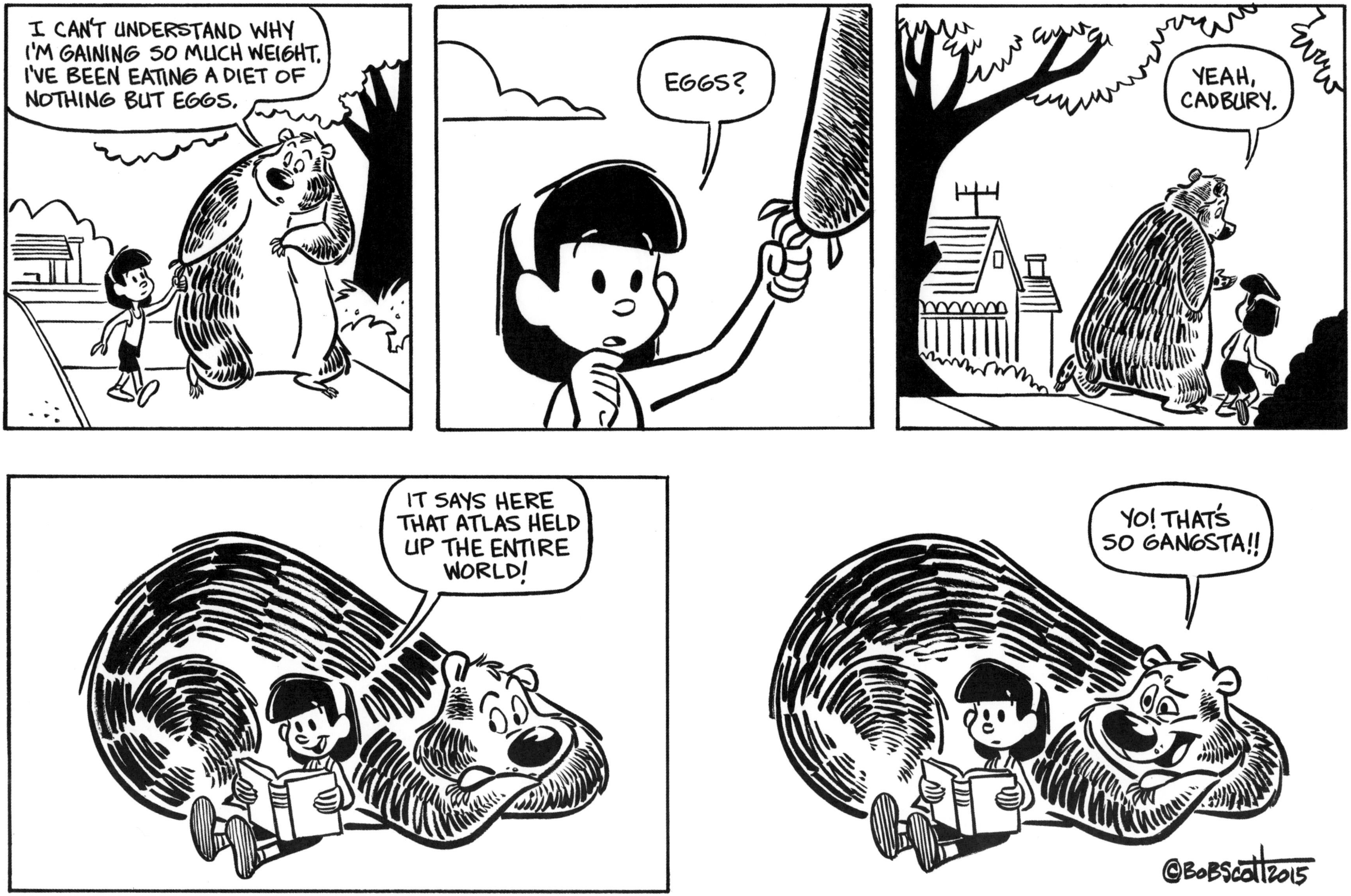
I CAN'T UNDERSTAND WHY I'M GAINING SO MUCH WEIGHT. I'VE BEEN EATING A DIET OF NOTHING BUT EGGS.
EGGS?
YEAH, CADBURY.
IT SAYS HERE THAT ATLAS HELD UP THE ENTIRE WORLD!
YO! THAT'S SO GANGSTA!!
©BOBSCOTT2015

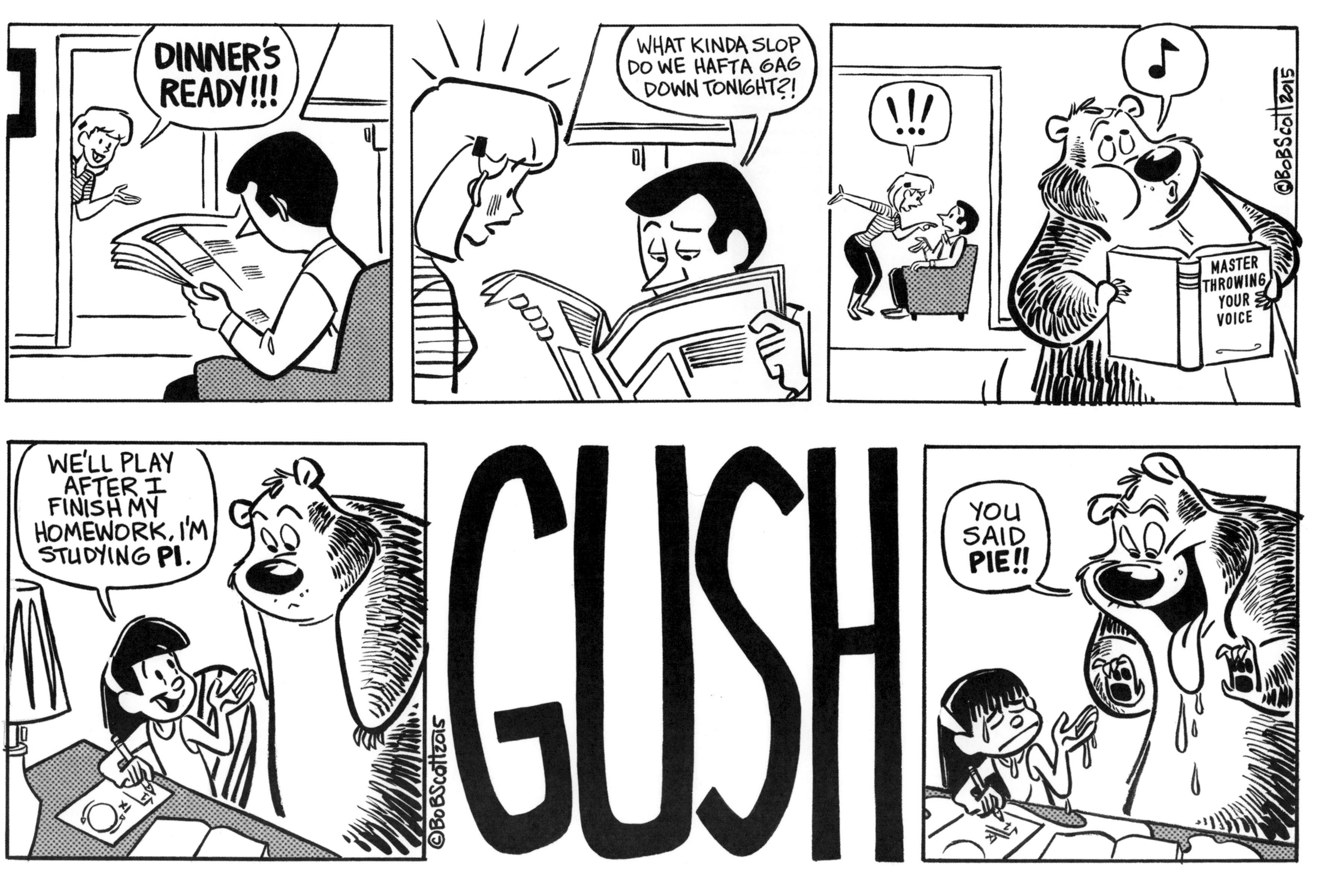
DINNER'S READY!!!
WHAT KINDA SLOP DO WE HAFTA GAG DOWN TONIGHT?!
!!!
MASTER THROWING YOUR VOICE
©BoBScott2015
WE'LL PLAY AFTER I FINISH MY HOMEWORK, I'M STUDYING **PI**.
©BoBScott2015
GUSH
YOU SAID **PIE**!!

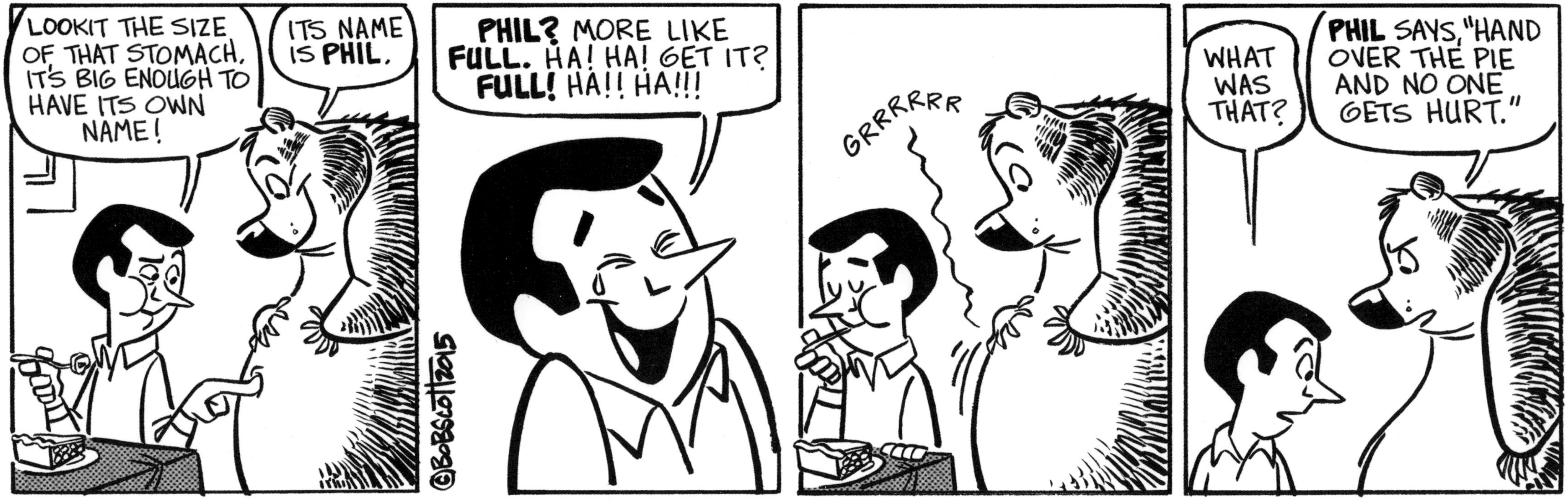
LOOKIT THE SIZE OF THAT STOMACH. IT'S BIG ENOUGH TO HAVE ITS OWN NAME!
ITS NAME IS **PHIL**.
PHIL? MORE LIKE **FULL.** HA! HA! GET IT? **FULL!** HA!! HA!!!
©BOBSCOTT 2015
GRRRRRR
WHAT WAS THAT?
PHIL SAYS, "HAND OVER THE PIE AND NO ONE GETS HURT."

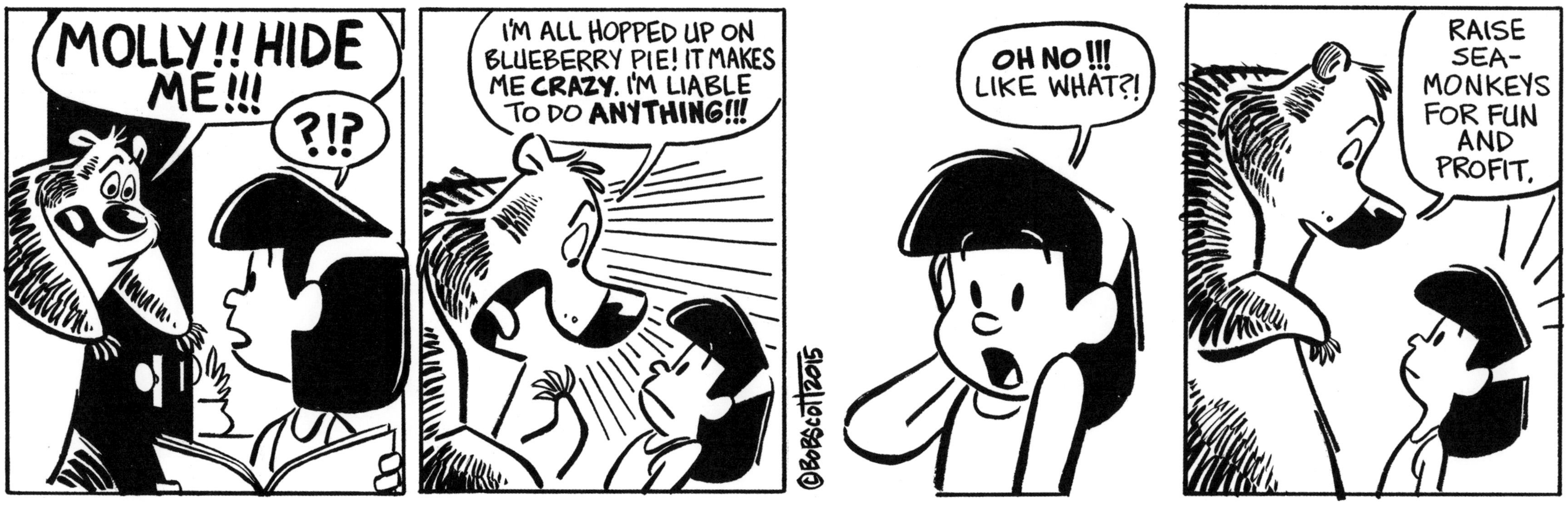
MOLLY!! HIDE ME!!!
?!?
I'M ALL HOPPED UP ON BLUEBERRY PIE! IT MAKES ME **CRAZY**. I'M LIABLE TO DO **ANYTHING**!!!
©BOBSCOTT 2015
OH NO!!! LIKE WHAT?!
RAISE SEA-MONKEYS FOR FUN AND PROFIT.

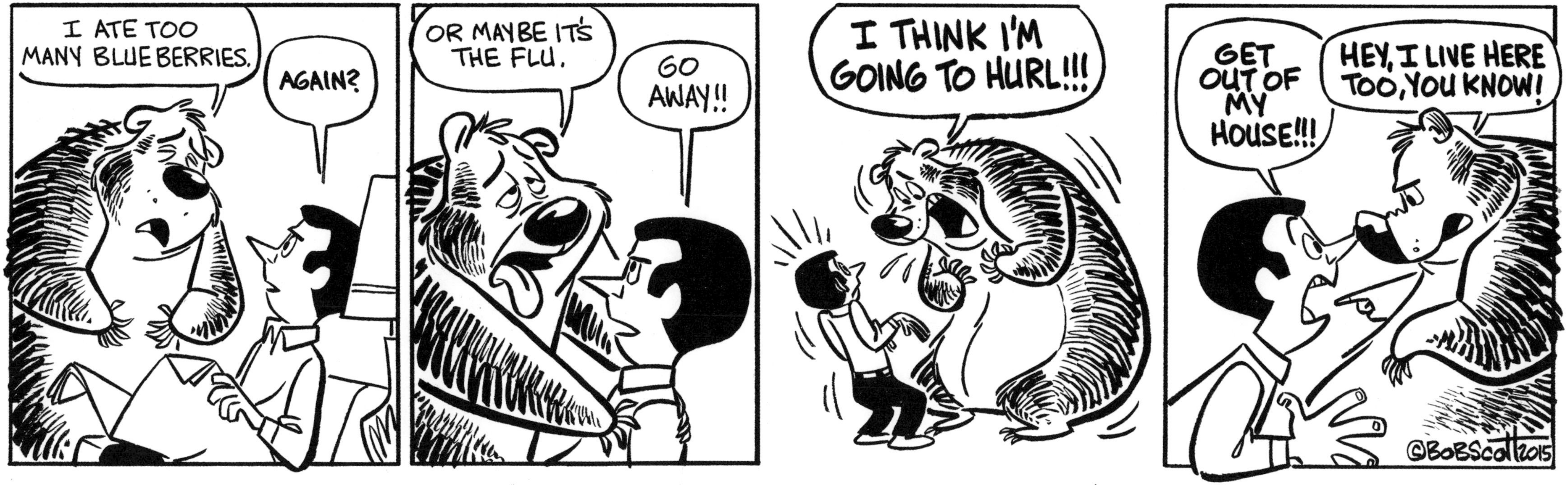
I ATE TOO MANY BLUEBERRIES.
AGAIN?
OR MAYBE IT'S THE FLU.
GO AWAY!!
I THINK I'M GOING TO HURL!!!
GET OUT OF MY HOUSE!!!
HEY, I LIVE HERE TOO, YOU KNOW!
©BOBSCOTT2015

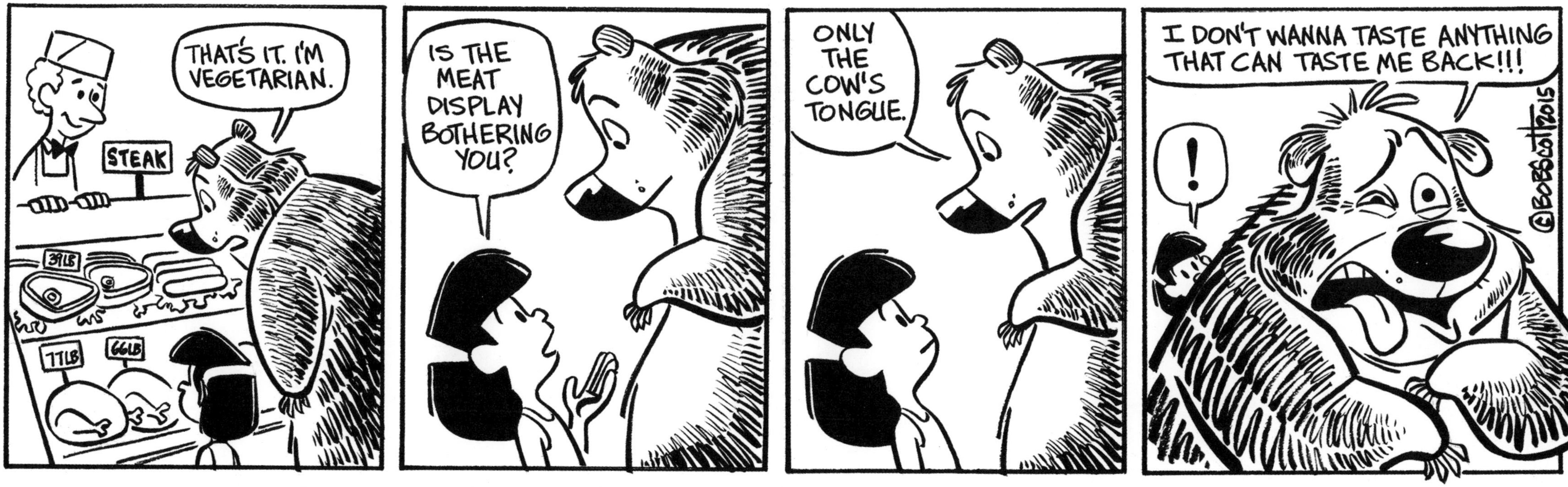
STEAK
THAT'S IT. I'M VEGETARIAN.
39LB
77LB
66LB
IS THE MEAT DISPLAY BOTHERING YOU?
ONLY THE COW'S TONGUE.
!
I DON'T WANNA TASTE ANYTHING THAT CAN TASTE ME BACK!!!
©BOBSCOTT2015

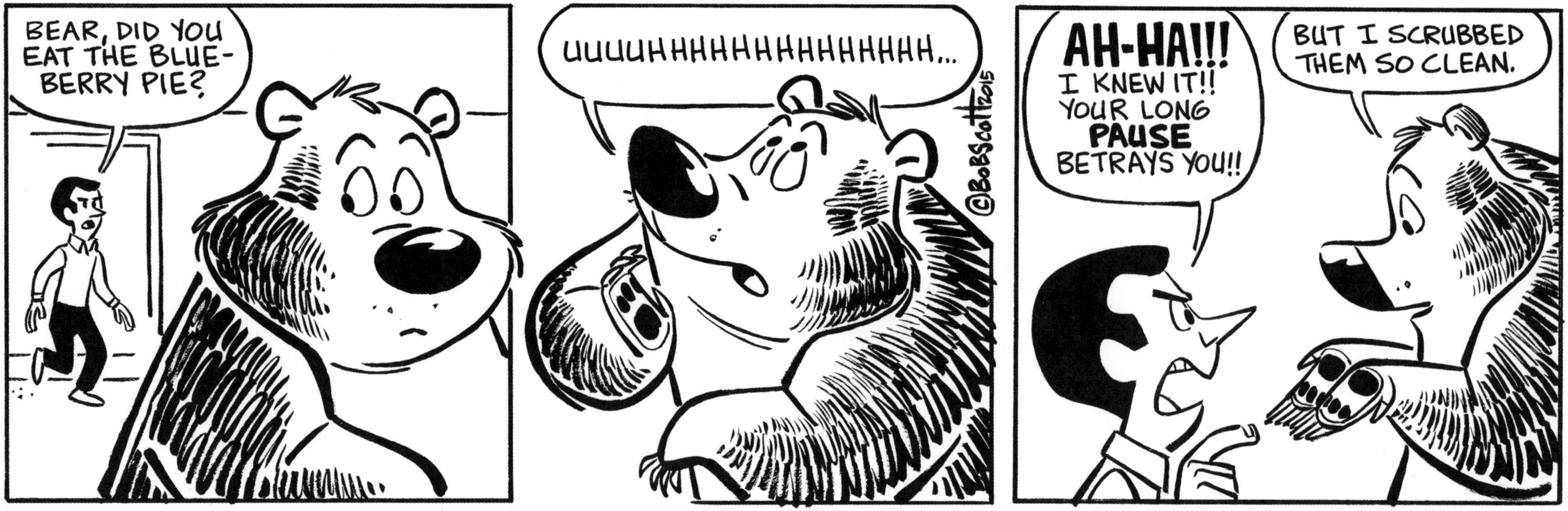
BEAR, DID YOU EAT THE BLUE-BERRY PIE?
UUUUHHHHHHHHHHHHHHH...
©BOBSCOTT2015
AH-HA!!! I KNEW IT!! YOUR LONG PAUSE BETRAYS YOU!!
BUT I SCRUBBED THEM SO CLEAN.

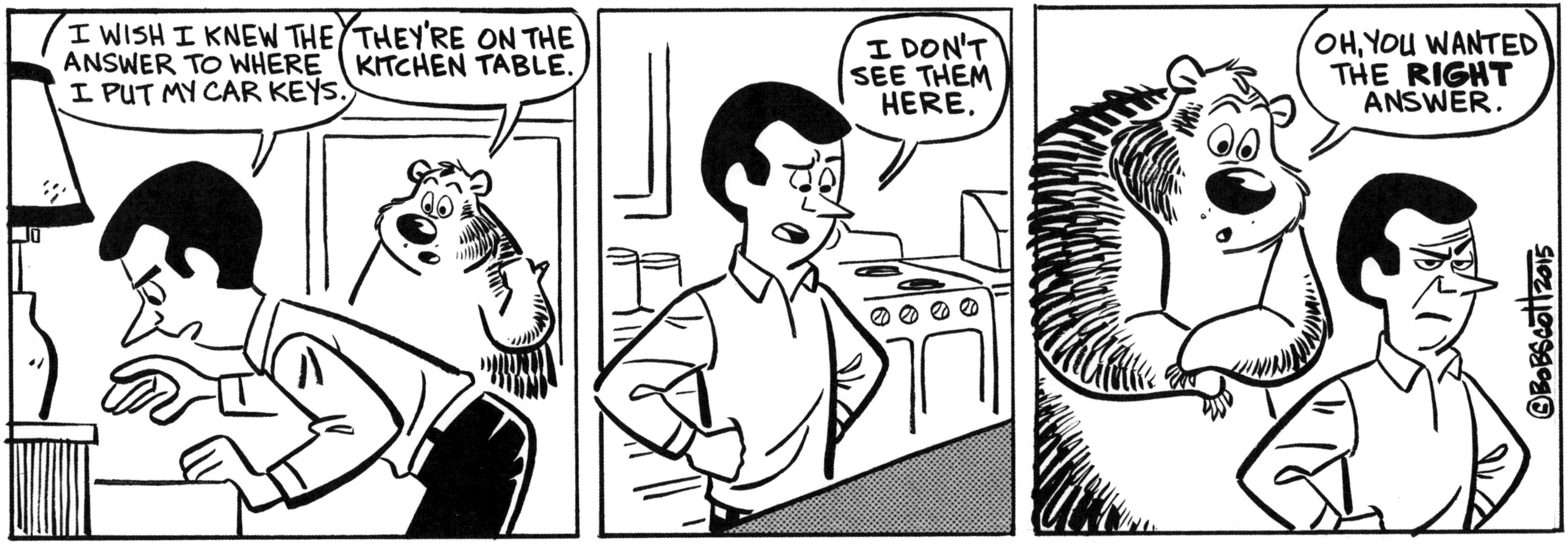
I WISH I KNEW THE ANSWER TO WHERE I PUT MY CAR KEYS.
THEY'RE ON THE KITCHEN TABLE.
I DON'T SEE THEM HERE.
OH, YOU WANTED THE RIGHT ANSWER.
©BOBSCOTT2015

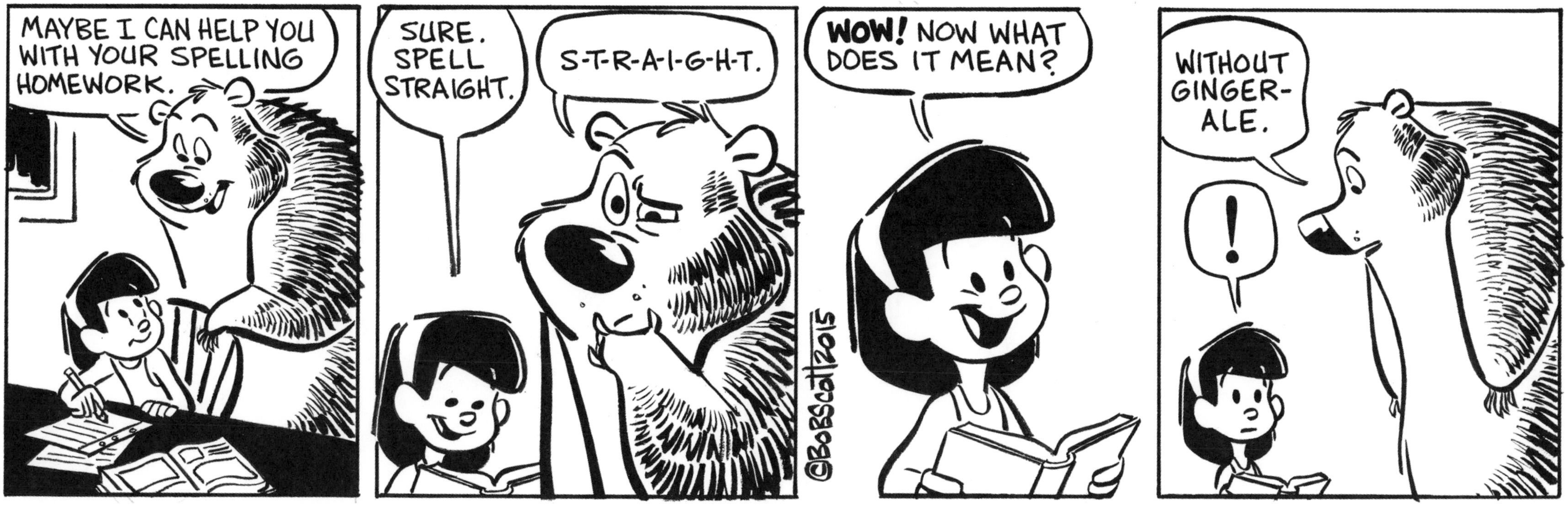
MAYBE I CAN HELP YOU WITH YOUR SPELLING HOMEWORK.
SURE. SPELL STRAIGHT.
S-T-R-A-I-G-H-T.
©BOBSCOTT2015
WOW! NOW WHAT DOES IT MEAN?
WITHOUT GINGER-ALE.
!

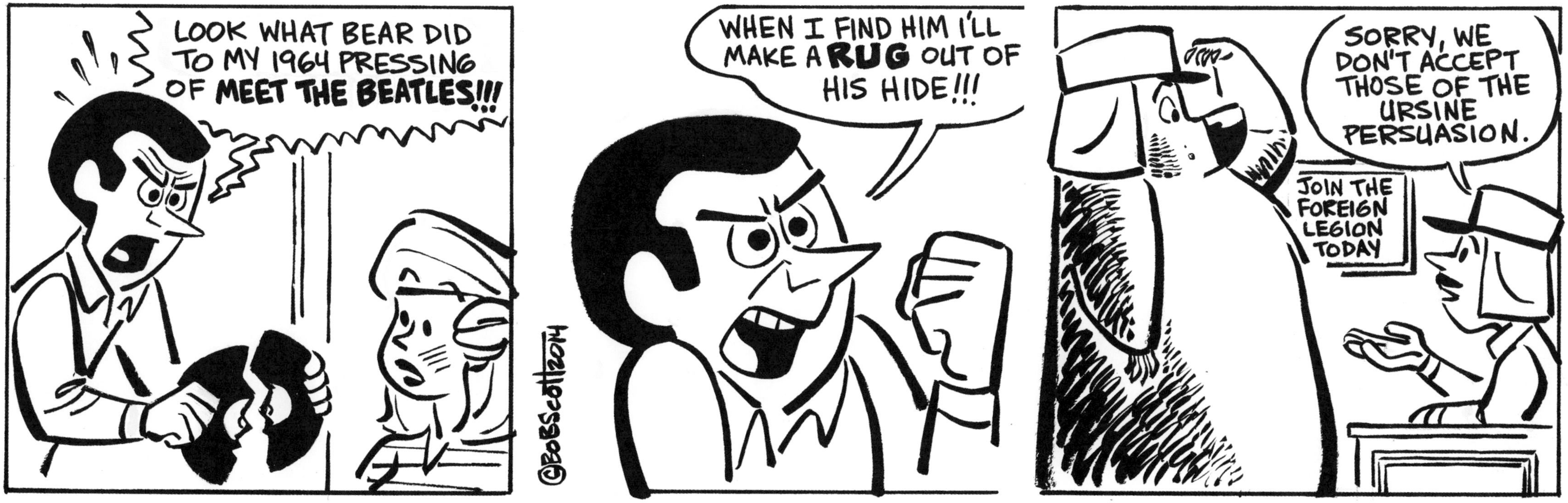
LOOK WHAT BEAR DID TO MY 1964 PRESSING OF MEET THE BEATLES!!!
©BOBSCOTT2014
WHEN I FIND HIM I'LL MAKE A RUG OUT OF HIS HIDE!!!
SORRY, WE DON'T ACCEPT THOSE OF THE URSINE PERSUASION.
JOIN THE FOREIGN LEGION TODAY

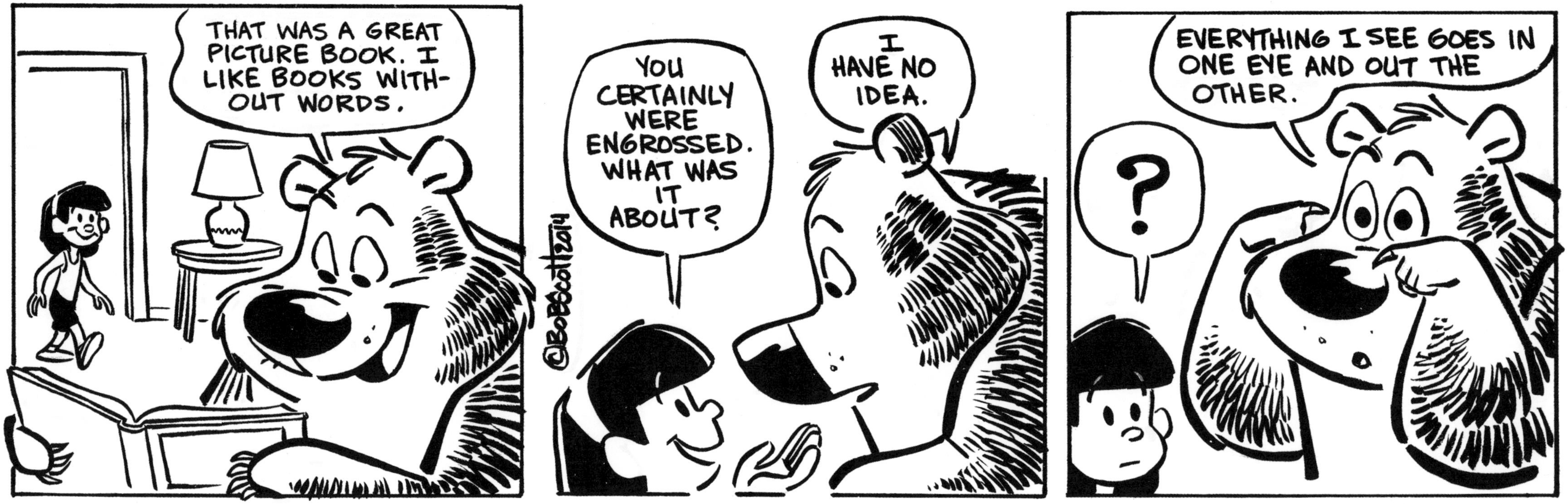
THAT WAS A GREAT PICTURE BOOK. I LIKE BOOKS WITHOUT WORDS.
YOU CERTAINLY WERE ENGROSSED. WHAT WAS IT ABOUT?
I HAVE NO IDEA.
©BOBSCOTT2014
?
EVERYTHING I SEE GOES IN ONE EYE AND OUT THE OTHER.

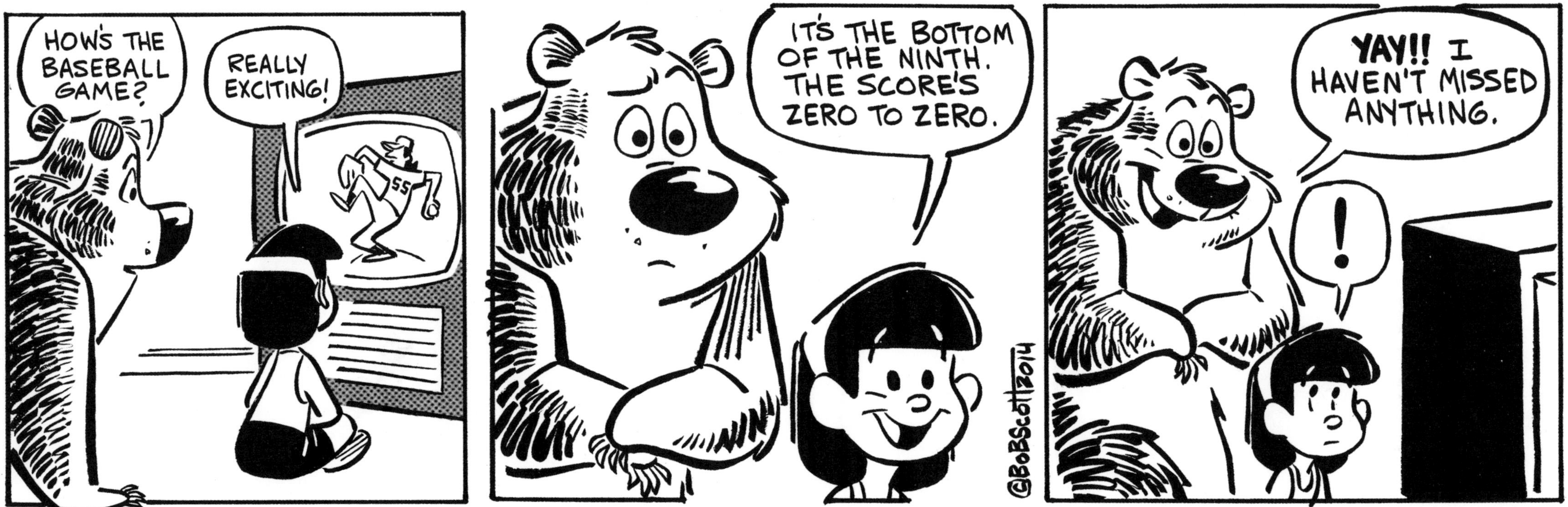
HOW'S THE BASEBALL GAME?
REALLY EXCITING!
55
IT'S THE BOTTOM OF THE NINTH. THE SCORE'S ZERO TO ZERO.
©BOBSCOTT2014
YAY!! I HAVEN'T MISSED ANYTHING.
!

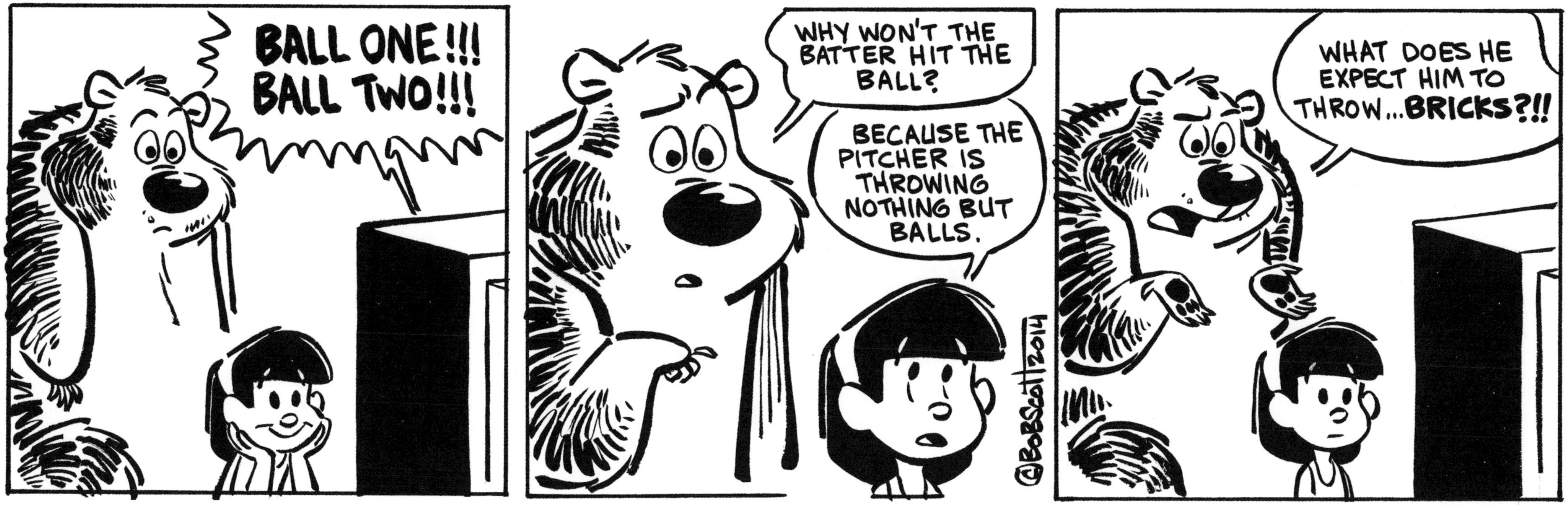
BALL ONE!!!
BALL TWO!!!
WHY WON'T THE BATTER HIT THE BALL?
BECAUSE THE PITCHER IS THROWING NOTHING BUT BALLS.
©BOBSCOTT2014
WHAT DOES HE EXPECT HIM TO THROW... **BRICKS?!!**

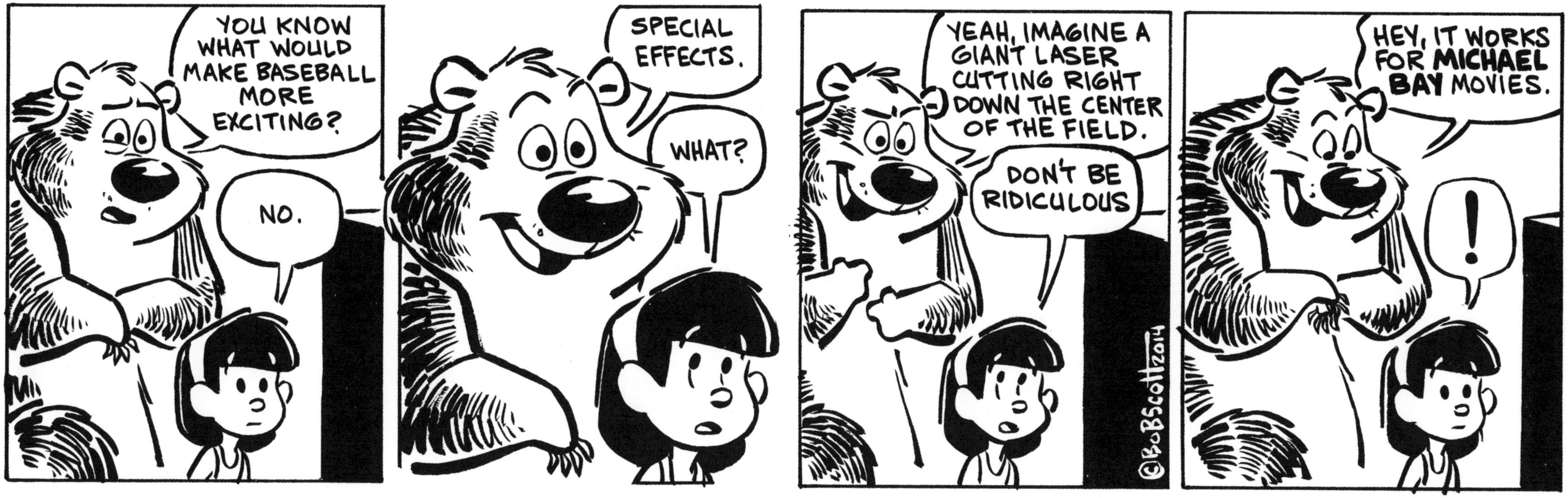
YOU KNOW WHAT WOULD MAKE BASEBALL MORE EXCITING?
NO.
SPECIAL EFFECTS.
WHAT?
YEAH, IMAGINE A GIANT LASER CUTTING RIGHT DOWN THE CENTER OF THE FIELD.
DON'T BE RIDICULOUS
©BOBSCOTT2014
HEY, IT WORKS FOR **MICHAEL BAY** MOVIES.
!

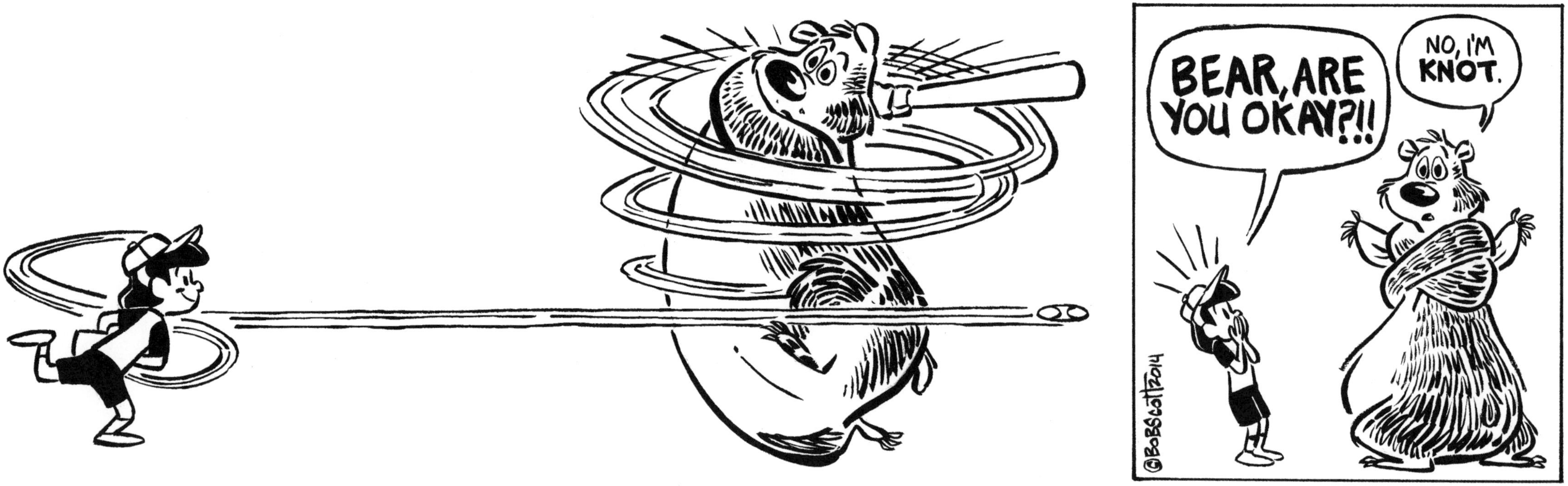
BEAR, ARE YOU OKAY?!!
NO, I'M **KNOT**.
©BOBSCOTT2014

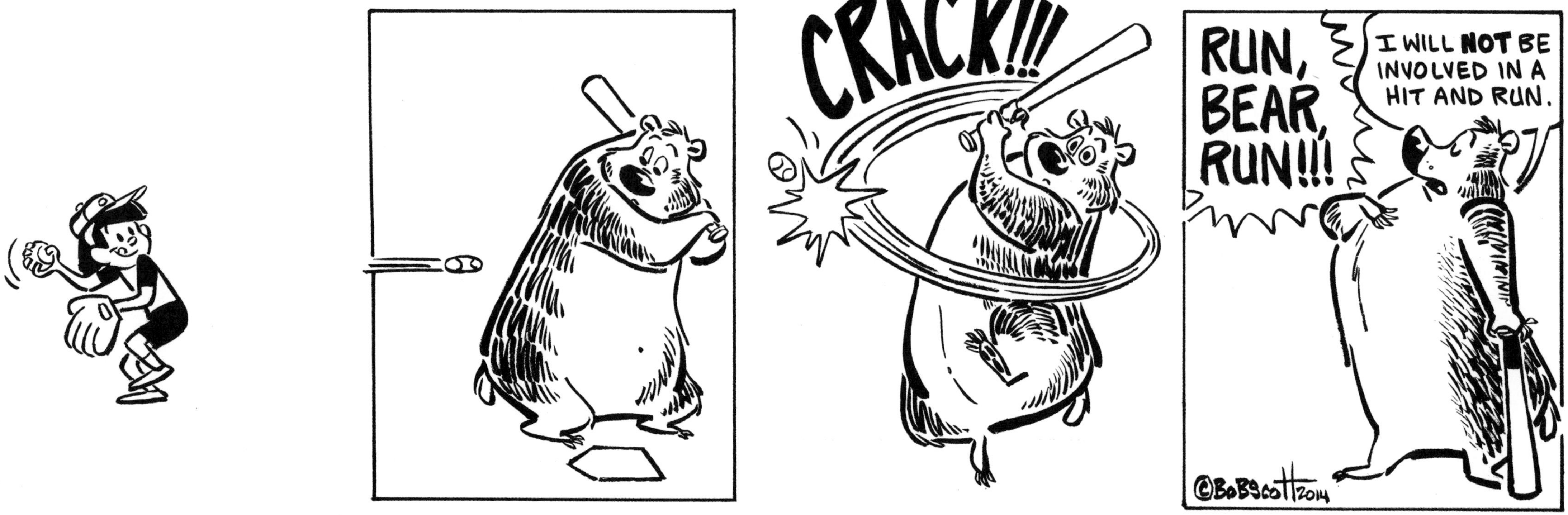
CRACK!!!
RUN, BEAR, RUN!!!
I WILL **NOT** BE INVOLVED IN A HIT AND RUN.
©BOBSCOTT2014

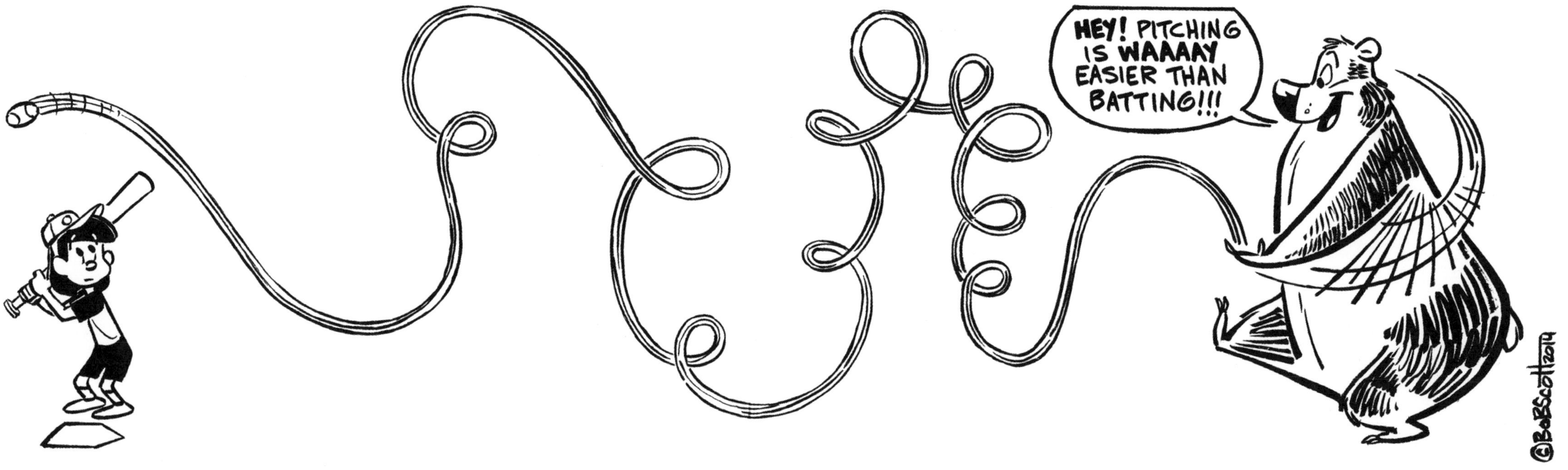
HEY! PITCHING IS WAAAAY EASIER THAN BATTING!!!
©BOBSCOTT2014

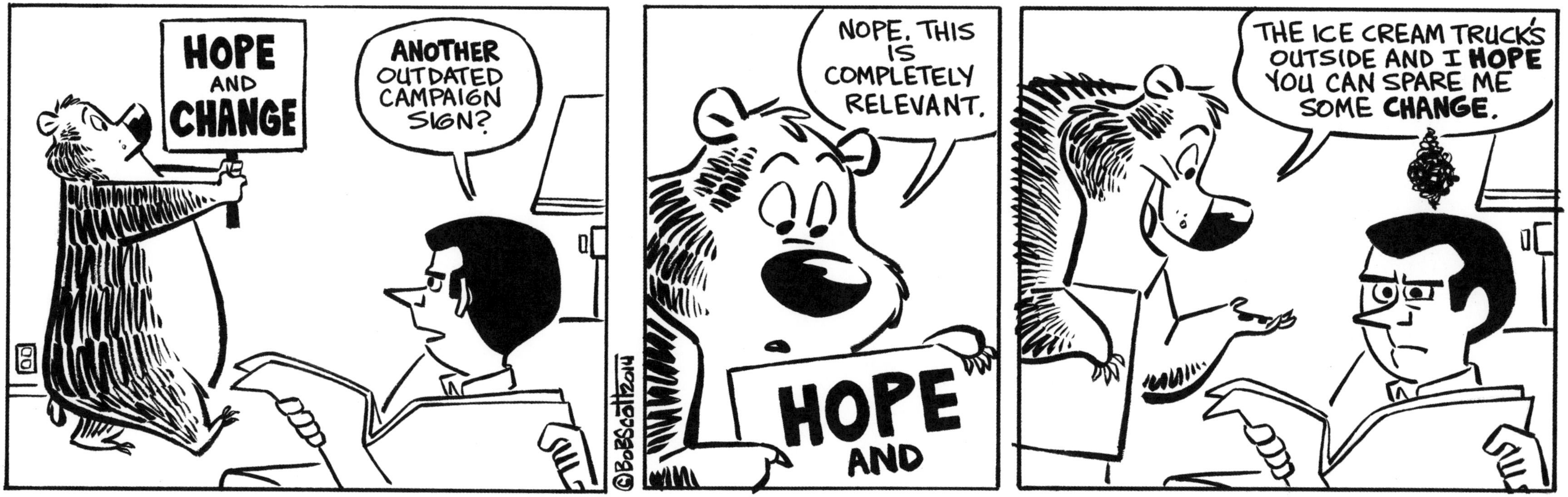
HOPE AND CHANGE
ANOTHER OUTDATED CAMPAIGN SIGN?
©BOBSCOTT2014
NOPE. THIS IS COMPLETELY RELEVANT.
HOPE AND
THE ICE CREAM TRUCK'S OUTSIDE AND I HOPE YOU CAN SPARE ME SOME CHANGE.

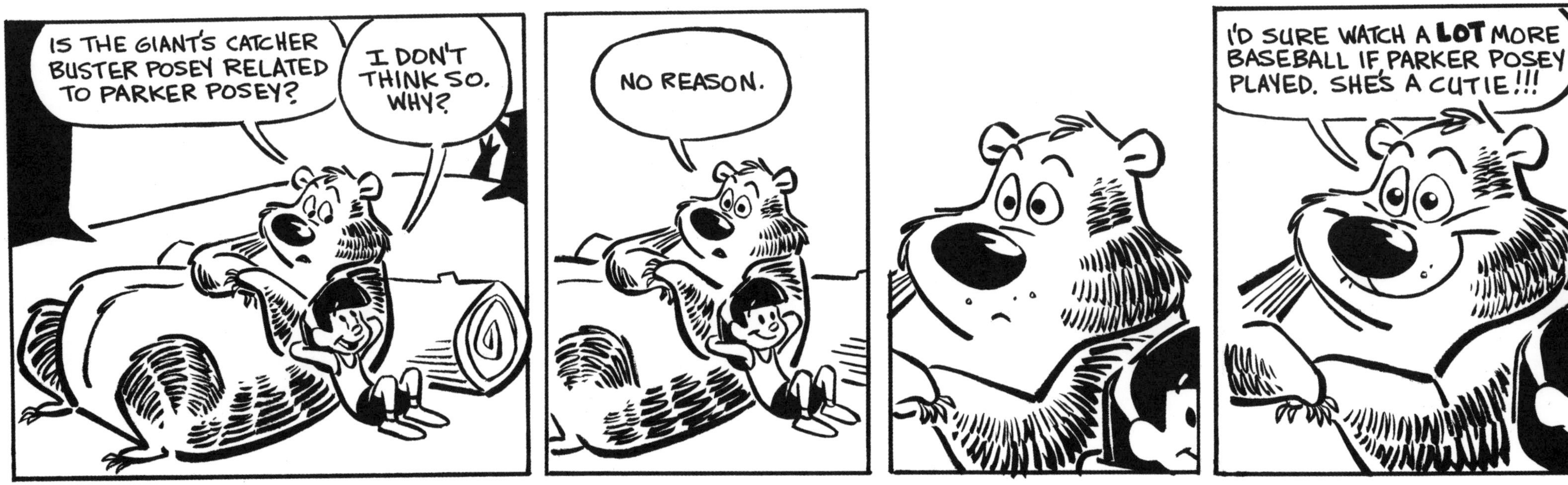
IS THE GIANT'S CATCHER BUSTER POSEY RELATED TO PARKER POSEY?
I DON'T THINK SO. WHY?
NO REASON.
I'D SURE WATCH A **LOT** MORE BASEBALL IF PARKER POSEY PLAYED. SHE'S A CUTIE!!!
!
©BOBSCOTT2014

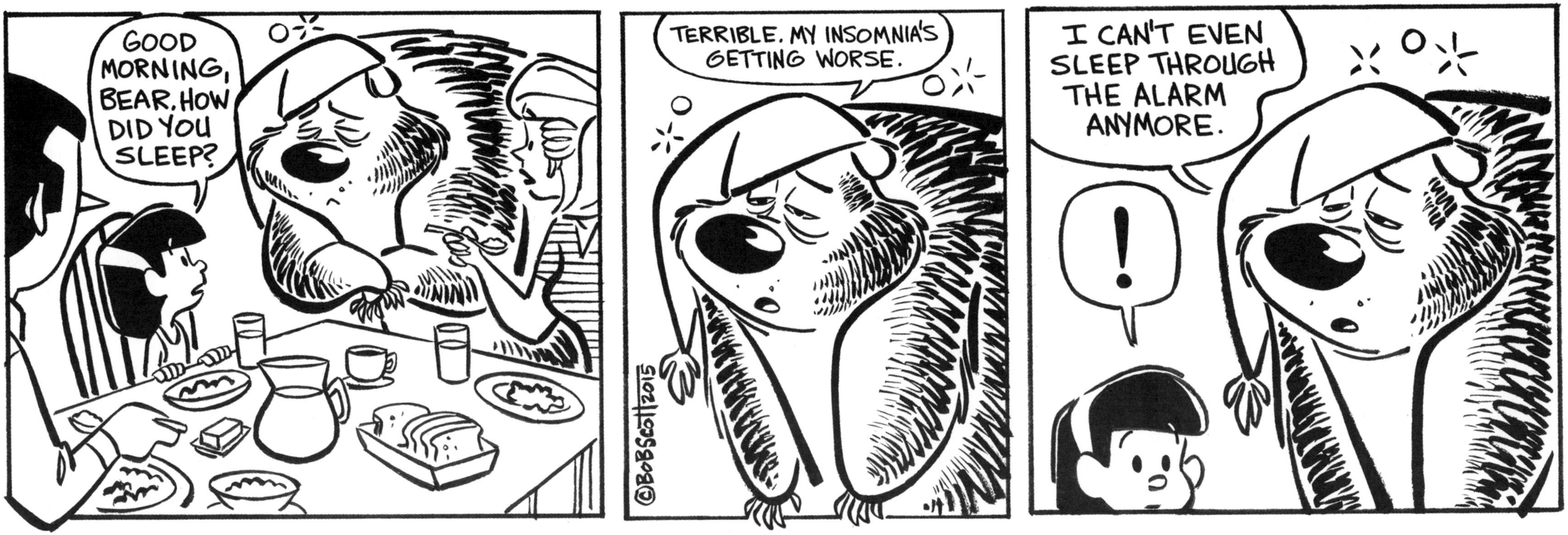
GOOD MORNING, BEAR. HOW DID YOU SLEEP?
TERRIBLE. MY INSOMNIA'S GETTING WORSE.
©BOBSCOTT2015
I CAN'T EVEN SLEEP THROUGH THE ALARM ANYMORE.
!

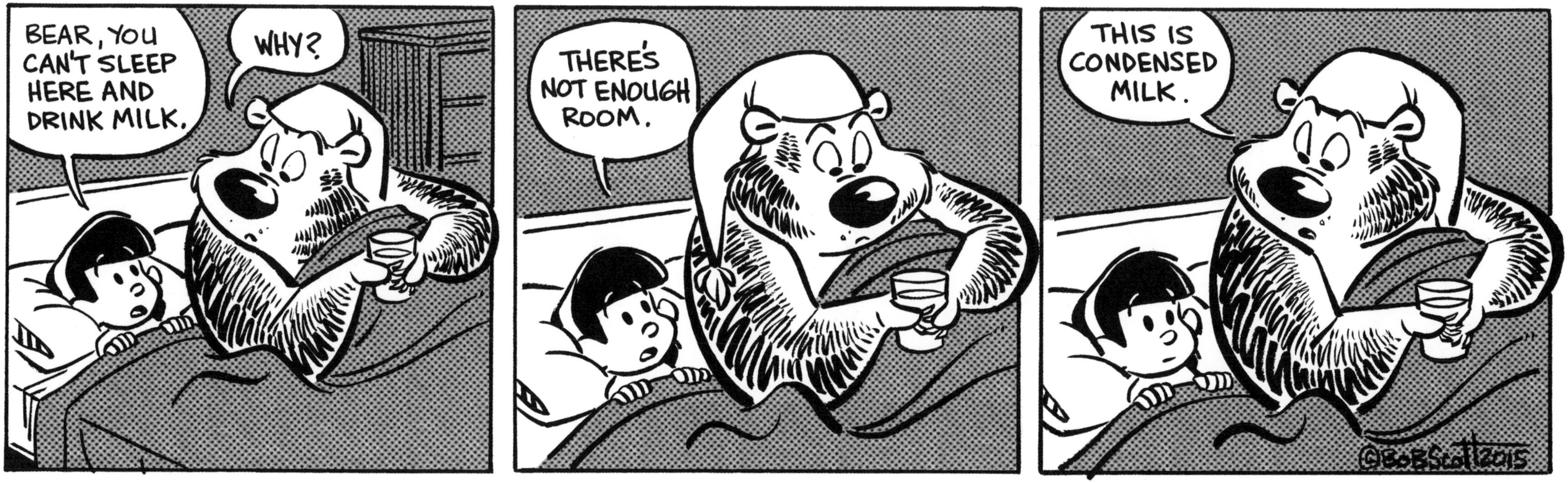
BEAR, YOU CAN'T SLEEP HERE AND DRINK MILK.
WHY?
THERE'S NOT ENOUGH ROOM.
THIS IS CONDENSED MILK.
©BOBSCOTT2015

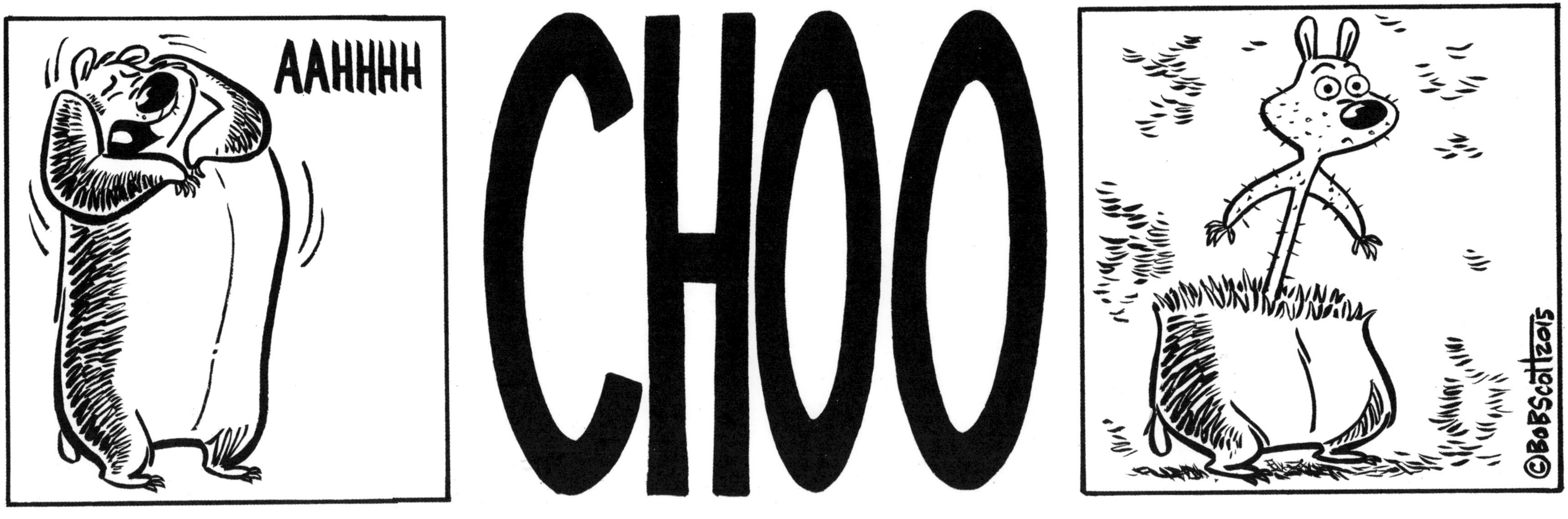
AAHHHH
CHOO
©BOBSCOTT2015

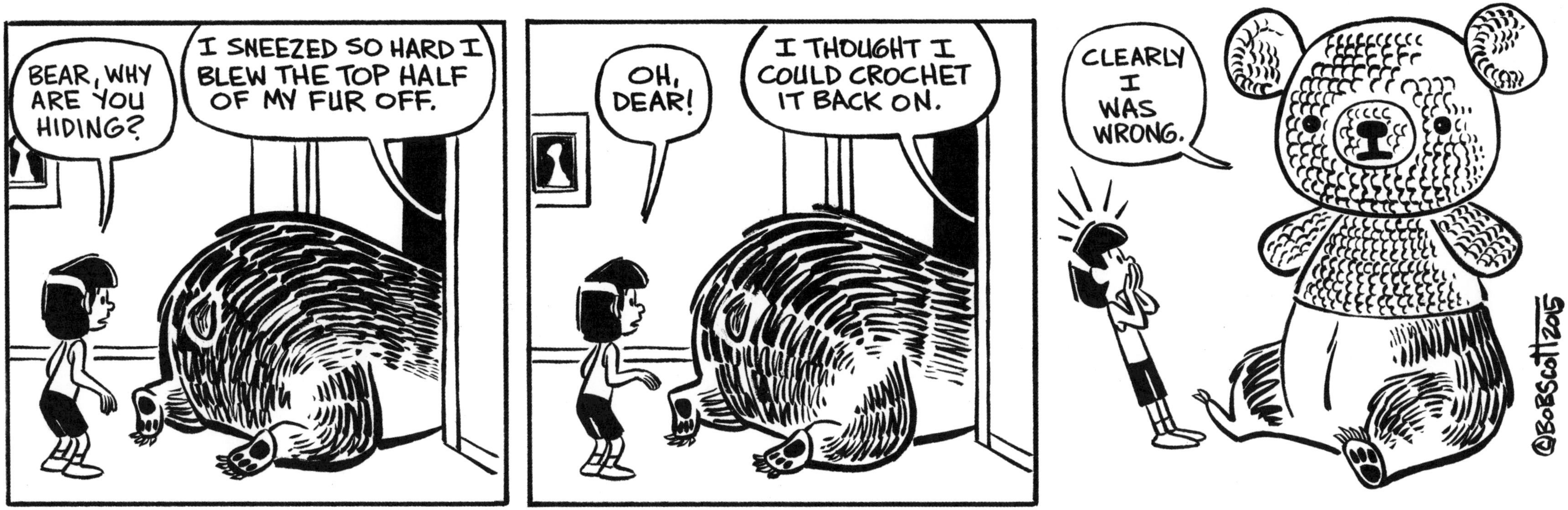
BEAR, WHY ARE YOU HIDING?
I SNEEZED SO HARD I BLEW THE TOP HALF OF MY FUR OFF.
OH, DEAR!
I THOUGHT I COULD CROCHET IT BACK ON.
CLEARLY I WAS WRONG.
©BOBSCOTT2015

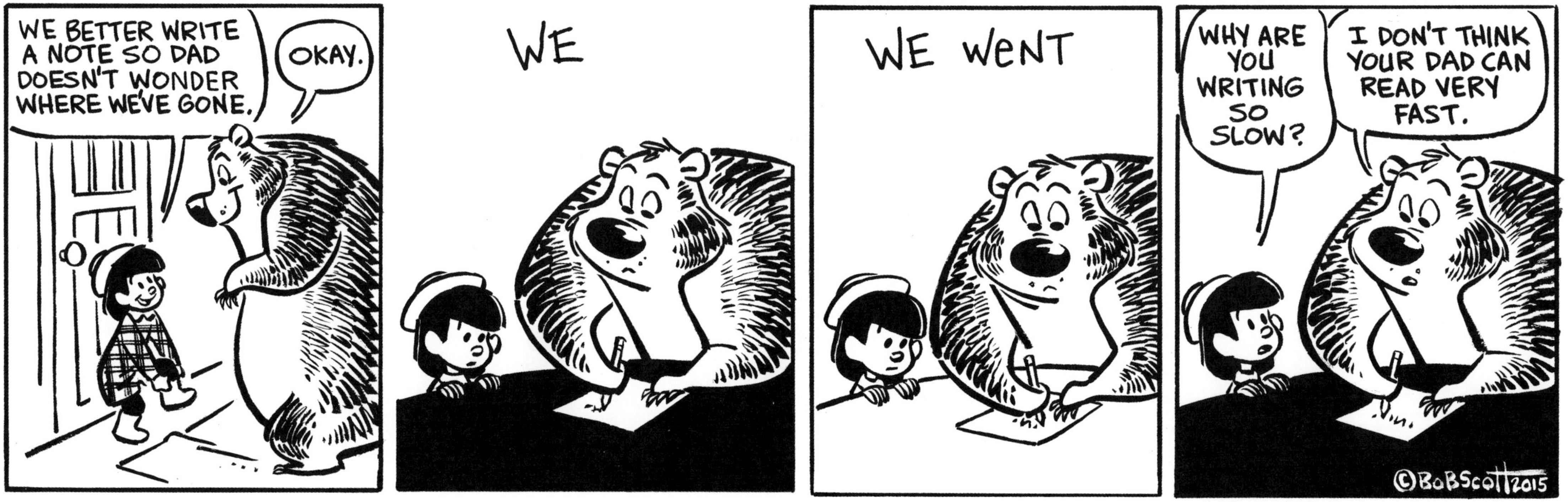
WE BETTER WRITE A NOTE SO DAD DOESN'T WONDER WHERE WE'VE GONE.
OKAY.
WE
WE WENT
WHY ARE YOU WRITING SO SLOW?
I DON'T THINK YOUR DAD CAN READ VERY FAST.
©BOBSCOTT2015

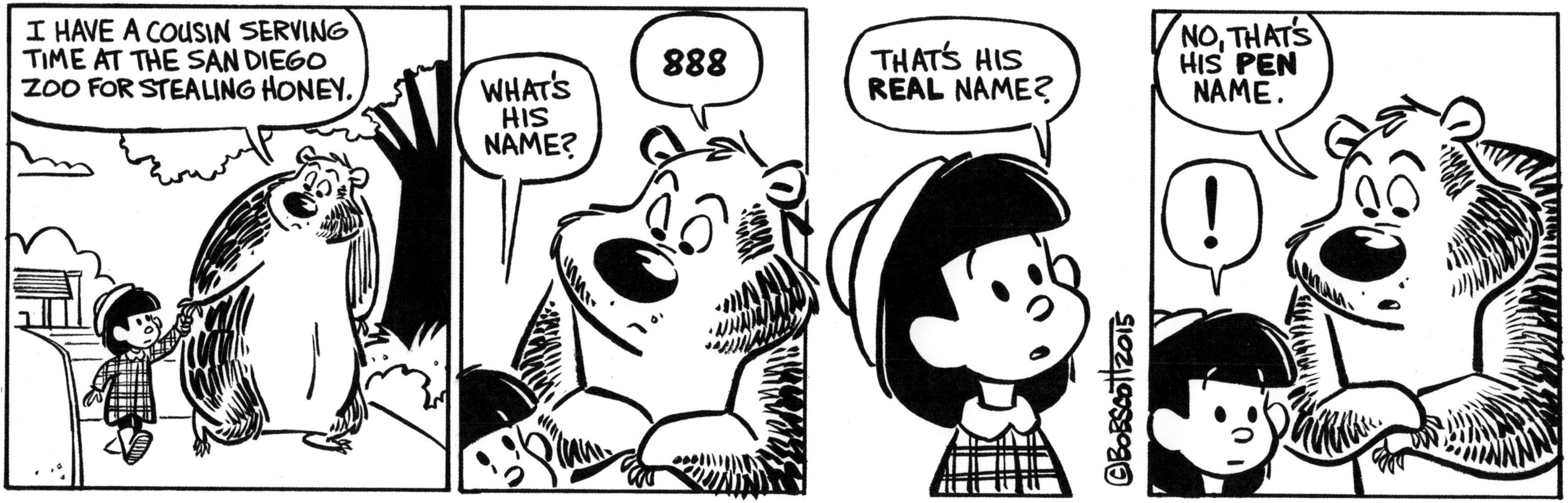
I HAVE A COUSIN SERVING TIME AT THE SAN DIEGO ZOO FOR STEALING HONEY.
WHAT'S HIS NAME?
888
THAT'S HIS REAL NAME?
©BOBSCOTT 2015
NO, THAT'S HIS PEN NAME.
!

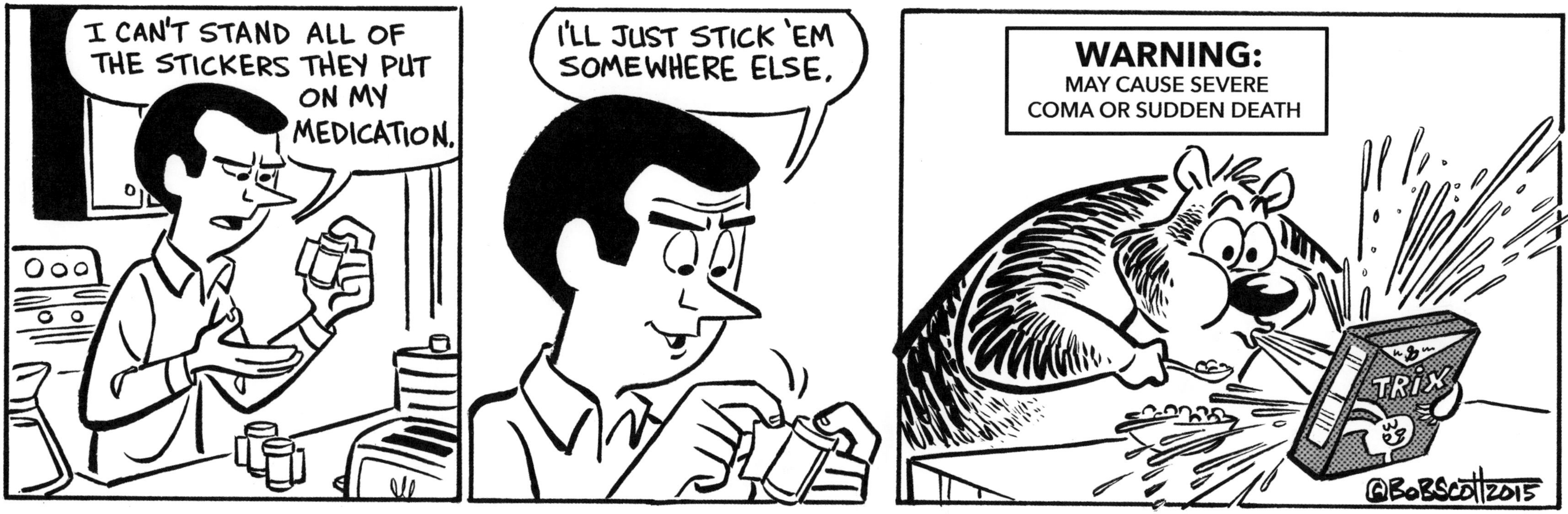
I CAN'T STAND ALL OF THE STICKERS THEY PUT ON MY MEDICATION.
I'LL JUST STICK 'EM SOMEWHERE ELSE.
WARNING:
MAY CAUSE SEVERE COMA OR SUDDEN DEATH
TRIX
©BOBSCOTT 2015

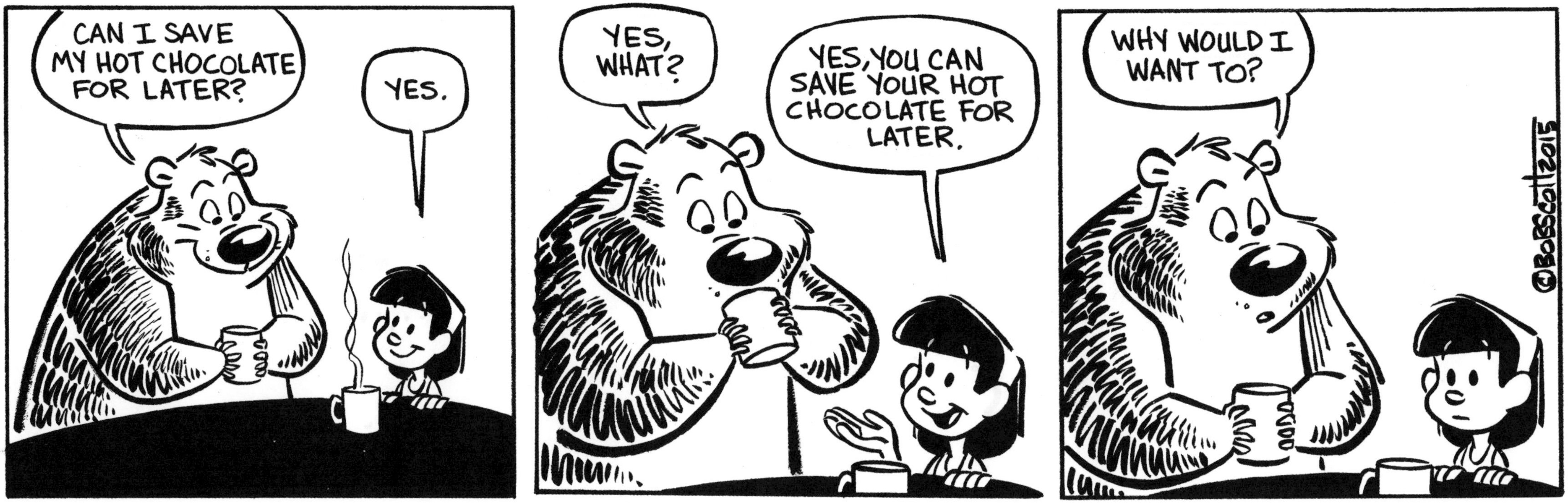
CAN I SAVE MY HOT CHOCOLATE FOR LATER?
YES.
YES, WHAT?
YES, YOU CAN SAVE YOUR HOT CHOCOLATE FOR LATER.
WHY WOULD I WANT TO?
©BOBSCOTT2015

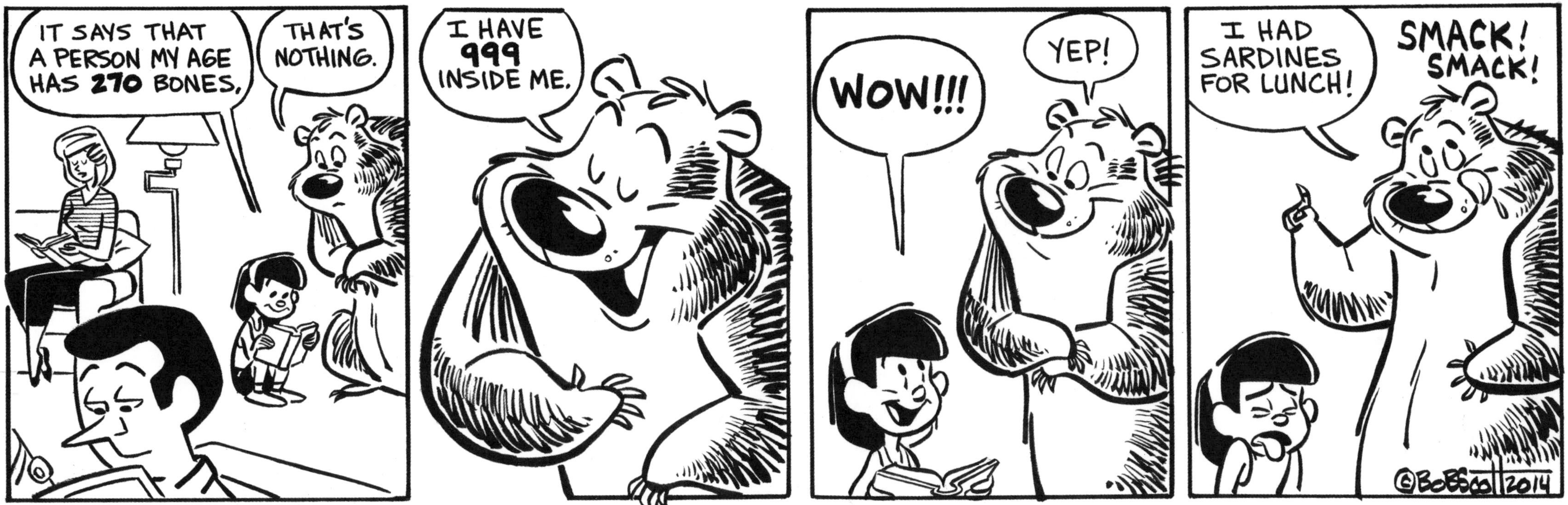
IT SAYS THAT A PERSON MY AGE HAS 270 BONES.
THAT'S NOTHING.
I HAVE 999 INSIDE ME.
WOW!!!
YEP!
I HAD SARDINES FOR LUNCH!
SMACK! SMACK!
©BOBSCOTT2014

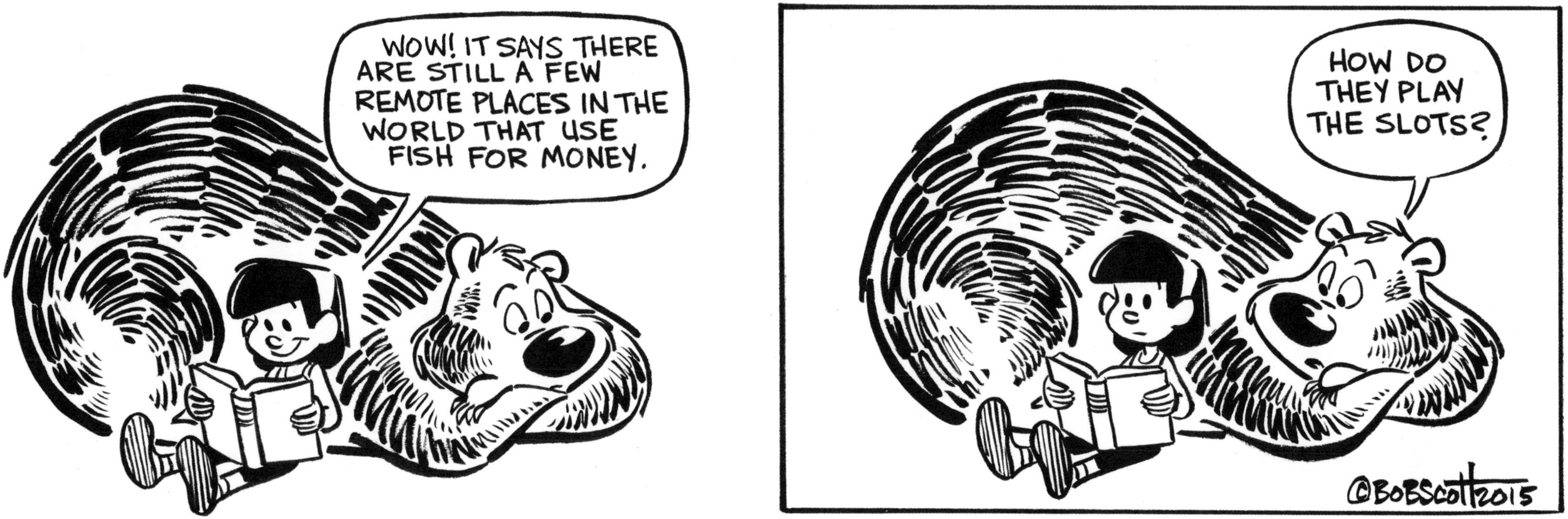
WOW! IT SAYS THERE ARE STILL A FEW REMOTE PLACES IN THE WORLD THAT USE FISH FOR MONEY.
HOW DO THEY PLAY THE SLOTS?
©BOBSCOTT2015

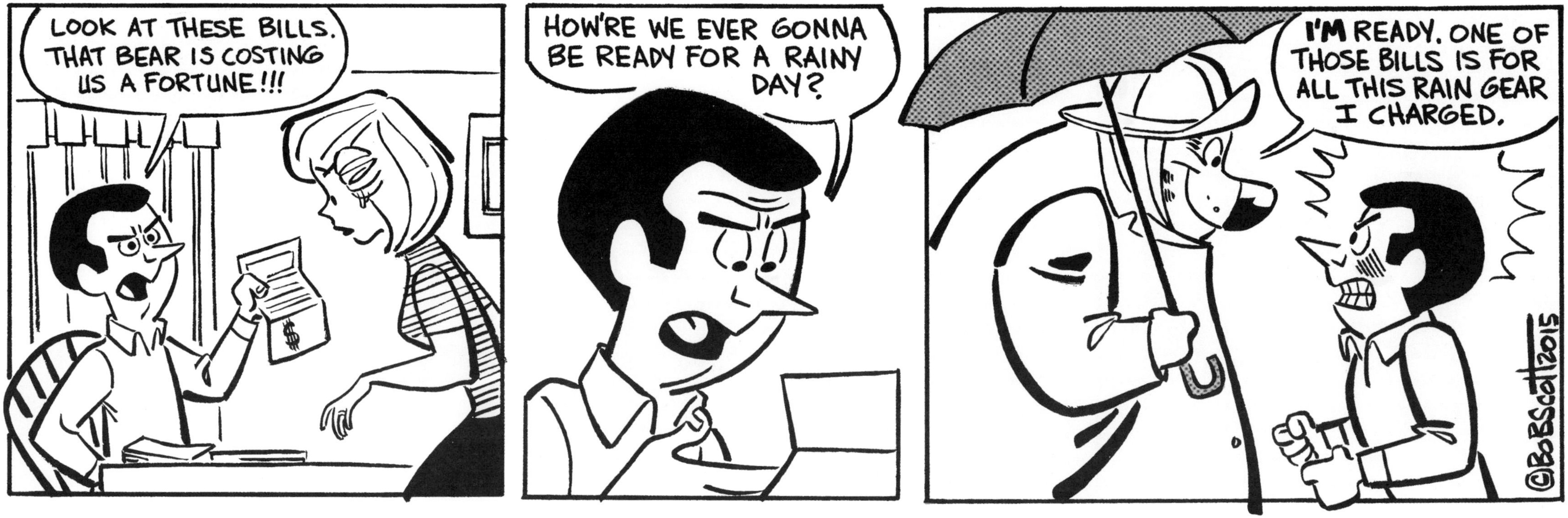
LOOK AT THESE BILLS. THAT BEAR IS COSTING US A FORTUNE!!!
HOW'RE WE EVER GONNA BE READY FOR A RAINY DAY?
I'M READY. ONE OF THOSE BILLS IS FOR ALL THIS RAIN GEAR I CHARGED.
©BOBSCOTT2015

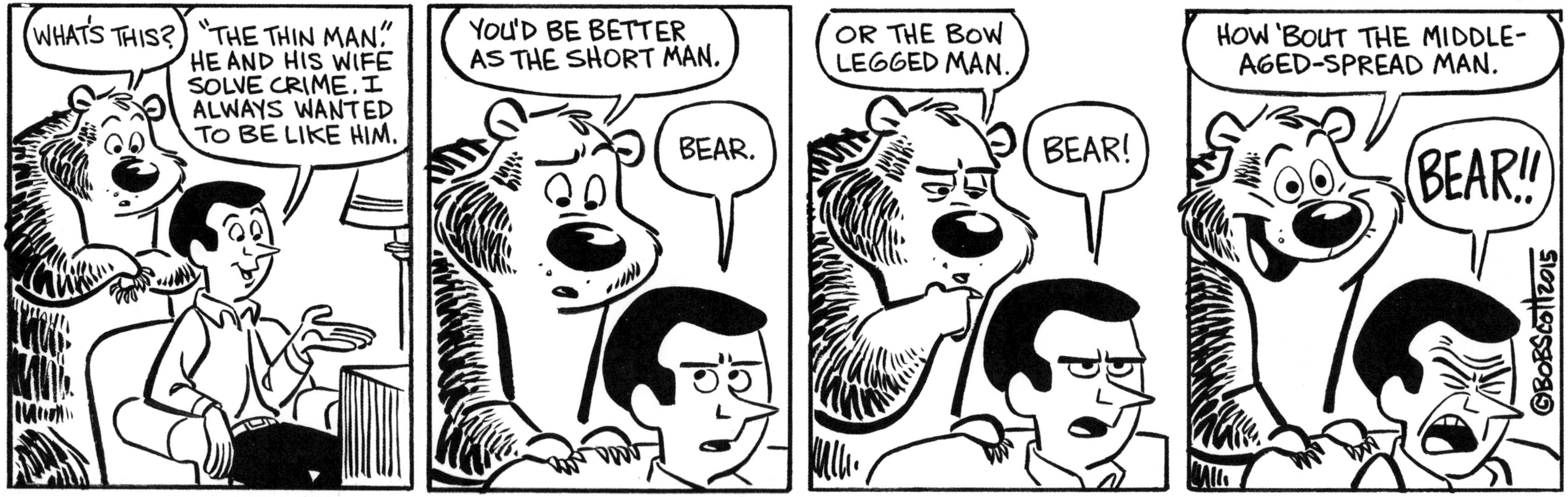
WHAT'S THIS?
"THE THIN MAN." HE AND HIS WIFE SOLVE CRIME. I ALWAYS WANTED TO BE LIKE HIM.
YOU'D BE BETTER AS THE SHORT MAN.
BEAR.
OR THE BOW LEGGED MAN.
BEAR!
HOW 'BOUT THE MIDDLE-AGED-SPREAD MAN.
BEAR!!
©BOBSCOTT2015

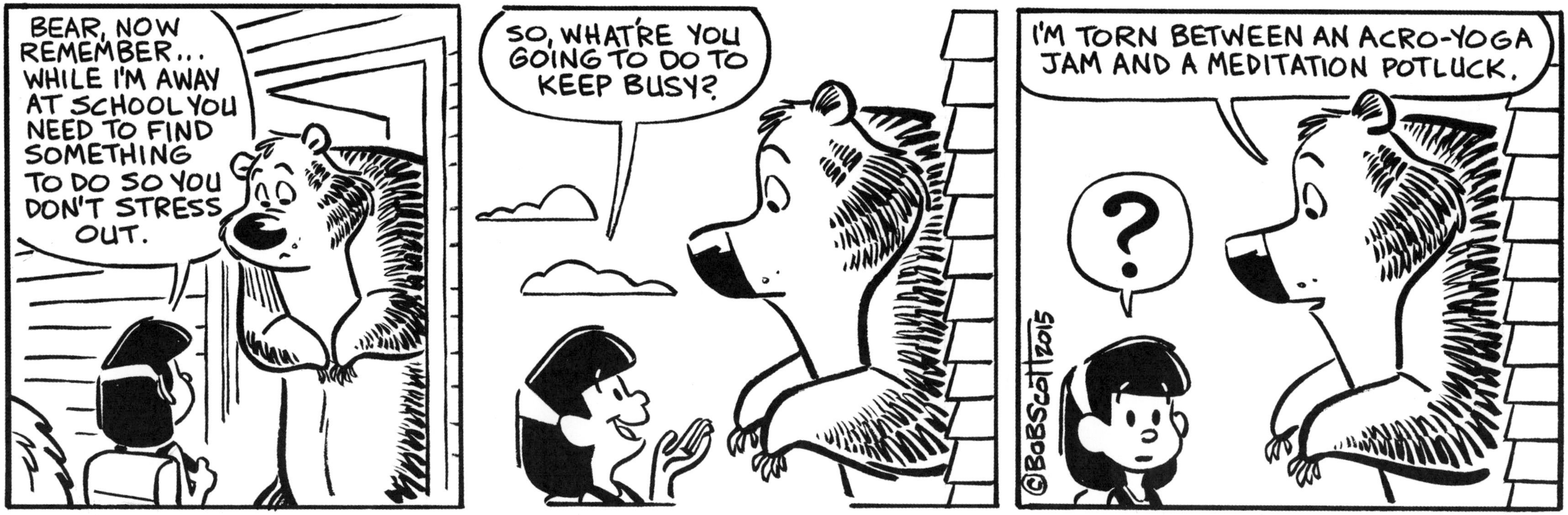
BEAR, NOW REMEMBER... WHILE I'M AWAY AT SCHOOL YOU NEED TO FIND SOMETHING TO DO SO YOU DON'T STRESS OUT.
SO, WHAT'RE YOU GOING TO DO TO KEEP BUSY?
I'M TORN BETWEEN AN ACRO-YOGA JAM AND A MEDITATION POTLUCK.
?
©BOBSCOTT2015

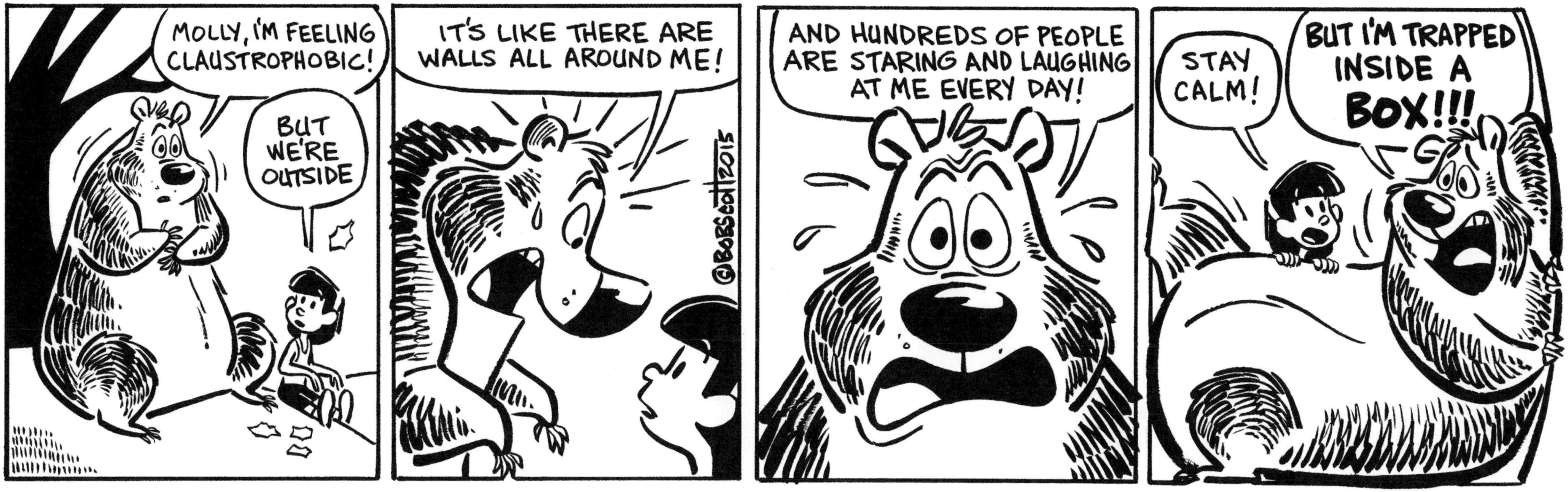
MOLLY, I'M FEELING CLAUSTROPHOBIC!
BUT WE'RE OUTSIDE
IT'S LIKE THERE ARE WALLS ALL AROUND ME!
©BOBSCOTT2015
AND HUNDREDS OF PEOPLE ARE STARING AND LAUGHING AT ME EVERY DAY!
STAY CALM!
BUT I'M TRAPPED INSIDE A BOX!!!

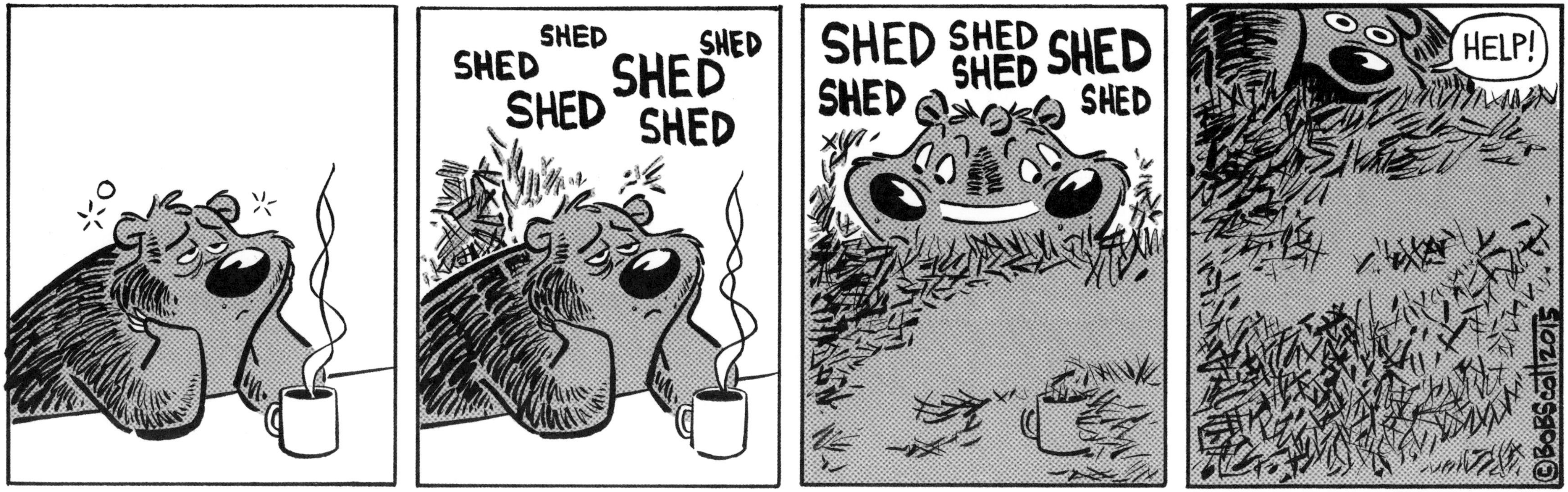
SHED SHED SHED SHED SHED SHED SHED
SHED SHED SHED SHED SHED SHED
HELP!
©BOBSCOTT2015

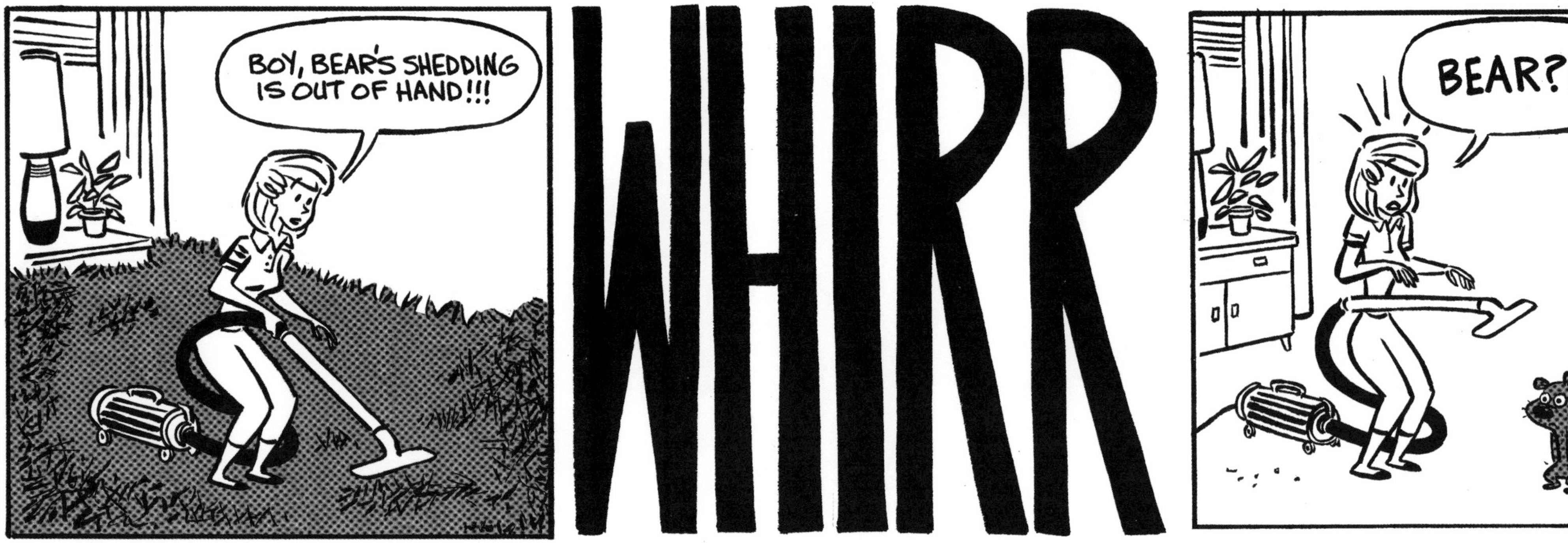
BOY, BEAR'S SHEDDING IS OUT OF HAND!!!
WHIRR
BEAR?!!
©BOBSCOTT2015

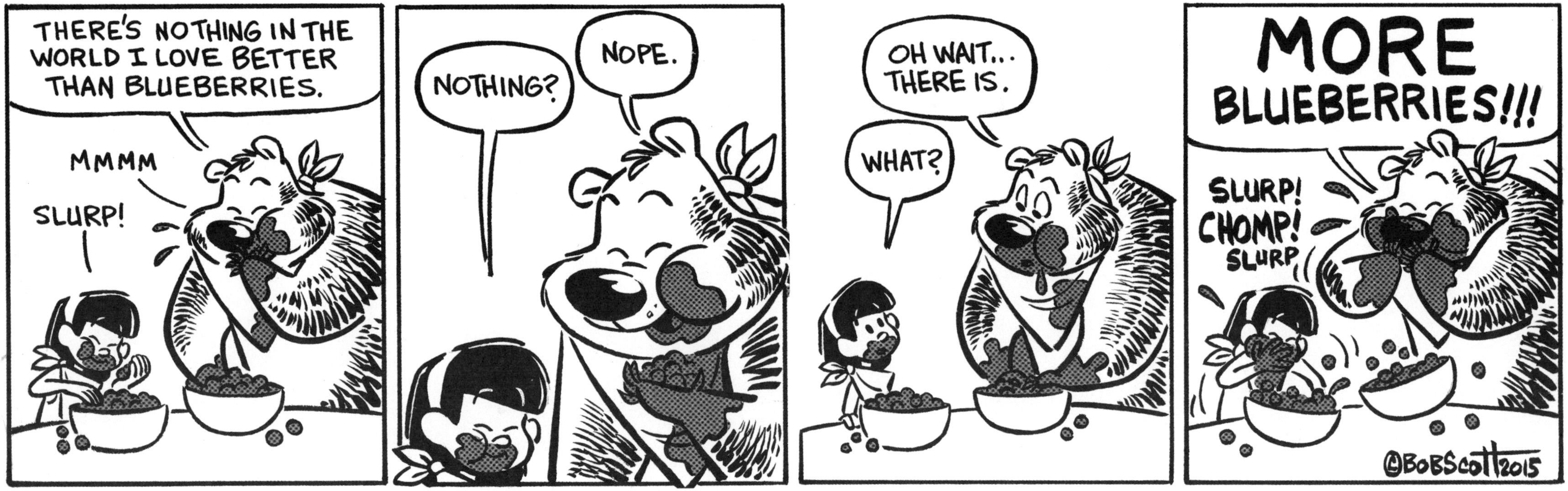
THERE'S NOTHING IN THE WORLD I LOVE BETTER THAN BLUEBERRIES.
MMMM
SLURP!
NOTHING?
NOPE.
OH WAIT... THERE IS.
WHAT?
MORE BLUEBERRIES!!!
SLURP!
CHOMP!
SLURP
©BOBSCOTT2015

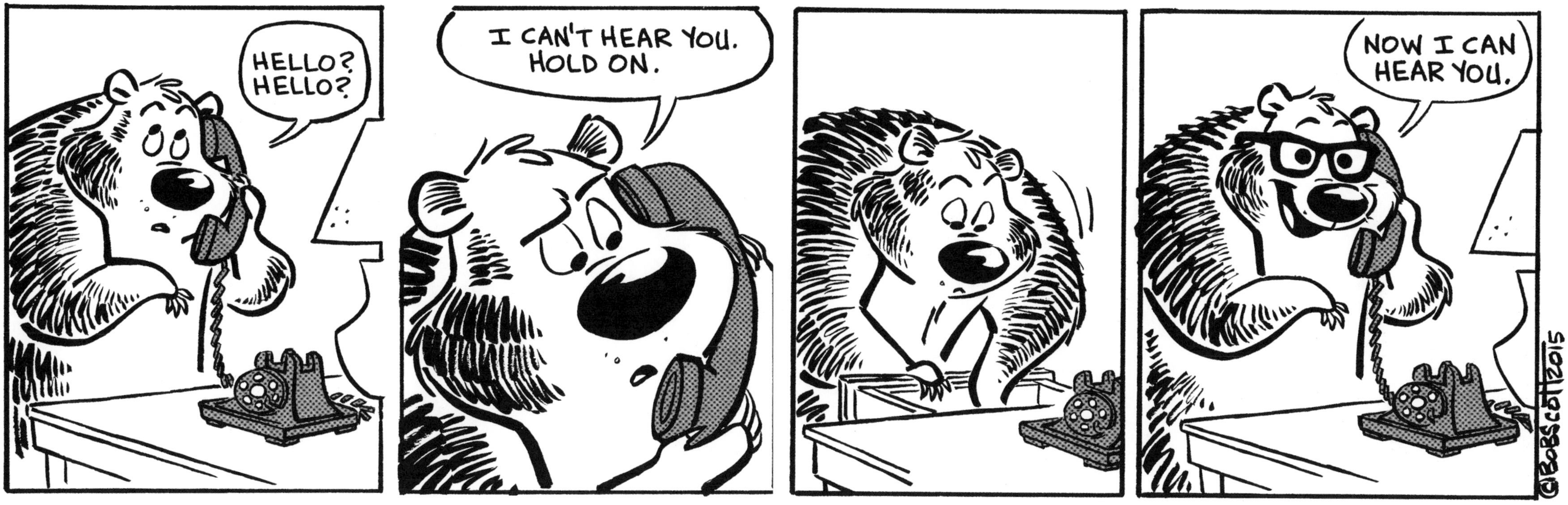
HELLO? HELLO?
I CAN'T HEAR YOU. HOLD ON.
NOW I CAN HEAR YOU.
©BOBSCOTT2015

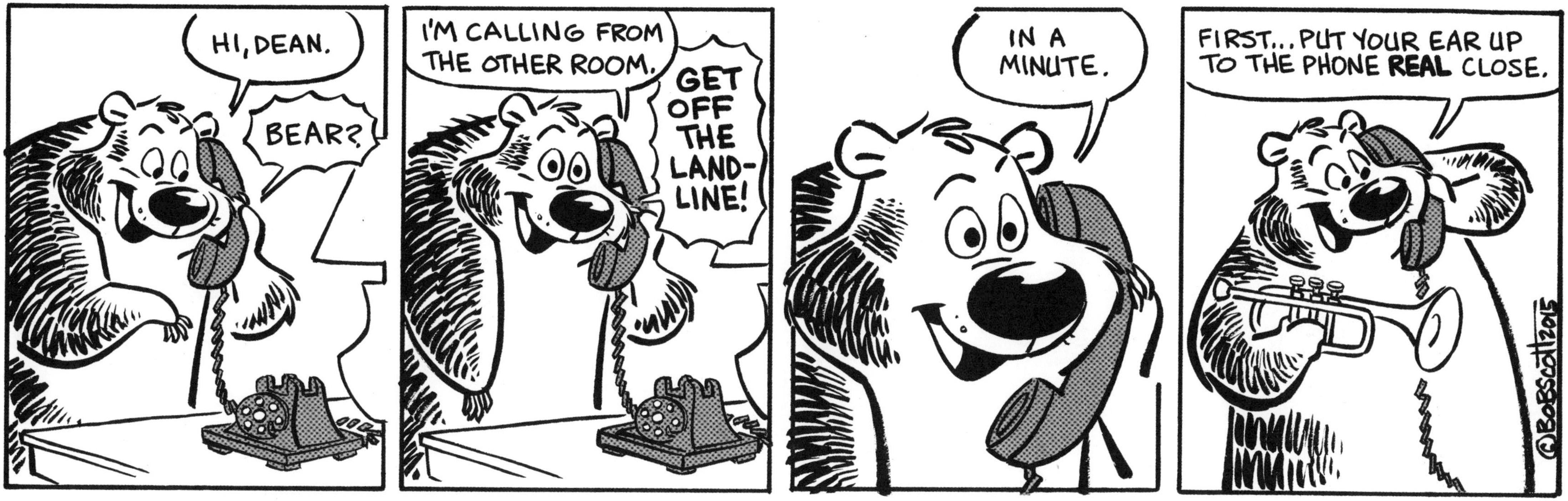
HI, DEAN.
BEAR?
I'M CALLING FROM THE OTHER ROOM.
GET OFF THE LAND-LINE!
IN A MINUTE.
FIRST... PUT YOUR EAR UP TO THE PHONE **REAL** CLOSE.
©BOBSCOTT2015

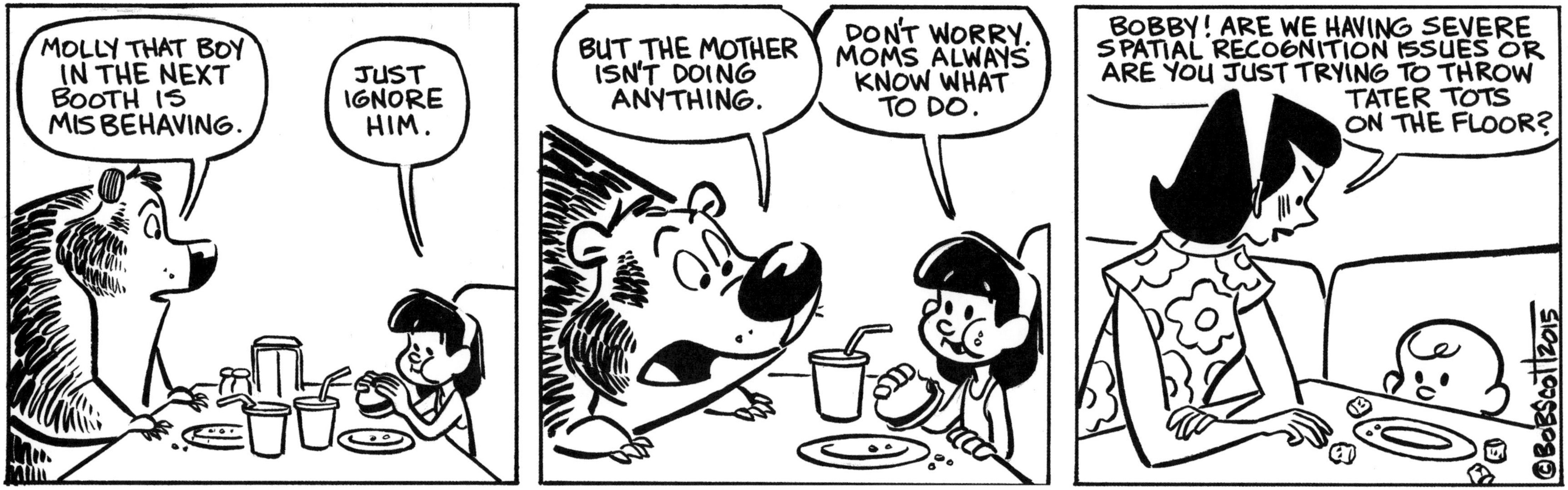
MOLLY THAT BOY IN THE NEXT BOOTH IS MISBEHAVING.
JUST IGNORE HIM.
BUT THE MOTHER ISN'T DOING ANYTHING.
DON'T WORRY. MOMS ALWAYS KNOW WHAT TO DO.
BOBBY! ARE WE HAVING SEVERE SPATIAL RECOGNITION ISSUES OR ARE YOU JUST TRYING TO THROW TATER TOTS ON THE FLOOR?
©BOBSCOTT2015

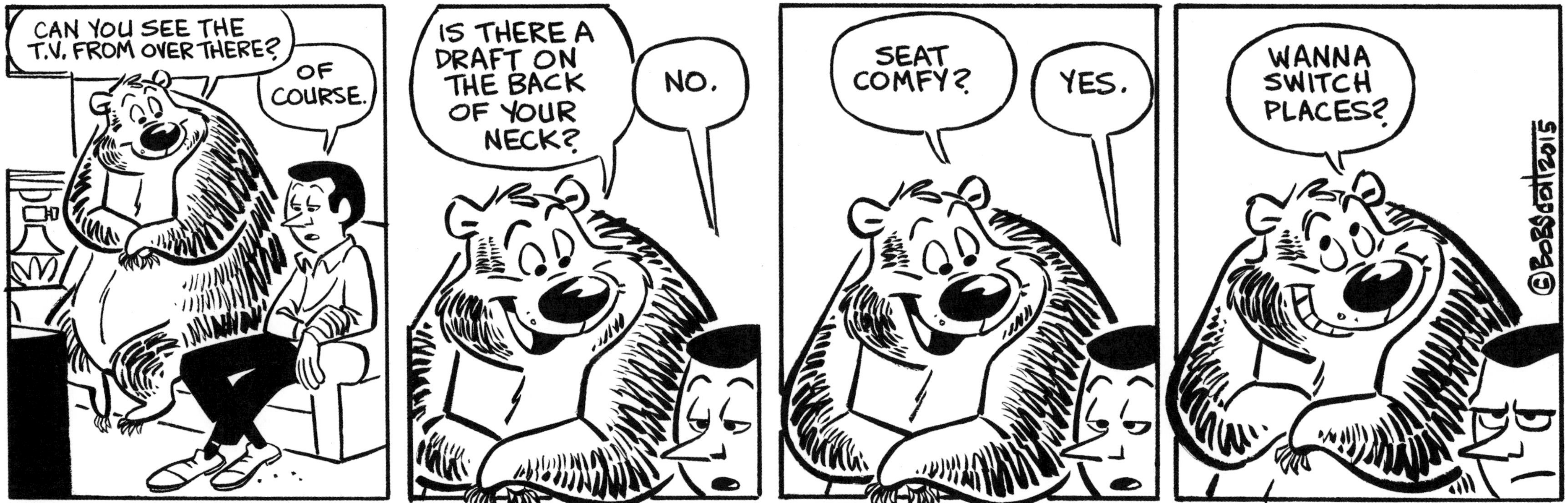
CAN YOU SEE THE T.V. FROM OVER THERE?
OF COURSE.
IS THERE A DRAFT ON THE BACK OF YOUR NECK?
NO.
SEAT COMFY?
YES.
WANNA SWITCH PLACES?
©BOBSCOTT2015

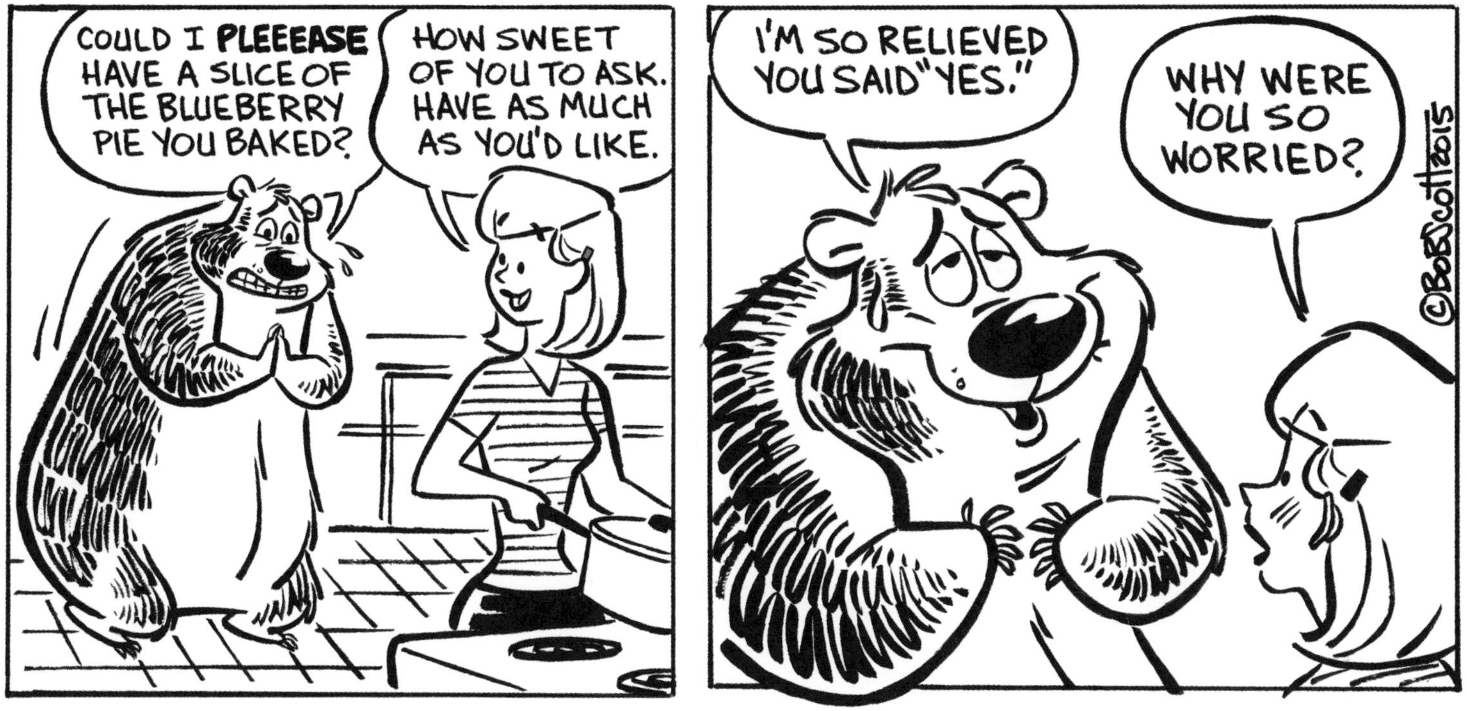
COULD I PLEEEASE HAVE A SLICE OF THE BLUEBERRY PIE YOU BAKED?
HOW SWEET OF YOU TO ASK. HAVE AS MUCH AS YOU'D LIKE.
I'M SO RELIEVED YOU SAID "YES."
WHY WERE YOU SO WORRIED?
©BOBSCOTT2015
BECAUSE I ALREADY ATE THE WHOLE THING.

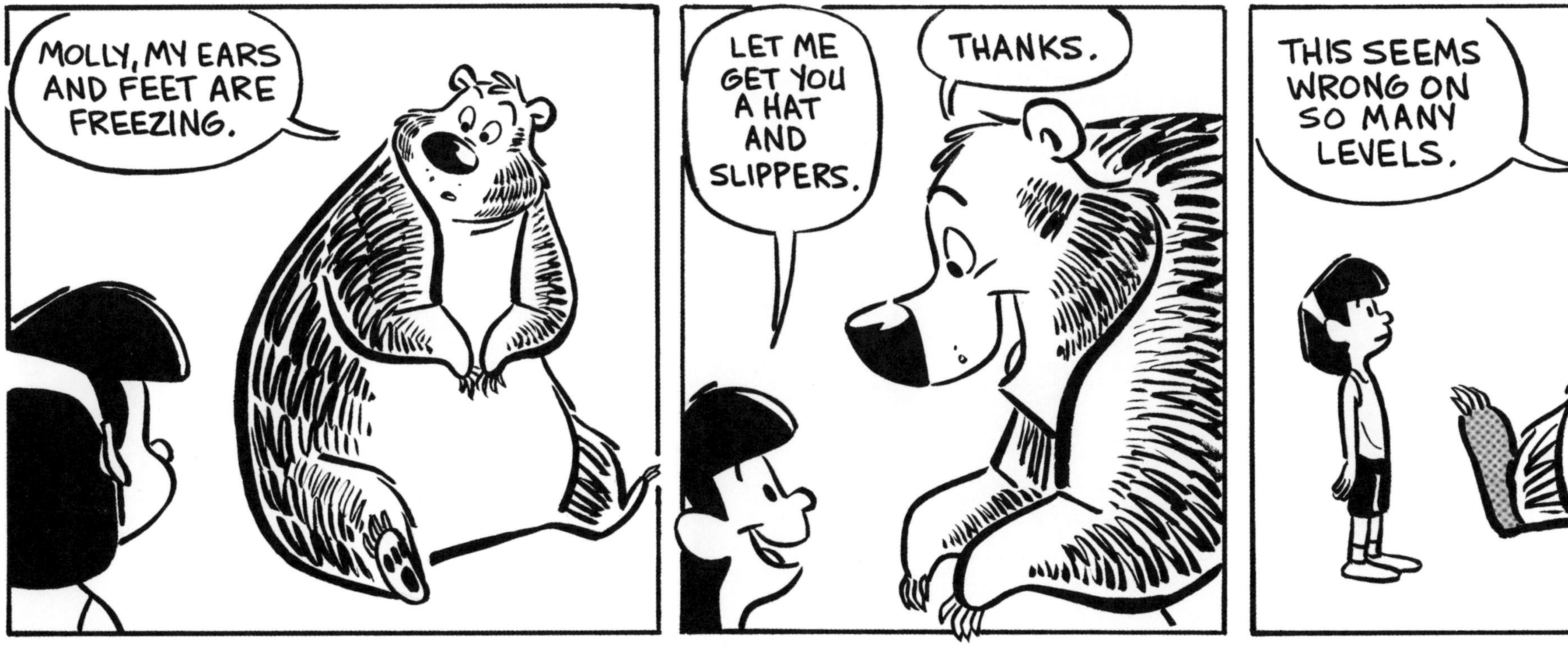
MOLLY, MY EARS AND FEET ARE FREEZING.
LET ME GET YOU A HAT AND SLIPPERS.
THANKS.
THIS SEEMS WRONG ON SO MANY LEVELS.
©BOBSCOTT2015

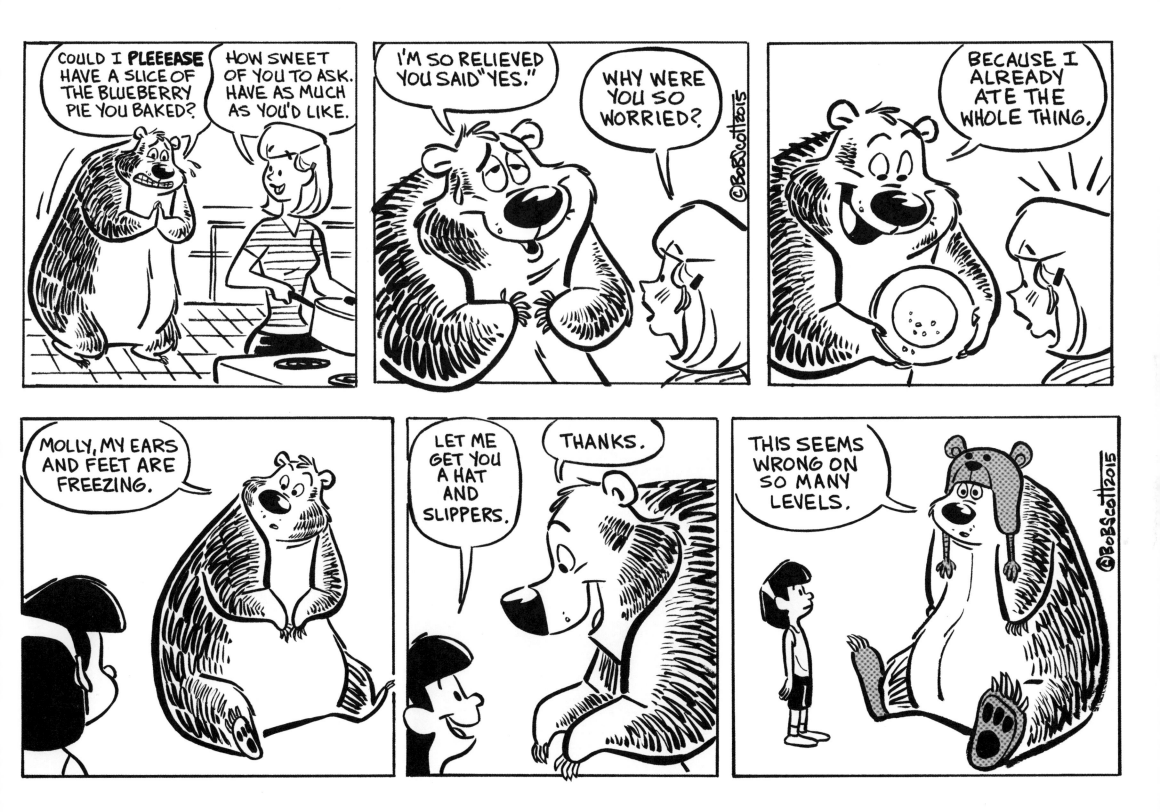

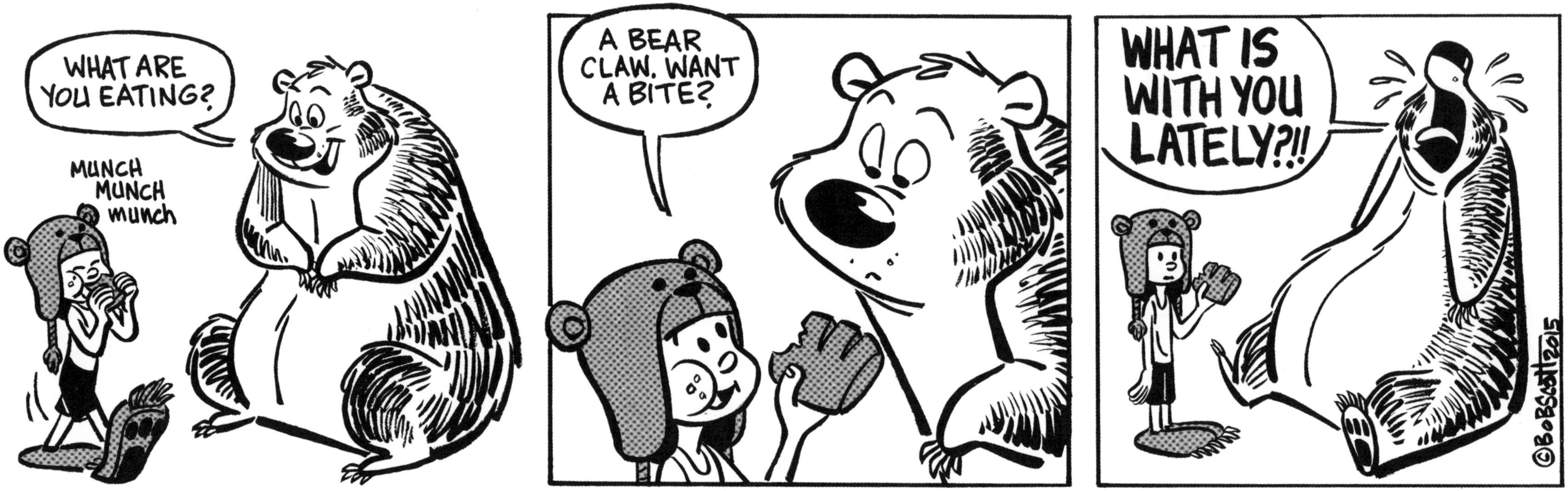
WHAT ARE YOU EATING?
MUNCH MUNCH munch
A BEAR CLAW. WANT A BITE?
WHAT IS WITH YOU LATELY?!!
©BoBSCOTT2015

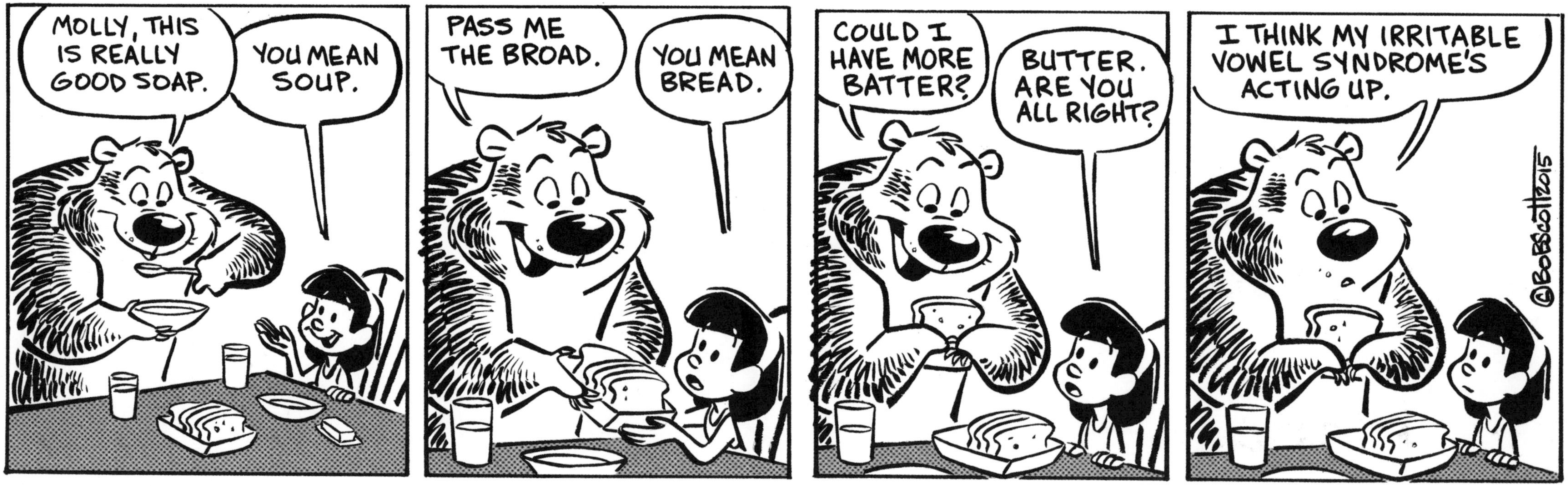
MOLLY, THIS IS REALLY GOOD SOAP.
YOU MEAN SOUP.
PASS ME THE BROAD.
YOU MEAN BREAD.
COULD I HAVE MORE BATTER?
BUTTER. ARE YOU ALL RIGHT?
I THINK MY IRRITABLE VOWEL SYNDROME'S ACTING UP.
©BoBSCOTT2015

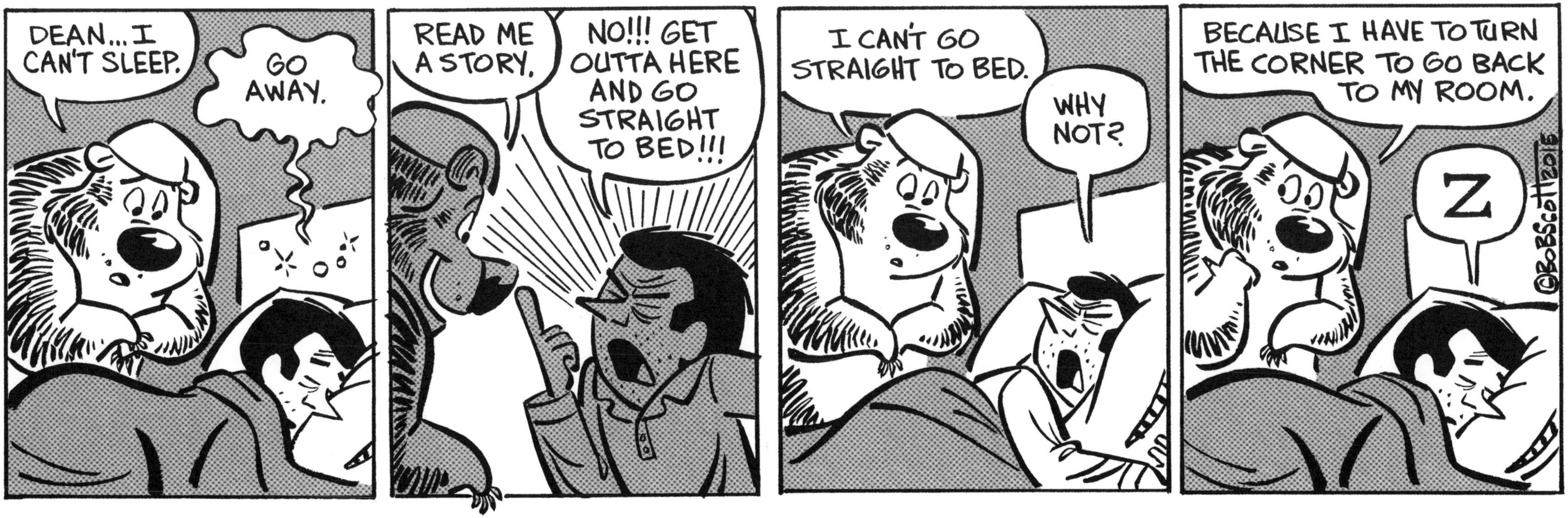
DEAN... I CAN'T SLEEP.
GO AWAY.
READ ME A STORY.
NO!!! GET OUTTA HERE AND GO STRAIGHT TO BED!!!
I CAN'T GO STRAIGHT TO BED.
WHY NOT?
BECAUSE I HAVE TO TURN THE CORNER TO GO BACK TO MY ROOM.
Z
©BOBSCOTT2015

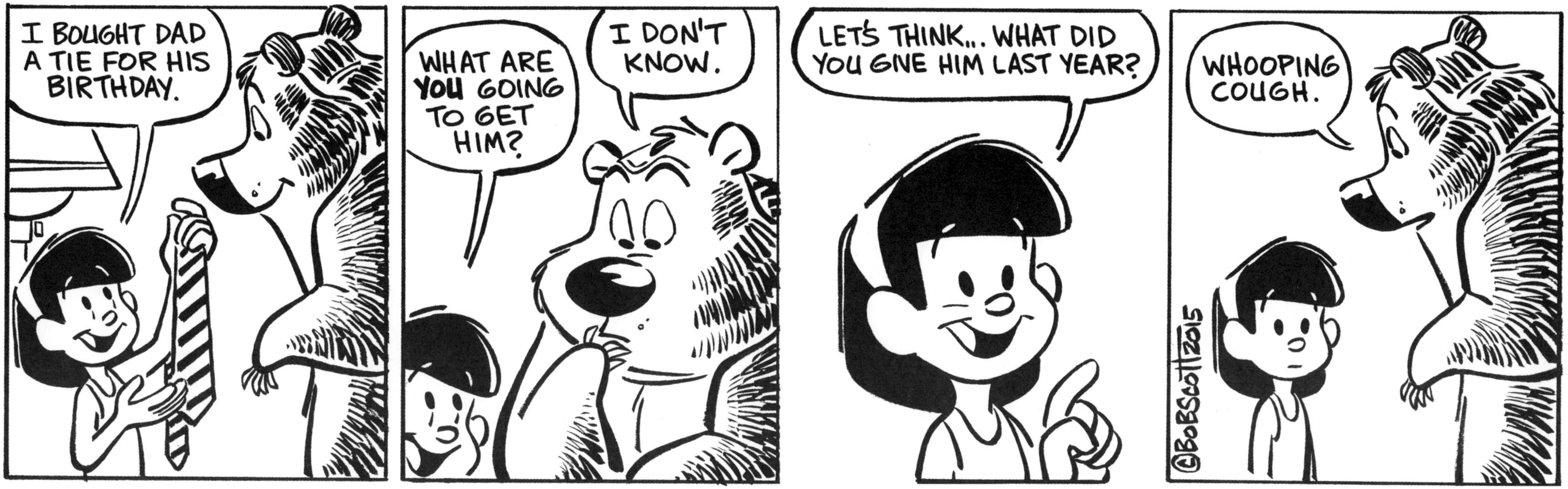
I BOUGHT DAD A TIE FOR HIS BIRTHDAY.
WHAT ARE YOU GOING TO GET HIM?
I DON'T KNOW.
LET'S THINK... WHAT DID YOU GIVE HIM LAST YEAR?
WHOOPING COUGH.
©BOBSCOTT2015

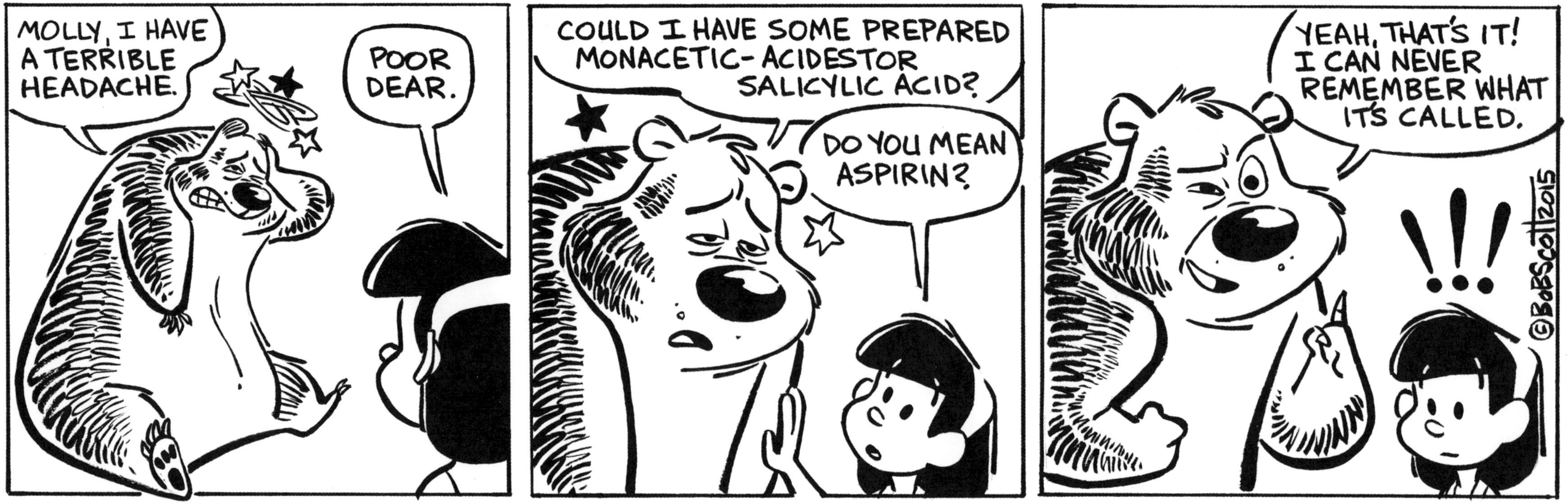
MOLLY, I HAVE A TERRIBLE HEADACHE.
POOR DEAR.
COULD I HAVE SOME PREPARED MONACETIC-ACIDESTOR SALICYLIC ACID?
DO YOU MEAN ASPIRIN?
YEAH, THAT'S IT! I CAN NEVER REMEMBER WHAT IT'S CALLED.
!!!
©BOBSCOTT 2015

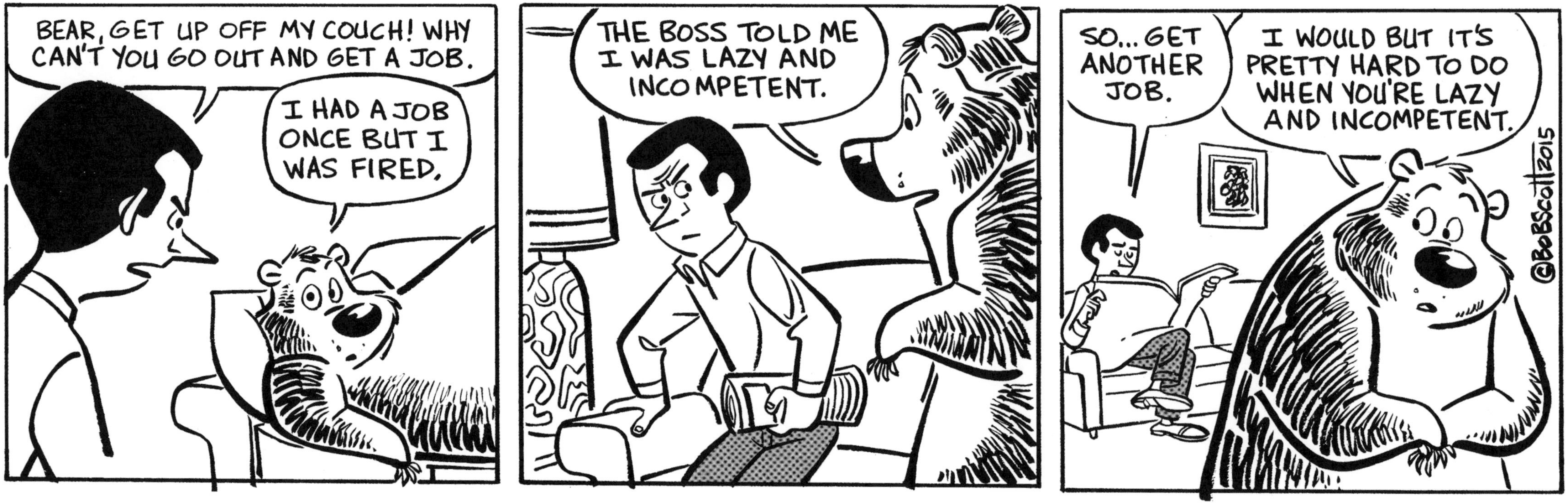
BEAR, GET UP OFF MY COUCH! WHY CAN'T YOU GO OUT AND GET A JOB.
I HAD A JOB ONCE BUT I WAS FIRED.
THE BOSS TOLD ME I WAS LAZY AND INCOMPETENT.
SO... GET ANOTHER JOB.
I WOULD BUT IT'S PRETTY HARD TO DO WHEN YOU'RE LAZY AND INCOMPETENT.
©BOBSCOTT 2015

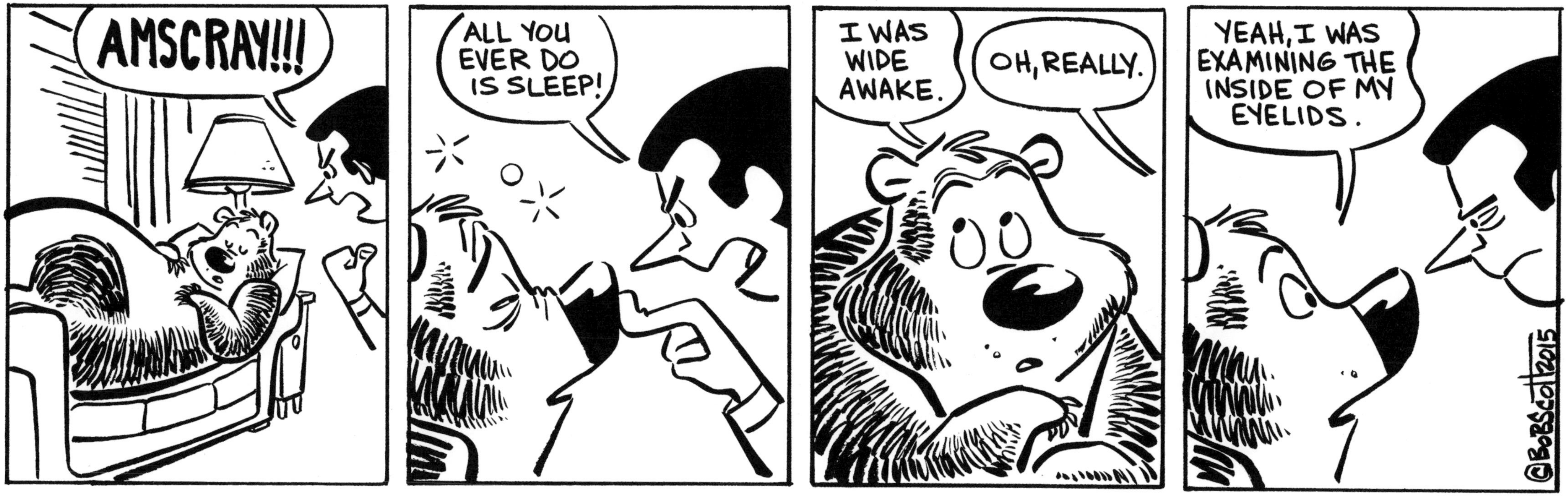
AMSCRAY!!!
ALL YOU EVER DO IS SLEEP!
I WAS WIDE AWAKE.
OH, REALLY.
YEAH, I WAS EXAMINING THE INSIDE OF MY EYELIDS.
©BOBSCOTT2015

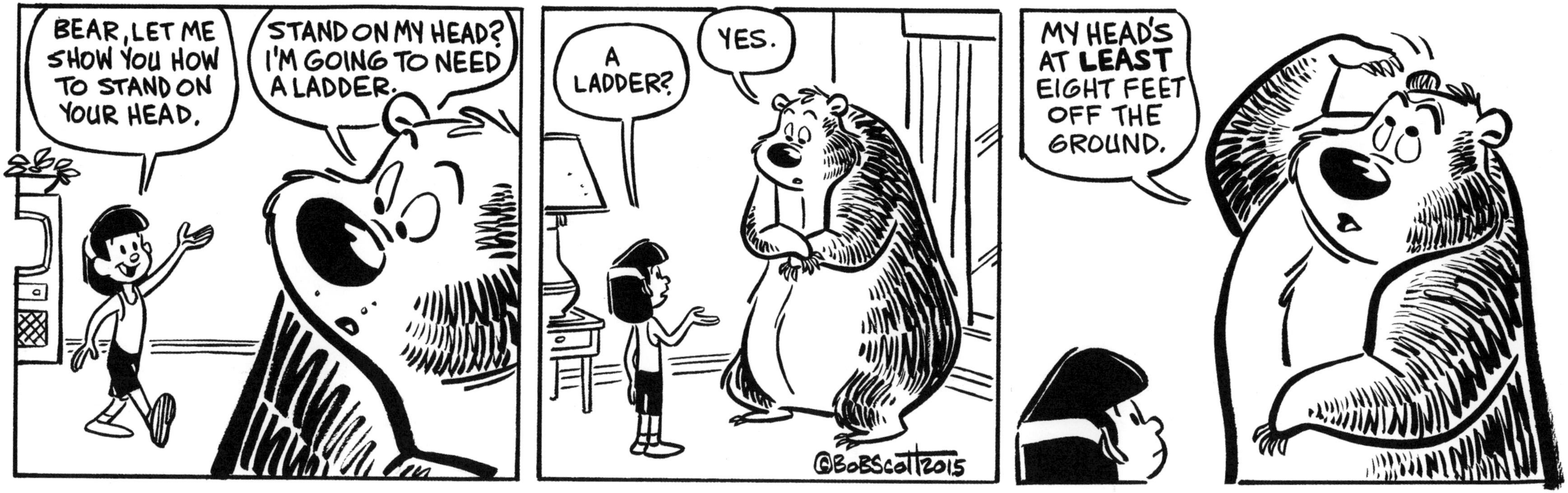
BEAR, LET ME SHOW YOU HOW TO STAND ON YOUR HEAD.
STAND ON MY HEAD? I'M GOING TO NEED A LADDER.
A LADDER?
YES.
©BOBSCOTT2015
MY HEAD'S AT **LEAST** EIGHT FEET OFF THE GROUND.

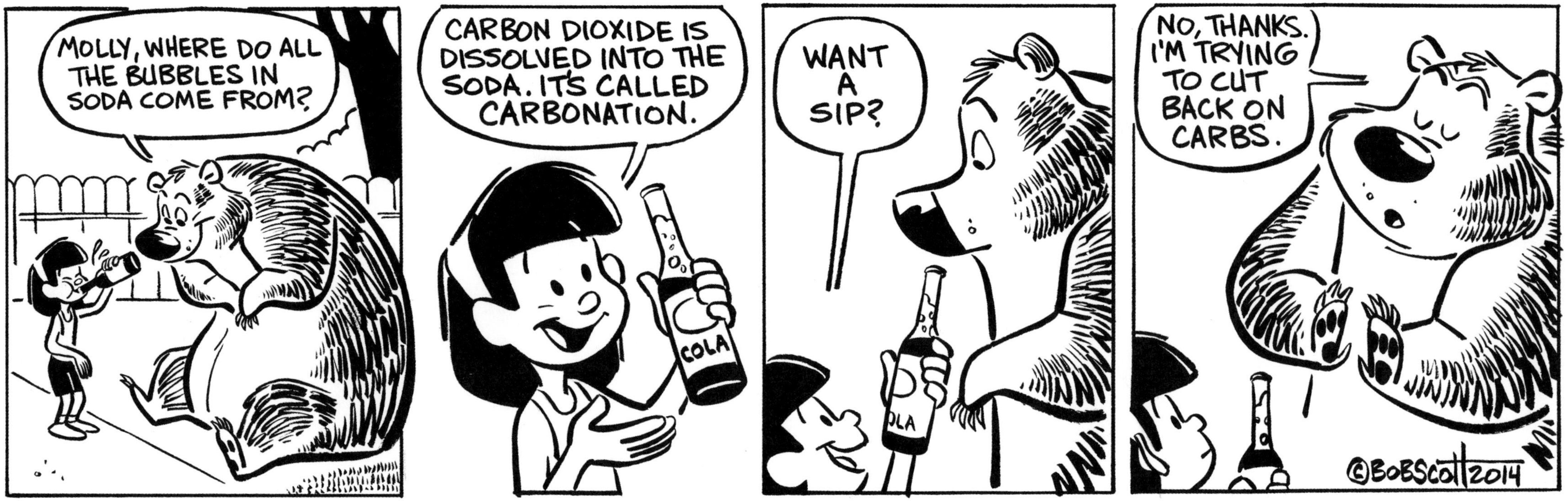
MOLLY, WHERE DO ALL THE BUBBLES IN SODA COME FROM?
CARBON DIOXIDE IS DISSOLVED INTO THE SODA. IT'S CALLED CARBONATION.
COLA
WANT A SIP?
NO, THANKS. I'M TRYING TO CUT BACK ON CARBS.
©BOBSCOTT 2014

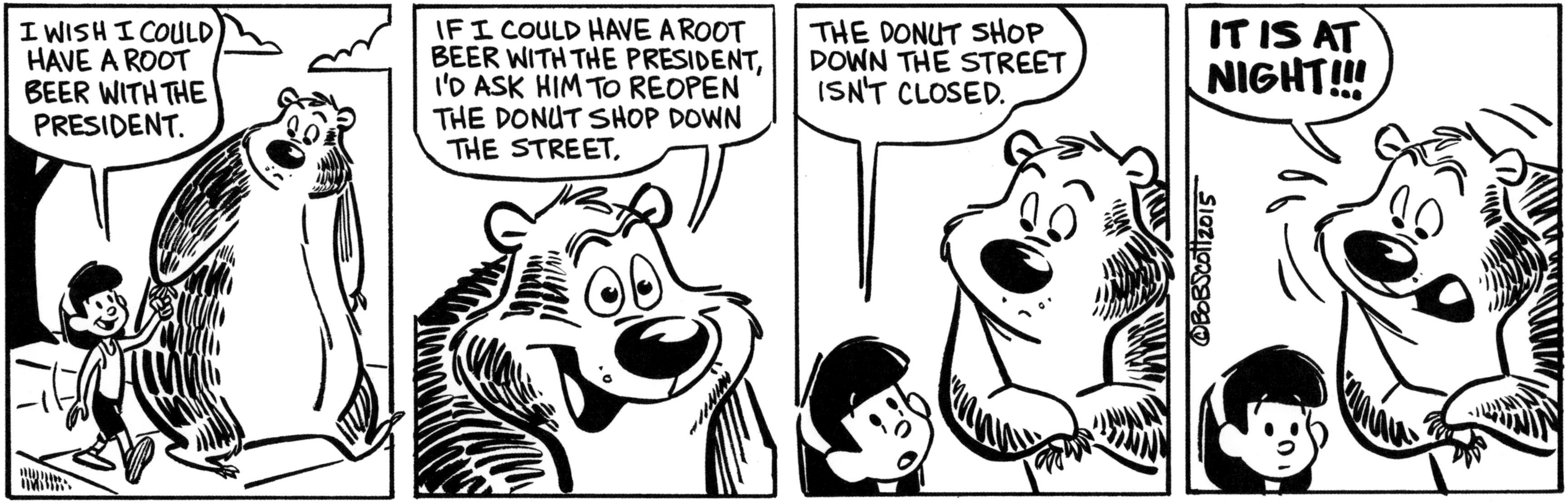
I WISH I COULD HAVE A ROOT BEER WITH THE PRESIDENT.
IF I COULD HAVE A ROOT BEER WITH THE PRESIDENT, I'D ASK HIM TO REOPEN THE DONUT SHOP DOWN THE STREET.
THE DONUT SHOP DOWN THE STREET ISN'T CLOSED.
©BOBSCOTT 2015
IT IS AT NIGHT!!!

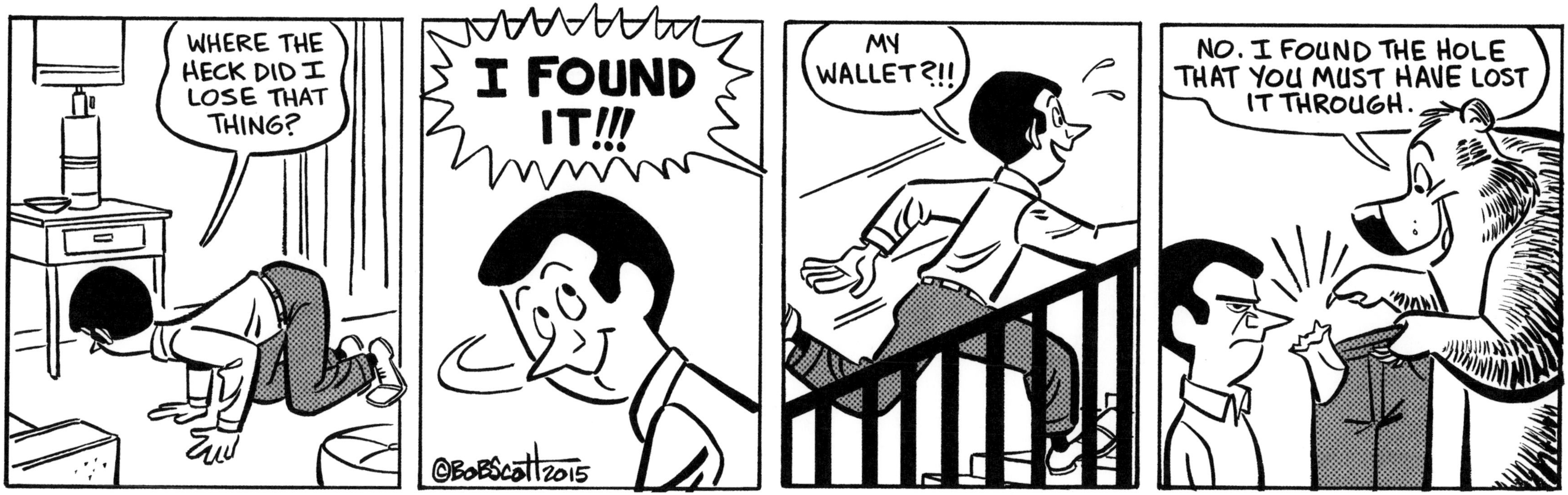
WHERE THE HECK DID I LOSE THAT THING?
I FOUND IT!!!
©BOBSCOTT 2015
MY WALLET?!!
NO. I FOUND THE HOLE THAT YOU MUST HAVE LOST IT THROUGH.

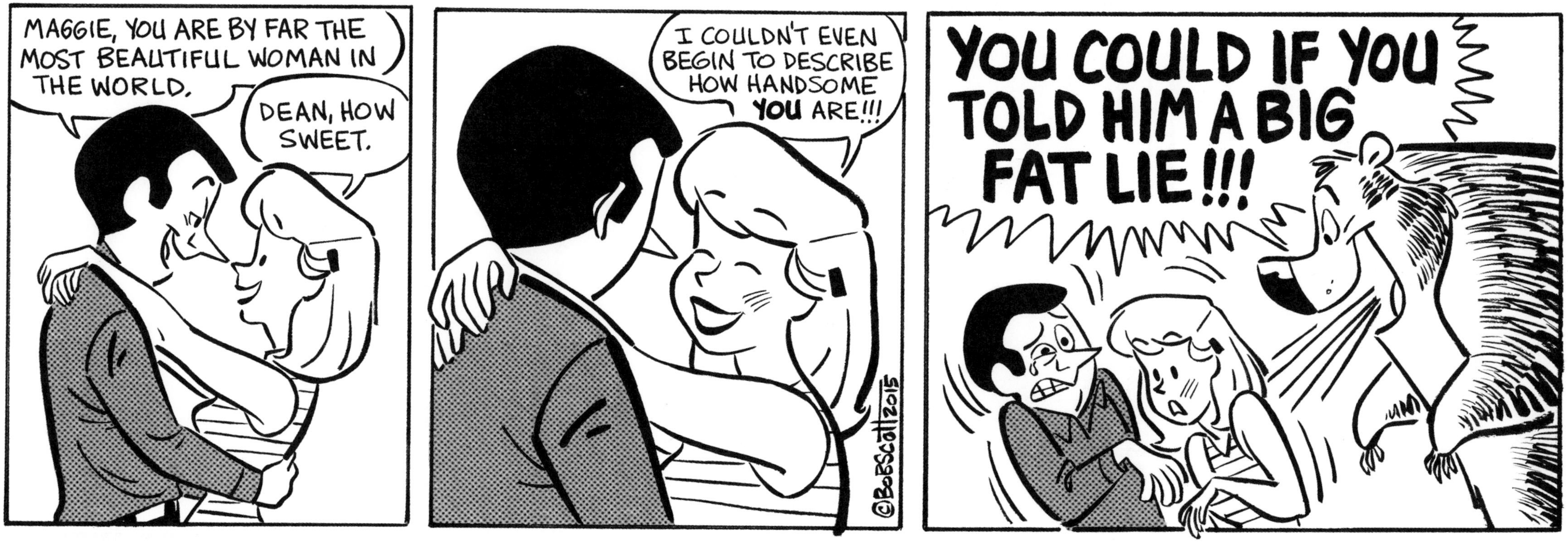
MAGGIE, YOU ARE BY FAR THE MOST BEAUTIFUL WOMAN IN THE WORLD.
DEAN, HOW SWEET.
I COULDN'T EVEN BEGIN TO DESCRIBE HOW HANDSOME YOU ARE!!!
©BOBSCOTT 2015
YOU COULD IF YOU TOLD HIM A BIG FAT LIE!!!

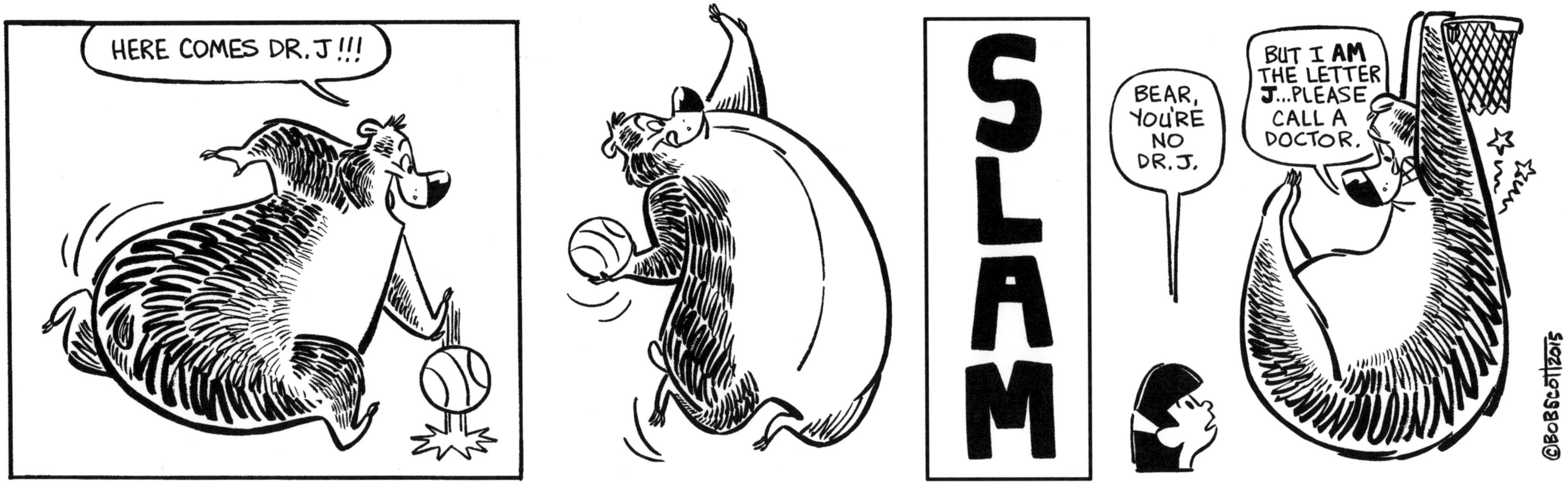
HERE COMES DR. J!!!
SLAM
BEAR, YOU'RE NO DR. J.
BUT I AM THE LETTER J...PLEASE CALL A DOCTOR.
©BOBSCOTT2015

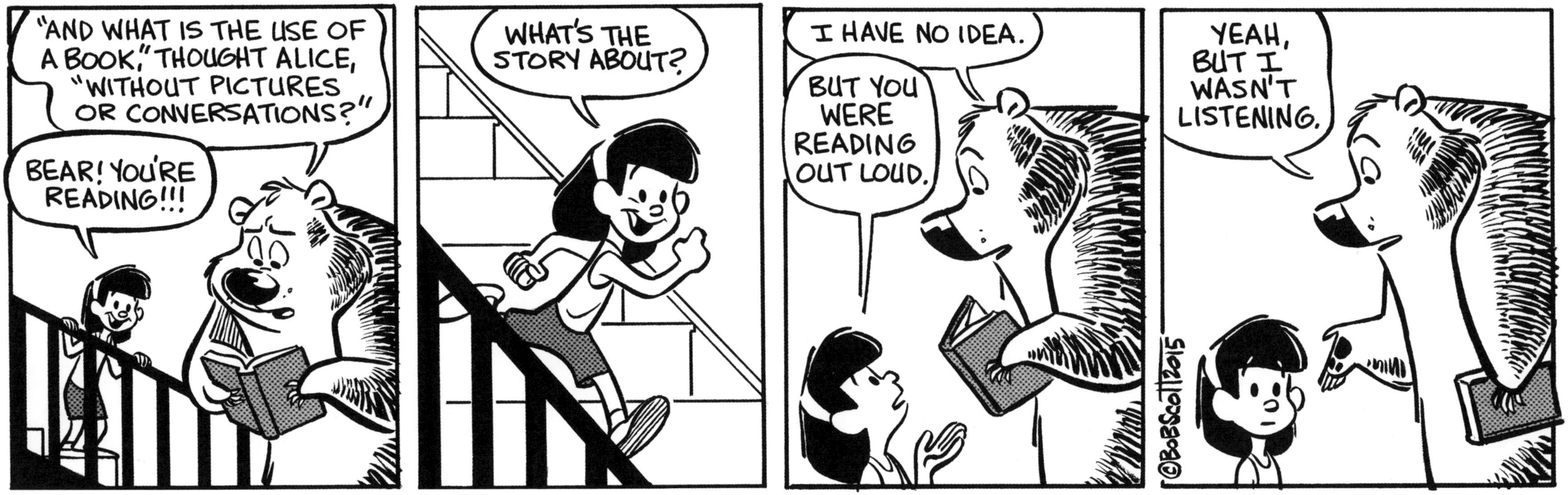
"AND WHAT IS THE USE OF A BOOK," THOUGHT ALICE, "WITHOUT PICTURES OR CONVERSATIONS?"
BEAR! YOU'RE READING!!!
WHAT'S THE STORY ABOUT?
I HAVE NO IDEA.
BUT YOU WERE READING OUT LOUD.
YEAH, BUT I WASN'T LISTENING.
©BOBSCOTT2015

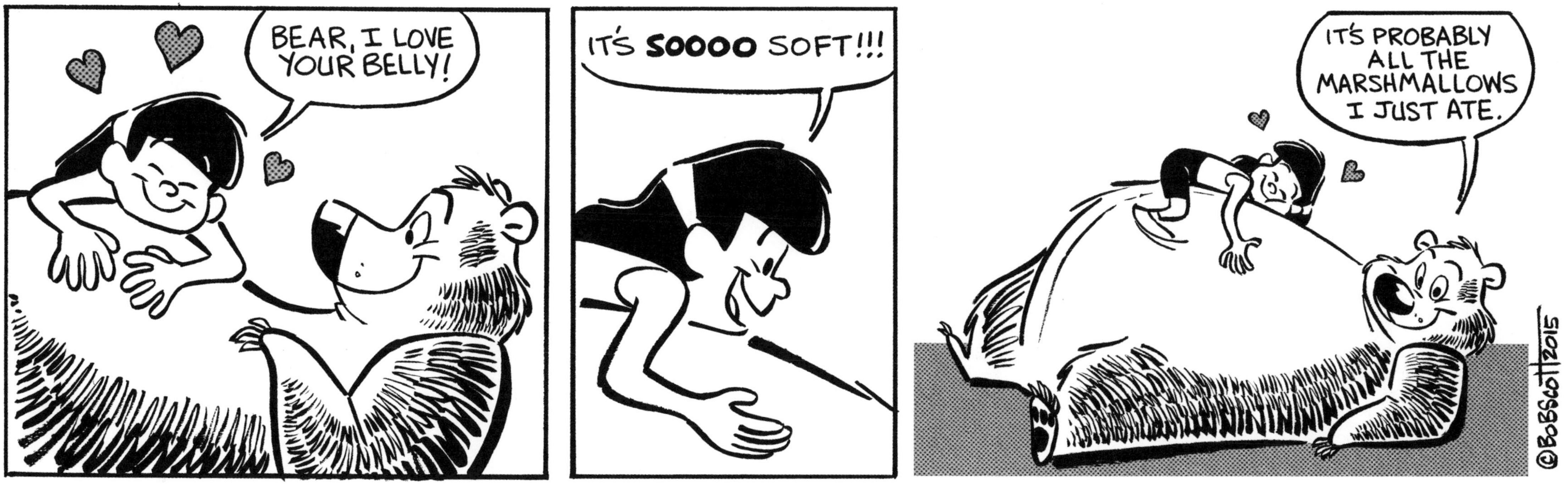
BEAR, I LOVE YOUR BELLY!
IT'S SOOOO SOFT!!!
IT'S PROBABLY ALL THE MARSHMALLOWS I JUST ATE.
©BOBSCOTT2015

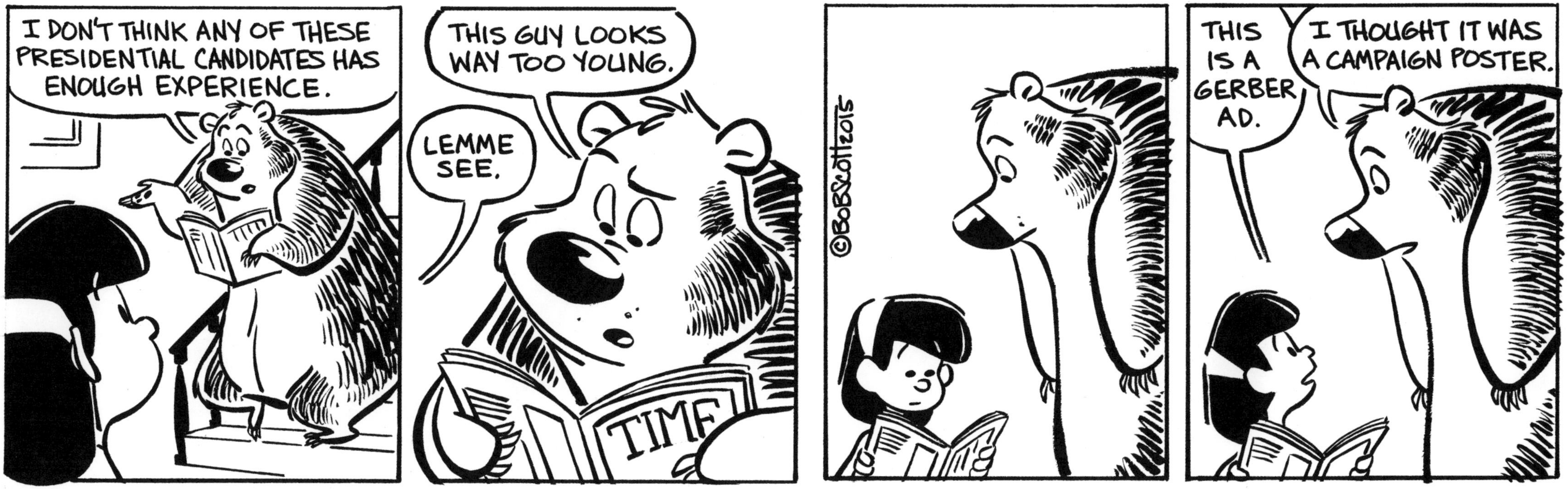
I DON'T THINK ANY OF THESE PRESIDENTIAL CANDIDATES HAS ENOUGH EXPERIENCE.
THIS GUY LOOKS WAY TOO YOUNG.
LEMME SEE.
TIME
©BOBSCOTT2015
THIS IS A GERBER AD.
I THOUGHT IT WAS A CAMPAIGN POSTER.

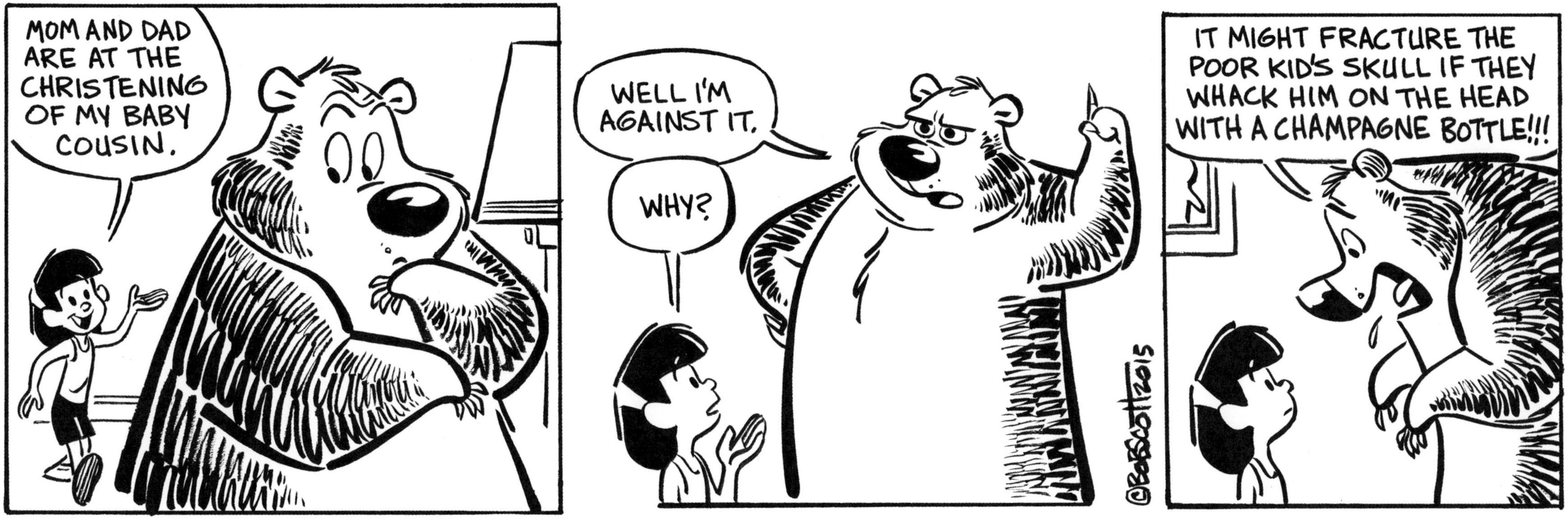
MOM AND DAD ARE AT THE CHRISTENING OF MY BABY COUSIN.
WELL I'M AGAINST IT.
WHY?
©BOBSCOTT2015
IT MIGHT FRACTURE THE POOR KID'S SKULL IF THEY WHACK HIM ON THE HEAD WITH A CHAMPAGNE BOTTLE!!!

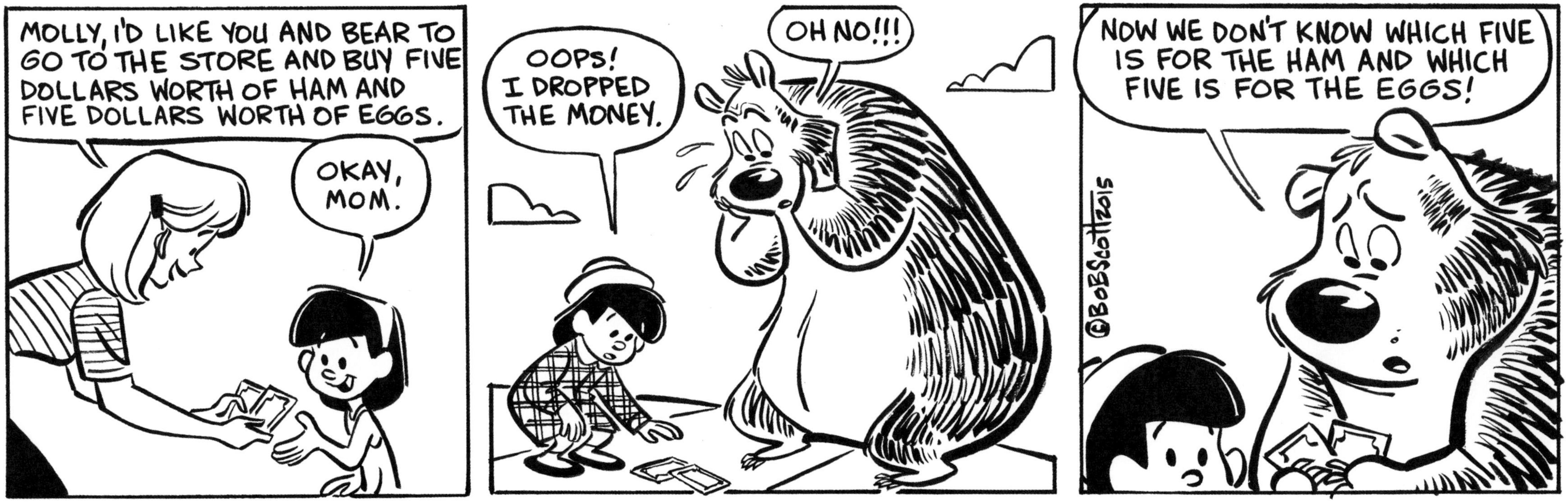
MOLLY, I'D LIKE YOU AND BEAR TO GO TO THE STORE AND BUY FIVE DOLLARS WORTH OF HAM AND FIVE DOLLARS WORTH OF EGGS.
OKAY, MOM.
OOPS! I DROPPED THE MONEY.
OH NO!!!
©BOBSCOTT2015
NOW WE DON'T KNOW WHICH FIVE IS FOR THE HAM AND WHICH FIVE IS FOR THE EGGS!

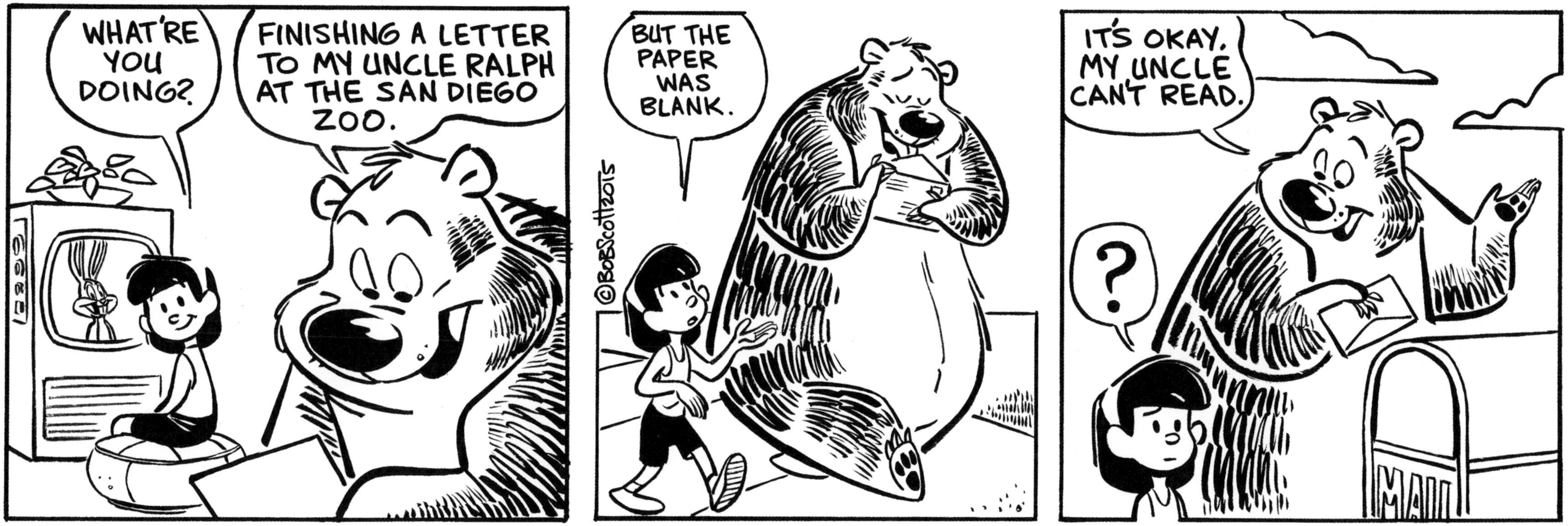
WHAT'RE YOU DOING?
FINISHING A LETTER TO MY UNCLE RALPH AT THE SAN DIEGO ZOO.
©BOBSCOTT2015
BUT THE PAPER WAS BLANK.
IT'S OKAY. MY UNCLE CAN'T READ.
?
MAIL

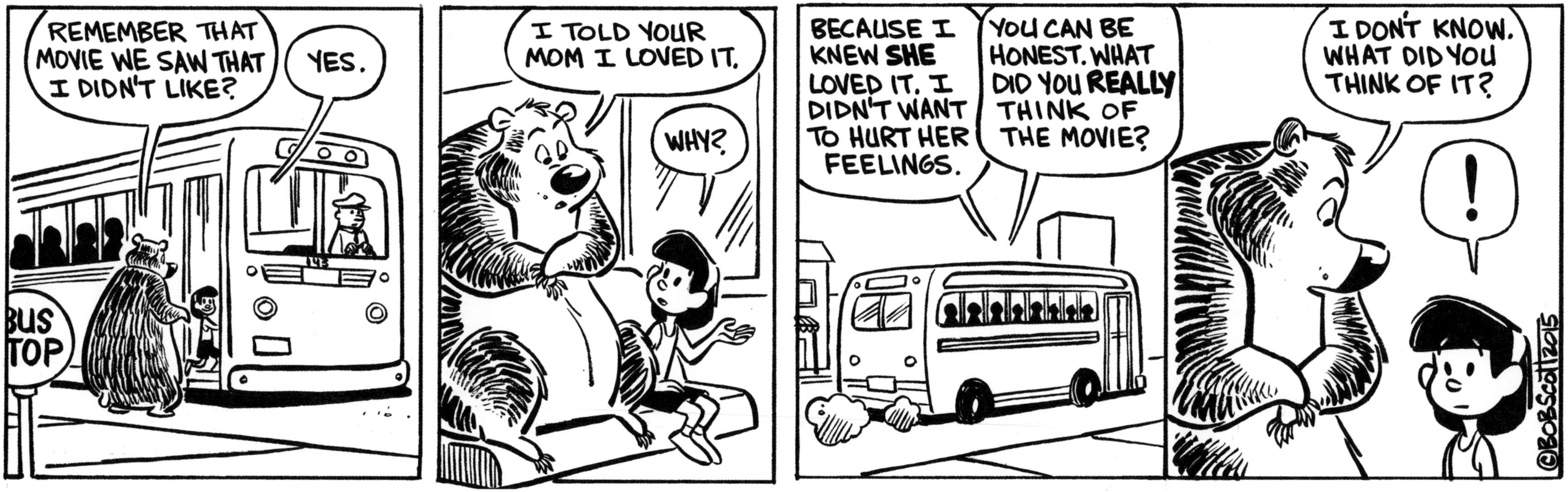
BUS STOP
REMEMBER THAT MOVIE WE SAW THAT I DIDN'T LIKE?
YES.
I TOLD YOUR MOM I LOVED IT.
WHY?
BECAUSE I KNEW **SHE** LOVED IT. I DIDN'T WANT TO HURT HER FEELINGS.
YOU CAN BE HONEST. WHAT DID YOU **REALLY** THINK OF THE MOVIE?
I DON'T KNOW. WHAT DID YOU THINK OF IT?
!
©BOBSCOTT2015

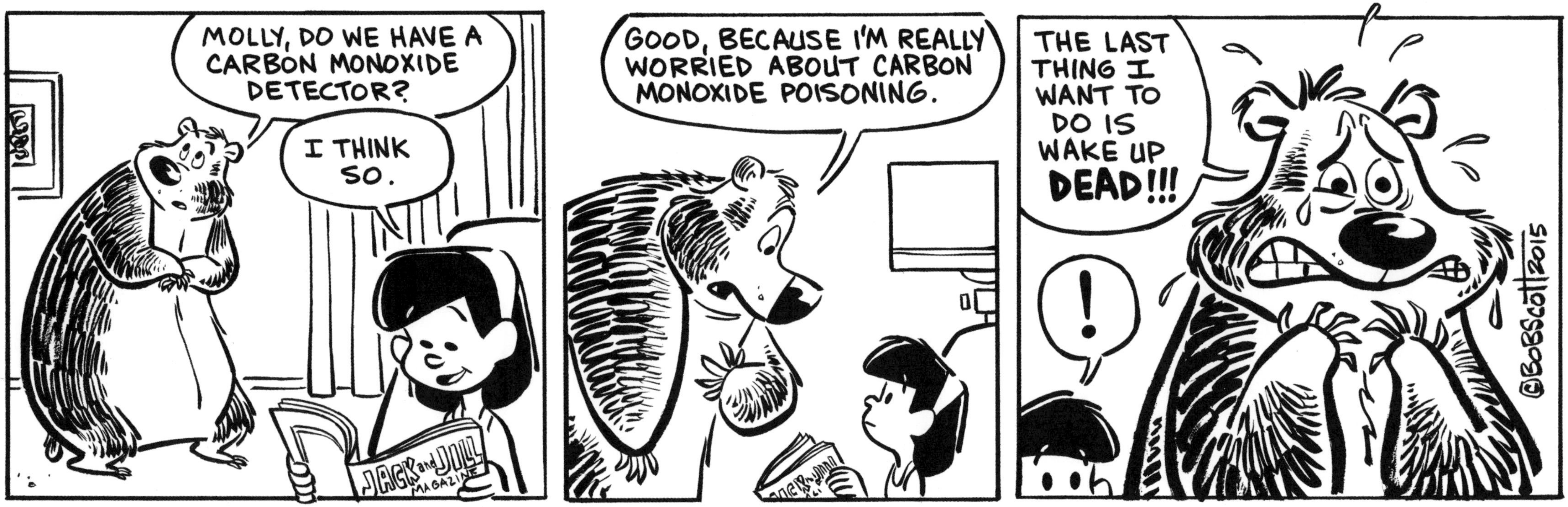
MOLLY, DO WE HAVE A CARBON MONOXIDE DETECTOR?
I THINK SO.
JACK and JILL MAGAZINE
GOOD, BECAUSE I'M REALLY WORRIED ABOUT CARBON MONOXIDE POISONING.
THE LAST THING I WANT TO DO IS WAKE UP **DEAD**!!!
!
©BOBSCOTT2015

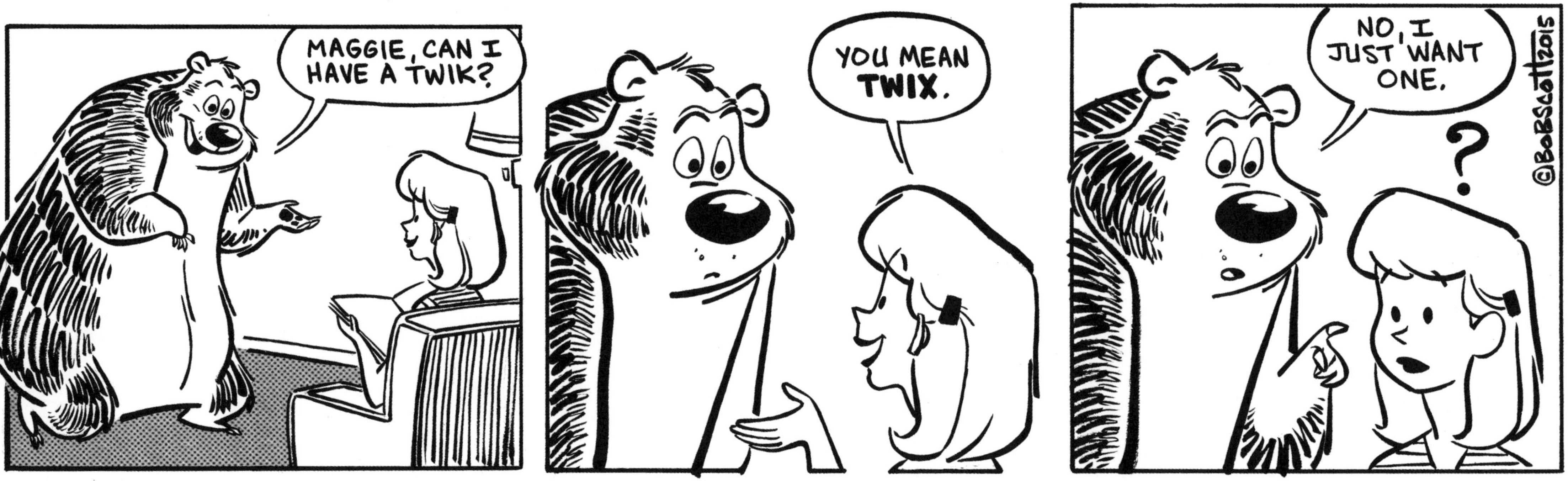
MAGGIE, CAN I HAVE A TWIK?
YOU MEAN **TWIX**.
NO, I JUST WANT ONE.
?
©BOBSCOTT2015

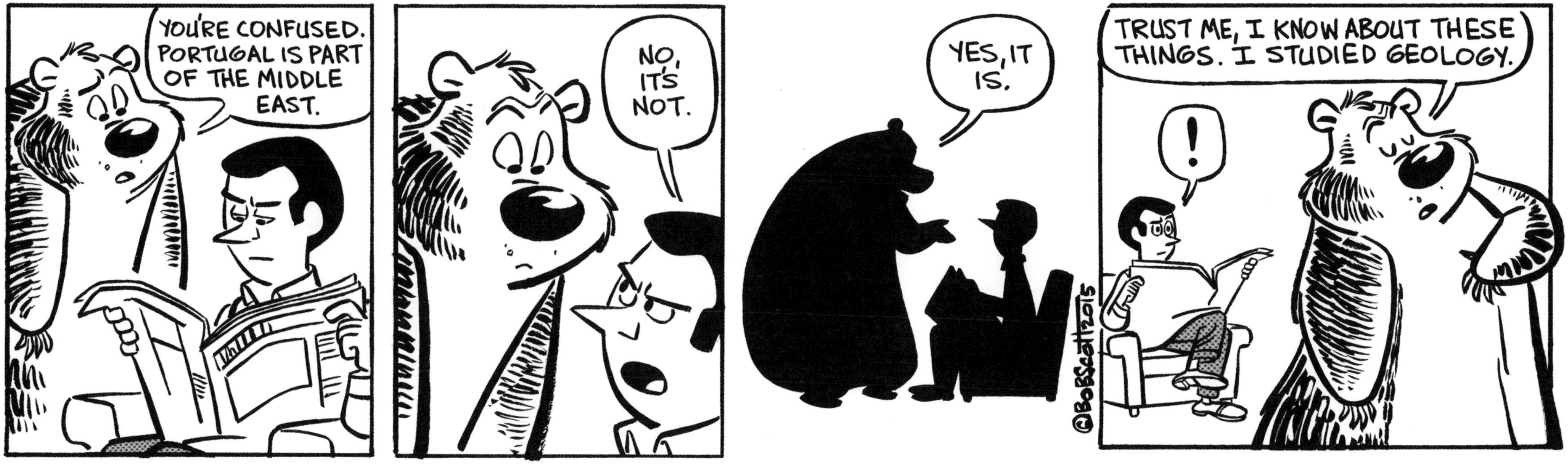
YOU'RE CONFUSED. PORTUGAL IS PART OF THE MIDDLE EAST.
NO, IT'S NOT.
YES, IT IS.
©BOBSCOTT2015
!
TRUST ME, I KNOW ABOUT THESE THINGS. I STUDIED GEOLOGY.

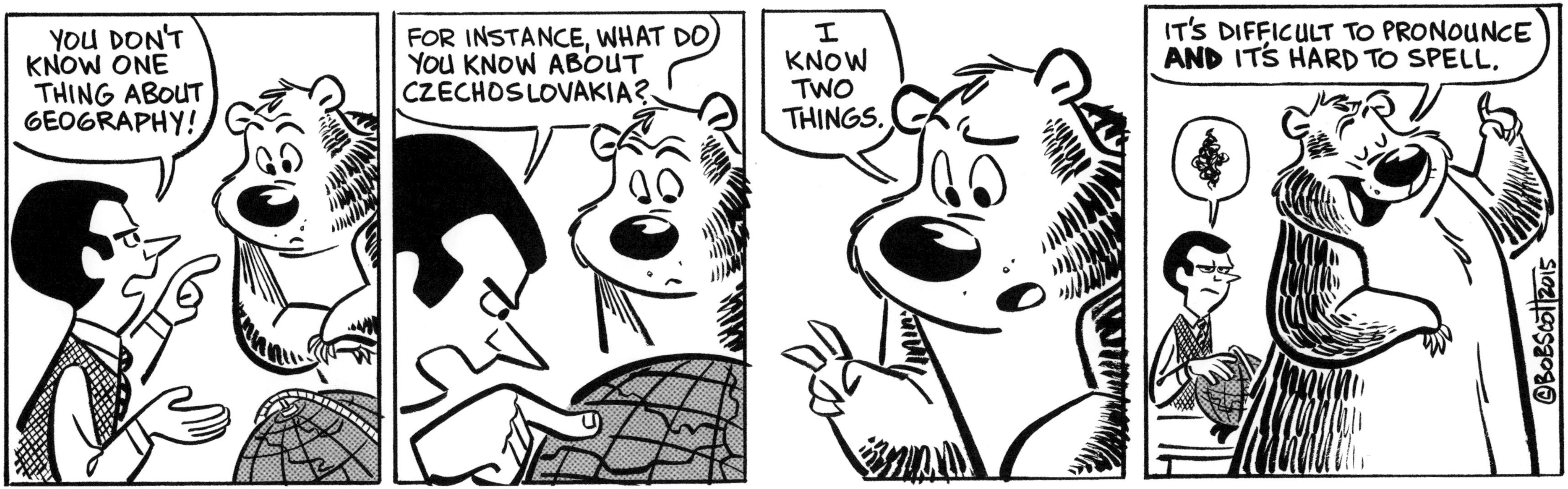
YOU DON'T KNOW ONE THING ABOUT GEOGRAPHY!
FOR INSTANCE, WHAT DO YOU KNOW ABOUT CZECHOSLOVAKIA?
I KNOW TWO THINGS.
IT'S DIFFICULT TO PRONOUNCE **AND** IT'S HARD TO SPELL.
©BOBSCOTT2015

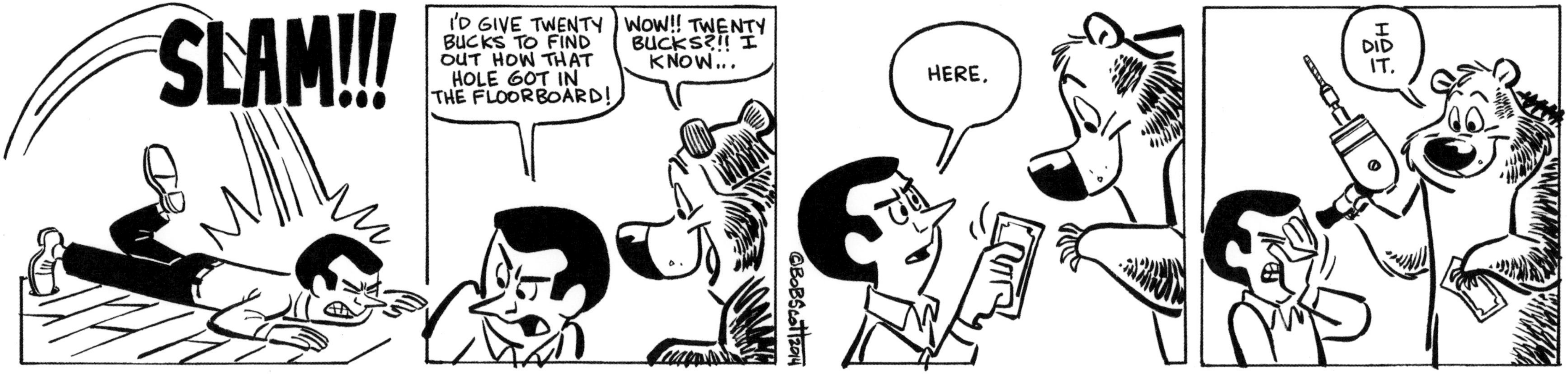
SLAM!!!
I'D GIVE TWENTY BUCKS TO FIND OUT HOW THAT HOLE GOT IN THE FLOORBOARD!
WOW!! TWENTY BUCKS?!! I KNOW...
©BOBSCOTT2014
HERE.
I DID IT.

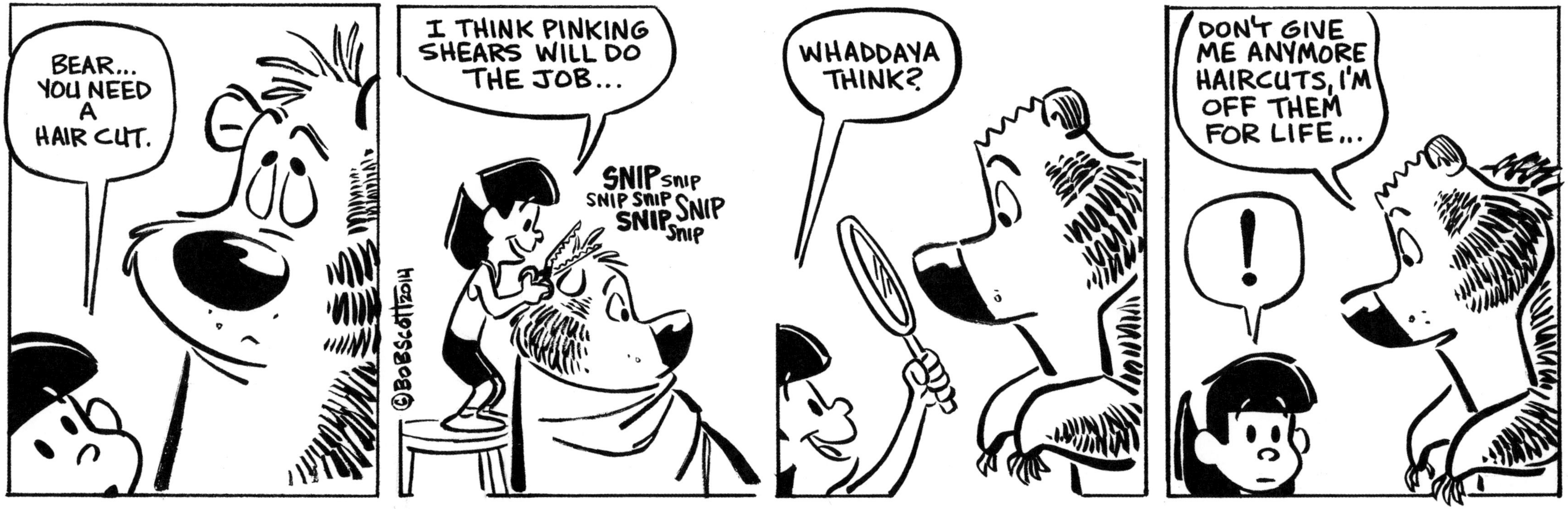
BEAR... YOU NEED A HAIR CUT.
I THINK PINKING SHEARS WILL DO THE JOB...
SNIP snip snip snip SNIP SNIP snip
©BOBSCOTT2014
WHADDAYA THINK?
!
DON'T GIVE ME ANYMORE HAIRCUTS, I'M OFF THEM FOR LIFE...

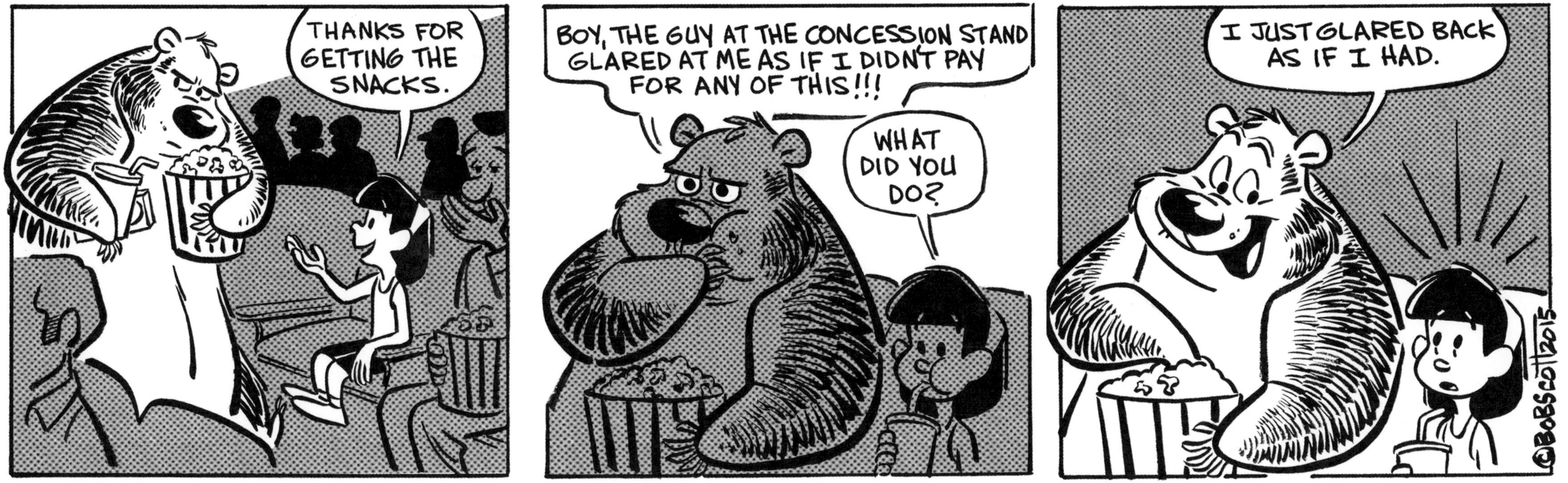
THANKS FOR GETTING THE SNACKS.
BOY, THE GUY AT THE CONCESSION STAND GLARED AT ME AS IF I DIDN'T PAY FOR ANY OF THIS!!!
WHAT DID YOU DO?
I JUST GLARED BACK AS IF I HAD.
©BOBSCOTT 2015

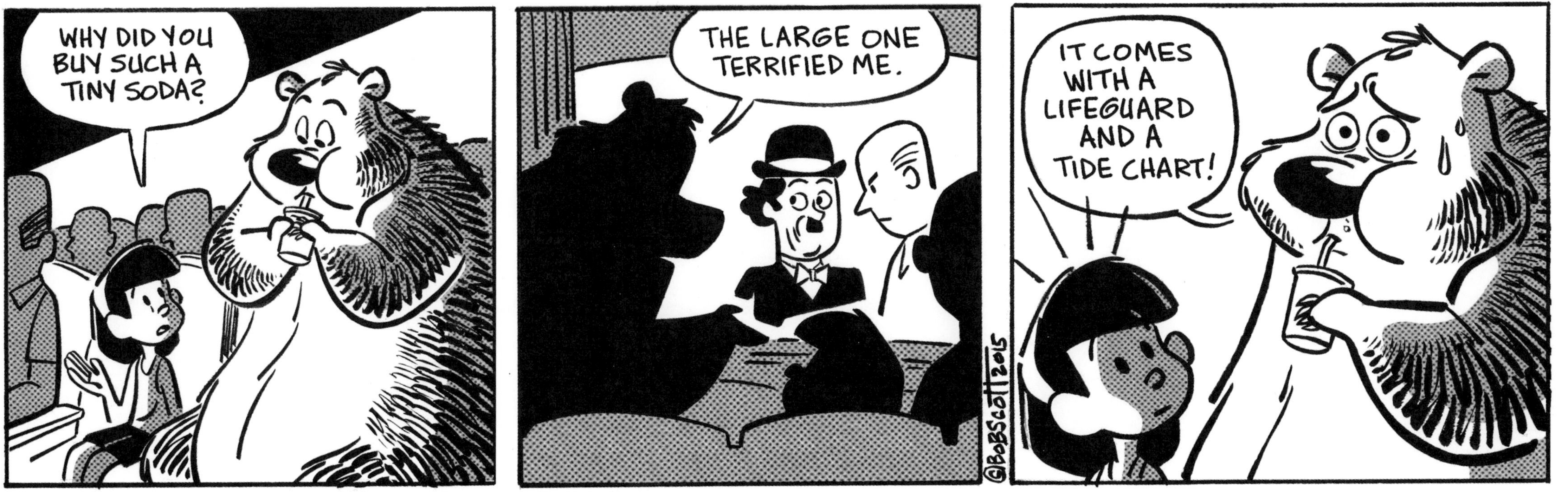
WHY DID YOU BUY SUCH A TINY SODA?
THE LARGE ONE TERRIFIED ME.
IT COMES WITH A LIFEGUARD AND A TIDE CHART!
©BOBSCOTT 2015

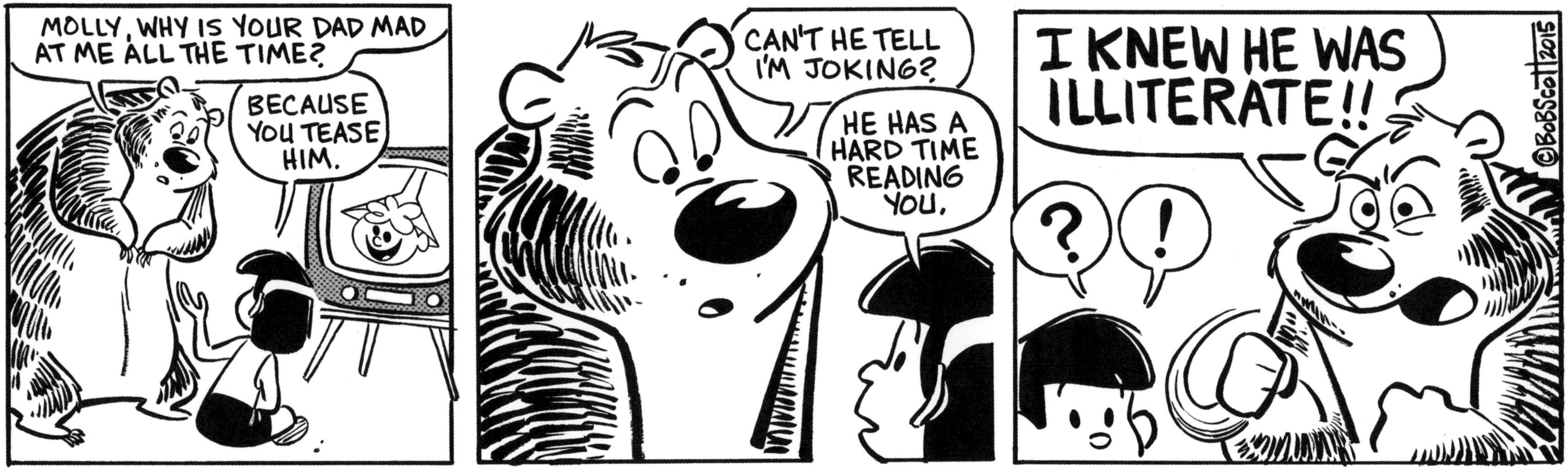
MOLLY, WHY IS YOUR DAD MAD AT ME ALL THE TIME?
BECAUSE YOU TEASE HIM.
CAN'T HE TELL I'M JOKING?
HE HAS A HARD TIME READING YOU.
I KNEW HE WAS ILLITERATE!!
?
!
©BoBScott 2015

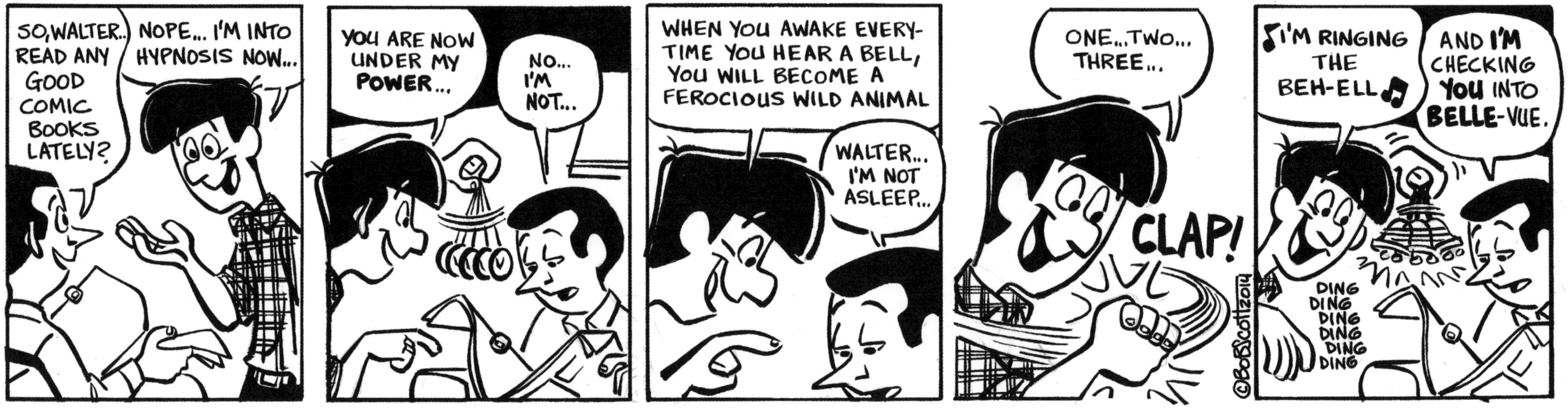
SO, WALTER.. READ ANY GOOD COMIC BOOKS LATELY?
NOPE... I'M INTO HYPNOSIS NOW...
YOU ARE NOW UNDER MY POWER...
NO... I'M NOT...
WHEN YOU AWAKE EVERY-TIME YOU HEAR A BELL, YOU WILL BECOME A FEROCIOUS WILD ANIMAL
WALTER... I'M NOT ASLEEP...
ONE... TWO... THREE...
CLAP!
©BoBScott 2014
♪I'M RINGING THE BEH-ELL♪
AND I'M CHECKING YOU INTO BELLE-VUE.
DING DING DING DING DING DING

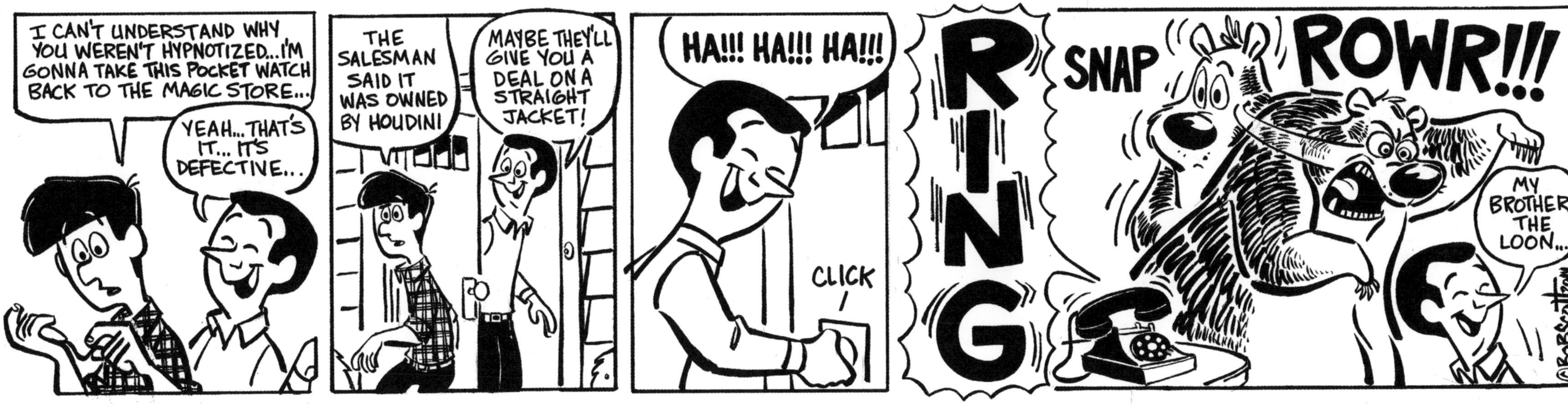
I CAN'T UNDERSTAND WHY YOU WEREN'T HYPNOTIZED...I'M GONNA TAKE THIS POCKET WATCH BACK TO THE MAGIC STORE...
YEAH...THAT'S IT... IT'S DEFECTIVE...
THE SALESMAN SAID IT WAS OWNED BY HOUDINI
MAYBE THEY'LL GIVE YOU A DEAL ON A STRAIGHT JACKET!
HA!!! HA!!! HA!!!
CLICK
RING
SNAP
ROWR!!!
MY BROTHER THE LOON...
©BOBSCOTT2014

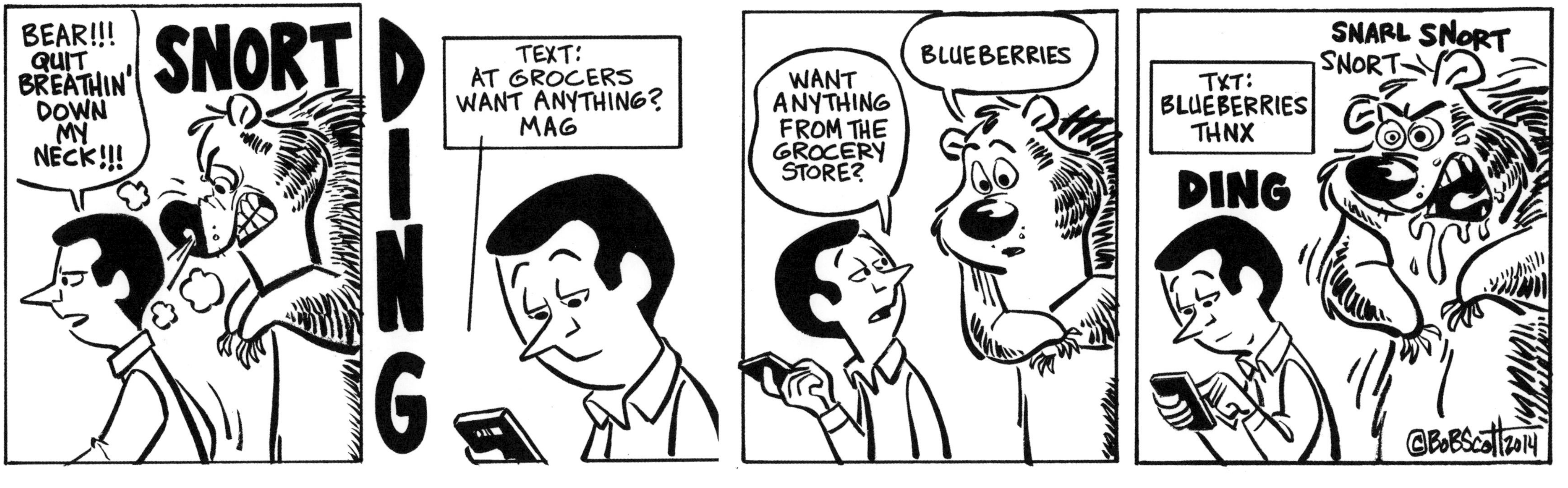
BEAR!!! QUIT BREATHIN' DOWN MY NECK!!!
SNORT
DING
TEXT: AT GROCERS WANT ANYTHING? MAG
WANT ANYTHING FROM THE GROCERY STORE?
BLUEBERRIES
SNARL SNORT
SNORT
TXT: BLUEBERRIES THNX
DING
©BOBSCOTT2014

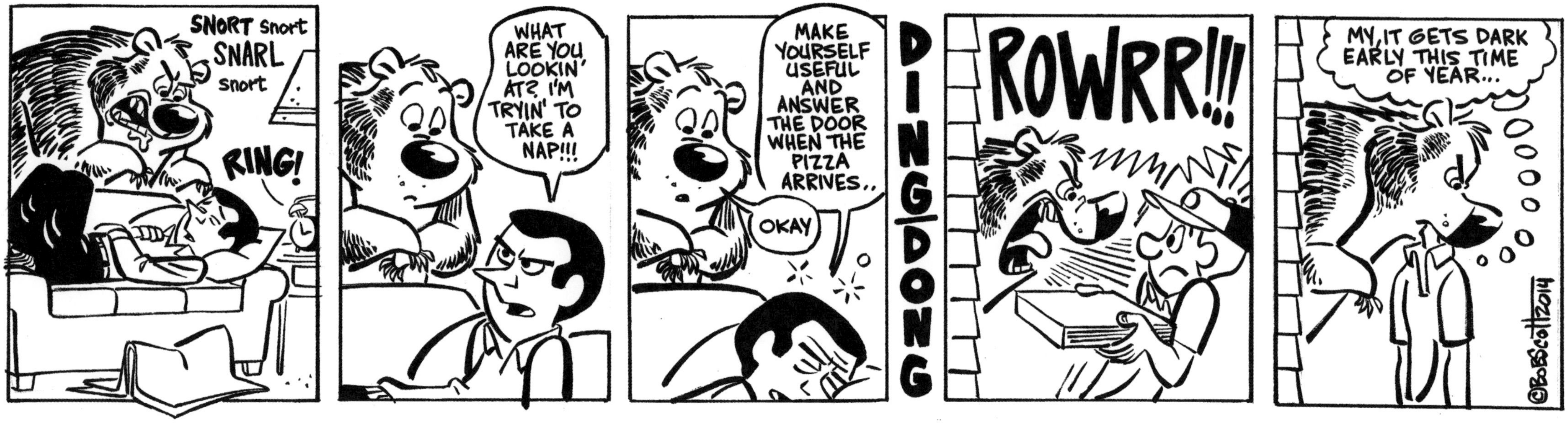
SNORT snort
SNARL
snort
RING!
WHAT ARE YOU LOOKIN' AT? I'M TRYIN' TO TAKE A NAP!!!
MAKE YOURSELF USEFUL AND ANSWER THE DOOR WHEN THE PIZZA ARRIVES..
OKAY
DING DONG
ROWRR!!!
MY, IT GETS DARK EARLY THIS TIME OF YEAR...
©BOBSCOTT2014

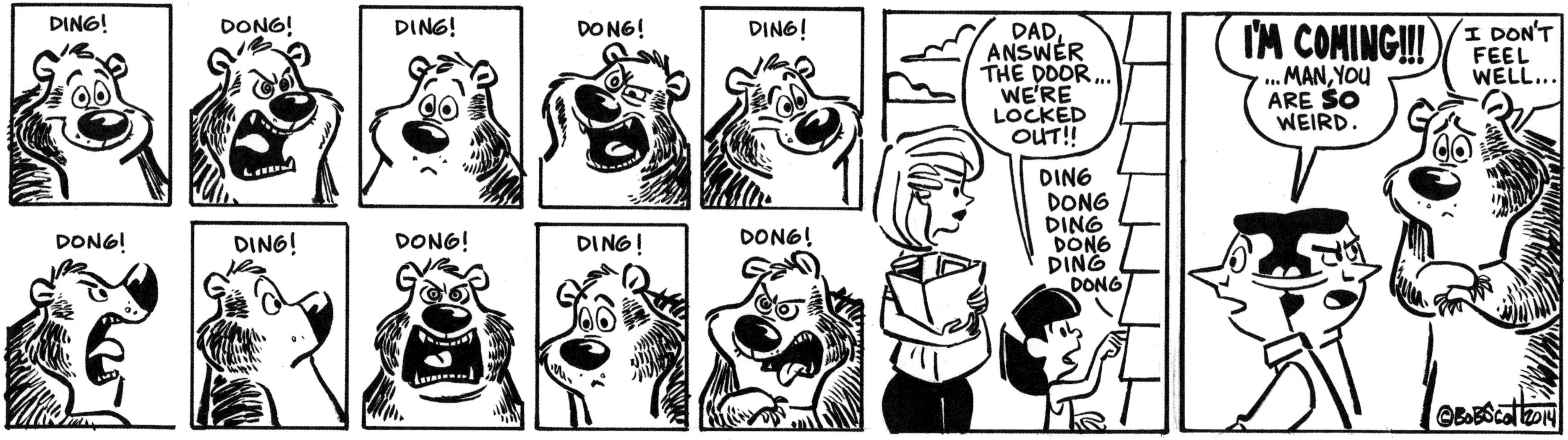
DING!
DONG!
DING!
DONG!
DING!
DONG!
DING!
DONG!
DING!
DONG!
DAD, ANSWER THE DOOR... WE'RE LOCKED OUT!!
DING DONG DING DONG DING DONG
I'M COMING!!! ...MAN, YOU ARE **SO** WEIRD.
I DON'T FEEL WELL...
©BOBSCOTT2014

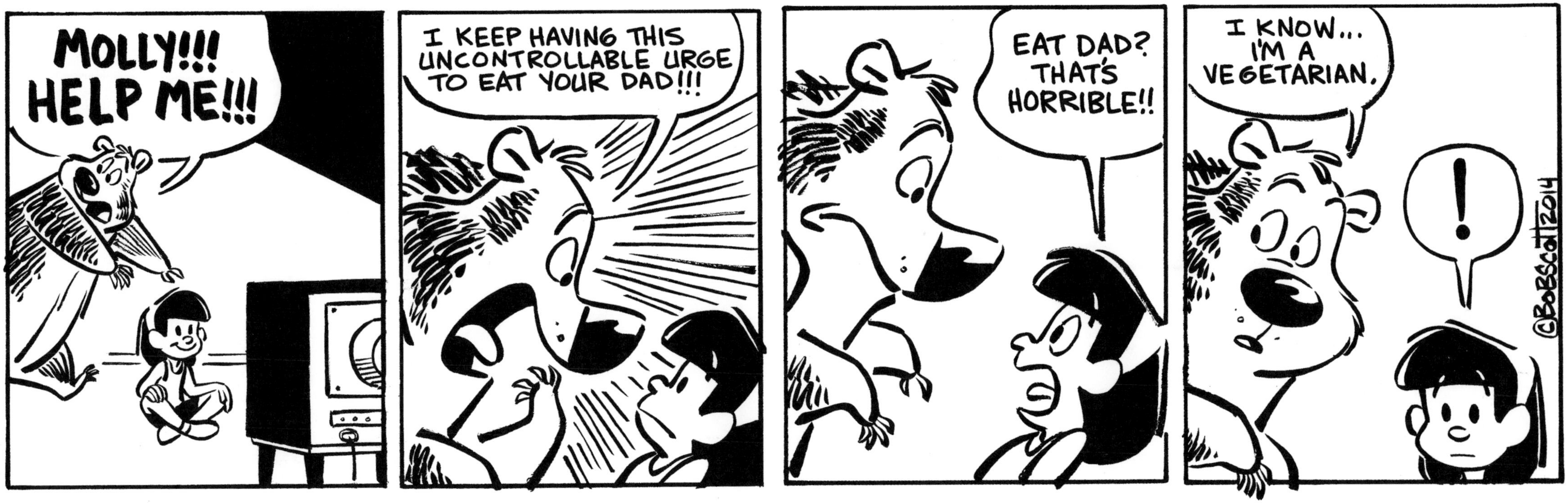
MOLLY!!! HELP ME!!!
I KEEP HAVING THIS UNCONTROLLABLE URGE TO EAT YOUR DAD!!!
EAT DAD? THAT'S HORRIBLE!!
I KNOW... I'M A VEGETARIAN.
!
©BOBSCOTT2014

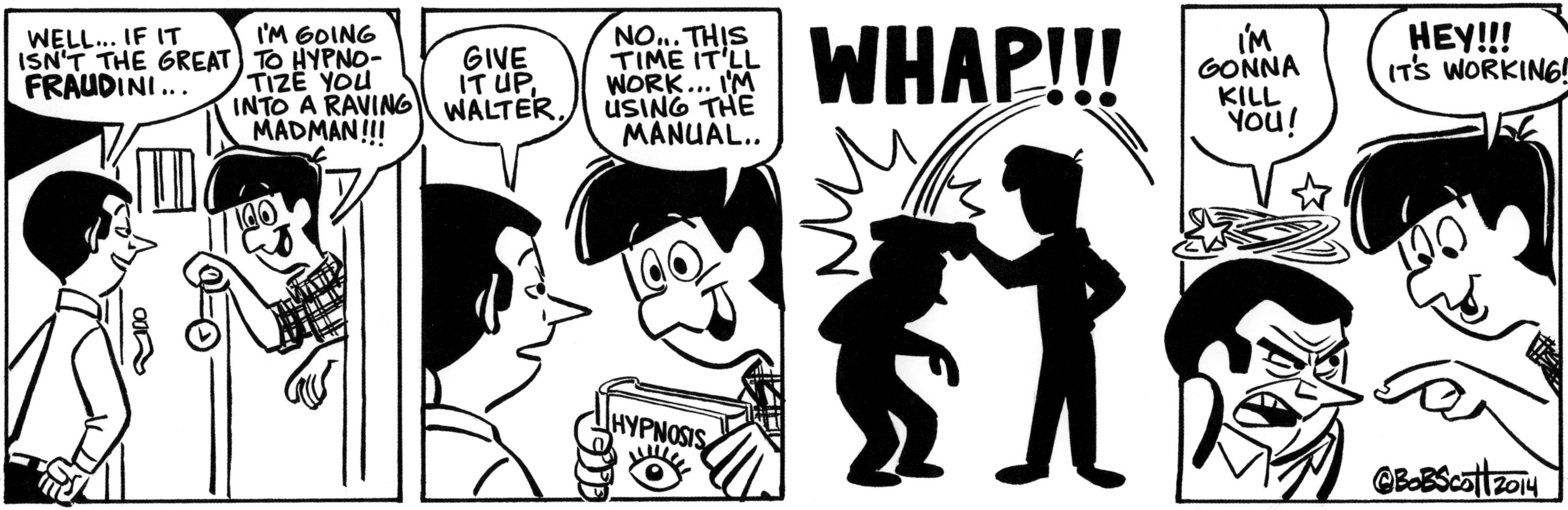
WELL... IF IT ISN'T THE GREAT FRAUDINI...
I'M GOING TO HYPNO-TIZE YOU INTO A RAVING MADMAN!!!
GIVE IT UP, WALTER.
NO... THIS TIME IT'LL WORK... I'M USING THE MANUAL..
HYPNOSIS
WHAP!!!
I'M GONNA KILL YOU!
HEY!!! IT'S WORKING!
©BOBSCOTT2014

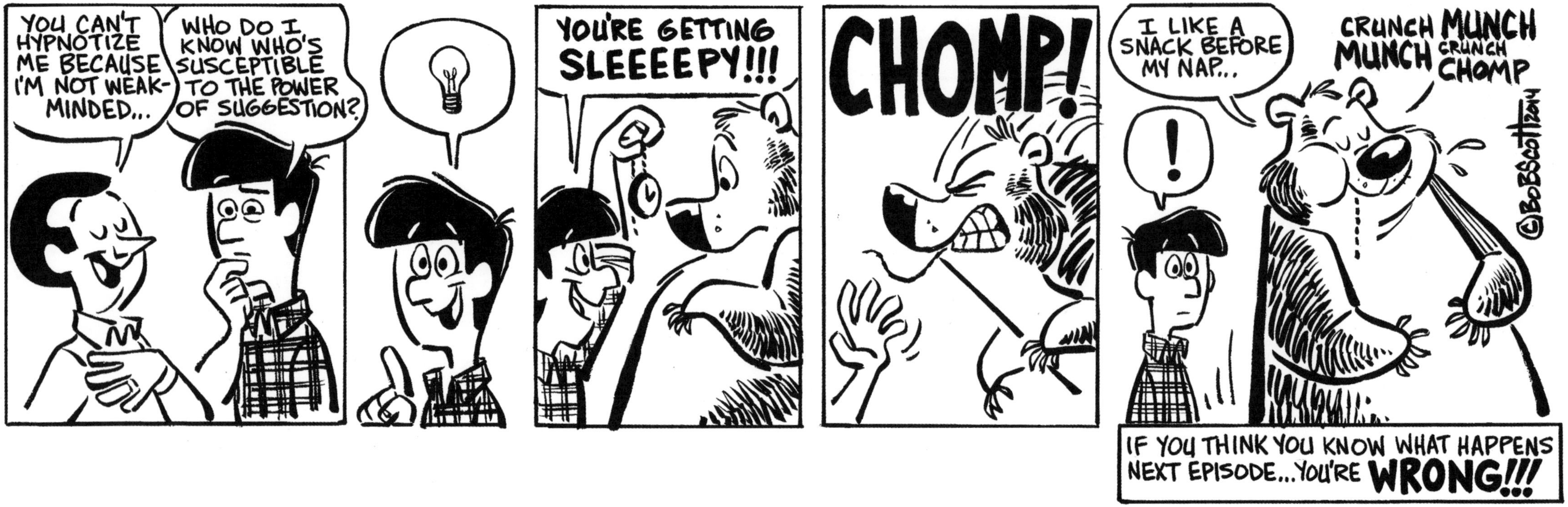
YOU CAN'T HYPNOTIZE ME BECAUSE I'M NOT WEAK-MINDED...
WHO DO I KNOW WHO'S SUSCEPTIBLE TO THE POWER OF SUGGESTION?
YOU'RE GETTING SLEEEEEPY!!!
CHOMP!
I LIKE A SNACK BEFORE MY NAP...
CRUNCH MUNCH MUNCH CRUNCH CHOMP
©BOBSCOTT2014
IF YOU THINK YOU KNOW WHAT HAPPENS NEXT EPISODE... YOU'RE WRONG!!!

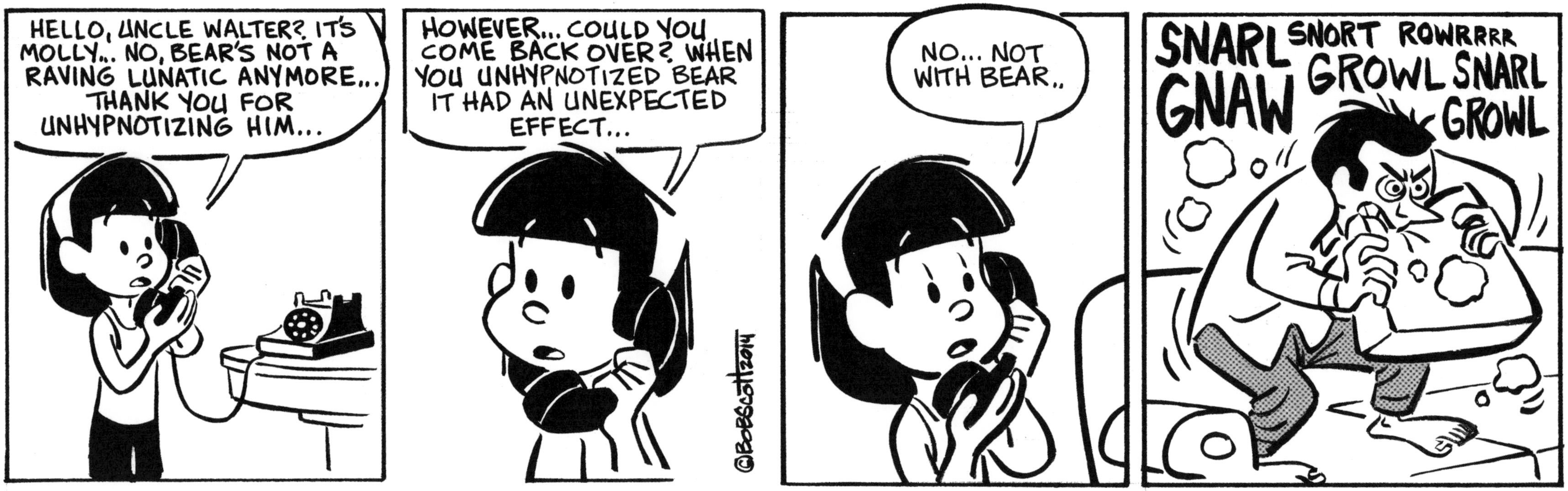
HELLO, UNCLE WALTER? IT'S MOLLY... NO, BEAR'S NOT A RAVING LUNATIC ANYMORE... THANK YOU FOR UNHYPNOTIZING HIM...
HOWEVER... COULD YOU COME BACK OVER? WHEN YOU UNHYPNOTIZED BEAR IT HAD AN UNEXPECTED EFFECT...
©BOBSCOTT2014
NO... NOT WITH BEAR..
SNARL SNORT ROWRRRR
GNAW GROWL SNARL
GROWL

BEHIND THE INK

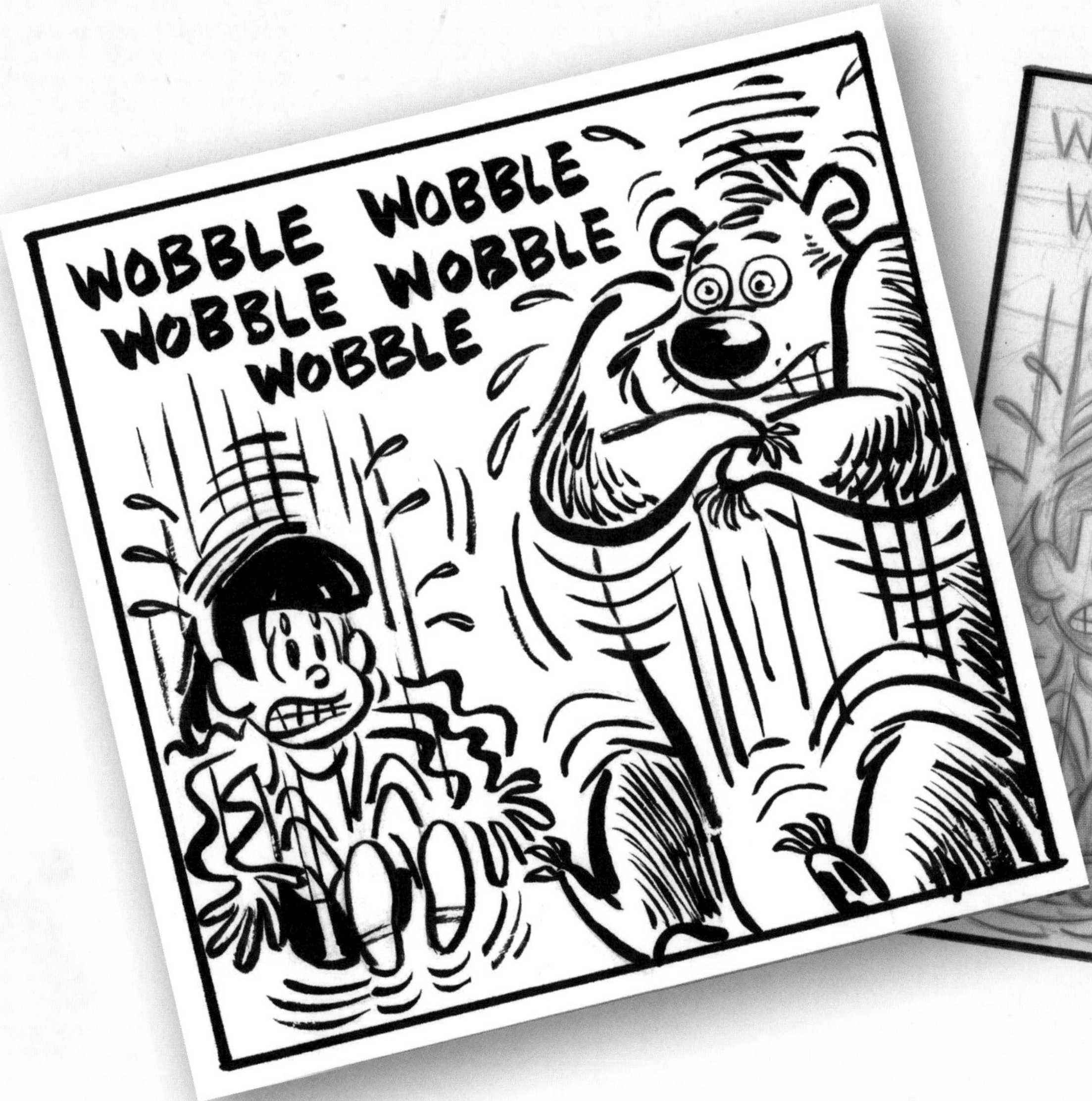
WOBBLE WOBBLE
WOBBLE WOBBLE
WOBBLE

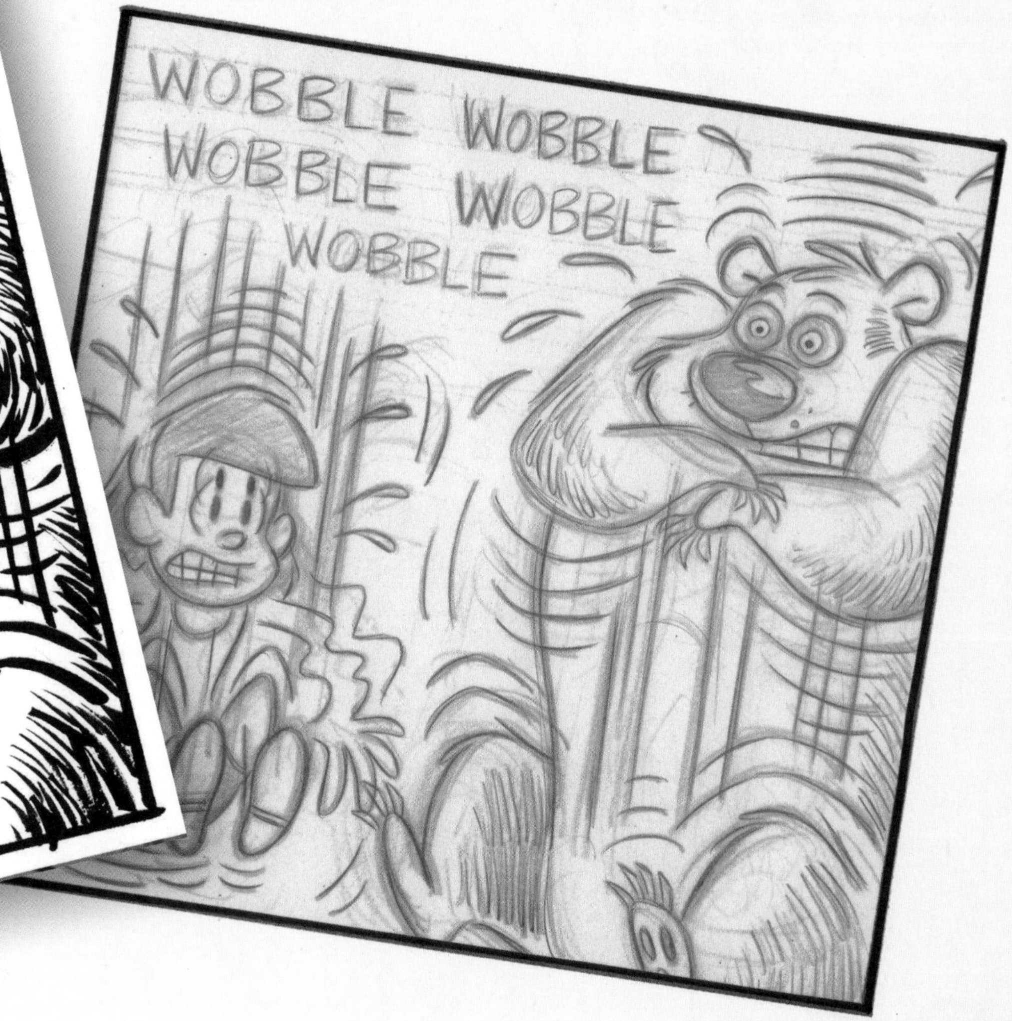
WOBBLE WOBBLE
WOBBLE WOBBLE
WOBBLE

I love comic strips! Ever since I was a little kid, I have loved reading comic strips. In those days, the newspapers carried pages and pages of daily comics and were conveniently delivered to everyone's homes. The strips that captured my young imagination were *Pogo* and *Dennis the Menace*, and they are still two of my favorites. I love the beautiful drawings as well as the wonderful humor. Today I find inspiration in strips that remind me of the golden era of comic strips, most notably *Diamond Lil* by Brett Koth.

I work as a story artist at Disney Features, and we toil away on the same project for a few years before it is done. Crafting a daily strip is the perfect creative relief from the long-running movie projects. I love the three-four panel format, each day presenting the elusive possibility of perfection, but also allowing forgiveness of a blunder, as a new strip is up the next day.

Because I love the golden era of strips, my creative process is the same as the masters'. I draw on bristol board with blue pencil and then ink the strips with a brush and India ink. I hand-letter each strip, and I find a lot of pleasure in the lettering. The writing inspiration comes from my life and my imagination, but mostly my jokes grow out of funny drawings from my sketchbook.

LEFT: Thumbnails exploring the best way to stage a gag.
BELOW LEFT: Character sketches. Sometimes the best gags come from a funny drawing or expression. I'm constantly doodling for inspiration.
BELOW: "Summer Blowout" Illustration used to announce 5 strips a week for the month of July 2011.
RIGHT: Early sketches of a much younger Molly.

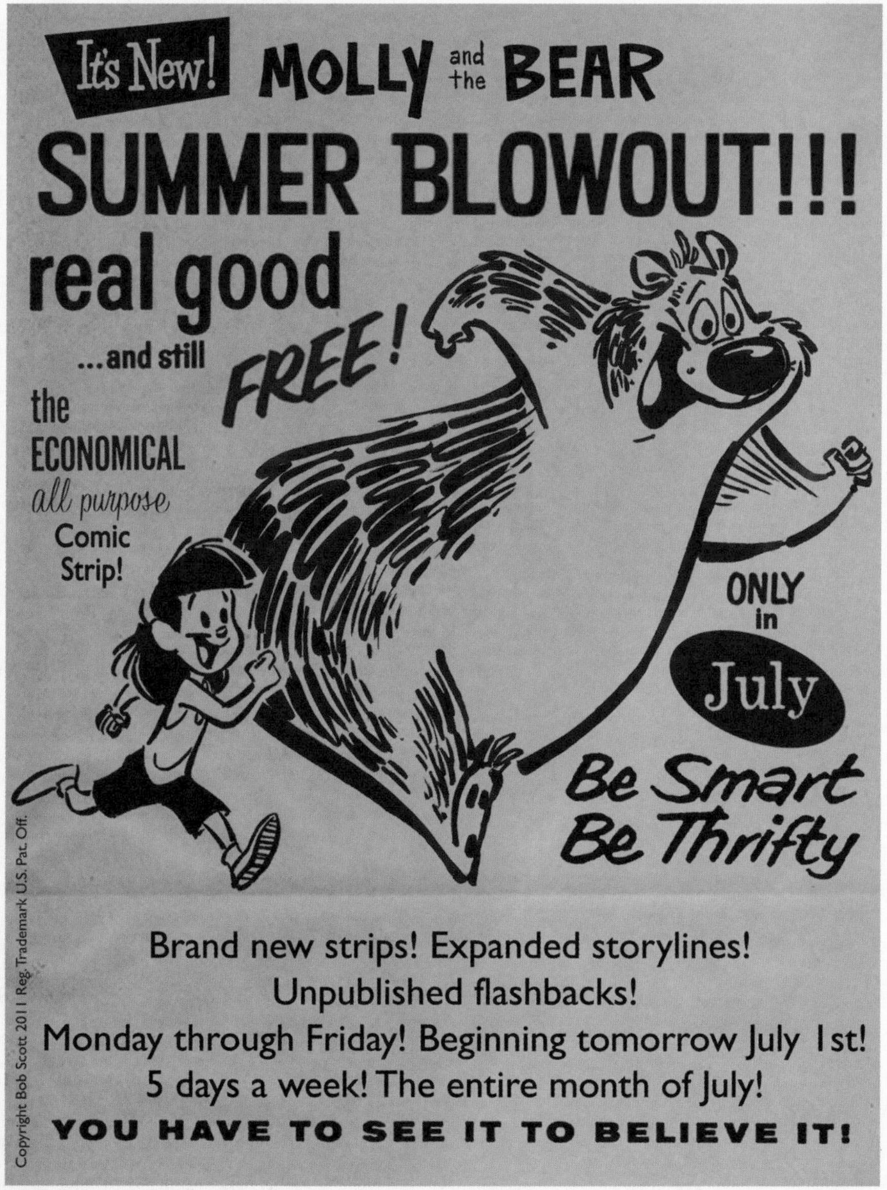

It's New!
MOLLY and the BEAR
SUMMER BLOWOUT!!!
real good
...and still
FREE!
the
ECONOMICAL
all purpose
Comic
Strip!
ONLY
in
July
Be Smart
Be Thrifty
Copyright Bob Scott 2011 | Reg. Trademark U.S. Pat. Off.
Brand new strips! Expanded storylines!
Unpublished flashbacks!
Monday through Friday! Beginning tomorrow July 1st!
5 days a week! The entire month of July!
YOU HAVE TO SEE IT TO BELIEVE IT!

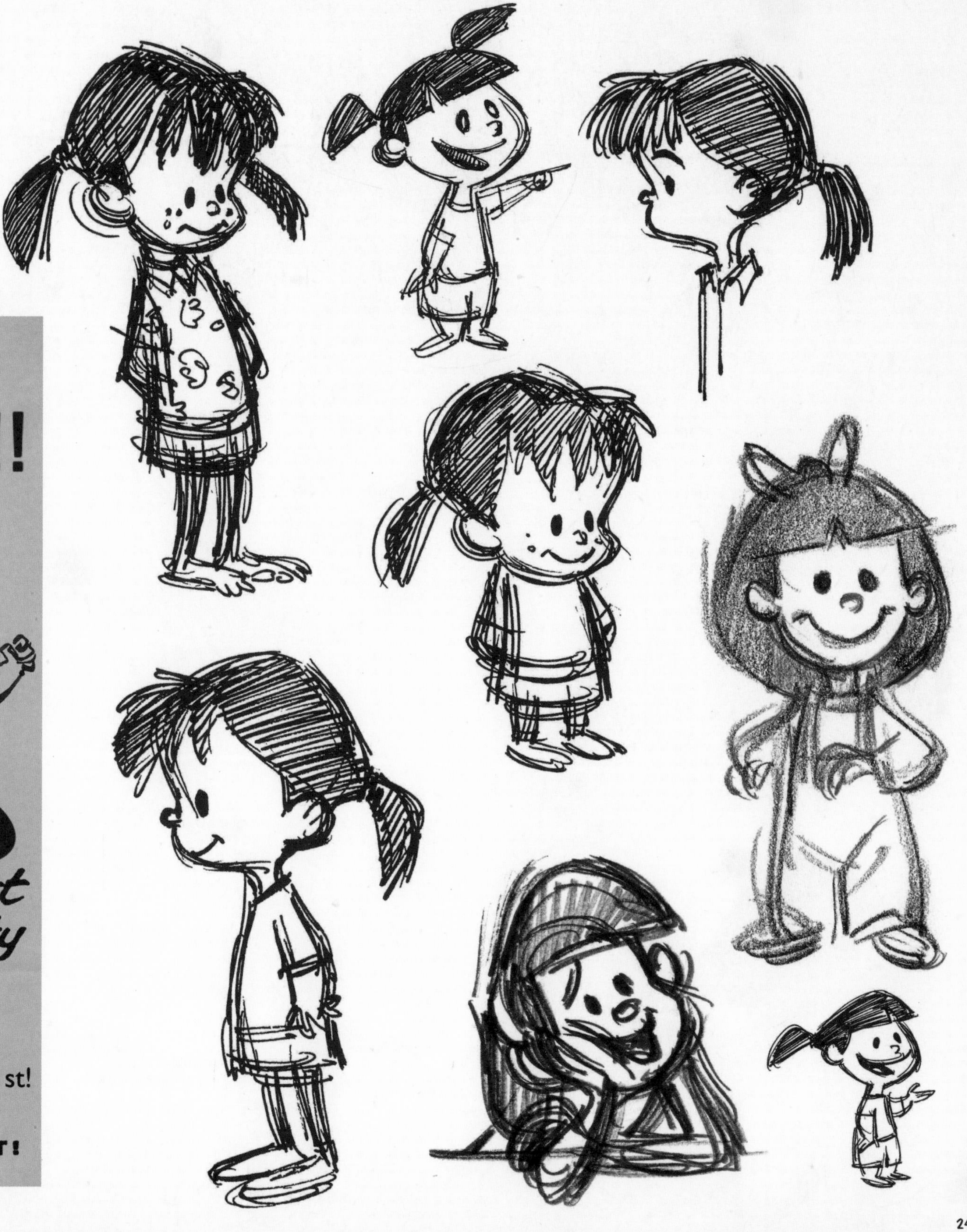

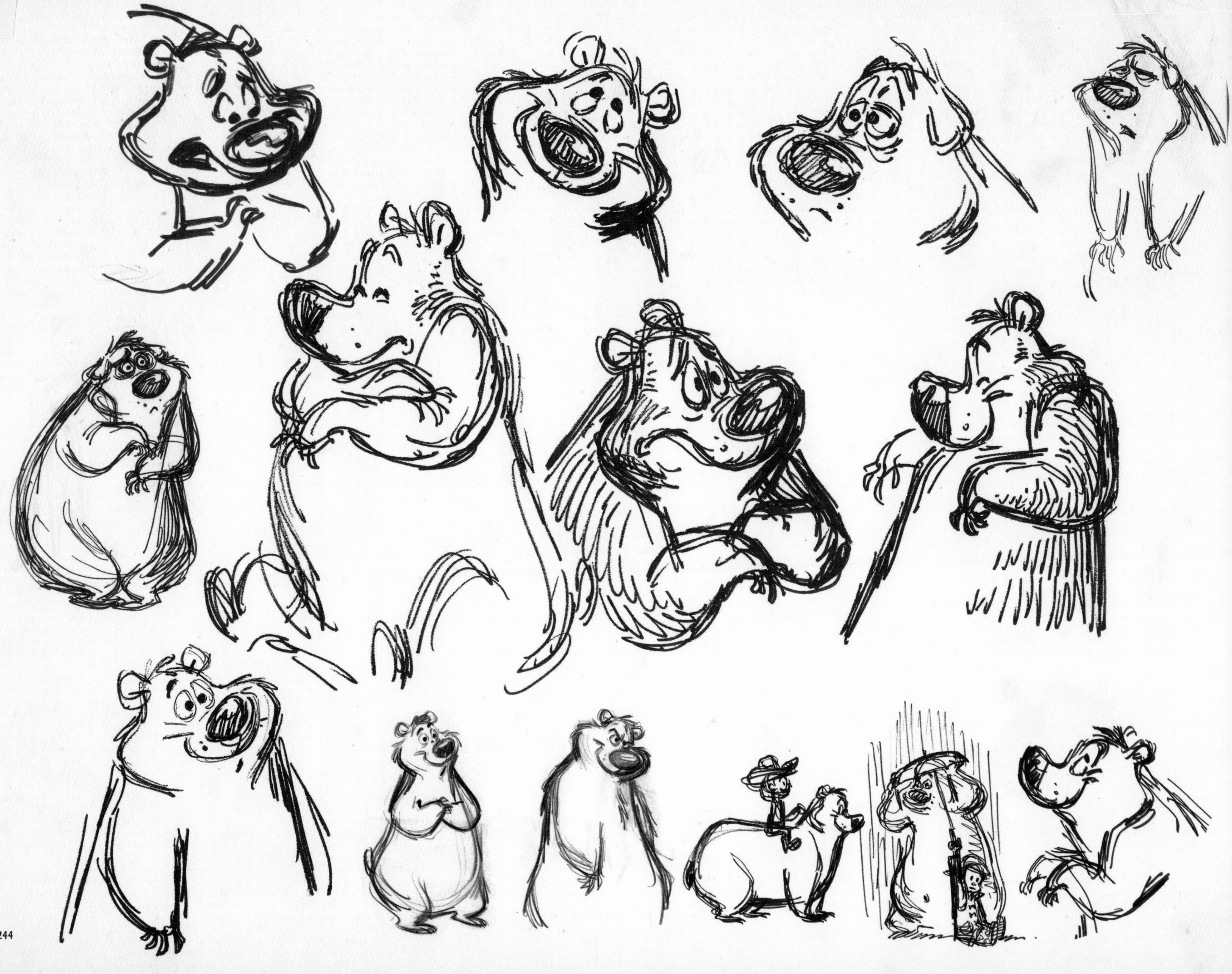

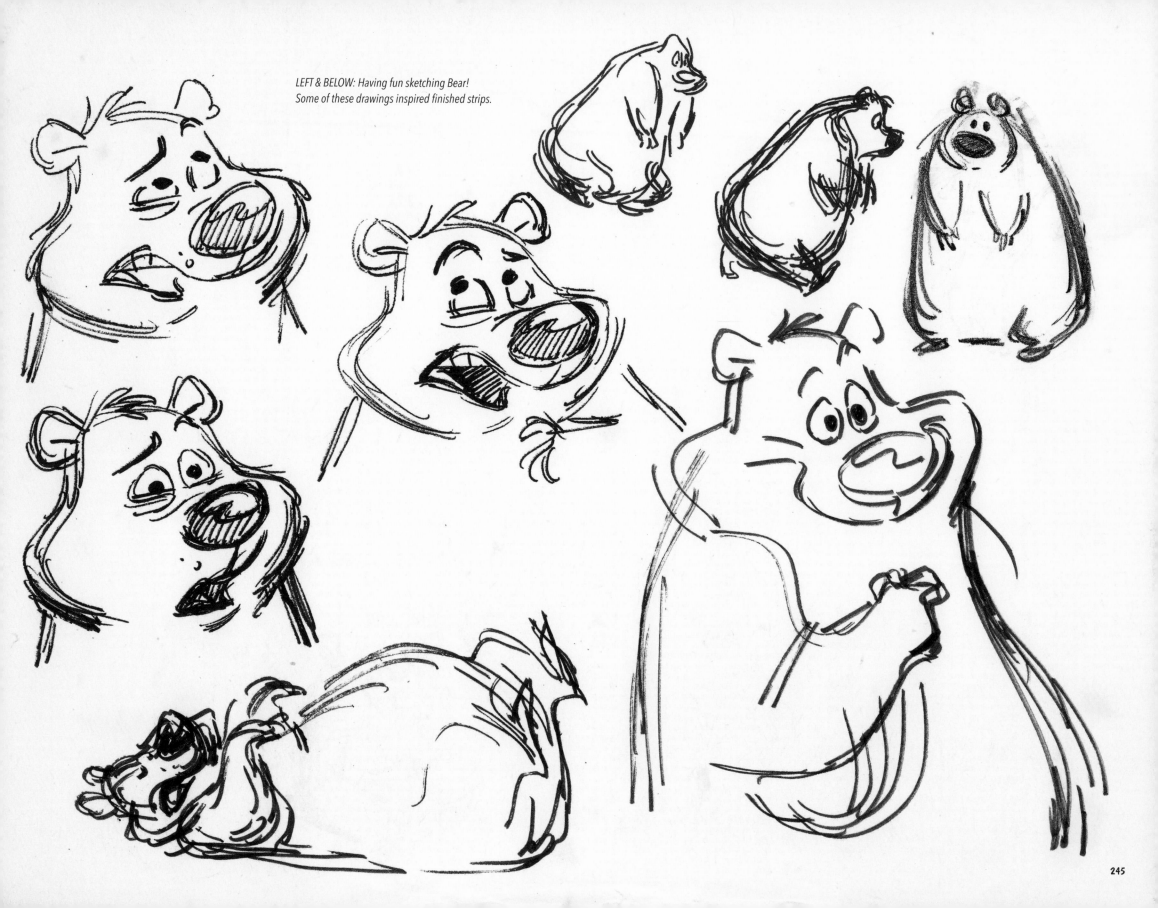

LEFT & BELOW: Having fun sketching Bear!
Some of these drawings inspired finished strips.

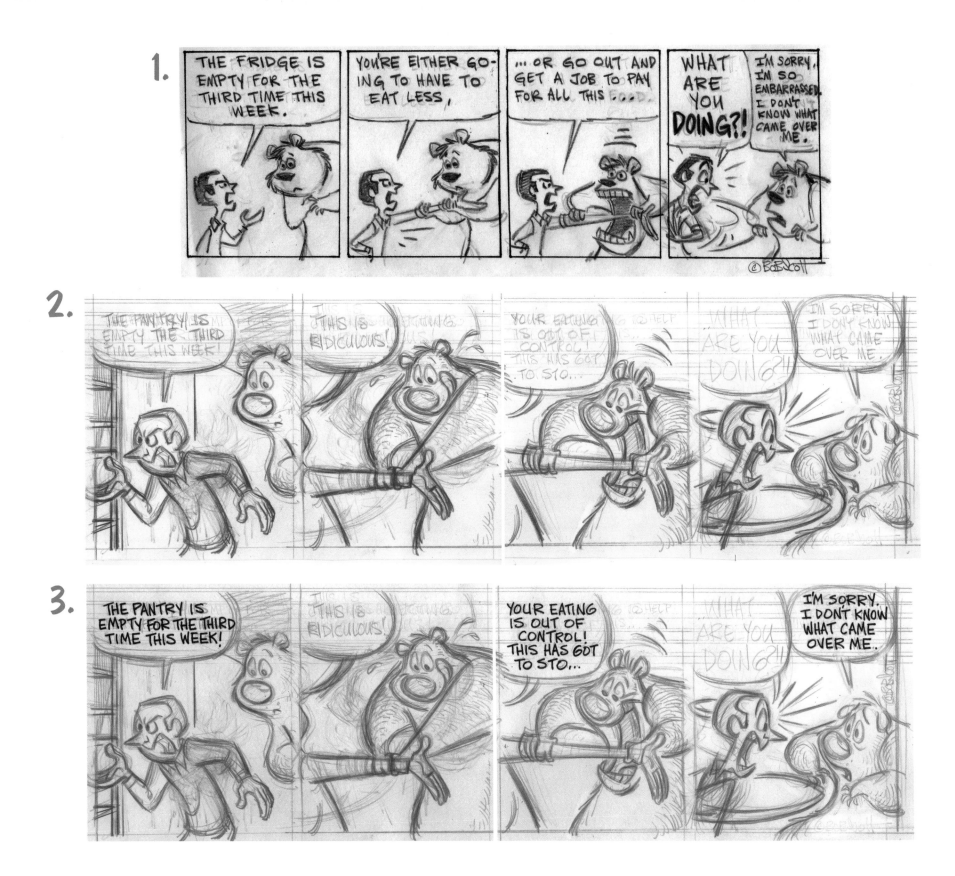

1. Rough thumbnail   **2.** Blue pencil sketch   **3.** Lettered with a pen   **4.** Inked with a brush   **5.** Final strip cleaned up in Photoshop

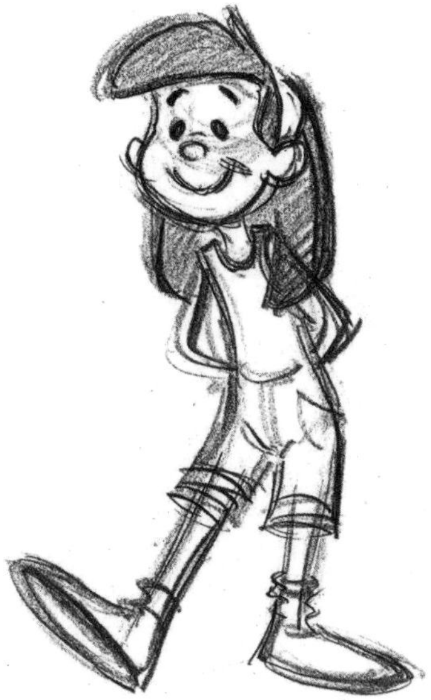

ABOVE: First drawing of the Molly we know. (1998)
BELOW: I seldom receive fan mail but when I do I like to respond. Especially when it's snail mail. This drawing was sent to a reader in the military.
RIGHT & FAR RIGHT: The strip is rarely in color. I always like to do something special for Christmas.

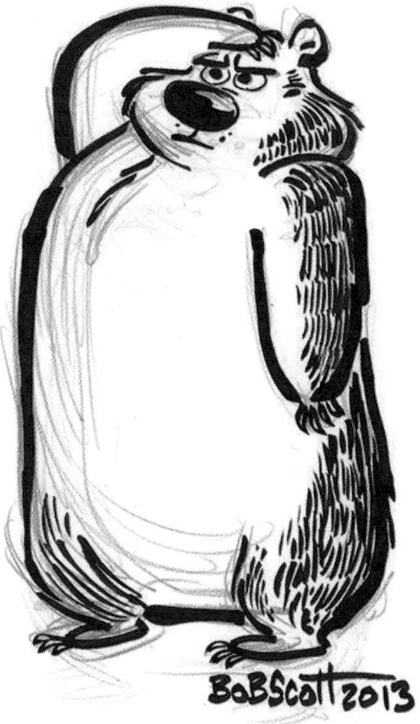

BoBScott 2013

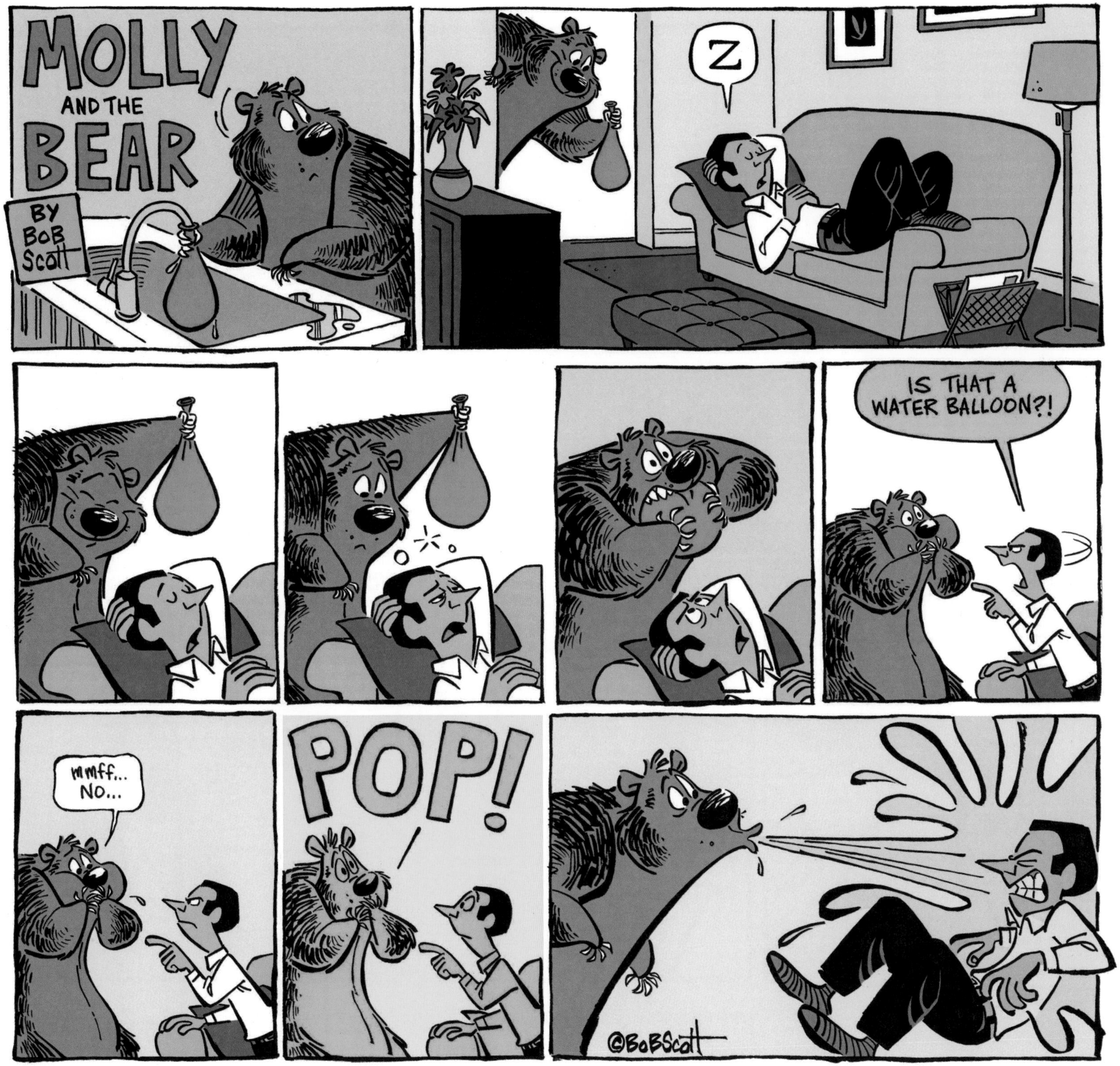

MOLLY AND THE BEAR
BY BOB SCOTT
Z
IS THAT A WATER BALLOON?!
mmff... NO...
POP!
©BoBScott

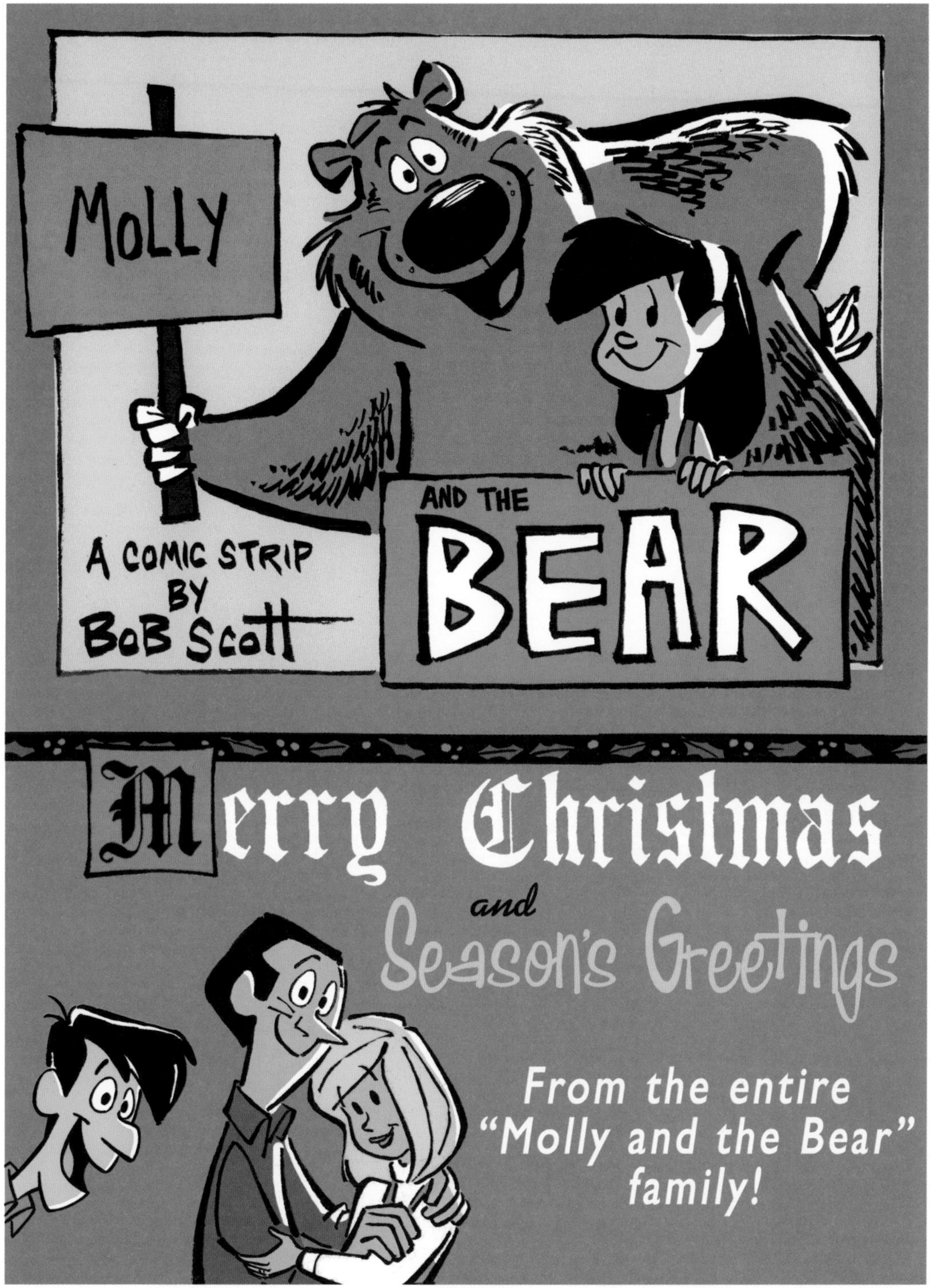
MOLLY
AND THE
BEAR
A COMIC STRIP BY BOB SCOTT
Merry Christmas
and
Season's Greetings
From the entire "Molly and the Bear" family!

Give this season: *Join* The MARCH OF DIMES
www.marchofdimes.com

A Molly and the Bear Flashback

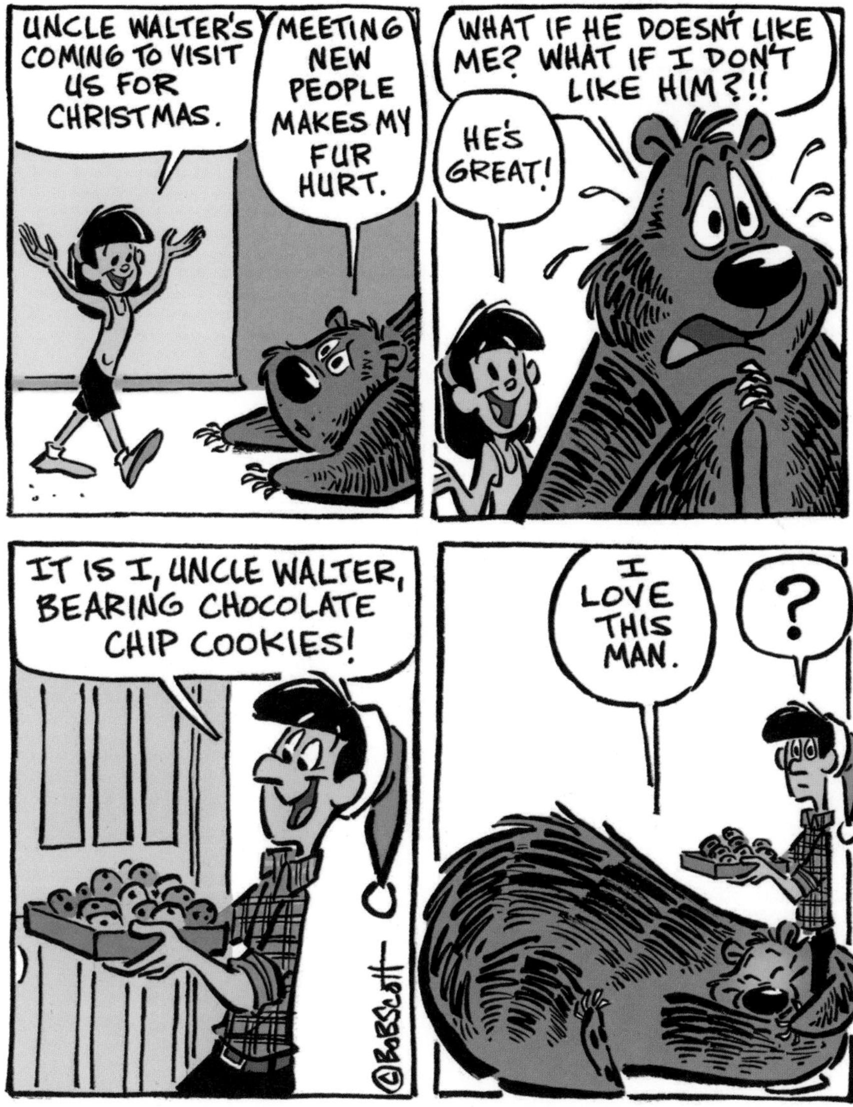
UNCLE WALTER'S COMING TO VISIT US FOR CHRISTMAS.
MEETING NEW PEOPLE MAKES MY FUR HURT.
WHAT IF HE DOESN'T LIKE ME? WHAT IF I DON'T LIKE HIM?!!
HE'S GREAT!
IT IS I, UNCLE WALTER, BEARING CHOCOLATE CHIP COOKIES!
©BoBScott
I LOVE THIS MAN.
?

Merry Christmas
And a Happy New Year!

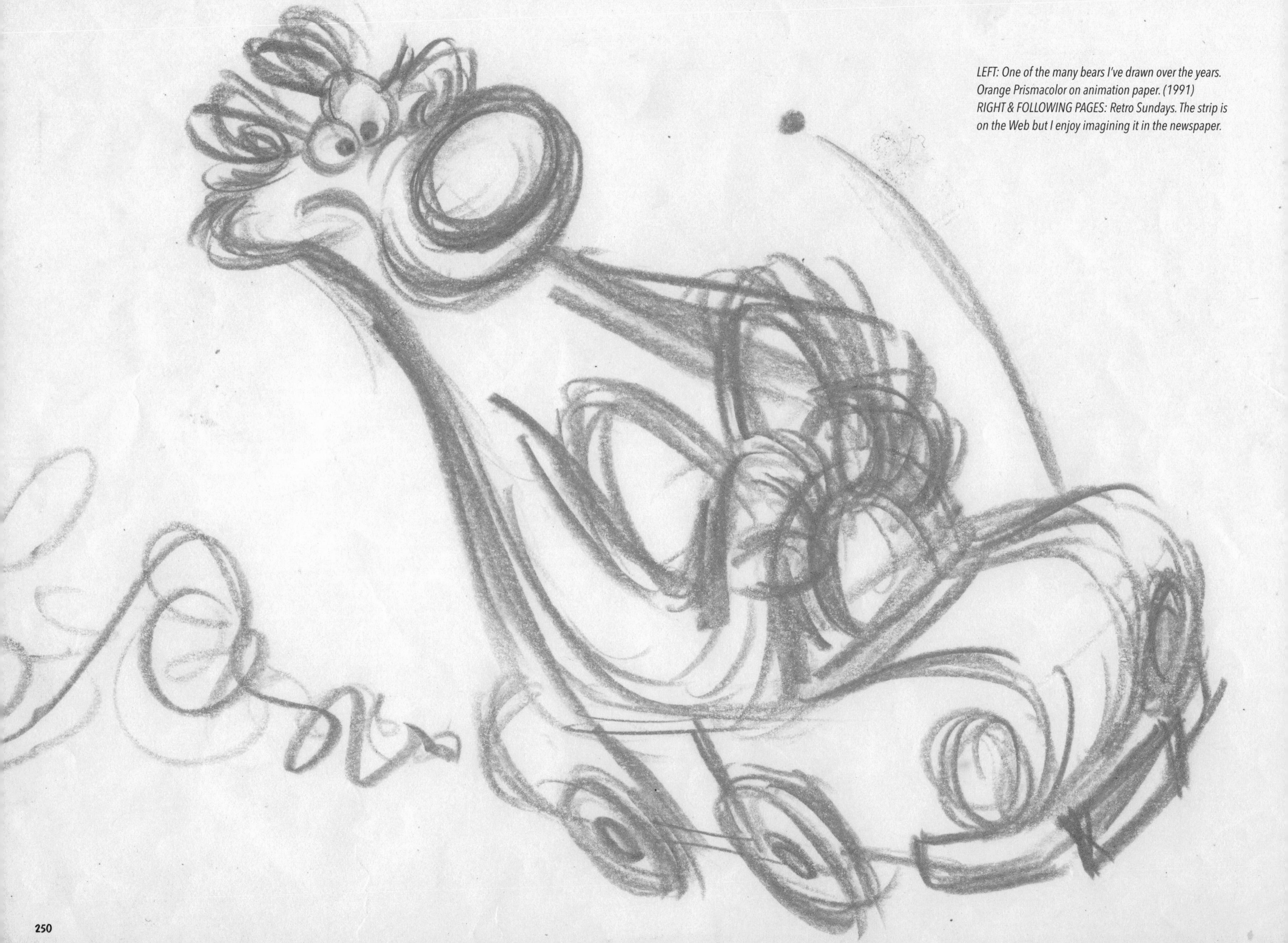

LEFT: One of the many bears I've drawn over the years. Orange Prismacolor on animation paper. (1991)
RIGHT & FOLLOWING PAGES: Retro Sundays. The strip is on the Web but I enjoy imagining it in the newspaper.

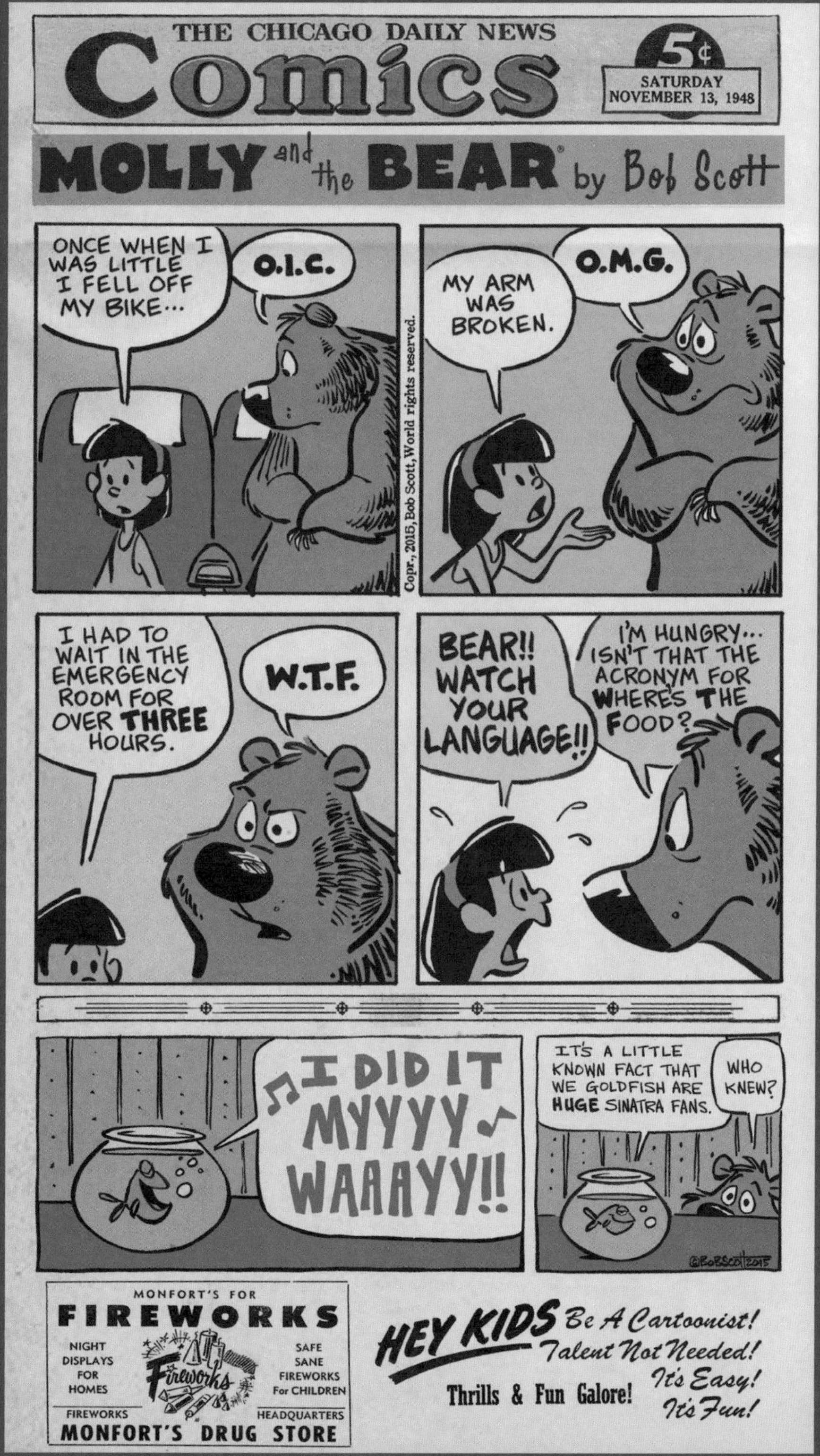
THE CHICAGO DAILY NEWS
Comics
5¢
SATURDAY NOVEMBER 13, 1948
MOLLY and the BEAR by Bob Scott
ONCE WHEN I WAS LITTLE I FELL OFF MY BIKE...
O.I.C.
MY ARM WAS BROKEN.
O.M.G.
Copr., 2015, Bob Scott, World rights reserved.
I HAD TO WAIT IN THE EMERGENCY ROOM FOR OVER THREE HOURS.
W.T.F.
BEAR!! WATCH YOUR LANGUAGE!!
I'M HUNGRY... ISN'T THAT THE ACRONYM FOR WHERE'S THE FOOD?
I DID IT MYYYY WAARYY!!
IT'S A LITTLE KNOWN FACT THAT WE GOLDFISH ARE HUGE SINATRA FANS.
WHO KNEW?
MONFORT'S FOR
FIREWORKS
NIGHT DISPLAYS FOR HOMES
Fireworks
SAFE SANE FIREWORKS For CHILDREN
FIREWORKS HEADQUARTERS
MONFORT'S DRUG STORE
HEY KIDS
Be A Cartoonist!
Talent Not Needed!
It's Easy!
It's Fun!
Thrills & Fun Galore!

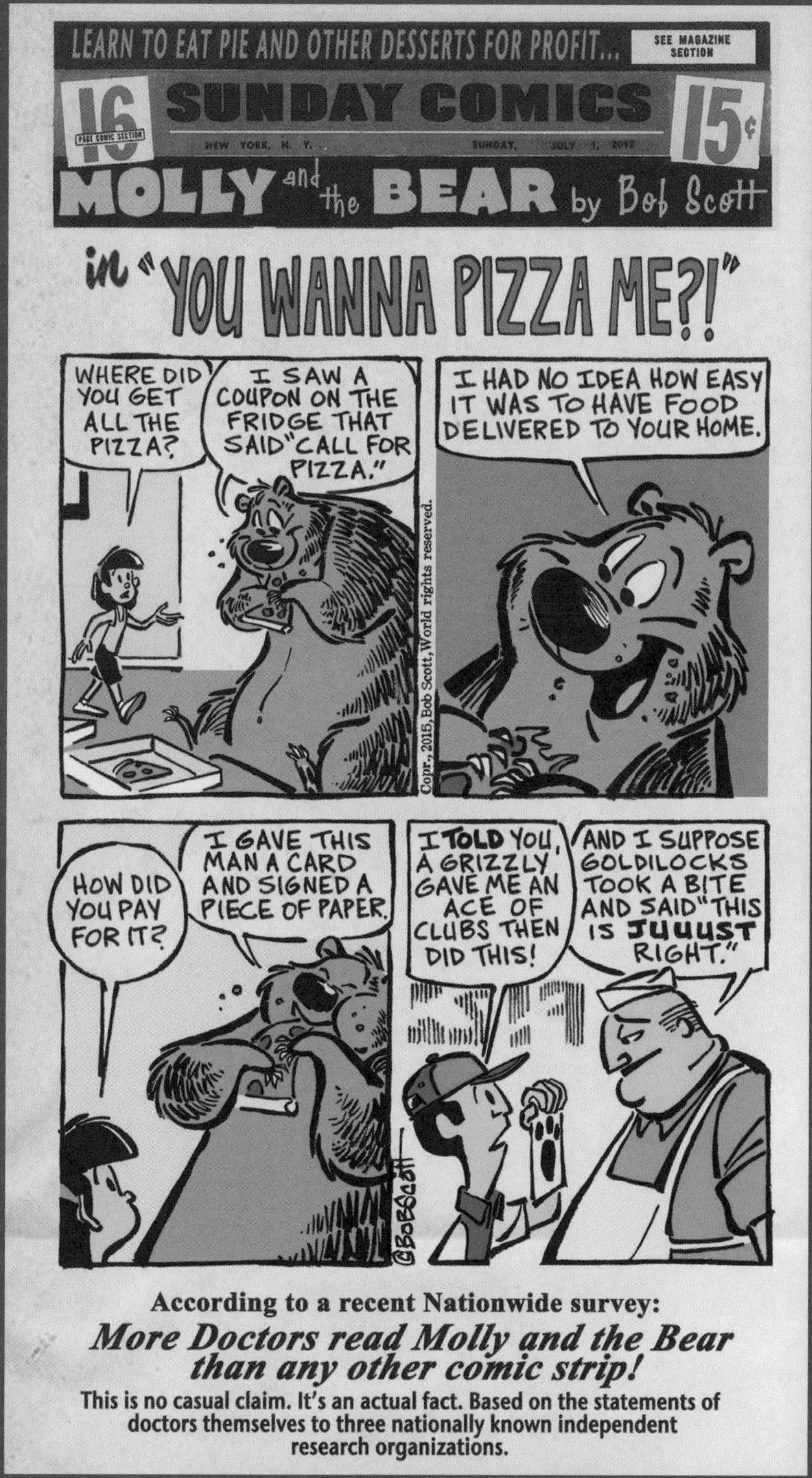
LEARN TO EAT PIE AND OTHER DESSERTS FOR PROFIT...
SEE MAGAZINE SECTION
16
PAGE COMIC SECTION
SUNDAY COMICS
15¢
MOLLY and the BEAR by Bob Scott
in "YOU WANNA PIZZA ME?!"
WHERE DID YOU GET ALL THE PIZZA?
I SAW A COUPON ON THE FRIDGE THAT SAID "CALL FOR PIZZA."
I HAD NO IDEA HOW EASY IT WAS TO HAVE FOOD DELIVERED TO YOUR HOME.
Copr., 2015, Bob Scott, World rights reserved.
HOW DID YOU PAY FOR IT?
I GAVE THIS MAN A CARD AND SIGNED A PIECE OF PAPER.
I TOLD YOU, A GRIZZLY GAVE ME AN ACE OF CLUBS THEN DID THIS!
AND I SUPPOSE GOLDILOCKS TOOK A BITE AND SAID "THIS IS JUUUST RIGHT."
According to a recent Nationwide survey:
More Doctors read Molly and the Bear than any other comic strip!
This is no casual claim. It's an actual fact. Based on the statements of doctors themselves to three nationally known independent research organizations.

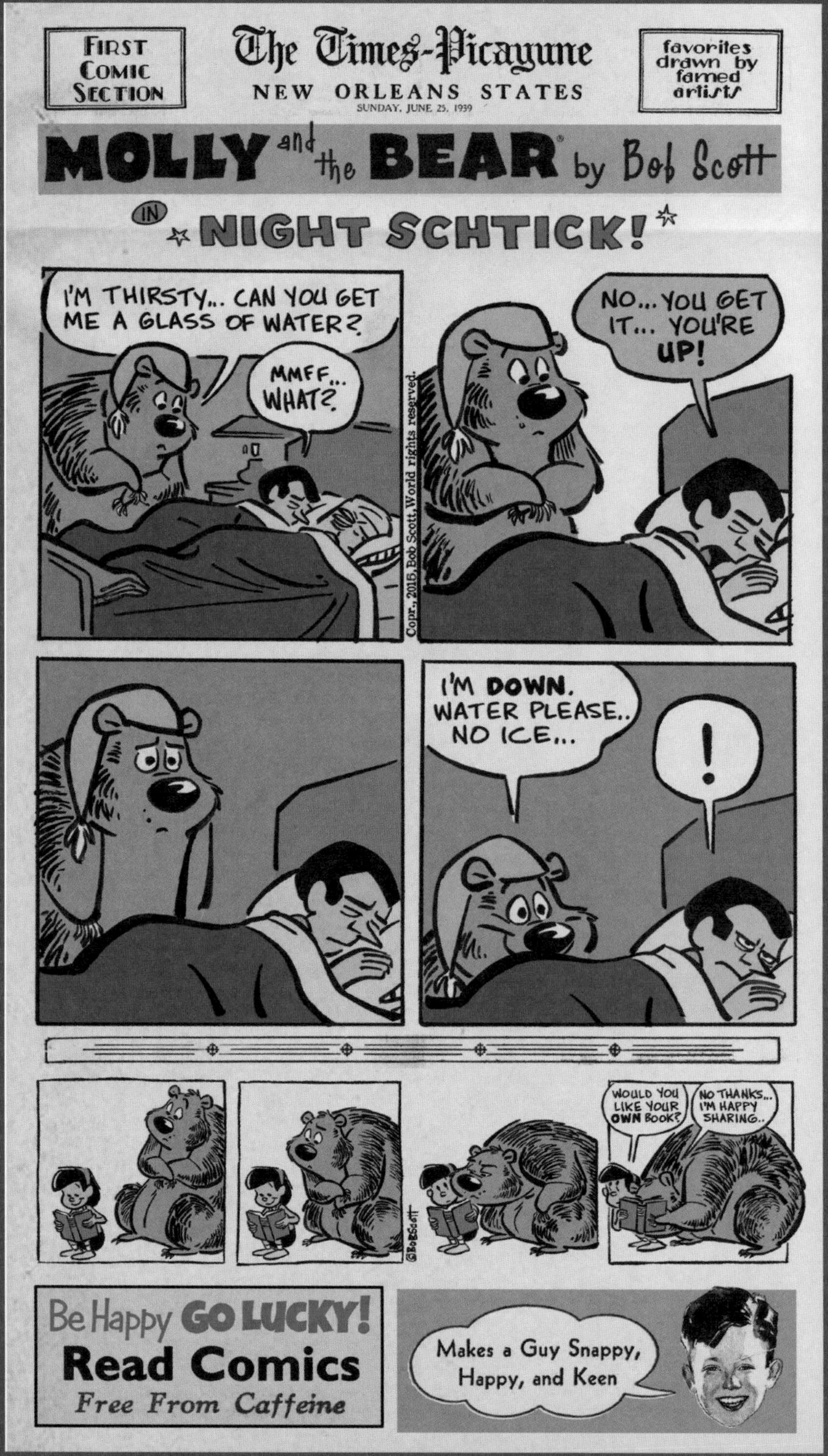
FIRST COMIC SECTION
The Times-Picayune
NEW ORLEANS STATES
SUNDAY, JUNE 25, 1939
favorites drawn by famed artists
MOLLY and the BEAR by Bob Scott
IN NIGHT SCHTICK!
I'M THIRSTY... CAN YOU GET ME A GLASS OF WATER?
MMFF... WHAT?
NO... YOU GET IT... YOU'RE UP!
Copr., 2015, Bob Scott, World rights reserved.
I'M DOWN. WATER PLEASE.. NO ICE...
!
WOULD YOU LIKE YOUR OWN BOOK?
NO THANKS... I'M HAPPY SHARING..
©BoBScott
Be Happy GO LUCKY! Read Comics Free From Caffeine
Makes a Guy Snappy, Happy, and Keen

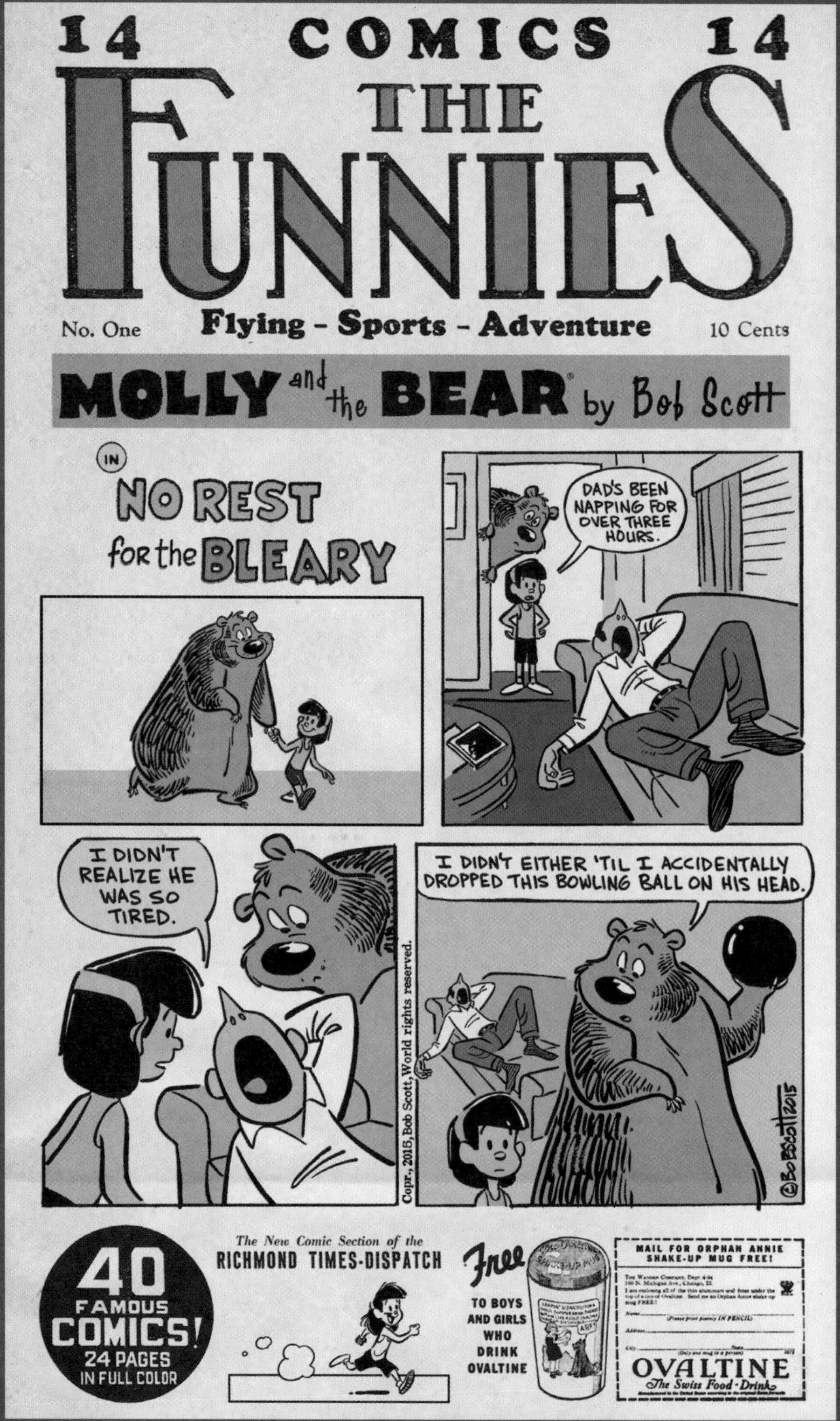
14 COMICS 14
THE FUNNIES
No. One
Flying - Sports - Adventure
10 Cents
MOLLY and the BEAR by Bob Scott
IN NO REST for the BLEARY
DAD'S BEEN NAPPING FOR OVER THREE HOURS.
I DIDN'T REALIZE HE WAS SO TIRED.
I DIDN'T EITHER 'TIL I ACCIDENTALLY DROPPED THIS BOWLING BALL ON HIS HEAD.
Copr., 2015, Bob Scott, World rights reserved.
©BoBScott2015
40 FAMOUS COMICS! 24 PAGES IN FULL COLOR
The New Comic Section of the
RICHMOND TIMES-DISPATCH
Free TO BOYS AND GIRLS WHO DRINK OVALTINE
MAIL FOR ORPHAN ANNIE SHAKE-UP MUG FREE!
OVALTINE
The Swiss Food-Drink

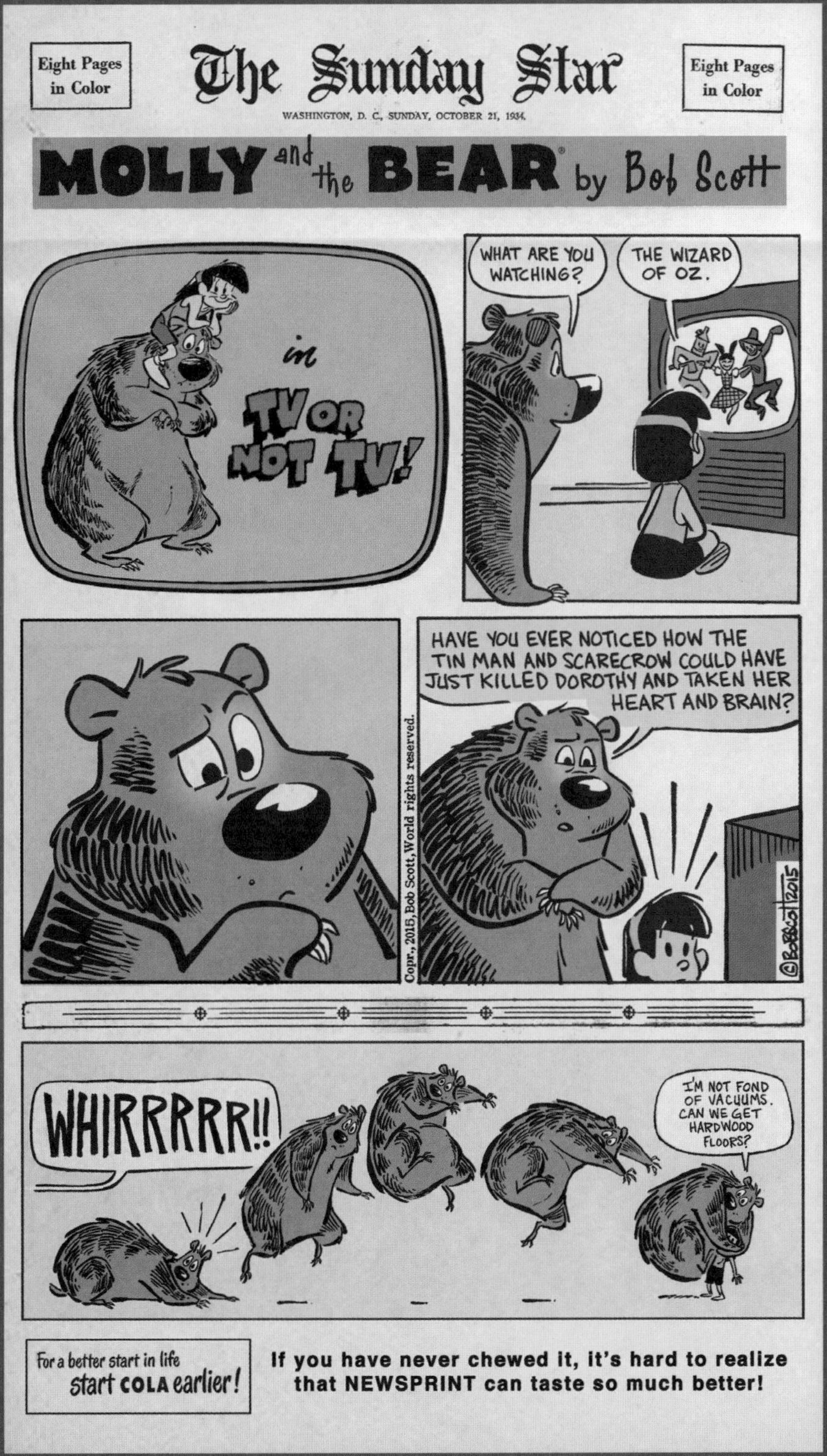
Eight Pages in Color
The Sunday Star
Eight Pages in Color
WASHINGTON, D. C., SUNDAY, OCTOBER 21, 1934.
MOLLY and the BEAR by Bob Scott
in TV OR NOT TV!
WHAT ARE YOU WATCHING?
THE WIZARD OF OZ.
HAVE YOU EVER NOTICED HOW THE TIN MAN AND SCARECROW COULD HAVE JUST KILLED DOROTHY AND TAKEN HER HEART AND BRAIN?
Copr., 2015, Bob Scott, World rights reserved.
©BOBSCOTT2015
WHIRRRRR!!
I'M NOT FOND OF VACUUMS. CAN WE GET HARDWOOD FLOORS?
For a better start in life start COLA earlier!
If you have never chewed it, it's hard to realize that NEWSPRINT can taste so much better!

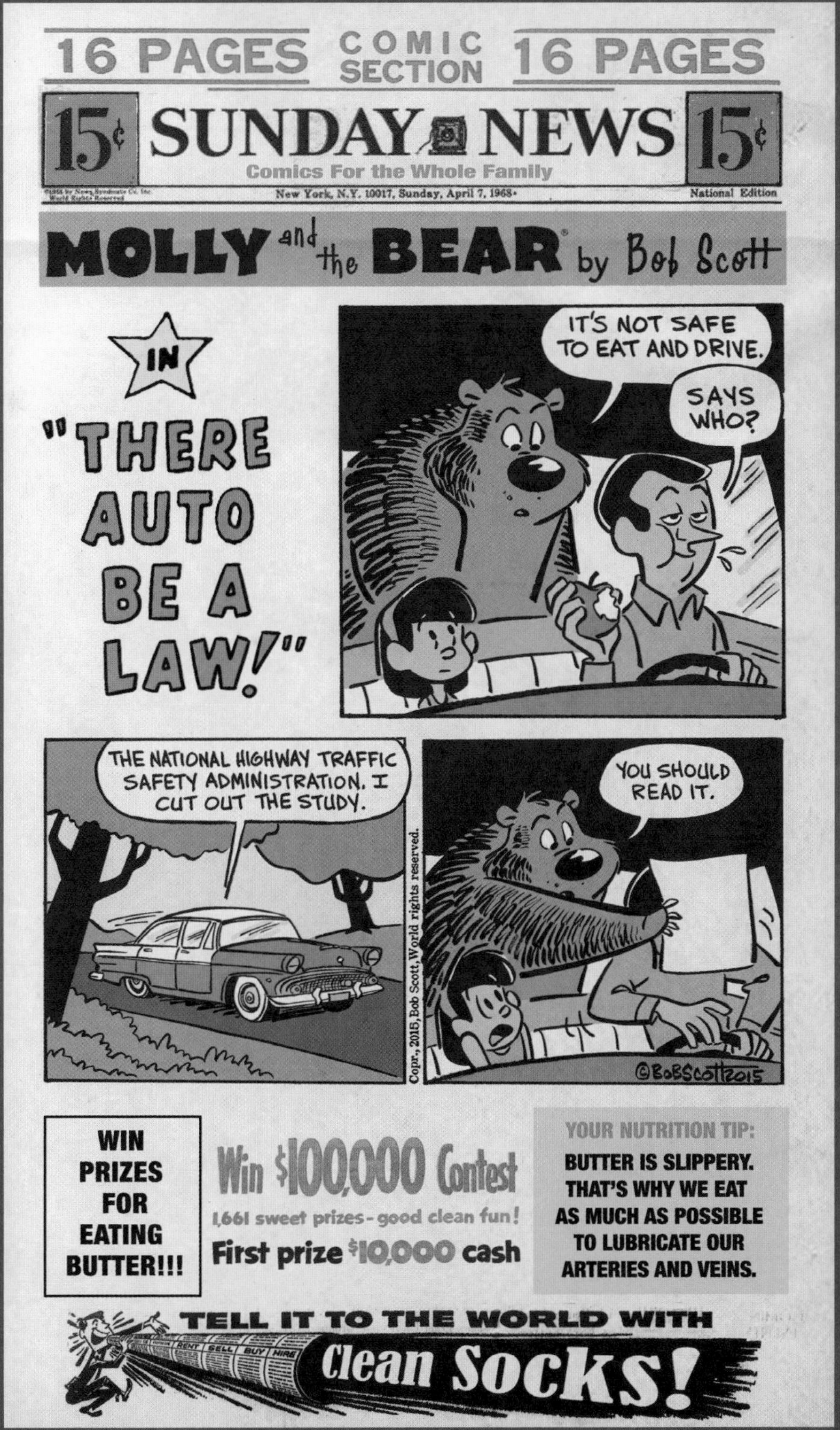
16 PAGES
COMIC SECTION
16 PAGES
15¢
SUNDAY NEWS
15¢
Comics For the Whole Family
New York, N.Y. 10017, Sunday, April 7, 1968
National Edition
MOLLY and the BEAR by Bob Scott
IN "THERE AUTO BE A LAW!"
IT'S NOT SAFE TO EAT AND DRIVE.
SAYS WHO?
THE NATIONAL HIGHWAY TRAFFIC SAFETY ADMINISTRATION. I CUT OUT THE STUDY.
YOU SHOULD READ IT.
Copr., 2015, Bob Scott, World rights reserved.
©BOBSCOTT2015
WIN PRIZES FOR EATING BUTTER!!!
Win $100,000 Contest
1,661 sweet prizes - good clean fun!
First prize $10,000 cash
YOUR NUTRITION TIP:
BUTTER IS SLIPPERY. THAT'S WHY WE EAT AS MUCH AS POSSIBLE TO LUBRICATE OUR ARTERIES AND VEINS.
TELL IT TO THE WORLD WITH Clean Socks!

ACKNOWLEDGMENTS

It's been a long road to the completion of this book, and there are so many people I want to thank. Without them it never could have turned out this well.

Thanks to Iain Morris for helping rescue this book when I was about to give up and for designing something better than I could have imagined. Thanks to Donna Almendrala for reformatting and laying out hundreds of strips. Thanks to Brett Koth for spending the time to write such a hilarious foreword in addition to the wonderful drawing of Lil and Bear.

I want to thank my wife Vicki for her input, brainstorming, and constant support on this project. Jim Davis for the extraordinary opportunity to work for you, right out of college. I learned so much! Thanks to David Stanford for his advice and editorial expertise. Thanks to Jason Lethcoe for the constant enthusiasm. To the always-encouraging Ron Zorman and Tony Fucile for keeping up with the strip. Thanks to my daughter, Lila, for being the inspiration for Molly and thanks to my son, Adam, for his laughter and constant pitching of ideas. And thank you to Cameron + Company for the privilege to publish with you.

Special thanks to Tim Hittle for his friendship, emails, and loyal readership.

–Bob Scott

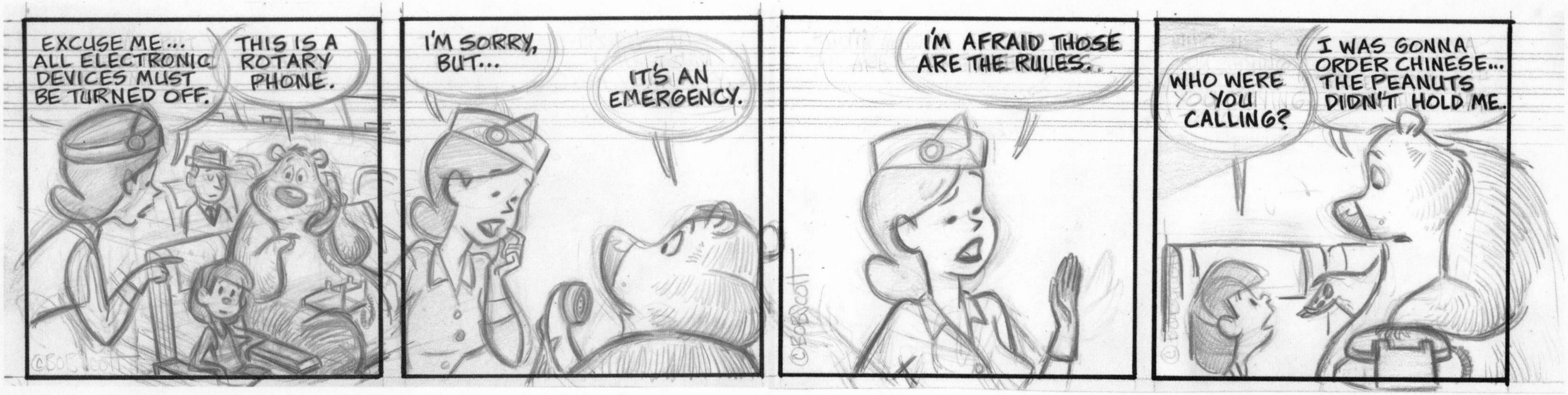
EXCUSE ME... ALL ELECTRONIC DEVICES MUST BE TURNED OFF.
THIS IS A ROTARY PHONE.
I'M SORRY, BUT...
IT'S AN EMERGENCY.
I'M AFRAID THOSE ARE THE RULES.
WHO WERE YOU CALLING?
I WAS GONNA ORDER CHINESE... THE PEANUTS DIDN'T HOLD ME.

ABOVE: Daily strip. Blue pencil. Hand-lettered with a felt pen.
RIGHT: Bob Scott photograph by Nick Winer.

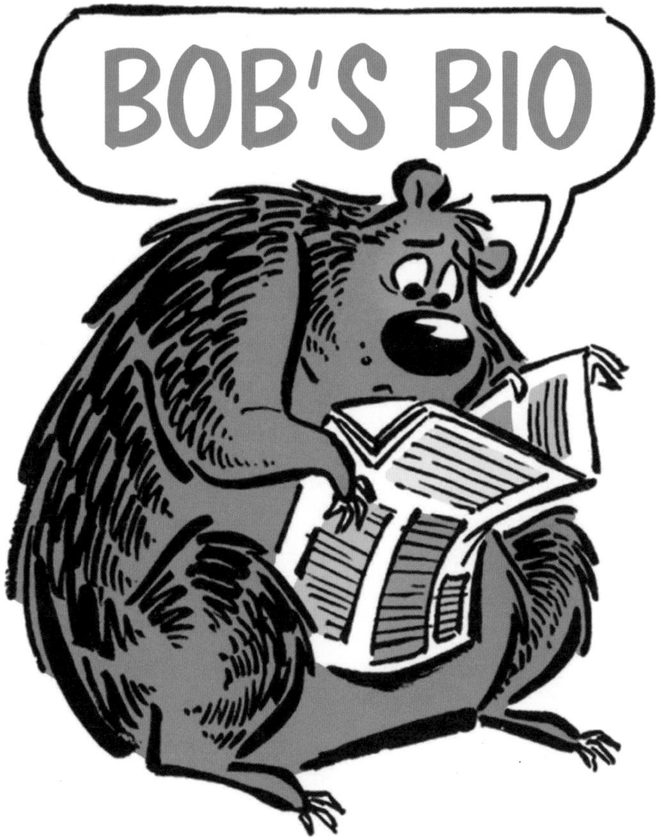
BOB'S BIO

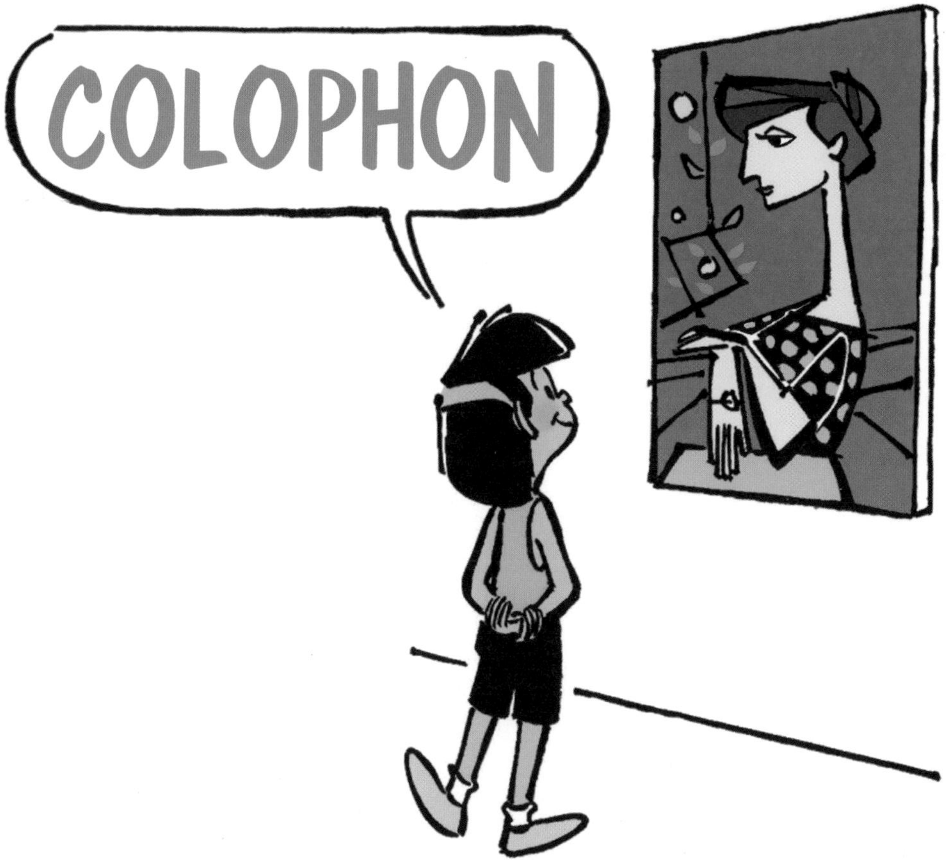
COLOPHON

Bob Scott lives in both the world of comic strips and animation. Born in Detroit, he taught himself cartooning, emulating the masters in the funny pages. Acceptance and graduation from California Institute of the Arts opened the world of character animation for Bob. He has worked over thirty years in the industry as an animator, character designer, storyboard artist, and voice talent. His credits can be found on projects from Marvel's *Muppet Babies*, Turner Animation's *Cat's Don't Dance* and Pixar's *The Incredibles*. He has worked for Jim Davis, co-penciling *U.S. Acres* and co-directing *Garfield: His 9 Lives*. His heart has always wanted a comic strip of his own, and so *Molly and the Bear* was born in 1997 and became a syndicated webcomic in 2010.

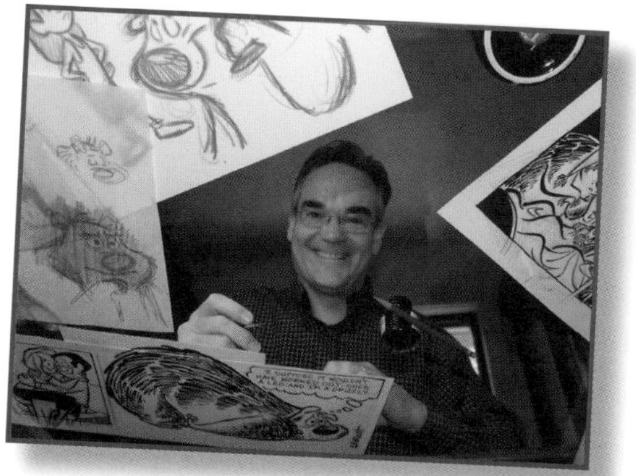

CAMERON + COMPANY, 6 Petaluma Blvd. North, Suite B-6, Petaluma, CA 94952
707-769-1617 • www.cameronbooks.com
Publisher: *Chris Gruener* • Creative Director: *Iain R. Morris*
Editor: *Jan Hughes* • Production Artist: *Donna Almendrala*

ISBN: 978-1-937359-85-0 • Printed and bound in China • 10 9 8 7 6 5 4 3 2 1
Library of Congress Catalog Control Number available upon request

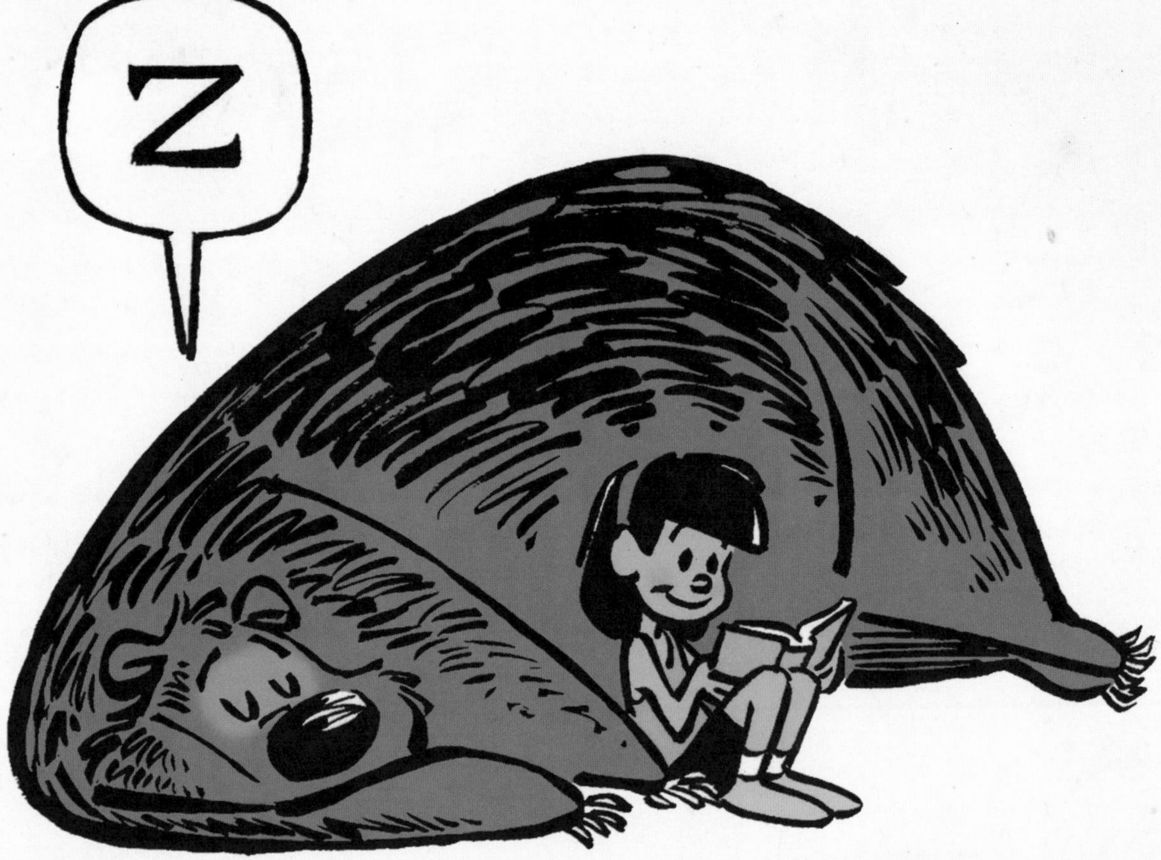
Z

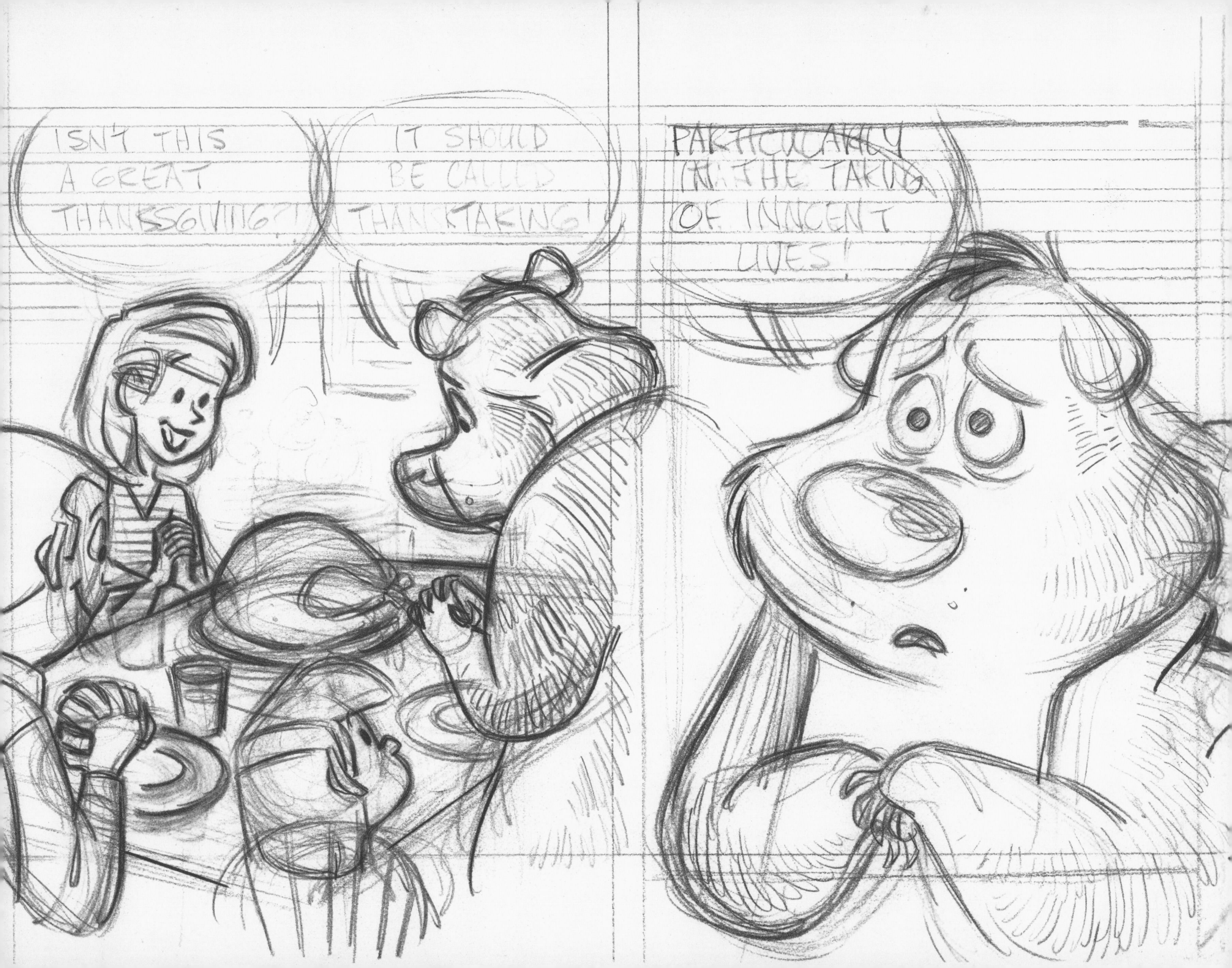
ISN'T THIS A GREAT THANKSGIVING?!
IT SHOULD BE CALLED THANKSTAKING!
PARTICULARLY THE TAKING OF INNCENT LIVES!